Crashed

ADAM TOOZE

Crashed

*How a Decade of Financial Crises
Changed the World*

ALLEN LANE
an imprint of
PENGUIN BOOKS

ALLEN LANE

UK | USA | Canada | Ireland | Australia
India | New Zealand | South Africa

Allen Lane is part of the Penguin Random House group of companies
whose addresses can be found at global.penguinrandomhouse.com.

First published in the United States of America by
Viking, an imprint of Penguin Random House LLC 2018
First published in Great Britain by Allen Lane 2018
003

Printed and bound in Great Britain by Clays Ltd, Elcograf S.p.A.

A CIP catalogue record for this book is available from the British Library

ISBN: 978–1–846–14036–5

www.greenpenguin.co.uk

MIX
Paper from
responsible sources
FSC® C018179

Penguin Random House is committed to a
sustainable future for our business, our readers
and our planet. This book is made from Forest
Stewardship Council® certified paper.

For Dana

Contents

Acknowledgments

This book was written with urgency and I am deeply grateful to those who have made it happen. Working with Sarah Chalfant and the Wylie Agency has been as smooth as ever. My editors Simon Winder and Wendy Wolf collaborated enthusiastically on the project. Melanie Tortoroli gave invaluable advice on early drafts. It is their work and that of the production team at Viking and Penguin that have carried this book across the line.

In getting the manuscript into shape I relied heavily on the careful editorial attention of Nick Monaco, Kevin James Schilling and Ella Plaut Taranto.

The project took shape as an undergraduate course taught at Yale and Columbia, where my teaching fellows included Ted Fertik, Gabe Winnant, Nick Mulder, Madeline Woker, David Lerer and Noelle Tutur. I am enormously grateful to all of them.

In addition, from an early stage, the manuscript was read and commented on by Ted Fertik, Grey Anderson, Stefan Eich, Anusar Farooqui, Nick Mulder, Hans Knundani and Nicholas Monaco. Wolfgang Proissel, Barnaby Raine and Dana Conley added their comments to particular chapters. These friends and interlocutors know individually and collectively how much I owe to them.

Pieces I cowrote with Stefan Eich and Danilo Scholz helped to further sharpen the argument.

In connection with the book I benefited enormously from conversations

with an array of colleagues, witnesses and participants in the drama described here.

As part of the research I was privileged to interview Mario Monti, Giuliano Amato, Timothy Geithner and Giulio Tremonti. I am extremely grateful for the time they devoted to our conversations.

Through my role as director of the European Institute at Columbia I have been fortunate to try out arguments with Frans Timmermans, Pierre Moscovici, Pierre Vimont, Marco Buti and Moreno Bertoldi.

François Carrel-Billiard is my indispensable collaborator at the institute. It is a privilege to work with him.

Nathan Sheets and Patricia Mosser, veterans of the Fed, gave generously of their time.

Erik Berglof helped me to think through the East European crisis.

A dinner with Mervyn King arranged by Peter Garber proved very illuminating.

Perry Mehrling, Brad Setser, Mike Pyle, Clara Mattei, Martin Sandbu, Nicolas Véron, Cornel Ban, Gabriella Gabor, Shahin Vallée and Eric Monnet all offered invaluable input.

As ever, my old friends David Edgerton and Chris Clark provided an indispensable sounding board.

I have been fortunate to try the arguments of the book at workshops, conferences and seminars hosted in Berlin courtesy of the Hamburg Stiftung für Sozialgeschichte, at the Heidelberg Center for American Studies, the American Academy Berlin, Brown University, Stanford, the Eisenberg Institute University of Michigan, the European University Institute, NYU Florence, the New School, UCLA, the MaxPo conference, the German Historical Institute Paris, the FPLH workshop in London, as part of the Science Po public debt project and at the NYU Kandersteg workshop. I am grateful both to my hosts and other participants at all these events.

A memorial conference for Francesca Carnevali in Birmingham heard a version of the argument about Europe's banks.

Presenting to a seminar of the Siemens Stiftung moderated by Knut Borchardt and attended by Jürgen Habermas was a particular honor.

Beyond the formal academy I have been extraordinarily fortunate to fall in with a brilliant and deeply informed crowd on Twitter and Facebook who

have changed my understanding of how an intense, real-time debate can develop in the twenty-first century.

In the trajectory of my work this project marks a double departure. I have moved forward in time into the field of contemporary history. At the same time I have moved backward to reengage with a youthful preoccupation with economics. This double movement has reminded me of debts I owe to two teachers.

Alan Milward, my doctoral supervisor, was a brilliant but difficult man. Given my personal makeup, the engagement with him was particularly high risk. But I survived and Alan remains a towering figure in the field of modern European history. I don't know whether he would have agreed with my take on the eurozone crisis, but I feel Alan's presence.

Wynne Godley was a mentor and teacher of a very different kind. Spontaneously warm and generous in spirit, he took me under his cape in my first year at King's and introduced me, and a group of my contemporaries, to what, at the time, was a highly idiosyncratic brand of economics. In so doing he provided a model of intellectual warmth and vitality. And he confirmed doubts that had been gestating in me about the IS-LM model that was my first great love in economics. Wynne introduced me to the importance of looking "beyond the flows" and insisting on stock-flow consistency in macro models. I don't think this book, written almost thirty years later, would have been the same without his early influence.

Writing a book is an emotional, intellectual and physical task. It is work I do at home and there I owe everything to my partner, Dana Conley, whose love and support energized and sustained this project from start to finish. To have such an engaged, deeply intelligent, courageous, vivacious and loving companion, so open to me and to my world, is a blessing beyond words.

Puppy Ruby—a marvelous gift from Dana—added joy, warmth, walks and endless distraction.

My daughter, Edie, has jolted dinner table conversation with a burst of political radicalism and sharp insights. When current events were robbing me of my senses, she offered precocious wisdom. Her energetic but grounded engagement with the world is a source of both inspiration and encouragement.

There is no doubt that these three forces are the keys to my current

emotional stability. The fact that this book has not driven us apart but brought us closer together and given us things to talk about is my greatest personal satisfaction.

The fact that I can say all this is due in large part to the wise counsel of an outstanding psychoanalyst. He shall remain nameless. But everyone should be so lucky.

As Nicolas Véron put it to me one evening in Washington Square Park, making sense of what has happened since 2008 is a collective undertaking. As a historian, it has been an extraordinary privilege to be included in that collective. I hope this book in some small way repays the welcome I have received.

New York City
January 2018

CRASHED

Introduction

THE FIRST CRISIS
OF A GLOBAL AGE

Tuesday, September 16, 2008, was the "day after Lehman." It was the day global money markets seized up. At the Federal Reserve Board in Washington, DC, September 16 began with urgent plans to sluice hundreds of billions of dollars into the world's central banks. On Wall Street all eyes were on AIG. Would the global insurance giant make it through the day, or would it follow the investment bank Lehman into oblivion? A shock wave was rippling outward. Within weeks its impact would be felt on factory floors and in dockyards, financial markets and commodity exchanges around the world. Meanwhile, in Midtown Manhattan, September 16, 2008, was the opening day of the sixty-third meeting of the UN General Assembly.

The UN building, on East Forty-second Street, is not where financial power is located in New York. Nor did the speakers at the plenary session that began on the morning of September 23 dwell on the technicalities of the banking crisis. But what they did insist on talking about was its wider meaning. The first head of government to speak was President Lula of Brazil, who energetically denounced the selfishness and speculative chaos that had triggered the crisis.[1] The contrast with President George W. Bush, who followed him to the rostrum, was alarming. Bush seemed not so much a lame duck as a man out of touch with reality, haunted by the failed agenda of his eight-year presidency.[2] The first half of his address spiraled obsessively around the specter of global terrorism. He then took solace in the

favorite neoconservative theme of the advance of democracy, which he saw culminating in the "color revolutions" of Ukraine and Georgia. But that was back in 2003/2004. The devastating financial crisis raging just a short walk away on Wall Street merited only two brief paragraphs at the end of the president's speech. The "turbulence" was, as far as Bush was concerned, an American challenge to be handled by the American government, not a matter for multilateral action.

Others disagreed. Gloria Macapagal Arroyo, president of the Philippines, spoke of America's financial crisis as having unleashed a "terrible tsunami" of uncertainty. It was spreading around the globe, "not just here in Manhattan Island." Since the first tremors had shaken the financial markets in 2007, the world had repeatedly reassured itself that the "worst had passed." But, again and again, "the light at the end of the tunnel" had revealed itself as "an oncoming train hurtling forward with new shocks to the global financial system."[3] Whatever America's efforts at stabilization were, they were not working.

One after another, the speakers at the UN connected the crisis to the question of global governance and ultimately to America's position as the dominant world power. Speaking on behalf of a country that had recently lived through its own devastating financial crisis, Cristina Fernández de Kirchner of Argentina was not one to hide her Schadenfreude. For once, this was a crisis that could not be blamed on the periphery. This was a crisis that "emanated from the first economy of the world." For decades, Latin America had been lectured that "the market would solve everything." Now Wall Street was failing and President Bush was promising that the US Treasury would come to the rescue. But was the United States in a fit state to respond? "[T]he present intervention," Fernández pointed out, was not just "the largest in memory," it was being "made by a State with an incredible trade and fiscal deficit."[4] If this was to stand, then the "Washington Consensus" of fiscal and monetary discipline to which so much of the emerging world had been subjected was clearly dead. "It was a historic opportunity to review behaviour and policies." Nor was it just Latin American resentment on display. The Europeans joined the chorus. "The world is no longer a unipolar world with one super-Power, nor is it a bipolar world with the East and the West. It's a multipolar world now,"[5] intoned Nicolas Sarkozy,

speaking as both president of France and president of the European Coun-
cil. "The 21st century world" could not be "governed with the institutions of
the 20th century." The Security Council and the G8 would need to be ex-
panded. The world needed a new structure, a G13 or G14.[6]

It was not the first time that the question of global governance and
America's role in it had been posed at the United Nations in the new mil-
lennium. When the French president spoke at the UN against American
unilateralism, no one could ignore the echoes of 2003, Iraq and the strug-
gles over that disastrous war. It was a moment that had bitterly divided
Europe and America, governments and citizens.[7] It had revealed an alarming
gulf in political culture between the two continents. Bush and his cohorts
on the right wing of the Republican Party were not easy for bien-pensant,
twenty-first-century citizens of the world to assimilate.[8] For all their talk of
the onward march of democracy, it wasn't even clear that they had won the
election that first gave them power in 2000. In cahoots with Tony Blair, they
had misled the world over WMD. With their unabashed appeals to divine
inspiration and their crusading zeal they flaunted their disregard for the
conception of modernity in which both the EU and the UN liked to dress
themselves—enlightened, transparent, liberal, cosmopolitan. That was, of
course, its own kind of window dressing, its own kind of symbolic politics.
But symbols matter. They are essential ingredients in the construction of
both meaning and hegemony.

By 2008 the Bush administration had lost that battle. And the financial
crisis clinched the impression of disaster. It was a stark historical denoue-
ment. In the space of only five years, both the foreign policy and the eco-
nomic policy elite of the United States, the most powerful state on earth,
had suffered humiliating failure. And, as if to compound the process of
delegitimatization, in August 2008 American democracy made a mockery
of itself too. As the world faced a financial crisis of global proportions, the
Republicans chose as John McCain's vice presidential running mate the
patently unqualified governor of Alaska, Sarah Palin, whose childlike per-
ception of international affairs made her the laughingstock of the world.
And the worst of it was that a large part of the American electorate didn't
get the joke. They loved Palin.[9] After years of talk about overthrowing Arab
dictators, global opinion was beginning to wonder whose regime it was that

was changing. As Bush the younger left the stage, the post–cold war order that his father had crafted was crumbling all around him.

Only weeks before the General Assembly opened in New York, the world had been given two demonstrations of the reality of multipolarity. On the one hand, China's staggering Olympic display put to shame anything ever seen in the West, notably the dismal Atlanta games of 1996, which had been interrupted, it is worth recalling, by a pipe bombing perpetrated by an alt-right fanatic.[10] If bread and circuses are the foundation of popular legitimacy, the Chinese regime, bolstered by its booming economy, was putting on quite the show. Meanwhile, as the fireworks flared in Beijing, the Russia military had meted out to Georgia, a tiny aspirant to NATO membership, a severe punishment beating.[11] Sarkozy came to New York fresh from cease-fire talks on Europe's eastern border. It was to be the first of a series of more or less open clashes between Russia and the West that would culminate in the violent dismemberment of Ukraine, another aspiring NATO member, and feverish speculation about Russia's subversion of America's 2016 presidential election.

The financial crisis of 2008 appeared as one more sign of America's fading dominance. And that perspective is all too easily confirmed, when we return to the crisis from the distance of a decade, in the wake of the election of Donald Trump, the heir to Palin, as president. It is hard now to read the UN speeches in 2008 and their critique of American unilateralism without Trump's truculent inaugural of January 20, 2017, ringing in one's ears. On that overcast Friday, from the steps of the Capitol, the forty-fifth president summoned the image of America in crisis, its cities in disorder, its international standing in decline. This "carnage," he declared, must end. How? Trump's answer boomed out: He and his followers, that day, were issuing a "decree, to be heard in every city, in every foreign capital, and in every hall of power. From this day forward, a new vision will govern our land. From this day forward, it's going to be only America first, America first . . ."[12] If America was indeed suffering a profound crisis, if it was no longer supreme, if it needed to be made "great again," truths that for Trump were self-evident, then it would at least "decree" its own terms of engagement. This was the answer that the right wing in American politics would give to the challenges of the twenty-first century.

The events of 2003, 2008 and 2017 are all no doubt defining moments of recent international history. But what is the relationship among them? What is the relationship of the economic crisis of 2008 to the geopolitical disaster of 2003 and to America's political crisis following the election of November 2016? What arc of historical transition do those three points stake out? What does that arc mean for Europe, for Asia? How does it relate to the minor but no less shattering trajectory traced by the United Kingdom from Iraq to the crisis of the City of London in 2008 and Brexit in 2016?

The contention of this book is that the speakers at the UN in September 2008 were right. The financial crisis and the economic, political and geopolitical responses to that crisis are essential to understanding the changing face of the world today. But to understand their significance we have to do two things. We have to place the banking crisis in its wider political and geopolitical context. And, at the same time, we have to get inside its inner workings. We have to do what the UN General Assembly in September 2008 could not do. We have to grapple with the economics of the financial system. This is a necessarily technical and at times perhaps somewhat cold-hearted business. There is a chilly remoteness to much of the material that this book will be dealing with. This is a choice. Tracing the inner workings of the Davos mind-set is not the only way to understand how power and money operated in the course of the crisis. One can try to reconstruct their logic from the boot prints they left on those they impacted or through the conformist and contradictory market-oriented culture that they molded.[13] But the necessary complement to those more tactile renderings is the kind of account offered here, which attempts to show how the circulation of power and money was understood to function—and not to function—from within And this particular black box is worth prizing open, because, as this book will show, the simple idea, the idea that was so prevalent in 2008, the idea that this was basically an American crisis, or even an Anglo-Saxon crisis, and as such a key moment in the demise of American unipolar power, is in fact deeply misleading.

Eagerly taken up by all sides—by Americans as well as commentators around the world—the idea of an "all-American crisis" obscures the reality of profound interconnection.[14] In so doing, it also misdirects criticism and righteous anger. In fact, the crisis was not merely American but global and,

above all, North Atlantic in its genesis. And in a contentious and problematic way it had the effect of recentering the world financial economy on the United States as the only state capable of meeting the challenge it posed.[15] That capacity is an effect of structure—the United States is the only state that can generate dollars. But it is also a matter of action, of policy choices— positive in the American case, disastrously negative in the case of Europe. Clarifying the scale of this interdependence and the ultimate dependence of the global financial system on the dollar is important not just for the sake of getting the history right. It matters also because it throws new light on the perilous situation created by the Trump administration's declaration of independence from an interconnected and multipolar world.

I

To view the crisis of 2008 as basically an American event was tempting because that is where it had begun. It also pleased people around the world to imagine that the hyperpower was getting its comeuppance. The fact that the City of London was imploding too added to the deliciousness of the moment. It was convenient for the Europeans to shift responsibility across the channel and then across the Atlantic. In fact, it was a script prepared ahead of time. As we will see in the first section of this book, economists inside and outside America critical of the Bush presidency, including many of the leading macroeconomists of our time, had prepared a disaster script. It revolved around America's twin deficits—its budget deficit and its trade deficit—and their implications for America's dependence on foreign borrowing. The debts run up by the Bush administration were the bomb that was expected to go off. And the idea of 2008 as a distinctively Anglo-American crisis received a backhanded confirmation eighteen months later when Europe experienced its own crisis, which appeared to follow a rather different script, centered on the politics and the constitution of the eurozone. Thus the historical narrative seemed to neatly arrange itself with a European crisis following an American crisis, each with its own distinct economic and political logic.

The contention of this book is that to view the 2008 crisis and its

aftermath chiefly through its impact on America is to fundamentally misunderstand and underestimate its economic and historical significance. Ground zero was America's housing market, for sure. Millions of American households were among those hit earliest and hardest. But that disaster was not the crisis that had been widely anticipated before 2008, namely, a crisis of the American state and its public finances. The risk of the Chinese-American meltdown, which so many feared, was contained. Instead, it was a financial crisis triggered by the humdrum market for American real estate that threatened the world economy. The crisis spilled far beyond America. It shook the financial systems of some of the most advanced economies in the world—the City of London, East Asia, Eastern Europe and Russia. And it went on doing so. Contrary to the narrative popular on both sides of the Atlantic, the eurozone crisis is not a separate and distinct event, but follows directly from the shock of 2008. The redescription of the crisis as one internal to the eurozone and centered on the politics of public debt was itself an act of politics. In the years after 2010, it would become the object of something akin to a transatlantic culture war in economic policy, a minefield that any history of the epoch must carefully navigate.

If mapping this misunderstanding, charting the global financial crisis outward from its hub in the North Atlantic and presenting the continuity between 2008 and 2012, is the first challenge of this book, the second is to account for the way in which states did and did not react to the turmoil. The impact of the crisis was uneven but global in its reach, and by the vigor of their reactions, emerging market governments spectacularly confirmed the reality of multipolarity. The emerging market crises of the 1990s—Mexico (1995); Korea, Thailand, Indonesia (1997); Russia (1998); and Argentina (2001)—had taught how easily state sovereignty could be lost. That lesson had been learned. After a decade of determined "self-strengthening" in 2008, none of the victims of the 1990s were forced to resort to the International Monetary Fund. China's response to the financial crisis it imported from the West was of world historic proportions, dramatically accelerating the shift in the global balance of economic activity toward East Asia.

One might be tempted to conclude that the crisis of globalization had brought a reaffirmation of the essential role of the nation-state and the emergence of a new kind of state capitalism. And that is an argument that

would gain ever greater force in the years that followed, as the political backlash set in.[16] But if we look closely not at the periphery but at the core of the 2008 crisis, it is clear that this diagnosis is partial at best. Among the emerging markets, the two that struggled most with the crisis of 2008 were Russia and South Korea. What they had in common apart from booming exports was deep financial integration with Europe and the United States. That would prove to be the key. What they experienced was not just a collapse in exports but a "sudden stop" in the funding of their banking sectors.[17] As a result, countries with trade surpluses and huge currency reserves—supposedly the essentials of national economic self-reliance—suffered acute currency crises. Writ spectacularly larger, this was also the story in the North Atlantic between Europe and the United States. Hidden below the radar and barely discussed in public, what threatened the stability of the North Atlantic economy in the fall of 2008 was a huge shortfall in dollar funding for Europe's oversized banks. And a shortfall in their case meant not tens of billions, or even hundreds of billions, but trillions of dollars. It was the opposite of the crisis that had been forecast. Not a dollar glut but an acute dollar-funding shortage. The dollar did not plunge, it rose.

If we are to grasp the dynamics of this unforecasted storm, we have to move beyond the familiar cognitive frame of macroeconomics that we inherited from the early twentieth century. Forged in the wake of World War I and World War II, the macroeconomic perspective on international economics is organized around nation-states, national productive systems and the trade imbalances they generate.[18] It is a view of the economy that will forever be identified with John Maynard Keynes. Predictably, the onset of the crisis in 2008 evoked memories of the 1930s and triggered calls for a return to "the master."[19] And Keynesian economics is, indeed, indispensable for grasping the dynamics of collapsing consumption and investment, the surge in unemployment and the options for monetary and fiscal policy after 2009.[20] But when it comes to analyzing the onset of financial crises in an age of deep globalization, the standard macroeconomic approach has its limits. In discussions of international trade it is now commonly accepted that it is no longer national economies that matter. What drives global trade are not the relationships between national economies but multinational corporations coordinating far-flung "value chains."[21] The same is true for the

global business of money. To understand the tensions within the global financial system that exploded in 2008 we have to move beyond Keynesian macroeconomics and its familiar apparatus of national economic statistics. As Hyun Song Shin, chief economist at the Bank for International Settlements and one of the foremost thinkers of the new breed of "macrofinance," has put it, we need to analyze the global economy not in terms of an "island model" of international economic interaction—national economy to national economy—but through the "interlocking matrix" of corporate balance sheets—bank to bank.[22] As both the global financial crisis of 2007–2009 and the crisis in the eurozone after 2010 would demonstrate, government deficits and current account imbalances are poor predictors of the force and speed with which modern financial crises can strike.[23] This can be grasped only if we focus on the shocking adjustments that can take place within this interlocking matrix of financial accounts. For all the pressure that classic "macroeconomic imbalances"—in budgets and trade—can exert, a modern global bank run moves far more money far more abruptly.[24]

What the Europeans, the Americans, the Russians and the South Koreans were experiencing in 2008 and the Europeans would experience again after 2010 was an implosion in interbank credit. As long as your financial sector was modestly proportioned, big national currency reserves could see you through. That is what saved Russia. But South Korea struggled, and in Europe, not only were there no reserves but the scale of the banks and their dollar-denominated business made any attempt at autarkic self-stabilization unthinkable. None of the leading central banks had gauged the risk ahead of time. They did not foresee how globalized finance might be interconnected with the American mortgage boom. The Fed and the Treasury misjudged the scale of the fallout from the bankruptcy of Lehman on September 15. Never before, not even in the 1930s, had such a large and interconnected system come so close to total implosion. But once the scale of the risk became evident, the US authorities scrambled. As we shall see in Part II, not only did the Europeans and Americans bail out their ailing banks at a national level. The US Federal Reserve engaged in a truly spectacular innovation. It established itself as liquidity provider of last resort to the global banking system. It provided dollars to all comers in New York, whether banks were American or not. Through so-called liquidity swap

lines, the Fed licensed a hand-picked group of core central banks to issue dollar credits on demand. In a huge burst of transatlantic activity, with the European Central Bank (ECB) in the lead, they pumped trillions of dollars into the European banking system.

This response was surprising not only because of its scale but also because it contradicted the conventional narrative of economic history since the 1970s. The decades prior to the crisis had been dominated by the idea of a "market revolution" and the rollback of state interventionism.[25] Government and regulation continued, of course, but they were delegated to "independent" agencies, emblematically the "independent central banks," whose job was to ensure discipline, regularity and predictability. Politics and discretionary action were the enemies of good governance. The balance of power was hardwired into the normality of the new regime of deflationary globalization, what Ben Bernanke euphemistically referred to as the "great moderation."[26] The question that hung over the dispensation of "neoliberalism" was whether the same rules applied to everyone or whether the truth was that there were rules for some and discretion for others.[27] The events of 2008 massively confirmed the suspicion raised by America's selective interventions in the emerging market crises of the 1990s and following the dot-com crisis of the early 2000s. In fact, neoliberalism's regime of restraint and discipline operated under a proviso. In the event of a major financial crisis that threatened "systemic" interests, it turned out that we lived in an age not of limited but of big government, of massive executive action, of interventionism that had more in common with military operations or emergency medicine than with law-bound governance. And this revealed an essential but disconcerting truth, the repression of which had shaped the entire development of economic policy since the 1970s. The foundations of the modern monetary system are irreducibly political.

No doubt all commodities have politics. But money and credit and the structure of finance piled on them are constituted by political power, social convention and law in a way that sneakers, smartphones and barrels of oil are not. At the apex of the modern monetary pyramid is fiat money.[28] Called into existence and sanctioned by states, it has no "backing" other than its status as legal tender. That uncanny fact became literally true for the first time in 1971–1973 with the collapse of the Bretton Woods system.

Under the Bretton Woods agreement of 1944, the dollar, as the anchor of the global monetary system, was tied to gold. This was itself, of course, no more than a convention. When it became too hard for the United States to live with—upholding it would have required deflation—on August 15, 1971, President Nixon abandoned it. This was a historic caesura. For the first time since the advent of money, no currency in the world any longer operated on a metallic standard. Potentially, this freed monetary policy, regulating the creation of money and credit as never before. But how much freedom would policy makers actually have after throwing off the "golden fetters"? The social and economic forces that had made the gold peg unsustainable even for the United States were powerful—at home the struggle for income shares in an increasingly affluent society, abroad the liberalization of offshore dollar trading in London in the 1960s. When those forces were unleashed in the 1970s without a monetary anchor, the result was to send inflation soaring toward 20 percent in the advanced economies, something unprecedented in peacetime. But rather than retreating from liberalization, by the early 1980s any restriction on global capital flows was lifted. It was precisely to tame the forces of indiscipline unleashed by the end of metallic money that the market revolution and the new neoliberal "logic of discipline" were inaugurated.[29] By the mid-1980s Fed chair Paul Volcker's dramatic campaign to raise interest rates had curbed inflation. The only prices going up in the age of the great moderation were those for shares and real estate. When that bubble burst in 2008, when the world faced not inflation but deflation, the key central banks threw off their self-imposed shackles. They would do whatever it took to prevent a collapse of credit. They would do whatever it took to keep the financial system afloat. And because the modern banking system is both global and based on dollars, that meant unprecedented transnational action by the American state.

The Fed's liquidity provision was spectacular. It was of historic and lasting significance. Among technical experts it is commonly agreed that the swap lines with which the Fed pumped dollars into the world economy were perhaps the decisive innovation of the crisis.[30] But in public discourse these actions have remained far below the radar. They have been displaced from discussion by controversies surrounding the bailouts of individual banks and subsequent waves of central bank intervention that went by the

name of quantitative easing. Even in the memoirs of Ben Bernanke, for instance, the transatlantic liquidity measures of 2008 receive little more than a passing mention by comparison with the fraught politics of the AIG takeover or mortgage credit relief.[31]

The technical and administrative complexities of the Fed's actions no doubt contribute to their obscurity. But the politics go beyond that. The bank bailouts of 2008 provoked long-running and bitter recrimination and for good reason. Hundreds of billions of taxpayer funds were put in play to rescue greedy banks. Some interventions yielded a return. Others did not. Many of the choices made in the course of the bailouts were highly contentious. In the United States they would exacerbate deep rifts within the Republican Party, with dramatic consequences eight years later. But the problem goes beyond individual decisions and party political programs to the way in which we think and talk about the structure of the modern economy. Indeed, it goes directly back to the analytical agenda of reimagining international economics, forced on us by the crisis and articulated by the proponents of the macrofinancial approach. In the familiar twentieth-century island model of international economic interaction, the basic units were national economies that traded with one another, ran trade surpluses and deficits and accumulated national claims and liabilities. Those entities were made familiar by economists, who gave them an empirical, everyday reality in statistics for unemployment, inflation and GDP. And around them an entire conception of national politics developed.[32] Good economic policy was what was good for GDP growth. Questions of distribution—the politics of "who whom?"—could be weighed up against the general interest in "growing the size of the cake." By contrast, the new macrofinancial economics, with its relentless focus on the "interlocking matrix" of corporate balance sheets, strips away all the comforting euphemisms. National economic aggregates are replaced by a focus on corporate balance sheets, where the real action in the financial system is. This is hugely illuminating. It gives economic policy a far greater grip. But it exposes something that is deeply indigestible in political terms. The financial system does not, in fact, consist of "national monetary flows." Nor is it made up of a mass of tiny, anonymous, microscopic firms—the ideal of "perfect competition" and the economic analogue to the individual citizen. The overwhelming majority of

private credit creation is done by a tight-knit corporate oligarchy—the key cells in Shin's interlocking matrix. At a global level twenty to thirty banks matter. Allowing for nationally significant banks, the number worldwide is perhaps a hundred big financial firms. Techniques for identifying and monitoring the so-called systemically important financial institutions (SIFI)—known as macroprudential supervision—are among the major governmental innovations of the crisis and its aftermath. Those banks and the people who run them are also among the key actors in the drama of this book.

The stark truth about Ben Bernanke's "historic" policy of global liquidity support was that it involved handing trillions of dollars in loans to that coterie of banks, their shareholders and their outrageously remunerated senior staff. Indeed, as we shall see, we can itemize precisely who got what. To compound the embarrassment, though the Fed is a national central bank, at least half the liquidity support it provided went to banks not headquartered in the United States, but located overwhelmingly in Europe. If in intellectual terms the crisis was a crisis of macroeconomics, if in practical terms it was a crisis of the conventional tools of monetary policy, it was by the same token a deep crisis of modern politics. However unprecedented and effective the Fed's actions might have been, even for those politicians whose support for globalization was unfailing, its practical implications were barely speakable. Though it is hardly a secret that we inhabit a world dominated by business oligopolies, during the crisis and its aftermath this reality and its implications for the priorities of government stood nakedly exposed. It is an unpalatable and explosive truth that democratic politics on both sides of the Atlantic has choked on.

II

It should not be surprising, given what has been said, that the Europeans were only too happy to forget the entanglement of their global banks in the transatlantic crisis. In 2008 the British had their own national catastrophe to digest. In the eurozone, led by France and Germany, the 2008 financial crisis has vanished down a memory hole, closed over by the "sovereign debt crisis" of 2010 and after.[33] There is no appetite for acknowledging the

dependence on the US Federal Reserve and little sense of obligation or deference either. In this respect too the Americans have lost their authority. The Europeans all too easily dismissed the American crisis fighting of 2008–2009 as yet another instance of the kind of improvisation and indiscipline that had got the world into trouble in the first place. It became the first stage in a transatlantic culture war over economic policy that culminated in the acrimonious debate about the crisis of the eurozone, which takes center stage in Part III of this book.

Given that they were essentially interrelated crises and that the first was much larger in scale and dramatic in speed, the contrast between the relatively effective containment of the global meltdown in 2008, described in Part II, and the spiraling disaster of the eurozone, narrated in Part III, is painful. Around Greek debt the Europeans constructed their own crisis with its own narrative. It had the politics of sovereign debt at its heart. But, as senior economic officials of the EU will now publicly admit, this had no basis in economics.[34] The sustainability of public debts may be a problem in the long term. Greece was insolvent. But excessive public debt was not the common denominator of the wider eurozone crisis. The common denominator was the dangerous fragility of an overleveraged financial system, excessively reliant on short-term market-based funding. The eurozone crisis was a massive aftershock of the earthquake in the North Atlantic financial system of 2008, working its way out with a time lag through the labyrinthine political framework of the EU.[35] As one leading EU expert closely associated with the EU's bailout programs has put it: "If we had taken the banks under central supervision then already [in 2008], we would have solved the problem at a stroke."[36] Instead the eurozone crisis expanded into a doom loop of private and public credit and a crisis of the European project as such.

How do we account for the strange morphing of a crisis of lenders in 2008 into a crisis of borrowers after 2010? It is hard not to suspect sleight of hand. While Europe's taxpayers were put through the mill, the banks and other lenders got paid out of money pumped into the bailout countries. It is a short step from there to concluding that the hidden logic of the eurozone crisis after 2010 was a repetition of the 2008 bank bailouts, but this time in disguise. For one sharp-tongued critic it was the greatest "bait and switch" in history.[37] But the puzzle is that if this were so, if what was happening in

the eurozone was a veiled rerun of 2008, then at least one might have expected to have seen American-style outcomes. As its protagonists were well aware, America's crisis fighting exhibited massive inequity.[38] People on welfare scraped by while bankers carried on their well-upholstered lives. But though the distribution of costs and benefits was outrageous, at least America's crisis management worked. Since 2009 the US economy has grown continuously and, at least by the standards set by official statistics, it is now approaching full employment. By contrast, the eurozone, through willful policy choices, drove tens of millions of its citizens into the depths of a 1930s-style depression. It was one of the worst self-inflicted economic disasters on record. That tiny Greece, with an economy that amounts to 1–1.5 percent of EU GDP, should have been made the pivot for this disaster twists European history into the image of bitter caricature.

It is a spectacle that ought to inspire outrage. Millions have suffered for no good reason. But for all our indignation we should give that point its full weight. The crucial words are "for no good reason."[39] In the response to the financial crisis of 2008–2009 there was a clear logic operating. It was a class logic, admittedly—"Protect Wall Street first, worry about Main Street later"—but at least it had a rationale and one operating on a grand scale. To impute that same logic to the management of the eurozone is to give Europe's leaders too much credit. The story told here is not that of a successful political conjuring trick, in which EU elites neatly veiled their efforts to protect the interests of European big business. The story told here is of a train wreck, a shambles of conflicting visions, a dispiriting drama of missed opportunities, of failures of leadership and failures of collective action. If there are groups that benefited—a few bondholders who got paid, a bank that escaped painful restructuring—it was on a small scale, totally out of proportion to the enormous costs inflicted. This is not to say that the individual actors in the drama—Germany, France, the IMF—lacked logic. But they had to act together and the collective result was a disaster. They inflicted social and political harm from which the project of the EU may never recover. But amid the outrage this shambles should inspire, we are apt to forget another of its long-term consequences. The botched management of the eurozone crisis coming on the heels of the transatlantic financial crisis of 2008–2009 was damaging not only for millions of Europe's citizens. It had dramatic

consequences for European business too, on whom willy-nilly those same people rely for jobs and wages.

Far from being beneficiaries of EU crisis management, business was one of its casualties, and the European banks above all. Since 2008, it is not just the rise of Asia that is shifting the global corporate hierarchy. It is the decline of Europe.[40] This might ring oddly to Europeans used to hearing boasts of Germany's trade surplus. But as Germany's own most perceptive economists point out, those surpluses are as much the result of repressed imports as of roaring export success.[41] The inexorable slide of corporate Europe down the global rankings is clear for all to see. Though we might wish otherwise, the world economy is not run by medium-sized "Mittelstand" entrepreneurs but by a few thousand massive corporations, with interlocking shareholdings controlled by a tiny group of asset managers. In that battlefield of corporate competition, the crises of 2008–2013 brought European capital a historic defeat. No doubt there are many factors contributing to this, but a crucial one is the condition of Europe's own economy. Exports matter, but, as both China and the United States demonstrate, there is no substitute for a profitable home market. If we take the cynical view that the basic mission of the eurozone was not to serve its citizens but to provide European capital with a field for profitable domestic accumulation, then the conclusion is inescapable: Between 2010 and 2013 it failed spectacularly. And not first and foremost as a result of missing eurozone institutions, but as a result of choices made by business leaders, dogmatic central bankers and conservatively minded politicians.

Of course, we may not welcome a world organized this way. Europeans may warm to the spectacle of the European Commission as a consumer champion taking on global monopolists like Google and challenging Apple's tax evasion.[42] But the fines levied on Silicon Valley are a tiny portion of those firms' cash hoards. A rather different vision of the balance of power is suggested by those moments in 2016 when the financial world waited with bated breath to learn the size of the settlement that the US Department of Justice was going to impose on Deutsche Bank for mortgage fraud. Deutsche's financial condition was understood to be so fragile that the US authorities held its fate in their hands.[43] A bank that for more than a century had been a powerhouse of Germany Inc. was at the mercy of the United

States. In the wake of the crisis it was the last European investment bank with any global standing.

Europeans may wish to opt out of the global battle for corporate domination. They may even hope that they may thus achieve a greater degree of freedom for democratic politics. But the risk is that their growing reliance on other people's technology, the relative stagnation of the eurozone and the consequent dependence of Europe's growth model on exports to other people's markets will render those pretensions to autonomy quite empty. Rather than an autonomous actor, Europe risks becoming the object of other people's capitalist corporatism. Indeed, as far as international finance is concerned, the die has already been cast. In the wake of the double crisis, Europe is out of the race. The future will be decided between the survivors of the crisis in the United States and the newcomers of Asia.[44] They may choose to locate in the City of London, but after Brexit even that cannot be taken for granted. Wall Street, Hong Kong and Shanghai may simply bypass Europe.

If this were simply a drama of Europe's self-inflicted wounds, it would be bad enough. But to write the history of the eurozone crisis as simply European would be barely less misleading than writing the history of 2008 as all-American. In fact, the eurozone crisis spilled over, repeatedly. At least three times—in the spring of 2010, in the fall of 2011 and then again in the summer of 2012—the eurozone was on the brink of a disorderly breakup with the distinct possibility of the sovereign debt crisis sucking in trillions of dollars of public debt. The idea that Germany or any other country would have been immune was fatuous. The resulting inversion of the fronts was spectacular. In 2008 it had been the worldly Europeans calling on the out-of-touch Bush administration to recognize the reality of globalism. Eighteen months later it was the centrist liberals of the Obama administration pleading for the eurozone to stabilize its financial system in the face of dogged and unheeding resistance from conservatives in Berlin and Frankfurt. Already in April 2010, in the judgment of the rest of the G20 and far beyond, the eurozone crisis was too dangerous and the Europeans too incompetent for them to be left to sort out their own affairs. To prevent Greece from becoming "another Lehman," the Americans mobilized the IMF, that quintessential creation of mid-twentieth-century globalism, to

rescue twenty-first-century Europe. That rescue in May 2010 stopped a further escalation, but it locked Europe, the IMF and the United States as an accessory into a nightmarish entanglement from which they still had not extricated themselves seven years later. Nor did it staunch the panic in bond markets. As late as the summer of 2012 the prospect of a major European sovereign debt crisis threatened the United States and the rest of the world economy. It was not until July 2012, with insistent urging from Washington and the rest of G20, that Europe stabilized, and it did so by means of what was generally taken to be the belated "Americanization" of the ECB.[45]

III

If one stopped the clock in the fall of 2012, the difference to the scene four years earlier in New York would have been remarkable. Despite the unpromising start, it would have been churlish to deny that American corporate liberalism, as embodied by the Obama administration, had prevailed once again. Indeed, even today, our sense that the financial crisis had an ending, that at some point in the not too distant past something like normality was restored, depends on looking back to the fall of 2012. At that point the acute threat of a comprehensive crisis was ended. And a sign of that restored normality was the fact that America had not been dethroned. Obama's reelection in November 2012 clinched it. The Palin tendency had been stopped in its tracks. Internationally, the emerging markets were booming, helped along by the Fed's generous supply of dollars. The EU was playing catch-up. Whereas in 2008 Obama had put distance between himself and the Bush-Cheney years by adopting a tone of modesty and caution, in 2012 he resumed a classic exceptionalist narrative. America was "indispensable." The phrase coined in the Clinton era had a new lease on life.[46] There was a revival in big-picture foreign policy thinking. The new frontier was the "trade" treaties of TTIP and TPP, in reality gigantic projects of commercial, financial, technical and legal integration with geopolitical intent. Insofar as the first Obama term had been disappointing, this could be laid at the door of conservative opposition. That was depressing but predictable. Modernity and the global capitalism that gave

it so much of its dynamic are demanding pacesetters; foot-dragging from conservatives is only to be expected. But in the end history moves on. Even in Europe, pragmatic managerialism in the end prevailed over conservative dogma.

If we are to understand the last ten years historically, we have to take this moment of renewed complacency seriously. Given subsequent events, our retrospective view is easily clouded by a combination of rage, indignation and fear. But at the time the sense of self-confidence restored was real enough and it left an intellectual legacy. It was the moment when the first surveys of the crisis began to be written. The most optimistic insisted that *The System Worked*.[47] Another declared that 2008 had turned out to be *The Status Quo Crisis*.[48] The more pessimistic version argued that we lived in a *Hall of Mirrors*.[49] Precisely because the crisis had been contained so early and effectively, it had produced a false sense of stability. That in turn had sapped the energy necessary for fundamental reform. And this meant that there was an acute risk of repetition. But repetition is not the same as continuation or extension. What all of these narratives took for granted—both the more and the less pessimistic versions—was the fact that the 2008–2012 crisis was over. That was also the basis on which this book was begun. It was intended to be an anniversary retrospect on a crisis that had reached closure. The tasks that seemed urgent in 2013 were to explain the interconnected history of Wall Street and the eurozone crisis, to do justice to the transnational quality of the crisis—its effects across Eastern and Western Europe and Asia—to highlight the indispensable role of the United States in anchoring the response to the crisis and the novel tools that the Fed had deployed, to chart the painful and protracted inadequacy of the European response and to cast light on an intense but underappreciated period of transatlantic financial diplomacy. All of that is still worth doing. But it has now taken on a new and more ominous meaning. Because it is only if we get to grips with the inner workings of the dollar-based financial system and its fragility that we can understand the risks that lurk in the situation of 2017. If Trump's presidency marks the nadir of American political authority, that is all the more troubling given the deep functional dependence on the United States revealed not only by 2008 but by the eurozone crisis as well.

What we have to reckon with now is that, contrary to the basic assumption of 2012–2013, the crisis was not in fact over. What we face is not repetition but mutation and metastasis. As Part IV of this book will chart, the financial and economic crisis of 2007–2012 morphed between 2013 and 2017 into a comprehensive political and geopolitical crisis of the post–cold war order. And the obvious political implication should not be dodged. Conservatism might have been disastrous as a crisis-fighting doctrine, but events since 2012 suggest that the triumph of centrist liberalism was false too.[50] As the remarkable escalation of the debate about inequality in the United States has starkly exposed, centrist liberals struggle to give convincing answers for the long-term problems of modern capitalist democracy. The crisis added to those preexisting tensions of increasing inequality and disenfranchisement, and the dramatic crisis-fighting measures adopted since 2008, for all their short-term effectiveness, have their own, negative side effects. On that score the conservatives were right. Meanwhile, the geopolitical challenges thrown up, not by the violent turmoil of the Middle East or "Slavic" backwardness but by the successful advance of globalization, have not gone away. They have intensified. And though the "Western alliance" is still in being, it is increasingly uncoordinated. In 2014 Japan lurched toward confrontation with China. And the EU—the colossus that "does not do geopolitics"—"sleepwalked" into conflict with Russia over Ukraine. Meanwhile, in the wake of the botched handling of the eurozone crisis, Europe witnessed a dramatic mobilization on both Left and Right. But rather than being taken as an expression of the vitality of European democracy in the face of deplorable governmental failure, however disagreeable that expression may in some cases be, the new politics of the postcrisis period were demonized as "populism," tarred with the brush of the 1930s or attributed to the malign influence of Russia. The forces of the status quo gathered in the Eurogroup set out to contain and then to neutralize the left-wing governments elected in Greece and Portugal in 2015. Backed up by the newly enhanced powers of the fully activated ECB, this left no doubt about the robustness of the eurozone. All the more pressing were the questions about the limits of democracy in the EU and its lopsidedness. Against the Left, preying on its reasonableness, the brutal tactics of

containment did their job. Against the Right they did not, as Brexit, Poland and Hungary were to prove.

IV

Distance in time, historians like to tell themselves, is a tonic. It permits the detachment and sense of perspective that are commonly touted as virtues of the discipline. But that depends on where time takes you. History writing does not escape the history it attempts to reconstruct. The more pertinent question to ask is not how much time must pass before history can be written, but what has happened in the interim and what, at the time of writing, is expected to happen next. This book, for one, would have been easier to write and might be clearer in its conclusions if it had been finished even closer to the time of the events it begins by describing. It may be easier to write a book like this ten years from now, though given the current train of events, that may be unduly optimistic. Certainly, the tenth anniversary of 2008 is not a comfortable vantage point for a Left-liberal historian whose personal loyalties are divided among England, Germany, the "Island of Manhattan" and the EU. Things could be worse, of course. A ten-year anniversary of 1929 would have been published in 1939. We are not there, at least not yet. But this is undoubtedly a moment more uncomfortable and disconcerting than could have been imagined before the crisis began.

Among the many symptoms of unease and crisis that have afflicted us in the wake of Donald Trump's victory is the extraordinary uncouth variety of postfactual politics that he personifies. He doesn't tell the truth. He doesn't make sense. He doesn't speak coherently. Power appears to have become unmoored from the basic values of reason, logical consistency and factual evidence. What has caused this degeneration? One can cite a complex of factors. Certainly unscrupulous political demagoguery, the debasement of popular culture and the self-enclosed world of cable TV and social media are part of the problem, as is Trump's personality. But to attribute our current state of postfactuality to Trump and his cohorts is to succumb only to further delusion.[51] As this book will show, what the history of the

crisis demonstrates are truly deep-seated and persistent difficulties in dealing "factually" with our current situation. It isn't just those denounced as populists who have a problem with truth. It goes far wider and far deeper and it affects the center as much as the margins of mainstream politics. We do not need to go back to the notoriously misleading and incoherent case made for the war against Iraq and its fawning media coverage. It was the current president of the European Commission who announced in the spring of 2011: "When it becomes serious, you have to lie."[52] At least, one might say, he knows what he's doing. If we believe Jean-Claude Juncker, a posttruth approach to public discourse is simply what the governance of capitalism currently demands.

The loss of credibility is flagrant and it is comprehensive. The damage goes deep. To say that liberals should simply "pick yourself up, dust yourself off, and start all over again," as the Depression-era song goes, that if America has failed we should look for leadership to a fresh-faced president of France or the relentlessly reliable chancellor of Germany, is either simpleminded or disingenuous. It does no justice to the scale of the disasters since 2008, or to the failure of the lopsided politics prevailing in both Europe and America to offer an adequate response to the crisis. It does no justice to the extent of our political impasse, with the center and the Right having failed and the Left massively obstructed and self-obstructing. Nor does it acknowledge that some losses are irreparable and that sometimes the appropriate response is not just to keep on going but, instead, to linger for a while, to pick over the ruin of our expectations, to tally up the broken identifications and disillusionments. There is a certain immobility in such an effort at reconstruction. But even as we look back, we can rely on the restless dynamic of global capitalism to force us onward. It is already tugging. As we shall see in the final chapter, the next moments of economic challenge and crisis are already upon us, not in America or in Europe but in Asia and the emerging markets. Looking back is not an act of refusal. It is simply a contribution to the necessary collective effort of coming to terms with the past, of figuring out what went wrong. To do that there is no substitute for digging into the workings of the financial machine. It is there that we will find both the mechanism that tore the world apart and the reason why that disintegration came as such a surprise.

Part I

GATHERING STORM

Chapter 1

THE "WRONG CRISIS"

O n April 5, 2006, the youthful junior senator from Illinois, Barack
Obama, took time out from discussion of an India nuclear deal on
Capitol Hill to attend the opening of a new think tank project at
Brookings.[1] The Brookings Institution is widely regarded as the most influ-
ential social science research center in the world. Obama's Brookings ap-
pearance was an audition that would define his presidency.[2] The keynote
he delivered was for a new initiative—the Hamilton Project—launched by
Robert Rubin, one of the kingmakers of the Democratic Party. Rubin per-
sonified the link forged in the 1990s between centrist Democrats and glob-
ally minded bankers that reshaped the American economic policy agenda.
In 1993 Rubin had moved from his position at the top of Wall Street, as
cochairman at Goldman Sachs, to serve as the first head of the National
Economic Council, which Bill Clinton had called into existence as a coun-
terpart to the National Security Council. Two years later Rubin was ap-
pointed Treasury secretary. Alongside Rubin presiding over the Brookings
meeting in April 2006 was a youthful economist by the name of Peter
Orszag, also a veteran of the Clinton administration, who would go on to
become Obama's budget director. It was from among the veterans of Ru-
bin's Treasury that Obama would recruit virtually his entire economics
team in 2008. Twelve months ahead of the financial crisis, two and a half
years before Obama took office, the launch of the Hamilton Project presents

the worldview of some of his most influential advisers in microcosm. It reveals both what they could see and what they could not.

I

Having returned to the business world in 1999, Rubin was worried about the drift in Washington. Globalization had been the central challenge of the 1990s. In the new millennium it was even more so. But two years into President Bush's second term, the policies of the Republican administration were putting America at risk. Rather than mitigating the pressures of global competition, they were dividing American society. This risked provoking both an antiglobalization backlash and a catastrophic financial crisis that would call into question America's monetary stability and the global standing of the dollar.

Not that Rubin and his circle were doing badly out of a world of globalization. After the Treasury, Rubin had retired to an influential sinecure as a nonexecutive chairman of the board at Citigroup. Orszag, who started his career bouncing back and forth among academia, government and consulting, would in due course end up at Citigroup too. But for average Americans the story was different. There had been good moments. The Clintonites still celebrated the 1990s and the twin booms of tech and Wall Street. But since the 1970s wages had not kept up with productivity. For the meritocrats of the Hamilton Project it was clear where the finger of blame pointed. America's schools were failing to give its young people the education essential to stay ahead of the game. The first reports issued by the Hamilton Project bristled with proposals to improve the recruitment of teachers and make better use of kids' summer vacations.[3] It was the kind of nuts-and-bolts, "evidence-based," nonideological approach to productivity improvement that dominated economic policy discussion of the era. Its purpose, however, was eminently political. As Obama put it in his keynote:

"When you invest in education and health care and benefits for working Americans, it pays dividends throughout every level of our economy. . . . I think that if you polled many of the people in this room, most of us are strong free traders and most of us believe in markets. Bob [Rubin] and I

have had a running debate now for about a year about how do we, in fact, deal with the losers in a globalized economy. There has been a tendency in the past for us to say, well, look, we have got to grow the pie, and we will retrain those who need retraining. But, in fact, we have never taken that side of the equation as seriously as we need to take it. . . . Just remember . . . [t]here are people in places like Decatur, Illinois, or Galesburg, Illinois, who have seen their jobs eliminated. They have lost their health care. They have lost their retirement security. . . . They believe that this may be the first generation in which their children do worse than they do."[4]

This was a betrayal of the American Dream of endless uplift, and that risked spilling over into a political backlash. As Obama put it: "Some of that, then, will end up manifesting itself in the sort of nativist sentiment, protectionism, and anti-immigration sentiment that we are debating here in Washington. So there are real consequences to the work that is being done here. This is not a bloodless process."[5]

Amid the fears about globalization and the risk of populist revolt already evident in 2006, there was one note of economic nationalism that Obama himself was not afraid to strike: "When you keep the deficit low and our debt out of the hands of foreign nations, then we can all win." Alongside global competitiveness, the other preoccupation that defined the Hamilton team was the question of debt.

As Clinton's Treasury secretary, Robert Rubin's great boast was to have turned the deficits of the Reagan era into substantial budget surpluses. Since then under the Republicans, America was headed fast in the wrong direction. In June 2001, in the wake of the dot-com bust and a disputed election, the Bush administration had delivered a tax cut estimated to cost the federal government $1.35 trillion over ten years.[6] This paid off key constituencies, but it also wiped out Rubin's surpluses and it did so deliberately. The Republicans had convinced themselves that surpluses tended to encourage more government spending. Their approach was the obverse, what Republican strategists of the Reagan era first dubbed "starving the beast."[7] By entrenching tax cuts and courting a fiscal crisis they would create an irresistible imperative to slash spending, curb entitlements to social welfare and shrink the footprint of government.

The problem was that the spending cuts that were supposed to follow

the tax cuts never happened. The terrorist attack of September 11, 2001, put America on a war footing. The Bush administration responded with a huge surge in defense and security spending. In a manner horribly reminiscent of Vietnam, it then plunged America into the Iraq quagmire. In 2006, as the Hamilton group met, Iraq was on the edge of a bloody sectarian civil war. The question now was how to get out. Iraq was not only demoralizing and humiliating. It was also hugely expensive. The Bush administration did its best to keep the costs of the war off the regular budget. So a cottage industry of Democratic Party experts set itself to doing the sums. By 2008 the bill for Afghanistan and Iraq alone was at least $904 billion. Less conservative estimates put the bill as high as $3 trillion. It was certainly more than the United States had spent on any war since World War II.[8]

Of course it could have been paid for.[9] America was far richer than it was at the time of Pearl Harbor. But the Bush administration was not only not going to reverse its tax cuts; in May 2003 it doubled down, introducing a further round of tax relief. Given that the military budget was sacrosanct and the rest of discretionary expenditure was not large enough to make a difference, the Republicans proposed to close the gap with grossly inequitable cuts

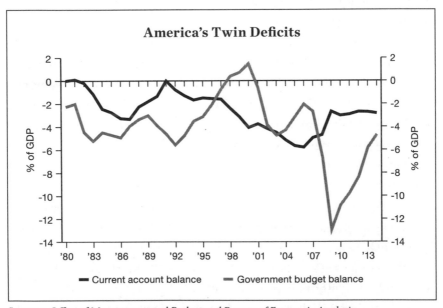

Sources: Office of Management and Budget and Bureau of Economic Analysis.

to welfare "entitlements." Those, however, could not pass the Senate, where the Republican majority was wafer thin and "moderates" held the balance. It was this logjam that turned Rubin's budget surplus of $86.4 billion in 2000 into a record deficit of $568 billion in 2004 with no end in sight.[10]

The original inspiration for the Hamilton Project was a paper written in 2004 by Orszag and Rubin sounding the alarm.[11] First, the Bush deficits would drive up interest rates and squeeze private investment. Further down the line lurked a far more serious scenario. "Substantial deficits projected far into the future can cause a fundamental shift in market expectations and a related loss of confidence both at home and abroad," Rubin and Orszag drily remarked. "The unfavorable dynamic effects that could ensue are largely if not entirely excluded from the conventional analysis of budget deficits. This omission is understandable and appropriate in the context of deficits that are small and temporary; it is increasingly untenable, however, in an environment with deficits that are large and permanent. Substantial ongoing deficits may severely and adversely affect expectations and confidence, which in turn can generate a self-reinforcing negative cycle among the underlying fiscal deficit, financial markets, and the real economy." Conventional analysis, in short, was not sufficiently alarmist. What it did not "seriously entertain" was the possibility that America was headed toward "fiscal or financial disarray."

Veterans of the Clinton administration knew what they were talking about when they invoked a "negative cycle" of "underlying fiscal deficit, financial markets, and the real economy." This, in their view, is what they had inherited from the high-spending Reagan and Bush administrations. In 1993, faced with a bond market sell, Clinton had shelved ambitious plans for a stimulus[12] Egged on by Rubin and Fed chair Alan Greenspan, deficit reduction became a mantra of the Clinton team. Chief political adviser James Carville was left to ruminate: "I used to think if there was reincarnation, I wanted to come back as the president or the pope or a .400 baseball hitter. But now I want to come back as the bond market. You can intimidate everybody."[13]

In the 1980s and 1990s, the so-called bond vigilantes had their day in the sun. Ten years later they were still in the market. Indeed, the bond funds were bigger than ever. But, as Obama had hinted, domestic investors

were not what most worried the Rubinite crowd. Foreign investors were the key concern. The Bush administration's deficits were financed overwhelmingly by bond buying from abroad. As Orszag and Rubin's paper remarked, United States Treasurys were still seen as the safest investment in the world. There was no chance of default or a sudden burst of inflation. "But if that expectation were to change and investors had difficulty seeing how the policy process could avoid extreme steps, the consequences could be much more severe than traditional estimates suggest." Nor was it just the Clinton crowd that worried. In 2003 the nonpartisan Congressional Budget Office saw fit to remind its audience of an extreme scenario in which foreign investors stopped buying US securities, the dollar plunged and interest rates and inflation shot up. "Amid the anticipation of declining profits and rising inflation and interest rates, stock markets could collapse and consumers might suddenly reduce their consumption. Moreover, economic problems in the United States could spill over to the rest of the world and seriously weaken the economies of US trading partners."[14]

The scale of America's deficits made it vulnerable to bond market pressure. The fact that foreign investors might suddenly turn away from Treasurys evoked the nightmare of a sudden stop to external financing of America's imbalances. But it was the identity of the foreign investors that infused the scenario with real terror. Until the 1980s the major foreign investors in the United States had been European. Then Japan, with its giant trade surpluses, had taken over. Still, in the new century it was one of America's largest creditors. But in the 1990s, with a surging yen and a domestic economy crippled by a devastating real estate bust, Japan's competitive threat had faded. Since the millennium, globalization had acquired a new Asian face. In April 2006, when Obama spoke about keeping our "debt out of the hands of foreign nations," everyone knew it was China and its Communist regime that he was talking about.

II

Since the 1970s China had been a cornerstone of US geopolitics. Nixon and Kissinger had unhinged the fronts of the cold war by breaking China out of

the Soviet embrace. Now the Soviet Union had faded from view, and the European theater of the cold war had faded along with it. The Pacific was the new horizon of American power and China the future rival. For the first time since the rise of Nazi Germany, the United States faced a power that was, at one and the same time, a potential geopolitical competitor, a hostile political regime type and a capitalist economic success story. The fact that Obama came to the Brookings meeting from talks about a nuclear deal with India was a telling coincidence. America was looking for new allies in Asia. But what mattered more than nukes, at least as far as the Hamilton crowd was concerned, was economics.

The Clinton administration had midwifed China into globalization. In November 1995, Washington encouraged Beijing's application to join the newly founded World Trade Organization (WTO). America had done this before, of course, with Western Europe after 1945, with Japan and East Asia in the 1950s and 1960s and with Eastern Europe in the 1990s. Opening markets was good for American business, for American investors and for American consumers. America's economic interests were so widespread that they were de facto identical with global capitalism.[15] By the mid-1990s Washington had abandoned any frontal challenge to the Chinese Communist regime over human rights, the rule of law or democracy. Instead, globalists of both the Democratic and Republican parties wagered that the powerful and impersonal force of commercial integration would in due time make China into a biddable and congenial "stakeholder" in the world order.[16]

China's growth was spectacular. Huge profits were to be made for American investors. American manufacturers like GM would stake their future on China.[17] After a brief storm over the Taiwan Strait in 1995–1996, diplomatic relations calmed. But China's sheer size made it a contender. With the Tiananmen crackdown of 1989, the Communist Party had signaled its intent not to abandon its one-party leadership. Since then it had fashioned a popular ideology that was as much nationalist as Communist.[18] If Washington was betting on international trade and globalization to "Westernize" China, the Chinese Communist Party took the other side of the bet.[19] The party's leaders wagered that supercharged growth would not weaken them but would consolidate their position as the successful helmsmen of their nation's spectacular comeback. Beijing took advantage of trading opportunities.

But it never subscribed to fully open markets. It decided who would invest and on what terms. It controlled movement of funds in and out. That, in turn, allowed the People's Bank of China to fix its exchange rate, and since 1994 it had done so by pegging against the dollar.

In choosing a dollar peg, China was far from unique. Despite the reigning narrative of market liberalization, the financial world was not flat. The global monetary system was hierarchical with the key currency, the dollar, at the top of the pyramid.[20] The twenty-first century began with a network of dollar-linked currencies accounting for c. 65 percent of the world economy (weighted by GDP).[21] Those currencies that were not pegged to the dollar tended to be hooked to the euro. Often pegging was a sign of weakness. In many cases the exchange rate was set at an aspirational, overvalued rate. This created short-term advantages. It made imports cheap. Local oligarchs could snap up prestige foreign real estate at a discount. But it also harbored huge risk. The peg could break and frequently it would do so with a bang. The appearance of stability offered by a fixed exchange rate encouraged a large inflow of foreign funds, which helped to stoke up domestic economic activity, creating an unbalanced trade account funded from abroad. Banks that acted as the conduit for foreign funds boomed. This set up the crisis.[22] When international investors lost confidence, the result was a devastating sudden stop. Then the central bank's foreign exchange reserves would drain and it would have no option but to let the currency peg go. Stability would give way to a disastrous devaluation. Those who got their money out first would be saved. Those who had borrowed in foreign currency would face bankruptcy.

This was the saga of the 1990s: 1994 in Mexico; 1997 in Malaysia, South Korea, Indonesia and Thailand; 1998 in Russia; 1999 in Brazil. It was containing these crises that earned US Federal Reserve chairman Alan Greenspan, Treasury secretary Robert Rubin, and Larry Summers, Rubin's number two, the accolade of the "Committee to Save the World."[23] What happened when the American superheroes were not on hand was revealed in 2001. With the Bush administration fully distracted by the terror attack of 9/11, financial speculation built against Argentina. Despite a $22 billion loan from the IMF, without American backing the Argentinian position became untenable; 80 percent of Argentine private debt was in dollars, whereas only

25 percent of Argentina's economy was export oriented.[24] In December 2001, with dollars draining out of the country, the Argentine government suspended access to bank accounts. Amid rioting that claimed the lives of twenty-four people, the government collapsed. On December 24, 2001, Argentina announced the suspension of payments on $144 billion of public debt, including $93 billion owed to foreign creditors. The peso plunged in value from 1:1 to 3:1 against the dollar, bankrupting the dollar debtors. The economy reeled backward to levels not seen since the early 1980s. As the twenty-first century began, more than half of Argentina's population fell below the poverty line.[25]

China had no intention of becoming either the victim of a sudden stop or the needy recipient of US assistance.[26] To reverse the balance of risk, when Beijing pegged its exchange rate it chose one that was not too high, but too low. This was what Japan and Germany had done in the 1950s and 1960s.[27] It was a recipe for export-led growth, but it created tensions of its own. Undervaluing the currency made imports more expensive than they needed to be, which lowered the Chinese standard of living. When it ran a trade surplus with the United States and bought American government bonds, poor China was exporting capital to rich America, funding American consumers to buy the products of its huge new factories. Moreover, maintaining the artificially low peg was a battle in its own right. With China's trade surplus with the United States surging from $83 billion in 2000 to $227 billion in 2009, to hold the value of the yuan down the Chinese central bank had to continually buy dollars and sell its own currency. To do so it printed yuan. In the normal course of things this would have unleashed domestic inflation, wiping out any competitive advantage and triggering social unrest. So, to "sterilize" the effects of its own intervention, the People's Bank of China required all Chinese banks to hold large and growing precautionary reserves, effectively removing the currency from circulation. It was a profoundly unbalanced situation and one that could be sustained only because of the extremely tight relationship between the Chinese regime and the business elite, a relationship built on common affiliation to the Communist Party, coercion and mutual profit. Chinese businesses and their owners, the emerging oligarchs, profited spectacularly from a gigantic export-led development boom.[28] Chinese peasants and workers chased the dream of

urban prosperity. Meanwhile, Beijing's giant foreign currency reserves were
the best guarantee an uncertain global economy could offer that in case of
a crisis, it would not be China's sovereignty that was violated.

With so many currencies fixed against the dollar, without the possibil-
ity of adjusting export competitiveness by means of devaluation or appre-
ciation, it was no surprise that the world economy polarized into export
surplus and import deficit countries. In the first three months of 2005
alone, the United States ran a current account deficit—an excess of out-
ward payments on trade in goods and services and investment income—of
almost $200 billion. For the year it came to $792 billion and was showing
signs of further deterioration in 2006. For those on the surplus side of the
"global imbalances," so-called sovereign wealth funds (SWF) became huge
repositories of capital. According to estimates by the Peterson Institute for
International Economics in Washington, DC, by 2007 emerging market

China's Foreign Reserve Accumulation (in $ billions)

Legend:
- Bank deposits
- Treasury bills
- Treasury notes
- Agencies
- Corporate bonds
- Equities
- ··· Total Chinese foreign holdings (dollar and nondollar)
- — Total Chinese dollar holdings reported worldwide, of which the various colored lines are the breakdown

Note: Estimates adjusted for Belgian holdings and UK flows.

Source: Brad Setser, "How Many Treasuries Does China Still Own?," *Follow the Money* (blog),
Council on Foreign Relations, June 9, 2016, https://www.cfr.org/blog/how-many-treasuries-does
-china-still-own.

sovereign wealth funds held at least $2 trillion in assets, in addition to the trillions in reserves held by their central banks.[29] The Saudi Arabian Monetary Authority was flush with cash, as were the SWF of Norway and Singapore. Some SWF made adventurous investments in equities. China's State Administration of Foreign Exchange looked for safe and predictable returns. Its safe assets of choice were long-dated US government debt and securities guaranteed by the US government.

The imbalances were worrying, but, at least as far the surplus countries were concerned, they promised that the first shock in the case of an unwinding would be borne by the other side. It was the United States, the world's great deficit economy, that would see its currency devalue and its interest rates surge as foreign investors abandoned American assets. It was this scenario that caused Orszag, Rubin and Senator Obama such concern. Nor were they alone. In the prestigious house journal of the Council on Foreign Relations, *Foreign Affairs*, Peter G. Peterson, chairman of the council, the Institute of International Economics and the Blackstone Private Equity Group, raised the alarm about America's twin deficits.[30] Economists Nouriel Roubini and Brad Setser warned that if investors were to lose confidence, the United States could face a very sudden depreciation of the dollar and a massive hike in interest rates.[31] It might well turn out to be the worst recession experienced since World War II.[32] And America would not only be depressed. It would be humbled at the hands of the rising power of Asia. Of course, if the United States suffered a crisis, China would be hurt too.[33] Niall Ferguson and Moritz Schularick came up with the term "Chimerica" to describe the Sino-American economic complex.[34] For Larry Summers, who had moved from the Treasury to an ill-fated stint as president of Harvard, it reawakened memories of cold war–era mutually assured destruction. At the heart of the world economy, he told Washington audiences, was a "balance of financial terror."[35] The difference was that in the cold war the economy had been America's strong suit. Now America's trump card consisted of the hope that it was simply "too big" for China to let it fail. It was hardly a reassuring diagnosis.

III

To ease these imbalances, the obvious solution, as the Hamilton Project demanded, was fiscal restraint. Reduce the federal deficit, squeeze domestic demand, reduce the import of Chinese goods and Chinese money. But the Bush administration didn't seem to care. In 2004 former Treasury secretary Paul O'Neill, fired from the cabinet in 2002, released his revealing exposé of the early Bush administration. It contained a nugget that haunted the economic policy community. In November 2002 O'Neill tried to warn Vice President Dick Cheney that the surging "budget deficits . . . posed a threat to the economy." Only for Cheney to cut him off with the following remark: "You know . . . Reagan proved deficits don't matter." The Republicans had won the congressional midterms; tax cuts were the Republican "due." Within the month O'Neill was fired.[36] From the perspective of the Rubinite Democrats, this was not just economically illiterate, it was also a political scandal. Following in the footsteps of George Bush senior, they had spent agonizing years working off Reagan's deficits. If Cheney's version of Republicanism prevailed, it undermined the basis for turn taking in America's two-party system. How could the Democrats conduct responsible "national" economic policy if the Republicans viewed the economy as a resource to be milked for the benefit of its privileged constituency? As Brad DeLong, deputy assistant secretary for economic policy in the Clinton-era Treasury, ruefully remarked: "Rubin and us spear carriers moved heaven and earth to restore fiscal balance to the American government in order to raise the rate of economic growth. But what we turned out to have done . . . was to enable George W. Bush's right-wing class war: his push for greater after-tax income inequality."[37]

The question was pressing because following the momentous November 2006 midterms, control of the House and the Senate changed hands. In a turn of events that can only be described as fateful, it would be the Democrats who held power in Congress during the greatest crisis of American capitalism since the 1930s. But that was in the future. In 2006 the question was whether the Democrats, as the new power on Capitol Hill, should once again take responsibility for cutting the deficit. Many in the party, especially

those on the Left, were wondering why they should accept the burden.[38] As one centrist remarked: "On fiscal responsibility, it takes two to tango, and insofar as the GOP doesn't want to dance, Democrats can't afford to take sole responsibility."[39] Perhaps the best way to prevent another "wealth-polarizing offensive" by a Republican Congress would be to spend so much on public works, welfare and job creation that even a Republican would not consider adding tax cuts on top. As DeLong resignedly observed, the "surplus-creating fiscal policies established by Robert Rubin and company in the Clinton administration would have been very good for America had the Clinton administration been followed by a normal successor. But what is the right fiscal policy for a future Democratic administration to follow when there is no guarantee that any Republican successors will ever be 'normal' again?"[40]

Given this dilemma, the disaster scenarios invoked by Orszag and Rubin take on a different meaning. They were as much about controlling the agenda within the Democratic Party as about winning over Republicans. If all that was at stake in the struggle over the deficit was a percentage point of economic growth here or there, why should the Democrats not put their own partisan priorities first? But if what threatened was a Weimar-style disaster, then, surely, the left wing of the Democrats would fall into line and prioritize budget cutting.

Given the political impasse over fiscal policy and the evident imbalances of the US economy, the other agents that one might have expected to swing into action were the mighty guardians at the Federal Reserve Board. Under the chairmanship of first Paul Volcker (1979–1987) and then Alan Greenspan (1987–2006), the authority of America's central bank soared to new heights. In terms of its expert authority and unassailable position within the structure of the US government, it came to rival the US security apparatus.[41] The irony, however, was that as the Fed's reputation and authority grew, its key tool of policy seemed to be losing its effectiveness. The short-term interest rate set by the Fed no longer seemed to be setting the pace for the rest of the economy.

Following the dot-com crash Greenspan had cut rates to 3.5 percent. After the 9/11 attacks there were further cuts, reaching 1 percent in the summer of 2003. Then, from 2004 on, the Fed started raising rates. Faced

with America's trade deficit and its rapid domestic boom, this was the standard prescription. It should increase private saving and restrict investment.[42] But to the Fed's dismay, the results were feeble. Most strikingly, as the Fed hiked short-term rates, rates in long-term bond markets failed to respond. There were too many buyers of long-term bonds, driving prices up and yields down. Nor should this have been a surprise.[43] By fixing their currencies against the dollar, many of America's trading partners prevented not only a downward movement of the dollar, which might have restored America's competitiveness. They also prevented an appreciation of the American currency, which would normally have followed on an interest rate increase. Under de facto fixed exchange rates, an increase in the interest rates would not reduce the supply of credit. It had the opposite effect of making investment in the United States more attractive, drawing in a greater flow of foreign funds.

The Fed found itself boxed in between China's determination to peg its currency and the refusal of Congress to curb America's budget deficit. China's unbalanced growth path created an excess of savings that needed to be invested abroad. AAA-rated US Treasurys were the reserve asset of choice. As a newly appointed member of the Federal Reserve Board, one of the first contributions to the policy debate by the Princeton economist Ben Bernanke was to coin the term "global savings glut" to describe this situation in which the Fed's principal policy instrument lost its leverage on the economy.[44] The availability of foreign funding negated Fed efforts to raise interest rates. At the same time it reduced the pressure on Congress to tighten fiscal policy. As capital surged in, this pushed down US interest rates, stoking the domestic economic upswing and sucking in imports, above all from China. But barring a change of heart on the part of Congress or a general liberalization of exchange rates, there was little the Fed could do. This was the ambiguous inheritance that Bernanke stepped into on February 1, 2006, as he took up the baton of Fed chair.

Bernanke's placid and undersized persona would soon come to occupy an outsized space in global economic history. He would turn out to be an unusual but highly significant case of the possibility of "learning lessons from history." In November 2002 at a birthday celebration for Milton Friedman and Anna Schwartz, Friedman's coauthor in the monumental *Monetary*

History of the United States, the bible of monetarism, Bernanke promised: "I would like to say to Milton and Anna: Regarding the Great Depression. You're right, we did it. We're very sorry. But thanks to you, we won't do it again."[45] Given the association forged in the 1970s between monetarism and inflation fighting, one could easily confuse Bernanke's promise with a conventional central banker's commitment to price stability. Indeed, Bernanke *was* making a commitment to price stability, but what he was promising to prevent was deflation, not inflation. The lesson of the 1930s was that the Fed must act promptly not just to prevent the money supply expanding excessively but also to prevent bank failures from causing it to implode.[46] On Bernanke's watch there would be no deflation. That single-minded determination, embodied by the new Fed chair but shared across the US policy-making establishment, would define the response of monetary policy to the crisis. In the process Bernanke would redefine what a central bank can do as an agency of modern government. Given the weight of this hindsight, it is easy to forget how unremarkable his appointment seemed at the time. He was a safe pair of hands, no outsized ego, a reliable middle-of-the-road Republican. In policy terms he was known, above all, for his belief that the best way to perpetuate the era of the great moderation, in which both unemployment and inflation were fluctuating much less than ever before, was a rules-based approach to policy making he described as "constrained discretion."[47]

As an economist steeped in the disastrous history of the 1920s and 1930s gold-exchange standard, Bernanke knew all too well the perils of a lopsided fixed exchange rate system. He was profoundly critical of China's currency policy.[48] But relations among central bankers are polite. It was not for the Fed to lecture the Chinese on currency policy. The same rules did not apply to the US Treasury or to Congress. In the early 2000s dozens of bills began to move through Congress accusing China of being a currency manipulator in violation of WTO norms and demanding sanctions. It was those initiatives that raised fears in circles like the Hamilton Project about "populist protectionism." In July 2005, to relieve pressure on the US economy, China began to allow a slow currency appreciation. In due course this would bring about a 23 percent revaluation. But it was painfully slow.

To speed things up, some in Washington favored activating the IMF.

Why was the global monetary watchdog not calling on China to address its lopsided balance of payments? In September 2005, Treasury undersecretary Tim Adams remarked in a widely reported speech that the IMF appeared to be "asleep at the wheel."[49] But to promote the IMF as an arbiter had serious implications. China could not be expected to take advice from the IMF until it had representation on the IMF's board that was commensurate with its size. Furthermore, Beijing would expect IMF monitoring to apply to the United States as well. That wasn't likely to appeal to a Republican White House.[50] Barring market-driven adjustment or international supervision, the balance of "financial terror" was managed by means of summit diplomacy in the manner of the cold war. And it was no coincidence that as his last Treasury secretary President Bush chose Hank Paulson. Paulson, like Rubin, moved to the Treasury from the CEO job at Goldman Sachs. But apart from his investment banking credentials, what recommended Paulson for the job was his reputation as an old China hand. He liked to boast that since the Tiananmen Square massacre, he had visited China seventy times.[51] He had no particular fondness for multilateral institutions like the IMF. Instead he preferred bilateral dialogue—what some had taken to calling the "G2" format.[52] One of Paulson's first moves was to initiate a US-China Strategic Economic Dialogue and to take personal charge of the US side.[53]

IV

In the fall of 2007, even as quite a different crisis loomed on the horizon, it was the dollar that was still at the center of attention. The *Economist* warned of a "Dollar Panic."[54] Germany's *Spiegel* magazine announced a "Pearl Harbor without a war." Bill Gross, the kingpin at bond trading giant PIMCO, was reported to be selling dollar assets, as was billionaire investor Warren Buffett. In November 2007 Bloomberg reported that the world's highest-paid supermodel, the Brazilian Gisele Bündchen, had demanded that Procter & Gamble pay her in euros for endorsing their Pantene brand. With a net worth of more than $300 million, Bündchen could not afford to ignore sentiment in the currency markets. Meanwhile, hip-hop star Jay Z took to thumbing wads of euros on MTV.

If the euro was the new bling, was the dollar really about to go out of style? In the summer of 2007, the year before he was awarded the Nobel Prize, Paul Krugman sketched the logic of what he described as a "Wile E. Coyote moment," in which foreign investors would suddenly realize that there was nothing holding the dollar up other than their own purchasing of it.[55] Like the cartoon character suspended in midair by the propeller motion of his own legs, the dollar was hanging above a precipice. It was comforting, Krugman reassured his readers, that most of America's debts were in its own currency, so the impact of the dollar collapse would be cushioned. It wouldn't be Argentina. But if the Fed was forced suddenly to hike interest rates, the United States would face a severe contraction. "This," Krugman concluded, "won't be fun."

The best and brightest in American economic policy were not wrong to worry about the Sino-American imbalance. If it had blown up, it would have been a disaster. Ten years on, the scenario still hangs over the world economy. The threat of crisis was contained in 2008 because there were deep interests engaged on both sides and because it was handled as a matter of top priority by both Washington and Beijing. From the outset, Sino-American financial relations were explicitly politicized and were understood as a matter of great power diplomacy. No one was under any illusion that it was simply a market relationship, a matter of business as usual. When Paulson was worried about a Chinese dollar sell-off, he knew whom in Beijing to call. Larry Summers's cold war analogy proved more apt than he realized. The balance of financial terror held.[56] But in the meantime, what became increasingly clear was that the US policy-making elite had been focused, as Bradford DeLong would put it, on the "wrong crisis."[57] The crisis that will forever be associated with 2008 was not an American sovereign debt crisis driven by a Chinese sell-off but a crisis fully native to Western capitalism—a meltdown on Wall Street driven by toxic securitized subprime mortgages that threatened to take Europe down with it.

Chapter 2

SUBPRIME

When the economists linked to the Hamilton Project envisioned disaster, they worried about excessive public debt, underperforming schools and a Chinese sell-off. What they did not put in question was the basic functioning of America's economy, its banks and financial markets. America's problems were its people, its society, its politics, not its economy as such. And yet by 2006, if one looked in the right place, it was evident that something was seriously amiss. Since the early 2000s the American economy had been buoyed not only by huge fiscal deficits but by a sustained surge in house prices. Now, in some of the most challenged neighborhoods in the country, tens of thousands of families who had recently taken out home loans were failing to make payments. In marginal ethnic minority communities in cities like Cincinnati and Cleveland, but also in ribbon developments in the sunshine states, mortgages were failing en masse. America's housing market bull run was about to come to a juddering halt. And as it did so, it would precipitate a global crisis.

For tens of millions of Americans this crisis hit them where it hurt most, at home. But compared with the grand sweep of global economic imbalances and the Sino-American relationship, the mechanics of American mortgage finance cannot but appear a parochial concern. How could this domestic drama shake the world's financial system and precipitate a global crisis? The simple answer is that real estate may be mundane, and McMansions may be nondescript, but they account for a huge share of total

marketable wealth worldwide. By one estimate, the share of American real estate in global wealth is as much as 20 percent.[1] American homes account for 9 percent of the total. At the time of the crisis 70 percent of American households owned their own home—more than 80 million in total. Those same households were the greatest source of demand for the world economy. In 2007 American consumers bought c. 16 percent of global output, and nothing made them feel better than surging real estate prices. As America's home prices almost doubled in the ten years leading to 2006, this raised household wealth by $6.5 trillion, delivering a giant boost not just to the United States but to the world economy.[2] As US consumer spending surged toward $10 trillion, it added $937 billion to global demand between 2000 and 2007.[3]

Fluctuations on such huge scales can clearly help account for a business-cycle downturn in 2007. But to explain how this could trigger a financial crisis, with bank failures spreading panic and a credit crunch across the world, there is one crucial thing to add: Real estate is not only the largest single form of wealth, it is also the most important form of collateral for borrowing.[4] It is mortgage debt that both amplifies the broader economic cycle and links the house price cycle to the financial crisis.[5] Between the 1990s and the outbreak of the crisis in 2007, American housing finance was turned into a dynamic and destabilizing force by a fourfold transformation—the securitization of mortgages, their incorporation into expansive and high-risk strategies of banking growth, the mobilization of new funding sources and internationalization. All four of these changes can be traced back to the transformation in world economic affairs between the late 1970s and the early 1980s in the wake of the collapse of Bretton Woods.

I

On October 6, 1979, after an unscheduled meeting of the Federal Reserve's key interest-rate-setting committee, the Federal Open Market Committee (FOMC), Paul Volcker, the Fed chair, announced that the Fed would henceforth attempt to tightly regulate bank reserves and that interest rates could be expected to rise.[6] It was the Fed's response to a wave of inflation that was

threatening domestic instability, America's global standing and the status of the dollar. Since Nixon had unhooked the dollar from gold, the world's currencies had floated against one another without a metallic anchor. Only political discipline prevented limitless printing of currency. Contrary to some fears, there was no runaway inflation. But with prices accelerating toward annual increases of 14 percent in 1979, Volcker and the Fed decided that it was time to apply the brakes. It was the moment the power of the modern Fed was born. The interest rate was its weapon. As Germany's outspoken chancellor Helmut Schmidt put it, Volcker pushed real interest rates (interest rates adjusted for inflation) to levels not seen "since the birth of Christ."[7] He did not exaggerate. In June 1981 the prime lending rate touched 21 percent.

The result was to send a shuddering shock through both the American and the global economies. The dollar surged, as did unemployment. Inflation collapsed from 14.8 percent in March 1980 to 3 percent by 1983. In Britain this was the crisis with which the Thatcher government began. In Germany it would contribute to Schmidt's unseating and his replacement by the conservative government of Helmut Kohl.[8] France's Socialist government under President François Mitterrand would be forced into line in 1983. Volcker's shock set the stage for what Ben Bernanke would later dub the great moderation.[9] It was an end not just to inflation but to a large part of the manufacturing base in the Western economies, and with it the bargaining power of the trade unions. No longer would they be able to drive up wages in line with prices. And there was another part of America's postwar political economy that did not survive the disinflationary shock of the 1980s: the peculiar system of housing finance that had emerged from the New Deal era.

Since the 1930s, America's housing finance had been based on commercial banks and local savings banks, so-called savings and loans, making long-term fixed interest loans. By the late 1960s thirty-year fixed interest loans had become normal, with as little as 5 percent in down payment.[10] The funding was provided by depository institutions, which offered government-insured savings accounts with capped interest rates. This was the basis on which home ownership had expanded to almost 66 percent of households

by the 1970s. For home owners on fixed interest, long-term mortgages, the inflation of the post–Bretton Woods era was a windfall. The real value of their loans was eaten up while their interest rates remained fixed. For the banks that lent to them it was a disaster. In an era of inflation and fluctuating interest rates, at the capped interest rates inherited from the 1950s they could not retain their depositors, let alone attract new ones. To borrow from money markets or issue bonds, they now faced the withering interest rates set by the Fed. Meanwhile, their portfolios of fixed interest mortgages were devalued as rates on new loans soared.[11] By the early 1980s the vast majority of the almost four thousand savings-and-loan banks still in operation were insolvent. Given the cost of cleaning them up and the prevailing free market ideology of the Reagan era, the path of least resistance was to deregulate and lower capital standards in the hope that they could grow themselves out of trouble. The commercial banks survived this trial by fire; the savings and loans did not. More than a thousand failed. Most of the rest were bailed out, bought up or amalgamated. The resolution costs to the taxpayer were around $124 billion in 1990s dollars.[12]

By the late 1980s the macroeconomic picture was stabilizing. Inflation was down and interest rates were falling. Whereas most bond investors did well in the new era, anyone who held mortgage loans had to reckon with another risk. American mortgage borrowers have the right to repay early and refinance at lower rates. This boosts the economy, as borrowers can reduce their mortgage payments and as borrowers they tend to have a higher propensity to consume than those they borrow from.[13] But for the lender it means that the US mortgage contract is highly one-sided. During a period of rising rates their fixed-rate loans will devalue. During a loosening of monetary policy, when rates fall, the borrowers refinance. Lending for thirty-year terms at fixed rates is a viable business proposition only under the kinds of conditions of stability that prevailed under Bretton Woods between 1945 and 1971. In a new age of flexible monetary arrangements it was dangerously one-sided, especially if the risks were concentrated in small mortgage lenders with limited means of funding themselves. The solution was to go for scale, to adopt a new market-based model of financing and to place government institutions at the center of the system.

The basic anchor of America's mortgage system in the aftermath of the savings-and-loans debacle was the so-called government-sponsored enterprise (GSE).[14] The mother ship of the GSEs was Fannie Mae, founded in 1938 to create a secondary market for lenders who were willing to issue the new type of government-insured Federal Housing Authority mortgages promoted by the New Deal. Fannie Mae did not issue mortgages. It bought them mainly from commercial banks across the United States that specialized in issuing FHA-insured mortgages. By acting as a backstop, Fannie Mae lowered the cost of lending and set a national standard for both lenders and "prime" borrowers. It helped to unify America through mortgage debt. Fannie Mae was able to fund its purchases of these standardized mortgages cheaply because its credit rating was that of a government agency that could not fail. So-called agency debt was equivalent to that of the Treasury. By the same token, the obligations of Fannie Mae featured on the federal government's balance sheet. To get them off at a time of fiscal stress during the Vietnam War, in 1968 Fannie Mae was privatized. The branch still devoted to making loans to public employees and veterans was split off as Ginnie Mae. "New Fannie Mae" was licensed to buy any mortgages, government guaranteed or not, that conformed to certain quality standards—so-called conforming loans. And in 1970 Congress legislated into existence a third agency, the Federal Home Loan Mortgage Corporation, or Freddie Mac, to level the playing field by buying up mortgage loans issued by savings and loans.

Despite this government guarantee, with their large portfolios of fixed interest loans, the GSEs were hit hard by the Volcker shock of the early 1980s. Fannie Mae came close to failure. But it survived, and as the housing market recovered in the 1990s, the GSEs flourished. Thanks to their residual tie to the federal government, the GSEs continued to enjoy a substantial discount in funding costs. By the end of the century Fannie Mae and Freddie Mac together were backstopping at least 50 percent of the total national mortgage market. Creating conforming loans—loans that qualified for GSE backstop—was the basis of the American home loan business. It is a deep irony that the era in which America is commonly thought of as leading the world in a market revolution saw its housing market become dependent on a government-sponsored mortgage machine descended from the New

Deal. It was also the source of deep and irreducible politicization of the mortgage issue in the United States.

American housing policy and mortgage practice since the war had systematically favored home ownership for the white majority.[15] In the 1990s promoting home ownership for lower-income and "underserved" minority communities became a congressional priority. The Federal Housing Enterprises Financial Safety and Soundness Act of 1992 called for lending goals to be set for the GSEs. In December 1995 the government issued targets for underserved areas and low-income housing. Many of the new home owners in the 1990s and 2000s were ethnic minority families who had been denied mortgages for decades under the regime of "redlining" institutionalized by New Deal housing policy. Viewed in this way the real estate boom was part of the rise of the diverse African American and Latino middle class on which the Democrats as a political party had a lot riding.[16] On the back of their influence over the Democratic Party, the GSEs built one of the most powerful lobbies in Washington, DC. Their political firepower was legendary. By the same token, the GSE mortgage regime always attracted the ire of the American Right. Deep down most free market advocates are convinced that the interferences of the GSEs were responsible for the disaster that was beginning to unfold in 2006. The GSEs had political mandates set by progressives to funnel money into underserved communities. They had a market-distorting funding advantage due to their attachment to the federal government. When you distort the market, crises are inevitable.[17] It was this conservative critique of the GSEs that shaped the Republican reaction when the crisis reached fever pitch in 2008. For many in Congress the bailout was not just of the banks—they at least were private businesses trying to make a buck. The bailout was also a desperate effort to make the taxpayer pay for the rescue of a Democrat-controlled parastate housing welfare apparatus designed to serve pampered minorities.

This was powerful mobilizing rhetoric for the Republican base. But as an explanation of the crisis that was brewing in 2006, this political critique is wide of the mark. Fannie Mae and Freddie Mac set a high minimum standard for the quality of loans they would buy. The GSEs didn't support the kind of low-quality, subprime loans that were beginning to fail in droves in 2005–2006. Those toxic loans were the products of a new system of mortgage

finance driven by private lenders that came into full force in the early 2000s. Though the GSEs met their government lending quotas, private lenders driven by the search for profit were far more adventurous in lending to underserved communities.[18] In this sense the GSEs did not create the crisis. But what they did contribute were two innovations without which the crisis is hard to imagine: the originate-to-distribute mortgage lending system and securitization.

From its origins in the 1930s, the GSE model of subsidy separated the origination of a mortgage from its ultimate funding. The commercial banks that issued the original loans to American families were repaid when they sold the mortgages to Fannie Mae. That enabled them to make more loans. It was the debt issued by the GSEs to finance the mortgages they were holding on their balance sheets that ultimately funded the loan. This was the basic structure of what became known as "originate to distribute." Mortgage lenders no longer needed to hold the mortgages on their balance sheets; they became brokers operating for a fee. The government-backed credit rating of the GSEs backstopped the entire system.

Starting in the 1970s, as they confronted the instability of interest rates and its damaging implications for America's mortgage model, the GSEs took a further critical step. Working with the help of investment banks, they pioneered securitization.[19] Rather than holding the locally originated mortgages on their own books and financing them by issuing bonds, they would sell the mortgages directly to investors. To do so they packaged the mortgages into pools, in which they sold shares—securities. The idiosyncratic risks of individual loans would be pooled. Investors looking to hold real estate could buy a portfolio of broadly based exposure without having to build a branch network necessary to make loans across the far-flung economy of the United States. They did so fully aware of the risks and returns generated by the fluctuation of interest rates. Rather than having small savings and loans gamble on what was a viable loan, securitization would let the collective process of market haggling determine funding costs.

In 1970 Ginnie Mae carried out the first securitization. It was a simple model—a so-called pass-through—under which the flows of revenue from a pool of mortgages were passed by way of the GSE to investors. Not satisfied that this should remain a public monopoly, Lewis Ranieri and his team

at hard-driving investment bank Salomon Brothers put together the first private securitization of mortgages for Bank of America in 1977.[20] But it took a brave investor to buy a package of fixed interest mortgages at that moment. It was in the aftermath of the interest rate shock of the early 1980s that securitization came to the fore. The mortgage lender stranded with portfolios of low-interest mortgages turned to the market to recover whatever value they would yield by securitizing them and selling them off. From the 1980s, the GSEs, working with the investment banks, created not just pass-through mortgage-backed securities (MBS) but so-called collateralized mortgage obligations (CMO) that allowed a pool of MBS to be tranched into separate risk tiers profiles. This was the origin of so-called structured finance. Those with the top-tier first claim on the revenue stream had low risk of both default and early repayment. Tranches lower down the pecking order could be sold off to investors looking for riskier investments. The top-tier senior tranches would pay out except in the highly unlikely event of massive, collective default. Those top tranches, even if they were based on a pool of high-yielding, high-risk debt, could be designated as low risk, and the ratings agencies obliged by classifying them as AAA (80 percent of most securitizations were designated as senior and given the AAA rating).

Not surprisingly, given the very high ratings they handed out for MBS, the role of the ratings agencies would later become highly controversial. By the 1990s, Moody's Investors Service and Standard & Poor's divided 80 percent of the global debt-rating business between them.[21] Fitch took another 15 percent of the market. They did not attain that control of the global market by freely handing out top AAA ratings. In 2008 there were only six AAA-rated corporations and no more than a dozen countries enjoying that ranking. This was despite the fact that since the 1980s it was issuers of debt who paid the ratings agencies to make their classifications, not the subscribers to their information services. Payment by the issuer created a conflict of interest. But the agencies had much to lose if they appeared to be selling good ratings and relatively little to gain if they showed favor to a client that was involved in only occasional bond issues. The mortgage securitization business changed that calculus. The sheer volume of mortgage-backed security issuance, involving tens of thousands of tranches, combined with the fact that the flow was concentrated in the hands of a few issuers,

gave the ratings agencies a significant incentive to be "helpful."[22] But even more important was the nature of MBS as such. What made rating MBS different was that the underlying assets were not bonds issued by a company facing the unpredictable force of global competition. The MBS bundled thousands of what were supposed to be predictable assets—regular domestic mortgages. The ratings agencies did not have to calculate the risks of default on the basis of more or less subjective evaluations of a company's business prospects. Nor did they have to render a judgment on a country's fiscal policy. Instead, they could apply standardized financial mathematics to a population of mortgages that was assumed to have well-known statistical properties. If you knew default rates and could make assumptions about the degree of correlation between them, once you assembled enough mortgages and tranched them, the likelihood of the top tranches not paying was infinitesimal. Tens of thousands of asset-backed securities thus qualified for ultrasafe AAA ratings. What happened to the tranches lower down the pile was another matter altogether. There the risk of failure was much higher than if one simply held the mortgage pool. But at the right yield they too would find a buyer.

The idea, in the wake of the savings-and-loans disaster, was to spread risk outward from those immediately involved in lending to mortgage borrowers and to attract investors by turning mortgages into securities that offered a wide range of yield-risk profiles. And it worked. In 1980, 67 percent of American mortgages had been held directly on the balance sheets of depository banks. By the end of the 1990s, the risks involved in America's system of long-term, fixed interest, easy repayment mortgages were securitized and spread across a much wider segment of the financial system than had been the case in 1979 when Volcker made his shock announcement. The GSEs held them. Banks held them. But so too did pension and insurance funds.[23]

Compared with the model of the savings and loan, securitization thus did its job in spreading risk. But did it by the same token reduce the incentive to carefully monitor the underlying loans? By splitting origination from funding, had the new system eliminated the incentive to monitor loans carefully? Whereas a local lender that held a mortgage for its entire thirty-year duration had every reason to monitor its customer very carefully, by

the 1990s American mortgages were passing through at least five differ-ent institutions—originators, wholesalers of packages of mortgages, under-writers who assessed risk, government-sponsored enterprises and servicers who managed the flow of interest income—before being sold to an investor. Along that chain, what confidence could an investor have that the job was being done correctly? At each step of the way the main concerns were vol-ume and fees. Who had an interest in maintaining quality? Perhaps it was not the government subsidy but these perverse incentives that led to the huge boom in bad lending and the crisis of 2007–2008.[24]

It is a theory that would have a superficial plausibility if the 1990s model of GSE-centered mortgage finance had still been dominant in the early 2000s. But, in fact, in the early 2000s, when the subprime boom un-folded, the industry had changed again. Securitization was more dominant than ever. The GSEs were still responsible for buying and securitizing the top-tier conforming mortgages. But as a new range of actors entered the mortgage market with a more dynamic and expansive agenda, their princi-pal business model was not to disaggregate and to spread the risk but to integrate every step of the process, including the holding of large quantities of securities on their own balance sheets.[25] It was this growth model, based on integration, not disintegration, that would blow the system up.

II

The path that led to the supercharged private mortgage industry of the early 2000s was twisted, but it too goes back to the breakdown of Bretton Woods in the 1970s and the unfettering of currencies, prices, interest rates and capital movements that followed. It was not just the savings and loans but the entire financial sector that was forced to rethink its business model, and this went for the investment banks of Wall Street as much as for the commercial banks.

It is barely too much to say that the new, deregulated world of national and international finance was made for the investment banks.[26] Through their business of trading on their clients' behalf and launching debt and other securities, they enjoyed an "edge" over all other participants in the

market.[27] In 1975 the abolition of fixed fees charged by Wall Street brokers for trading stocks led to fierce competition, wiped out smaller firms and forced the integration of trading, research and investment banking. In the 1980s, with interest rates coming down and bonds beginning their long bull run, trading in so-called fixed-income securities—as opposed to equities—became ever more important. Drexel Burnham Lambert pioneered the market in high-yield corporate bonds, also known as junk bonds. Meanwhile, Salomon Brothers helped the GSEs devise the securitization model and launch each new batch of mortgage-backed securities. For other clients, the investment bankers were hard at work figuring out how to hedge against fluctuations in currencies and interest rates. They developed swaps, for instance, that allowed clients to trade excessive exposures in currencies. They made instruments that allowed one client to take on the risk of fluctuating interest rates while another client opted for fixed rates. In the 1990s a team at J.P. Morgan devised the credit default swap (CDS), which offered protection against the risk of nonpayment and allowed lenders to fine-tune their lending risk.[28] At the same time, the investment banks progressively increased their own trading activity. They discovered the profits to be made through volume and leverage. The returns were extraordinary. In the early 1980s America's investment banking elite earned returns of more than 50 percent on equity.

But achieving scale raised the question of funding. Investment banks don't have deposits. They borrow the money they lend on wholesale markets from other banks or institutional funds. In the aftermath of the inflation and interest rate shocks of the late 1970s and early 1980s, this put them in a sweet spot. If investment banks didn't have depositors, that suited savers, who, in the wake of the inflation, no longer wanted to put their money in bank deposits either. They opted instead for money market mutual funds (MMF), that characteristic financial institution of the new age.[29] These were highly attractive to affluent households looking for better rates than those on offer from bank deposits. The money market mutual funds offered instantly accessible accounts without official government guarantee, but pledged by their private sector operators to return at least a dollar on the dollar plus an attractive rate of interest on top. Bypassing the bankrupt savings and loans and the struggling commercial banks, cash deposits flowed

into huge pools of professionally managed cash looking for good yields on Wall Street.

Nor were the MMFs the only ones. Corporations began to manage their cash pools more professionally. Ultrarich individuals who became more and more numerous from the 1970s onward had billions of dollars that were managed by funds and family offices. By the end of the 1990s perhaps as much as a trillion dollars had accumulated in these institutional cash pools, looking for highly liquid, interest-yielding investment opportunities that were absolutely, or close to absolutely, safe.[30] Lending against security, or buying the commercial paper of well-known investment banks, was precisely the kind of safe short-term asset that the managers of the cash pools wanted. And acting as the banker to the funds, so-called prime brokerage, was ideal business for the investment banks.

These institutional cash pools and the liquidity they brought to wholesale funding markets were the rocket fuel for the rise of the modern investment bank. The more resources they mobilized, either by borrowing in the wholesale market or on deposit, the bigger the turnover, the larger the profits. Until the 1980s, investment banks were relatively small operations, partnerships, well known and respected on Wall Street and the City of London but not household names. The belief in the ability to manage risk inspired by the new derivative instruments, combined with access to the institutional cash pools, enabled them to scale up their size, creating the "New Wall Street."[31] Firms like Goldman Sachs, Morgan Stanley and Merrill Lynch went from obscurity to star status. Originally built as partnerships, the huge scaling up of trading activity and the derivatives business meant that they needed to issue shares and go public. Merrill Lynch had done so already in 1971. Bear Stearns followed in 1985, Morgan Stanley in 1986. Goldman Sachs was the last to launch its IPO in May 1999.[32] With Robert Rubin a classic exponent of this new Wall Street, the investment banks even had their man in government. Goldman Sachs began to earn its nickname as "government Sachs."

Since the 1980s the investment banks had built their businesses on navigating uncertainty. As asset market booms they leveraged up.[33] But sometimes uncertainty bites back. Between 1994 in Mexico and 1998 in Russia the globalized American banks faced a series of major crises. In

September 1998, but for concerted action by the major Wall Street firms, the implosion of Long-Term Capital Management triggered by the uncertainty spreading from Russia might have brought down the entire hedge fund industry.[34] That was followed by the dot-com boom and bust in 1998– 2001—a creation of the new Wall Street as much as of Silicon Valley. Finally there was the spectacular accounting scandal at Enron, which took down once legendary accountants and management consultants Arthur Andersen. By the early 2000s, after two decades of dramatic growth, Wall Street was facing a political and regulatory backlash and urgently needed the "next big thing." Given the expertise of the investment banks in bond trading and their role in the securitization of mortgages on behalf of the GSEs, it was not hard to foresee where scrappy investment banks like Lehman and Bear Stearns would look next.

For the commercial banks, the post-Volcker age was tougher. They lost deposits. They lost mortgage business. Might they go the way of the savings and loans?[35] To reestablish profitability in the 1990s America's high street banks underwent spectacular consolidation. The top ten banks increased their share of total assets from 10 to 50 percent between 1990 and 2000. In addition they looked for a new business model.[36] Rather than thinking of themselves as maintaining lifelong relationships with clients and their communities, they repurposed themselves as service providers for a fee. They had always originated mortgages but had generally sold them to the GSEs. Given the pressure that they were now under, the mortgage market, with its multiple layers of origination, securitization, selling and servicing, seemed like a natural bridge between their familiar high street banking business and their aspirations to high finance. But to engage in that full range of activities they needed regulatory relief. The New Deal–era regulations that separated retail from investment banking had to fall. The Clinton Treasury, first under Rubin and then under Larry Summers, gave them what they needed. In 1999 the last remnants of 1930s banking regulations were swept aside. Citigroup and Bank of America rushed through the opening to a new era of American universal banking. Stretching from the high street to Wall Street, it was a model more familiar from Continental Europe now applied to America.

The third group of actors in the mortgage boom of the early 2000s was

already in the business in the 1990s. They were banks like Washington Mutual, a survivor of the savings-and-loan disaster, and specialized mortgage lenders like Countrywide.[37] As feeders to the GSEs they were restricted to mortgage origination. But why limit their ambitions? Why not integrate the entire chain? By the late 1990s and early 2000s all three groups of banks—investment banks, commercial banks and mortgage lenders—were following this logic. Rather than organizing their mortgage business around the GSEs, they set out to build integrated mortgage securitization businesses. Countrywide expanded from origination to securitization. A giant bank like Citi could envision itself as a provider at every stage, originating, securitizing, selling, holding and dealing in MBS. Even more remarkable was the evolution of investment banks like Lehman and Bear Stearns that had previously defined themselves through their remoteness from ordinary retail customers. Already in the 1990s Bear added the mortgage originator and servicer EMC to its portfolio and Lehman added four small mortgage lenders to its investment bank.

By the early 2000s the corporate strategies centered on private mortgage securitization were fully in place. But Fannie Mae and Freddie Mac still enjoyed a dominant position in the market thanks to their funding advantage. What gave the private mortgage securitization machine its chance was another interest rate shock combined with a hiccup at the GSE.[38]

When the dot-com bubble was followed by the shock of 9/11, the Fed dropped interest rates to 1 percent. As Alan Greenspan clearly intended, this unleashed a scramble among borrowers to refinance as many long-term mortgages as possible at lower rates. This was painful from the point of view of the original lenders. But it triggered an immediate wave of consumer spending, and for the mortgage industry it generated a huge surge in fees. The industry churned as it had never churned before. As compared with $1 trillion in new mortgages issued in 2001, in 2003 mortgage origination soared to $3.8 trillion, of which $2.53 trillion were for refinancing. In this huge boom the GSEs were still the major players. They continued to monopolize the prime mortgage segment. Their share of the market reached its maximum point in 2003 at 57 percent. But at that point it stalled. In the huge surge of business in the early 2000s not everything at the GSEs was aboveboard. Accounting and regulatory irregularities piled up. Fearful of

another Enron, regulators subjected first Freddie Mac and then Fannie Mae to capital surcharges. They either had to raise new capital or contract their balance sheets. To make sure it was the latter, caps were imposed on their total balance-sheet size.[39] The door to the private issuers was opened.

During Greenspan's refinancing boom of 2000–2003, it wasn't just the GSEs that were busy. The huge surge in issuance meant that there was plenty of unconventional, "nonconforming" business to go around too. But the decisive thing was what happened in early 2004 when interest rates had reached rock bottom, the refinancing boom had run its course and the GSEs were stopped in their tracks. With the pipeline ready and waiting, it was at this point that the private mortgage industry took over. Leaving behind the GSE-centered model of the 1990s, they deprioritized conforming mortgages in favor of private label "unconventional" lending—subprime, slightly better Alt-A and oversized jumbo loans.

What the private issuers discovered was that if scrutinizing conventional mortgages was profitable, subprime was even more so.[40] The financial engineering was more elaborate and one could charge more money for the services. The techniques of the fixed-income investment bankers were now brought fully into play. A surprisingly large share even of nonconforming private label MBS could still attract an AAA rating once combined in structured products. To manage the risks, the production of credit default swaps (CDS), once the preserve of bespoke investment banks, was industrialized. Mainline insurers like AIG offered CDS insurance on exotic securitized products. Given the quality of the underlying mortgages, not all the tranches were good. But that stimulated the investment banks to expand the collateralized debt obligation (CDO) business. CDOs were derivatives based on repackaged middle-ranking "mezzanine" tiers of other securitized mortgage deals. By combining them together and tranching, you could make a large pool of BBB assets yield further tranches of AAA securities. Once you had done that you could then go one step further. You could take the low-rated mezzanine slices of the CDO and pool and tranche them once more to create CDO-squared. And once again by the logic of independent risks and the good graces of the ratings agencies, a portion even of those securities would warrant an AAA rating.

III

By the early 2000s, the private mortgage industry was waiting for the starter's gun. It had its new raw material—securitized mortgages. It had its mechanics and its engineers at the ready. The end of the refinancing boom of 2003 in conventional mortgages triggered the push into unconventional lending. To unleash the final phase of the boom, it needed one last ingredient. Someone had to be interested in buying the hundreds of billions of dollars in securities that were being produced. If there had been no demand to meet the supply, the price of MBS would have fallen, yields would have surged leading borrowing rates to rise, choking off the mortgage boom. Not only did this not happen, but long-term interest rates remained flat and the spread—the premium that nonconforming borrowers had to pay—declined. This points to the third historic transformation that made possible the 2000s boom, a change not on the supply but on the demand side: the surging demand for safe assets and the mobilization of institutional cash pools for mortgage finance.[41] It is at this point that the technical mechanics of mortgage banking reconnects with the grand theme of the rise of China, the emerging markets and the mounting inequality and wealth polarization in the Western world.

To understand this connection, the best place to start is to go back to the most scandalous thing about MBS, their credit rating. The AAA label was important because it placed them in a class of assets like Treasurys that attracted investors looking for safe assets.[42] AAA was a badge of quality, and, like any certificate of this type, it signaled that if what you were looking for was safety, you had to look no further. Such assets constitute as close as the unstable capitalist economy can offer to a neutral safe position. They are desired and in some cases legally required by all investors with a particular aversion to risk and little capacity for independent research or evaluation—pension funds, cash funds, insurance funds and so on. As one of the key economists in the field has remarked: "[A]lmost all human history can be written as the search for and the production of different forms of safe assets."[43] This may be true, but it begs the question of what was

happening in the late 1990s and early 2000s to drive a huge surge in the demand for safe assets.

The first part of the answer is the development of the emerging market economies from the 1990s. As a result of their trade surpluses and their desire to self-insure against the risk of a repeat of the 1994–1998 crises, they wanted reserve assets that they could liquidate in an emergency. And the assets that best fit that description were US Treasurys, long- and short-dated. In the early 2000s, China and other emerging market sovereigns bought all the Treasurys that even the gaping budget deficits of the first Bush administration could provide. Macroeconomists worried about the current account imbalance that resulted and the possibility of a catastrophic sudden stop unwinding. What they did not pay attention to, because they

Foreign Reserves and Institutional Investors Compete for US Short-Term Safe Assets (in $ billions)

Outstanding Amounts:	2005	2006	2007	2008	2009	2010
Short-term Treasury securities*	1,146	1,173	1,192	1,909	2,558	2,487
Short-term agency securities**	568	489	560	903	844	618
Total	1,714	1,662	1,752	2,812	3,402	3,105
(–) Foreign Official Holdings:						
Short-term Treasury securities	216	193	181	273	562	na
Short-term agency securities	112	110	80	130	34	na
Total	328	303	261	403	596	na
(–) Demand from Institutional Cash Pools:						
Institutional cash pools (based on available data)	1,771	2,120	2,216	1,834	2,041	1,911
Institutional cash pools (estimate of total volume)	3,120	3,735	3,852	3,467	3,596	3,432
Average	2,445	2,927	3,034	2,650	2,818	2,672
= Deficit of safe, liquid, short-term products	(1,059)	(1,568)	(1,543)	(241)	(12)	na

*Includes Treasury bills and Treasury securities with a remaining maturity of one year or less.

**Includes agency discount notes.

Source: Zoltan Pozsar, "Institutional Cash Pools and the Triffin Dilemma of the US Banking System," *Financial Markets, Institutions & Instruments* 22, no. 5 (2013): 283–318, figure 5.

did not dirty their hands with technicalities like MBS, was the effect the influx of emerging market funds might have in financial markets. Emerging market investors bought first Treasurys and then GSE-issued agency debt. This left other institutional investors looking for alternatives. What filled the gap was financial engineering. If pension funds, life insurers and the managers of the gigantic cash pools accumulated by profitable corporations and the ultrawealthy needed safe assets, AAA-rated securities were a product America's mortgage machine knew how to synthesize.

But once again we have to be careful. The shuffling of global demand for dollar-denominated safe assets helps to explain why the mortgage pipeline did not result in an oversupply of AAA securities. But to the extent that private label asset-backed securities were actually sold off to investors, little more was heard of them. When the market turned bad, they would sit on balance sheets as an illiquid entry. They were no longer counted as safe assets. There would be lawsuits against investment banks that had knowingly repackaged unsafe mortgages. Certainly the losses would have an impact on investment allocation and on the spending decisions of millions of pensioners. But this would not by itself create a financial crisis, with bank failures rippling out across the world. The comparison with the dot-com bubble is instructive. It created a huge surge in wealth followed by a collapse. It triggered a severe recession. But it did not lead to banking crises. The subprime mortgage boom of the early 2000s led to a financial crisis because, contrary to the professed logic of securitization, hundreds of billions of private label MBS were not spread outside the banking system, but were stockpiled on the balance sheets of the mortgage originators and securitizers themselves.[44]

Why did the securitizers end up holding their own product? In part it was a matter of the production system itself. Securitization produced some attractive tranches and some less so. The less attractive tranches needed to be held off the market. Furthermore, the banks operating the pipeline believed their own business proposition. Holding MBS was very profitable at prevailing funding costs. The banks in the mortgage supply chain were at the source of the profit. So why not get rich too? It was a choice. Not every bank did it. Those that took the biggest risks were large mortgage originators and the most aggressively expansive commercial banks—Citigroup, Bank of

America and Washington Mutual—and the two smallest and scrappiest investment banks—Lehman and Bear Stearns. By contrast, J.P. Morgan began throttling back its mortgage pipeline already in 2006 and bought as much protection as it could in the CDS market. Goldman Sachs went beyond hedging to place a large bet on an imminent housing market collapse.[45]

Their caution was easy to justify given the kind of business that subprime lending involved. But it also reflected a more basic banking consideration. Building a big balance sheet of MBS didn't just involve risk on the asset side. It also involved expanding the liabilities of the bank on the funding side. And this brings us to the true heart of the 2007–2008 crisis. If the mortgage production line was holding hundreds of billions of private label MBS and ABS on its own balance sheet, how were those holdings funded? Here too it was the new model of investment banking that provided the answer. If an upstart mortgage lender like Countrywide didn't have depositors, neither did Lehman. Lehman got its funding wholesale by tapping the cash pools and so too would the new mortgage lenders, including Lehman. This was the truly lethal mechanism at the heart of the crisis. Funds from money market cash pools were channeled into financing the holding of large balance sheets of MBS.

The largest mechanism for funding mortgage holdings was asset-backed commercial paper (ABCP).[46] The three biggest American issuers of ABCP were Bank of America, Citigroup and J.P. Morgan. The vehicles for managing this operation were so-called structured investment vehicles (SIV), legal entities provided with a minimum layer of capital by their "sponsors," but otherwise separate from the balance sheets of their parent banks. Onto these SIVs the parent bank would offload a large portfolio of mortgage bonds, securitized car loans, credit card debt or student debt. The SIV would pay the parent bank for the securities with funds raised by issuing ABCP. These were three-month notes backed by the assets in the SIV and the good name of the parent bank. Though the SIV had no track record, it could issue the commercial paper at competitive rates because of the value of the securities it held and because it was assumed that it enjoyed the backing of the sponsoring bank. Remarkably, under the bank regulations prevailing until the early 2000s, assets parked off balance sheet in the SIV could be backed by a fraction of the capital that would be required if they

were on balance sheet. Inflating the balance sheet was risky but it raised rates of return on capital. Further profits were to be made by trading on the spread between long-term returns and short-term funding costs. Typically, an ABCP vehicle would hold a portfolio of securities with maturities of three to five years and would fund those securities by selling commercial paper repayable between three months and as little as a few days. For the managers of cash pools, the commercial paper was more attractive than the underlying securities, because it was very short term and backed by a top-rated commercial bank. For the parent banks, the spread between the return from the high-risk cocktail of assets held in the SIV and the low rate paid on the highly rated ABCP was handsome.

If the SIV-ABCP model involved a degree of maturity mismatch, the investment banks pushed this to extremes. The entire business model of investment banks was based on wholesale funding. The most elastic vehicles for this were so-called repurchase agreements, or repo. In a repo transaction a bank would buy a security and pay for the purchase by immediately reselling it for a period of as little as one night or as long as three months, with a promise to repurchase at a certain price. It was in effect a collateralized short-term funding agreement. The investment bank would buy $100 million in securities and repo them with a mutual fund or another investment bank, with the party repoing the paper paying a small interest charge to the investor it was repoing with. It also accepted a haircut. In exchange for $100 million in Treasurys, it did not receive full value, but only $98 million in cash. It would also repurchase them for $98 million. In the meantime, the haircut determined how much of its own money the investment bank would have to put into holding the securities, and thus the leverage in the deal.[47] A 2 percent haircut meant that to fund the purchase of $100 million of securities and to receive the interest paid on those bonds, a bank would need $2 million of its own money. The rest it could get out of the repo transaction. Using this mechanism, a small amount of capital could support a far bigger balance sheet, provided, of course, that the repo could be repeatedly "rolled" and that the haircut did not suddenly increase.

By the 2000s the collateral posted in repo markets in New York ran to several trillions of dollars a day. It was split into two markets—bilateral and

triparty repo. Both were over-the-counter professional markets, which were only loosely monitored by the central banks or regulators. The best data we have is for trilateral repo where the trade was managed by a third party—either JPMorgan Chase or Bank of New York Mellon—which held the collateral for the duration of the repo.[48] In triparty repo the collateral used was of top quality—almost exclusively Treasurys or agency MBS. Given the additional layer of protection, triparty repo was where institutional cash pools like MMFs did their repo. Triparty was not used to fund private label MBS. It was in the bilateral repo market that they could be funded. The best available data suggest that the bilateral repo market was three times larger than the triparty segment.[49] Because the players in the bilateral market tended to be investment banks and hedge funds, the types of assets acceptable as collateral were more wide ranging. It is here, along with ABCP and various types of interbank and unsecured borrowing, that the investment banks financed their holding of private label MBS and CDO portfolios. Given the wide range of collateral, haircuts in the bilateral repo market ranged in the spring of 2007 from 0.25 percent on US Treasurys to 10 percent or more for asset-backed loans of inferior quality.

As in commercial paper, repo was exposed to serious funding risk. You might not be rolled over. Specifically, the risk was that if an investment bank like Lehman or Bear was thought to have suffered major losses on some big part of its portfolio—whether that was funded by commercial paper, bilateral repo or other types of interbank borrowing—it would suffer a general loss of confidence. It would then be considered ineligible as a counterparty in the triparty market and would find itself shut out from critical funding. The scale of the potential risk was huge. At Lehman at the end of fiscal year 2007, of its balance sheet of $691 billion, 50 percent was funded through repo. At Goldman Sachs, Merrill Lynch and Morgan Stanley, the share was 40 percent.[50] If any one of these investment banks was to lose access to the repo markets, at a stroke its business model would collapse, taking its entire balance sheet—not just its MBS business, but its derivatives book, currency and interest swaps—down with it.

IV

With so many interests engaged, the expansion in US mortgage lending in the final burst of the boom was spectacular, not to say grotesque. Between 1999 and 2003, 70 percent of the new mortgages issued in the United States were still conventional GSE-conforming. With the end of the refinancing boom, that balance shifted. By 2006, 70 percent of new mortgages were subprime or other unconventional loans destined for securitization not by the GSE, but as private label MBS. In both 2005 and 2006, $1 trillion in unconventional mortgages were issued, compared with $100 billion in 2001. Fannie Mae and Freddie Mac were scrambling to keep up, purchasing $300 billion in nonagency securitized mortgages to hold in their own portfolios. The GSEs were driven. They were not the drivers. They were competing with upstarts like Countrywide, which in 2006 was responsible for originating 20 percent of all mortgages in the United States.[51] They were competing with an ultrasophisticated investment bank like

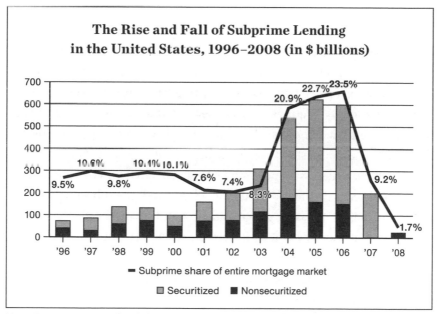

The Rise and Fall of Subprime Lending in the United States, 1996–2008 (in $ billions)

Note: Percent securitized is defined as subprime securities issued divided by originations in a given year. In 2007 securities issued exceeded originations.

Source: Inside Mortgage Finance.

Lehman Brothers that had assembled an entire pipeline. In 2005 two thirds of the mortgages contained in Lehman's issuance of $133 billion in MBS/CDO were sourced from its own subprime loan originators. A top Wall Street name was scraping the very bottom of the credit barrel.

The message that this communicated down the food chain was simple: We want more mortgage debt to process, and the worse the quality, the better. By the magic of independent probabilities, the worse the quality of the debt that entered into the tranching and pooling process, the more dramatic the effect. Substantial portions of undocumented, low-rated, high-yield debt emerged as AAA. In any boom, irresponsible, near criminal or outright fraudulent behavior is to be expected. But the mortgage securitization mechanism systematically produced this race to the bottom in mortgage lending quality. It was the difference between the high yield of the underlying securities included in the collateral pool and the low interest that was paid to the investors who bought the AAA-rated asset-backed securities that generated the profit. From 2004, fully half the subprime mortgages being fed into the system had incomplete or zero documentation, and 30 percent were interest-only loans to people who had no prospect of making basic repayment.[52]

The ratings agencies would subsequently face penetrating questions about their complicity in this process. It did not help that they were paid by the banks for which they rated the bonds and that the big three ratings agencies competed with one another to offer the most streamlined and cheap route to AAA ratings. In their defense they would argue that they were operating tried-and-tested formulae that had the stamp of approval of the smartest economists in the land. But payment was by results. Fitch, which applied a risk assessment model that generated fewer of the coveted AAA-rated securities, found itself largely cut out of the subprime securitization business.[53] As later congressional inquiries revealed, the ratings agency staff at Moody's and S&P were clearly aware of the monster they were creating. As one ratings expert remarked to another in an e-mail in December 2006: "Let's hope we are all wealthy and retired by the time this house of cards falters. :o)."[54]

Certainly some people were getting wealthy. The profits of the 1980s

and late 1990s had been good in investment banking. Now everyone was making money. In the early 2000s 35 percent of all profits in the US economy were earned by the financial sector. At the very top it was dizzying. Though in the course of the 1990s they had converted to public companies selling shares to investors, the Wall Street firms continued to operate effectively as partnerships. The rule was that half of net revenue after interest costs was reserved for staff payments, the other half being paid to shareholders. The 2006 business year generated $60 billion in bonuses for the finance crowd in New York, and 2007 topped that with $66 billion in bonuses.[55] For senior staff at the investment banks, that translated into payments in the tens of millions of dollars each. Richard Fuld, who drove Lehman's dramatic growth as CEO from 1994, earned $484.8 million in salary and bonus between 2000 and 2008. That was staggering enough, but to understand the psychology of those operating the system, one has to appreciate that even the top investment bankers knew that they were not the real kings of the money game. Their remuneration paled by comparison with that of the hedge fund managers with whom they dealt in the prime brokerage, repo and ABCP markets. At the hedge funds and private equity groups, individuals could earn hundreds of millions, or even billions, of dollars per annum. In 2007 the six top hedge fund managers earned at least a billion dollars each in compensation.

Nor was the greed confined to the top. No doubt many mortgage borrowers were victimized by a process that systematically misled them and had every interest to do so. But once a real estate market shifts from a state of equilibrium to one of boom, everyone becomes a speculator willy-nilly. As capital appreciation came to be expected, the meaning of home ownership changed. Home owners, whether they liked it or not, were taking a speculative position. At the bottom, those who got on the housing ladder by taking out adjustable-rate, low-credit-score mortgages were speculating that their properties would rise in value so much that their equity would be sufficient to refinance on better terms. Those further up the ladder engaged in a fiesta of real estate speculation. In 2006 fully a third of new mortgages issued in the United States were for second, third or even fourth properties. In what became known as the "bubble states"—Florida, Arizona, California—the

Funding of Outstanding US Private-Label ABS and Corporate Bonds in 2007 Q2 (in $ billions)

	Private-label ABS		Corporate bonds	
	Amount	%	Amount	%
Total outstanding	5,213	100%	5,591	100%
Short-term funding				
ABCP	1,173	23%		
Direct holdings				
MMF	243	5%	179	3%
Securities lenders	502	10%	369	7%
Repo				
MMF	31	1%	42	1%
Securities lenders	165	3%	121	2%
Total short term	**2,113**	**41%**	**711**	**13%**

Source: Arvind Krishnamurthy, Stefan Nagel and Dmitry Orlov, "Sizing Up Repo," *Journal of Finance* 69, no. 6 (2014): 2381–2417, table II.

percentage was as high as 45 percent.[56] Obviously, these were not the fortunes being made on Wall Street or on the Gold Coast of Connecticut, but real estate speculation had become a mass sport.

All told, if we focus on that section of the market that was truly a product of the bubble, by the summer of 2007, $5.213 trillion in private-label asset-backed securities had been issued—that is, MBS generated from unconventional mortgages and credit card, student loan and auto debt. Of this total, the most dangerous mortgage component, subprime mortgage MBS, amounted to $1.3 trillion. Though this was "only" 12 percent of the total American mortgage market, the $1.3 trillion had been produced in a single surge since 2003. Of the total sum of $5.13 trillion, more than $3 trillion had been placed with long-term investors and $700 billion were placed directly with investment funds or investment banks. But $1.173 trillion were held by banks that funded them off balance sheet by issuing ABCP. As a result, ABCP had become the largest short-term money market instrument for investors looking to park cash for less than three months. The market for ABCP was larger even than for the short-term Treasury bills issued by

the US government to manage its cash flow. If there was a channel through which the crisis in real estate could ramify outward to unleash the global financial crisis, this was it—ABCP, the place where private label MBS met wholesale funding.

V

Every year in August the elite of the central banking and monetary economics world gathers at a resort in Jackson Hole, Wyoming. In August 2005 the theme of the conference was not the crisis brewing in the US housing market but a celebration in honor of the outgoing Fed chairman, Alan Greenspan. Most of the presentations were appropriately upbeat. But one rang an off note. It was given by Raghuram G. Rajan, an Indian by birth but a fully paid-up member of the American economics elite, professor at the Chicago Booth business school and chief economist at the IMF. His paper bore the heretical title "Has Financial Development Made the World Riskier?"[57] Rajan worried that the dramatic expansion of modern financial intermediation was building up a dangerous new appetite for risk. At Greenspan's farewell party, the message was not welcome. Rajan was slapped down by Larry Summers. Wielding his full authority as former Treasury secretary, Summers introduced himself as "someone who has learned a great deal about this subject from Alan Greenspan . . . and . . . who finds the basic, slightly Luddite premise of this paper to be largely misguided."[58] To highlight risks in a complex, modern financial system, as Rajan was tactlessly doing, was to invite "restriction" and other "misguided policy impulses." It would be like giving up air travel for fear of crashes.

This response from Summers—his warning that even to discuss risks within the system was to incite dangerous political reactions and tantamount to resisting technological progress—was emblematic of the attitudes that had driven a forty-year deregulatory push. The truly decisive early moves went back to the reemergence of a global capital market in the 1960s, the collapse of Bretton Woods, the deregulation of interest rates and capital flows in the early 1980s.[59] It was those moves that unleashed monetary instability

and precipitated Volcker's interest rate shock. It was that turmoil which forced innovation in the housing market and gave rise to the hyperactive new breed of Wall Street investment banks. The competitive flows of capital thus unleashed drove all that followed. Rubin and Summers added a personal touch with the 1999 Financial Services Modernization Act, which released the final restraints on the fusion of commercial and investment banking. Within months of departing the Treasury, Rubin had returned to banking at Citigroup. Summers took slightly longer to join Wall Street, but barely a year after the clash with Rajan at Jackson Hole he had joined hedge fund D. E. Shaw as a part-time managing director.

Summers's reaction to Rajan is all the more telling because the signs of stress in the world economy were so obvious. At the level of macroeconomic policy, Summers himself was willing to sound the alarm with his talk of a balance of financial terror. The commonplace recommendation to tighten fiscal policy might have helped. But this pointed the finger away from where the stress really was, in the financial system. Indeed, from the point of view of financial stability it might have been desirable if more of the AAA securities in circulation had been genuine US government debt rather than the products of financial engineering. In the final analysis, it was convenient to make the case at the level of macroeconomic aggregates. It was particularly easy to demand that a Republican president change his course. It was far less comfortable to question the house price boom and the giant Wall Street edifice erected on top of it.

The boosters far outnumbered the Cassandras and not just at Jackson Hole. The mortgage industry lobby did its job. David Lereah, the chief economist for the National Association of Realtors, chipped in with a book titled *Why the Real Estate Boom Will Not Bust*.[60, 61] Conservative pundits such as Larry Kudlow, economics editor of the *National Review,* railed against "all the bubbleheads who expect housing-price crashes in Las Vegas or Naples, Florida, to bring down the consumer, the rest of the economy, and the entire stock market."[62] Kudlow need not have worried. There was little sense of any urgency on the part of the authorities about limiting the boom.

Briefly, following Enron, there was a push for greater regulation. There was talk about requiring the parent sponsors of the off balance sheet SIVs to put more capital behind them. The threat alone was enough to bring

growth in the ABCP industry to a halt. Moody's warned investors that banks might soon face the end of one of their easiest funding sources. But in July 2004, as subprime was really hitting its stride, the regulators agreed to provide a permanent exemption that effectively allowed assets held in SIVs to be backed by only 10 percent of the capital that would have been required if the assets were held on the balance sheets of the banks themselves. This was particularly attractive for big commercial banks, like Citigroup and Bank of America, that were subject to relatively tight capital regulation, putting them at a huge disadvantage to the lightly regulated investment banks. It was following that regulatory shift that the ABCP market exploded from $650 billion to in excess of $1 trillion.[63] By the summer of 2007 Citigroup alone was guaranteeing $92.7 billion in ABCP, enough to wipe out its entire Tier 1 capital.

More than the grand gestures of deregulation, like the 1999 act, it was this kind of apparently small-scale regulatory change that unfettered the growth of shadow banking. The same was true for repo. Traditionally, repo had been limited by the fact that the categories of assets that were exempt from the automatic stay in case of bankruptcy included only US government and agency securities, bank certificates of deposits and bankers' acceptances. If those classes of security were offered as collateral in repo, in cases of bankruptcy they could be seized without delay and any losses made good. In 2005 the Bankruptcy Abuse Prevention and Consumer Protection Act gave creditors much stronger protection against defaulting borrowers, which ironically increased their willingness to lend. But it also expanded the repo collateral provided with special protection to include mortgage loans and mortgage-related securities. Not surprisingly, in the wake of the act there was a surge in bilateral repo secured on nonstandard assets.[64]

Could the Fed have contained the bubble through tougher interest rate policy? Greenspan's cuts of the early 2000s had triggered the lending surge. Indeed, it had clearly been Greenspan's intention to unleash a refinancing boom to help the recovery from the dot-com bust and the shock of 9/11. But what the Fed did not appreciate was the structural change in the mortgage machine the refinancing boom would trigger. Certainly by 2004 it was clear that it was time to raise rates. In seventeen tiny steps the Fed inched rates from 1 percent in June 2004 to 5.25 percent in June 2006. It was fine-tuning,

not shock and awe. The mortgage boom continued undeterred, as did global demand for American safe assets and the expansion of the shadow banking sector. By the spring of 2006, to the alarm of many commentators, the result was that the yield curve was inverted. Long-term rates were below the short-term interest rates set by the Fed. This was usually a signal for trouble. It meant that the normal bank-funding model of borrowing short to lend long no longer made any sense.

In due course, the inversion of the yield curve might by itself have produced a recession. But it wasn't Greenspan or Bernanke who killed the mortgage boom. It killed itself. By 2005 at the latest it was clear that low-quality mortgage debt was a ticking bomb. Many of the subprime mortgages were on balloon rates that would rapidly increase after a period of two or three years. In 2007 the typical adjustable-rate mortgage in the United States favored by low-income borrowers was resetting from an annual rate of 7–8 percent to 10–10.5 percent.[65] As traders such as Greg Lippmann at Deutsche Bank realized, between August 2006 and August 2009, $738 billion in mortgages would experience "payment shock."[66] As the escalated interest payments hit, a wave of defaults was more or less inevitable. Once that began it was only a matter of time before house prices stopped increasing and the market turned. At that point, millions of speculative real estate investments would go bad. Families would lose their homes. Thousands of MBS would suffer default and whoever held insurance would get rich. Nowhere in Lippmann's extensive document arguing for Deutsche Bank to short MBS was there any mention of Fed tightening. The subprime mortgage machine had a self-tightening timer built in. Unless house prices continued to rise at record rates, it would activate mercilessly and stop the boom in its tracks.

It was the first round of that tightening that was beginning to make itself felt in the most stressed communities across the United States already in 2006. Default rates were rising. It would not be long before the AAA rating granted to the lowest-quality CDO would be in doubt. To take advantage a growing band of contrarian investors began to build the "big short" positions that would make them famous. Those making the play included Lippmann at Deutsche Bank, J.P. Morgan and Goldman Sachs as well as a cluster of hedge funds. To build the position they bought CDS,

derivatives designed to provide protection against default. Anticipating shipwreck, the holders of the big short were making advanced bookings in the lifeboat. They could either hold their insurance until the bonds failed and their payouts were due or they could sell their positions at a huge profit to lenders who were desperate for default protection. The question was one of timing and the problem was funding. Going long in CDS when majority opinion was still driving the market up was an expensive and nerve-racking proposition. You were on the other side of the last surge in ABCP and repo deals. At Citigroup in the summer of 2007, CEO Chuck Prince was still telling journalists that "as long as the music is playing, you've got to get up and dance. We're still dancing."[67] The question was what would happen when the music stopped.

Chapter 3

TRANSATLANTIC FINANCE

Americans liked to think of their problems as American and outsiders were only too happy to concur. As the mortgage meltdown spread like a lethal virus across urban America in 2007–2008, European commentators took up the narrative of an American national crisis. "Feral" financial capitalism, like the Iraq war and climate change denial, was part of a toxic Anglo-American variant on modernity.[1] When the storm broke in 2008, the Schadenfreude among European politicians was palpable. The polite phrases at the UN only scratched the surface. On September 16, 2008, as Wall Street unraveled, Peer Steinbrück, Germany's tough-talking SPD finance minister, went before the Bundestag to announce that the global financial system faced a crisis originating in America from which Germany had so far been spared. "America's laissez-faire ideology," as practiced during the subprime crisis, "was as simplistic as it was dangerous," he later told Germany's parliamentarians. He confidently expected that America would soon forfeit its role as financial superpower.[2] French president Sarkozy chirped along with him. Just returned from New York on September 25, Sarkozy, who had formerly been regarded as a true disciple of Atlantic capitalism, told a crowd in Toulon that "the idea that the markets were always right was mad . . . laissez-faire is finished. The all-powerful market that always knows best is finished."[3] And just in case anyone wondered where the home of that mad idea was, Giulio Tremonti, Silvio Berlusconi's outspoken finance minister, boasted that Italy's banking system would be fine because

"it did not speak English."[4] It was convenient, but it was a self-deception. America's securitized mortgage system had been designed from the outset to suck foreign capital into US financial markets and foreign banks had not been slow to see the opportunity.

I

Since the 1980s Americans had grown used to the idea that Asians—first the Japanese, now the Chinese—owned their government debt. That was the anxiety that haunted the Hamilton Project. What they did not reckon with was that foreigners owned a large portion of America's houses. By 2008 roughly a quarter of all securitized mortgages were held by foreign investors. Fannie Mae and Freddie Mac funded $1.7 trillion of their portfolio of $5.4 trillion in mortgage-backed securities by selling securities to foreigners. China was by far the biggest foreign investor in these "Agency bonds," with holdings estimated at $500–600 billion.[5] But in the riskier segment of the securitized mortgage business it was Europeans, not Asians, who led the way.[6]

For nonconforming high-risk MBS, those not backed by Fannie Mae or Freddie Mac, the share held by European investors was in the order of 29 percent.[7] In 2006, at the height of the US mortgage securitization boom, a third of newly issued private label MBS were backed by British or European banks.[8] The segment of the securitization chain in which European banks were of truly crucial importance was also the weakest link in the chain, ABCP. In the summer of 2007, though it was Citigroup that had the largest off balance sheet SIV exposure, it was European banks that dominated the market. Overall, two thirds of the commercial paper issued had European sponsors, including 57 percent of the dollar-denominated commercial paper. Europe's banks had good standing with the ratings agencies, but they did not have large dollar-denominated depositor bases. If they wanted to get in on the MBS boom, they needed to go to the wholesale market.

Among the European sponsors, German financial institutions were particularly prominent, and what was remarkable was the kind of German bank that was involved. Germany's giant, Deutsche Bank, was a leading

ABCP Sponsor Location and Funding Currency (in $ millions)

Currency / Sponsor location	US dollars	Euro	Yen	Other	Total
Belgium	30,473	4,729	0	0	35,202
Denmark	1,796	0	0	0	1,796
France	51,237	23,670	228	557	75,692
Germany	139,068	62,885	0	2,566	204,519
Italy	1,365	0	0	0	1,365
Japan	18,107	0	22,713	0	40,820
Netherlands	56,790	65,859	0	3,116	125,765
Sweden	1,719	0	0	0	1,719
Switzerland	13,082	0	0	0	13,082
United Kingdom	92,842	62,298	0	3,209	158,349
United States	302,054	0	0	2,996	305,050
Total	**714,871**	**219,441**	**22,941**	**12,444**	**969,697**

Source: Viral V. Acharya and Philipp Schnabl, "Do Global Banks Spread Global Imbalances? Asset-Backed Commercial Paper During the Financial Crisis of 2007–09," *IMF Economic Review* 58, no. 1 (2010): 37–73, figure 15. Based on data from Moody's.

player on Wall Street. It is not for nothing that it featured as prominently as it did in Michael Lewis's bestselling narrative of the crisis, *The Big Short*, or in the subsequent Senate investigation.[9] Dresdner Bank, Germany's number two, was also heavily involved in the United States. But it was Germany's smaller regional banks, the Landesbanken, that threw themselves head over heels into the American adventure. In the early 2000s, at the insistence of Brussels, the Landesbanken were stripped of the local state guarantees that lowered their funding costs. They responded by taking a punt on adventurous financial engineering. Banks from the former industrial heartland of Germany, such as Sachsen-Finanzgruppe, WestLB and IKB of Düsseldorf, took huge gambles on real estate investments in the United States. At least four German sponsors—Sachsen, WestLB, IKB and Dresdner—had ABCP exposure large enough to wipe out their equity capital several times over.

Nor did European banks confine themselves to dealing in the securities. The Europeans went native, joining their American counterparts in integrating down the supply chain so as to control mortgage origination

itself. After all, if a Wall Street investment bank could do it, why not a European bank with some experience in retail banking? From the mid-1990s banks like Britain's HSBC aggressively bought into the American mortgage market. By 2005 HSBC could boast of having serviced 450,000 mortgages to a total value of $70 billion.[10] Credit Suisse built an American mortgage-servicing department that fed one of the largest ABS CDO operations of the early 2000s.[11] Deutsche Bank had close relationships with the giant mortgage-generating machines at Countrywide and AmeriQuest. In 2006 the German bank bought the subprime specialists MortgageIT Holdings and Chapel Funding LLC. As a Deutsche Bank press release glowed, ownership of these operations at the bottom of the US credit pyramid would "provide significant competitive advantages, such as access to a steady source of product for distribution into the mortgage capital markets."[12] From the point of view of generating high-yielding CDOs, it was precisely the bottom of the mortgage barrel that was most attractive.

II

How was this possible? It was easy enough to understand how China acquired claims on the United States. It had a gigantic trade surplus, the dollar proceeds of which were bought up by its financial authorities and invested in US Treasurys, giving rise to Larry Summers's scenario of a "balance of financial terror." But among those who worried about global macroeconomic imbalances, Europe was rarely mentioned. The EU current account surplus with the United States was modest compared with that of China. With the world as a whole, Europe's current account was in modest deficit. The Europeans did not peg their currencies against the dollar. There was no agency in Brussels accumulating foreign assets as part of a currency stabilization effort, no German sovereign wealth funds. So how did European banks end up owning such a large slice of American mortgage debt?

The answer is that European banks operated just like their adventurous American counterparts. They borrowed dollars to lend dollars. And the scale of this activity is revealed if we look not at the *net* flow of capital in and out of the United States (inflows minus outflows), which has its

Gross Capital Flows to the US by Region (% US GDP)

Source: Claudio Borio and Piti Disyatat, "Global Imbalances and the Financial Crisis: Link or No Link?," BIS Working Paper 346 (2011), graph 6.

counterpart in the trade deficit or surplus, but at the gross flows, which record how many assets were bought and sold in each direction. As the gross inflow data show, by far the largest purchasers of US assets, by far the largest foreign lenders to the United States prior to the crisis, were not Asian but European. Indeed, in 2007, roughly twice as much money flowed from the UK to the United States as from China.

Before 2008 the net financial flow from Asia to the United States could reasonably be construed as the financial counterpart to America's trade deficit with Asia. By contrast, the financial flows between Europe and the United States made up a financial circulatory system quite independent of the trade connections between the two. Across the Pacific, from Asia to the United States, money flowed one way. In the North Atlantic financial system it flowed both ways, both in and out of the United States. This was in the logic of the market-based banking model. Europe's banks did not have branches spread across the United States. But a Wall Street firm like Lehman didn't either. This was the beauty of the market-based model of banking. You borrowed the dollars on Wall Street to fund your holdings of mortgages from all over the United States.

The ABCP market was a showcase for this transatlantic system. The ABCP conduits organized bundles of securitized assets from the United States and Europe.[13] With those securities as collateral they then issued short-term commercial paper, which was bought by the managers of cash pools in the United States. In 2008, $1 trillion, or half of the prime nongovernment money market funds in the United States, were invested in the debt and commercial paper of European banks and their vehicles.[14] A large portion of this simply moved from one office on Wall Street to another, with one address being adorned with the name of a European bank. But hundreds of billions of dollars took a more circuitous route. They flowed out of the United States from the branches of foreign banks in New York to the head offices of European banks, from which they returned for investment in the United States, sometimes by way of an offshore tax haven such as Dublin or the Cayman Islands.[15] It was the spinning motion of this transatlantic financial axis that impelled the surge in financial globalization in the early twenty-first century.

In managing these flows, the multicurrency balance sheets of European banks played a crucial role. To understand the nature of these flows, take the example of a German bank keen to participate in the lucrative American mortgage business. The bank did not have an existing depositor base in dollars. Its existing liabilities—deposits, bonds issued and short-term borrowing—were in euros. This meant that the German bank had a funding problem if it wanted to lend in dollars. But in that respect it was no different from a Wall Street investment bank. To participate in the profitable American securitization wave, European banks exchanged part of their euro funding for dollars (option 1), holding a long dollar position or hedging by way of swap agreements (option 2). Or the German bank could borrow directly in the United States (option 3), for instance from an American money market fund eager to earn slightly more than the returns offered by Treasurys, now that the Chinese were buying them. The result would be a German bank with a balance sheet that featured liabilities and assets of different maturities and denominated in a variety of currencies. And its counterparts would include a bank or other business that had lent dollars in exchange for euros (if it had chosen funding options 1 or 2), or an American money market fund holding dollar-denominated debt issued by

a German bank (option 3). In the national balance of payments statistics one would see both borrowing from and lending to America happening within the accounts of the same bank. One could net the flows out to identify how much, on balance, flowed one way rather than the other, but that would give no idea of the scale of the commitments on each side. It would be akin to noting that two elephants on either end of a circus seesaw leave a net balance of zero. It would be true, but it would not be a very adequate description of the forces in play.

The rise of China dominated contemporary perceptions of early twenty-first-century globalization. And the axis of imbalance that attracted most attention was that between China and the United States. Worries about geopolitics, Larry Summers's balance of financial terror, Ben Bernanke's

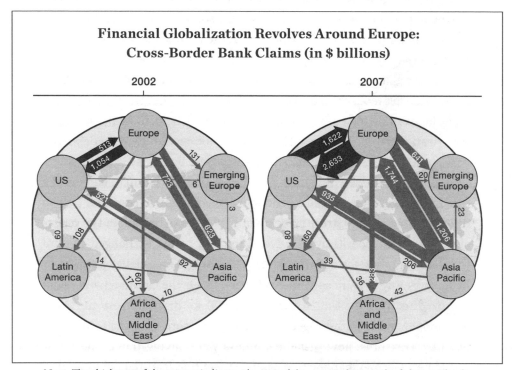

**Financial Globalization Revolves Around Europe:
Cross-Border Bank Claims (in $ billions)**

Note: The thickness of the arrows indicates the size of the outstanding stock of claims. The direction of the arrows indicates the direction of the claims: Arrows directed from region A to region B indicate lending from banks located in region A to borrowers located in region B.

Source: Stefan Avdjiev, Robert N. McCauley and Hyun Song Shin, "Breaking Free of the Triple Coincidence in International Finance," *Economic Policy* 31, no. 87 (2016): 409–451, graph 6.

savings glut, all pointed the finger in that direction. But if we map not annual flows but cross-border banking claims, this gives further proof of how one-sided the Sino-American view of the buildup to the crisis was. The central axis of world finance was not Asian-American but Euro-American. Indeed, of the six most significant pairwise linkages in the network of cross-border bank claims, five involved Europe.

European banking claims on the United States were the largest link in the system, followed by Asian claims on Europe and American claims on Europe. European claims on Asia exceeded the much commented upon Asian-American connections. Indeed, West European claims on emerging Eastern Europe alone were more than three times the size of American claims on Asia. It was also noticeable that oil- and gas-rich Middle Eastern investors preferred to channel their funds through Europe rather than directly to the United States. This was a pattern already established in the 1970s and only reinforced by the aggressive politics of Bush's "War on Terror." The European financial centers offered a safe channel through which funds from Asia and the Middle East were then sluiced into more speculative investments in the United States. It was not for nothing that China preferred to channel many of its claims on the United States through Belgium. In the process, the European financial system came to function, in the words of Fed analysts, as a "global hedge fund," borrowing short and lending long.[16]

What this suggests is a further crucial development of the argument. If it is misleading to construct our image of financial globalization around the Sino-American trade balance, to imagine it as centered on US securitization with outsiders being "sucked in" misses the point too. In fact, the entire structure of international banking in the early twenty-first century was transatlantic. The new Wall Street was not geographically confined to the southern end of Manhattan. It was a North Atlantic system. The second node, detached from but integrally and inseparably connected to New York, was the City of London.[17] In the nineteenth century, in the age of the gold standard and the British Empire, London had been the capital of global finance in its own right. From the 1950s, the City of London made a new role for itself as the main hub for offshore global dollar financing.

III

In the aftermath of World War II, the Bretton Woods monetary system had sought to restrict speculative capital flows. This gave the US Treasury and the Fed controlling roles. The aim was to minimize currency instability and to manage the global shortage of dollars. But it meant that the US authorities had to operate the kinds of controls that we now associate with China. This was a fetter on private banking. From the 1950s, with connivance of the UK authorities, the City of London developed as a financial center that sidestepped those constraints.[18] British, American, European and then Asian banks too began to use London as a center for unregulated deposit taking and lending in dollars. Among the first to avail themselves of these "eurodollar" accounts were Communist states that wanted to keep their export earnings safe from meddling by the US Treasury. They set a trend. By the 1960s eurodollar accounts in London offered the basic framework for a largely unregulated global financial market. As a result, what we know today as American financial hegemony had a complex geography. It was no more reducible to Wall Street than the manufacture of iPhones can be reduced to Silicon Valley. Dollar hegemony was made through a network. It was by way of London that the dollar was made global.[19]

Driven by the search for profit, powered by bank leverage, offshore dollars were from the start a disruptive force. They had scant regard for the official value of the dollar under Bretton Woods and it was the pressure this exercised that helped to make the gold peg increasingly untenable. When the final collapse of Bretton Woods coincided in 1973 with the surge in OPEC dollar revenue, the rush of offshore money through London's eurodollar accounts became a flood. By the early 1980s both Britain and the United States had abolished all restrictions on capital movements and this was followed in October 1986 by Thatcher's "Big Bang" deregulation. The City of London was thrown open to outside investment, sacrificing guild-like structures that dated back centuries to the imperative of creating a genuinely global financial center. Within a decade the UK's own investment banks had been swallowed by their American and European competitors.[20] American, Asian and European capital flooded in. This involved not

only regulatory change and huge financial flows but the physical reconfiguration of the medieval heart of the City of London. To house the gigantic new offices and electronic trading desks needed by global banks, Canadian real estate moguls undertook the construction of a massive new office complex in the abandoned postindustrial docklands of Canary Wharf. In April 2004 Chancellor Gordon Brown ceremonially opened the new Lehman offices at 25 Bank Street.[21] Meanwhile, the emerging hedge fund industry found a comfortable new home in Mayfair, where the American insurer AIG would choose to locate its later notorious Financial Products division.

For many of the most fast-paced global transactions, it was London, not Wall Street, that was the location of choice. By 2007, 35 percent of the global turnover in foreign exchange, running at a staggering $1 trillion per day, was conducted between computer systems in the City of London.[22] European banks were the biggest players in the business. London was also the hub for the over-the-counter (OTC) interest rates derivatives business, a means of hedging against the risk of interest rate fluctuations and an essential complement to repo deals. Of an annual turnover in interest rate derivatives in excess of $600 trillion, London claimed 43 percent, to New York's 24 percent.[23]

A decade after Thatcher's Big Bang, with Britain's native banking industry under intense competitive pressure, Tony Blair's New Labour government set about further streamlining the City's regulatory system.[24] Nine specialist regulators were combined into a single agency, the Financial Services Authority (FSA). It set a new low bar for financial oversight. Tony Blair's chancellor, Gordon Brown, boasted that the FSA offered "not only light but limited regulation."[25] The FSA was mandated to achieve its "goals in the most efficient and effective way." "[N]ot damaging the competitive position of the United Kingdom" was its top priority.[26] The FSA was required to apply cost benefit analysis to its own interventions and benchmark its operations against other countries.[27] Perhaps not surprisingly, given this mandate, the FSA's staff was a fraction of that of its US counterparts. As Howard Davies, the FSA's first chair, put it in the libertarian language of the day: "The philosophy of the F.S.A. from when I set it up has been to say, 'Consenting adults in private? That's their problem.'"[28] The sort of thing that you could do in London but not in New York is exemplified by "collateral rehypothecation."

In a repo, the main flexible source of funds for investment banks, other banks acting as "broker-dealers" took securities as collateral in exchange for cash. What were they to do with their large stockpiles of collateral? Why not use this collateral as collateral in further repo loans, this time on behalf of the broker itself, a so-called reverse repo? In the United States, under regulations that went back to 1934, such rehypothecation of collateral was strictly limited to no more than 140 percent of the collateral being held. In the UK there was no limit on rehypothecation. As a result, according to investigations by a team of analysts from the IMF, the City of London came to function as a "platform for higher leveraging not available in the United States." The scale of this activity was enormous. According to the IMF team, trading in and out of London the main European and US banks achieved a collateral multiplication of 400 percent, amounting to roughly $4.5 trillion in additional funding, effectively out of thin air.[29]

The UK's liberalization not only freed up UK markets but acted as a crowbar to dislodge regulation worldwide. A transatlantic feedback loop drove regulation down on both sides.[30] The notorious US deregulation decisions taken by the Clinton administration in the late 1990s, which overturned the last remaining financial restrictions of the New Deal era, were not taken in a vacuum. The 1999 law was not called the Financial Services Modernization Act for nothing. There was a distinct vision of modern finance that the US industry was chasing and it was defined by global competition, above all by the City of London. In promoting the legislation, Senator Charles Schumer (D-NY) insisted "the future of America's dominance as the financial center of the world" was at stake. If Congress did not pass the bill, London, Frankfurt or Shanghai would take over.[31] New York, certainly, stood to benefit, but that should not mislead one into thinking in terms of national champions. No one had been more active in shaping the global marketplace in London than expat American bankers working for the London offices of the major Wall Street firms. What Wall Street wanted was license to bring back home the adventurous practices developed among "consenting adults" in London.

Nor was it only Americans in London. European politicians and cultural critics might be skeptical of freewheeling "Anglo-Saxon" finance. But this downplays the extent to which Europeans coconstructed global finance.

From the 1980s onward, Swiss, German, French and Dutch banks began to buy into the City of London with aggressive acquisitions. It was, more often than not, their springboard for a venture into US markets. In 1989 Deutsche Bank acquired Morgan Grenfell Group before buying Bankers Trust in the United States in 1999, and Scudder Investments, a US asset management firm, in 2002. Shortly thereafter, Germany's leading bank declared English to be its official working language. Credit Suisse was unusual in starting with the acquisition of First Boston in 1990 before reorganizing itself as CSFB in 1996–1997, the same year that it acquired the London firm BZW from Barclays. Germany's Dresdner Bank bought Kleinwort Benson in 1995 before buying the small but highly influential New York investment bank Wasserstein Perella in 2001. In the 1980s City of London insider Hoare Govett sold out to Security Pacific before being snapped up by the expansive Dutch bank ABN AMRO, which would become the leading European issuer of ABCP before being acquired and dismembered by a pan-European consortium. The Swiss bank UBS-SBC acquired S. G. Warburg in London in 1995. In 1997 it followed this with the purchase of Dillon, Read & Co., an investment bank in New York. After abortive merger talks with Merrill Lynch in 1999, UBS bought out the asset manager PaineWebber. With its fixed-income and currency businesses booming, in June 2004 UBS's CEO, Marcel Ospel, announced that his ambition was to make the Swiss bank into not only the premier wealth manager but the leading investment bank in the world.[32] UBS never reached that objective, but its giant Connecticut-based office did manage to make the bank into the third-largest issuer of CDO based on private label MBS after Merrill and Citigroup, and the leader in the riskiest mezzanine ABS segment.

All told, in 2007 the City of London was home to 250 foreign banks and bank branches, twice as many as operated out of New York.[33] But the European footprint in Wall Street was very substantial. Of the top twenty broker-dealers in New York, twelve were foreign owned and held 50 percent of the assets.[34] These were the competitors in the top tier. But European financial adventurism came in all shapes and sizes. And it was not confined to the City of London–Wall Street axis. From the 1980s Dublin set out to establish itself as a low-tax, low-regulation jurisdiction, attracting bankers

from Europe and North America. A case in point was the German bank Depfa. Founded in 1922 at the time of the Weimar Republic by the government of Prussia to make subsidized housing loans, Depfa moved to Dublin's International Financial Services Center in 2002 to take advantage of Ireland's welcoming tax laws. Depfa soon became known across the world as an adventurous financer of infrastructure, providing credits to the Spanish city of Jerez, giving financial advice to Athens and financing a conference center in Dublin and a toll road between Tijuana and San Diego. The Irish-German bank invested the retirement fund of the teachers of the state of Wisconsin, as well as funding Vancouver's Golden Ears Bridge project. By the time of the crisis, Depfa's total assets as reported by credit-rating agency Moody's had swollen to $218 billion, one-third the size of Lehman.[35] This astonishing expansion was not from Depfa's own resources. It had precious few to begin with. Depfa grew like other market-driven modern banks. It borrowed to lend. And it made handsome profits doing so. So much profit, in fact, that it attracted the attention of Hypo Real Estate, the Munich-based mortgage lender. Hypo was looking to diversify its risk profile and in July 2007 finalized plans to buy out Depfa, taking the combined balance sheet of the two banks to more than 400 billion euros.[36]

IV

As they had grown up in the nineteenth and twentieth centuries across the United States and Europe, modern banks had been regional and national in scope. They lived in close and often incestuous relations with national Treasuries, central banks and regulators. The reglobalization of banking unleashed from the 1950s raised basic questions of governance. The original impetus was to create zones of financial activity that were lightly regulated in offshore centers like London. But by the early 1970s at the latest it was clear that this transatlantic financial system had the potential for dangerous instability.[37] Furthermore, the competitive race for profit and market share among the banks in turn unleashed a regulatory race to the bottom. In 1984 Fed chair Paul Volcker proposed new rules to set minimum standards for bank capital, hoping thereby to prevent undercutting of relatively

robust banks by less well-capitalized competitors, notably from Japan. For the resilience of a bank in the face of losses on its loan book, capital is the crucial criterion. The more capital a bank has, the more it is able to absorb losses. However, the larger a bank's book of loans relative to its capital, the higher the rate of return it will be able to offer investors. That was the point of the elaborate legal structures designed to hold securitized assets off balance sheet, to minimize the capital invested and to maximize its leverage. Capital ratios were, therefore, one of the neuralgic points of bank governance. After years of deadlock, in September 1986 the Fed and the Bank of England reached a deal, which in July 1988 finally brought the Basel Committee to agreement on what was known as the Capital Accord, or Basel I. Henceforth, the minimum level of capital that a large international bank should aim to hold against normal business loans was set at 8 percent.[38]

Almost as soon as the standard was set, the argument over its definition, implementation and consequences began. If the 8 percent rule had been imposed as a simple percentage, the effect would have been to encourage banks to make the most high-risk investments available in a frantic attempt to milk every cent of profit from every dollar of capital. It would have incentivized risk taking. So the Basel Committee provided for a basic system of risk weights, requiring no capital to be held against the low-risk, short-term debt of governments that were members of the OECD, the exclusive club of rich countries.[39] Mortgages and mortgage-backed securities were also favored with low-risk weights. But at the margin, the system continued to encourage risk taking. Furthermore, the lax provisions of Basel I enabled banks to hold substantial parts of their portfolio off balance sheet in special purpose vehicles (SPV) financed by ABCP. This was one of the main reasons why European banks were so active in ABCP. Their national regulators interpreted Basel I in such a way as to allow them to hold hundreds of billions of dollars of securities and fund them with short-term commercial paper, without needing to commit much of their capital. Not only was their capital stretched thin but the maturity mismatch was terrifying.

The obvious inadequacies of Basel I set in motion the search for a new framework that finally emerged in 2004 with the Basel II accord. But the transition from one regime to the other was telling. Whereas Basel I had been a conventional regulation aiming to impose standards on the industry

from the outside, the chief ambition of Basel II was to align risk regulation with "best business practice" as defined by the bankers themselves. Basel II did require off balance sheet risks to be brought onto the banks' own accounts. But at the same time, they were encouraged to apply their own risk-weighting models to those assets to decide how large their capital buffer needed to be. Far greater reliance was placed also on the credit evaluations issued by the private credit rating agencies.[40] Though Basel II notionally maintained the 8 percent capital requirement, once the big banks applied their proprietary risk-weighting models, they found that they could sustain larger balance sheets than ever before. Under Basel I mortgage assets had been rated as relatively safe and counted only 50 percent for purposes of calculating the necessary capital. Rather than tightening those regulations as a way of moderating the real estate boom, Basel II cut the capital weight of mortgage assets to 35 percent, which made it far more attractive to hold high-yielding mortgage-backed assets.[41] Precisely as the private label securitization boom was about to accelerate, the regulations lightened.[42]

One method of massaging the figure down was to purchase default insurance against risky assets in the portfolio. The key supplier of default insurance for "regulatory capital relief" was the American insurance giant AIG and its Financial Products offices in London and Paris. By the end of 2007 it was providing insurance for $379 billion in assets held by major European banks, led by ABN AMRO ($56.2 billion), Danish bank Danske ($32.2 billion), German bank KfW ($30 billion), French mortgage lender Crédit Logement ($29.3 billion), BNP Paribas ($23.3 billion) and Société Générale ($15.6 billion).[43] AIG's insurance allowed them to save a total of $16 billion in regulatory capital, further increasing leverage, profits and bonus payments.[44]

Rather than imposing intrusive inspections and external audits, Basel II placed heavy emphasis on self-regulation, disclosure and transparency. "Well-informed" market judgments would do the work of oversight better than "arbitrary" regulatory decisions. After all, rational investors could have no interest in exposing themselves to the risk of catastrophic loss, or so the reasoning went. They would price bank shares accordingly, sending a clear signal as to which banks were safe and which were not. The regulators were utterly subservient to the logic of the businesses they were supposed to be

regulating. The draft text of what would become the Basel II regulations was prepared for the Basel Committee by the Institute of International Finance, the chief lobby group of the global banking industry.[45]

Nor was the Basel framework well designed to drive standards upward. Both Basel I and Basel II enshrined the principle of "home country rules." This required signatories to the system to accept the regulations of all other parties as adequate. So banks from lax areas of supervision were free to operate according to their domestic norms in lucrative American and European markets. By the same token, it excused the City of London and New York from responsibility for onerous oversight of the hundreds of foreign banks that congregated in their precincts.[46] The Fed further amplified the effect by declaring in January 2001 that the US banking operations of foreign financial holding companies that were considered adequately capitalized in their home countries would not need to meet separate capital adequacy rules in the United States.[47] Despite the huge scale of their American operations, the European banks were not required to hold adequate capital actually in the United States.

Not surprisingly, given how forgiving its provisions were, European regulators encountered little resistance as they pushed ahead to implement Basel II. It was a framework that Europe's expansive banks could happily live with. The SEC and the New York Fed, which oversaw America's investment banks, took a similar view. Tellingly, it was the FDIC, the American deposit insurance agency that oversaw medium and small American banks, that raised objections. The FDIC's chair, Sheila Bair, an outspoken midwestern Republican appointee, was incredulous that big banks were effectively being given license to "set their own capital requirements."[48] It would give them a huge competitive advantage over their smaller competitors. The FDIC estimated that the introduction of Basel II would permit big banks to reduce their capital by 22 percent. In 2006 Blair threw whatever political weight she could muster into a delaying action. With Bernanke as the new Fed chair she negotiated a compromise under which the short-term reduction in capitalization due to the introduction of Basel II should not exceed 15 percent per bank before 2011.[49] Partly, as a result, if we take leverage— the ratio of bank balance sheet to bank capital—as the basic indicator of banking risk, a considerable gap emerged between the United States and

the Europeans ahead of the crisis. According to the calculations of the Bank for International Settlements (BIS), Deutsche Bank, UBS and Barclays, three of the most aggressive European players in global financial markets, all boasted leverage in excess of 40:1, compared with an average of 20:1 for their main American competitors. In 2007, even before the crisis struck with full force, leverage at Deutsche and UBS touched 50:1.[50] Even allowing for differences in the ways in which Europeans and Americans account for bank balance sheets, the gap was significant.

To the American banks this did not seem fair. In response their industry lobby pushed hard to level the playing field. In February 2007 New York mayor Michael Bloomberg traveled to London, where he met with the chair of the UK's FSA, and used the London platform to lobby for further deregulation in the United States. "The FSA is an example of the kind of streamlined and responsive regulatory framework Congress must implement if New York City is to remain the financial capital of the world," the mayor intoned. Bloomberg wasn't the only one making the trip. That same month the *Financial Times* reported that Citigroup had "reshuffled its management in a move that gave greater influence to London-based executives, with five receiving global responsibility for their areas and the global head of commodities moving to London. Merrill Lynch, J.P. Morgan and Lehman Brothers also gave global management roles to executives based in the UK."[51] It was with these pressures in mind that Bloomberg and Senator Charles Schumer in May 2007 put their names to a McKinsey & Company report warning that New York's position as the world's leading financial center was under threat unless it fell into line with international standards. "The findings are clear: . . . our regulatory framework is a thicket of complicated rules, rather than a streamlined set of commonly understood principles, as is the case in the United Kingdom and elsewhere."[52]

Of course at every stage in the construction of global capital markets, think tanks, economists and lawyers contributed ideas and argumentation to justify the next move. Technological change gave banks massive new information-processing capacity. The complex financial instruments they produced exuded an energizing charisma.[53] The clannish society of the bankers created a social force field of common assumptions and an overweaning superiority complex. They were the masters of the universe. They could not

fail. But the basic driver of expansion and change was the competitive search for profit, played out in the force field of financial engineering, transnational capital movement and competitive deregulation between Wall Street, the City of London and Basel. It was not that the key players were completely oblivious to risk. But they believed in their capacity to manage it and were totally committed to maximizing the rate of return. So every regulation and every restriction on leverage was subject to second-guessing and subversion by the overwhelming force of competition and the unfettered movement of capital that had been gathering steam since the 1960s.

What if the regulations failed? What if there was a comprehensive crisis of the transatlantic financial system? No one wanted to ask that question. In the rescue of the emerging markets in the 1990s it was Washington that had taken the lead. The US Treasury and the IMF acted in concert. Though they had faced determined criticism and foot-dragging from the Europeans, their resources were up to the task of bailing out Mexico or South Korea.[54] Would that be the case if it were the transatlantic financial system that suffered a circulatory failure? The sums involved were enormous, denominated not in the billions or even hundreds of billions but in trillions. In the last instance, US banks could expect support from the bottomless resources of the Fed. But the question was particularly pressing for European banks operating a multicurrency balance sheet. In case of emergency, where would they get the dollars they needed? Who would be their lender of last resort?

The global Financial Stability Forum (FSF), a group set up in the wake of the 1990s financial crises, had been edging around the question since 2000. At the Bank of England, John Gieve was keen to run "table exercises" to game the scenario of a major international banking failure. But he met with little enthusiasm. Bank of England governor Mervyn King, a thoroughbred macroeconomist, was little interested in the technical issues of financial stability. "There was no real appetite on the US side to get into discussing particular examples. We were offering to put HSBC or Barclays on the table, with real balance sheets, and maybe in return, they would do Citi or Lehman. But that never got off the ground."[55] Would Europe's central banks have the dollar reserves necessary to backstop the European financial system? It was an old-fashioned question, seemingly out of season

in a world of limitless global liquidity.[56] But when the question was put by analysts from the BIS, the answer was sobering. In the balance sheets of the European banks at the end of 2007 there was a mismatch between dollar assets (lending) and dollar liabilities (funding by way of deposits, bonds or short-term money market borrowing) of $1.1–1.3 trillion.[57]

The only central banks that held these kinds of sums were in China and Japan. Against the backdrop of a sanguine view about financial markets, their "hoarding" of dollars was widely seen as a sign of insecurity, an after-effect of the trauma of the 1997 crisis.[58] It is telling that no one troubled to ask the question of what the adequate level of reserves would be for a European country with a gigantic globalized banking system. As it turns out, given the scale of the banking business in their jurisdictions, the level of foreign exchange reserves held by the Swiss and British central banks was astonishingly low—less than $50 billion each. To backstop the sprawling banking system of the eurozone, the European Central Bank had little more than $200 billion on hand. What did this say about their assumptions about both financial risk and financial sovereignty? When asked later how he justified such minimal reserve holdings prior to the crisis, one of the most outspoken central bankers of the period paused for a minute, smiled at a point well taken and then said quite simply: "Given our long history of relations with the Fed, we didn't expect to have any difficulty getting hold of dollars." In other words, there was a presumption that collaboration would be forthcoming and in an emergency the Fed would provide Europe, and London in particular, with the dollars it needed. Given the scale of the offshore dollar business there could be no other answer. But for that same reason, it was also an astonishingly audacious assumption, an expectation so exorbitant that it was better left unspoken.

Chapter 4

EUROZONE

If Europe preferred not to highlight its role in the "American" financial crisis of 2008, covering its tracks was made easier by the fact that from 2010 Europe was consumed by its own "authentically" European crisis. The eurozone crisis followed directly on the footsteps of Wall Street and the US mortgage bust. But as conventionally understood, it is as if the Wall Street crisis and the eurozone disaster belong to different worlds. Whereas the US crisis involved overextended banks and mortgage borrowers impelled by greed and financial excess, the eurozone crisis would revolve around quintessentially European themes of public finance and national sovereignty. It would pit Greeks against Germans and reawaken memories of World War II. Both crisis narratives play to type: mercenary Americans, squabbling European nationalisms. But was it merely bad luck that the two crises followed so closely upon each other? Was it merely bad luck that the same banks were involved in both? If the buildup to the American crisis was less all-American than is generally credited, how "European" were the problems of the eurozone?

I

As the twenty-first century began, the Europeans could certainly be forgiven for being preoccupied with questions of politics and institution building.

With the introduction of the euro as a single currency between 1999 and 2002 and the expansion of the EU to include much of Eastern Europe in 2004, they were embarked on truly dramatic experiments, which were driven as much by political and geopolitical considerations as by economics.[1]

As far as the euro is concerned, the story again goes back to the early 1970s and the collapse of Bretton Woods. Between 1945 and 1971, the Europeans did not have to worry about intra-European currency issues. The dollar tied to the gold reserve in Fort Knox was the anchor of the global system. Once Nixon abandoned the gold peg in August 1971, Europe faced a problem. Fluctuating exchange rates would disrupt the tightly integrated trading networks that had brought Europe together. On the other hand, efforts to create a zone of exchange-rate stability by pegging the European currencies against one another reopened the basic question of power. In a European Monetary System, whose currency would replace the dollar as the anchor, as the "key currency"? The stresses might have been manageable if capital movement had been constrained, limiting speculative attacks. But by the early 1980s the freewheeling habits of the eurodollar business had become the global norm. Huge surges of hot money between currencies put extreme pressure on the more financially fragile states and conferred an intolerable degree of influence on Germany's conservative central bank. From the early 1970s the Budesbank's anti-inflationary stance and the resulting strength of the Deutschmark constrained not only Germany's own government in Bonn but the governments of all of the rest of Europe too. By 1983 even France's Socialist administration under François Mitterrand was forced to give in. After a series of messy devaluations between 1981 and 1983, Paris abandoned its effort at social democracy in one country and adopted instead a hard-currency policy of "franc fort." Interest rates would be set at whatever level was necessary to hold the franc against the Deutschmark, even if that meant borrowers paying 18 percent or more. Far from seeking to restrict capital movement, European officials at international organizations like The OECD pushed for further liberalization. The pressures generated by unrestricted capital movements across Europe's fixed exchanges in turn provided a powerful argument for those who favorerd ever closer European integration.[2] How else were the weaker members of the European Monetary System to regain even a modicum of control over the conduct of monetary policy? By

the late 1980s plans were afoot, driven above all by Jacques Delors, the president of the European Commission, and his supporters in the French Socialist Party, for another round of negotations over monetary integration. Given the national interests at stake those would most likely have gone nowhere had it not been for the sudden end to the cold war. The fall of the Berlin Wall in 1989 and German chancellor Helmut Kohl's irresistible push for national reunification threatened to make Germany even more dominant. A currency union and irrevocable economic unification seemed to both Kohl and Mitterrand the best way of securing a much larger Germany in a peaceful and stable continent.[3] As a price of surrendering the Deutschmark, the Germans exacted the promise that the new European Central Bank would continue the conservative heritage of the Bundesbank. But a joint central bank board would give a voice to all the other member states, and monetary union would end the ruinous cross-country pressure exercised by financial markets.

It was a spectacularly ambitious undertaking. The monetary union came into full effect in 2001. There was a single European central bank. There were fiscal rules limiting deficits and setting debt ceilings (known as the Stability and Growth Pact). But the euro was clearly unfinished.[4] There was no unified economic policy. No unified regulatory structure for banking. Nor, however, was there much urgency in moving to further integration. In its early years, the new currency zone performed tolerably well. European growth accelerated. After an initial hike in prices following the adoption of the single currency, inflation remained moderate. Capital markets were calm.

Despite this benign atmosphere, there were two problems that preoccupied experts both inside and outside the eurozone. The first was whether preexisting imbalances in intra-European trade would narrow or expand over time.[5] The fear was that the lack of currency adjustment could lead to cumulative divergence as less competitive regions fell further and further behind. Second, there was the risk of asymmetric external shocks.[6] A bust in tourism would hurt Greece far more than Germany. A collapse in Chinese import demand would damage Germany in a way that it would not hurt Ireland. American critics, in particular, warned that Europe's labor markets did not have the flexibility or mobility of their American counterparts.[7] And if people would not move, faced with a crisis, Europe would need a common system of benefits, taxes and spending to allow funds to flow from the more

prosperous to the more hard-hit regions. Along with labor mobility, it was this backbone of social security, disability and unemployment benefits that held the gigantic diversity of the US economy from Alabama to California together. Worryingly, there was plenty of self-congratulation in Brussels in the early 2000s but little urgency about building the overarching mechanism of fiscal redistribution and burden sharing that would be necessary to see the eurozone through a recession, let alone a major financial crisis.

Getting to the moment of unification had required huge efforts from many members of the eurozone. Italy, in particular, imposed severe belt tightening.[8] The collective effort of the 1990s to stabilize Italy's finances shaped a generation of Italian technocrats and politicians who would go on to play a key role in European politics, among them Mario Monti, economist, EU commissioner and future prime minister of Italy, and Mario Draghi, the future head of the ECB.[9] It was another Italian economist, Romano Prodi, who as president of the commission oversaw the introduction of the new currency. But having mastered Italy's acute financial political crisis of 1992–1993 and achieved euro membership, there was little energy left in Rome for further initiatives. The victory of Silvio Berlusconi's Forza Italia in the 2001 elections was a sign of the times. Far from making progress toward further European integration, holding the line on the budget criteria set in the Maastricht Treaty was hard enough. In 2003 France and Germany both exceeded the agreed limit of a 3 percent budget deficit, but Brussels shrank from imposing sanctions on such heavyweights. To fiscal disciplinarians this raised the alarm. Would the EU's central institutions ever have the political courage to impose themselves on larger members? For others the more pressing question was what was wrong with Germany.

Germany's entry into the euro did not go well. The other members made sure to settle on competitive exchange rates against the Deutschmark. Germany's exports took a hit. Its rule-busting budget deficits reflected its anemic growth. The world's media labeled Germany the "sick man of Europe."[10] Germans themselves talked of a "blockierte Gesellschaft" (blocked society).[11] The response from Gerhard Schroeder's Red-Green coalition, which governed Germany from 1998 to 2005, was unexpectedly energetic. For years Germans had suffered from painfully high levels of long-term unemployment, exacerbated by the sudden deindustrialization of the former GDR. In 2005

joblessness would peak at 10.6 percent. To combat this scourge, between 2003 and 2005 the Schroeder government announced a national restructuring program titled Agenda 2010. Its main thrust was a multiphase program of labor market liberalization and benefit cuts, designed by a committee headed by VW's head of human resources, Peter Hartz.[12] The fourth and final phase of cuts, Hartz IV, became synonymous with a new German "reform" narrative. The unemployed were returned to work. Wage restraint restored German competitiveness. The reward came already in 2003 when Germany could boast of being the world export champion (Exportweltmeister).

Agenda 2010 would come to define a new bipartisan self-understanding of Germany's political class.[13] Having accomplished the enormous task of reunification, Germany had overcome its internal difficulties and "reformed" its way back to economic health. It is a narrative that is superficially compelling and it would have significant implications for how Berlin approached the crisis of the eurozone, but it does not withstand close scrutiny. Hartz IV certainly drove millions of people more or less willingly off long-term unemployment benefits into a range of insecure jobs. This helped to hold down wages for unskilled workers, such as cashiers and cleaning workers. In the first ten years of the euro, despite soaring productivity, half of German households experienced no wage growth at all. This shortened unemployment rolls. It also increased pretax inequality and lowered Germany's wages relative to its European neighbors. But as to the competitiveness of German exporters, the significance of Hartz IV is far less obvious.[14] German companies do not win export orders by shaving the wages of unskilled workers. A far more important source of competitive advantage came from outsourcing production to Eastern Europe and Southern Europe. Added to which there was the boost from the global recovery of the early 2000s.

While its economic impact has been exaggerated, what Hartz IV did transform was German politics. The blue-collar electorate and the left wing of the SPD never forgave Schroeder for Hartz IV.[15] The left wing split from the SPD to unify with the former Communists of the East. The result was a new party known as Die Linke, which gathered almost 10 percent of the electorate. Together, Die Linke, the SPD and the Greens were a powerful political force. Red-Red-Green was capable of winning a majority. But the bitter divisions between them over Agenda 2010 made a broad-based

center-left coalition difficult to imagine. The result was to hand the political initiative to their opponents. The decisive force in European politics for the next decade and beyond would be German Christian Democracy and its leader, Angela Merkel.

Merkel has come to be seen as the figurehead of Europe's political center—oscillating between conservative stances on economic and financial policy and cultural modernization.[16] When she first emerged on the political scene her profile was harder edged. In the 2005 election that brought her to power, Merkel ran on a strong promarket platform. It was unpopular and she subsequently softened her stance. But there is little doubt that the 2005 agenda expressed the chancellor's basic personal vision. It can be summarized in three numbers: 7, 25 and 50. As Merkel is fond of pointing out, Europe has 7 percent of the world's population and 25 percent of global GDP. But it is responsible for 50 percent of global social spending.[17] This, as Merkel sees it, is not sustainable. Germany's growth is steady, but slow at best. Germany's population, along with that of much of Europe, is aging. What has to give is government spending. Fiscal consolidation is the deep continuity of Merkel's administrations. As she announced in her first speech at Davos in January 2006: "To understand the social market economy as a NEW social market economy in the twenty-first century we must first of all reorder the priorities of politics toward an understanding of politics that is directed ahead, toward future generations. For us in Germany that means first of all clearing up our financial situation, our budgets. We have a demographic problem. We know that we have too few young people and nevertheless we live at the expense of the future by running up debts. That means that we rob future generations of their room for investment and development and that is immoral."[18]

Needless to say, this was music to the ears of business lobbyists concerned to see taxation and state spending held in check. But Angela Merkel's first government was a grand coalition with the defeated SPD.[19] Fiscal consolidation, like Hartz IV, commanded a consensus across the center ground of German politics. The finance ministry was claimed by Peer Steinbrück, an acolyte of the legendary SPD chancellor of the 1970s and 1980s, Helmut Schmidt.[20] Steinbrück was profoundly committed to a supply-side, anti-Keynesian vision of economic policy. For him restoring "fiscal room" was

not merely a matter of financial stability. The ossification of the government budget under the impact of quasi-automatic entitlement spending and interest payments was indicative of a broader problem affecting the developed world: the crisis of democratic politics and democratic participation. What choice could political parties offer to voters if the room for budgetary maneuver was restricted by "entitlement spending," debt service and low tax rates to 1 percent of GDP one way or another? One could of course go the route of the Cheney wing of the Republicans and simply blow up the deficit. But if one was not willing to take that risk, one was forced into the center ground. In a proportional representation system like Germany's, this led to disaffection among the voters and the splintering of the party political landscape, with the once-dominant CDU and SPD huddling together in the center. Merkel's grand coalition was indicative of the impasse. It was not for nothing that "postdemocracy" became one of the buzzwords of German political discussion in the early 2000s.[21] For Steinbrück, paradoxically, present-day discipline was a promise of freedom to come.

Beyond these high-minded considerations, German fiscal strategy was also driven by more basic calculations of electoral advantage. Over the two decades since unification, West Germany had poured more than a trillion euros into reconstruction and regional subsidies for the East.[22] In 2005–2006, as Merkel's grand coalition took office, the mood in the western Länder, and particularly the rich southern states, was resentful. They had been conscripted into a gigantic act of solidarity with the East. Now they had had enough. Capping deficits was a not-so-covert promise to the rich southern states to rebalance priorities away from the needy and indebted eastern and northern members of the Bund. Fatefully for the future of the eurozone, the problem of fiscal control was cast by German politics already from the early 2000s as one of equity within a federal transfer union. Well before the Greek crisis broke, the most prosperous regions of West Germany had made clear their refusal to take responsibility for other people's debts, German or otherwise. The argument that the debts "shouldered by the West" to pay for spending "in the East" had generated huge orders for West German business—in effect exports within Germany from West to East—cut no ice. After 2010 the same argument would cut no ice at the European level either. What the most influential voters and voices in German public

opinion wanted was simple: discipline all around. In 2006 a commission was set up to devise a new federal fiscal settlement. The idea, following the Swiss example of 2001, was to adopt a "debt brake" to block any further expansion of debt at the Bund, Länder or Commune level. Hammering out the multilevel political deal was slow work. But Steinbrück and the Federal Ministry of Finance were sanguine. As the global economic horizon began to darken in 2007–2008, the German finance ministry was projecting a budget surplus by 2011.[23]

Of course, national politics and the drama of reunification gave a particular hue to the German discussions. But there is no need to construct a new narrative of the peculiarities of German history, or to search for some particular German trauma that will explain Berlin's newfound preoccupation with fiscal rectitude. In fact, there are striking similarities between the debates in Germany and those in Rubinite circles in the United States. On both sides of the Atlantic, globalization, competitiveness and fiscal sustainability were key issues. Nor should this be surprising. The rise of China and the funding problems of the modern welfare state were common challenges. The Bush administration might have been political poison in Europe. But in the late 1990s, Clinton's Democrats had been an inspiration for Gerhard Schroeder's Red-Green coalition.[24] Merkel was nothing if not an Atlanticist. But if there was a common agenda, there were common blind spots too. For all the focus in the eurozone on the need to make labor responsive to the demands of global competition, for all the calls for common fiscal discipline, there was an almost total lack of recognition of the destabilizing forces unleashed by global finance. In Europe, as in the United States, it was politicians, workers and welfare recipients who were seen as the problem, not banks or financial markets.

II

If Europe did not have a common fiscal policy or labor market policy, it did at least have a common monetary policy. Its guardian was the ECB, headed from November 2003 by Jean-Claude Trichet.[25] This was precisely the

bargain that Mitterrand had hoped for: a Frenchman in charge of Europe's money. But the other side of the bargain was that the ECB's operational DNA came from the Bundesbank. And Trichet was perfectly suited to play this dual role. He was a deeply conservative former head of the Banque de France. The ECB's independence was his highest value and he guarded it jealously. The ECB's constitution provided plenty of safeguards. Its deliberations were shielded from public scrutiny by minimal transparency requirements. To prevent it from being put to work as a vehicle of fiscal policy, it was banned from monetizing newly issued government debt. Unlike the Fed, which had a dual mandate for price stability and maximum employment, the ECB had price stability as its only target.

All this made the ECB the most remote of all the modern central banks.[26] To call it apolitical would be a misnomer, because it, in fact, entrenched a conservative bias against inflation as the unquestionable doxa of Europe. Nor would it be fair to say that anti-inflation politics were the ECB's only ambition. It also wanted to promote Europe as a financial center and the euro as a reserve currency, and that meant actively developing European debt markets. Specifically, it meant importing to Europe the American model of a repo market for government debt. Being able to repo government securities made them much more attractive as assets. This was a lesson that France had learned in the 1980s. Faced with the financial pressures exercised by Germany, France had actively promoted the market for its own debt by offering American-style repo facilities.[27] The easier it was to trade French debt for instant liquidity, the more actively it would be purchased and the more accepting the market would be of France's borrowing requirements. Over the resistance of the Bundesbank, repo was adopted as a core operational model by the ECB. Unlike the more traditional central banks, like the Bank of England or the Fed, the ECB did not hold large quantities of government debt. It managed Europe's financial system by repoing a wide range of bonds including both private debt and public bonds.[28] Rather than the ECB, it was Europe's banks that bought their governments' debt. But they did so with the understanding that if they needed cash in a hurry, the bonds could be exchanged with the ECB on a repurchase basis. The terms of the repo and the size of the ECB haircut were the basic regulating

variables in the unified financial system of the eurozone. In this respect, market logic was internal to the operation of the ECB to a degree that was not the case at either the Fed or the Bank of England.

If it had wished to maximize pressure on Europe's government to preserve fiscal discipline, the ECB could have adopted a discriminatory system of nationally specific repo haircuts, imposing tougher conditions on less credible peripheral eurozone borrowers. Haircuts in the bilateral repo market in the United States varied widely across different types of bonds. A higher haircut would require banks to hold more capital against their bond holdings and shrink their portfolios of that debt. In Europe in the late 1990s, Greece had had to offer far higher interest rates to attract lenders than had Germany. But instead of discriminating, the ECB took the view that a single currency implied a single rate. It would repo the bonds of all European sovereigns on the same terms.[29] Unsurprisingly, this produced a dramatic convergence of yields as investors bid up the price of higher-yielding debts from countries like Greece, Italy, Portugal and Spain, which in the eyes of the ECB were now equivalent to Bunds, Germany's rock-solid government bonds. The result was a self-reflexive loop in which the ECB relied on markets to exercise discipline over public borrowers while the markets came to assume that the ECB's "one bond" policy implied an implicit European guarantee for even the weakest borrowers.

The result was that Greece and Portugal could borrow on terms that were better than ever before in their history, and one might have expected this to produce a huge surge in new public borrowing. Reading some commentary on the eurozone crisis, one might imagine that this was indeed what happened.[30] But, despite the unprecedentedly low interest rates, there was, in fact, no public debt boom after 2001. Certain countries borrowed more than others. But overall, the Maastricht rules limiting deficits exercised an effective restraint, especially when one considers the inducement to borrow provided by the convergence of yields. Despite the profound ambiguity of the institutional structure, the sense of calm was preserved by the fact that no major public borrower was grossly abusing the situation. Indeed, as economic growth moved into a higher gear, the ratio of public debt to GDP across the eurozone fell by 7 percent.[31]

The countries that failed to meet the eurozone's budget rules were a

mixed bag. Portugal had the most rapidly rising public debt ratio and its budgeting was undeniably lax. But when it joined the euro, its debt was at a low level. Unfortunately, Lisbon made the mistake of entering at an uncompetitive exchange rate. The sharp deterioration in the debt-to-GDP ratio that followed was due as much to a deceleration in growth as it was to irresponsible borrowing.[32] Greece was the other reprobate. In the 1990s, to qualify for eurozone membership, Greece, like Italy, had eked out primary surpluses (on the budget excluding debt service). Even with interest costs running at 11.5 percent of GDP, this had held the deficit in check. After the formation of the eurozone, Greek borrowing costs and debt service charges fell by more than half. It could have been the opportunity for a substantial fiscal consolidation. Instead, Athens let its tax revenue decline. The primary surpluses evaporated and the deficit expanded to 5.5 percent, twice the Maastricht limit. This was bearable only because nominal income growth was so rapid.[33] What made Greece's situation dangerous, however, was not the pace of borrowing after 2001 but the debts built up in the 1980s and 1990s, when modern Greek democracy had been established on the back of a huge surge in government spending and expensive borrowing.[34] In 2000 Greece's debt already amounted to 104 percent of GDP.

Though the degree of Greece's problems was not fully appreciated, it was a known problem case and it was small fry. More politically significant in the early 2000s was the violation of the Growth and Stability Pact rules by France and Germany. This definitely eroded the authority of fiscal discipline. But what were the economic consequences? There was ample demand in financial markets for German Bunds and France's Treasurys, also known as OATs. Interest rates remained low. France maintained a level trade balance. Germany's government ran up debt, but combined it with consumer and investment spending so repressed that it produced an ever-larger current account surplus. From the point of view of the eurozone's macroeconomic balance, it would have been better if Germany had broken the fiscal rules more comprehensively.

It may fly in the face of conservative assumptions about "democratic deficits" and the spendthrift habits of irresponsible politicians, but the formation of the eurozone without an ironclad fiscal constitution did not lead to a festival of unrestrained sovereign borrowing. The backdrop to the eurozone

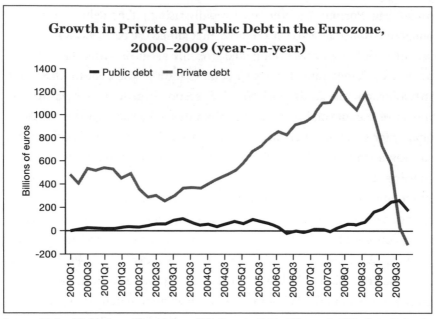

Growth in Private and Public Debt in the Eurozone, 2000–2009 (year-on-year)

Source: Richard Baldwin and Daniel Gros, "The Euro in Crisis: What to Do?," in *Completing the Eurozone Rescue: What More Needs to Be Done* (2010), 1–24, figure 3, http://voxeu.org/sites/de fault/files/file/Eurozone_Rescue.pdf.

crisis was, indeed, a gigantic surge in debt, but it was in the private, not the public, sector. The eurozone played host to the same runaway, market-driven process of credit creation that European banks were contributing to so actively in the North Atlantic economy.

III

As the *Financial Times*'s economic commentator Martin Sandbu has re-marked, it was the euro's "great misfortune" to be born "into the greatest private credit bubble of all time."[35] To which one might add that it was not entirely a matter of bad luck. Giving Europe the scale necessary to cope with the wild fluctuations of global capital unleashed in the early 1970s was always the chief raison d'être of the European Monetary Union. But the global credit expansion of the early 2000s put anything hitherto experi-enced in the shade, and Europe's banks were at the leading edge of the boom. French, German, Italian, Benelux, Spanish, Irish and British banks

poured credit into profitable hot spots of growth. The eurozone allowed them to do so without regard to borders or currency risk. Cross-border lending within the eurozone exploded, rising even more rapidly than cross-border finance globally.[36] Europe's bankers used the same array of modern banking techniques in the eurozone that they were putting to such profitable use in London and New York. Securitization had long been a method of mortgage finance in Europe. Notably in Germany, the Pfandbrief model had been a staple since the eighteenth century. But from the early 2000s, American-style securitization took off in Europe as well. In 2007 more than $500 billion in loans were securitized in Europe. In 2008 the total reached $750 billion in European asset-backed security issuance with UK and Spanish banks particularly active.[37]

Once again, as in the case of America's international finances, it is easy to deceive oneself about the direction of these intra-European flows. We have a clear map of the economic hierarchy of Europe in our heads. We know where the loans went—Greece, Spain, Ireland. We know that Germany was the main "surplus" and "creditor" nation. So does that mean that Germany financed the credit boom? Certainly it had the largest trade surplus and was thus the largest net exporter of capital. But as far as overall financial flows within Europe are concerned, that simple mental map is as misleading as the exclusive focus on Sino-American financial relations is on a global scale.

Thanks to the work of economists at the European Commission, we can map the flow of funds within Europe as part of the broader circulation of funds throughout the world economy. In the bottom right-hand quadrant of the following table, we see the outline of the world economy that we have mapped in previous chapters. But if we focus on intra-European flows, it is clear that Germany, despite its export prowess, did not dominate the European financial system. Germany was the largest net lender. Its status was like that of China in relation to the US economy. But financial flows within Europe no more mapped onto trade than they did in the world economy. Germany was a champion exporter of cars and machinery, but in banking and finance others led the field. The UK, France, the Benelux and Ireland (the latter hidden within the category "Rest of Euro area") were the key hubs for financial flows. The City of London, home to banks from around

Cross-Border Financial Flows Within the Eurozone and the World Economy: Annual Averages, 2004–2006 (in billions of euros)

from \ to	Germany	Greece	Spain	France	Italy	Austria	Portugal	Benelux	Rest of EA	Poland	Sweden	UK	Rest of EU	Non-EU	US	Japan	Switzerland	Rest of OECD	OFFSHORE	Hong Kong	Rest of world	Total
Germany	–	3	41	27	23	20	5	56	38	4	4	84	15	61	29	-5	12	15	18	1	-11	382
Greece	1	–	0	0	0	0	0	2	1	0	0	7	1	9	1	0	0	1	1	0	6	20
Spain	2	0	–	16	7	3	5	23	5	1	0	34	4	54	8	0	1	6	-2	0	40	154
France	27	4	29	–	35	7	3	69	45	1	1	95	5	126	43	11	13	13	32	-1	13	445
Italy	20	3	8	15	–	6	1	39	8	1	-1	30	1	5	-10	-3	-1	1	5	-1	9	131
Austria	13	1	2	3	5	–	0	6	9	2	0	4	11	15	1	0	1	2	4	0	3	68
Portugal	1	1	4	2	0	0	–	4	1	0	0	2	0	5	1	0	0	1	1	0	2	21
Benelux	48	9	43	78	38	9	4	–	47	6	4	155	6	167	100	14	14	36	38	3	-46	602
Rest of euro area	20	3	17	15	24	3	9	25	–	2	6	67	7	110	51	11	0	13	25	1	9	308
Poland	1	0	0	1	0	1	0	2	6	–	0	1	1	4	0	0	1	0	0	0	2	11
Sweden	6	0	2	2	0	0	0	6	13	0	–	12	7	16	5	1	0	10	6	0	-7	63
United Kingdom	24	3	41	110	1	2	-3	64	64	2	7	–	14	562	228	59	35	53	102	9	69	884
Rest of EU-27	7	0	1	3	1	1	1	2	3	0	6	16	–	17	16	1	-14	4	2	0	7	57
Rest of world non-EU	72	7	27	181	33	17	8	275	78	1	12	431	9	–	816	80	-4	165	19	61	0	2287
US	-6	1	8	68	9	4	-1	40	30	2	8	156	-2	427	–	64	16	75	82	8	56	738
Japan	5	1	2	18	1	0	0	21	2	1	-1	36	1	130	44	–	1	12	60	2	-18	212
Switzerland	9	1	0	9	1	2	0	4	4	0	0	60	2	24	-1	5	–	8	-7	0	-53	111
Rest of OECD	16	2	4	11	3	1	1	26	9	0	2	26	4	178	82	4	5	–	–	2	73	262
OFFSHORE	7	0	-18	29	-1	2	4	29	9	0	5	90	0	-10	173	4	23	9	64	-16	-58	323
Hong Kong	0	0	0	2	0	0	0	7	2	0	0	10	0	71	6	-2	2	12	-6	–	-11	71
Rest of world	9	1	23	40	14	4	2	134	15	-2	-4	19	4	0	443	-11	-56	21		31	–	682
Total	211	33	209	447	162	66	32	559	305	20	39	904	82	1973	1219	155	51	290	627	71	87	

Note: Estimated gross flows (net asset acquisitions) of direct, portfolio and "other" investments (excluding financial derivatives).

Source: A. Hobza and S. Zeugner, "The 'Imbalanced Balance' and Its Unravelling: Current Accounts and Bilateral Financial Flows in the Euro Area," *European Commission Economic Papers* 520 (2014): table A.2.

the world, including all the leading German banks, stands out as the major financial partner for every eurozone member, even though it was not a member of the currency union. France and the Benelux were particularly important because they served as channels through which funds flowed into the eurozone from the outside. American and other lenders from the rest of the world clearly preferred to do business with well-known French, Dutch and Belgian counterparties, who then channeled the funds to the European periphery. France was a major financial hub, not because it had a huge trade surplus but because it had large, ambitious banks that were willing to borrow to lend: 445 billion euros flowed out of France and 447 billion flowed in, leaving a net imbalance of merely 2 billion euros. At the same time, 602 billion euros flowed out of the Benelux banking centers and 559 billion flowed in. The Dutch trade surplus made up the difference.

The flow of funds around Europe, as around the global economy, was driven not by trade flows but by the business logic of bankers, who sought out the cheapest funding and the best returns. The upward spiral of asset prices and balance sheets that drove the US boom was even more pronounced in Europe. Between 2001 and 2006, Greece, Finland, Sweden, Belgium, Denmark, the UK, France, Ireland and Spain all experienced real estate booms more severe than those that energized the United States. In Ireland and Spain, the combination of credit growth and house price inflation was truly explosive.

It was these credit-fueled booms that drove the trade and fiscal imbalances of the eurozone, rather than the other way around. The huge influx of credit from all over the world to a hot spot like Spain inflated economic activity there. This generated healthy tax revenues for Madrid, which proudly boasted a fiscal surplus. It also generated export orders for Germany. Foreign demand gave a boost to the languishing German economy, raising incomes and profits.[38] But German households and businesses did not want to spend their income increment in Germany, on either consumption or investment. The German government borrowed, but not enough to soak up the difference. Through interbank markets, surplus liquidity in the north helped to fund business ventures around Europe. Some of that, not surprisingly, went to Spain. At the end of the day the accounts balanced. Germany's savings appear as the counterpart to Spain's trade deficit.

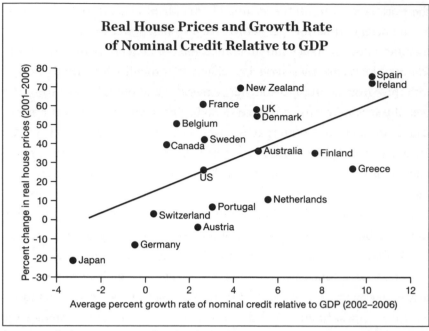

Real House Prices and Growth Rate of Nominal Credit Relative to GDP

Source: Prakash Kannan, Pau Rabanal and Alasdair M. Scott, "Macroeconomic Patterns and Monetary Policy in the Run-up to Asset Price Busts," IMF Working Papers (November 2009), figure 2.

But accounting identity is not the same as causal relationship. It wasn't Germany's excess savings, or its exports, that produced the boom in Spain. It was the lopsided credit-fueled boom that produced the demand imbalances, the trade flows and the savings imbalances. Europe's banking system provided elastic intermediation. Had Germany's domestic economy been in more robust shape, Germany's demand for imports would have been larger, and the trade imbalances within the eurozone might have been smaller. A somewhat larger fraction of the Spanish economy might have been directed toward producing goods for export to Germany rather than supplying the domestic boom. But there is no reason to think that a smaller flow of net savings from a more rapidly growing Germany would have done much to slow the credit-fueled upswing in Ireland or Spain. In modern finance, credit is not a fixed sum constrained by the "fundamentals" of the "real economy." It is an elastic quantity, which in an asset price boom can easily become self-expanding on a transnational scale.

Where does Greece, the country that would become the epicenter of

the eurozone crisis, fit in this picture? It is present, but vanishingly small. Of the annual flux in cross-border funding within the eurozone between 2004 and 2006, which on average came to c. 1.8 trillion euros, Greece accounted for 33 billion euros. That is less than 2 percent, proportional to Greece's weight in eurozone GDP. Of that flow of funds, a larger share than was the case in Ireland and Spain went to the Greek state. But Greece too experienced a property boom on a par with the United States. The red flag in Greece was not the annual inflow of capital after 2001 but the fact that the new borrowing was being added to huge stocks of debt already accumulated in prior decades. What would happen if the flow of funds was abruptly cut off was a worrying question, but given Greece's tiny size, it was hardly headline grabbing.

It would later be said that the ECB should have done more to dampen the boom in Ireland and Spain. And it is clearly true that this was made more difficult by the fact that it set one interest rate for the entire eurozone. In effect, by setting low rates, the ECB prioritized the need to stimulate the German economy over restraining the boom in the periphery. It was a reasonable decision. Germany's economy is far bigger. Furthermore, given the rates of return that beckoned in the hot spots of the European economy, it is wishful thinking to imagine that the ECB could have curbed the boom with a rate hike. If the EU's business statistics are to be believed, investment in Spanish tourism and real estate offered rates of return of 30 percent or more. Little wonder that investment crowded in.[39] In a world of globalized finance, the ECB could no more limit the flow of funds to such a hot spot than the Fed could choke off the capital inflow to the United States. Ireland's banks were a case in point. They sourced their funding wholesale in the City of London, outside the ECB's immediate purview.[40]

To have slowed the booms would have required not a mild tweak of ECB interest rates but a full-scale economic policy mobilization by the governments of the boom countries. This might have included tougher lending rules, throttling back growth in the banking system and even tighter fiscal policy. In the case of Spain, the larger, internationalized banks were, in fact, held on a tight leash. Foreign investors expected high governance standards. And they came through the crisis well.[41] But the same cannot be said for the local mortgage lenders, the *cajas* that made up 50 percent of the

credit market.[42] They were tightly connected with local politics and deeply immersed in the real estate boom. Between 2002 and 2009 their business grew by a factor of 2.5, resulting in a combined balance sheet of 483 billion euro, or 40 percent of Spanish GDP.[43] But efforts to restrict their lending were easily seen as a centralizing power grab by Madrid. And why should Spain's politicians undertake such unpopular action? One of the side effects of a bubble is that it makes balance sheets look good. Tough governance reform seems unnecessary and punitive.[44] Spaniards were enjoying their long overdue return to the spotlight. Firms like Telefónica, Ferrovial and Banco Santander were emerging as global players. Fashion giant Zara made its owner Amancio Ortega the richest billionaire in Europe. Prime Minister José Luis Rodríguez Zapatero was lobbying for Spain to be invited to join

Increase in Indebtedness in the Eurozone (% of GDP), 2000–2007

	Households	Nonfinancial corp.	Financial corporations	Government	Total debt increase	Real home price index
Belgium	7	57	124	−26	162	48.7
Germany	−10	0	33	5	27	−14.0
Ireland	54	−13	612	−8	645	52.8
Greece	32	13	41	4	90	37.2
Spain	34	78	74	−24	162	73.1
France	15	20	113	5	152	81.7
Italy	17	23	22	−7	55	37.6
Netherlands	32	−42	217	−12	195	14.4
Austria	7	68	72	−7	140	1.2
Portugal	26	12	71	13	122	−11.2
Finland	23	−77	70	−11	4	37.7
Eurozone-11	21	12	132	−6	159	28.3
Denmark	37	60	145	−26	216	57.9
Sweden	24	49	70	−10	133	55.3
UK	31	−34	367	1	365	63.4
Average	23	15	145	−7	176	38.3

Source: Calculated from Eurostat and OECD data (for the real home price index) from S. T. H. Storm and C. W. M. Naastepad, "Myths, Mix-ups and Mishandlings: What Caused the Eurozone Crisis?," Annual Conference Institute for New Economic Thinking, "Liberté, Égalité, Fragilité," Paris, France, April 2015, https://www.ineteconomics.org/uploads/papers/The-Eurozone-Crisis.pdf.

the top table in an expanded G8. With lean social services and booming tax revenues, Spain's public budget was in far better shape than that of France or Germany. Why put the brakes on such a healthy-looking burst of private sector growth?

Among Ireland's tiny political elite a similar spirit of ebullience prevailed. Coddled by EU investment and incestuously connected with bankers and developers, politicians boasted of the global attractions of Dublin's International Financial Services Center. Ireland's tax system enabled foreign corporations to spirit hundreds of billions of dollars in profit past tax authorities in the United States and the rest of Europe. Though a member of the eurozone and benefiting enormously from Brussels subsidy payments, the Irish liked to regard themselves as an "outpost of American (or Anglo-American) free-market values on the far edge of a continent where various brands of social democracy were still the political norm."[45] In the American presidential election of 2008, the world was treated to the incongruous spectacle of Phil Gramm, chief champion of deregulation in Congress in the 1990s and economic adviser to Republican hopeful John McCain, touting Ireland as the beau ideal of a low-tax economy. Disgraced former prime minister Bertie Ahern toured the world selling audiences on the benefits of "extreme economic globalisation, low personal and corporate taxes, 'business-friendly' government and light regulation."

IV

There are many risks involved in forming a currency union and it would no doubt have made sense for Europe to have added a fiscal constitution. But Europe's chief problem was not the lack of a fiscal fire code. Its problem was the lack of a financial fire department.[46] The failure of state building that mattered most was not fiscal union but the failure to build the capacity to handle a banking crisis. Coping with highly integrated financial capitalism requires a state that is disciplined, has the capacity to act and has the will to do so. Coping with a banking crisis on the scale that was brewing in Europe required a very capable state indeed.

How badly such a facility was needed becomes clear only when we put together the local and global activities of Europe's banks, to get a full view of their spectacularly overinflated growth. America's banks were very big and very important to global finance. But it was in Europe that bank finance had grown most disproportionately.[47] Europe's banks had always been large. Unlike the United States, where equity and bond markets were the main sources of business finance, Europe's economies had long relied heavily on bank lending. But spreading out across the EU and feeding off the transatlantic financial circuit, the European banks had grown to gargantuan size. In 2007 the three largest banks in the world by assets were all European—RBS, Deutsche Bank and BNP. Combined, their balance sheets came to 17 percent of global GDP. The balance sheet of each of them came close to matching the GDP of its home country—Britain, Germany and France—the three largest economies in the EU.[48] In tiny Ireland the situation was far more extreme. The liabilities of its banks added up to 700 percent of GDP. France and the Netherlands rivaled each other, with liabilities at 400 percent of GDP. The banks of Germany and Spain had liabilities amounting to 300 percent of GDP. By this standard every member of the eurozone was at least three times more "overbanked" than the United States. Furthermore, Europe's banks were far more dependent on volatile "wholesale," market-based funding than their US counterparts.

Given the size of the balance sheets and the complexity of Europe's banking businesses, it was foreseeable that only collective action would be sufficient to bail out a crisis that could spread across the eurozone. To call for unified action to tame, discipline and make safe a particular sector of business activity was hardly out of keeping with Europe's history. Indeed, the origin of European integration was the realization that Europe's coal and steel industries were sources of conflict and instability. Out of that logic had emerged the European Coal and Steel Community as the first step toward the "European rescue of the nation-state."[49] Likewise, the Common Agricultural Policy had been devised in the 1960s to contain the spillover costs of national farm support policies. It was only in the 1980s that this sectoral vision of the EU went out of fashion, displaced by the deceptive simplicity of the single market. This was the true deficit of the eurozone. It was a monetary union that unified financial markets but provided none of

the institutions of governance required for a banking union. If there was one urgent reason why Europe truly did need a fiscal constitution it was to provide the financial underpinning for a giant deposit insurance and bail-out fund.

In the late 1990s, as European Monetary Union approached, Larry Summers had the temerity to ask an international gathering of financial experts: "Could the Europeans here explain to me what happens if a bank in Spain gets into serious trouble? What are the respective responsibilities of the Spanish supervision authorities, the Spanish central bank, the ECB, and Brussels?" The question silenced the meeting. After an embarrassed pause there followed a "chaotic argument among the Europeans, which ended without resolution but with only a sense that they didn't want to air their linen in front of the rest of us."[50] Looking back on the incident, Summers attributed the chaos and embarrassed silence to the usual disunity of European politics. But in truth it was not that different from the United States. No one in the United States wanted to think about bank failures either, not in 1997 and not in 2007. Indeed, as his reaction to Rajan's

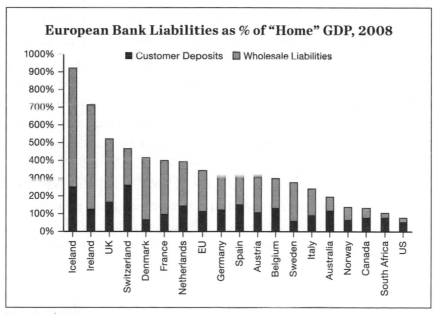

Note: As of 2008.

Source: https://qz.com/19386/europe-is-still-massively-overbanked-by-the-way/. Based on data from Barclays Research.

impolitic remarks at the Jackson Hole conference in August 2005 made only too clear, Summers was one of the "very serious people" enforcing that taboo. The state of denial was common. The difference was that when the unthinkable happened, the United States had a structure of federal government within which to improvise a response. The misfortune of the EU was that when the crisis struck, it not only lacked such structures. The crisis came at a moment when the EU's efforts to build a more robust constitutional framework had run up against basic political limits.

Up to the early 2000s, the EU operated against a backdrop of what political scientists called a "permissive consensus."[51] Europe's population accepted the gradual push for ever closer union without enthusiasm but also without protest. The EU is not an obtrusive presence. Contrary to prevailing myth, the EU is by no means a gigantic bureaucracy. The EU employs fewer people than most medium-sized cities. But it was a sprawling, incoherent constitutional structure lacking in democratic accountability. It was clearly unsatisfactory and would become even more so once the EU expanded in 2004 to include new East European members. In December 2001 the European Council charged a European Convention with drafting a constitutional document that would ensure efficiency, clearer lines of responsibility and prepare the way for Europe's expansion. The convention consisted of a commission of bigwigs headed by that old warhorse of French Europeanism former president Giscard D'Estaing.[52] The proposal enshrined a new balance between centralized decision making by majority vote and the irreducible role of the European nation-states. It subordinated all the various institutions and treaties that had made up the pillars of European integration into a single overarching European Union. Europe's ambition was defined as being a "social market economy" that prioritized full employment, "social justice" and "solidarity between generations" as well as the fight against "social exclusion and discrimination," while also promising to be "highly competitive."[53]

The constitution was a pleasing portmanteau of all the nostrums of good governance of the early 2000s. The European Trade Union movement gave its approval. Tony Blair and Britain's New Labour government were enthusiastic. In Washington, DC, the Hamilton Project would probably have been pleased to put its name to it. But on May 29, 2005, the constitution was rejected by popular referenda in France and then, in June, in the

Netherlands. Left-wing hostility to the promarket character of the EU and nationalist hostility to Brussels united to deliver solid majorities against it. It was a profound shock. The permissive consensus was dead. Whatever the rights and wrongs of the constitution, popular democracy had asserted itself and Europe's elite were left in disarray.[54] Given the reality of increasingly close economic and financial integration and the extension of the EU to Eastern Europe, the project of reorganizing Europe could not simply be abandoned. A substitute had to be found. If a true constitution was no longer a viable proposition, Europe would have to proceed by the tried-and-tested formula of intergovernmental treaty. This gave a key role to Germany, and from November 2005 this meant Chancellor Angela Merkel.

Merkel's relationship to Europe was quite different from that of her mentor Helmut Kohl.[55] Given her upbringing in cold war East Germany, her early fascination with the outside world was directed first to Russia and then to Britain and the United States. This was of a piece with her embrace of globalism and its causes of the 1990s, including environmental politics and climate change. The unified Germany is what made her. Beyond that, Merkel's world was larger than Europe. The crucial implication is that in European affairs the German chancellor did not look to Brussels for solutions. She was no federalist. Rather than seeing the future of Europe in the construction of common European institutions and machinery directed from Brussels, Merkel advocated intergovernmentalism. She looked for grand bargains between the European nation-states. There are those who suspect that this is merely a disguise for a project of German domination.[56] There were nationalists on the fringes of German politics of whom this might truly be said. But Merkel was not one of them, nor were other key figures in the CDU leadership, such as her interior minister, Wolfgang Schäuble, who would in 2009 replace Steinbrück as finance minister in Merkel's second government. Unlike Merkel, Schäuble was a federalist, eager to move the hard core of Europe to a higher stage of integration. What they shared was not a desire to dominate Europe. There was no grand hegemonic project in early-twenty-first-century Berlin. What they had in common was their belief that it is not just Germany's right but its proper historical role to act as a self-confident veto player in European affairs. Germany's terrible history forbids strategies of domination or even overly assertive leadership. But the success of the Federal

Republic gives it the right to insist that European solutions meet its standards, and Berlin will apply those standards as it sees fit. It was a minimal, demanding and sometimes arbitrary and self-serving posture. The position of "Madame Non" that Merkel only too readily assumes in European affairs was strongly backed by the domestic electorate. If it was a blind spot, it was not a repressed desire for domination but a tendency to underestimate the extent to which Germany's success and international prominence were in fact interdependent with Europe. It also arrogated to Germany the right to set the pace. A veto costs time, and in an urgent crisis, whether in financial or foreign affairs, time lost can exact a heavy price. The more acute the crisis, the more decisive is the control over the clock exercised by the veto player. As Europe entered rough waters it was predictable that both the fear of "German domination" and calls for German leadership would intensify. So too would Berlin's determination to control the pace of events.

It was a fateful coincidence that in the wake of the constitutional debacle of 2005, it was Germany that took the rotating presidency of the council of the EU. At this moment, early on in her career as chancellor, Merkel assumed responsibility for redrafting and driving through a replacement for the failed constitution. The result, after months of meticulous high-pressure preparation by Berlin, was the Lisbon Treaty of December 2007. Like the constitution it replaced, the Lisbon Treaty merged the multiple pillars of the European integration project into a single European Union with a population of 500 million. It created a new foreign and security policy for the EU. It streamlined the commission and established the principle of majority voting that was essential to make the vastly expanded structure manageable. But above all, it institutionalized the council as the representation of Europe's national governments and created a presidency of the council as its standing representative. It ended any pretension on the part of the European Commission and its president to executive leadership.[57] Many of the key provisions of the original constitutional treaty were thus maintained. But the defeat of 2005 left a lasting mark. The paramountcy of Europe's national governments was reaffirmed. For the foreseeable future there would be no further steps toward federal integration. Policy in Europe would be made not centrally by Brussels but by intergovernmental bargain.

As the first financial boom of the twenty-first century began to unravel

in 2007, Europe was in a conflicted situation. It was deeply economically integrated, with the ECB presiding from a distance over a hyperactive financial system that linked the eurozone to the City of London and Wall Street. And yet the wider politics of European integration were in retreat. The Lisbon Treaty enshrined intergovernmentalism and Europe's voters had shown their willingness to exercise a veto over steps beyond that. How, given this disequilibrium, the EU would respond to an unforeseen crisis was anyone's guess. And that observation went beyond finance.

IV

If one compares American and European policy discussion in the early 2000s, one sees that they shared many preoccupations. Policy experts on both continents were focused on fiscal discipline and international competitiveness, supply side incentives, efficient government spending, deficits, evidence-based welfare policy, education reform and flexible labor markets. These were the shibboleths of the watered-down, supply-side market economics inherited from the days of Reagan and Thatcher and the Washington Consensus of the 1990s. The policy communities on both sides of the Atlantic also shared blind spots. Sharing a deep faith in markets, neither realized the threat posed by the new, market-based model of banking. On both sides of the Atlantic they were oblivious to the risks accumulating in overleveraged banks, relying on vast quantities of wholesale funding. Why, then, did both sides find it so hard to recognize the risks that they shared? And why have crisis narratives on either side of the Atlantic diverged so sharply since 2008?

If we are looking for one crucial difference it is surely this: From the morning of September 11, 2001, America was a superpower at war. Not only that, under the Bush administration, it was a regime pursuing a global war on terror. The initial European reaction to the attacks of 9/11 was one of solidarity. The ouster of the Taliban from Kabul enjoyed general support. But over the winter of 2002–2003, as Washington and London pushed toward the invasion of Iraq, that sense of common commitment evaporated. The German and French governments came out in opposition to war, as did

millions of European citizens who filled the streets in some of the largest demonstrations in Europe's history. This was the moment in which the American neoconservative Robert Kagan coined his famous phrase that Americans were from Mars and Europeans from Venus.[58] Europe's leading intellectuals responded in kind. The unlikely pairing of Jürgen Habermas and Jacques Derrida issued a counterblast. Significantly, for them, the transatlantic divide went far beyond foreign policy. It extended to social policy and political culture. In the early twenty-first century it amounted to nothing less than a civilization divide, a bifurcation within modernity, between the chastened postimperial world of Europe and the expansive, imperially aggressive Anglosphere.[59]

A wide gulf conventionally separates accounts of global geopolitics in the wake of 9/11 from our narratives of the genesis of the financial crisis. But if we listen closely it is clear that the quagmire of Iraq haunted the Washington policy-making elite in the early 2000s, awakening nightmarish memories of Vietnam and the crisis of American power and authority of the 1930s. The rise of China added to the sense of menace. Larry Summers's description of the Sino-American trade balance as a balance of financial terror was telling. That was not how the Germans or the Dutch thought about their trade surpluses. The pervasive militarization of the language of national leadership in the United States would become even more glaring once the crisis began. Both in rhetoric and self-conception it would mark a fundamental transatlantic divide.

In terms of political culture the differences are undeniable. But to take the loudly proclaimed transatlantic alienation of the early 2000s at face value as a description of economic or geopolitical reality would be self-deceiving in a double sense.[60] The idea that "social Europe" had deviated in any essential way from the logic of turbocharged "financial capitalism" as exemplified by America was an illusion. In fact, Europe's financial capitalism was even more spectacularly overgrown and it owed a large part of its growth to its deep entanglement in the American boom. Furthermore, whatever the differences over Iraq, Europe's pose of geopolitical innocence is a historically recent phenomenon. Though it balked at Iraq, France remains a hardened postcolonial war fighter. Nor does Europe only do "small wars." As recently as the 1980s the European members of NATO had been

active participants in winning the cold war and making the victory stick. Given the dramatic escalation of tension with the Soviet Union, the stakes could hardly have been higher. Particularly notable was the Federal Republic's commitment to hard power. At its peak, the Bundeswehr had a standing strength of 500,000, with a mobilization strength of 1.3 million. The deployment of nuclear-armed cruise and Pershing missiles to Europe in 1983 was a transatlantic effort that bonded a generation of Atlanticists in the face of concerted opposition from the Left in both Europe and the United States.[61] The high priests of Europe's twenty-first-century cult of innocence reside, of course, in Brussels. But though the EU might prefer to deny the fact, in the post–cold war world, it was far from geopolitically inert. It entertained complex relations with its neighbors in the Mediterranean and in Eastern Europe that could not easily be disentangled from the hard power of the NATO alliance or coercive border policing. And this would matter, because whereas the EU kept its distance from the Middle East imbroglio and refused to see the rise of China as a geopolitical threat, it would be on Europe's doorstep that a violent great power confrontation would erupt, and it did so just as the world banking system began to unravel. In August 2008, as the financial markets hurtled toward disaster, Russia went to war with Georgia, a Western-backed proxy.

Chapter 5

MULTIPOLAR WORLD

Russia's return to the world stage in the early 2000s owed even more to global economic growth than did the rise of China. Russia poured oil and gas into world markets. Its banks and industrial corporations borrowed enthusiastically in Europe and the United States. Like China it held a huge reserve of dollars, but unlike China its financial and economic interrelationship with the United States was indirect. Russia did not earn its dollars by exporting to the United States. It sold its gas and oil to Europe and Asia. Furthermore, whereas the Chinese Communist Party approached the West with self-confidence, the wounds of the Soviet Union's defeat in the cold war were still fresh. There were no fond memories of a "Nixon-Kissinger" moment in the Kremlin. It was not by accident, therefore, that it would be Russia's president Vladimir Putin, the cold war KGB operative, who would pose the question that China and America preferred not to speak out loud. What, Putin demanded to know, were the implications of a rebalanced and reintegrated world economy for the geopolitical order? Putin not only posed the question. In so doing he exposed a deep lack of agreement within the West—inside Europe and between Europe and the United States—over what kind of international architecture should frame economic and financial development, not just in the world at large but in particular on Europe's very doorstep, in Eastern Europe, the showcase for capitalist transition in the post–cold war world.

I

In Europe, unlike in Asia, the triumph of "the West" over communism was absolute. It was a triumph of both hard and soft power, military, political and economic might. Though Germans might give more credit to Gorbachev and détente diplomacy, and Americans more to Reagan and Star Wars, the Atlantic alliance was united in victory. No one benefited more from the end of the cold war than a newly reunified Germany, and it was German-American cooperation that secured the win. In 1990 French president François Mitterrand favored a conciliatory vision of embracing the former Soviet bloc in a common European security policy that would supersede NATO as well as the Warsaw pact.[1] But neither Helmut Kohl nor George Bush wanted anything to do with that. The West had won. It would set the terms for Europe's reunification.

The fall of the Wall and the dissolution of the Soviet Union in December 1991 left Russia shrunken and isolated. Not since the dark days of Lenin's ruinous peace of Brest-Litovsk in 1918 had Russia been so humbled. Under Yeltsin, Moscow's relations with the West were friendly. But Russia's economy was a shipwreck. In the words of George Soros, Russia was "a centrally planned economy with the centre knocked out."[2] In the so-called transitional recession, inflation soared and Russia's real GDP fell by 40 percent between 1989 and 1995. On "Black Tuesday," October 11, 1994, in one single session of frantic currency trading, the ruble lost more than a quarter of its value against the dollar. It was not until 1995 that Russia's economy stabilized. A modest revival fueled by large imports of foreign capital enabled Russia to catch its breath, only to be thrown off balance yet again by the Asian financial crisis of 1997.[3] Struggling to hold the exchange rate, the Russian central bank introduced exchange controls and begged an emergency IMF loan.[4] But in August 1998 Yeltsin's government lost its grip. On August 17 Moscow devalued and declared a ninety-day moratorium on the payment of foreign debts owed by Russian banks. The ruble went into free fall, plunging from 7 to the dollar to 21. The cost of imports surged. Russians who had borrowed abroad faced bankruptcy. Then on August 19 the

Russian government defaulted on its ruble-denominated domestic debts. By October 1998, with 40 percent of the population counted as living below the subsistence minimum, Moscow was reduced to appealing to the international community for assistance to pay for food imports. As inflation soared to an annualized rate of 84 percent, Russians lost confidence in their national currency. As the new millennium began, dollars made up 87 percent of the value of all currency in circulation in Russia. Outside the United States, Russia was the largest dollar economy in the world. International investors in Russia were required to pay their local taxes in American currency. Russia became the ultimate experiment in dollarization, a nuclear-armed, former superpower with a currency supplied from Washington.[5]

With the exception of newly independent Ukraine, Russia was the worst hit of the post-Soviet countries, but the early 1990s were tough

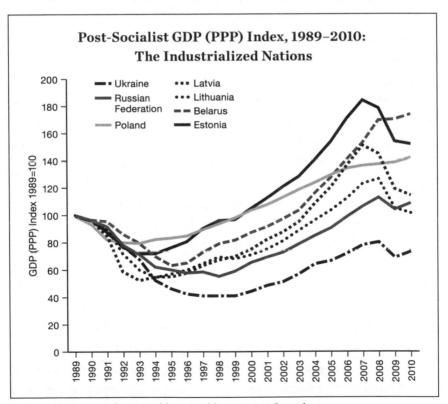

Source: http://www.ggdc.net/maddison/maddison-project/home.htm.

across the former Eastern bloc.[6] As they stripped away the institutional structure of planning, the economies of Eastern Europe and the former Soviet Union experienced economic trauma. On average between 1989 and 1994, output fell by more than 30 percent. Inflation, unemployment and social inequality rocketed as real wages plunged and Communist-era welfare systems disintegrated. In the Baltic states, the hit to the wage level in the 1990s was staggering. Wages fell by 60 percent in Estonia and 70 percent in Lithuania. For many millions, emigration was the best option, illegal if need be.

This was the backdrop against which NATO and the EU decided on enlargement to the East, stabilizing the immediate crisis, offering a future direction and permanently redrawing the geopolitical map.[7] The double expansion of EU and NATO was not a coordinated affair. It was driven as much by the East Europeans themselves as by Washington, Berlin and Paris. Poland, Hungary, the Czechs and the Slovaks—the Visegrád group—began pushing for NATO membership as early as February 1991. The EU followed up with an association agreement. But the EU's decision for enlargement did not follow until 1993, with its conditions being spelled out in detail only in 1997. While some outside observers called for a Marshall Plan to launch economic development, what the EU offered to aspirant members in Eastern Europe was technical and expert assistance as they embarked on the transformation of everything from public finances to transport infrastructure, property rights and the legal system. Focusing only on the military dimension, NATO could move more quickly. Already in 1999 the Poles, Hungarians and Czechs were admitted as full members. The really big bang came in 2004. On April 1, 2004, Bulgaria, Estonia, Latvia, Lithuania, Slovakia, Slovenia and Romania joined NATO. A month later all but Bulgaria and Romania also joined the EU. The two stragglers were judged ready for EU membership in 2007.

It took fifteen years from the end of the cold war. There were second thoughts in Washington, and many West European governments were reluctant to embark on the eastward expansion. The costs were likely to be huge. The risk of provoking Russia was obvious. In 2003 the divisions over the invasion of Iraq were deep and embarrassing.[8] The East Europeans who

were candidates for both NATO and EU membership had to choose. On one side stood Berlin and Paris in opposition to the war. On the other side were Washington, London and their supporters in Madrid and Rome. Eastern Europe opted overwhelmingly for war and US defense secretary Donald Rumsfeld did not hesitate to rub salt in the wounds, playing the "new Europe" against the "old," leaving France and Germany resentful and isolated.[9] Habermas and Derrida's 2003 vision of a distinct "European identity" was directed as much against the East Europeans as it was against the Anglo-Americans. It was core Western Europe that counted. It was left to the European Commission to put a brave face on things. Commission president Romano Prodi was fond of announcing that the fall of the Wall in 1989 and the reunification of Germany and Europe marked not the end of history but a new beginning.[10] Whereas Europe's history had once meant conflict and penury, now Europe had nothing to fear and the world had nothing to fear from Europe. The EU had overcome both the classic power politics of the nineteenth century and the armed truce of the cold war. As a bringer of stability, prosperity and the rule of law, the EU was realizing Kant's dream of perpetual peace.

Prodi talked as though the EU would soon emerge as a fully featured state, combining both soft and hard power. But, in fact, the geopolitical configuration of the post–cold war world was more uncertain and ramshackle than that. The EU never developed its own hard-power capabilities. Not only was European military cooperation factious and frowned upon by Washington, but the European states all took the peace dividend. In light of Russia's weakness, what reason was there not to run down their substantial cold war military establishments? It was this decision that laid the basis for the transatlantic divide on security policy in the 2000s. It also left the East Europeans all the more dependent on the Americans, whose military preponderance grew ever more massive as the new century progressed. At the same time, after the first round of financial assistance in the early 1990s, the United States played no more than a peripheral role in shaping the wider integration of Eastern Europe. On the ground it was the EU that set the pace in erasing the legacy of the Soviet experiment.

II

The incorporation of Eastern Europe into the EU and NATO was an encompassing geopolitical, political and bureaucratic process. But the first mover was not officialdom, but West European business.[11] With wages less than one quarter of those prevailing in Germany in the 1990s, the attraction of the highly skilled East European labor force was irresistible. The process of integration was even more dramatic than that taking place among Canada, the United States and Mexico under the NAFTA agreement. Within a decade of the fall of communism, around half of all East European manufacturing capacity was in the hands of European multinationals.[12] East European motor vehicle production, which soon accounted for 15 percent of European output, was 90 percent foreign owned, with VW's acquisition of Škoda as the emblematic case. Meanwhile, the biggest single foreign investor in Poland in the 1990s was FIAT, followed by Korea's Daewoo.[13]

If private capital led the way, it was followed by a rising tide of public funding. All over Eastern Europe, highways and public buildings were emblazoned with the blue badge of the EU and its ring of stars. Though the initial levels of spending were quite modest, after 2000 through the Cohesion Fund, the European Regional Development Fund and the EU's agricultural subsidy schemes, tens of billions of euros flowed from West to East. In the last funding period, 2007–2013, 175 billion euros were earmarked in structural funds for Eastern Europe, 67 billion euros for Poland alone.[14] The Czechs received 26.7 billion euros, and 25.3 billion went to the Hungarians. Across the region, the EU's money was sufficient to fund between 7 and 17 percent of gross fixed capital formation over a seven-year period. The sums that were poured into the new member states in Eastern Europe by Brussels were comparable in scale to the famous Marshall Plan launched in 1947 to rescue ruined postwar Western Europe. Whereas after World War II it took until the late 1950s before private capital began to flow abundantly across the Atlantic, in the transition economies of Eastern Europe the impact of the EU's public funding was immediately multiplied by private investment.

Western European Banks' Claims on
Central and Eastern Europe (in $ billions)

	Austria	Belgium	France	Germany	Italy	Netherlands	Sweden	Western Europe
Bulgaria	5.7	2	3.6	2.8	8.1	0.7	0	41.5
Czech Rep	65.1	56.7	38.6	12.7	19	6.2	0.2	205.7
Hungary	38.3	18.7	11.9	37.9	29.3	5.6	0.3	153.3
Poland	17.2	25.2	22.9	55.4	54.4	41.2	8.1	287.4
Romania	46.5	1.2	17.6	3.8	12.9	11	0.2	124.1
Slovakia	33.2	10.9	6.4	4.1	23.6	6.7	0.2	87.3
Estonia	0.3	0.1	0.1	1.1	0.4	0	32.7	40.2
Latvia	0.8	0	0.4	4.8	1.4	0	25.0	43.3
Lithuania	0.3	0.1	0.4	3.8	0.7	0	28.9	45.5
Belarus	2.1	0.1	0.2	0.9	0.2	0.1	0	3.8
Russia	23.9	10.3	34.7	49.5	25.7	25.5	9.9	222.6
Ukraine	12.9	0.8	10.6	5	4.9	3.7	5.4	52.8
Total	246.3	126.1	147.4	181.8	180.6	100.7	110.9	1307.5

Source: Danske Bank Research, "Euro Area: Exposure to the Crisis in Central and Eastern Europe," February 24, 2009, table 1.

The takeover of Eastern Europe's industrial base in the 1990s was just the beginning. By the end of 2008 Western-owned banks in the post-Soviet economies had extended $1.3 trillion in credits. These huge figures were not only the result of "foreign loans" but amounted to the wholesale incorporation of the local banking system. Whereas in the eurozone French, Dutch, British and Belgian banks channeled funds into hot spots like Ireland and Spain, in the former Communist world it was Dutch banks like ING, Bavaria's Bayerische Landesbank, the Austrian Raiffeisen Bank or Italy's UniCredit that took the lead.

Across Eastern Europe, financial integration went "all the way down." To an extraordinary extent, foreign currency loans were used to finance mortgages, credit cards and car loans. In Hungary, the most extreme case, between 2003 and 2008, the entire 130 percent increase in household debt was made up of foreign currency credit. What could signify your arrival in

the West more clearly and in a more personal way than the fact that your newly privatized home was financed in Swiss francs?

The impact of this simultaneous financial, political and diplomatic incorporation was transformative. In the main cities of Eastern Europe the material standard of living converged rapidly with norms in the West. And it is hardly surprising that this should have made an impression on the less-favored ex-Soviet republics farther to the east. By the early 2000s, many of the former Soviet republics seemed locked in a time warp. As Gorbachev's foreign minister, Eduard Shevardnadze had been a darling of the West. By the early 2000s his personal regime in Georgia was so riddled with corruption that it could not borrow even from the IMF. Ukraine had suffered almost as badly as Russia in the economic collapse of the 1990s and showed little sign of recovering. The contrast to its Polish neighbor was painful. The "color revolutions" in Georgia and Ukraine in 2003 and 2004 were driven, above all, by the determination not to fall further behind and miss out on the dramatic changes going on farther west.[15] The title of the main Ukrainian protest group PORA translates as "It's time." Its symbol was a ticking clock.[16] The post-Soviet laggards had no more time to lose. In Ukraine the revolutionaries of 2004 were careful to preserve a geopolitical balance, opting for neither Russia nor the West. In Georgia things were simpler. Having turfed Shevardnadze out, by 2006 the new Western-backed government in Georgia headed by Mikhail Saakashvili was glorying in its new status as "Top Reformer" accredited by the World Bank. Georgian soldiers were soon on their way to support the coalition in Iraq.[17] Brussels might profess that "the EU does not do geopolitics," and that slogan suited policy makers in old Europe, particularly Berlin. But to the bevy of new accession states that joined both NATO and the EU between 1999 and 2007 this made little sense. European integration and NATO were born together in the cold war. Their joint eastward expansion since 1989 was the result of the defeat of the Soviet Union. As far as the new accession states were concerned, the historical logic linking the EU to NATO and thus to the United States was undeniable. Western integration promised security and prosperity. But it also harbored risks, both financial and geopolitical.

III

In the financial integration of Eastern Europe as across the emerging market economies, the currency question was paramount. There was no uniformity of currency regime in the former Communist countries.[18] In the Baltics, Latvia opted for a straight peg against the euro managed and defended by the central bank. Lithuania and Estonia opted for currency boards under which the entire domestic monetary system was tied to the stock of euros held by the board. The Poles and the Czechs opted for free floats. Hungary allowed the forint to move within bands. Bulgaria adopted a currency board and Romania a managed float, under which the central bank intervened periodically to guide the movement of the foreign exchange markets within adjustable bands.[19] What they had in common were the optimistic expectation of convergence with the EU and, in due course, eurozone membership. And these hopes were not merely paper dreams. The preemptive adaptation of Eastern Europe economies to EU conditions changed their way of doing business, how markets operated and who owned what. No less significant was the adaptation of their policy-making institutions and their cadres. Thanks to active involvement by the Bank of England and the ECB, the Eastern European states were, by the early twenty-first century, equipped with Westernized central banks, staffed by professional economists.[20] No one was more enthusiastic about the prospect of eurozone accession than the central bankers. Alignment with Brussels and Frankfurt not only raised their status. It also shielded them against unwanted domestic political pressure. Soon they would be joining the global elite of central bankers.

The result was that Eastern Europe reproduced on Europe's doorstep the configuration of overoptimistic expansion that had led to the emerging market crises of the 1990s. Success stories of market reform and privatization, combined with freedom of capital movement and relative stability of exchange rates, led to a huge inward surge of capital. Capital inflow led to upward pressure on exchange rates. All the indicators looked good. But the entire constellation—the booming domestic economy, the appreciating exchange rate, the rising reserves—could all be traced back to a common factor:

the huge inward surge of foreign capital. What if that surge reversed? What if there was a sudden stop?

Under top-secret conditions, the IMF ran a simulation exercise in February 2007 role-playing its response to a reversal in Hungary, which was among the most exposed East European economies. So anxious were they to preserve secrecy and avoid a panic that the IMF's IT department created a separate SimulationMail e-mail system to avoid notes from the game leaking to the outside.[21] Hungary's own central bank duplicated the simulation. Its results, it breezily informed a conference at the ECB in the summer of 2007, were reassuring. If there was one note of caution, it was a reminder that 60 percent of Hungary's banking sector was in the hands of Belgian, Austrian, Italian and German banks. In the event of a crisis, if Budapest was to cope, it would need the closest possible cooperation from its West European counterparts.[22]

Hungary's situation was grossly unbalanced, but the situation in the Baltic states was even more extreme. In early 2008 the IMF noted that Latvia's economy was overheating so badly that its imports exceeded its exports by an amount equivalent to 20 percent of GDP.[23] According to the IMF's models, its currency was overvalued by between 17 and 37 percent. While China and the United States were in deadlock over their trade imbalances, the IMF's staff thought it might be less contentious to single out Latvia as a country with an undeniably "fundamental imbalance." That turned out to be a miscalculation. Any public pronouncement on irrational exuberance in the Baltic was blocked by the Europeans on the IMF board. They wanted to keep the Baltics on track for euro membership and did not want to risk an IMF warning unleashing a chain reaction of uncertainty across Eastern Europe. The Swedes in particular were deeply concerned. Their banks had lent so heavily to Latvia that a crisis could easily spill back across the Baltic. Over the winter of 2007–2008, the Scandinavian representative on the IMF board went so far as to block the dispatch of the IMF delegation to Riga to complete Latvia's regular Article IV report.

No one in Europe wanted to burst the bubble. Latvia was enjoying a recovery from the doldrums of the 1990s. In the fall of 2007 its foreign ministry moved into the newly renovated building it had last occupied in the 1930s, when Latvia first enjoyed its independence from czarist Russia.[24]

As one retrospective commentator noted, there were high hopes that "Latvia would be able to extend its foreign policy presence beyond the transatlantic space and facilitate the development of closer ties between post-Soviet states such as Ukraine, Georgia and Moldova and the EU and NATO. It was estimated that Latvia's development cooperation budget would grow rapidly, that Latvia would open new embassies in faraway places and that entering Africa in order to help poorer nations to develop was only a matter of time."[25] To say that this was a transformation in the fortunes of tiny Latvia would be an understatement. It was a vision both expansive and fragile. It depended on two crucial conditions—the continuation of Latvia's feverish economic boom and the acquiescence of its hulking neighbor to the east. Russia had watched as Latvia reclaimed its independence in May 1990. It had watched as Latvia conducted a referendum on EU membership in the autumn of 2003 that overrode the no vote of the ethnic Russian minority, and it had watched as Latvia, along with its Baltic neighbors, joined NATO in April 2004. Would Russia continue to watch as Latvia, and other countries like it, set about rolling back the Soviet-era boundaries of power even farther to the east?

IV

If the 1990s had been terrible for Russia's economy, the new millennium brought a period of recovery. Vladimir Putin, who was confirmed as president by a landslide election victory in May 2000, will forever claim credit for Russia's restoration. In fact, the turnaround in Russia's financial fortunes already had been initiated in 1999 by austere former Communist Yevgeny Primakov, Putin's political mentor. The collapse in the external value of the ruble jolted Russia's export industries into life and curbed imports. But the key driver of the recovery was the global boom in oil and other commodities, which began months after Putin took office in the latter half of 2000. From $9.57 per barrel in 1998, the spot price of Urals crude would soar by 2008 to $94 per barrel. It would have taken catastrophic mismanagement for the Russian economy and Russian public finances not to

have flourished. The questions were who would benefit from the boom and how would it affect Russia's relationship with the outside world.

Whereas in the 1990s large parts of Russia's economy had been privatized, under Putin the energy sector was brought back under the control of the state, which in effect meant the oligarchic group around the president. In the energy sector, the corporate giants Gazprom and Rosneft were the battering ram of state industry. In October 2003 respectable opinion in the West looked on aghast as Mikhail B. Khodorkovsky—who, in the 1990s, had installed himself as the billionaire owner of private oil giant Yukos in a particularly egregious privatization deal—was arrested and imprisoned on charges of tax evasion.[26] A year later, Yukos's main assets were snapped up in a fire sale by a shell company that turned out to be a front for state-owned Rosneft. Meanwhile, Gazprom consolidated its grip on the giant gas industry by buying up Sibneft from Roman Abramovich, who retired out of harm's way to London to enjoy life at the top of the Premier League as owner of Chelsea FC. In 2006 threats of prosecution forced Anglo-Dutch oil major Shell to sell its valuable Sakhalin assets to Gazprom. In 2007 the TNK-BP joint venture was leveraged out of another promising gas field. Though Rosneft and Gazprom were never merged, together they gave the Russian state a powerful corporate underpinning. By one calculation the share of government-owned firms in oil production in Russia rose from 19 percent in 2004 to 50 percent in 2008.[27]

With the force of a booming, state-controlled energy business behind them, Putin and his team built on the measures put in place in the 1990s to restore Russia's finances. Of Russia's state revenues, just under 50 percent were accounted for by taxes and revenues from oil and gas. The profits would have been even larger if growth in output of oil and gas had not slowed disappointingly after 2005. Nevertheless, as the profits of the oil and gas boom rolled in, household consumption by ordinary Russians surged back to precrisis levels, rising at a rate of 10 percent per annum. By 2007 the percentage of the population below the subsistence minimum had fallen to 14 percent. And this was no longer the feverish, dollarized speculation of old. Prices were stable and were no longer set in dollars. Taxes were paid in rubles. The Russian parliament passed a law imposing fines on public officials

who lapsed into the bad old habits of using dollars as a unit of account.[28] On one occasion even Putin found himself embarrassingly caught out. From 2003, the Russian Treasury, headed by the technocrat economist Alexei Kudrin, used oil and gas earnings to accumulate a gigantic strategic reserve of international assets. By early 2008 these had reached $550 billion. After China and Japan, Russia was now the third-largest holder of dollar reserves in the world. On Putin's orders a special staff assembled a national reserve of food and vital raw materials.[29] Russia would never again suffer the kind of humiliating crisis that it had lived through in 1998.

Russia could thus seem the very model of a national economic power-house, with a huge trade surplus, surging foreign reserves and a strong state. But the paradox of Russia's position was that its new prosperity was associated not with independence from the world economy but with entanglement with it.[30] And this entanglement extended beyond the export of oil and gas. Money was even more liquid and the pipelines connecting the off-shore banking system were ready laid. Tens of billions of dollars in oil and gas export earnings never returned to Russia. Russia's oligarchs behaved like the masters of a 1970s petrostate, harboring their wealth in offshore havens like Cyprus, from where it cycled back to London and its convenient eurodollar accounts. From the early 2000s the pattern was further complicated by a large flow of funds back to Russia. In 2007 this peaked at an annual total of $180.7 billion, of which only $27.8 billion was foreign direct investment (FDI).[31] The rest flowed through international banks such as Sberbank and VTB into the Russian financial system. To prevent a sharp appreciation, Russia's central bank, like that of China's, found itself having to sterilize the dollar inflow by buying it up with freshly minted rubles. Having driven dollars out of domestic circulation, Moscow was now assuming an unfamiliar position as a de facto creditor to the United States.

With the global commodity boom fueling Russia's resurgence at the same time as West European money flooded eastward into the territory of the former Warsaw Pact, it was as if the two great weather fronts of global capitalism were charging toward each other across Eurasia. Did the contradictory geopolitical consequences of global growth, strengthening both Russia and its former satellites, make conflict inevitable? Certainly not from an economic point of view. The growth of the Polish and Baltic economies and

the development of Ukraine, Georgia and Russia did not preclude each other. European exports to Russia flourished and all of Europe relied heavily on Russian gas. The question was whether a shared and interconnected prosperity could be given a common political meaning. Would it be cast as a foundation for a stable and prosperous international order? Or would the uneven but dramatic growth serve as fuel for a new arms race? Would interdependence come to be seen not as productive and efficient but as a source of vulnerability and threat? In the dark years of the 1990s the former Communist economies had experienced a common emergency. Exhaustion and disorder were shared. The common boom, ironically, would prove far more explosive.

Given his background, Putin had far less reason to look favorably to the West than had Boris Yeltsin. But early in his term as president even his critics acknowledge that Putin seemed to be looking to Washington for acceptance.[32] After 9/11 Putin overrode the hostile impulses of many Russian nationalists and gave ostentatious backing to the American invasion of Afghanistan. But the rapprochement was one-sided. Under Bush, Washington never took Russia seriously as an ally and refused to treat Moscow's brutal war in Chechnya as part of the common fight against terrorism and "Islamic extremism." Rebuffed by Washington, the divisions over the Iraq War provided Russia with leverage. Playing Germans against Americans was a game Putin was familiar with from his old days as a KGB resident in Dresden. Nor was it only Germany and America that were at odds. Germany's preference for détente with Russia was a source of alienation also between Berlin and the East Europeans. When Germany and Russia signed the first Nord Stream pipeline deal in 2005, enormously increasing the flow of Gazprom's gas to the West, it was denounced by Poland's foreign minister as a second coming of the Hitler-Stalin Pact that had sealed Poland's fate in 1939. When Moscow tweaked Ukraine's gas prices over the winter of 2005–2006, it only confirmed the Poles' worst fears. By early 2006 Warsaw and Washington were calling for a new division of NATO to confront Russia on its chosen terrain of energy security.[33]

But it wasn't just gas supplies that were in play. In April 2006 at the meeting of the IMF and the World Bank in Washington, with central bankers Mario Draghi, Ben Bernanke and Jean-Claude Trichet looking on, Putin's

finance minister, Alexei Kudrin, shook hands with the American Treasury secretary. Kudrin had come to announce the repayment of a large tranche of international debt still owed to the Paris Club of creditors from the bad old days of the 1990s. But he had also come to deliver a less friendly message. The dollar, Kudrin declared, was in danger of forfeiting its status as the "universal or absolute reserve currency."[34] It was simply too uncertain in value. "Whether it is the U.S. dollar exchange rate or the U.S. trade balance, it definitely causes concerns with regard to the dollar's status as a reserve currency." Eight years on from the humiliation of 1998, when Russia's finance minister spoke, the markets listened. Kudrin's words were enough to send the dollar down against the euro by almost half a cent.

On the streets of Moscow the language was more inflammatory. In 2006 Nashi, the Russian nationalist movement, rallied its rent-a-mob following for street demonstrations against dollar hegemony. The lingering attachment of ordinary Russians to the greenback was not just a sign of psychological weakness. "Buying one hundred dollars," its leaflets informed passersby, "you invest 2,660 rubles in the US economy. This money finances the war in Iraq, this money finances the construction of US nuclear submarines. Various estimates say that the US dollar is worth 15 percent to 20 percent of its face value. The secret of the dollar's stability is the continued expansion of the dollar zone. . . . [T]his is a financial pyramid based on nothing but simpletons believing in the dollar."[35]

In February 2007 President Putin made his first appearance at the prestigious Munich Security Conference. Attended by heads of government and ministers from around the world, the Munich conference is for security policy what Davos is for business and economics. The speech Putin delivered forced into the open the question of the power politics in an age of globalization.[36] Looking back at the decades since the end of the cold war, Putin asked: What kind of world organization did the West want to see? It talked of rights and international law, but "today we are witnessing an almost uncontained hyper use of force—military force—in international relations, force that is plunging the world into an abyss of permanent conflicts. . . . One state and, of course, first and foremost the United States, has overstepped its national borders in every way. This is visible in the economic, political, cultural and educational policies it imposes on other nations.

Well, who likes this? . . . [O]f course this is extremely dangerous. It results in the fact that no one feels safe. I want to emphasise this—no one feels safe! Because no one can feel that international law is like a stone wall that will protect them. Of course such a policy stimulates an arms race." Once upon a time America had won an arms race against the Soviet Union on the back of its strong economy. In the new millennium, the United States still commanded huge stockpiles of nuclear weapons and missile systems. America's military power was undeniable. But in light of contemporary economic developments, any claim to omnipotence was simply unrealistic. "[T]he international landscape is so varied and changes so quickly—changes in light of the dynamic development in a whole number of countries and regions. . . . The combined GDP measured in purchasing power parity of countries such as India and China is already greater than that of the United States. And a similar calculation with the GDP of the BRIC countries—Brazil, Russia, India and China—surpasses the cumulative GDP of the EU. And according to experts this gap will only increase in the future. . . . There is no reason to doubt that the economic potential of the new centres of global economic growth will inevitably be converted into political influence and will strengthen multipolarity." Under such circumstances, for the West to imagine that a global order could be based on its own organizations—the EU and NATO—rather than the truly comprehensive authority of the UN was either self-deceiving or in profoundly bad faith. Nor could the West reasonably claim that NATO expansion into Eastern Europe had "any relation with the modernisation of the Alliance itself or with ensuring security in Europe," unless it presumed Russian hostility. How, then, could Moscow not interpret such expansion as a "serious provocation"?

Energy was an object of contention between Europe and Russia, Putin admitted. But what was the answer? Prices, he proposed, should be "determined by the market instead of being the subject of political speculation, economic pressure or blackmail." With global demand booming, Russia had nothing to fear from the judgment of the market. Its experts were gleefully predicting a future in which oil prices would hit $250 a barrel.[37] Gazprom was surging up the global corporate rankings. Within a few years it was projected that it would overtake ExxonMobil as the world's largest publicly traded company.[38] Nor was it reasonable to suggest that Russia was

not open for business. Certainly the Russian state had asserted its legitimate national interest, but "26 percent of the oil extraction in Russia is done by foreign capital. Try, try to find me a similar example where Russian business participates extensively in key economic sectors in Western countries. Such examples do not exist!" Russia submitted itself to the judgment of the credit-rating agencies and celebrated the improvement in its standing. It was hoping to gain full membership in the WTO. What Russia would not tolerate, however, and here Putin's tone harshened, was the repurposing of organizations such as the Organization for Security and Cooperation in Europe (OSCE) "into a vulgar instrument designed to promote the foreign policy interests of one or a group of countries." Moscow deeply resented the critical commentary on the rigged Russian elections of 2004. It would stand for no repeat of the Western-backed revolutions in Georgia and Ukraine in 2003–2004.[39]

As one of Russia's leading commentators, Dmitri Trenin, noted, Putin was driving home the reality of multipolarity: "Until recently, Russia saw itself as a Pluto in the Western solar system, very far from the center but still fundamentally part of it. Now it has left that orbit entirely: Russia's leaders have given up on becoming part of the West and have started creating their own Moscow-centered system." Russia was establishing itself as a "major outside player that is neither an eternal foe nor an automatic friend."[40] The question of course was who Russia meant to include in its new "solar system." In particular, what were the implications for the post-Soviet and East European states? What did it mean for a state like Latvia, with its newly redecorated foreign ministry and its ambitions to spread its model of market economics to other former Soviet republics? At Munich in February 2007 the response of the Czech foreign minister, Karel Schwarzenberg, was immediate. "We must thank President Putin," he remarked facetiously, "who has not only shown concern about the publicity for this conference, but has clearly and convincingly demonstrated why NATO had to enlarge."[41] Schwarzenberg spoke in the past tense. But the real question was the future. In the face of Putin's challenge, could the West be content with upholding the status quo in Eastern Europe, or would that imply a tacit acceptance of Putin's line in the sand? Was the only way for the West to respond to Putin's challenge to push for even further enlargement of the EU

and NATO? The urgency on the part of the smaller ex-Communist states was obvious. Their vulnerability in both security policy and economic terms was only too evident. But how would the big players in the European and transatlantic system—Washington, Berlin and Paris—respond? The question would explode embarrassingly into the open at the NATO summit hosted in Bucharest on April 2–4, 2008.

V

The venue for the meeting was in itself symbolic. Romania, as an eager exponent of the new Europe, had joined NATO in 2004 and the EU in 2007. Romanian soldiers were doing policing duty in the former Yugoslavia, Angola and Iraq. Meanwhile, EU accession triggered a subsidy payment of 19.8 billion euros to Romania's population of 21 million. It also enabled freedom of movement and a massive migration of Romanians to the West, notably to Italy, where the Romanian population topped 1 million in 2007, triggering local anti-immigrant resentment that the Prodi government struggled to contain.[42] Meanwhile, at home, Romania's GDP growth was running at 6 percent, projected to rise to 7 percent in 2008. The Romanians dubbed themselves the "Tigers of the East."[43] There was talk of Romania joining the rich country club of the eurozone as soon as 2012. In Bucharest, its newly renovated capital, the Europe Real Estate Yearbook reported a vacancy rate for prime office space of no more than 0.02 percent.[44] As US subprime was imploding, international investors like ING Real Estate were snapping up Romanian assets to add to their East European property portfolios.[45] As host of the NATO summit in April 2008, Bucharest was the perfect stage for the last major effort by George W. Bush to burnish his presidential legacy. And there was no issue more decisive for the future of Russian and Western relations than NATO membership for Georgia and Ukraine.

In February 2008 both Georgia and Ukraine formally applied to be put on a NATO fast-track Membership Action Plan (MAP).[46] After the Baltics they would be the fourth and fifth Soviet republics to join the Western alliance. Georgia, like the Baltics, was touchy but small. Ukraine was in a different league. With its population of 45 million, its substantial economy,

its strategic location on the Black Sea and its historic significance for the Russian Empire, for Ukraine to join the Western coalition would be a terrible blow to Russia, precisely at a moment when Putin had announced his intention to stop the slide. Despite, or perhaps because of, its spectacularly provocative nature, President Bush immediately threw his authority behind the NATO membership bid. Welcoming Ukraine and Georgia into the MAP would send a signal throughout the region, the White House announced. It would make clear to Russia that "these two nations are, and will remain, sovereign and independent states." It was a proposal that was bound to please the new Europe. Poland's government was delighted. The fact that Berlin and Paris had reservations was not off-putting. Nor was Bush in any mood to spare their sensibilities. En route to Bucharest in early April, the American president paid a flying visit to Kiev, where he announced: "My stop here should be a clear signal to everybody that I mean what I say: It's in our interest for Ukraine to join."[47] As one US official remarked, the outgoing president was laying "down a marker."[48]

At the NATO meeting in the Romanian capital the fallout was predictable. Putin, who was attending the joint Russia-NATO session for the first time before handing over the Russian presidency to his associate Dmitry Medvedev, was in no mood to compromise. In February 2008 the West had rubbed salt in the wounds of Russian resentment by extending recognition to an independent Kosovo, overriding the claims of Serbia, which Russia regarded as its client. When, at the NATO meeting, the conversation turned to Ukraine and Georgia, Putin stalked out in protest. This left it to Berlin and Paris to fight the idea of the MAP to a standstill. In so doing they could count on the backing of Italy, Hungary and the Benelux countries against the East European and Scandinavian advocates of NATO expansion. The Americans looked on. As one senior Bush administration official commented to the *New York Times*: "The debate was mostly among Europeans. . . . It was quite split, but it was split in a good way."[49] Condoleezza Rice was less sanguine. The clashes she witnessed between the Germans and the Poles were disturbing. The arguments in Bucharest were, in her words, "one of the most pointed and contentious debates with our allies that I'd ever experienced. In fact, it was the most heated that I saw in my entire time as

secretary."[50] No formal process of membership application was initiated. But Merkel conceded that the summit should issue a statement endorsing the aspirations of Georgia and Ukraine and boldly declaring, "These countries will become members of NATO."[51] It was a fudge, and a disastrous one at that. It invited the Russians to ensure that Georgia and Ukraine were never in a fit state to take the next step toward NATO accession. It invited Georgia, Ukraine and their sponsors to force the pace. Ambiguity was a formula for escalation. And both sides responded accordingly.

In May, at the urging of Poland, the EU adopted the idea of an Eastern Partnership for Ukraine as one of the key elements of the new EU foreign policy to be developed under the terms of the Lisbon Treaty.[52] Despite the opposition they had voiced at Bucharest, there was no counter steer from Berlin or Paris. The EU and NATO stayed locked in step. Meanwhile, Russo-American relations took a sharp turn for the worse. Though he liked to present himself as a modernizer, Putin's successor as president, Medvedev, continued to steer a hard line. As the financial markets in the United States convulsed in the summer of 2008, dark rumors circulated that Moscow was about to move from verbal attacks on dollar hegemony to concerted action. US Treasury Secretary Paulson had not named his sources, but in the run-up to the Olympics, his Chinese contacts informed him that they "had received a message from the Russians which was, 'Hey let's join together and sell Fannie and Freddie securities on the market.'"[53] The fragility of America's mortgage market was about to be turned into a geopolitical weapon. China, which was celebrating its global coming-out party as the host of the Olympic Games, had too much at stake in the US economy to take this suggestion seriously. But over the course of 2008, Russia did unload its portfolio of $100 billion of Fannie Mae and Freddie Mac bonds. As Reuters reported it, the decision was motivated primarily by domestic political concerns.[54] "The holdings have met hostility from some Russian media and the public, who are wary of risky investments." By the summer of 2008, one didn't need to be a Russian nationalist to view American mortgage securities as a bad investment. The GSE were at the heart of the mortgage crisis and were on the point of spectacular failure. Patriotic Russians saw no reason why they should be propping up the United States, which so

openly flouted Russia's national interests. Looking back, Treasury Secretary Paulson ruefully admitted: "[I]t just drove home to me how vulnerable I felt."[55]

Whereas China refused to participate in a move that would upset the international order, America's friends in Tbilisi were less cautious. In early August 2008, with Russian encouragement, irregular forces in the rebel province of South Ossetia began shelling positions of the Georgian army.[56] On August 7, apparently believing that they had Washington's approval, the Georgian government took the bait. A sudden counterstrike by Georgia's American-trained army would subdue Ossetia and Abkhazia, settle the outstanding territorial questions and clear the way for a successful NATO membership application. As the awe-inspiring opening ceremony of the Beijing Olympics exploded across Western TV screens, Georgia launched its army and air force into an invasion of South Ossetia. Moscow's response was devastating. In a matter of days the Russian army crushed Georgia's undersized forces, inflicting hundreds of casualties. According to Georgian sources, 230,000 civilians were put to flight. After a rapid advance, Russian tanks halted on the Gori-Tbilisi highway, an hour's drive from the capital.

While President Medvedev announced to his Security Council that August 8, 2008, marked a turning point in the international order and that henceforth the world would have to reckon with Russian power, in the West the reaction was opprobrium.[57] The presidents of Poland, Ukraine and the Baltics flew into Georgia to express their solidarity. Estonia demanded sanctions against Russia, including the expulsion of Russian students studying at Western universities and travel bans on oligarchs.[58] Poland called for urgent action to break Gazprom's grip on Europe's energy supplies. And Warsaw moved hastily to sign an agreement allowing the deployment of the US missile shield to Poland. But the response was not so unambiguous everywhere. On August 12, 2008, while the United States was preoccupied with Wall Street and the presidential election, President Sarkozy shuttled from Paris to Moscow in the hope of patching up a cease-fire. Though Chancellor Merkel now came out in favor of admitting Georgia to NATO, on September 1 at a special EU summit, any drastic anti-Russian moves were blocked by a united front of France, Germany and Italy. Russia was given three months to withdraw its forces. But Moscow had made its point.

In conversation with Western experts as part of the Valdai Discussion Club in Sochi on September 11, Putin remarked that any effort to push Ukraine toward NATO membership would result in severe countermeasures.[59] Meanwhile, $25 billion in foreign capital fled Russia. But that was no cause for panic. This was not 1998. Moscow had ample reserves to deal with such a minor market mood swing. It was America, not Russia, whose financial system looked to be imploding.

VI

Splits within the transatlantic alliance were not new. The disagreements among Berlin and Paris and the Bush administration over the Iraq War in 2002–2003 had been headline grabbing. But Russia and post-Soviet Europe were far closer to home, far more fundamental to the future of Europe and far more directly linked to the advance of financial and political integration over the previous decades. When added to the incomplete project of the eurozone and the missing political frame for the North Atlantic financial system, the unresolved geopolitics of Europe's "Eastern Question" completed a trifecta of unanswered political questions that hung over Western power in the summer of 2008.

This was the backdrop of the sixty-third meeting of the UN General Assembly assembled in New York in September 2008. Heedless of the precariously balanced state of the global economy, for the first time since the end of the cold war, Russia and the Western powers had engaged in a proxy war. Russia had announced that it would resist any further extension of Western influence and it had made good on that threat. For its part, the West was disunited. For all the saber rattling in Warsaw and Washington, there was neither the political will nor the resources to back up further eastward expansion. It was against this backdrop that President Sarkozy declared to the UN General Assembly: "Europe does not want war. It does not want a war of civilizations. It does not want a war of religion. It does not want a cold war. . . . The world is no longer a unipolar world with one super-Power, nor is it a bipolar world with the East and the West. It's a multipolar world now."[60] He was, in effect, conceding the point Putin had made eighteen

months earlier in Munich. Even if there had been the capacity or the will to further escalate the geopolitical clash, by the fall of 2008 the giant wave of capital that had carried Western political influence deep into Eastern Europe was receding fast. A generation of globalization under the sign of Western power and money had reached its limit. For the immediate future, the sheer shock of the financial crisis would tend to dampen geopolitical tensions. But the damage done by the escalation of 2007–2008 would prove to be long lasting.

Part II

THE GLOBAL CRISIS

Chapter 6

"THE WORST FINANCIAL CRISIS IN GLOBAL HISTORY"

America's real estate prices peaked in the summer of 2006 and began, slowly at first, to ease. In Ireland the turning point came in March 2007. By the summer construction sites began to close in Spain. October 2007 saw the first dip in UK house prices. Tens of millions of home owners now felt the force of asset valuation go into reverse gear.[1] As house prices fell, equity dwindled, and the hardest hit slid into negative equity. Families scrambled to slash spending and pay down credit card and other short-term debt. The result was a smothering recession in consumer demand. Whatever else happened, a large part of the North Atlantic economy was headed into a downturn. On the face of it, this was precisely the sort of contingency that financial engineering was supposed to deal with. Through securitization, risks were supposed to have been spread so that even severe losses would be absorbed across the broad base of the economy. That was the theory. By the late summer of 2007 it was evident that the reality was different. Though mortgage-backed securities had indeed been sold far and wide, lethal pockets of risk were concentrated in some of the most vulnerable nodes of the shadow banking system.

The first mortgage issuers to die were in the bottom tier.[2] The aptly named Ownit Mortgage Solutions, one of the feeders for Merrill Lynch's securitization pipeline, was the first to go, on January 3, 2007. On February 8, 2007, the crisis moved up the food chain when HSBC, whose offices spanned Hong Kong, Shanghai and London, announced it was making a $10.6 billion

provision for losses on mortgage investments. On March 7, Ben Bernanke was still in a sanguine mood, declaring that he thought the subprime problem was contained. But the bad news kept coming. In April New Century Financial, the largest stand-alone subprime lender, folded. May saw Swiss megabank UBS announce that it was closing its Dillon Read Capital Management hedge fund.[3] On June 22, Bear Stearns was forced to bail out two funds that had made heavy losses on MBS. By then it was clear that the foundations were shaking. It was in the late summer that the full scale of the financial fallout began to become clear. On July 29, 2007, the small German lender IKB had to be bailed out by a consortium of banks with public backing.[4] On August 8, 2007, another of Germany's overextended regional banks, WestLB, announced outsized losses on a real estate fund and stopped payouts. Within days it was followed by Sachsen LB. But the really decisive break in market confidence came on the morning of August 9, 2007, when BNP Paribas, France's most prominent bank, announced that it was freezing three of its funds.[5] The explanation Paribas offered marked a decisive moment in the opening of the crisis: "The complete evaporation of liquidity in certain market segments of the U.S. securitisation market has made it impossible to value certain assets fairly regardless of their quality or credit rating."[6] Without valuation the assets could not be used as collateral. Without collateral there was no funding. And if there was no funding all the banks were in trouble, no matter how large their exposure to real estate. In a general liquidity freeze, the equivalent of a giant bank run, no bank was safe. As the implications of the announcement from Paris sank in, around noon Central European Time on August 9, 2007, the cost of borrowing on European interbank markets surged.[7] As one senior bank executive commented, the event was disorientating: "It was something none of us had experienced. It was as if your entire life you had turned the spigot and water came out. And now there was no water."[8]

The ECB did not at this point have data on the subprime exposure of Europe's banks. But the stress in the interbank lending market was all too obvious. In response Jean-Claude Trichet and his colleagues opened the liquidity tap, offering funds at attractive rates in unlimited quantities. By the end of the day on August 9, Europe's banks had taken 94.8 billion euros,

and they took another 50 billion on August 10. It was the scale and urgency of this action that finally brought home to Ben Bernanke and Hank Paulson the true severity of the situation. As Larry Elliott, economics editor of the *Guardian,* commented: "As far as the financial markets are concerned, August 9 2007 has all the resonance of August 4 1914. It marks the cut-off point between 'an Edwardian summer' of prosperity and tranquility and the trench warfare of the credit crunch—the failed banks, the petrified markets, the property markets blown to pieces by a shortage of credit."[9] Quite how bad things were soon going to get was suggested three weeks later, when on September 14, Northern Rock, one of Britain's largest mortgage lenders, failed. On TV screens, the Northern Rock panic looked like a classic bank run. Anxious depositors queued up outside beleaguered bank branches to retrieve their funds. News photographers and camera crews had a field day. But off camera something even worse was happening. The trillion-dollar global funding market was shutting down.[10]

I

Northern Rock was a product of Britain's overheated housing bubble. Formed in the 1960s through amalgamation of two nineteenth-century building societies (thrifts) and headquartered in gritty Newcastle, it had by the 1990s acquired fifty-three competitors across the north of England. To create the platform for further growth in October 1997, it converted from thrift status to a public limited company and floated on the London Stock Exchange. Then, between 1998 and 2007, in a gigantic surge of growth, it quintupled its balance sheet. As house prices faltered, some of its more marginal loans were primed to go bad. It was no surprise that "the Rock" got into trouble. But the obviousness of this connection is deceptive. What triggered the collapse in 2007 were not the loans on its balance sheet but the mechanism of their funding. Northern Rock was the model of a modern highly leveraged bank: 80 percent of its funding was sourced not from deposits but wholesale, at the lowest rates global money markets would offer. The bank's 2006 annual report gives an idea of this far-flung funding operation:

"During the year, we raised £3.2 billion medium term wholesale funds from a variety of globally spread sources, with specific emphasis on the US, Europe, Asia and Australia. This included two transactions sold to domestic US investors totalling US$3.5 billion. In January 2007, we raised a further US$2.0 billion under our US MTN [medium-term notes] programme. Key developments during 2006 included the establishment of an Australian debt programme, raising A$1.2 billion from our inaugural issue. This transaction was the largest debut deal in that market for a single A rated financial institution targeted at both domestic Australian investors and the Far East."[11]

Northern Rock had minimal exposure to US subprime. But that didn't matter, because it sourced its funding from markets heavily used by banks that did. The bad news from Paribas on August 9 was enough to shut down the interbank lending markets and the market for asset-backed commercial paper. It was the seizure in the funding market that poleaxed the entire securitization business and in particular the European side, which had been most actively involved in the issuance of ABCP. Given Northern Rock's extreme dependence on wholesale funding, it took only two working days after the markets dried up for the bank to notify the Financial Services Authority of an impending crisis.[12] But the Bank of England was in no mood to help. Governor Mervyn King took the view that the overextended mortgage lender should suffer the consequences of its irresponsible expansion. By the end of August Northern Rock's liquidity problems had become life threatening. But it wasn't until September 13, after the BBC reported the story and the government acted to address the crisis by announcing a guarantee, that the retail depositors panicked. After that, the main damage to Northern Rock's balance sheet was done by online withdrawals. The elderly savers queuing in the streets made for alarming TV footage. But it was not their panic that was bringing down the bank. It was a bank run operating on an altogether different scale at the speed of computer terminals in money markets across the world. It was a bank run without deposit withdrawals. There had been no deposits. There was nothing to withdraw. For banks to find themselves a trillion dollars short, all that needed to happen was for major providers of funding to withdraw from the money markets.

ABCP was always the weakest link in the shadow banking chain. Repo,

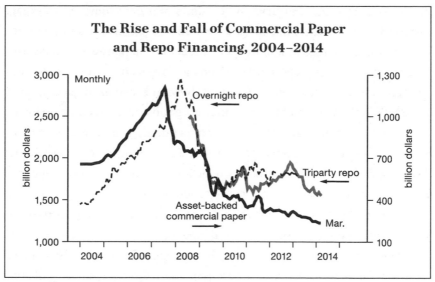

Source: Tobias Adrian, Daniel Covitz and Nellie Liang, "Financial Stability Monitoring," *Annual Review of Financial Economics* 7 (2015): 357–395, chart 15.

as fully collateralized lending, was supposed to be safe. Initially, that expectation was borne out. Bear Stearns, the smallest of the US investment banks, reported the first loss in the firm's history in the first quarter of 2007.[13] As was common knowledge, it was heavily involved in mortgage securitization. That was enough to restrict its access to commercial paper markets. The bank's ABCP issuance plunged from $21 billion at the end of 2006 to $4 billion a year later. Initially, Bear was able to make up for this shortfall by increasing its repo funding from $69 billion to $102 billion. To back this up, as late as Monday, March 10, 2008, Bear still held an $18 billion "pool" of ultraliquid, high-quality securities. But then collateralized borrowing began to fail too.

Unlike the implosion of ABCP, the "run on repo" was a surprise.[14] Under British and American law, the holder of repo collateral is entitled to seize it ahead of any other claimant in the bankruptcy queue. So even allowing for Bear's large portfolio of toxic mortgage-backed securities, its repo ought to have been good. A Treasury security is a Treasury security. Unfortunately for Bear, given that there were plenty of other counterparties to engage in repo trades with, no one wanted to take the risk of having to seize collateral from a failing bank, even if the collateral was as highly rated

and as liquid as US Treasurys. When news of a new round of mortgage failures hit the markets in March 2008 and hedge funds began emptying their prime brokerage accounts, quite suddenly the haircuts Bear Stearns faced in the bilateral repo market steepened and access to trilateral repo funding was shut off. A bank that in early March had easily been able to raise $100 billion overnight in exchange for good collateral could no longer fund itself. On Thursday, March 13, with its liquidity reserve down to only $2 billion, Bear's directors were told that $14 billion in repos would not "roll" the next day and that they were at imminent risk of running out of cash. This was a modern bank failure. There were no queuing depositors. Bear did not cater to pensioners. It died, because doubts about its business led it to be cut out of wholesale funding markets.

Then something even worse began to happen. The uncertainty spread from individual weak banks to the entire system. First in the spring of 2008 and then in June, the haircuts on bilateral repo took a severe step up across the board, for all asset classes, for all parties.[15] This meant that the amount of capital that was required to hold the outstanding stock of bonds leaped upward, across the entire banking system. Repo in US Treasurys and GSE-backed mortgage-backed securities was the least badly affected. As top-quality collateral they were reserved mainly for use in triparty repo overseen by JPMorgan Chase and Bank of New York Mellon. As long as a counter-

Haircuts on Repo Agreements (%)

Securities	April '07	August '08
US Treasurys	0.25	3
Investment-grade bonds	0–3	8–12
High-yield bonds	10–15	25–40
Equities	15	20
Senior-leveraged loans	10–12	15–20
Mezzanine-leveraged loans	18–25	35+
Prime MBS	2–4	10–20
ABS	3–5	50–60

Source: Tobias Adrian and Hyun Song Shin, "The Shadow Banking System: Implications for Financial Regulation," Federal Reserve Bank of New York Staff Reports 382, July 2009, table 9. Based on IMF Global Financial Stability Report, October 2008.

party remained in good standing and had top-quality collateral, that repo market remained open and stable. But in the interbank bilateral repo market where private label ABS was used as collateral, funding terms were getting stiffer and stiffer.[16]

The step up in haircuts would put huge pressure on the investment banks that relied most heavily on short-term funding markets. And it was clear which of those, after Bear, was most vulnerable. The warning signs at Lehman were unmistakable.[17] Like Bear, it was known to have taken huge risks on real estate in the hope of catapulting up the Wall Street league table. It had fully integrated its business with the mortgage securitization pipeline. Since the beginning of 2008, the bank's stock had lost 73 percent of its value. As at Bear, commercial paper issuance by Lehman fell from $8 billion in 2007 to $4 billion in 2008. Nevertheless, on May 31, 2008, its liquidity pool, which was intended to cover cash outflows over a twelve-month period, was as high as $45 billion.[18] In June 2008 investors were sufficiently confident to commit $6 billion in new share capital. What pushed Lehman over the edge were collateral calls by anxious lenders. Given the falling value of its stock, J.P. Morgan demanded large postings of collateral to back up daytime triparty repo risks. By Tuesday, September 9, allowing for liens on its assets, Lehman's liquidity pool was down to $22 billion. Two days later, on Thursday, September 11, Lehman was still posting $150 billion as collateral in the repo market.[19] But then confidence broke. S&P, Fitch and Moody's all downgraded Lehman. Its share price fell and with that went its standing in the repo markets; $20 billion in repo did not roll and J.P. Morgan demanded $5 billion in collateral to sustain even the most essential part of Lehman's triparty repo business. Within a matter of hours on Friday, September 12, the Lehman liquidity pool was down to $1.4 billion and it was clear that, barring a weekend rescue, it would be forced to file for bankruptcy.

On Monday, September 15, as Lehman's staff around the world stumbled dazed out onto the pavement, the question was who might be next. Bear and Lehman were badly run. Under intense competitive pressure they made high-risk bets on some of the worst parts of the mortgage securitization business. But they were not exceptional. Merrill Lynch too had huge real estate exposure, and it was funding $194 billion of its balance sheet on

a short-term basis in the summer of 2008.[20] In total, prior to the Lehman bankruptcy, $2.5 trillion in collateral was posted in the triparty segment of the repo market alone on a daily basis. This gigantic pile of claims and counterclaims could become destabilized in a matter of hours. Market analysts recognized the bimodal quality of this experience. It was a "massive game theory," one commented.[21] In trilateral repo, given the unimpeachable quality of the collateral used, there was effectively no price adjustment mechanism. One day the investment banks, dealers and those they borrowed from and lent securities to all functioned as a gigantic trillion-dollar machine based on confidence and widely acceptable collateral. The next day even a very large player in the system could be shut out.

After Lehman, the next link in the shadow banking chain to come under acute pressure was AIG, the insurer. In a dramatic burst of expansion from the 1990s onward, the Financial Products division of AIG had developed into a major player in the derivatives markets. In total in 2007 it had a book of $2.7 trillion in derivatives contracts.[22] Of this total, credit default swaps accounted for $527 billion. Of these, $70 billion were on

Source: Adam Copeland, Antoine Martin and Michael Walker, "Repo Runs: Evidence from the Tri-Party Repo Market," Federal Reserve Bank of New York Staff Reports 506, July 2011 (revised August 2014).

mortgage-backed securities, and of those, $55 billion had exposure to dangerous subprime. Given its inside knowledge of the property market, AIG had stopped writing new CDS already in 2005. But given the relatively small size of the portfolio and the AAA rating of the assets it had written CDS on, it had not thought it necessary to insulate itself against losses. It was a fatal mistake. Out of a total of 44,000 derivatives contracts on the books of AIGFP, there were, it turned out, a cluster of 125 CDS on mortgage-backed securities that were about to go bad in a spectacular way. Those 125 contracts would inflict book value losses on AIG of $11.5 billion, twice what the ill-fated AIGFP unit had earned between 1994 and 2006. This was a heavy blow, but given its enormous global business, AIG could absorb portfolio losses on this scale. In due course the market would bounce back. Nor was AIG facing demands to pay out on MBS that had actually defaulted. As at Bear and Lehman, it was not the slow-moving crisis in real estate markets that threatened AIG. An avalanche of defaults and foreclosures would in due course grind its way through the system. But that would take years. The first credit default event on which AIG had to pay out did not occur until December 2008. The problem was the anticipatory reaction of financial markets and the fast-moving revaluation of securitized mortgages and the derivatives based on them. In the case of AIG, as it lost its top-tier credit rating, this triggered immediate margin calls from the counterparties to AIG's insurance contracts. They wanted collateral to prove that AIG could meet its obligations if the mortgages did go bad. It was these collateral calls, running into tens of billions, that threatened to tip AIG over the edge.

AIG's troubles did not end there. It had made life much harder for itself by engaging in the securities lending business. A group within AIG specialized in pooling the high-quality Treasurys and other securities held by AIG's insurance funds. It lent those assets to other investors in exchange for cash, a trade akin to a repo. AIG's securities-lending business then looked to maximize returns by investing the cash it received from the securities loan in higher-yielding but more risky mortgage-backed securities. Perversely, the securities lending office of AIG began to take those risky bets in 2005 precisely at the moment that AIG's own Financial Products division decided it was too risky to continue writing CDS on mortgage-backed

securities. By the summer of 2007, AIG's securities lending program had $45 billion invested in high-yield private label MBS. As the securitization business collapsed, those assets became virtually unsalable, leaving AIG scrambling to find funds with which to repay the securities borrowers who now wanted their cash back. In search of profit, a cash-rich insurance company sitting on a giant portfolio of high-quality securities had turned itself into a dangerously leveraged shadow bank with a serious maturity mismatch. And to make matters worse, it was dealing with some of the most heavy-hitting players in global finance.

Taking the lead in making collateral calls against AIG was Goldman Sachs.[23] It was one of the sharpest operators in the market. But it was also an investment bank with no FDIC-insured deposit base. Like Bear, Lehman and Merrill, Goldman was acutely vulnerable to a loss of confidence. One of the plays that would see Goldman through the crisis was the big short position it had built, betting against mortgage-backed securities. A big piece of that bet was placed by buying CDS from AIG. Already by June 30, 2008, Goldman had called $7.5 billion in collateral. When AIG was downgraded on September 15, there was a new surge in margin calls. Of the total claim against AIG, which now topped $32 billion, Goldman Sachs and its partner Société Générale accounted for $19.8 billion.[24] For AIG the consequences were drastic. It was scrambling for cash at the worst possible moment. With its rating on the downgrade it could not borrow tens of billions through ordinary channels. It could raise the funds only through fire sales, and that meant recognizing the losses on its balance sheet, which would make its position only even more precarious. By the morning of September 16, AIG was hours away from default.

With ABCP, repo and CDS having gone into crisis, the next link to snap in the shadow banking chain was the money market funds. On September 10, ahead of the Lehman failure, MMF collectively administered $3.58 trillion in savings and cash resources for individuals, pension funds and other investors.[25] An essential part of their appeal was that while they offered better returns than ordinary savings accounts, they also promised that the principal invested was safe. They would return a dollar on the dollar whatever happened. The day after Lehman, on September 16, that illusion burst. The Reserve Primary Fund, one of the oldest and most respected

in the business, with more than $62 billion under management, alerted the Fed that it was about to "break the buck." It could no longer guarantee a payout of one dollar for every dollar invested. In August 2007 the Reserve Primary Fund had been under intense competitive pressure. To improve its yield and attract more investors it had committed 60 percent of its funds to buying ABCP just as other investors pulled out.[26] The high yields on offer from desperate borrowers catapulted the fund from the bottom 20 percent to the top 10 percent in the performance league and doubled its assets under management in a single year. But it also exposed its investors to serious risks. In general its managers picked well. But 1.2 percent of its funds were invested in high-yielding Lehman ABCP, and by September those had plunged in value. The eventual losses at Reserve Primary were tiny. By 2014 the fund would pay out 99.1 cents on the dollar, but in the days following September 15, with investors no longer certain that they would get full reimbursement, half a trillion dollars fled out of exposed mutual funds looking for the safety of US Treasurys.[27]

The events of September 2008 brought the spectacular contraction of wholesale funding markets that had begun in August 2007 to crisis point. An index of haircuts on lower-quality collateral used in the biparty repo market surged from the elevated level of 25 percent it had reached over the summer of 2008 to 45 percent.[28] This had the effect of doubling the amount of money an investment bank would have to mobilize to hold anything other than top-quality securities on its books. Even at Goldman Sachs, the strongest of the stand-alone investment banks, its vital liquidity reserve, which it had pumped from $60 billion in 2007 to $113 billion by the third quarter of 2008, plunged on September 18 to a nominal total of $66 billion.[29] If that slide continued, the game would soon be up.

Meanwhile, the run for safety contracted balance sheets, which had the effect of withdrawing credit from the rest of the system. Loans by banks, investment banks, hedge funds and mutual funds to big businesses in the United States—so-called syndicated loans—fell from $702 billion in the second quarter of 2007 to as little as $150 billion in the fourth quarter of 2008. Interest rates demanded from high-yield, high-risk corporate borrowers surged to 23 percent, shutting out all but the most desperate borrowers.[30] This put a huge squeeze on all business activities. At the same

time, corporations that were finding it hard to gain credit elsewhere increased the draw down on their existing credit lines, putting further pressure on the banks.[31]

As money market mutual funds, repo, ABCP and AIG's credit default swaps all came into question, the shock waves spread far beyond the United States. Among the investments most favored by the money market funds were European bank debts. They were a key source of dollar funding for the European megabanks.[32] With the mutual funds pulling back, how were the European banks to fund their large books of dollar assets? With interbank lending shutting down, the European banks resorted to a variety of roundabout mechanisms to obtain dollar funding. A measure of their desperation was the price that they were willing to pay to borrow in euro, sterling, yen, Swiss francs and Australian dollars, and then to swap those loans into dollars. Normally, since these were close to risk-free transactions, the premium was zero. As dollar funding shut down, it soared to 2–3 percent. Applied to balance sheets running into the trillions of dollars, that spread was enough to threaten an avalanche. If the Europeans couldn't fund their dollar portfolios at affordable rates, they would be forced to sell. But as the Paribas announcement had made clear already in August 2007, there simply was no market for assets, which once had been valued at hundreds of billions of dollars. On Tuesday, September 16, 2008, the day after Lehman, Europe's funding issues were judged to be so serious that they were first order of business for the Fed's Open Market Committee meeting, even before Bernanke and his colleagues turned to the problems of AIG.[33]

Nor was it just the Fed that was preparing for the end of the world. By conference call early in the morning on Saturday, September 13, Jamie Dimon of J.P. Morgan commanded his astonished senior staff to prepare for Armageddon. While J.P. Morgan would retreat to the safety of its legendary "fortress balance sheet," they should brace for the bankruptcy of every investment bank on Wall Street, not just Lehman, but Merrill Lynch, Morgan Stanley and Goldman too.[34] Meanwhile, on the other side of the Atlantic, the impact of the funding crisis on a string of big European lenders was devastating. HBOS and RBS in Britain, Fortis and Dexia in the Benelux, Hypo Real Estate in Munich, Anglo Irish Bank, UBS, Credit Suisse and dozens of others all faced failure. Given that there weren't any deposits, no

one needed to run. You just stopped transacting in money markets and pulled in your horns. The result of the collective flight to safety, not by households but by the largest actors in the global financial system, was a trillion-dollar disaster.

II

Beyond Manhattan and the City of London, the economic news was devastating. Real business activity was collapsing on both sides of the Atlantic. In Europe no less than in the United States it was the crisis of 2008, not the later eurozone debacle, that marked the decisive break in investment, consumption and unemployment. From the second half of 2007, as banks great and small in Germany, France, Britain, Switzerland, and the Benelux began to acknowledge the scale of their losses, lending collapsed. The banking sector felt the pressure first because it was most dependent on the daily churn

Source: http://macro-man.blogspot.co.uk/2016/06/a-broad-scan.html.

of vast volumes of credit. But soon the crunch extended to nonfinancial corporations and households too. In the eurozone, after running at between 10 and 15 percent, growth in new lending plummeted to zero. It wasn't the sovereign debt crisis of 2010 that halted Europe's growth, it was the transatlantic banking crisis of 2008.

As new mortgage borrowing contracted, the slide in the housing market accelerated. Falling house prices and collapsing financial markets slashed personal wealth. In Spain net wealth per person fell by at least 10 percent between 2007 and 2009. Within five years personal wealth would plunge by 28 percent, or 1.4 trillion euros, more than a year's worth of output.[35] In the UK, as the stock market and house prices slumped, household wealth losses in 2008–2009 were estimated by the IMF at $1.5 trillion—50 percent of GDP in a matter of twelve months. Ten percent of home owners found themselves mired in negative equity.[36] In Ireland, house prices, having quadrupled between 1994 and 2007, halved between 2008 and 2012, taking household wealth with them.[37] These were severe shocks, but for sheer scale the US crisis trumped them all. An early IMF estimate in the summer of 2009 put US household wealth losses at $11 trillion.[38] By 2012 the US Treasury would raise that to $19.2 trillion.[39] Independent estimates put the figure closer to $21–22 trillion—$7 trillion from real estate, $11 trillion in the stock market and $3.4–4 trillion in retirement savings.[40] From their peak in 2006, by 2009 US house prices had fallen by a third. At the worst point in the crisis, 10 percent of home loans across the United States would be seriously in arrears and 4.5 percent of all mortgages crashed into foreclosure. More than 9 million families would lose their homes. Millions more suffered years of anxiety as they struggled to make payments on homes that were no longer worth the mortgages secured on them. At the worst point in the crisis more than a quarter of US homes had negative equity.[41]

And the pain was compounded by the distribution of losses between wealthier and poorer households. Between 2007 and 2010 the mean wealth of American households fell from $563,000 to $463,000. But those figures are elevated by the huge fortunes of the very wealthy. If we look instead at the median household—the household that sits at the 50 percent mark in the wealth distribution—it saw its net worth halved from $107,000 to

$57,800.[42] And as bad as these figures are, the experience of America's minority populations was worse. The median wealth of the Hispanic population, which had participated particularly actively in the housing boom, plunged by 86.3 percent between 2007 and 2010.[43] The median African American household saw virtually its entire housing wealth wiped out, and African American home owners were twice as likely to suffer foreclosure as white borrowers.[44] It did not produce the memorable imagery of the 1930s Dust Bowl, but the housing crisis that began in 2007 forced the largest mass movement of people in the United States since the Great Depression. And as minority home ownership collapsed, the result was resegregation along racial lines.[45]

With households suffering, in America's economic downswing of 2008 it was consumption that led the way.[46] As demand fell, so did production and employment. In the Central Valley in California, which witnessed a collapse of 50 percent in home values, consumption was cut by 30 percent.[47] Every kind of expenditure that could be postponed was cut back. For America's long-ailing motor vehicle industry it was the coup de grâce. Car and light vehicle sales plunged from an annual rate of 16 million units in 2007 to as few as 9 million per annum in 2009. By December 2008 it was clear that both Chrysler and General Motors would fail. In the early twenty-first century GM was no longer the national totem that it had once been. Its total worldwide employment in 2007 was 266,000, compared with a peak of 853,000 in 1979. But as 2008 began it was still the largest car company in the world. GM paid $476 million in salaries each month as well as the health-care and pension benefits for 493,000 retired workers. Its production operations generated $50 billion in orders for parts and services supplied by 11,500 vendors.[48] In total, industry lobbyists claimed that c. 4.5 percent of all US jobs were supported by the auto industry, paying more than $500 billion annually in wages and generating more than $70 billion in tax revenues.[49] On November 7, 2008, GM declared that, barring government aid, it would face insolvency by the summer of 2009.

The imminent failure of GM and Chrysler was an exclamation point on the long-running decline of the American auto industry. One version of the American Dream was dying. But Detroit's crisis sent shock waves around

the world. The future of GM's long-established UK and German divisions, Vauxhall and Opel, was in doubt.[50] So too were Detroit's operations in Mexico. Under the NAFTA free trade system, interconnected production systems, known as value chains, had been stretched from one end of North America to the other. As a result, Mexico's dependence on the United States was overwhelming. In 2007, 80 percent of Mexico's exports were sent to the United States. As the American crisis hit, Mexico's GDP fell by almost 7 percent, a worse contraction even than during the homegrown financial crisis of 1995—the so-called Tequila Crisis.[51] Mexico's nonoil exports fell by 28 percent between May 2008 and May 2009. Automotive exports fell by 50 percent.[52] In the northern industrial cities of Ciudad Juárez and Tijuana, the great *maquiladora* export processing centers, employment in manufacturing fell by more than 20 percent. Together with the surging violence of the drug wars, the recession led more than 100,000 desperate workers and their families to abandon Juárez. As unemployment surged north of the border, remittances dried up and hundreds of thousands of migrants returned home, making the situation of the poorest Mexicans progressively more desperate. Meanwhile, the inflow of new foreign investment in Mexico halved and the peso plunged in value from 11 to 15 to the dollar, driving up the cost of living.

Nor was the pain confined to North America. For decades GM's great global rival was Toyota, and 2008 would be the year in which Toyota claimed the title of the world's leading car producer. It paid a heavy price. In 2009 Japan was rocked by a "Toyota shock" as its national champion reported its first loss in seventy years and cut global production by 22 percent.[53] From a profit of $28 billion in 2007–2008, Toyota slid to a loss of $1.7 billion in 2008–2009. In the words of its president, Katsuaki Watanabe, "The change in the world economy is of a magnitude that comes once every hundred years. . . . We are facing an unprecedented emergency."[54] As inventories of unsold cars piled up in the United States and Europe, Japanese car exports fell by two-thirds.[55] Japan's investment industries stopped in their tracks. Hitachi, the giant producer of capital goods and electronics, was worst hit, facing a record loss for a Japanese industrial company of $7.87 billion.[56] Consumer electronics icon Sony announced a loss of $2.6 billion.

Toshiba expected to lose $2.8 billion, Panasonic $3.8 billion.[57] All in all, in January 2009 Japan's economy contracted at a rate of 20 percent per annum and exports by 50 percent year on year.[58] The largest part of this was accounted for by a fall in exports to the United States, followed by Japan's immediate Asian neighbors, China, Taiwan and Korea, all of which were plunged into recession.

As the shock of 2008 revealed, with supply chains synchronized to perfection, "factory Asia" responded within a matter of weeks to any hesitation of demand in Europe and America. Nor were they the only ones to be hit. Germany suffered a 34 percent fall in exports between the second quarter of 2008 and 2009, with its machinery and transport equipment sector taking a deep dive. It was the most severe economic shock suffered by the Federal Republic since its foundation in 1949. As one bank economist remarked: "One has to go back to the 1930s during the Great Depression to find comparably horrible figures."[59] Meanwhile, emerging markets were hit too. Turkey, which had joined the club of rapidly growing economies after its financial stabilization in 2004, suffered a sudden and jarring stop. By the first quarter of 2009, Turkey's GDP was falling by 14.7 percent on an annualized basis. Unemployment rocketed from 8.6 percent in the summer of 2008 to 14.6 percent in the first winter of the crisis. It was the worst affected of any of the emerging markets outside Eastern Europe. Turkey had not seen a situation so bad as this since the disastrous financial crisis of 2001.[60] Istanbul's stock market plunged by 54 percent between December 2007 and November 2008.[61]

What made the collapse of 2008 so severe was its extraordinary global synchronization. Of the 104 countries for which the World Trade Organization collects data, every single one experienced a fall in both imports and exports between the second half of 2008 and the first half of 2009. Every country and every type of traded goods, without exception, experienced a decline.[62]

If in manufacturing the downturn was in the volume of trade—the number of cars shipped or the number of cell phones exported—in commodities the shock was to prices. In the worst six months of 2008, oil prices fell by more than 76 percent. That in turn wreaked havoc with the budgets

of the petrostates. Saudi Arabia swung from a budget surplus of 23 percent of GDP in 2008 to a substantial deficit.[63] Kuwait was rocked by the crisis at Gulf Bank, which faced losses on currency trades.[64] But nowhere was worse affected than the boomtown of Dubai. Driven by surging commodity prices, heavily backed by international banks such as RBS and Standard Chartered, Dubai's real estate sector had become the center of a global construction frenzy.[65] By 2008 the city bristled with construction cranes. Its palatial malls boasted floor space four times the per capita level in the United States. In the autumn of 2008 the bubble burst. New credit was slashed. By February 2009 Dubai's rip-roaring six-year construction boom had come to a halt. Half of a portfolio of $1.1 trillion in construction projects being undertaken in the Gulf Cooperation Council was canceled in a matter of months. Luxury cars were abandoned in droves as Western contract workers scuttled to the airport to escape debtor's prison. An airlift of charter flights repatriated tens of thousands of migrant guest workers to India.[66]

As both household consumption and business investment plummeted, of the sixty countries that supply the IMF with quarterly GDP statistics, fifty-two registered a contraction in the second quarter of 2009.[67] Not since records began had there been such a massive synchronized recession. Tens of millions of people were thrown into unemployment. Though it was dazed bankers with boxes of belongings stumbling out of office towers in London and New York that attracted the TV cameras, it was young, unskilled blue-collar workers who suffered the worst.[68] In the United States, the epicenter of the crisis, the month-on-month fall in employment over the winter of 2008–2009 was breathtaking. In the worst period, the monthly rate of job losses topped 800,000. Among the African American population the surge was particularly dramatic, with unemployment rising from 8 percent in 2007 to 16 percent by early 2010.[69] Young black workers were particularly hard hit, with their unemployment rate surging to 32.5 percent by January 2010. At the very bottom of the pile were young African American men with no high school diploma. In New York City in 2009 their unemployment rate was more than 50 percent.[70] Precisely how many people lost their jobs across the global economy depends on our guess as to joblessness among China's giant migrant workforce. But reasonable estimates range between 27 million and something closer to 40 million unemployed worldwide.[71]

III

The situation was clearly bad. But in historical terms, how bad was bad? Trying to find his bearings, in the spring of 2009 Paul Krugman concluded that the situation was dire. But at least as far as the industrial economy of the United States was concerned, it was less grim than it had been in the Great Depression of the 1930s.[72] It was, he quipped, only "half a Great Depression." It was not a judgment that stood for long. As critics scrambled to point out, Krugman's assessment was deeply parochial. The Great Depression of the 1930s was not confined to the United States, and neither was the crisis that struck in 2008. On a global level, industrial output, stock markets and trade were all falling at least as fast in 2008–2009 as they had in 1929.[73]

We now know that urgent and massive countermeasures would forestall the kind of agonizing depression that the world experienced in the early 1930s. But that relatively sanguine perspective depends on the safety of hindsight. In September 2008 the scale of the response was an index of the desperation felt by those at the epicenter of the crisis in the United

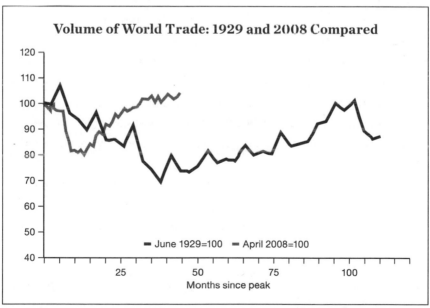

Source: Barry Eichengreen and Kevin O'Rourke, "A Tale of Two Depressions Redux," http:// voxeu.org/article/tale-two-depressions-redux.

World Industrial Production, Now Versus Then

— June 1929=100 — April 2008=100

Months since peak

Source: Barry Eichengreen and Kevin O'Rourke, "A Tale of Two Depressions Redux," http://voxeu.org/article/tale-two-depressions-redux.

States. Ben Bernanke at the Fed, Tim Geithner at the New York Fed and Hank Paulson at the Treasury all recounted the experience as traumatic. After Lehman collapsed, Paulson confronted his staff with the prospect of an "economic 9/11."[74] On the morning of September 20, the US Treasury secretary alerted Congress to the fact that unless they acted fast, $5.5 trillion in wealth would disappear by two p.m. They might be facing the collapse of the world economy "within 24 hours."[75] In private session with congressional leadership, Bernanke, who is not given to overstatement, warned that unless they authorized immediate action, "we may not have an economy on Monday."[76]

As far as America was concerned, this was clearly an exaggeration. Bernanke was trying to scare Congress into action. But if one looks at data on international investment flows, the picture is truly astonishing. Across the world before the crisis hit, inflows and outflows of capital came to just under 33 percent of world GDP. The vast majority of this was accounted for not by transactions between the advanced world and emerging markets but by flows between advanced economies. At the height of the crisis, between the last quarter of 2008 and the first quarter of 2009, those flows collapsed

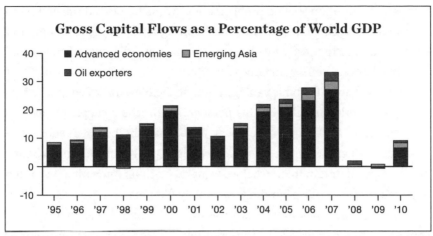

Source: Claudio Borio and Piti Disyatat, "Global Imbalances and the Financial Crisis: Link or No Link?," BIS Working Paper 346 (2011), graph 5.

by 90 percent to less than 3 percent of global GDP.[77] In the second half of 2008 capital flows between rich countries plunged from $17 trillion to barely more than $1.5 trillion. No other aggregate in the global economy was affected on anything like this scale or with this suddenness. It was as though a gigantic stabilizing flywheel suddenly came crashing to a halt, sending a shuddering jolt through the entire financial system.

In public, Ben Bernanke knew it was essential for him to keep a straight face: "Financial panics have a substantial psychological component. Projecting calm, rationality, and reassurance is half the battle," he would later opine.[78] But as an economist and an economic historian, Bernanke understood the scale of what he was up against. What threatened in 2008 wasn't 1929. What threatened was something even bigger and quite possibly even worse. As he was to affirm on several occasions afterward, for Bernanke, "September and October of 2008" was clearly the "worst financial crisis in global history, including the Great Depression."[79] In the 1930s there was no moment of such massive synchronization, no moment in which so many of the world's largest banks threatened to fail simultaneously. The speed and force of the avalanche was unprecedented. As Bernanke later admitted to the readers of his memoirs, "[I]t was overwhelming, even paralyzing, to think too much about the high stakes involved, so I focused as much as I could on the specific task at hand. . . . [A]s events unfolded I repressed my

fears and focused on solving problems."[80] Only as he neared the end of his second term was he ready to unwind. Looking back, it was like being in a car wreck. "You're mostly involved in trying to avoid going off the bridge; and then later on you say, 'oh my god!'"[81]

Tim Geithner, from his vantage point at the New York Fed, gave a typically hard-boiled insight into his perspective on the struggle to save the financial system: "I didn't have a way to explain the terror of those days until later, when I saw *The Hurt Locker*, the Oscar-winning film about a bomb disposal unit in Iraq. What we went through on interminable conference calls in fancy office buildings obviously did not compare with the horrors of war, but ten minutes into the movie I knew I had finally found something that captured what the crisis felt like: the overwhelming burden of responsibility combined with the paralyzing risk of catastrophic failure; the frustration about the stuff out of your control; the uncertainty about what would help; the knowledge that even good decisions might turn out badly; the pain and guilt of neglecting your family; the loneliness and the numbness."[82]

There is no reason to doubt the sincerity of these professions. It was a fearful situation. But the metaphors—terrorist attack, car wrecks and unexploded improvised explosive devices—are telling. They position the crisis-fighting team as first responders facing a compelling emergency. And they place us, their audience, by their side. Who would not root for the fatherly Ben Bernanke trying to keep the family car on the bridge, or Geithner's heroic bomb disposal team? Politics is set aside as we anxiously watch our heroes struggle to rescue us from disaster. There is no time to ask why this is happening. We are "all in this together." But it is precisely with that assertion that a political economy of the crisis begins.[83] Which system was it that needed to be saved in the autumn of 2008? Who was being hurt? Who was included in the circle of those who needed to be protected? And who was not?

As the crisis spiraled toward September 2008 the first responders performed a substitution. It had all started with the predictable but devastating bursting of the housing bubble. That crisis was affecting millions of households on both sides of the Atlantic. But starting with the rash of bank failures and fund failures in the late summer of 2007, the real estate crisis

was gradually displaced from the center of attention. What now mattered was the possible failure of an investment bank. By September 2008 it was no longer individual banks but the entire financial *system* that had to be saved at all costs. It was entire markets and sectors—the repo market, ABCP, the mutual funds—that needed life support. It was the implosion of the financial system, imagined as something akin to a massive electrical power failure that threatened the entire economy.

It was crucial to fix Wall Street, so the slogan went, to help Main Street. The mantra was repeated in local idiom all over the world. And for the purposes of ongoing business activity, it clearly was crucial to maintain business credit. In September even blue-chip businesses could not get short-term funding. McDonald's could no longer get an overdraft from Bank of America.[84] Engineering giant GE and Harvard University were rumored to be having liquidity issues.[85] But beyond such immediate rescue measures, did the all-out focus on the financial system really serve the interests of the real economy?[86] Was the inability to borrow causing a failure of investment and thus the ongoing depression? Or were the collapsed housing market and cash-strapped households curtailing economic activity such that there was no incentive to invest and thus no demand for loans?

These might seem like academic questions. The bomb was ticking. The car was hurtling off the bridge. Amid a global catastrophe, did it really matter which way the arrow of causation was pointing? Amid the intensity of the financial crisis, why should anyone care? Because the decision made by the American crisis fighters to take those questions off the table and to give absolute priority to saving the financial system shaped everything else that followed. It set the stage for a remarkable and bitterly ironic inversion. Whereas since the 1970s the incessant mantra of the spokespeople of the financial industry had been free markets and light touch regulation, what they were now demanding was the mobilization of all of the resources of the state to save society's financial infrastructure from a threat of systemic implosion, a threat they likened to a military emergency.

Chapter 7

BAILOUTS

The ferocity of the financial crisis in 2008 was met with a mobilization of state action without precedent in the history of capitalism. Never before outside wartime had states intervened on such a scale and with such speed. It was a devastating blow to the complacent belief in the great moderation, a shocking overturning of prevailing laissez-faire ideology. To mobilize trillions of dollars on the credit of the taxpayer to save banks from the consequences of their own folly and greed violated maxims of fairness and good government. But given the risk of contagion, how could states not act? Having done so, however, how could they ever go back to the idea that markets were efficient, self-regulating and best left to their own devices? It was a profound challenge to the basic idea that had guided economic government since the 1970s. It was all the more significant for the fact that the challenge came not from the outside. It was not motivated by some radical ideological turn to the Left or the Right. There was precious little time for thought or wider consideration. Intervention was driven by the financial system's own malfunctioning and the impossibility of separating individual business failure from its wider systemic repercussions. Martin Wolf, the *Financial Times*'s esteemed chief economic commentator, dubbed March 14, 2008, "the day the dream of global free-market capitalism died."[1] That was the day the Bear Stearns rescue was announced. It was only the beginning.

I

Bailout battles were fought all along the contours of the integrated Atlantic financial economy—in the United States, Iceland, Ireland, Britain, France, Germany, the Benelux, Switzerland. The financial firepower deployed was immense and accounting for it became a field of political argument in its own right. But whichever metrics we use, it is clear that there had never before been anything so extensive or massive in scale. Commitments were made in excess of $7 trillion.

The main mechanisms for intervention were fourfold: (1) loans to banks; (2) recapitalization; (3) asset purchases; and (4) state guarantees for bank deposits, bank debts or even for the entire balance sheet. Everywhere the crisis struck, states were forced to take some combination of these measures. The agencies involved were central banks, finance ministries and banking regulators. What summary statistics cast as cool enumerations were, in fact, frantic, improvised solutions that emerged from barely coordinated sessions of all-day, all-night problem solving. As the crisis intensified it put the financial and political resilience of states to the test. Broadly speaking, this produced four types of outcome, which reflect the degree of immersion in global finance, the resources of the states at risk, the shape of the governing elite and the balance of power within the financial sector itself.[2]

In the most extreme cases the crisis overwhelmed the state. Ireland and Iceland simply did not have the resources, the institutions or the political capacities to deal with the gigantic shock to their overgrown financial sectors. They would suffer a comprehensive crisis, as would the worst-hit emerging market economies of Eastern Europe. Others were better placed. Despite having a grossly overgrown financial sector, Switzerland survived intact. It did so through early, intense and unrelenting attention to its one failing megabank, UBS.[3] Though it was never nationalized, it became in effect a ward of the state. The larger European states and those with less excessive banking systems—the UK, Germany, France, Belgium and the Netherlands—presented a more mixed bag. Despite the scale of the crises they faced, they had the resources to cope. They attempted comprehensive

Government Support Measures to Financial Institutions Since October 2008, as of End of May 2010 (in billions of euros unless stated otherwise)

	Capital injections			Liability guarantees, bonds		Other guarantees		Asset support			Total commitment
	committed in schemes	used	outside schemes	committed	used	committed	used	committed	used	outside schemes	% as 2008 GDP
Austria	15	5.8	0.6	75	21.8						32
Belgium	40		19.9	32	34		90.8			16.8	47
Germany	99	29.4	24.8	400	110.8		75	40	17	39.3	25
Spain	21	11	1.3	100	56.4		9	50	19.3	2.5	24
France	5	8.3	3	320	134.2						18
Greece	10	3.2	0	30	13.3			8	4.4		18
Ireland	12	12.3	7	485	72.5			90	8		319
Italy	20	4.1	0	0	0			50			4
Netherlands	13	10.2	16.8	200	54.2		50			21.4	52
Denmark	5	3.5	2.2	0	36.9						23
Sweden	55	0.5			142	25.4					49
UK	4	33.7	35.8	300	157.2					217.8	25
Switzerland								41	41.2		13
Australia				602	118.6						97
USA	580	216.2	19.1	1066	369.8	534	26.7	1148	40	74.9	30
Total	879	338.2	130.5	3610	1321.7	559.4	251.5	1427	129.9	372.7	

Source: Based on Stéphanie Stolz and Michael Wedow, "Extraordinary Measures in Extraordinary Times: Public Measures in Support of the Financial Sector in the EU and the United States," Bundesbank Series 1 Discussion Paper 13, 2010.

organizational and financial solutions, including abortive proposals to co-
ordinate a common European response to the crisis. But efforts to achieve
consistency and coordination were undermined by national political calcu-
lation and the uncooperative behavior of leading banks that fancied them-
selves large enough to survive without the humiliation of taking state aid.
There was no spiraling disaster, but containing the crisis was hugely expen-
sive and success was partial at best.

Out of this trial of strength the United States emerged as the one
nation-state with the capacity not only to backstop the biggest financial
sector in the world but also to impose a comprehensive solution. Not for
nothing, America's crisis fighters liked to speak in military terms, about
"big bazookas" and "shock and awe." Geithner went furthest in this respect.
For inspiration he invoked the war-fighting doctrine developed in the after-
math of the Vietnam debacle by America's chairman of the Joint Chiefs,
Colin Powell: Strike with massive force and plan a clear route out.[4] It was
an analogy that had first been invoked by Larry Summers at the time of the
Mexico financial crisis in 1994. Now it became Geithner's mantra. For him,
the "Powell Doctrine applied to international finance" meant "the over-
whelming use of force, with a clear strategy for resolution." As Geithner
insisted, "There is more risk and greater cost in gradualism than in aggres-
sive action." For Geithner and his cohorts it was clear that swift and deci-
sive action paid dividends. Compared with the disastrous performance of
the European economy, the United States was set back on track.[5] The lead-
ership of American finance renewed itself. Even when viewed narrowly in
accounting terms, many of the Treasury and Fed support programs made
a profit for the American taxpayer.[6] The benefits of preventing a second
Great Depression were vast.

By contrast with the European experience it is not hard to see how this
self-congratulatory American narrative gained purchase. But its economic
merits are not so obvious as its proponents presume. And it offered no
comfort to the advocates of laissez-faire. Gone were the days when eco-
nomic policy was about shrinking the state to set free the spontaneous
order of market liberty. No longer did wisdom lie in devising predictable
rules to curtail the arbitrary discretion of policy makers. Economic pol-
icy modeled on warfare was a matter of will, vigilance, tactical nous and

firepower. And despite the populist appeal of the military rhetoric, there was a political price to pay.[7] The crisis fighting of 2008–2009 scrambled American politics. The Bush administration lost the backing of much of the congressional Republican Party. The crisis snapped the fragile bond between the GOP's managerial, big-business elite and its right-wing mass base. As the popular wing of the party, backed by maverick oligarch donors, moved increasingly toward indignant antiestablishment opposition, mainline conservatives like Bernanke and Paulson were left to complain that it was not they who left the party, but the party that left them.[8] The Bush administration's crisis-fighting effort was carried by the Democratic Party's majorities in Congress. That contradiction would be resolved by Barack Obama's election victory on November 4, 2008, only weeks after the crisis reached its peak. But the fracture of the American Right would in due course have profound consequences both for America and for the wider world.

II

In 2007 the best hope of the authorities was still that the private sector might rescue itself. J.P. Morgan's consortium of 1907 was the stuff of Wall Street legend. In late October 2007, with the help of the US Treasury, the three largest banks—Citigroup, Bank of America and JPMorgan Chase—agreed to collaborate in creating a so-called Master Liquidity Enhancement Conduit that would help to stabilize the market for mortgage-backed securities and revive the ABCP market.[9] Not surprisingly, Treasury Secretary Paulson loved the idea. But any private sector arrangement was vulnerable to problems of collective action. Though bankers detested government intervention, they also wanted to avoid the stigma of joining a cartel of ailing firms, especially one including Citigroup, whose balance sheet was particularly toxic.[10] When major global competitor HSBC announced that it would absorb the full amount of $45 billion in losses suffered by its SIVs onto its balance sheets, its largest American rivals could not be seen to be settling for a second-best option.[11] By December 2007 the private bad bank plan had collapsed.

When collective action failed, the state could step in, acting as a match-

maker in chief, brokering takeover deals between individual banks. In Britain in 2008, the Scottish conglomerate HBOS would be sold off to Lloyds Bank with encouragement from Downing Street.[12] Germany's number two bank, Dresdner, would be amalgamated with Commerzbank, the number three.[13] As both deals would reveal, the risk was that the bank that was in trouble would pull its rescuer down with it. In the United States the amalgamations began in earnest with Bear Stearns, which came to the point of failure on the night of March 13–14, 2008.[14] If it had unloaded its portfolio of $200 billion in asset-backed securities and CDO at fire sale prices, the effect would have been catastrophic. It would have forced all the other banks to recognize crippling losses, spreading the panic. To the relief of the Treasury and the Fed, J.P. Morgan was interested in buying out Bear. Its hard-charging CEO, Jamie Dimon, was confident that his robust balance sheet put him in a position to safely pick over the carcass. But to finalize the deal, Dimon needed the right inducement. Under the emergency powers provided by section 13(3) of the Fed's statutes, $30 billion in the most toxic assets were taken off Bear's books by a SIV funded by the New York Fed.[15] Then, at five a.m. on the morning of March 14, with the repo markets closed to Bear, the New York Fed lent $12.9 billion to J.P. Morgan, which J.P. Morgan then lent to Bear. After that, the die was cast. J.P. Morgan initially agreed to pay the laughable price of $2 per share for what was left of Bear. This compared with a valuation of $159 per share only one year earlier. When Bear's shareholders protested, the price was raised to $10 per share. Whether at $2 or $10, J.P. Morgan was confident it would make a profit.

The Fed's actions forestalled what might have been a disruptive and chaotic bankruptcy. But the inducements that J.P. Morgan had extracted were debatable, to say the least. Paul Volcker, the legendary ex-chairman of the Fed, would characterize them as extending "to the very edge of its lawful and implied powers."[16] Strict advocates of moral hazard logic would forever after argue that it was the Bear rescue that set up the Lehman disaster.[17] With one investment bank having been rescued, Lehman's management felt safe. A solution for their problems would be found too. They could afford to take their time finding the best possible deal, an attitude that would cost them dearly.

Whether it was legal or wise, rescuing investment banks by means of

obscure balance sheet transactions was a technical business that could be kept out of the political headlines. That changed with Fannie Mae and Freddie Mac. As the indispensable government-sponsored backdrop to the American housing market, they were at the center of one of the most formidable political networks in Washington. By the summer of 2008, with private securitization stalled, they were also responsible for backstopping 75 percent of new mortgages in the United States. The vast bulk of the Fannie Mae and Freddie Mac balance sheet consisted of top-quality conforming mortgages. If they had had conventional balance sheets, they ought to have been able to ride out the storm. The problem was they did not. In June 2008 Fannie Mae and Freddie Mac held MBS valued at $1.8 trillion and guaranteed another $3.7 trillion on the basis of shareholder equity, which in the case of Fannie Mae came to only $41.2 billion, and in the case of Freddie Mac, to $12.9 billion.[18] It was a leverage ratio that would have made even the boldest investment banker blush. It was conceivable only because Fannie Mae and Freddie Mac were government-sponsored enterprises. In the summer of 2008 the meaning of that term was going to be put to the test. Allowing for only minimal losses, the capital of both Fannie Mae and Freddie Mac would be completely wiped out. If they folded they would take down the last remaining lenders in the mortgage market and put in doubt the credit of the United States. They would put in jeopardy a huge portfolio of securities widely held by foreign investors. In the summer of 2008 foreign investors held $800 billion in debt issued by the GSEs. Fannie Mae and Freddie Mac were, as the influential blogger Brad Setser quipped, "too Chinese to fail."[19]

Desperate to gain a grip on the situation, in the spring of 2008 Hank Paulson's Treasury began to broker a deal between congressional Democrats and Republicans that would give the federal government the powers necessary to overhaul the mortgage giants.[20] But over the summer Congress dragged its heels. The Republicans were uncooperative and the Democrats insisted that if they were to carry the bill, it must include support for struggling home owners and the transfer of block grants to hard-hit states to buy up foreclosed properties. By mid-July the situation was becoming critical. Given the scale of the crisis and the opacity of the GSEs' financial situation, the capital injection might need to be huge.[21] The Treasury favored an authorization limited only by the federal government's borrowing

ceiling, putting the full financial clout of the American state behind the GSE. As Paulson famously put it to the Senate Banking Committee, "[I]f you've got a squirt gun in your pocket, you may have to take it out. If you've got a bazooka, and people know you've got it, you may not have to take it out."[22] Paulson's request was meant to sound impressive, and his bazooka comment echoed around the world. The US Treasury secretary was desperate to reassure foreign bondholders. Beijing was increasingly alarmed.[23] In his memoirs, Paulson recorded: "I was talking to them [Chinese ministers and officials] regularly because I didn't want them to dump the securities on the market and precipitate a bigger crisis. . . . And so when I went to Congress and asked for these emergency powers [to stabilize Fannie and Freddie], and I was getting the living daylights beaten out of me by our Congress publicly, I needed to call the Chinese regularly to explain to the People's Bank of China, 'listen this is our political system, this is political theatre, we will get this done.' And I didn't have quite that much certainty myself but I sure did everything I could to reassure them."[24]

The Chinese might be excused their confusion. The political theater being played in Washington, DC, was new and strange. A conservative, free-market administration led by businessmen was proposing unlimited state spending to nationalize a large part of the housing finance system. The Republican electorate was outraged by the thought of assisting undeserving mortgage borrowers and the New Deal machinery that had aided and abetted their fecklessness. But to Paulson the systemic imperative was obvious. And President Bush stood behind him. "It was a tremendous act of political courage," Paulson gushed, "It was as if, in the last days of his administration, the president were suddenly switching sides, supporting Democrats and opposing Republicans on matters that went against the basic principles of his administration. But he was determined to do what was best for the country."[25] Paulson was registering a basic rift within American conservatism. The right wing of the party could not be counted on to give support to measures that were unpopular and distasteful, but were clearly necessary to save "the system." Paulson recognized that the authorization he was asking for was unprecedented. "I don't know if any executive branch agency had ever before been given the authority to lend to or invest in an enterprise in an unlimited amount. All I could do was argue that the

extraordinary and unpredictable nature of the situation warranted the authority in this case."[26] He also knew that it was only the Democrats, the party with relatively less inhibition about expanding the scope of government, who were willing to go along with this logic of absolute and unlimited necessity, dictated not by a national security emergency but by a financial crisis.

Paulson's extraordinary plenipotentiary authorization to rescue Fannie Mae and Freddie Mac passed Congress on July 26, with three quarters of House Republicans voting against. It was signed into law on July 30. The White House thought it best to forgo the usual festive Oval Office ceremony. There was no reason to goad the Republicans and no time to lose. With a team recruited from Morgan Stanley on a pro bono basis, the Treasury plunged into weeks of forensic investigation and negotiations with the GSEs' failed regulators. The results were dispiriting. Both of the GSEs were insolvent. Liquidity support would not be enough. On Sunday, September 7, 2008, Fannie Mae and Freddie Mac were placed under conservatorship. It was nationalization in all but name. If necessary, the Treasury would replenish their capital to make up any gap between assets and liabilities up to an initial maximum of $100 billion each. The Fed provided credit lines and undertook to buy whatever MBS the ailing GSEs needed to offload. It wasn't so much a bazooka as the nuclear option.

The crucial effect of this intervention was to reassure bondholders, especially those abroad, that Fannie Mae and Freddie Mac would not fail. Despite the machinations of Russia, the breakdown of America's government-sponsored mortgage machine did not spill over into a global crisis. But the political fallout was dire and it had serious implications for the future course of the crisis. On the right wing of the Republican Party, fully mobilized for the hotly contested presidential election, the nationalization of Fannie Mae and Freddie Mac unleashed a firestorm.[27] The Treasury did its best to ward off allegations of cronyism by imposing a punitive dividend for the capital it contributed, wiping out the GSEs' existing shareholders. The American Bankers Association rallied to the administration, calling on Republicans to support the rescue effort. But it was immediately countered by the conservative Club for Growth, a key right-wing lobby group funded by the Koch brothers. House leader John Boehner and former speaker Newt

Gingrich spoke out against Paulson's bailout. John McCain personally was thought to favor a rescue. But on August 29 he nominated the populist Alaskan governor Sarah Palin as his vice-presidential running mate. Palin did not have coherent views on the GSEs or the financial crisis. But her bluff persona fired up the passions of the Republican base. As the crisis deepened, the Bush administration was terrified that they might find themselves facing an insurgency from within their own party led by a presidential candidate on the warpath against bailouts. What made the Republican brush fire so worrying was that by early September it was clear that the rescue of Fannie Mae and Freddie Mac was only the first round, and that the next phase of the battle would be decided not in Washington but on Wall Street.

For months the Treasury had been anxiously watching as Lehman Brothers looked for a buyer. By the second week of September options were running out. Talks with a potential Korean suitor had stalled. In frantic negotiations hosted by Geithner's New York Federal Reserve and personally overseen by Paulson, the search for a private sector solution failed. The culminating moment came on the weekend of September 13–14. What exactly happened in those forty-eight hours will remain forever a matter of controversy. What is beyond dispute is that Bank of America, the giant commercial bank that had been expected to act as the white knight for Lehman, bought Merrill Lynch instead.

Merrill was bigger than Lehman. It too was heavily exposed to the real estate bust. Like Lehman it was an investment bank that could not function without access to the repo market. After Lehman it would certainly have been the next to fail.[28] But unlike Lehman, Merrill's management was nimble and saved its bank by pushing for direct talks with Bank of America. It was well known that Bank of America CEO Ken Lewis had long wanted to emulate Citigroup in integrating an investment bank with his commercial banking business. On the desperate weekend of September 13–14, 2008, Bank of America's hundreds of billions of retail deposits guaranteed by the FDIC were one part of the financial system that was not running. That funding base gave Bank of America the platform to buy out Merrill Lynch. But on what terms? On the face of it Merrill was a prize. One of the biggest names on Wall Street, at the end of 2007 it was valued at $150 billion, with $1.02 trillion in assets and more than sixty thousand employees worldwide.

But given the potential losses on its books and its precarious wholesale funding, what was Merrill worth in September 2008? In the event, under huge pressure from Paulson and Bernanke, Bank of America paid $50 billion, $29 per share, a third of what Merrill had recently been worth, but 40 percent more than its market valuation the previous week.

After Bank of America took Merrill, for Lehman, the last remaining hope was a transatlantic deal with the British bank Barclays, where the expat American Bob Diamond, formerly of Morgan Stanley and Credit Suisse, was calling the shots. But Prime Minister Gordon Brown and Chancellor Alistair Darling refused to loosen regulations to allow the takeover to go ahead without full shareholder approval and without commitments of support from the US Treasury. If Bank of America had chosen Merrill, what was wrong with Lehman? They told Paulson that London did not want to "import America's cancer."[29]

The basic question is why the options for Lehman were so narrow? Why were the Fed and the Treasury unwilling to sweeten the Lehman deal in the way that they had J.P. Morgan's takeover of Bear Stearns?[30] Why, following the failure of the private option, was some other kind of backstop not worked out, of the kind that they would provide so liberally in the weeks to come? Geithner, Paulson and Bernanke have all insisted that the question is otiose. The problem was not that the Treasury and the Fed lacked the will, but that they lacked the means. The Lehman collapse was not the result of a deliberate intention on the part of the authorities. "We hadn't done it on purpose," Geithner insisted. "We had run up against the limits of our authority and the fears of the British regulators."[31] The Fed could not lend to Lehman, Bernanke maintains, because the Fed lends only against good collateral to solvent banks.[32] Lehman was insolvent and, due to the nature of its investment banking business, its lack of depositor base and alternative income streams, it lacked the collateral. But these are retrospective justifications. At the time Lehman's failure was seen as the result of a deliberate decision, and a welcome one. On September 17, Democratic congressman Barney Frank declared in a hearing with Treasury officials that Monday, September 15, the day of Lehman's failure, would long be celebrated as "Free Market Day."[33] Frank was joking. But others were not. As one of Paulson's assistants remarked, September 15 felt like a "good day at the Treasury."

They had let markets do their work.[34] A *New York Times* editorial declared that it was "oddly reassuring" that Lehman had been allowed to fail.[35] The *Wall Street Journal* congratulated Paulson on not blinking. "[T]he government had to draw a line somewhere."[36] For Geithner at the New York Fed, this was no comfort: "We hadn't chosen to draw a line. We had been powerless, not fearless. We had tried but failed to prevent a catastrophic default."[37]

On this interpretation of the crisis, Geithner would go on to base an entire program of state building. If in 2008 what had been missing were adequate state powers of intervention, the answer was to equip the Fed and the Treasury with the right tools. What Geithner could not admit is the possibility that "Hank and Ben" had, in fact, made a mistake. That they might have underestimated the severity of the fallout that Lehman's failure would cause. Or that Paulson, as a Republican Treasury secretary, might, in fact, have been constrained by politics. But this is what subsequent forensic reconstruction suggests. The best available contemporary evidence, rather than the self-justifications that the actors fashioned for themselves after the catastrophic consequences of Lehman's failure became apparent, suggests that the basic constraint on the Lehman rescue was Paulson's refusal, from the outset, to consider another bailout.[38] British chancellor Alistair Darling was in frequent contact with New York throughout the critical weekend. His perspective is telling: "What was worrying was that it was becoming more evident that the US Treasury was reluctant to provide the financial support to make the deal work. I was not entirely surprised. . . . I didn't think he had enough political capital to persuade the Republicans to nationalize another bank."[39] It was a judgment that would be borne out two weeks later in the desperate battle to pass the Troubled Asset Relief Program (TARP). Though it was Paulson who took the lead in the Lehman talks in New York, from Washington Bernanke was fully in agreement. The Fed was notably uncooperative in the desperate efforts of Lehman's management to buy time. Contrary to the impression created by Bernanke's retrospective testimony, the Fed concertedly pushed Lehman toward bankruptcy. The argument made at the time was that ending uncertainty by means of bankruptcy would help to calm the markets. It is easy to say with hindsight, but it was a spectacular error of judgment.

The scale of that error became clear within hours as the shock wave

from the Lehman failure impacted the American and the world economy. A day later, Paulson, Bernanke and Geithner had to face the question of what to do about the insurance giant AIG.[40] Here too their first impulse was to look for a private solution, with J.P. Morgan and Goldman Sachs leading "frenetic" discussions throughout Monday, September 15. But by seven p.m. any hope of a private rescue had evaporated. When the bailout team had reached a similar conclusion about Lehman twenty-four hours earlier, they had started preparing for bankruptcy. This time, the conclusion was the opposite. The financial markets would not withstand a second shock, and AIG's level of interconnectedness through derivatives, repo and securities lending was even greater than that of Lehman. Letting AIG fail would, in the words of one Wall Street player, have been an "extinction-level" event. Instead, the Fed stepped in. As it had done with Bear Stearns, the Fed declared a section 13(3) emergency. The New York Fed would offer a secured credit facility of up to $85 billion. On the early afternoon of Tuesday, September 16, Fed security personnel rushed to the offices of AIG at 80 Pine Street in Lower Manhattan to gather up tens of billions of dollars of share certificates to serve as collateral. With the deeds to the world's second-largest insurance company safely stashed in the vaults of the New York Fed, the first phase of the rescue was announced at 3:30 p.m. The Fed backstopped AIG's credit default swap portfolio and its securities lending business. In exchange it would take stock in AIG and its subsidiaries that would give the US government a 79.9 percent equity stake in AIG's global insurance business. Following the template established with the Fannie Mae and Freddie Mac nationalization, the deal inflicted a huge loss on AIG's existing shareholders. The securities lending business was unwound, with the New York Fed purchasing from AIG its depreciated portfolio of MBS, enabling it to pay off its securities-lending counterparties. Most generous of all was the resolution of the CDS portfolio, which was accomplished by buying out the dangerous CDO on which AIG had written insurance. In effect, together with the collateral they had already claimed from AIG, the counterparties received payment at 100 percent of par on $62.2 billion in toxic mortgage-backed securities, the market value of which was closer to $27.2 billion. How little they would have been worth if AIG had been driven into bankruptcy is anyone's guess. In any case, the subsidy

to the counterparties and their clients clearly ran into the billions. Nor was it only the American financial system that benefited. In the course of the bailout, the Fed made sure to leave in place the insurance contracts that AIG had offered to European banks to provide "regulatory relief." If they had been voided, the Americans estimated that the European banks would have faced calls for at least $16 billion in additional capital. "For fear of shouting 'Fire!' in a crowded theater," the New York Fed later told Congress, it thought it best not even to mention this potential fallout from AIG's crisis to European regulators.

III

If systemic stability was the goal, the kind of improvisations that had let Lehman fail and rescued AIG would not suffice. Having realized the scale of what they were up against, Bernanke and Paulson decided on September 17 that they must appeal to Congress for additional resources and the authority to use them.[41] Paulson knew it was a serious political risk. But they were now faced with the collapse of the entire Wall Street system, and the resources at their disposal to meet it were stretched to the limit. With money hemorrhaging out of the money market funds, the Treasury made the extraordinary decision on September 19 to offer a guarantee to any fund willing to pay an insurance fee, with the coverage to be backed by $50 billion in the Exchange Stabilization Fund. It was another improvisation. The Exchange Stabilization Fund was a creation of the New Deal era. It was established in 1934 to enable FDR's Treasury to manage the exchange rate of the dollar after the abandonment of the gold standard. The fund was tiny compared with the scale of the trillion-dollar cash pools that were running in September 2008. But using it to back an insurance fund allowed it to be leveraged, and, more important, it was the only pot of money immediately available to the Treasury.

Meanwhile, Morgan Stanley and Goldman, the two investment banks left standing, were under immense funding pressure. One week after Lehman, they were rescued by the transparent expedient of redesignating them as commercial bank holding companies so that they might benefit from the

protection of FDIC deposit insurance. But that only increased the burden on the FDIC, which had problems of its own. On September 25 the FDIC closed, broke up and sold off Washington Mutual. With $244 billion in mortgages on the balance sheet, WaMu was the largest commercial bank in American history to fail. J.P. Morgan promptly snapped up WaMu's network of 2,239 retail branches and their deposits.[42] Nor was J.P. Morgan the only buyer that could see the prizes on offer in the giant fire sale. The Japanese bank Mitsubishi was poised to rescue Morgan Stanley by taking a 20 percent stake. Warren Buffett was about to prop up Goldman Sachs with a $5 billion capital injection. But both deals were contingent on the promise of a government backstop.

On September 20 the Treasury sent Congress a three-page legislative proposal asking for authority to spend up to $700 billion to stabilize securities markets. After the unlimited bailout authorization for the GSEs, the Treasury was now asking to spend the equivalent of the entire US defense budget on bad mortgage securities. But what was truly audacious about Paulson's bill was the nature of the power he was asking for.

As the three crucial sentences of the bill read:

"The Secretary is authorized to purchase, and to make and fund commitments to purchase, on such terms and conditions as determined by the Secretary, mortgage-related assets from any financial institution having its headquarters in the United States. . . . The Secretary's authority to purchase mortgage-related assets under this Act shall be limited to $700,000,000,000 outstanding at any one time. Decisions by the Secretary pursuant to the authority of this Act are non-reviewable and committed to agency discretion, and may not be reviewed by any court of law or any administrative agency."[43]

Paulson was asking for legal carte blanche.

Sketchy though it was, the proposal did not come out of the blue. Already in mid-April 2008 Paulson and a Treasury team had met with Bernanke and his staff to discuss what they called a "Break the Glass" memo outlining different options for emergency action.[44] They had considered large-scale guarantees for mortgages but had shied away because the liability was uncertain and potentially huge. Recapitalization was a more direct way of intervening in a bank. It was also efficient. Every dollar of bank

capital was leveraged. So a dollar of government capital would support ten, twenty or thirty times as much in lending. But recapitalization was rejected on political grounds. Paulson had no desire to go down in history as the Treasury secretary who nationalized America's banking system. And even if Paulson had been willing to pay the personal price, an open call for government recapitalization would never have passed Congress. The Republicans would have voted en bloc against nationalization, and without bipartisan cover the Democrats could not take the risk.[45] Already in the spring of 2008 the Treasury team thus decided that asset purchases were the path of least resistance. Buying debts did not involve ownership of banks. It did not raise issues of control or corporate governance. It could all be done through "the market." An auction mechanism could be used to determine the price. It was also, admittedly, slow moving and expensive: $700 billion would cover barely more than half the outstanding subprime securitization. It wasn't the perfect solution. But after Lehman, AIG and WaMu, the Treasury and the Fed were desperate. They needed something that might pass, and pass quickly.

Legislation that would ordinarily spend months in Congress needed to be passed in a matter of days. It was "hyperdrive blitzkrieg," one lobbyist flippantly remarked, and it ran into trouble from the start.[46] As Geithner recorded in his memoirs: "Congressional leaders, who had seemed shell-shocked but willing to act after Hank and Ben warned them about a second depression . . . now just seemed angry." "This proposal is stunning and unprecedented in its scope—and lack of detail, I might add," said Senate Banking Committee chairman Chris Dodd. "I can only conclude that it is not just our economy that is at risk, but our Constitution as well."[47] Dodd was a Democrat and at least willing to consider the possibility of action. Republicans were less measured. Jim Bunning of Kentucky described the proposal as "un-American financial socialism."[48] Ted Poe, a Texas Republican, lambasted the plan: "New York City fat cats expect Joe Sixpack to buck up and pay for all of this nonsense. . . . Putting a financial gun to the head of every American is not the answer."[49]

By 2008 the Bush administration had a credibility issue when it came to emergency powers. "This is eerily similar to the rush to war in Iraq," declared Representative. Mike McNulty, a Democrat from upstate New York.

"We have been told repeatedly by this administration that the economy is fundamentally sound, and then all of the sudden they say the economy is going to collapse. That is unacceptable."[50] Representative Pete Stark (D-CA) recalled how General Colin Powell, Bush's secretary of state during the Iraq crisis, had "tried to scare us some years ago by saying if we didn't vote for an ill-conceived war we'd see terrorists on the streets."[51]

In the *Financial Times* the economist and blogger Willem Buiter remarked that Paulson's bill read "as though it was personally written by Dick Cheney, the prince of absolute executive authority, no checks and balances, no accountability, no recourse. No administration that brought us WMD in Iraq and the torture camps of Guantanamo Bay and Abu Ghraib should expect anything but hysterical giggles in response to such a request."[52] The left-wing filmmaker Michael Moore weighed in with an incendiary e-mail to his mass following, entitled "The Rich Are Staging a Coup This Morning." As the British journalist Paul Mason remarked, Paulson's cack-handed proposal triggered an "accidental synergy between the right-wing populist opposition to the bailout and the left-liberal stance."[53] History would prove it to be more than accidental.

In the midst of a presidential election it was explosive stuff. The Democratic candidate Barack Obama was not the problem. Not only was Obama backed by an economics team recruited by way of Robert Rubin and the Hamilton Project but his personal entourage included top bankers from UBS and Merrill Lynch.[54] The problem was John McCain. If McCain threw in his lot with the rebel Republicans, it would not only threaten the proposed legislation, it would force the Democratic presidential campaign into a devastatingly unpopular choice. House Republican leader John Boehner was not helpful. One third of the Republican congressional party was so ideologically opposed to any more bailouts that there was no hope of their support. Another third were in tight races and could not risk alienating their base. "You were being asked to choose between financial meltdown on the one hand and taxpayer bankruptcy and the road to socialism on the other and you were told do it in 24 hours," Representative Jeb Hensarling of Texas, head of the conservative Republican Study Committee, indignantly told journalists.[55] Rising stars from the right wing of the Republican Party,

like Paul Ryan of Wisconsin and Eric Cantor of Virginia, rallied around the resistance to the Bush administration's "sellout."

With the Republicans deeply divided, on September 24 McCain suspended his campaign and announced he was returning to Washington to take the lead in "fixing" the crisis. In the Treasury and the White House this caused panic. The markets were in a febrile mood. No one knew what McCain had in mind. What was certain was that it would stir up the Republican base. Startled at the news, Paulson screamed into his Motorola, demanding that the White House get a grip on "their" candidate.[56] Bernanke was so alarmed by the intensity of the political power play that he thought it better to withdraw to the safety of the Fed. In the end it took interventions by the White House chief of staff and major Republican donors, including Henry Kravis, the private equity billionaire, J.P. Morgan vice chair James Lee and John Thain of Merrill Lynch, to hold McCain in line.[57] But this left McCain tongue-tied, torn between the demands of "the system" and the populist groundswell that Palin was rallying to his cause. In the climactic meeting of the two candidates with the Bush administration on September 25, a meeting called at McCain's request, the Republican candidate literally had nothing to say.[58]

By Sunday, September 28, it seemed that Paulson and the congressional Democrats had a deal. Paulson agreed to caps on remuneration, a phased release of the TARP aid, multiple layers of oversight and a commitment that if the taxpayer made a loss, the cost would be covered by a tax on the financial industry. To speed TARP along it was tacked on to House Resolution 3997, also known as the Defenders of Freedom Tax Relief Act, providing tax breaks for members of the armed services, volunteer firefighters and peace corps members. On the morning of the vote, Monday, September 29, the president gave a press conference hailing agreement on the Paulson bill. Later that same day he was hosting embattled President Yushchenko of Ukraine. It was a moment to demonstrate that the leader of the free world was still firmly in charge. Markets needed all the help they could get. The news from Europe was terrible. On Wall Street trading was jittery. All eyes were on the screens, waiting for the news from Capitol Hill.

The scene in the House of Representatives was not reassuring. After a

morning of polemical speeches, voting started after lunchtime. On screens around the world one could see the grinding process of congressional democracy in action. At 1:49 p.m., at the end of the normal voting period, the votes stood 228 to 205, against. The party leadership on both sides were staring into the abyss. To give the whips a chance to rally their troops, the voting period was extended and the TV cameras followed "as top lieutenants in both parties clutching lists of votes . . . clustered in the well and made unusual forays into what is normally enemy territory across the aisle."[59] Five minutes later it was clear that they had come up short. The gavel came down minutes before two p.m. and the bill failed. Tellingly, of the 205 votes in favor of Hank Paulson's TARP plan, 140 came from the Democrats and only 65 from the Republicans. Of those opposed, 133 were Republicans and 95 Democrats.

After the Fed and the Treasury had allowed Lehman to fail, America's elected representatives had refused to back their own government's emergency rescue effort. The reaction in the markets was one of terror. The Dow Jones index plummeted by 778 points, wiping $1.2 trillion off the value of American businesses in a matter of hours. It was the biggest loss on record, worse than on 9/11, when the index had plunged by 684 points.[60] The shock to global confidence was devastating. It produced a terrifying synchronization of the crisis on both sides of the Atlantic.

III

As the Americans were trying and failing to patch together the first TARP deal, in London Gordon Brown's government was frantically trying to persuade Spain's Santander to buy out the branch network of mortgage lender Bradford & Bingley and its £22 billion in deposits. That would leave the UK Treasury holding £41 billion in mortgages that no one wanted to touch.[61] When the UK had bailed out Northern Rock a year earlier, it had still seemed as though it might be an isolated incident. Now it was clear that the entire British financial system was at stake. It was lethally dependent on the wholesale funding market and that was shutting down.

The fear was that panic would soon spread from specialized mortgage

The Fragile UK Banking System:
Mortgage Exposure and Sources of Funding
(figures are % of assets/liabilities)

	Mortgage	Deposits	Wholesale	Equity
Abbey National	53	34	21	1.7
Alliance & Leicester	55	45	52	3.0
Barclays	6	26	19	2.5
Bradford & Bingley	62	51	44	3.2
Halifax Bank of Scotland	37	38	36	3.6
HSBC	4	48	17	6.2
Lloyds TSB	28	42	27	3.4
Northern Rock	77	27	68	3.1
Royal Bank of Scotland	8	43	24	4.8
Standard Chartered	17	58	20	7.1
Average	**34.7**	**41.2**	**32.8**	**3.86**

Source: Tanju Yorulmazer, "Case Studies on Disruptions During the Crisis," *Economic Policy Review* 20, no. 1 (February 2014). Available at SSRN: https://ssrn.com/abstract=2403923.

lenders like Northern Rock to bigger banks like HBOS and from there to the commercial bank RBS, whose balance sheet, on paper at least, had recently ranked as the largest of any bank in the world. On the Continent, the Belgian-Dutch-Luxembourgeois giant Fortis was on the point of being shut down. Its balance sheet matched that of Lehman.[62] The French government was struggling to keep the Franco-Belgian lender Dexia alive. Angela Merkel and her finance minister, Peer Steinbrück, were in knife-edge negotiations over Hypo Real Estate, which was being dragged down with Depfa, its adventurous Dublin affiliate.[63] Each rescue involved a combination of writing down losses, recapitalizing with public money, guaranteeing private borrowing, deal making with other banks and emergency liquidity from the central bank.

The Europeans were putting out one fire after another, bank by bank. But on the night of September 29, with the failure of TARP roiling the markets, Dublin cracked.[64] The three main Irish banks—Anglo Irish Bank, Bank of Ireland and Allied Irish Bank—were all on the brink of collapse.[65] The balance sheets of the banks registered in Ireland came to 700 percent of the country's GDP. The Irish state did not have the financial resources to

handle a general bank run. After a panic-stricken night of discussion, early in the morning of September 30 the Dublin government announced that for fear of dying it would commit suicide. As Europe turned on the morning news it learned that the Irish government was fully guaranteeing not just the deposits but all the liabilities of six major Irish banks for a period of two years. No other government had been advised in advance, nor had the ECB, nor had the Irish taxpayers.[66] It stopped the run, but it left Ireland, with a population half the size of New York City, guaranteeing 440 billion euros in bank liabilities. The losses the banks incurred would bankrupt the Irish state. They would become the telltale link connecting the banking crisis of 2008 to the eurozone sovereign debt crises of 2010. But that was music of the future. The issue on September 30 was the immediate impact on the rest of the world. If Ireland was offering a safe haven, would the run now extend to the rest of Europe?

Given how tightly the Irish banks were integrated with the British financial system, it was in London that the pressure was most acute. The UK was forced immediately to raise its deposit insurance limit. London and Paris were conferring urgently, as were the Dutch. The Germans were less cooperative. When the UK Treasury tried to reach Berlin to discuss a common European response, they could not get the German finance minister, Steinbrück, to pick up the phone. So anxious did Chancellor Darling become that he resorted to calling on the foreign office to find out whether the British embassy in Berlin could make contact with the German government.[67] And Berlin was not merely evasive. In the last days of September the Dutch government, reeling from the experience of bailing out Fortis, made a bold proposal.[68] The European states should all establish bank rescue funds on a common basis, each amounting to 3 percent of GDP. In total the fund would come to 300 billion euros. The French government was enthusiastic. To address the crisis Sarkozy invited the G4—France, Germany, Italy and the UK—to Paris. Ahead of the meeting French finance minister Christine Lagarde spoke to the German business daily *Handelsblatt* about the need for joint measures.[69] After the fraught transnational negotiations to rescue Dexia and Fortis, she was seriously concerned about the ability of small countries to cope with the crisis. "What would happen

if a little European Union state confronted a bank collapse?" she asked rhetorically. "Maybe the government would not have the means to save the institution in question. So the question arises of a solution at the European level."[70] The Italians liked the idea.[71] So too did the influential head of Deutsche Bank, Josef Ackermann.[72] Europe needed something on the scale that Paulson was asking for in the United States. Suddenly, Berlin sprang to life. There must be no talk of joint bailouts, Steinbrück announced. Merkel let it be known that she would not attend the summit in Paris if it was labeled a crisis meeting. As if to bind herself, the chancellor gave an interview to the popular tabloid *Bild-Zeitung*, soon to become notorious for its nationalist coverage of the crisis, denouncing any blank check for bankers.[73] And Berlin could count on support from Frankfurt. Jean-Claude Trichet of the ECB told journalists that a common European solution was inappropriate because the eurozone wasn't a fiscal union. Likewise, Jean-Claude Juncker, prime minister of Luxembourg and long-serving chair of the Eurogroup, told German radio: "I see no reason why we should mount a US-style programme in Europe." The crisis came from the United States. It was deeper there. Europe could get by with national solutions.

Sarkozy retreated, saving face by dismissing the idea as an unauthorized personal initiative on Lagarde's part. But the French and the Dutch were right. Within twelve months, precisely the scenario that Lagarde had sketched for *Handelsblatt* would come to haunt the eurozone. Crippled banks and ailing government borrowers would pull one another down. But prescient though the French might have been, nothing could be done without Berlin. On October 4 Sarkozy, Merkel, Brown and Berlusconi convened in Paris. The result was disappointing. Gordon Brown came away impressed by the sense that the Europeans thought the crisis to be an American problem.[74] As one disillusioned British official remarked, the Europeans "didn't see it coming. They didn't understand the economics. They didn't understand how collective action could work."[75] Sarkozy commented resignedly, "If we cannot cobble together a European solution then it will be a debacle. . . . But it will not be my debacle; it will be Angela's. You know what she said to me? 'Chacun sa merde!' (To each his own shit!)." According to the German side, the chancellor's language had been less vulgar. "Merkel had quoted a

proverb taken from . . . Johann Wolfgang Goethe: 'Ein jeder kehre vor seiner Tür, und rein ist jedes Stadtquartier' (Everyone should sweep in front of his door and every city quarter will be clean)."[76]

Why were the Germans so resistant? After all, Germany had its fair share of ailing banks that might have benefited from a common fund. But the hard truth was that German taxpayers did not want to pay for other people's bailouts, inside Germany or out. In a broader sense, the question of national versus federal solutions was for Merkel not just a matter of euros and cents. Since 2005 she had been toiling amid the wreckage of Europe's failed effort to give itself a constitution. The Lisbon Treaty, enshrining the grand retreat to a nation-state–based vision of the EU, had been signed only in December 2007. In June 2008 it had suffered a serious setback when it was rejected by a referendum in Ireland. As the financial crisis hit, the Lisbon framework was undergoing emergency surgery. A case in the German constitutional court was pending. With the basic political frame of the EU in flux, Berlin was not going to support a huge increase in the powers of the European Commission to enable a bank bailout.[77] Whatever solution was found would be based on intergovernmental agreement, not enhanced federal powers.

The most that the summit on October 4 could agree on was a statement calling for coordinated action, rebuking Ireland for its unilateral action the previous week. All the more shocking was what happened next. As the European heads of government made their way home from Paris, the news broke that the rescue of Hypo Real Estate had broken down. Depfa's condition was worse than had been realized. An expert team dispatched by Deutsche Bank to Dublin had found that Hypo would need to come up not with 35 billion but with 50 billion euros to fill the gap at Depfa. The banks that Merkel and Steinbrück had enlisted in the bailout to support Hypo immediately reneged. As one German banker later put it to the investigative inquiry of the Bundestag, if Lehman's failure had been a tsunami, then the bankruptcy of Hypo Real Estate would have been Armageddon for the German economy. Axel Weber, the head of the Bundesbank, spoke of a nuclear meltdown (Kernschmelze). Somewhat melodramatically, Germany's bank regulator, Jochen Sanio, invoked *Apocalypse Now.*[78] What really worried Berlin were rumors that German savers were panicking. As cash

withdrawals spiked, the Bundesbank registered unprecedented demand for large-denomination euro notes. Abruptly, less than twenty-four hours after returning from Paris, Merkel decided that she must make a statement. It was all Steinbrück could do to persuade her that she should not do it entirely alone.[79] On the afternoon of Sunday, October 5, Merkel and Steinbrück went before the TV cameras. They didn't have a legislative mandate from the Bundestag. They were deliberately vague about the details. But the leaders of the two political parties that had ruled Germany since 1949 jointly declared that all savings deposits were safe.

This was directed at a German audience. But it had far wider implications. Germany was not Ireland. Even on the most restrictive definition, Merkel and Steinbrück had given a guarantee in the order of at least a trillion euros. Was Germany positioning itself to take advantage of a global bank run? Berlin gave neither London nor Washington prior warning. Within hours of the Merkel-Steinbrück performance, Prime Minister Brown convened an emergency meeting in Downing Street to consider London's response. British officials "tried frantically to reach the Germans," but once again Berlin wasn't answering the phone.[80] In the absence of a clear European policy, smaller countries with big banks, such as Denmark, were forced to make unilateral decisions and to extend guarantees of their own. In Washington, Paulson's team was also scrambling to establish what Merkel had in mind. Was it a "moral guarantee," or the kind of binding two-year obligation that Ireland had entered into? It felt as though the US authorities were losing their grip on the situation. "[T]his is going to move quick and force us to do some things we may or may not want to do," Paulson told his staff.[81] If Germany felt it necessary to issue a guarantee, where was America's guarantee? On Monday, October 6, equity markets shed $2 trillion in value. With the finance ministers of the world converging on Washington for the autumn meetings of the IMF and the World Bank, the Americans decided to call an impromptu gathering of the G7 and G20 finance ministers at the US Treasury for October 10 and 11.

It was reassuring that the Treasury had realized the need for coordination. But a week was a very long time in a financial crisis and London could not wait. Gordon Brown's government was facing the collapse of two giant banks—HBOS and RBS. Lloyds had agreed to buy out HBOS already on

September 18. But the ailing mortgage lender was losing access to wholesale funding markets.[82] Its credit rating was dropping, and as panic spread, retail and corporate customers withdrew £30 billion. If it failed before the takeover was complete, it would be a catastrophe to dwarf Northern Rock.[83] Given its sheer size, RBS was even more dangerous. Since September 26, separate teams at the UK Treasury and Downing Street had been working on a bailout plan. To coordinate the crisis fighting, on October 3 Brown declared the establishment of a National Economic Council (NEC). The *Daily Telegraph* immediately dubbed it an "economic war cabinet," an idea encouraged by the fact that it met in the underground, high-security conference room usually reserved for the government's COBRA emergency-response committee.[84] Despite the uncomfortable and ominous surroundings, the meetings were productive. Whereas Paulson's TARP model was based on the idea of buying bad assets, London brought together two ideas: guarantees and recapitalization. Like Ireland and Germany, London would offer guarantees. The Bank of England and the Treasury would underwrite debt issuance by the banks. But these guarantees would be conditional on recapitalization either through market investment or from public funds. The details were worked out in frantic meetings in Whitehall and road tested with focus groups of investment bankers who were sworn to secrecy. On the morning of October 7, while Chancellor Darling was in conference with Europe's finance ministers trying to hammer out an agreed policy on deposit insurance, the share price of RBS collapsed and trading had to be suspended. The bank that had been touted as the largest in the world as recently as the spring of 2008 was hours away from failure.[85]

The UK bank bailout package launched on October 8, 2008, after a night of cliff-edge negotiation with the leading banks, was an accomplished piece of political theater. Compared with Paulson's struggles with Congress, Brown and Darling had the huge advantage of a solid majority in the House of Commons. Though Brown's position at the head of the Labour Party was far from secure, he did not have to fear the parliamentary mutiny faced by President Bush. Altogether the commitments by the UK Treasury and the Bank of England matched or even exceeded those of TARP. Relative to the much smaller UK economy they were far larger.

The British scheme consisted of three parts:

1. The UK's eight major banks were required to draw up plans for recap-
 italization. It was left up to them to decide whether they drew on a
 government fund of £50 billion (i.e., c. $75–85 billion), or raised re-
 sources privately.
2. £250 billion ($374–420 billion) would be used to guarantee new debt
 issued by participating banks.
3. A £200 billion ($300–350 billion) extension of the Bank of England's
 Special Liquidity Scheme would allow banks to trade unsalable asset-
 backed securities for Treasurys.

The issue that had kept bankers and Treasury officials up all night was
whether the £50 billion recapitalization should be forced through at a
stroke, or whether this might spook the markets. Would it be better to
proceed in stages? Perversely, the ailing banks resisted to the bitter end.
None of them wanted to become a ward of the state. On the brink of failure
they were still angling for whatever margin of advantage they could extract.
In the end, £15 billion in government funds were put into RBS (a 57.9 per-
cent stake) and £13 billion into Lloyds TSB-HBOS (a 43.4 percent stake).[86]
Barclays and HSBC, Britain's strongest banks, ostentatiously opted out of
the schemes. They took neither the capital nor the guarantees. The UK gov-
ernment never mustered the authority or even made the attempt to impose
recapitalization on either of them. HSBC, with its large base in Asia, was
strong enough to raise funds through the markets. Barclays resorted to
a highly irregular deal with a gulf sovereign wealth fund to which it lent
the funds to recapitalize itself, a transaction for which it was later to pay a
substantial fine and for which its senior management would face criminal
charges.[87]

Against the backdrop of the TARP debacle and the shambles in Europe,
Gordon Brown's scheme looked like a breakthrough. From New York, Paul
Krugman lavished praise on Britain's Labour government. Britain's Social
Democrats had figured out how to rescue financial capitalism.[88] It cer-
tainly helped that the Labour government was less averse to nationalization
than Hank Paulson was. Less charitably it might be said that since the
1990s, New Labour, like the Democrats in the United States, had entered
into an enthusiastic partnership with the City of London. It was, therefore,

no coincidence that it was now Labour in Britain and the Democrats in the United States who were showing such energy in the struggle to fix the banking crisis. It was a monster they had helped to create. In any case, given the enormous burden that UK taxpayers were going to have to bear in supporting HBOS and RBS, it was hard to see that there was ever any alternative to nationalization.

The reaction of investors was not so enthusiastic as that of the pundits. When the G7 finance ministers assembled on Friday, October 10, global markets were in a state of panic. That afternoon in the famous wood-paneled cash room of the US Treasury, the mood was less than amicable. Italy's finance minister, Giulio Tremonti, and Shōichi Nakagawa for Japan hammered home the damage that had been done by the US decision to let Lehman fail. Steinbrück repeated his line about the end of Anglo-American capitalism.[89] Jean-Claude Trichet indulged in a little theatrics by handing around a single graph showing the surge in the Libor-OIS spread since the Lehman failure. It was a benchmark of the funding pressure the European banks were under. The Americans, seconded by Mervyn King of the Bank of England, held their cool and insisted that though Lehman might be the proximate cause, it was hardly the fundamental source of all the world's problems. To turn the discussion in a more positive direction they proposed a short five-point plan:

1. There would be no more failures of systematically important institutions.
2. There would be measures to assist recapitalization.
3. They would work to unfreeze liquidity in interbank markets.
4. They would provide adequate deposit insurance.
5. They would rebuild markets for securitized assets.

As a surprise treat for the finance ministers, President Bush made an impromptu appearance to add some easy charm to the discussions. Unfortunately, Bush's remarks were not well calculated to reassure his guests. "You folks don't need to worry," he told them. "Hank's got a handle on this. He's going to freeze that liquidity."[90] Given that TARP was still in limbo and

that freezing liquidity was the last thing anyone needed, it can hardly have been comforting.

Back in Europe three days later, the agreements in Washington set the tone for a meeting of the eurozone heads of government in Paris. Sarkozy was the host, but the lead part belonged to Gordon Brown. Though the UK was not a eurozone member, the City of London was the financial capital of Europe and the British bank bailout plan was now being touted as the model. Politically, Sarkozy hoped to use Brown's weight to push the Germans into a more cooperative attitude.[91] Though what emerged from the meeting on October 12 was a huge headline figure for bank guarantees, it was less than a European plan. There was no agreement on a common European response. The European Commission issued a permissive license to member states to issue debt guarantees as long as they were extended to all banks in the country, both domestic and foreign. There must be no discrimination. For the duration of the crisis European states were free to pump capital into the banks. The EU would act as an agency of oversight and try to minimize the extent to which the European common market would be torn apart. But it was not a crisis fighter in its own right. In total, the commission would review and approve twenty schemes for bank-debt guarantee and fifteen for recapitalizations.[92] On top of that came applications for support for individual banks—forty-four from Germany alone. But it was case by case, country by country. Merkel's veto was decisive. It would be three long years before a common European bailout was back on the agenda.

On Monday, October 13, 2008, the UK nationalized Lloyds-HBOS and RBS. That same day Germany announced that it was putting up 400 billion euros in guarantees and 100 billion euros for recapitalization. France guaranteed 320 billion euros in medium-term bank debt and set up a 40 billion euro capitalization fund. Italy budgeted 40 billion euros for capitalization and "as much as necessary" in guarantees. In the Netherlands the guarantees came to 200 billion euros. Spain and Austria each put up 100 billion euros.[93] In proportion to GDP, the largest program was that in Ireland. But Belgium and the Netherlands also made huge commitments.

Europe's national programs were defined by the circumstances of the

banks and local politics. France's large banks were in relatively good shape. Société Générale was fortunate that the so-called "Kerviel scandal" involving 50 billion euros in unauthorized positions and losses of almost 5 billion euros, unwound in January 2008, rather than six months later at the height of the crisis.[94] Société Générale managed to recapitalize and avoid a takeover, which might have ended as badly as the other shotgun weddings of the period. In addition, the French bank, which acted as a close partner of Goldman Sachs, was a particular beneficiary of the generous terms of the AIG bailout. But even if the other major French banks were robust, no one was exempt from the loss of confidence in the fall of 2008. On October 16 an emergency recapitalization and refinancing program was ramrodded through the French parliament. The urgency was commonplace. What was different in France was the response of the private sector. All of the major banks, led by BNP Paribas, agreed to take capital from the Société de Prise de Participation de l'État (SPPE). A second tranche followed in January 2009. Again, all the banks took the capital. Even more unusual was the refinancing scheme headed by the Société de Financement de l'Économie Française (SFEF). This entity was legally entitled to issue state-guaranteed bonds on behalf of banks up to a total of 265 billion euros, but 66 percent of its shares were subscribed by the six major French banks. Even HSBC France signed on. It was an elegant construction. With the French state holding only a minority stake, the SFEF's liabilities were not counted toward the French public debt. At the same time, thanks to a special arrangement with the banking regulators, the SFEF was not required to meet Basel II capital rules, so the actual financial call on the banks was minimal. It was an efficient mechanism for restoring confidence made possible both by the relative lack of pressure on France's biggest banks and close cooperation within France's extraordinarily tight-knit elite.[95] Though they work in very different ways, business and government are every bit as interconnected in Paris as they are in New York and Washington, DC, enabling that rarest of things under conditions of market competition—an uncoerced agreement on collective action.

For sheer scale, only Germany's program rivaled that in Britain. On October 17 the legislation establishing the Sonderfonds Finanzmarktstabili-

sierung was bounced through the Bundestag.[96] But as in Britain, any possibility of a general solution was spoiled by the power of the dominant player. With the regional Landesbanken ailing and Commerzbank struggling with the ill-advised takeover of Dresdner, Deutsche Bank saw the opportunity to put distance between itself and the rest. In an internal discussion, which was clearly intended to be leaked, CEO Josef Ackermann stigmatized the national bailout package. He would be ashamed, he let it be known, to see his bank requesting help from Berlin. As Barclays was to do in the UK, Deutsche preferred to rely on accounting tricks and investments from gulf state sovereign wealth funds to see it through the crisis. It too would later face legal action over its makeshift crisis management, but in the United States, not in Germany.[97] Meanwhile, Steinbrück was livid. Ackermann, he said, had paved the way "for a two-class society in the banking sector: into those that don't need help and those that are at risk of relegation. This is dangerous, because the markets respond to it."[98] It was the same problem that at the same moment was preoccupying Washington.

IV

After the setback in Congress on September 29 there was never any option but for the Treasury to make a second attempt to get the TARP legislation on the books. To get TARP passed, Paulson abandoned his demand for a blank check. The $700 billion in bailout funds were split into three tranches, a first of $250 billion, a second of $100 billion and $350 billion conditional on presidential request and congressional approval. Support for the banks would be balanced by tax breaks for the middle class and support for home owners. Section 109 of the act specifically empowered the Treasury secretary to "facilitate loan modifications to prevent avoidable foreclosures."[99] Rather than immunity for the Treasury secretary, the law now provided for multiple overlapping layers of oversight. On October 3 TARP passed into law, carried by 74 percent of the Democratic votes in the House, but only 46 percent of the Republicans.

But by the first week of October, with events in the US markets and in

Europe moving at a rapid pace, it was clear that TARP as originally conceived would not work. The Treasury faced the sheer impracticality of making markets for hundreds of billions of dollars' worth of dubious assets at a time of market terror. Either it overpaid and sacrificed the taxpayer interest, or it drove a hard bargain and risked ruining the banks it was trying to help. Meanwhile, the British had tipped the discussion in favor of recapitalization. Rather than buying bad assets or guaranteeing more borrowing by the banks, government should inject share capital. Having obtained the funds from Congress for asset purchases, TARP would now be repurposed as a vehicle for injecting capital. At the same time, events in Ireland, Germany and the UK had changed the conversation about deposit insurance. According to Paulson, it was the risk of a shift in funds from the United States to Europe that led him and Bernanke to converge on the FDIC and to demand that its head, Sheila Bair, should offer even more comprehensive guarantees.[100]

The new package was worked out between the Treasury, the Fed and the FDIC over the weekend of October 11–12, in the shadow of the G7/G20 meetings. It was presented to the stunned CEOs of America's nine largest banks on the afternoon of Monday, October 13, just as the Europeans were rolling out their guarantees.[101] It was a take it or leave it offer. In rations fixed by Tim Geithner as president of the New York Fed, all nine major banks would be required to take slices of government capital. The shares would be preferred shares. The guaranteed dividends that the federal government would require were low, but would escalate after five years to give the banks an incentive to repay early. In exchange for accepting the capital injection, the banks would receive an FDIC guarantee on all business checking accounts and a guarantee on any new debt issued by the summer of 2009, up to a total of 125 percent of the debt maturing by the end of that year. The two were linked. No FDIC guarantee without government capital injection. Characteristically, Ben Bernanke sought to calm the fraying nerves in the room by appealing to everyone to consider their common interests. They were all in it together. "I don't really understand why this needs to be confrontational," he said soothingly.[102] The bankers stared at him in disbelief. The core of American financial capitalism was about to be partially nationalized.

Beyond the general sense of shock, the reactions came down to business logic. For the weakest in the group it was evidently a great deal, and Vikram Pandit of Citigroup said so. Given the state of his balance sheet, he couldn't afford to be fussy. As he blurted out: "This is cheap capital." Indeed, it was. The yield on Citigroup bonds that day was 22 percent. Paulson was asking for 5 percent.[103] A better-placed bank, like J.P. Morgan, could have got by without the TARP money. But Dimon understood the systemic logic and was among the first to sign, though he made his signature conditional on the rest of the group agreeing. It was California's Wells Fargo that forced the government side to show its hand. When Wells objected to bailing out New York banks, Paulson coolly pointed out that Wells Fargo was sitting opposite its regulator. If they did not take the capital on offer that afternoon, they would be notified the following morning that they were undercapitalized. They would find themselves locked out of capital markets. When they came back to Paulson for help, the terms would be less attractive than those available that afternoon. The CEOs were then dismissed to call their boards. Within a matter of hours they had all agreed. Under the Capital Purchase Program facility, America's nine largest banks took $125 billion in preferred stock from the government.

By comparison with the less encompassing effort in Europe, America's recapitalization would come to look very impressive. And this judgment was reinforced by hindsight. America's banks recovered from the crisis more quickly and comprehensively than their European counterparts. The meeting of October 13, 2008, it seems, is when the great transatlantic divergence began.[104] Advocates of strong executive branch prerogatives would later celebrate these actions as an essential assertion of sovereign authority. As it had done after 9/11, the American state had declared a state of exception and it had risen to the occasion.[105] But comforting as it may be to invoke sovereign power at moments of great uncertainty, this is a mystification of the events in September and October of 2008. The path from Lehman to TARP was less one of a sovereign state rising to a crisis than of a dysfunctional power struggle within the social and political network that tied Washington, DC, to Wall Street and to the European financial system beyond. In September political and commercial considerations had prevented a deal to save Lehman. It took a month of panic, political confusion and

unprecedented financial turmoil to reach the point in mid-October when the barons of Wall Street would listen when Paulson thumped the table and declared that everyone must take the Treasury's money. Even then, the executive branch had the power that it appeared to do in large part because J.P. Morgan swung behind the Treasury proposal. If this was an act of sovereignty, whose sovereignty was it? The American state's, or that of the "new Wall Street"—the network personified by figures like Paulson and Geithner who tied the Treasury and the Fed to America's globalized financial sector?[106]

The Treasury's act of power would have been more impressive if the injection of capital had been on onerous terms. But the opposite was the case. Vikram Pandit was right. The capital the Treasury was "forcing" on the banks was cheap, in every respect. As Phillip Swagel, assistant secretary for economic policy at the Treasury and a key architect of Paulson's bailout, has described it: "[T]o ensure that the capital injection was widely and rapidly accepted, the terms had to be attractive, not punitive. . . . [T]his had to be the opposite of the 'Sopranos' or the 'Godfather'—not an attempt to intimidate banks, but instead a deal so attractive that banks would be unwise to refuse it."[107] The Treasury was far from being a difficult shareholder. Designating itself a "reluctant shareholder," the US government abstained from claiming any voting rights.[108] Whereas in the UK and Germany the nationalization of Lloyds-HBOS, RBS, Hypo and Commerzbank was akin to bankruptcy restructuring and led to wholesale changes in management, America's more comprehensive approach was necessarily light touch.[109] If robust J.P. Morgan was to participate in the scheme alongside ailing Citigroup, the terms could not be too onerous. The participants in TARP were allowed to go on paying dividends. The dividend to be paid on the capital provided from TARP was no more than 5 percent, half of what Goldman Sachs paid to Warren Buffett when he "rescued" them. The Treasury's aim was to persuade all banks to participate en masse so as to ensure that state support was not taken as a signal of weakness that would attract the attention of short sellers. As Steinbrück had spelled out in his furious reaction to Deutsche Bank, at a moment of crisis, defense of the system involved both treating everyone as though they were healthy and the healthier banks being willing to play along. They had to recognize that in the event of a

truly comprehensive crisis their cherished margin of superiority would not save them from disaster.

The result of the Treasury's "sovereign" intervention was to extend a huge subsidy to the banks, increasing the value of their businesses by perhaps as much as $131 billion.[110] The biggest beneficiaries were the fragile investment banks and the sprawling colossus of Citigroup. Citigroup received $25 billion from the Treasury in exchange for securities valued at $15.5 billion and soon to be worth much less. In contrast, Wells Fargo, widely regarded as one of the banking industry's stronger players, gave approximately $23.2 billion worth of securities for its $25 billion in government capital.[111] J.P. Morgan did not need the money, and by agreeing to go along with the government's efforts to stop the run, Dimon passed up the opportunity to predate any more of his weaker competitors. For critics of the bailout, like Sheila Bair of the FDIC, it seemed that the entire process was a smoke screen put up to hide a bailout of Citigroup.[112] The Clinton-era network was still at work. Citi was not just too big to fail. It was too well connected. Whatever one thinks of this interpretation, it is undeniable that as soon as the extreme panic of early October had passed, the pretense of equal treatment was dropped.

The October stabilization was not enough for Citigroup. In November it disclosed huge losses and announced fifty-two thousand layoffs. By Friday, November 21, 2008, Citi's market valuation was $20.5 billion, down from $250 billion in 2006. As fear spread, the death knell sounded. Citi was losing access to repo markets. The end, it seemed, was nigh. Given Citi's immense size and entanglement in global markets, the consequences did not bear contemplating. In an urgent series of negotiations culminating with "Citi weekend" on November 22–23, another deal was patched together. A second capital injection of $20 billion reinforced Citi's balance sheet while a so-called loss protection plan protected it against losses on $306 billion in toxic assets. In exchange the government received $7 billion in preferred shares paying 8 percent.[113] Bank of America was struggling too and that put Merrill Lynch in jeopardy. As the takeover proceeded, the full scale of Merrill's mortgage losses was becoming apparent and CEO Ken Lewis and his team at Bank of America were desperate to pull out of the deal that had saved the investment bank on September 14. No one wanted

to go back to Lehman weekend. Under heavy pressure from Paulson and Bernanke, Lewis pressed on with the deal, withholding crucial information from Bank of America's shareholders, but taking another $20 billion in government capital and a "loss-protection arrangement" on $118 billion of Merrill's troubled assets.[114]

The financial crisis was not yet contained. But at least in political terms, Wall Street was reassured. On November 4 Barack Obama won the presidency and the Democrats consolidated their grip on both the House and the Senate. American progressives celebrated a historic victory. Obama appeared as an almost messianic figure and he occupied not just the White House. He had the congressional majority necessary to actually change America. And in a remarkable historical twist, the election of the first African American president on the Democratic Party ticket was good news for Wall Street too. It was Obama and the Democrats who had provided the Bush administration with the political backing they needed for the extraordinary crisis-fighting measures of 2008. And they clearly intended to continue that line. On November 23, the same day that the Treasury announced the latest round of support for Citi, Obama's team made public their nomination for Treasury secretary. The rumor mill had been churning for weeks. Perhaps not surprisingly given his long-standing connections to Obama, Rubin was on the short list, as was Larry Summers, his coarchitect of Clinton-era deregulation. Paul Volcker, Greenspan's predecessor as Fed chair, godfather of disinflation in the Carter-Reagan era, was an Obama favorite. But he was too old. The others were too politically toxic. The man picked for the Treasury was none other than the hard-driving head of the New York Fed, Tim Geithner, a protégé of Summers and Rubin. Summers was made head of the National Economic Council while he waited to replace Bernanke as Fed chair. Rubin would serve as an éminence grise behind the scenes—a "Harry Hopkins" role, Rubin liked to call it—while another of his protégés and partners in the Hamilton Project, Peter Orszag, would take the role as director of the budget. The keeper of the lists in the transition team was Michael Froman, Rubin's former chief of staff at the Treasury. Froman continued to draw a salary as Citigroup's head of emerging markets strategy while he moonlighted for the Obama campaign.[115] In 2009 he joined the Obama administration as deputy assistant to the

president and deputy national security adviser for international economic affairs. The only figure on the Obama economics team who did not belong to the Clinton-era "old boys" networks was Christina Romer, a "new Keynesian" economist from Berkeley and noted expert on the history of the Great Depression, who was appointed to be chair of the Council of Economic Advisers.[116] The market liked the news. As one investment adviser noted, "Geithner assures a smooth transition between the Bush administration and that of Obama, because he's already co-managing what's happening now."[117]

Indeed, even to talk in terms of a transition from the Bush administration to Obama is to exaggerate the break. Well before November 4, the baton had already passed. The political party that had demonstrated its willingness to mobilize the full resources of the US government to fight the financial crisis was the Democratic Party. The Republicans weren't so much a partner in managing the crisis as a symptom of it. In the course of the crisis the GOP had shown itself to be less a party of government than a political vehicle through which conservative, white Americans expressed their alarm at the earthquakes shaking their world.

Chapter 8

"THE BIG THING": GLOBAL LIQUIDITY

In retrospect it can seem as though it was the decisions taken in the first weeks of October 2008 that decided the future course of events. The United States moved concertedly toward recapitalizing its banks. In Europe, proposals for a common approach were vetoed by Berlin. From there the crisis unfolded as a series of national struggles that after 2010 became once again entwined in the form of the eurozone crisis. In the end Europe could not escape a common solution, but it would take years of economic uncertainty and distress before it arrived at that point. As the eurozone crisis would reveal, the national approach insisted on by Berlin was fundamentally unfit for purpose. But by focusing attention on the European dimension of interdependence, that judgment in fact understates the case. The banks and the borrowers of Europe were indeed interdependent. But even more basic and far more pressing in the fall of 2008 was their dependence on the United States. The closure of interbank and wholesale funding markets created huge pressures in the dollar-funding markets all over the world, and it was in Europe that the pressure was most acute. This was a shortfall that even the strongest European states were powerless to address. That it did not result in a spectacular transatlantic crisis was decided not in Europe but in the United States, where the Fed, acting in the enlightened self-interest of the US financial system, acknowledged the compelling force of financial interconnectedness and acted on it. At a moment when Paulson and the Treasury were struggling with Congress to

mobilize political support for a backstop for the American financial system, the Fed, without public consultation of any kind, made itself into a lender of last resort for the world. When the music in the private money markets stopped, the Fed took up the tune, providing a stopgap of liquidity that, all told, ran into trillions of dollars and was tailored to the needs of banks in the United States, Europe and Asia. It was historically unprecedented, spectacular in scale and almost entirely unheralded. It transformed what we imagine to be the relationship between financial systems and national currencies.

I

The wholesale funding stop had hit the European banks already in August 2007. It was no coincidence, therefore, that it was the ECB that led the way in providing 95 billion euros in liquidity to overnight interbank markets on August 9.[1] Trichet was not the central banker to take such dramatic action without due cause.[2] By the autumn of 2008 both the ECB and the Bank of England were pumping liquidity on a huge scale. This did not involve parliamentary votes or unusual long-term capital investments. These were not bailouts but money market transactions, of the type that central banks routinely conduct to tighten and ease financial conditions, but now on a scale never seen before. As they lent cash or cash equivalents against collateral—good and bad—the balance sheets of all the major central banks began to expand. Potentially, at least, this could be done without limit within a closed national economy, or a large currency zone like that of the euro or the dollar. But what such operations could not conjure up was liquidity in foreign currencies. The Bank of England supplied sterling, the ECB euros. This domestic currency constraint was a crucial limit on the power of central bank operations and particularly so in 2008, because what the European banks desperately needed were dollars. It was into this breach that the Fed stepped with a program of liquidity provision that matched the global reach of the offshore dollar banking system.

Starting from a conventional trade-based view of international economics, it is not easy to see how a shortage of dollars could have been so

threatening to Europe. In September 2008 the eurozone as a whole was running a trade surplus with the United States. Germany, in particular, was a champion exporter. Surely, if European banks needed dollars they could buy or borrow them from global exporters like Audi, VW and Mercedes-Benz. But this is where the disparity between the trade-based view of the economy and global financialization becomes starkly evident. In 2007 Germany's exporters earned a trade surplus with the United States of roughly $5 billion per month. According to calculations by economists at the Bank of International Settlements, what the European banks needed was not $5 billion, or even $10 billion. Prior to the crisis they had funded their dollar operations with c. $1 trillion in commitments from US money market funds. On top of that they had borrowed $432 billion in the interbank market, $315 billion on the foreign exchange swap markets and $386 billion in short-term funding from those monetary authorities that were managing dollar cash pools. In total this added to more than $2 trillion.[3] The precise figure depended on how much of Europe's gigantic bank balance sheet needed to be refinanced and how quickly.

What the 2008 crisis exposed was a dangerous imbalance in the business model of the European banks. As the American money markets shut down, all the European banks were scrambling for dollar funding. They tried to borrow from one another, which led to a painful surge in short-term funding costs as measured by the so-called Libor-OIS spread.[4] At the same time, the market for currency swaps was becoming dangerously congested, with Europeans bidding for dollar credits and ever fewer counterparties willing to take the other side of the trade. The cross-currency basis swap spread, which measures the interest rate spread that European banks were willing to pay to transfer euro or sterling funding into dollars, became strongly negative, indicating that it was extremely difficult to access dollar funding directly. When markets are functioning normally, this premium should be close to zero. In September 2008 it exceeded 200 basis points. When the FOMC met on September 16, the day after Lehman's bankruptcy, with AIG teetering on the brink, its first item of business was the funding difficulties not of American but of European banks. As Bill Dudley of the New York Fed put it, "The big thing,

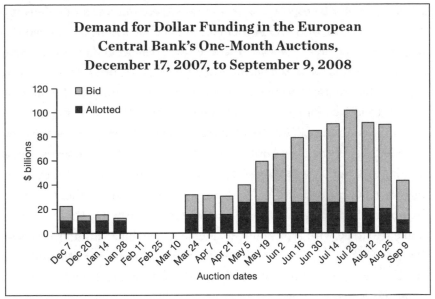

Demand for Dollar Funding in the European Central Bank's One-Month Auctions, December 17, 2007, to September 9, 2008

Source: Michael J. Fleming and Nicholas J. Klagge, "The Federal Reserve's Foreign Exchange Swap Lines," *Current Issues in Economics and Finance* 16, no. 4 (2010): 1.

where there has probably been the most severe stress in the market, is in dollar liquidity for foreign banks."[5]

Where could more dollar funding come from? One might think of central banks as a possible source of foreign exchange. But the dollar reserves of the European central banks were, by themselves, nowhere near large enough to meet the funding needs of the banks.[6] As the crisis worsened in the autumn of 2008 and the City of London convulsed, the Bank of England had as little as $10 billion on hand.[7] Throughout July, in the dollar auctions held regularly by the ECB, the bids exceeded the allotted sums by a factor of four. Little wonder that as the crisis deepened, the dollar was not falling in value, as standard macroeconomic models had predicted, but rising.

Lesser countries in this kind of predicament would be directed to the IMF. And in the fall of 2008, in close dialogue with the US Treasury and the Fed, the Fund was scrambling to devise a new genre of short-term liquidity facility to offer support for countries under acute funding pressure, which did not require a full IMF adjustment program.[8] But for the ECB or the Bank of England to have resorted to the IMF would in 2008 have been a

disaster of historic proportions. In any case, the Fund was still defined by the basic rationale of the 1944 moment in which it was born and had the proportions to match. The IMF financed trade deficits and handled public debt crises. It was not in the business of filling gigantic private sector funding gaps. Its programs were denominated in tens of billions of dollars. It was not conceived for an age of trillion-dollar transnational banking.

In the autumn of 2008 the stark truth could no longer be escaped. As Tim Geithner of the New York Fed told the FOMC, the Europeans "ran a banking system that was allowed to get very, very big relative to GDP with huge currency mismatches and with no plans to meet the liquidity needs of their banks in dollars in the event that we face a storm like this."[9] As Bernanke remarked with typical understatement, the dollar funding needs of Europe's banking system were "a novel aspect of the current situation."[10] It was a novel aspect with potentially drastic implications for the United States. If the Fed did not act, what threatened was a transatlantic balance sheet avalanche, with the Europeans running down their lending in the United States and selling off their dollar portfolios in a dangerous fire sale. It was to hold those portfolios of dollar-denominated assets in place that from the end of 2007 the Fed began to provide dollar liquidity in unprecedented abundance not only to the American but to the entire global financial system, and above all to Europe. In 2008 that flow of dollars grew to such proportions that it rendered any effort to write a separate history of the American and European crises anachronistic and profoundly misleading.[11]

II

The Fed labeled its liquidity facilities in a bamboozling array of acronyms— among insiders the programs were known collectively as the "hobbits." But when broken down by function, they mapped directly onto each of the key elements of the shadow banking system: the asset-backed commercial paper market, repo lending, the market for the mortgage-backed securities, currency swaps. As Fed economists observed, this was no longer conventional monetary policy in which the Fed manipulated interest rates to affect market behavior. Instead, the "Federal Reserve's balance sheet expansion"

was an "emergency replacement of lost private sector balance sheet capacity by the public sector."[12] The Fed was inserting itself into the very mechanisms of the market-based banking model. The relationship between the state, as represented by the central bank, and the financial markets was nakedly revealed. The Fed was not just any branch of government. It was the bankers' bank, and as the crisis intensified, the money market reorganized itself accordingly, taking on the shape of spokes with the Fed as the hub.

The scale of the Fed's liquidity actions was so large and varied that it poses problems of accounting. How should one measure the Fed's huge programs? As a stock at the point of maximum exposure? As a rate of flow over a given period during the crisis? Or should one simply compile the sum total of all lending from the beginning to the end of the crisis? The first measure will tend to minimize the image of intervention. The last measure will yield the largest figure. Each measure has its uses.[13] Thanks to records extracted from the Fed by legal action, we can compile all three numbers.[14]

The point where distressed banks normally accessed central bank assistance was the discount window. At the discount window, the central bank bought and sold securities for cash. As a classic sign of stress, it was generally reserved for banks in dire need of emergency liquidity. The list of the largest customers at the discount window in 2008 included all the most prominent American casualties of the crisis—AIG, Lehman, Countrywide, Merrill Lynch, Citigroup. If anything, the stigma of using the discount window was less severe for non-American banks. So alongside the American strugglers, the Fed's accounts also prominently featured two of the European basket cases: Franco-Belgian bank Dexia and the ill-fated Irish branch of Hypo Real Estate, Depfa.[15]

As the ABCP market shut down in the autumn of 2007, the Fed realized that it needed to add new facilities. The first was the Term Auction Facility (TAF), which provided banks with access to short-term funds they could no longer acquire on the ABCP markets. Avoiding stigma was a key concern. A wide range of collateral, including ABS and CDO, were accepted, and the more banks participated, the more popular TAF became. Between December 2007 and March 2010 TAF expanded on a gigantic scale. The maximum outstanding balance in the spring of 2009 was almost $500 billion. If TAF loans of varying duration are converted to a common twenty-eight-day basis,

the total sum loaned came to a staggering $6.18 trillion in twenty-eight-day loans. Hundreds of smaller American banks took advantage of TAF, but the biggest beneficiaries were the giant American and European banks with Bank of America, Barclays, Wells Fargo and the Bank of Scotland heading the list. Among the large borrowers the foreign share was well over 50 percent.[16]

Following the Bear Stearns crisis, it was not just ABCP but the collateralized repo markets that shut down. In the summer of 2008 the Fed, therefore, stepped into the breach, setting itself up as a repo dealer of last resort, offering twenty-eight-day repo against prime collateral (single-tranche open market operations, or ST OMO). A total of $855 billion were lent by December 2008, of which over 70 percent was taken by foreign banks, with five European banks dominating the entire program. Just one bank, the Swiss giant Credit Suisse, was the recipient of 30 percent of the liquidity the Fed provided.

Because the collateral that was preferred by triparty repo markets was Treasurys, in the spring of 2008 the Fed instituted another program, the Term Securities Lending Facility, under which it lent out top-rated US Treasurys on twenty-eight-day terms in exchange for a variety of mortgage-backed securities, including private label. In total through this mechanism, $2 trillion in superior collateral was flushed into the system, with the program reaching its peak in the wake of Lehman in September and October 2008. Of the collateral provided by the Term Securities Lending Facility, 51 percent was lent to non-American banks, with RBS, Deutsche and Credit Suisse alone taking up more than $800 billion.

The largest backstop for the repo market that the Fed operated during the crisis was the Primary Dealer Credit Facility (PDCF).[17] It was introduced after the run on Bear Stearns under the emergency 13(3) powers of the Fed. The PDCF offered the key operators in the repo market discreet and unlimited access to overnight Fed liquidity in exchange for a wide range of collateral. Not surprisingly, the dealers took ample advantage. Total lending under PDCF came to $8.951 trillion. This was a huge amount, but the loans were made overnight and they should be seen in relation to the daily collateral posting in repo markets that peaked at $4.5 trillion in March 2008. The maximum amount outstanding on the PDCF was on

September 26, 2008, at $146.57 billion. PDCF had the distinction of being the only large Fed liquidity program to have supported predominantly American banks. Merrill Lynch, Citigroup, Morgan Stanley and Bank of America were the heaviest users. But appearances were to a degree deceiving because the Fed allowed the London-based subsidiaries of Goldman Sachs, Morgan Stanley, Merrill Lynch and Citigroup to take advantage of the program. The Fed was thus remotely backstopping the City of London repo market.

When the crisis in the money market funds knocked the last remaining support out from under the commercial paper market, the Fed took the unprecedented decision not just to backstop banks and the mutual funds but to enter the lending business directly. It established its own SPV, the Commercial Paper Funding Facility, to buy top-quality short-term commercial paper. In total it provided $737 billion in funding through this facility, with a peak outstanding in January 2009 of $348 billion. The largest user of the system was the troubled Swiss giant UBS, which soaked up 10 percent of the Fed's funds. Another 7.3 percent went into Dexia, and 5 per cent each into Fortis and RBS. Some of the most severely stressed European banks received 27 percent of the entire program. In total, the European share cannot have been much less than 40 percent.

Alongside the mortgage market, the broader market for asset-backed securities had frozen up. To reenergize lending, on November 25, 2008, the Fed introduced the Term Asset-Backed Securities Loan Facility, which became the vehicle for the most mixed bag of lending sponsored by the Fed and the Treasury. It offered five-year nonrecourse loans to a select group of borrowers collateralized through the purchase of highly rated securitizations of consumer credit, such as auto loans, student loans, credit card loans and lending to small businesses for equipment and building construction. It was never the Fed's largest program. Total lending came to $71.09 billion. But the program accommodated some of the most adventurous support actions undertaken by the Fed. The firms taking advantage were exclusively American, with Morgan Stanley, PIMCO and CalPERS in the lead.

Finally, in early 2009, the Fed began to move from emergency liquidity

provision to what would subsequently become known as QE1—the buying up and holding on the Fed balance sheet of large quantities of mortgage-backed securities. For a central bank, buying securities was a conventional mechanism of monetary policy. But it would now be done on a far larger scale than ever before and with a wider array of assets. On top of the conventional purchase of Treasury securities, the Fed bought $1.85 trillion in GSE-backed mortgage-backed securities by July 2010. The busiest week of purchases was the third week of April 2009, and holdings (net of sales) peaked in June 2010 at $1.129 trillion. Crucially, what the Fed was doing was not just pumping liquidity into the system. It was also absorbing onto its balance sheet the maturity mismatch, which had done such damage in markets like ABCP. The Fed took the long-term asset in exchange for immediate liquidity.

Quantitative easing, or QE, is generally thought of as the quintessential "American" policy, the symbol of the Fed's adventurousness. It would earn Bernanke regular scolding by conservative policy makers in Europe. But after what we have already said, it will come as no surprise that 52 percent of the mortgage-backed securities sold to the Fed under QE were sold by foreign banks, with Europeans far in the lead. Deutsche Bank and Credit Suisse were the two largest sellers, outdoing all their American rivals by a healthy margin. Barclays, UBS and Paribas came in eighth, ninth and tenth. Having kept open the basic institutions of transatlantic shadow banking during the most acute phase of the crisis in 2008, the Fed now worked hand in glove with the European megabanks to unwind the transatlantic balance sheet.

III

Not everyone in the network of Atlantic finance could take advantage of the facilities that the Fed offered to the top tier of international banks in New York. Nor did everyone have the kind of collateral the Fed demanded. To have lent to the most fragile European banks without adequate collateral would have exposed the Fed to serious risk. But to deny the weakest banks liquidity assistance was to court disaster. So from 2007 the Fed repurposed

an instrument that was first developed in the age of Bretton Woods. To manage the fixed currency system in the 1960s the central banks had developed a system of so-called currency swap lines that allowed the Fed to lend dollars to the Bank of England against a reverse deposit of sterling in the accounts of the Fed.[18] Having gone out of use in the 1970s, the swap lines had been briefly revived in 2001 to deal with the aftermath of 9/11. In 2007 faced with the implosion of the transatlantic banking system, they were repurposed and expanded on a gigantic scale to meet the funding needs not of sovereign states but of Europe's megabanks. As Geithner explained to his Fed colleagues:

"We have a bunch of U.S. affiliates of some of the weakest European institutions that have faced very substantial dollar funding needs and have come to us and asked for substantial ongoing access to liquidity. When they have a substantial amount of . . . collateral with substantial market value relative to the needs, we have been comfortable meeting those needs [above all through the TAF program discussed above]. When their needs have substantially exceeded or might potentially exceed the market value of their eligible collateral, then we have talked to the home central bank. We have said that, in effect, if you want us to be able to meet those needs and they have collateral in your market that is substantial relative to those needs, then the better way for us to do this is for the home country central bank to meet their dollar liquidity needs against the collateral there . . . and we provide the dollar's' [sic] worth of guarantees from the central bank."[19]

Having reached the limit of the dollars it could provide directly to Europe's tottering banks, the Fed now lent to the ECB, the Bank of England, the National Bank of Switzerland and the central banks of Scandinavia. They then channeled the precious dollar liquidity to the European megabanks at one remove.[20] The Fed and the central banks it was supporting agreed on an exchange rate. The European central bank needing the dollars deposited the required amount of local currency in an account in the name of the Fed. The Fed credited the European central bank with the equivalent amount in dollars. The two sides agreed to reverse the trade at a future date at the agreed exchange rate. The terms were spelled out with a minimum of fuss in a contract running to no more than seven pages.[21] The Fed received an interest premium that ensured that the swap lines would be used only if

market funding was not available. The European central banks passed that cost on to the banks that were the ultimate recipients of the dollars.

The initiative for the swap line program came from the Fed. In the aftermath of the disastrous Paribas announcement in August 2007, the Fed was seeing regular early-morning spikes in European dollar funding costs that were causing disruption when the US markets opened in the middle of the European trading day. Tellingly, the ECB's initial reaction was skeptical. As one American journalist put it, the Fed's proposal "ran up against a strong effort," on the part of the ECB, "to pin the Great Panic on the United States." The ECB's reply to the Fed was blunt: "[I]t's a dollar problem. It's your problem."[22] As Bernanke was later to remark, the ECB "had some difficulty coming to the realization that Europe would be under a great deal of stress and was not going to be decoupled from the United States."[23] With regard to the swap lines, that attitude did not last much beyond 2007. The first agreements were reached with the ECB and the Swiss National Bank in December 2007.[24] As the crisis became critical in September 2008, the swap facilities were rapidly expanded to a total capacity of $620 billion. On October 13, 2008, as the Europeans rolled out their guarantee programs and Paulson, Bernanke and Geithner persuaded America's bankers to take their dose of TARP capital, even that cap was lifted. Four central banks—the ECB, the Bank of England, the Bank of Japan and the Swiss National Bank—were given unlimited access to dollars.

The swap lines helped to reassure markets. But they also threw a shadow of doubt over those central banks that had not been so favored. The shutdown in the money market was affecting the entire financial system. Where were major emerging market central banks to get their dollars from? For a nation like South Korea to have approached the IMF was out of the question given live memories of the Asian financial crisis of 1997–1998.[25] So on October 29 the Fed's favor was extended to four key emerging market central banks: Brazil, Korea, Mexico and Singapore.[26] All told, fourteen central banks would be included in the program.[27]

The total amount outstanding on the network of dollar swap lines reached its peak in December 2008 at $580 billion. Briefly, the swaps touched 35 percent of the Fed's balance sheet. But even these gigantic figures do not do justice to the scale of the program. The essence of the swap line was to

provide easy access to short-term dollar funding. With the New York Fed and its counterparts across the world working on a hectic schedule, new dollar funding was flushed into the system on a daily basis. In a single week in late October 2008, as dollars previously sourced from American money markets hemorrhaged out of the global banking system, the Fed lent $850 billion through the swap lines. It was this circulation of funds that allowed the Bank of England, the ECB and the Swiss National Bank to meet huge demands for dollars without running down their exchange reserves to even more critical levels. But for the swap facilities, between September 2008 and May 2009, monthly demand for dollars at the auctions organized by the ECB would have wiped out its reserves several times over.

The absence of a euro-dollar or a sterling-dollar currency crisis was one of the remarkable features of 2008. It was no accident. It was the swap lines

Running Low: Eurosystem Foreign Exchange Reserves and Foreign Currency Provided to Commercial Banks

	US dollars provided to commercial banks by the ECB ($ billions)	Swiss francs provided at auctions reported by the ECB ($ billions equivalent)	Eurosystem foreign exchange reserves ($ billions)
End of			
Sep '08	150.7	0	210.3
Oct '08	271.2	17.4	210.2
Nov '08	244.0	19.2	204.2
Dec '08	265.7	25.8	202.0
Jan '09	187.3	27.8	191.1
Feb '09	144.5	32.5	186.4
Mar '09	165.7	33.1	189.2
Apr '09	130.1	33.0	187.9
May '09	99.7	35.4	191.9
Jun '09	59.9	29.9	192.5
Jul '09	48.3	18.6	197.9
Aug '09	46.1	15.4	197.8
Sep '09	43.7	10.1	195.0

Source: William A. Allen and Richhild Moessner, "Central Bank Co-operation and International Liquidity in the Financial Crisis of 2008–9," BIS Working Paper 310 (May 2010), table 12.2.

that did the trick. What the Fed had done for money markets, the central banks now did for the global provision of dollar bank funding. They absorbed the currency mismatch of the European bank balance sheets directly onto their own accounts. Compensating public action ensured that private imbalances did not spill over into a general crisis.

The scale of the compensating credit flow was staggering. By September 2011 total lending (and repayment) under the terms of the swap facility came to $10 trillion at varying lengths of maturity. Standardized to a twenty-eight-day term, the sum was equivalent to $4.45 trillion in one-month loans. On either measure, by far the largest beneficiary of the swap lines was the ECB. Every cent of this staggering flow of funds was repaid in full. Indeed, the Fed made profits of c. $4 billion on its swap lending in 2008–2009. But this sober accounting understates the drama of this innovation. Responding to the crisis in an improvised fashion, the Fed had reaffirmed the role of the dollar as the world's reserve currency and established America's central bank as the indispensable central node in the dollar network. Given the even vaster volume of daily transactions in global

The Fed as Global Lender of Last Resort: Central Bank Liquidity Swap Lines, December 2007 to August 2010 (in $ billions)

	Raw swap amount	Standardized to 28-day swap
ECB	8,011	2,527
Bank of Japan	387	727
Bank of England	919	311
Swiss National Bank	466	244
Sveriges Riksbank	67	202
Bank of Korea	41	124
Reserve Bank of Australia	53	122
Danmarks Nationalbank	73	95
Norges Bank	30	68
Bank of Mexico	10	30
Total	**10,057**	**4,450**

Source: Federal Reserve.

financial markets, it is not the sheer size of the effort that mattered. The Fed's programs were decisive because they assured the key players in the global system—both central banks and large multinational banks—that if private funding were to become unexpectedly difficult, there was one actor in the system that would cover marginal imbalances with an unlimited supply of dollar liquidity. That precisely was the role of the global lender of last resort.

IV

Prior to the crisis, the transatlantic offshore dollar system had lacked a manifest center of leadership. Indeed, it had developed "offshore" so as to avoid national regulation and control. After 2008 it was openly organized around the Fed and its liquidity provision. "In a way," one European central banker remarked, "we became the thirteenth Federal Reserve district."[28] But if that was the case, the American public was not informed about the extension of their country's monetary territory. Not the least remarkable thing about the Fed's crisis response was its politics, or rather the lack of explicit political legitimation. The emergency liquidity provision to the international economy by the Fed between 2007 and 2009 was shrouded in as much obscurity as possible. In July 2009, when Bernanke was challenged by campaigning Democratic congressman Alan Grayson of Florida to explain "who got" the swap line money, the chairman of the Fed could reply "I don't know."[29] The ultimate destination of the trillions of dollars that had flushed back and forth between the central banks of the global system was not under direct American oversight. There was little doubt, of course, that the Swiss National Bank channeled the dollars it received from the Fed to its ailing giants, UBS and Credit Suisse.[30] But from the point of view of the Fed, it was far better that the swap be done with a central bank than with the fragile banks themselves.

As Neil Irwin describes it, "[T]he scale of lending to foreign banks . . . was a closely guarded secret even by standards of the always secretive Fed. . . . During the panic, this information was so closely held—and had it been known publically, so potentially explosive—that only two people at

Backing the Banks: Fed Liquidity Facilities and Their Users

	Commercial paper funding facility 3 month ABCP/CP	Term auction facility $ billions per month	Single tranche open market operations $ billions per month	Term securities lending facility $ billions per month	Primary dealer credit facility overnight
Bank of America	15	487	40	87	716
Citigroup	33	195	8	297	1,757
Citigroup (London)					263
Wells Fargo		304			
Wachovia		224			
JPMorgan Chase		171	3	60	
State Street		79			
Bank of NY Mellon		0			
Goldman			53	186	434
Goldman (London)					156
Lehman			31	87	83
Merrill Lynch			12	154	1,487
Merrill Lynch (London)					594
Morgan Stanley	4		41	101	1,364
Morgan Stanley (London)				548	
Bear Stearns				2	960
Barclays	39	313	67	159	410
RBS	39	153	70	250	
HBOS		262	66		
Credit Suisse		0	259	225	
UBS	72	94	57	109	35
Deutsche Bank		115	101	239	
Commerzbank	4	119			
Dresdner	9	171	5		
Depfa		52			
BNP		63	97	35	66
Société Générale		217			
Dexia	54	132			
Fortis	39	108			
Total	**737**	**6,180**	**910**	**2,006**	**8,951**
Total large	**253**	**3,259**	**910**	**2,006**	
Large non-American	**201**	**1,799**	**656**	**1,017**	**2,072**
% non-American	**79**	**55**	**72**	**51**	**23**

Source: Federal Reserve and my own calculations.

each of the dozen reserve banks were allowed access to it."[31] The Fed used every legal means at its disposal to prevent detailed information about its support programs to both domestic and foreign banks from leaking to the general public. The vociferous libertarian and gold standard advocate Congressman Ron Paul ran a vigorous campaign for Fed transparency, which Bernanke did his best to ward off. Only in June 2009 did the Fed begin publishing regular reports on the uptake of swap lines. The fuller records of the Fed's emergency programs, on which this chapter is based, were not opened to the public until December 2010 and March 2011. They were produced as a result of the Dodd-Frank legislation of 2010 and a Freedom of Information suit brought by the Bloomberg news organization and contested by the Fed and the New York Clearing House Association, a banking lobby group, all the way to the Supreme Court.[32] In defense of its secrecy, the Fed argued that revealing the information demanded by Bloomberg would jeopardize its efforts to calm financial markets, because full disclosure would reveal which banks were most in need of its liquidity assistance. The courts ruled in favor of Bloomberg and the Fed grudgingly complied. The forced disclosure offered an unprecedented glimpse into the operations of the world's key central bank at a moment of maximum stress. The data are a quantified ultrasound of the convulsions of the Atlantic financial system. No such records are available for either the ECB or the Bank of England. Beyond the generalities of "systemic stress and stability," they reveal the significance of individual banks, the extent of the pressure that they were under and the scale of the relief the Fed provided.

At the top of the Fed's list were Citigroup and Bank of America and the two highly stressed US investment banks, Merrill Lynch and Morgan Stanley, with their respective London operations. Then came a comprehensive list of the big European and American players in the global dollar banking business. Of the liquidity on one-month or three-month terms that the Fed provided to big banks, European banks took the majority. European banks and the London operations of the major US investment banks accounted for 23 percent even of the overnight primary dealer credit facility. When this support is added to the gigantic swap line facilities provided for the European central banks, the conclusion is inescapable. What the Fed was struggling to contain in 2008 were not two separate American and European

crises but one gigantic storm in the dollar-based North Atlantic financial system.

These data are explosive not only in revealing what was required by the Fed to keep a globalized financial system on the rails. They are remarkable also for the light that they shed on the politics of the bailouts in Europe. In Europe, the bullish CEOs of Deutsche Bank and Barclays claimed exceptional status because they avoided taking aid from their national governments. What the Fed data reveal is the hollowness of those boasts. The banks might have avoided state-sponsored recapitalization, but every major bank in the entire world was taking liquidity assistance on a grand scale from its local central bank, and either directly or indirectly by way of the swap lines from the Fed. Using the Fed's records we can track the liquidity support provided to a bank like Barclays on a daily basis, revealing a first hump of Fed borrowing during the Bear Stearns crisis and a second in the aftermath of Lehman.

The anatomy of the Fed's hidden liquidity support measures also casts in a rather different light the widespread discussion in 2008 about the future of the dollar system. Not surprisingly, in 2008 the United States faced a global chorus of criticism. Advocates of reform argued that at the root of global financial instability was the overreliance on the dollar as a reserve currency. This conferred on America an exorbitant privilege, which it exploited irresponsibly, running up deficits and borrowing abroad. In 2009 the head of China's central bank and a special commission of the United Nations would advance proposals for a new global currency system.[33] The Russians liked the idea, and so too did the West Europeans.[34] In September, Peer Steinbrück told journalists, "When we look back 10 years from now, we will see 2008 as a fundamental rupture. I am not saying the dollar will lose its reserve currency status, but it will become relative."[35] Two months later, President Sarkozy declared ahead of the G20 summit, "I am leaving tomorrow for Washington to explain that the dollar—which after the Second World War under Bretton Woods was the only currency in the world—can no longer claim to be the only currency in the world. What was true in 1945 cannot be true today."[36]

Clearly, the dollar-based financial system had experienced an existential crisis. For avowed skeptics and critics of American power it was an

unmissable opportunity to score points against Anglo-Saxon finance. But given the extraordinarily heavy dependence of both individual banks, such as Deutsche and Paribas, on Fed support and the huge swap line facility provided to the ECB, it is hard to see how either Steinbrück or Sarkozy could have been more out of touch with reality. By the early twenty-first century, the dollar's dominance did not rest on the Bretton Woods Agreement of 1944 or the institutions, like the IMF, that issued from it. The foundation of the global dollar was the private banking and financial market network, materialized in the Wall Street–City of London nexus. This was a cocreation of American and European finance, deliberately erected beyond state control. What happened in the fall of 2008 was not the relativization of the dollar, but the reverse, a dramatic reassertion of the pivotal role of America's central bank. Far from withering away, the Fed's response gave an entirely new dimension to the global dollar.

Steinbrück and Sarkozy may perhaps be forgiven for failing to recognize the significance of the moment, because the Fed had acted without fanfare and without seeking public legitimacy either at home or abroad. The sporadic global debate about alternatives to the dollar was the price that the Fed paid for keeping its stabilization campaign below the radar. On Capitol Hill, while controversy swirled around TARP, there was silence about the Fed's gigantic global liquidity effort. As one senior New York Fed official remarked, it was as if a "guardian angel was watching over us."[37] If some members of Congress understood what was going on, they thought better of discussing the Fed's actions openly. The reality of global financial policy disappeared in a "spiral of silence," in which it suited both the Fed and its collaborators to bury the reality of massive and explicitly hierarchical interdependence.

Chapter 9

EUROPE'S FORGOTTEN CRISIS: EASTERN EUROPE

By October 2008 the Fed's swap line facilities defined a relationship of dependence and interdependence between the US central bank and an exclusive club of privileged central bank counterparties. But that posed a question. Who was in and who was out? What were the criteria of membership in the swap line club?[1] On October 28, 2008, Nathan Sheets, the director of the Division of International Finance at the Fed, set out a short list of three criteria.[2] The recipients of swap lines must be:

"1. Of significant economic and financial mass so that there can be spill-over to the US.

2. Well-managed with 'prudent' policies so that the problems they have encountered are clearly the result of contagion from US and 'other advanced economies' and therefore warrant US assistance.

3. The problem faced by local banks should be one of dollar funding stress so that swap lines would actually make a difference."

Ultimately, the Fed had to justify its measures in terms of benefits to the US economy. There were economies that were too small to warrant action. There were countries that were experiencing stress as a result of a collapse of trade or commodity prices that could not be helped by swap lines. But it was point 2, with its stress on "prudent policy," that offered the

scope for political discrimination. What was a prudent policy was very much in the eye of the beholder. As two US analysts attached to the National Intelligence Council remarked at the end of 2009: "Artificial divisions between 'economic' and 'foreign' policy present a false dichotomy. To whom one extends swap lines" is as much a "foreign policy as economic decisions."[3] The Fed was well aware that with the swap lines it was treading onto the terrain of geopolitics. Each of the fourteen European, Latin American and Asian central banks included in the swap network was approved by the Treasury and the State Department. They were clearly safe bets. The Fed did everything it could to dissuade further applications. Nevertheless, two further countries did apply and were denied. Their identities are shrouded in secrecy. But there were clearly some countries that were never going to make it onto the Fed's list, no matter how large or hard hit by the crisis they were.

I

On November 14, 2008, Sarkozy hosted President Medvedev of Russia, who was en route to the first leader-level G20 summit in Washington. Sarkozy and Medvedev exchanged congratulations over the peace settlement that Sarkozy had brokered in Georgia in August. But this was not the only topic of Franco-Russian backslapping. Sarkozy also expressed his agreement with recent initiatives from Moscow on the currency question.[4] Over the summer, with the price of oil at all-time highs, Medvedev had been pushing for a diversification of reserve currencies and a greater use of the ruble. Days before arriving in France, Medvedev had given a speech to the Russian parliament in which he drew parallels between the crisis in Georgia and the global financial debacle. They were "two very different problems," as Medvedev told the Federal Assembly in November 2008, but they had "common features" and a "common origin": the presumption of an American government that "refuse[d] to accept criticism and prefer[red] unilateral decisions."[5] This played well with the nationalist gallery in Russia, but there was not much dissent from the European side either. At their summit in Nice, Medvedev noted that on currency issues "the Russian and European positions

were practically the same." What he did not mention was that whereas France's banks could count on limitless dollar liquidity from the Fed, the Russians were on their own.

If Moscow's increasing assertiveness had been buoyed by oil prices surging to $145 per barrel, the crisis was a severe setback. By the end of 2008 oil prices had plunged, reaching their nadir at $34 on December 21. With natural resource rents accounting for 20 percent of Russian GDP, the impact of the commodity price crash was devastating. Tax revenue per metric ton of oil fell by 80 percent.[6] But the Russian state had the resources to cope. Unlike in 1998, by 2008 Moscow had accumulated enough financial reserves to withstand the pressure of the global crisis. At their peak, Russia's foreign currency holdings were estimated at $600 billion. It was not the state but Russia's globalized business sector that was in trouble.

As oil prices plunged, so did the Russian stock market. By September 15 the Russian market was already 54 percent off its peak in May 2008. In the days after Lehman, trading was so jumpy that Moscow regulators took the

Russian Stock Market and Oil Prices, 2008

Source: World Bank in Russia, *Russian Economic Report* 17 (November 2008), figure 2.1. Data: RTS, Thomson Datastream.

decision to suspend trading. When the markets reopened on September 19, jitters continued, with October 6 seeing a single-day fall of 18 percent.[7] According to one widely quoted estimate, Russia's oligarchs saw their combined wealth slashed from $520 billion at the beginning of 2008 to a mere $148 billion by early 2009.[8] What was spooking investors, apart from oil, was the likely impact of a sharp ruble devaluation on Russian balance sheets. It was the private, not the public, sector that was in danger.

By the third quarter of 2008, Russia's banks, raw material producers and industrial conglomerates had run up external debts of $540 billion, half owed by Russian industrial corporations and the rest by banks. This debt mountain matched Russia's official reserves and was roughly equivalent to Lehman's balance sheet. A substantial fraction was short-term debt. Having adopted the market-based banking model, Russia's banks were particularly at risk, needing to refinance as much as $72 billion due by the end of 2008.[9] Apart from the banks, the list of stressed dollar borrowers included all the major Russian oligopolies: Gazprom ($55 billion), Rosneft ($23 billion), Rusal ($11.2 billion), TNK-BP ($7.5 billion), Evraz ($6.4 billion), Norilsk ($6.3 billion) and Lukoil ($6 billion). Collapsing commodity prices slashed their revenues and a slide in the ruble would put even heavier pressure on those that billed in local currency rather than dollars—a major issue for Gazprom, Russia's largest gas supplier.

As in the West, the crisis and the terms of the bailout opened the question of the balance of power. To some it seemed that the Kremlin was bent only on saving the skins of its cronies at the expense of the Russian taxpayer.[10] On this reading, the Russian story was an even more corrupt and brutal version of the drama played out in America.[11] Like the barons of Wall Street, Russia's oligarchs needed state aid and the regime came to their rescue. It is certainly true that Russia avoided dramatic bankruptcies, and considerable state resources were deployed to make sure of that. But putting events in Russia side by side with those in the United States or Europe, one is struck less by the self-dealing of Russian crisis management than by the frankness with which the question of power was ventilated in Russia and the obvious willingness of President Medvedev and Prime Minister Putin to use the occasion to shift the balance in their favor. Since the

breakup of oil conglomerate Yukos in 2003, none of the oligarchs had dared to challenge the Kremlin. Now Medvedev and Putin were turning the screw. They offered financial protection, but they exacted a price.

The cornerstone of the Kremlin's crisis-fighting strategy was to prevent a death spiral of devaluation and bankruptcy. In the first phase of the crisis, the central bank deployed its ample foreign currency reserves to stem the fall in the ruble. As a result, as oil prices plunged by 64 percent between October and December 2008, the ruble lost only 6 percent against the dollar.[12] Only in January did Moscow let the ruble go, allowing it to devalue by 34 percent before stabilizing in February. Like any successful rearguard action, it came at a price. The central bank burned $212 billion of its reserves, 35 percent of the total, to slow the slide. But by so doing it bought time, allowing dollar-exposed borrowers to pull in their horns and giving the state some time to launch its own response.[13]

A key element of this program was a demand from the Kremlin that the oligarchs sink a large part of their fortunes into stabilizing the stock market. There were rumors of an "all-night mandatory meeting held in the Kremlin" on September 16, the day of the AIG rescue, at which "oligarchs were ordered to plunge cash into their own faltering stocks, buy collapsing financial institutions directly, or simply fork over the cash and/or shares."[14] Following this "bail-in" of the oligarchs, the government targeted takeovers and bailouts at the smallest and weakest Russian banks. Coordination was provided by state-owned Vneshekonombank (VEB), where Putin, as Russian prime minister, served as chairman of the board. Five billion dollars was used to take over Sviaz Bank, Globex bank and Sobinbank. Then the deposit insurance fund was recapitalized and the insurance limit raised to $28,000. A $50 billion central bank facility put VEB bank in a position to act as the backstop, with a further $35.4 billion in subordinated debt available at tough rates for troubled oligarch enterprises. The loans would be repayable within a year and otherwise convertible into controlling shares.[15] It was not a government takeover, but a conditional threat and a stark demonstration of where power lay.

VEB pumped $4.5 billion into Rusal, the aluminum company majority owned by Oleg Deripaska, to allow it to unwind foreign financing, which it had used to buy a 25 percent stake in mining giant Norilsk Nickel. VEB also

put $2 billion into Mikhail Fridman's Alfa Group to help it to pay off Deutsche Bank and rescue Alfa's large stake in Russia's number two mobile phone firm, VimpelCom, which might otherwise have been forfeited as collateral. As investment plunged and domestic economic activity began to spiral downward, unemployment rates doubled. This was particularly worrying in the so-called monotowns—the urban legacy of Stalinist industrialization.[16] On October 16, 2008, Igor Sechin, Putin's right hand, convened an industrywide brainstorming session on the car industry at Togliatti, the company town of AvtoVAZ, the bankrupt inheritor of the Soviet car industry. He announced an immediate $1 billion loan for AvtoVAZ from VEB that would keep the factory and its staff of 100,000 working.[17] By the end of the crisis, $1.7 billion would be pumped into the Russian auto bailout.

In the wake of the oil price shock, the Russian federal budget was reset on the assumption of an average oil price of $41 per barrel by contrast with the June 2008 budget, which had assumed $95 per barrel. With tax revenues plunging, Putin, as prime minister, took credit for a large fiscal stimulus. A quarter of the government's 9.7 trillion ruble budget was dedicated to crisis spending on work creation, industrial subsidies and tax cuts. Relative to the size of its economy, commonly compared with that of Spain and roughly comparable to that of Texas, the Russian crisis response was one of the largest in the world, dwarfing those undertaken by West European governments.[18] It was heavily skewed toward the largest, best-connected corporations that were included in a list of 295 nationally important corporations and 1,148 regionally important firms. It was a top-down, corporatist stimulus, and Moscow made clear that it expected the oligarchs to reciprocate. Indeed, it was unafraid to call them out by name. On one notable occasion, Putin singled out four of them as follows: "Vladimir Potanin (Interros Holding), Leonid Lebedev (Sintez Group), Mikhail Prokhorov (Onexim Group), and Viktor Vekselberg (Renova Group) . . . I have known all of you for many years; in essence, we have been working jointly. Let me repeat that during the difficult conditions of the crisis we have made every effort to support you in the various directions of your business. The crisis is waning. It's not yet over, but it's on its way." Now Putin expected them to make good on their commitments. "We agreed to meet you half-way in this area as well. We postponed the deadlines for investments. There will be no more

such adjustments of schedules. Please focus your utmost attention on meeting your commitments."[19] What would happen if an oligarch failed in his responsibilities was demonstrated in June 2009 when Putin descended on Pikalevo, a small town south of St. Petersburg dominated by the metallurgical empire of Oleg Deripaska. Deripaska, who had once been listed as the richest man in Russia, with a fortune estimated at $28 billion, had seen it reduced to $3.5 billion. But that was no excuse for not paying wages.[20] Indignant workers were blockading the Moscow highway, causing a 250-mile traffic jam. In front of the TV cameras Putin upbraided Deripaska. Tossing him a pen, the premier demanded that the oligarch sign the paychecks there and then. It was economic management by personal intimidation of the telegenic tub-thumping variety.[21] The message was clear. Ten years on from the humiliation of 1998, there were men in charge who would see to it that things "got done."

In its way, it was effective. It demonstrated leadership. It humbled the oligarchs. It rallied Russian social interests around the state that provided for them. It kept Prime Minister Putin in the limelight. But was it a long-term strategy for growth? Liberal economists were skeptical. So too was Medvedev, who had succeeded Putin as president in 2008. Even before the crisis, the expert advisers that Medvedev cultivated in his personal entourage had been calling for a new course.[22] In the wake of the crisis their message was even louder. What had made Russia so vulnerable in 2008 was its lopsided integration into the world economy: on the one hand, its excessive reliance on oil and gas; on the other hand, the corrupt culture of capital flight, in which Russian oligarchs sluiced money in and out of the country through the off-shore banking system. How else could one account for the bizarre anomaly that made tiny Cyprus into one of Russia's main sources of foreign investment? What Russia needed was modernization. As Medvedev remarked on September 10, 2009: "Can a primitive economy based on raw materials and economic corruption lead us into the future?"[23] Two-fisted crisis fighting was not enough. A mere recovery from the shock of 2008 would lead "nowhere. We need to get out of the crisis by reforming our own economy."[24] What Russia needed was economic transformation, and for that it needed not less but more interaction with the world economy, and above all with its technological leaders. And this had wider implications.

After the shocking confrontation with the West in August 2008, Moscow needed to change course. With the crushing of Georgia, the Kremlin had made its point. In the future, Medvedev asserted, the success or failure of Russian foreign policy should be judged by a single criterion: "whether it contributes to improving living standards in our country." Rather than "puffing out its cheeks" to threaten others, Russia should concentrate on attracting foreign technology and capital.[25] It was a message of modernization and partnership that was eagerly taken up both in European capitals and by the new administration in Washington.

II

It might be tempting to conclude that by taming Russia, the effect of the crisis was to calm international relations. And in the short run this was surely true. But in the international sphere, power is judged by relative standards. And if Russia was hard hit by the 2008 crisis, the impact on Eastern Europe was even worse. The shock to the most highly leveraged transition states of the former Communist bloc was staggering. If we compare the forecasts for 2010 made in October 2007 with the expected outturn two years later, we see how radically the crisis changed the outlook for the worst-hit countries in the region.

The most extreme case was Latvia. One year into the crisis, in October 2009, the IMF's forecast for Latvia's GDP in 2010 was 39 percent lower than it had been in October 2007. Over the same two-year period, Estonia's and Lithuania's GDP expectations were revised downward by a whopping one-third. Slovenia, the Czech Republic, Slovakia, Hungary, Bulgaria and Romania all experienced downward shocks of between 15 and 18 percent, more than twice that suffered by the United States. In the adjoining post-Soviet Commonwealth of Independent States (CIS), the downward revision of growth expectations ranged from 18 percent for Russia to 32 percent for Armenia. The pattern was not uniform. Poland, notably, escaped largely unscathed.[26] But all the most severe casualties of the 2008–2009 crisis are to be found among the transition economies of the former Eastern bloc.

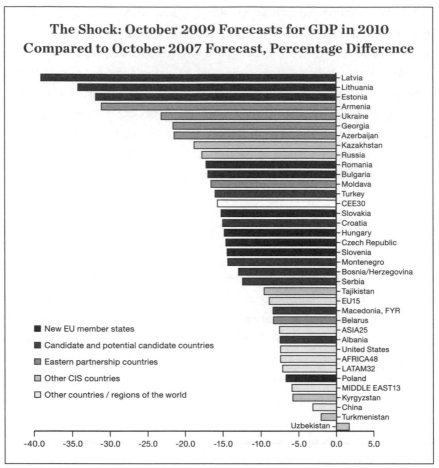

The Shock: October 2009 Forecasts for GDP in 2010 Compared to October 2007 Forecast, Percentage Difference

Source: Zsolt Darvas, "The EU's Role in Supporting Crisis-Hit Countries in Central and Eastern Europe," Bruegel Policy Contribution 2009/17 (December 2009), figure 1.

Individually, the East European states are not big economies. But taken together they formed a substantial unit comparable in economic heft to France or the state of California. They were the pride of Europe's transformation process, and the battleground in the new confrontation with Russia that had taken shape between 2007 and 2008. They were eager disciples of market liberalization and financial globalization. That put them especially at risk as global financial markets collapsed. The situation was made even worse, however, by the source of the capital that fueled their growth: the overleveraged banks of Western Europe. In total, the West European banks and their local branches had $1.3 trillion at stake in emerging Europe, $1.08

trillion excluding Russia.[27] As the balance sheets of the European banks were being crushed on the other side of the Atlantic, the risk was that they would dramatically curtail their operations in Eastern Europe.

Before the crisis struck it was normal to see an average of $50 billion flowing into the emerging markets of Eastern Europe and the post-Soviet world every quarter. In the last quarter of 2008 that suddenly reversed, with an outflow of $100 billion and a further $50 billion in the first quarter of 2009.[28] The pyramid of credit established over the previous fifteen years was shaking. In a "natural" process of adjustment, the floating currencies of Eastern Europe plunged. The result was a catastrophic increase in the local currency cost of servicing international loans.[29] In Bulgaria, Romania, Hungary and Lithuania, foreign loans made up more than half of all credit. As the forint plunged, in a matter of weeks Hungarian families saw their mortgage and car loan bills surge by 20 percent. The worst affected were the Hungarian families whose debts were denominated in Japanese yen. They faced a 40 percent increase in their debt burden as the yen soared.[30]

Whereas Russia had reacted to its humiliation in the 1990s by accumulating a substantial currency reserve, the East European states had no such defense. For them security lay in integration with the West, or at least so they imagined. With the Fed having used swap lines to stabilize a core group of economies in which American interests were undeniable, one might have expected the ECB to extend similar support to the East European neighbors of the eurozone. Certainly this was the expectation of the Fed. If one applied the three criteria set out by Nathan Sheets to Eastern Europe, the case for ECB assistance was clear-cut.[31] The East Europeans were EU members and aspired to future eurozone membership. As such, the respectability of their economic policy was vouched for in general terms. The crisis in Eastern Europe was immediately caused by a sudden stop in foreign credit supply. And the eurozone's own banks were deeply involved and stood to suffer substantial losses. The risk of blowback was acute. As Sheets remarked to the FOMC: "I think it is very appropriate for all the European EMEs to report to the ECB for their liquidity needs."[32] But whereas the Fed had effectively licensed the ECB to issue dollars, the ECB had no intention of extending equivalent privileges to Poland or Romania. With Sweden and Denmark the ECB established publicly announced swap

lines. Their banks would supply liquidity to Eastern Europe. Meanwhile, the central banks of Poland and Hungary were fobbed off with repo arrangements that treated them no better than stressed commercial banks in need of extra liquidity. The only assistance that the ECB was willing to provide was to give them short-term funding in exchange for first-class euro-denominated securities. When the problem was a shortage of euro funding, that was not a great help. What they needed was a swap facility for Hungarian forint or Polish zloty. Even the limited facilities offered by the ECB were extracted only thanks to urgent pressure from the Austrian and French central banks, which had particular reason to worry about the losses their banks might suffer on their East European portfolios.[33] Austria's banks were in particular difficulty because they had made loans in Swiss francs, funding them with borrowing in Switzerland, where interest rates were low. Now the Swiss franc was soaring and funding was scarce. To tide them over, the Swiss Central Bank offered full currency swap lines in exchange for euros, but not for Polish zlotys or Hungarian forints.[34]

Membership in the EU and NATO was supposed to have promoted Eastern Europe from their inferior status in the global pecking order. Ex-members of the Warsaw Pact and former Soviet republics had eagerly refashioned themselves as exponents of Donald Rumsfeld's new Europe. They now found their prospects for growth shattered and their governments thrown back to where their post-Communist careers had begun, as lesser sovereigns, and more or less resentful supplicants for international financial assistance. The IMF was their last resort. This was traumatic. No one in Eastern Europe wanted to relive the bitter aftermath of the collapse of communism, with which the IMF was indelibly associated.

The first and most desperate application for assistance from within the EU was Hungary's.[35] On October 27, 2008, Budapest reached agreement with the IMF and the EU (as opposed to the ECB) on a $25 billion loan package. At 20 percent of Hungarian precrisis GDP, it was a very substantial commitment and an unusually generous multiple of Hungary's IMF capital quota.[36] The IMF considered the program to be unusually lenient. Unsurprisingly, the Hungarians did not see it in such favorable terms. Hungarian politics polarized as the austerity program bit. The nationalist daily *Magyar Hírlap* described Hungary as being slowly garroted by a "credit

IMF Crisis Programs (as of August 2009)

				Burden sharing			Total financing ($ millions)	
		Date	Amount of arrangement ($ millions)	Amount drawn Aug 2009	EU ($ millions)	World Bank ($ millions)	Other ($ millions)	
Stand-by arrangements	Georgia	15-Sep-08	1,172	452	184	328	606	2,290
	Ukraine	5-Nov-08	17,253	10,979	1,000	1,750	1,250	21,253
	Hungary	6-Nov-08	16,529	11,900	8,400	1,300	0	26,229
	Seychelles	14-Nov-08	28	12	0	0	0	28
	Iceland	19-Nov-08	2,196	878	100	0	9,000	11,296
	Pakistan	24-Nov-08	11,349	7,376	0	3,400	6,800	21,549
	Latvia	23-Dec-08	2,387	840	4,382	565	3,251	10,585
	Belarus	12-Jan-09	3,560	1,499	0	200	1,000	4,760
	El Salvador	16-Jan-09	806	0	0	450	900	2,156
	Serbia	16-Jan-09	4,108	1,100	411	350	0	4,869
	Armenia	6-Mar-09	838	416	0	525	637	2,000
	Mongolia	1-Apr-09	240	120	0	60	125	425
	Costa Rica	11-Apr-09	772	0	0	500	500	1,772
	Guatemala	22-Apr-09	989	0	0	393	361	1,743
	Romania	4-May-09	17,948	6,854	6,550	1,310	1,310	27,118
	Bosnia & Herzegovina	8-Jul-09	1,592	287	137	259	74	2,062
	Sri Lanka	24-Jul-09	2,594	325	0	0	0	2,594
	Total		84,361	43,038	21,164	11,390	25,814	142,729
Flexible credit lines	Mexico	17-Apr-09	49,451	-				49,451
	Poland	6-May-09	21,472	-				21,472
	Colombia	11-May-09	10,926	-				10,926

Source: IMF, Review of Recent Crisis Programs (September 14, 2009), Appendix I, https://www.imf.org/external/np/pp/eng/2009/091409.pdf.

noose around our necks."[37] For the extremists of Hungary's Far Right it was a short step back in time from the "neocolonialism" of the EU and the IMF to the Treaty of Trianon, which had eviscerated Hungary after World War I.

In 2010 the right-wing Fidesz party would reap the benefits with a crushing electoral victory, setting Hungary on the path to a self-declared illiberal democracy.

The IMF's Hungarian aid package of October 2008 was followed by programs for Iceland, Latvia, Ukraine and Pakistan.[38] In 2009 Armenia, Belarus and Mongolia would be forced to apply to the IMF for help. Less than a year after it had played host to the contentious NATO summit, Bucharest found itself negotiating an IMF program. Precautionary credits would be offered to Costa Rica, El Salvador, Guatemala, Serbia, and Bosnia and Herzegovina. Additionally, at the urging of Washington, a new, minimally invasive flexible credit facility, offering a total of more than $80 billion in ready cash, was made available to Mexico, Poland and Colombia. Mexico thus had the singular distinction of receiving both a swap line and an IMF credit facility.

Thanks to the IMF and EU intervention, an immediate meltdown was avoided on the East European periphery of Europe in the fall of 2008.[39] But the situation remained extremely precarious. And it was dangerous not only to the borrowers. Austria's adventurous banks had since the 1990s accumulated claims on Eastern Europe equal to more than 55 percent of Austrian GDP. The exposure of Austrian banks to Hungary and Romania, the countries with flexible exchange rates that seemed most likely to suffer payment shock, came to 20 percent of Austria's GDP. German, French and Italian banks all had large claims on Eastern Europe, but these were manageable in relation to domestic resources. The other lender that was seriously exposed was Sweden, whose banks had almost entirely monopolized the banking markets of the Baltics, feeding a roaring real estate boom. There was acute anxiety on the part of international agencies such as the World Bank and the Bank for European Reconstruction and Development that an abrupt withdrawal by one or more stressed West European banks could precipitate a chain reaction that would overwhelm the modest resources provided by the IMF and the EU Commission. Desperate to reduce leverage on all fronts, West European banks would pull out of Eastern Europe en masse, unleashing a ruinous rush to the exit. Bob Zoellick, George Bush's nominee to head the World Bank, was deeply concerned about Europe's future. "It's 20 years after Europe was united in 1989," Zoellick reminded the readers of the *Financial Times* in early 2009, "what a tragedy if

you allow Europe to split again."[40] The new Europe, which the United States and the two Bush presidencies in particular had been fostering since the end of the cold war, was in jeopardy. Evoking a different chapter in Europe's history, the Viennese press was warning of a "monetary Stalingrad" that threatened Austria's and Italy's banks.[41]

The situation was serious. But the alarmist talk in Central Europe was also a reflection of the fact that Western Europe wasn't listening. Berlin was no more enthusiastic about a collective European solution in Eastern Europe than it had been in the eurozone. Germany shot down Austrian and Hungarian initiatives for a common support fund.[42] "Not our problem," Peer Steinbrück announced. East Europeans did not fail to notice that as a eurozone member, Greece seemed to be weathering the storm rather better than Hungary, even though its financial fundamentals were no better.[43] In early 2009 there were calls, ironic in light of later events, for Poland and other East European EU members to be put on a fast track to eurozone membership, thus bringing them under the protective umbrella of the ECB.[44] A confidential IMF staff report backed the proposal arguing that "[f]or countries in the EU, euro-isation offers the largest benefits in terms of resolving the foreign currency debt overhang [accumulation], removing uncertainty and restoring confidence. Without euro-isation, addressing the foreign debt currency overhang would require massive domestic retrenchment in some countries, against growing political resistance."[45] But no help was to be expected from the ECB. It had no interest in entangling itself in Eastern Europe.

In December 2008 the most exposed Italian and Austrian banks began clamoring for a concerted program of international assistance. Finding the door closed in Brussels, they turned to Vienna, which, given the extent of Austria's entanglement, could not afford to let things slide. Circumventing Brussels, the Austrian government announced what became known as the Vienna Initiative. This multilateral scheme committed the World Bank, the European Bank for Reconstruction and Development and the European Investment Bank to a program of 24.5 billion euros in new lending and capital injections. Crucially, it was flanked by an agreement with at least some of the leading private banks. On a case-by-case basis the Vienna Initiative extracted pledges from the leading lenders that they would maintain

their lines of credit to the region, thus preventing an even more dramatic credit stop.[46] UniCredit and Banca Intesa of Italy, Raiffeisen of Austria and Swedbank of Sweden all participated. Commerzbank of Germany and Deutsche Bank did not.[47]

As it turned out, the most important battleground for East European stabilization was a long way from Vienna. As the twenty-first century began, Latvia, Lithuania and Estonia had seemed like the lucky ones. Unlike other former Soviet republics, such as Ukraine, Georgia or Belarus, they had successfully transitioned to full membership in both the EU and NATO. Furthermore, unlike Hungary or Poland, the Baltics were eager to join the euro as soon as possible. In anticipation they had pegged their currencies. In 2008, despite the sudden stop to foreign capital inflows, they were under great pressure to remain on their convergence track. But as foreign credit dried up, maintaining their fixed exchange rates became ever more painful. When in early 2008 the IMF had contemplated the possibility of a crisis triggered by macroeconomic imbalances, Latvia, with its yawning current account deficit, had been singled out as particularly vulnerable.[48] Then it had been viewed in isolation as a national problem case. Now Latvia faced the unwinding of its huge deficits in the context of a comprehensive global crisis that had forced its regional competitors in Poland, Hungary and Romania to devalue. If the Baltics did not follow suit, how were they to keep up? How would they cope without foreign funding? How could they regain export competitiveness and shrink imports if they could not adjust their currencies against the euro? Without devaluation the only way to right the trade balance was by rebalancing domestic demand, cutting wages, raising taxes and slashing government spending. This was painful, but given the advanced stage of financial integration that the Baltic countries had already reached, devaluation was dangerous too. With 80 percent of credit outstanding sourced from their European neighbors, any substantial depreciation was likely to trigger wholesale default. The cost of servicing their debts in euros would simply have become prohibitive. Though they were not yet members of the eurozone, in early 2009 the Baltics faced a predicament that was a grim precursor of things to come.

Because of the scale of its debts and the deep involvement of Scandinavian banks, Latvia was commonly seen as the key to stability in the

Baltics.[49] If it abandoned its peg, contagion would most likely spread to Estonia and Lithuania, and from there to Slovakia and Bulgaria, which were also struggling to hold their currencies in line with the euro.[50] Once a wave of further devaluations began, it would be impossible to uphold the defenses put in place by the Vienna Initiative. Fire sales would sweep Eastern Europe. Some might get out alive. But for two of Sweden's most important banks, Swedbank and Nordea, the entanglement with the Baltics was existential.[51] If their loans were written off, the capital of both banks would be completely wiped out. As a BNP Paribas analyst put it, "Latvia may be a small country but it has vast repercussions."[52] One Central European minister of finance, who preferred to remain anonymous, predicted that the chain reaction across Central and Eastern Europe would take down at least half a dozen European banks. Latvia would play the role of a Lehman, or, even more ominously, that of the infamous Austrian Kreditanstalt in the financial crisis of 1931, the failure of which had precipitated Weimar Germany's final slide toward disaster.

For the IMF, the standard prescription for a country in Latvia's position was a one-off devaluation followed by debt restructuring or rescheduling. But the European Commission dug in its heels. Latvia was en route to eurozone membership. It must stay the course. If it needed to rebalance its current account it must do so through deflation and austerity. The results for Latvia were drastic. By the summer of 2009 house prices had plunged by 50 percent. Civil servants, including one-third of the country's teachers, were fired and public salaries were slashed by 35 percent. Unemployment surged from 5 to 20 percent.[53] Remarkably, Latvia clung on, as did its neighbors. In mounting its defense, Latvia received aid totaling 32 percent of its precrisis GDP: 3.1 billion euros came from the European Commission; the IMF provided 1.7 billion; 0.8 billion came from the World Bank and the European Bank for Reconstruction and Development; and 1.9 billion came from Sweden, Denmark, Finland, Norway and Estonia.[54] They all preferred to fight the crisis in Latvia rather than bailing out their banks at home. Significantly, the ECB absented itself from the crisis-fighting coalition.

The financial austerity course imposed a huge pressure on the new democracies of the Baltics.[55] In Latvia popular discontent with the new austerity line and accusations of corruption against the political class led to

two referenda calling for protection of pensions and a public right to dissolve the parliament by plebiscite. In January 2009 Riga was rocked by mass protests that escalated into rioting and a night of street battles with police. In February a conservative coalition government took office under the high-profile member of the European Parliament Valdis Dombrovskis. His government's objective was to stay the course of austere conformity. "We are facing national bankruptcy. It's going to be tough,"[56] Dombrovskis told the nation. What, after all, was the alternative? The legacy of the Soviet period hung over Latvia. Georgia was a reminder. For the Baltics the choice was between a Western or an Eastern hegemon. Since the 1990s they had managed miraculously to navigate their way under the umbrella of the EU and NATO. At least as far as the Latvian political class was concerned, they intended to stay there.

IV

Faced with the double crisis of 2008 the reaction of Eastern Europe was not uniform. The Baltics stayed the course. Hungarian nationalism rebelled. But nowhere was the double shock more jarring than in Ukraine. The coincidence of the escalation of geopolitical tension between Russia and the West with the financial crisis dealt a shuddering blow to its fragile polity. The route to the Ukraine crisis of 2013 was twisted. But the path that it would travel down was mapped out already five years earlier.

In the spring of 2008 the decision by Ukrainian president Viktor Yushchenko to apply for NATO membership—eagerly applauded by the Bush administration, Poland and the other East Europeans—split Ukrainian politics. Whereas President Yushchenko threw in his lot with the West, Prime Minister Yulia Tymoshenko favored the policy of balance between Russia and the West that Kiev had pursued since independence and that had made her personal fortune as a kingpin in the gas trade. The war in Georgia in August 2008 divided what was left of the political legacy of the revolution of 2004.[57] Then, before the cease-fire in the Caucasus had more than a few weeks to settle, Kiev was rocked by the financial crisis.

Since the 2004 revolution, Ukraine's economic growth had come to

rely on foreign borrowing. By early 2008, foreign funds made up 45 percent of all corporate financing and 65 percent of household loans in Ukraine.[58] Altogether, European banks had lent Ukraine at least $40 billion, with Austrian and French banks responsible for almost half. The onset of the crisis stopped the credit flow. And it hit Ukraine's exports hard. As one of the legacies of the Soviet era, steel accounted for 42 percent of Ukraine's foreign currency earnings. No sector was worse hit by the crash in global investment spending than steel. Prices plunged and industrial output by January 2009 was falling at an annualized rate of 34 percent.[59] As Ukraine's economy slid into recession, millions were left without pay, if they were not actually thrown out of work. Of all economies in the world, only Latvia would suffer a more severe contraction.

In October 2008 Ukraine had no option but to follow Hungary to the IMF. Kiev signed up to a $16.4 billion loan package. The IMF's approach was not demanding by its usual standards. It asked for Ukraine to fully fund its budget, to set a realistic exchange rate and to ensure that its financial system was stable. But even this was more than Kiev could manage. The exchange rate was allowed to devalue from the overvalued rate of 5 hryvnia to the dollar to 7.7, though unofficially it traded as low as 10 to the dollar. The tax increases and subsidy cuts necessary to balance the budget were ruinously unpopular.[60] Asked in 2009, "Who bears the most responsibility for the difficult socioeconomic situation in Ukraine?" 69 percent blamed the heroes of 2004, with 47 percent singling out Yushchenko and 22 percent naming Tymoshenko. Yushchenko's personal approval rating hovered between 2.5 and 5 percent.[61] The upshot was paradoxical. On the one hand, the impasse in Ukraine's post–cold war development was more evident than ever. What hope there was of economic development lay in further integration with the West even at the expense of painful structural adjustment. On the other hand, by the autumn of 2009 the most popular politician in Ukraine was Viktor Yanukovych, the representative of the Russian-oriented "party of the regions" with its base in eastern Ukraine, the thuggish dinosaur of the transition era whose rigged election victory in 2004 had triggered the Orange Revolution.

The one point of relief for Ukraine in 2009 was that geopolitical tension between East and West seemed to be subsiding. With Medvedev in the

Kremlin, the West scrambled to "reset" relations with Russia. But the fragility of the situation was painfully exposed in January 2009 when a dispute between Russia and Ukraine over unpaid bills and gas prices left Ukraine without heat in the depth of winter and interrupted flow through the pipelines running west to Europe.[62] The dispute was resolved only with EU mediation and a price increase for Gazprom that would become an albatross around the neck of Prime Minister Tymoshenko. Though Ukraine was far from being headline news, it was already in 2008–2009 drifting into an explosive state. As Austrian foreign minister Josef Proell presciently remarked in February 2009: "Ukraine is a very important keystone country and we must avoid a domino effect inside the EU, if there is economic and political catastrophe in such a huge neighbouring country. . . . We don't see this scenario developing now. But we must prepare and keep an eye on Ukraine."[63]

Chapter 10

THE WIND FROM
THE EAST: CHINA

I f the immediate impact of the financial crisis was to impose an uneasy truce on the old battlefields of the European cold war, the shocking realization of 2008 was how far both sides were willing to go. In Moscow, NATO's heedless attempt at expansion and the clash with Georgia would not be forgotten. Russia had made good on Putin's announcement at Munich that the unipolar moment was passing. And the Americans knew it was true. But when they thought of multipolarity, they did not think first and foremost of Putin's ramshackle regime. They thought of China. And so, in fact, did Russia's own best analysts.[1] The possibility of a Sino-American crisis was obvious to both sides. And the unexpected storm in the North Atlantic financial system further heightened tension.[2] But Beijing and Washington avoided disaster. Neither side wanted to take the kinds of risks that produced the violent clash in the Caucasus.

In 2008 Chinese opinion was alarmed to discover that their prized portfolio of dollar assets contained not just actual Treasurys but GSE debt, issued to finance the expansion of American mortgage lending. As in Russia, public opinion in China was indignant. Why was poor China financing America's excess? As a sign of its impatience, Beijing allowed its spokesmen to make dramatic and unusually frank statements. If the United States allowed the GSE to fail it would be a "catastrophe," China let it be known.[3] Toward the end of 2008 the *Atlantic* magazine garnered an interview with a fast-talking manager of China's sovereign wealth fund.[4] The result was

a startling insight into a topsy-turvy world. Over recent months, Gao Xiqing remarked, the world had watched as America, "after months and months of struggling with your own ideology, with your own pride, your self-righteousness," had finally applied "one of the great gifts of Americans, which is that you're pragmatic." The Fed and the Treasury had intervened on a massive scale to stabilize the financial economy, so now, Gao quipped, when the Chinese looked to the United States, what they saw was not capitalist democracy, but "socialism with American characteristics."

Cutting though it might have been, Gao's analysis was not Marxist enough. It hadn't been only ideology and vanity that stood in the way of a solution in September and October 2008. Interests had been at stake. Convening the "executive committee of the bourgeoisie" was never going to be a simple task. But, then, Gao was not a party theorist. He was an alumnus of Duke Law School and sported a CV including time spent working for Richard Nixon's Wall Street law firm. But with or without the theory, his sense of the shifting balance of power was acute. "This generation of Americans is so used to your supremacy. Your being treated nicely by everyone. It hurts to think, Okay, now we have to be on equal footing to other people. 'On equal footing' would necessarily mean that sometimes you have to stoop to appear to be humble to other people. . . . The simple truth today is that your economy is built on the global economy. And it's built on the support, the gratuitous support, of a lot of countries. So why don't you come over and . . . I won't say kowtow [with a laugh], but at least, be nice to the countries that lend you money. Talk to the Chinese! Talk to the Middle Easterners! And pull your troops back!"

As Barack Obama's stunning election victory demonstrated, many Americans agreed with Gao. And, in fact, the outgoing Bush administration was doing its very best to be "nice." What the Chinese really wanted was a total government guarantee for Fannie Mae and Freddie Mac debt. That would have had truly dramatic implications for the US government fiscal position, adding more than $5 trillion to the public debt at a stroke. Fannie Mae had been privatized during the Vietnam War for a reason. But in taking the GSE into conservatorship, Treasury Secretary Paulson did the next best thing. Even if it outraged the right wing of the Republican Party,

the managerial elite knew that it was essential. Nor was President Bush too proud to phone Beijing to deliver the message personally.[5]

The Chinese cut back their GSE holdings but they did not offload them like Russia, they merely reduced them to their level in the summer of 2007 before Gao and his colleagues had embarked on their ill-advised program of reserve diversification. Chinese purchases of Treasurys, meanwhile, increased. China's total holding of US securities continued to rise from $922 billion in June 2007 to $1,464 billion two years later.[6] Nor was this surprising. Panic and crisis, turned US Treasurys into the most desirable asset in the world. Everyone wanted safety. Treasury prices were rising, yields soaring, so too was the dollar. If China had wanted to diversify out of its dollar assets, this was the moment to do it. There was insatiable global demand for safe dollar assets. But what the crisis revealed was that China's options were limited. What other safe assets were there to buy? For China to have bought Japanese bonds would have created an entanglement that was potentially even more explosive. European bond markets weren't deep enough. China and America were locked together willy-nilly. Their interdependence was structurally conditioned and this went not only for foreign investments, but for trade too.

I

Given the scale of Chinese export success and its accumulation of foreign assets, Western observers are apt to believe that China's growth must be "export dependent." But this is an optical illusion that reflects our recalcitrant Western-centric view. Exports are important to China, and its insertion into the world economy has transformed global trade. But even before the crisis China's domestic economy was large and it was growing extraordinarily rapidly, far more rapidly than China's markets abroad. China had made itself into an export champion, but in so doing it had also fostered imports—of commodities and components from Australasia, the Middle East, Africa, the rest of Asia and Latin America, as well as technology and advanced machinery from the West. A large part of the value in China's

world-beating exports was accounted for by imported raw materials and subcomponents. As a result, net exports accounted for a smaller share of Chinese GDP growth before 2008 than one might imagine. In fact, no more than one third of China's growth from 1990 was driven by exports, with two thirds coming from domestic demand.[7] This was a very different balance from that of a truly export-dependent economy, of which Germany was the quintessential example. With slow domestic investment and consumption, the vast majority of Germany's growth after 2000 was accounted for by foreign demand. In China, far and away the main driver of growth was its enormous wave of domestic investment. As China's cities expanded and its infrastructure modernized at a staggering rate, the physical reconstruction of the country sucked the entire Chinese economy up with it.

By 2008 the immense dynamism of China's domestic demand and its central position as a regional trading hub in East Asia suggested to some analysts that Asia might be on the point of "decoupling" from America and Europe.[8] In the spring of 2008, as the rest of the world slid toward recession, Beijing's main worry was that China's economy was expanding too fast. Growth in consumption was roaring along at more than 20 percent per annum. The People's Bank of China raised interest rates and government fiscal policy was tightened to choke off the boom. Meanwhile, China's government machine was reorganized to concentrate responsibility for more balanced national growth in centralized superministries.[9] What no one reckoned with was the sheer force of the global trade collapse. Whereas in July 2008 Chinese exports were growing by 25 percent, imports by 30 percent and FDI by 65 percent per annum, six months later China's exports were falling by 18 percent, imports by more than 40 percent and FDI by 30 percent. It was an astonishing switchback. Even if net exports normally accounted for only a third of China's growth, the impact was severe. In the fall of 2008 South Korean and Taiwanese corporations suddenly began to shutter their Chinese operations.[10] At the same time, cash-hungry Western banks such as Bank of America, UBS and RBS sold up and pulled out. But these were pinpricks when compared with the impact of falling export orders on China's labor market. As the winter of 2008–2009 approached, 30 percent of China's gigantic annual surge of college graduates—5.6 million per annum—were unable to find work. The reserve army of tens of millions

of rural migrants fared even worse. For the Mid-Autumn Festival in October 2008, 70 million returned to their homes in the provinces, of whom only 56 million made the trip back to the cities after the break. Of those, according to World Bank estimates, 11 million were without jobs. Altogether, at least 20 million, and perhaps as many as 36 million, Chinese workers were left idle.[11]

Ever watchful for signs of domestic social unrest, Beijing knew that it had to react. Already on November 5 the State Council convened an emergency meeting to agree on a 4 trillion yuan ($586 billion) spending program. This amounted to a remarkable 12.5 percent of 2008 GDP. It was supplemental to existing investment plans and was to be disbursed by the end of 2010. It was the first truly large-scale fiscal response to the crisis worldwide. On Sunday, November 9, 2008, as the plan was revealed to the press, the State Council declared: "Over the past two months, the global financial crisis has been intensifying daily. . . . In expanding investment, we must be fast and heavy-handed."[12] And the declaration by the State Council was given additional force by a party instruction, Central Document No. 18, which called for a "package *plan* to counter the global financial crisis." The word used to refer to the crisis-fighting measures was the old Mao-era term *jihua*, or plan, rather than the newfangled word for softer government programs or initiatives, *guihua*, which had come into widespread currency since 2006.[13] Instructions to the press required reporting to "stay upbeat, to avoid panic and contribute to consumer confidence."[14]

In November 2008 fiscal policy was pushed in China with the kind of urgency that the West reserved for central bank initiatives and bank bailouts. It was Tim Geithner's "maximum force" approach but applied to public spending rather than monetary policy. The National Development and Reform Commission, the lead agency for Chinese economic policy, called on local government to "make every second count." Central Document No. 18 shocked the local party apparatus into action. In the words of a leading American analyst, Document No. 18 "added to the sense of urgency, communicating the sense that it was OK to overturn ordinary obstacles to spending the money." Over the days that followed, across China, provincial party meetings were hurriedly convened to "seize the favorable opportunity created by expansionary fiscal policy and the 'appropriately loose'

monetary policy," as one Shandong committee declared. On the evening of November 11 in Wugong County in Shaanxi Province, a "County Leadership Small Group for Implementing Central Document No. 18" was convened, to make the most of "an extremely rare and precious opportunity." The aim, the county leadership group declared, was to "concentrate our forces and act quickly, strengthen our links with the provincial and municipal authorities, and make sure that more keypoint investment projects come to our county. . . . Getting more project funding is our top current task." Within a year this party-led mobilization got 50 percent of China's stimulus projects under way.

Reconstruction following the terrible Sichuan earthquake of May 2008, which had left more than seventy thousand dead and millions homeless, provided one obvious focus of attention. In the aftermath there had been an upsurge of public criticism and popular activism criticizing the inadequacy of many of China's public buildings and demanding redress. For the party's local leaders, crash stimulus spending offered a chance to reassert their authority.[15] A wider programmatic frame was provided by the National Development and Reform Commission's promise of "scientific developmentalism."[16] Funds were to be concentrated in ten sectors, including health care, education (particularly in the relatively deprived and politically contested western regions of China), low-income housing on the edges of China's gigantic new cities, environmental protection, technological innovation, superhighways, urban electrification, the coal distribution network and railways. The popularly minded leadership team of President Hu Jintao had opened discussions of health-care reform already in 2005 in the wake of the SARS crisis. Something needed to be done about the glaring disparities in health coverage between rural and urban areas.[17] After several years of debate, the economic emergency of 2008 swung the decision quite suddenly toward a system centered on central government spending. On April 7, 2009, Beijing announced that health insurance coverage would be extended from 30 to 90 percent of China's population and that central funds would be allocated to pay for the construction of two thousand county hospitals and five thousand township-level clinical centers. It was the largest expansion in health-care provision in world history to date and

it was "inextricably interwoven with the stimulus package." Beijing was happy to approve spending on hospitals, clinics and public insurance subsidies "because concerns about short-run deficits" had "evaporated. . . . The economic crisis . . . opened a window in which a more aggressive fiscal approach to social policy has become possible."[18]

The gigantic surge in stimulus spending also paid for what is perhaps the most spectacular infrastructure project of the last generation anywhere in the world, the construction of China's high-speed rail network (HSR). In the first phase of Chinese growth, priority had been given to motorization and highway construction. Now rail came to the fore. After "borrowing" technology from the pioneers of HSR—Japan, Germany and France—China embarked on a program that dwarfed all previous efforts. Between 2008 and 2014 the network of rail lines suitable for traffic at speeds of 250 kilometers per hour or more was expanded from 1,000 kilometers to 11,000 kilometers. Journey times from Beijing to Shanghai were cut to 4.5 hours for an 819-mile trip, compared with the 7 hours that the Acela—the pride of America's Amtrak—takes to cover the 454 miles from Boston to Washington, DC. Not only did China pioneer ultrafast trains capable of cruising at 360 kilometers per hour. The economies of scale opened up by the gigantic construction program also made China into the technological leader in rail-line and viaduct construction.[19] Gigantic snail-like machines would lay the track in a continuous length, mile after mile, across endless arrays of standardized, prefabricated concrete pillars. According to World Bank estimates, even allowing for lower labor and land costs, China's costs of construction were a fraction of those in Europe and North America.

Following the spectacular 2008 Olympics, the promptness and scale of China's fiscal stimulus was further proof of the mobilizing capacity of the Communist regime. Compared with the sluggishness of many Western states, it is hard to avoid invidious comparisons. Both as presidential candidate and newly inaugurated president, Barack Obama referred frequently to China's great strides in infrastructure.[20] But this well-deserved credit should not obscure the tensions that lurked beneath the surface. In China the stimulus was deeply controversial. To many observers it seemed that, driven by a crisis in the West, the Chinese economy was being sucked in

precisely the wrong direction. Was the stimulus a spectacular demonstration of state power, or further proof of the addiction of the Chinese power elite to an unsustainable growth model?[21]

II

China's growth rate was the envy of the world. But at home, given the huge social and environmental costs, reviews were more mixed. The aim of the Hu Jintao leadership when it took office in November 2002 had been to give new priority to consumption and the household standard of living. After a decade of superrapid growth, the Chinese had had enough of heavy industrial development.[22] But investment-driven heavy industrial growth is a hard habit to break. Five years later, in March 2007, in a remarkably frank assessment delivered to the National People's Congress, Premier Wen Jiabao warned that "the biggest problem with China's economy" was still that growth was "unstable, unbalanced, uncoordinated, and unsustainable."[23] When announcing its stimulus response to the 2008 crisis, Beijing pushed high-tech railways and health care as hard as it did because it wanted to escape associations with clichés of heavy industrial growth. The government was determined to avoid "frivolous or speculative investments." "There won't be a penny spent on enlarging mass production, or highly polluting and resource intensive sectors," Zhang Ping, director of the National Reform and Development Commission, stressed. All its efforts would be directed so as to "target spheres that would promote and consolidate the expansion of consumer credit."[24] In December 2008 the State Council followed the November stimulus announcement with an "Opinion on Stimulating Circulation and Expanding Consumption," itemizing twenty measures to boost consumption. China's 220 million rural households were offered state-funded discounts on the purchase of two large household appliances, such as televisions, air conditioners, washing machines and refrigerators.[25] As the average rural household earned less than 16,000 renminbi (RMB—though used interchangeably with yuan, RMB refers to the Chinese currency as such, whereas yuan are the units in which sums are measured) in 2008, buying a computer or color TV for

7,000 RMB was a big step. But over a two- to three-year time horizon, the 140 billion RMB promised by Beijing was a powerful inducement.[26]

The aims of China's leadership were thus clear. And it is tempting to imagine these priorities being rolled out across the country by an all-powerful one-party state. But in practice, Chinese central government is stretched thinly across the giant bulk and complexity of the world's most populous nation. Though responsibility for revenue collection falls heavily on central government, government expenditure directly controlled from Beijing has amounted to no more than 4 to 5 percent of GDP since the 1990s, a very small figure by comparison with its American or European counterparts. In China, 80 percent of government spending is done at the regional and local levels, where expenditure has surged between 1994 and 2008 from 8 to 18 percent of GDP, even as China's national income quintupled.[27] The regime thus operates through decentralization and indirect mechanisms, which amplify its power and extend its reach, but also distort and distend Beijing's intentions.

Of the 4 trillion yuan stimulus announced by the center in November 2008, only 1.18 trillion yuan would be delivered directly from central funds. The rest were to come from local government, a ratio of 1:3, corresponding roughly to the general balance between central and local expenditure. It was the decentralized nature of the state apparatus that made the mobilization of the Communist Party and its nationwide apparatus so vital. Central Document No. 18 energized the networks that linked the Communist Party, local government and business interests. It was precisely this nexus that over the last generation had combined to supercharge China's spectacular economic growth. But it was that same combination that also went a long way to explaining the lopsided character of China's growth. To meet a central target or quota, there was always some regional highway connection, housing complex, bridge or industrial park to be built and profits to be made doing so. When the stimulus was launched it was precisely this chain reaction that worried those who advocated a more balanced model of growth. The centrally ordained stimulus would unleash the bulldozers of the infrastructure machine. The results confirmed the critics' worst fears. In Hubei province, with a population of 57 million and a regional GDP of $225 billion in 2009, there were projects under construction by 2010 notionally costed at $363 billion.[28] A further $390 billion and $450 billion were planned for 2011

and 2012. Taken at face value, this meant that a single Chinese province with a population the size of the UK and a GDP the size of Greece was engaging in a program of investment larger than any stimulus ever attempted in the United States. Across China, within a month of the State Council's November initiative, eighteen provinces had proposed projects with a total budget of 25 trillion RMB, six times greater than the original proposed stimulus, accounting for more than 80 percent of Chinese GDP.[29] Not only was this proposed spending gargantuan, but within the corporate sector, it was the State Owned Enterprises (SOE) that took charge. Since the 1990s the thrust of central policy had been to shed labor and to streamline these vehicles of Communist economic development policy.[30] Now, under the sign of the stimulus, the SOEs lurched once more to the forefront of Chinese growth.

Clearly the impetus for spending was massive. But from an economic point of view the vital question was how it was to be financed. This is the

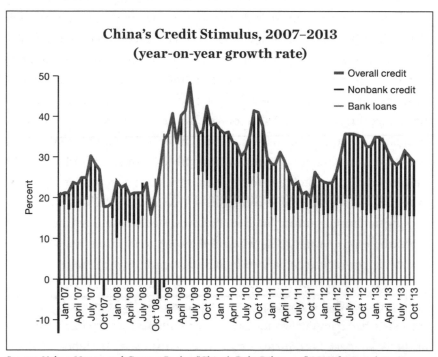

Source: Yukon Huang and Canyon Bosler, "China's Debt Dilemma," 2014, figure 1, http://carneg ieendowment.org/2014/09/18/china-s-debt-dilemma-deleveraging-while-generating-growth -pub-56579. Data: UBS.

key question in any fiscal policy "stimulus." If spending is paid for by tax increases, this negates any increase in purchasing power. Borrowing by issuing bonds will soak up private savings, which may divert the portfolios of private wealth holders away from other investments. Credit creation is the one surefire way to fund stimulus spending if the aim is immediately to revive an underemployed economy. Beijing's stimulus was particularly effective precisely because it combined huge government spending with a spectacular loosening of monetary policy.

In China, not only were many major industrial firms state controlled but the banking sector was under the direct influence of the central bank as well.[31] When it wants to control credit, the People's Bank of China (PBoC) not only sets the interest rates. It set quotas for credit issuance for each of the major banks. To further manipulate the credit flow it can use higher or lower reserve ratios and greater degrees of "sterilization" of its foreign exchange interventions. All of these mechanisms were once commonplace in the West as well, legacies of the World War II era. But from the 1970s onward, direct regulation of bank credit was progressively abandoned in the West. In facing the 2008 crisis these tools of banking control gave Beijing remarkable leverage. In September and November of 2008 the PBoC reversed its tightening of the spring by slashing its interest rate by almost 5 percent. Then it announced that for 2009 it was doubling the banks' lending target from 4.7 trillion RMB to 10 trillion RMB. Reserve ratios were cut by up to 25 percent for smaller banks. It was, as the PBoC's Monetary Policy Committee declared in April 2009, an "appropriately loose monetary policy" to sustain the priorities of the stimulus.[32]

The banks responded. The Bank of China alone wrote 1 trillion yuan of loans in the first half of 2009, with the Agricultural Bank of China, China Construction Bank and the Industrial and Commercial Bank of China not far behind. Together in the first quarter of 2009 credit issuance came to 4.6 trillion yuan, with the top four being responsible for 3.433 trillion yuan. More new credit was issued in three months than the official fiscal stimulus would provide for the next two years. Meanwhile, provincial and city governments were enjoined to work with local banks. The main mechanism for financing their local spending were so-called city investment companies,

or local government financing vehicles—the "shock troops of the stimulus." These SPVs were endowed with parcels of municipal land against which they borrowed to fund development projects.[33] Between 2008 and 2010 local government debt would rocket from 1 trillion RMB ($146 billion) to an estimated 10 trillion RMB ($1.7 trillion).[34]

At the height of the stimulus drive, in the first half of 2009, 7.37 trillion RMB were issued in new loans. This was a 50 percent increase on the year before, which had also been a year of booming economic activity. By the end of the year the total volume of lending hit 9.6 trillion yuan.[35] If we add the government deficit at all levels to the growth in bank credit *beyond* the 15 percent per annum expansion that had been the norm in China over the previous years, we get a measure of the true scale of China's stimulus. In 2009 its dimensions were extraordinary—950 billion yuan in deficit, 467 billion in additional bond finance and 5 trillion in bank loans beyond the previous growth norm, for a total stimulus of 6,487 billion RMB, or 19.3 percent of GDP.[36]

This huge additional growth boost was delivered through a variety of channels. But it was state directed from the top down and supplemental to China's already enormous growth rate. When the entire complex is ac-

Big Bang: China's Bank Lending and Fiscal Stimulus Programs, 2008–2010

Stimulus (RMB billions)	2008	2009	2010
Fiscal deficit	111	950	650
Net new bank loans	252	5070	1936
Net new bond finance	251	467	-232
Total	614	6487	2354
Stimulus (% GDP)			
Fiscal deficit	0.4%	2.8%	1.6%
Net new bank loans	0.8%	15.1%	4.9%
Net new bond finance	0.8%	1.4%	-0.6%
Total	2.0%	19.3%	5.9%

Source: C. Wong, "The Fiscal Stimulus Program and Problems of Macroeconomic Management in China," (2011), table 4, https://ora.ox.ac.uk/objects/uuid:4b8af91e-89c7-4a25-be7c-2394cd3c4e9b. Data: China Data Online.

Drivers of World Growth (in percentage points)

Source: S. Barnett, "China: Size Matters," IMF (blog), https://blogs.imf.org/2014/03/26/china-size-matters/.

counted for, this was an intervention comparable in scale to anything ever undertaken in the Mao era, or under Soviet communism. The Western capitalist economies had witnessed such huge mobilizations only in times of war. The rate of investment in the Chinese economy surged toward 50 percent of GDP, a level rarely, if ever, seen before. It was enough to offset even the worst shock to global trade.[37] At 9.1 percent, China's growth rate in 2009 was barely lower than it had been in 2008 and vastly higher than anywhere else in the world. And given the size to which the Chinese economy had expanded, this was decisive. In 2009, for the first time in the modern era, it was the movement of the Chinese economy that carried the entire world economy. Together with the huge liquidity stimulus delivered by the US Federal Reserve, China's combined fiscal and financial stimulus was the main force counteracting the global crisis. Though they were not coordinated policies, they made real the vision of a G2: China and America leading the world.

III

Given the geopolitical conclusions that are apt to be drawn from China's "overtaking" of the United States, it is worth noting that the 2008 mobilization was not part of any master plan. It was a hyperactive response to an unforeseen emergency that struck China from the outside. The origin of that negative shock was in the West. It unleashed forces within China that took its economy in directions that the Beijing leadership had been struggling to counteract and that were widely unpopular in China. And the dramatic impact of the stimulus had consequences that were political and geopolitical as well as economic.

The spectacular state action fit well within popular narratives of China's rise. As the twenty-first century began Chinese audiences were hooked on a massive diet of TV and film offerings preoccupied with the question of the rise and fall of great powers.[38] On the Internet there was a spectacular surge in public discussion of "Chinese greatness" and the "China model."[39] In the wider world, surveys conducted by the authoritative US polling center the Pew Charitable Trusts registered a dramatic shift in popular understanding of the global center of gravity. As the impact of the economic crisis sank in, the number of respondents identifying the United States as the dominant economy in the world began to decline sharply. By 2010 pluralities of respondents in both the United States and Europe would identify China as the "world's leading economy."[40] In material terms it empowered the Communist Party and the growth coalitions built around it. Because of the decentralized nature of power, those coalitions came in different colorations, ranging from Shanghai's hypermodernity to the neo-Maoism of Bo Xilai's "Chongqing Model." What was striking, however, was that these were overwhelmingly civilian coalitions. Unlike other historical examples of great growth spurts, China's stimulus was not a military-industrial push.

Unlike subordinate parts of America's global network, like Japan or Germany, for instance, China had a conventional view of national power. It took for granted that national autonomy implied autonomy in security policy. Given China's booming economy, spending on defense increased with spending on everything else. Already in 1999 the military-industrial complex

had been restructured to increase competition. In 2005–2006 the Chinese military formulated a major technological modernization program.[41] But this was merely a recognition of how far China lagged behind. The army was oversized and underpowered in technological terms. A society entering into mass affluence as rapidly as China was doing does not offer a congenial habitat for the underpaid profession of soldiering. Rather than raw recruits, the Chinese military needed technologists, but they were scarce and expensive. China's military equipment and infrastructure were far behind those of Western militaries and behind the standard set by China's booming business sector. And though it was increasing rapidly in absolute terms, as a share of GDP, China's military spending remained flat at 2 percent throughout the crisis—half the level that the United States had sustained since 9/11. As the civilian-centered stimulus program hit in 2008–2009, the share of military expenditure in total public spending halved from 12 to 6 percent.[42]

These facts were public knowledge, but Washington's seismograph reacts sensitively to any challenge. When in March 2009 a flotilla of Chinese trawlers harassed an American naval reconnaissance vessel off Hainan island, the incident was promptly declared to be a sign of escalating confrontation.[43] The Obama administration's first encounters with the Chinese were frosty. Treasury Secretary Geithner provoked laughter from nationalist students at Peking University when he declared that American debt was "very safe."[44] As one American analyst remarked, "2009–2010 will be remembered as the years in which China became difficult for the world to deal with."[45] Whether this reflected geopolitical ambition was not yet clear. But as far as strategists in Washington, DC, were concerned, this was incidental.[46] It was the economy itself that was decisive. Washington was convinced that China's military potential would grow with time, as would its ambition. What underpinned both was its spectacular economic growth, and what was decisive was Beijing's ability to control it. In this sense the financial crisis marked a moment of transition, as much on the Western side as in China itself. Given Beijing's response to the crisis of 2008, its emergence as a decisive force in world affairs was undeniable. As was the other realization taught by 2008: If China was not export dependent, it was massively interdependent with the West. It had a measure of control but not

insulation. Since the early 2000s, Washington's ambition had been to develop China as a "responsible stakeholder" in the world economy. Now the question was reversed. In the wake of the crisis what Beijing needed to know was what to expect from America. As Gao remarked to the interviewer at the *Atlantic*: "Why don't we get together and think about this? If China has $2 trillion [in US assets], Japan has almost $2 trillion, and Russia has some, and all the others, then—let's throw away the ideological differences and think about what's good for everyone. We can get all the relevant people together and think up what people are calling a second Bretton Woods system, like the first Bretton Woods convention did."[47]

Chapter 11

G20

China's stimulus benefited all its trading partners, from Australia to Brazil.[1] Across the world the share of China trade increased.[2] But, having recognized the scale and significance of the Chinese effort, it is important not to fall into the trap of allowing it to overshadow everything else. If we replace a narrowly Western view with a one-eyed focus on China, we fail to grasp the drama and complexity of the transition to a truly multipolar world. Ten years on from the emerging market debt crises of 1997–1998, what was impressive about 2008 was the policy response across the emerging economies. At the UN General Assembly meeting in New York in September 2008 it was the Latin Americans who were the most vociferous. But in responding to the crisis, it was "emerging Asia" that set the pace.

I

In the summer of 1997 the Asian financial crisis had started in Thailand and had spread from there across Southeast Asia to Indonesia, Malaysia and Singapore, before ricocheting two thousand miles to the northeast to unleash havoc in South Korea. After a year of severe recession, by 2000 Thailand, Indonesia, Malaysia and Korea were all growing again. From a combined GDP in 1997 of $2.3 trillion in purchasing power parity (PPP)

terms, by 2008 the output of these four economies had nearly doubled to $4.4 trillion.[3] This gave them a weight in the world economy comparable in PPP terms to France and Italy combined, or California plus Texas. In terms of economic policy, the East Asian economies were model students. Learning the lessons commonly prescribed after the crises of the 1990s, they adopted tight fiscal policies and built up huge currency reserves. Indonesia, where the 1998 crisis had triggered the fall of Suharto's dictatorship, went so far as to adopt a fiscal straitjacket modeled on the EU's Maastricht criteria.[4] Though this discipline was restrictive and particularly so for a developing economy in need of public investment, when the crisis struck in 2008, the regions of Southeast and East Asia had room to maneuver.[5] And they needed it. Though the crisis did not originate in Asia, they were acutely vulnerable to global shocks.

Most at risk in 2008 was South Korea, whose famous corporate export champions, the *chaebol*—Daewoo, Hyundai, Samsung—and their giant steel plants, shipyards and car factories suffered a shuddering blow. "We are collateral damage in a crisis that is not our doing," observed one professor at Korea University in Seoul. "We live in an unfair world."[6] But however real this sense of victimization, it does not capture the complex reality of South Korea's situation. What set South Korea apart in Asia, and gave it a vulnerability akin to that of Eastern Europe or Russia, was the global integration of its financial system.[7] After the shock of the 1990s the South Korean central bank had made sure to accumulate ample foreign reserves—$240 billion by the summer of 2008. But this did not cancel out the vulnerabilities in the Korean financial system. Unlike in Europe, subprime wasn't the issue. South Korean holding of toxic US mortgage securities amounted to only $850 million.[8] The problem was not on the asset, but on the funding, side of the balance sheet. Since the early 2000s, Seoul had promoted itself as a regional financial hub for Northeast Asia. It had liberalized currency and capital flows. A large part of South Korean banking was owned by foreign investors, and Korea's banks had shifted to the unstable new model of wholesale funding, borrowing short term on global dollar markets to invest long term at higher interest rates in Korea. This was made all the more attractive by South Korea's export success and the steady appreciation of the Korean won against the dollar. The problem for the *chaebol* was to hedge

their dollar export earnings against devaluation. One way to do this was to borrow in dollars and invest in Korean assets, repaying the dollar loan at more favorable exchange rates in the future.[9] The trade was profitable if short-term dollar funding remained cheap and exchange rates continued to move as expected. By June 2008, as a result of this hedging tactic, South Korean businesses had $176 billion in short-term dollar loans outstanding, an increase of 150 percent since 2005. The banking sector owed $80 billion, which had to be rolled over by the summer of 2009.

When short-term dollar lending markets shut down across the world and the dollar surged, the logic of the won-dollar carry trade went abruptly into reverse. As Korean businesses scrambled to cover their dollar exposure, a disastrous cycle ensued. Preemptive buying of dollars led to an immediate collapse in the value of the won. When national currency holdings slid perilously close to the psychological threshold of $200 billion, that added to the panic.[10] Between the summer of 2008 and May 2009 the won plunged from 1,000 to 1,600 to the dollar, increasing the local cost of US dollar loans by 60 percent. Only tiny bankrupt Iceland suffered a more drastic depreciation. The cost for Korean borrowers of insuring dollar bonds against default (CDS premiums) surged from 20 basis points (0.2 percent of the value of the loan) in the summer of 2007 to 700 by October 2008.[11] Adding 7 percent to the interest burden of a bank bond ruled out further borrowing for the foreseeable future. Even banks with government backing, such as Woori, found themselves shut out of repo markets.

Nowhere else in Asia experienced the full combination of plunging exports, devaluation and a massive liquidity squeeze that hit South Korea in 2008. But the impact on the entire region was dramatic. In Thailand the financial meltdown coincided with an escalating political crisis that culminated in huge demonstrations, the occupation of the Bangkok airport by middle-class protesters and, in December 2008, the removal by judicial means of the government headed by the People's Power Party, affiliated with the exiled oligarch and ex–prime minister Thaksin Shinawatra. With exports of goods and services, notably tourism, accounting for almost 70 percent of GDP, the civil disorder left Thailand's economy vulnerable.[12] Year on year to the third quarter of 2009, Thai exports fell by 25 percent. In Malaysia's case the export dependence was even greater: 103 percent of

GDP.[13] That the value of exports exceeded GDP was possible because Malaysia, even more than China, was an assembly hub for global manufacturers fed by imported raw materials and subcomponents. By the winter of 2008–2009 Malaysia's globalized manufacturing sector was contracting by 17.6 percent. Malaysia's electronics assembly plants were experiencing a 44 percent year-on-year contraction. By contrast with Thailand and Malaysia, in Indonesia, the largest and poorest of the ASEAN group, exports accounted for only 20 percent of GDP. But its exports consisted of commodities, whose prices plunged from the summer of 2008.

For those Asian economies hit mainly by the export shock, the policy response was simple: fiscal and monetary stimulus. None of the reactions was on the scale of China, but they were impressive nevertheless. In Thailand, following the "judicial coup" of December 2008, a new government took office, closely associated with the Bangkok establishment, the royal family and the military. It was headed by Abhisit Vejjajiva, who was educated at Eton and Oxford. Given the impact of the crisis on Thailand's highly open economy and his need to build legitimacy, Abhisit immediately embarked on a stimulus program. The first phase, announced in January 2009, amounted to 116.7 billion baht, or 1.3 percent of GDP, with priority given to popular consumption, including "saving the nation checks" distributed by way of the Social Security Administration, bonuses for senior citizens and subsidies for public education. At the same time, the Bank of Thailand slashed interest rates to 1.25 percent—compared with the 12.5 percent they had reached during the 1998 crisis—and directed six government-owned banks to rush loans, especially to small businesses. But the January plan was only the beginning. As the severity of the crisis deepened, Abhisit upped the scale of the stimulus to a remarkable 17 percent of 2009 GDP—$40 billion—to be spent over the next four years. In 2009 the budget deficit surged from 1 percent to 5.6 percent of GDP.[14]

Compared with its massively export-dependent neighbors, Indonesia enjoyed a degree of insulation from the global shock. But it was also by far the largest state in the region and it was extremely difficult for its central government to deploy resources effectively across its sprawling island territories. With former minister of finance and governor of the Bank of Indonesia Boediono leading the way as vice president, Jakarta opted for a

stimulus based largely on tax cuts rather than on government spending.[15] This meant that out of Indonesia's working population of 97 million and its teeming mass of 48 million small businesses, only the 10 million workers and 200,000 firms that were registered for tax would benefit. But within that sector the impact was considerable. The tax cuts amounted to 1.4 percent of GDP at PPP. This may not sound like much, but given the modest scope of the Indonesian central government budget, it amounted to 10 percent of public expenditure.

As in Thailand, the crisis struck Malaysia at a moment of political flux. The ruling nationalist party was going through a succession crisis. As the government of Prime Minister Abdullah Ahmad Badawi disintegrated, it was no coincidence that the man who moved to replace him was the forceful minister of finance Najib Razak. He did not take long to claim credit for a $16.4 billion stimulus that was launched in the spring of 2009. This was "the biggest economic stimulus initiative Malaysia has ever taken," which, when tax cuts and guarantees were included, amounted to 9 percent of GDP.[16] It was marketed as a major step toward rejuvenating the New Economic Model, which had supposedly guided Malaysia's development since independence. Fueled by foreign investment and the petrochemical boom, Malaysia hoped to catapult to the status of a fully developed economy on a par with Singapore, its enviable neighbor. There were tax cuts and reductions in interest rates by the central bank, but the main drivers of the program were the finance ministry and the Khazanah Nasional, Malaysia's sovereign wealth fund. One of the main vehicles for their lending was 1Malaysia Development Berhad (1MDB), a fund designed to channel gulf petrodollars into Malaysian national development and to act as a counterpart for infrastructure development projects by China's electricity grid, called State Grid. At the time of its launch, Najib's program met with wide international acclaim. Malaysia was promoted from eighteenth to tenth place in the global ranking of competitiveness issued by the International Institute for Management Development and attracted major investments from Goldman Sachs and Citigroup. Goldman's Singapore office was particularly eager to help, with a gigantic $6.5 billion bond issue by 1MDB. Only later, thanks to investigations by the *Wall Street Journal* and the *New York Times*, would it emerge that 1MDB was not just a vehicle for Malaysian economic

development and mouthwatering fees for Goldman. It also served as a conduit for billion-dollar corruption on the part of Malaysia's prime minister.[17]

All of Asia had to deal with the export shock. What set South Korea apart was the emergency in its financial sector. To help offset the closing of dollar funding markets, the Korean state was forced in October 2008 to provide $100 billion in foreign loan guarantees and at least $30 billion in other liquidity and support measures. Korea's crisis-fighting mobilization in the autumn of 2008 was not limited to the government. Major Korean exporters, such as steelmaker Posco, Hyundai Motor and Samsung Electronics, flushed hundreds of millions of dollars into the Seoul exchanges so as to ease pressure on the won.[18] The Korean state pension system volunteered to buy bank bonds to ease funding difficulties. Meanwhile, Korea's president, Lee Myung-bak, a former CEO at Hyundai's construction division, called on his citizens to save on imported fossil fuels and to commit their personal dollar savings to rescuing the won. The queues at the exchange booths were both a gratifying display of patriotism and an alarming sign of the extremity of the situation. Meanwhile, the Bank of Korea intervened actively in foreign exchange markets, desperately trying to stem the collapse of the won. But what was most effective in stopping the run against was help from the outside.[19] On October 30 the Bank of Korea announced the opening of a $30 billion swap line with the Fed, allowing it to auction dollars in generous amounts. With the foreign exchanges no longer in panic mode, Seoul could set about restoring the banking sector. In early 2009 the South Korean government issued a further $55 billion in liquidity backstops for interbank lending and set aside $23 billion for restructuring banks and nonperforming loans. It then added a $7.8 billion bond market stabilization fund and a $31.3 billion fund for corporate restructuring. Meanwhile, President Lee was true to his nickname—"the Bulldozer"— kicking off 2009 with a gigantic construction program, budgeted at $94 billion over a four-year period.[20] Headline projects included large investments in nuclear power, upgrades to the railway system and the president's favorite, the $15 billion Four Major Rivers Restoration Project, to restore riverbeds and construct a new dam system.[21] South Korea, Lee promised, would not just achieve 7 percent growth, a per capita income of $40,000 and claim the seventh spot in the global ranking of national

economies—"7-4-7" was his slogan—it would also establish itself as a pioneer of "green growth."

Across East and Southeast Asia, the response to the 2008 crisis set down a historical marker. Against the backdrop of their humiliating reliance on the IMF and the Clinton administration in the 1997 crisis, countries like Thailand, Malaysia and South Korea had reached a new level of autonomy. No more than in China or in the West was this merely a matter of technocratic competence, though they had plenty of that. Major stimulus efforts were political through and through. But whatever the local interests that mobilized in each case, the policy responses of the Asian emerging markets were effective. And this new resilience was acknowledged in Washington. One of the reasons why Fed officials advocated a swap line for South Korea was that they did not believe Seoul was willing to have recourse to the IMF any longer. Better to welcome South Korea discreetly to the top table rather than to risk a politicized clash that might upset fragile global markets.[22] The Asian economies rebounded quickly and they would soon attract new foreign capital flows. In addition, two of them, South Korea and Indonesia, emerged from the crisis as full members of a new organization designed specifically to reflect the complex reality of a multipolar global economy.

II

The G20 owed its existence to an initiative launched in December 1999 by then US Treasury secretary Larry Summers and Canadian prime minister Paul Martin. Their vision was to create a forum for global governance that was more representative than the Bretton Woods institutions, such as the IMF and the World Bank, but not so unmanageable as the United Nations. Twenty members seemed like a round number. As the story is told, the list was drawn up by Summers's assistant, Timothy Geithner (then in charge of international affairs at the Treasury), and Caio Koch-Weser, former managing director at the World Bank and then at the German finance ministry. With data for GDP, population and world trade to hand, they went down the list "ticking some countries and crossing others: Canada in, Spain out,

South Africa in, Nigeria and Egypt out, Argentina in, Colombia out, and so on."[23] Once the list had been approved by the G8, the invitations were then dispatched to the relevant finance ministries and central banks. There was no prior discussion or consultation. The rich countries decided to form a bigger club and asked twelve new members to join. It was global governance made simple.

Throughout the 2000s the G20 functioned as a top-level forum of technical experts.[24] The meetings were often perfunctory and some busy Treasury ministers chose not to attend. But Paul Martin was indefatigable in his efforts to have the G20 upgraded to a full leadership summit. To no one's surprise he was blocked by the Bush administration, which preferred to deal bilaterally with China and otherwise to assemble self-selecting coalitions of the willing. It was far from a foregone conclusion, therefore, that this ad hoc intergovernmental forum should become the global platform through which the world's leading economies responded to the financial crisis. When President Sarkozy addressed the UN General Assembly in September 2008, he called for the G8 to be expanded to a G13 or G14, adding China, India, South Africa, Mexico and Brazil. Both France and Japan preferred a smaller group, because this maximized their leverage. It was Britain's prime minister, Gordon Brown, who took up the proposal and, following the General Assembly meeting in September 2008, convened an impromptu gathering in New York to formulate a joint approach to the White House. The questions were how to get the United States on board and whom to include. Britain favored the larger G20 format, as did Australia, Canada and the Latin Americans. After the uncoordinated shambles of the bank bailouts in September and early October, the Bush administration had a new appreciation of the need for cooperation. What the White House wanted to avoid was a global assembly in New York under UN auspices, which was sure to be packed with critics of the Bush administration. The Americans preferred a meeting in Washington, where the IMF could put a dignified gloss on proceedings. Though it was by tradition headed by a European, IMF voting rights were weighted by financial contribution, giving the United States a veto. That was a global design with which the Bush administration could live. The invitation to the first G20 heads of government meeting finally went out on October 22, calling a gathering for

November 14. On his way out of office, Bush's administration, which had given unilateralism a bad name, would reluctantly inaugurate a new chapter in global multilateralism.

For new members of the elite circle, such as Australia, Brazil, Korea and Indonesia, the G20 was an exciting departure. For the United States it promised at least minimal coordination across the major economies. For China it was a convenient mechanism for gaining global influence without having to accept an excessive burden of responsibility. But the G20 was far from meeting with universal approval. As *Der Spiegel* reported, for Norway's foreign minister Jonas Gahr Støre, the formation of an oligarchy of globally significant states was one of the greatest setbacks to international organization since World War II.[25] In his words, "The spirit of the Congress of Vienna [1814–1815], where great powers assembled to effectively govern the world, has no place in the contemporary international community. The G20 is sorely lacking in legitimacy and must change." They were strong words, but to a degree beside the point. The Congress of Vienna was a reactionary convention reinstating the ancien régime in the wake of the French Revolution and Napoleon. The G20 was an exclusive club, for sure, but it was a new club, with new members, whose promotion to global prominence a small European state like Norway might well resent. The G20's organizing principle was not the ancien régime logic of the balance of power or traditionalist legitimacy, or, for that matter, the logic of globalism as it appealed to Rooseveltian New Dealers in 1945. The G20 was a reflection of the new world created since the 1970s by globalized economic growth. The nations represented at the G20 might represent only 10 percent of UN member states and 60 percent of the world's population, but they were responsible for 80 percent of trade and 85 percent of global GDP and their share was increasing. There was no pretense of equality within the G20, let alone with states beyond. But the members of the G20 did at least recognize one another as elements of the global economic system that were too significant to ignore. At the UN the exclusivity of the G20 provoked something of a countermovement. But when in 2009 the UN General Assembly convened its own committee on the global economic crisis, the G20 ignored it.[26]

The knock on the UN was that it was either an empty talking shop or

a stage for global grandstanding. Creating an expanded council of the "big 20" with all the principals in the room promised a more businesslike approach. But would global governance à la G20 be any different? The first G20 meeting in Washington on November 15, 2008, was not encouraging. The time allowed was too short. The leaders went around the table delivering prepared statements. After the twenty participants had each had their fifteen minutes, the allotted five hours were up. The statements were of varying levels of discipline, relevance and sophistication. The Germans, Australians and Canadians were on point. Sarkozy grandstanded and demanded action on the Doha trade round, despite the fact that France's defense of European agriculture was one of the greatest obstacles to progress on world trade liberalization. Italy's Prime Minister Berlusconi had nothing to say about the economy, but he did at least offer warm wishes to the outgoing President Bush. For a "global" forum there were still too many Europeans around the table.[27] Brazil and Argentina enjoyed their moment in the spotlight. They had axes to grind and wanted to fire off parting shots in the direction of President Bush.

Rather than any substantive discussion, the leaders gave their approval to a laundry list of ninety-five precommitments, including an agreement to a second gathering in the spring. Perhaps most important, there was strong language about the need to maintain open global trade. There would be no protectionist free-for-all, as in the 1930s. There was also an agreement to abandon a narrow view of fiscal propriety and not to discourage deficits, but no agreement on a coordinated worldwide stimulus. Why the G20 would matter, it seemed, was that it would be the channel through which the "great powers" set the agenda for change in other global institutions. In November 2008 there was an agreement between the FSF—the global assembly of bank regulators—and the IMF for the FSF to define new standards for financial regulators, for the IMF to oversee their implementation and for all financial organizations to widen their membership to include the assertive new emerging economies.

III

One reason that the first G20 could not do more was that it met ten days after the US election. After eight years of Republican control of the White House, president-elect Barack Obama was expected to set a new tone. But Obama refused to upstage the incumbent president. What Obama's approach to international economic affairs would be when he took office was unclear. This left it up to others to project their fantasies onto the next American administration. Gordon Brown had lobbied hard to get the right to host the second G20 in London. As the slogans of Tony Blair's "New Labour" had faded, Brown and his staff were desperate to associate themselves with the charisma of the new president and his promise of hope.[28] But Brown had visions that went beyond that. In the summer of 1933 London had hosted a World Economic Conference. Called to heal the wounds of the Great Depression, it had been blown apart by posturing from Nazi Germany, divisions between Britain and France and the isolationist turn of the early Roosevelt New Deal. London in 1933 had symbolized the descent into disintegration and economic nationalism that blighted the decade that followed. Brown was determined to avoid that fate. Instead, London did its best to sell the 2009 G20 as a new Bretton Woods.[29] With an eye to the history books, Brown and his staff consulted with experts on FDR and the New Deal. Biographies of John Maynard Keynes were on Downing Street bedside tables. What London needed to make real this historical romance was for the rest of the G20 to play along. And the signs were not good.

The new team in the White House did not welcome the solicitations lavished on them by the British. They had no patience for talk of a "special relationship." The Obama administration was focused on the Pacific, not on Europe. The first foreign visitor received at the White House was the Japanese prime minister, Tarō Asō. But overriding everything was the need to focus on domestic policy. Obama might not even have made time to attend the G20 meeting, but for the fact that his aides had written in his diary that he had to be in Strasbourg on April 4 to mark the sixtieth anniversary of the founding of NATO. Brown's team scheduled the London G20 for two days earlier to fit around the president's travel plans.[30] To prepare the

ground, on March 3, 2009, Gordon Brown arrived in DC for meetings with Obama and a triumphant speech to both houses of Congress. He spoke in bathetic terms of a "grand bargain" being struck in London and the sealing of "a global new deal."[31] What he had in mind was a "trillion-dollar summit," a giant orchestrated stimulus to lift the world economy out of recession. Unfortunately for the Labour Party's control-obsessed PR machine, the rest of the world was not cooperating. On March 14, 2009, as the G20 finance ministers assembled in London for a presummit meeting, Chancellor Angela Merkel dropped in for a visit. The result, to the embarrassment of Gordon Brown, was a concerted pushback orchestrated between Merkel and Christine Lagarde. Not only did Germany and France think that stimulus on the scale being rumored was unwarranted, but they suspected it was being used to push more sensitive issues off the global agenda. "The French and Germans worried that the villain of the piece—Anglo-Saxon market behaviour—was being let off the hook because the focus was now on the world economy."[32] America would want to talk about other people's trade surpluses and not its dangerous banks.

Even more disconcerting was the reaction from China. By the spring of 2009, Beijing was growing impatient with the lack of discipline in the West. In Beijing's view, it was reckless American deficits that had driven the global imbalances. Now, instead of retrenching, Britain and America were talking about even more spending. With a week to go to the G20, on March 23 the Chinese central bank chairman, Zhou Xiaochuan, surprised the world by launching his own call for a new Bretton Woods.[33] The Chinese had been at the original meeting in 1944 and they knew their economic history.[34] As far as Zhou was concerned, it was time to revisit the fundamental decisions made in 1944. It was thanks to America's overweening power at the end of World War II that the dollar had been established as the global reserve currency. Ever since, America had been free to spend at will while accumulating huge deficits. To ensure true stability, as John Maynard Keynes had argued for the British delegation in 1944, the world needed a global monetary unit independent of any national currency. The obvious candidate, Zhou suggested, was the IMF's unit of accounting and credit, the Special Drawing Rights (SDR). With this in place there would be a true anchor of stability that was not at the mercy of a single superpower. On that basis one

could then talk about rules binding on both deficit and surplus nations, the United States as well as China.

One might wonder why the Chinese regime would wish to change a system from which it had benefited so spectacularly. After all, it was Beijing that had pegged its currency against the dollar since the 1990s, creating what some economists had already dubbed "Bretton Woods 2."[35] The conventional reading in Washington was that China was free riding at America's expense. But that would be to view the situation with Western eyes. China had fixed its exchange rate in 1994 as a defensive measure at a time when the United States was running a responsible fiscal policy. If since 2000 gigantic imbalances had begun to appear, that, in Beijing's view, had more to do with America's fiscal recklessness than with China's currency manipulation. China's export surplus was far from being an unmitigated blessing. As far as Beijing was concerned, the surplus reinforced China's excessively investment-driven growth path and led it deeper into a lopsided entanglement with the United States. A more balanced trade account was a natural concomitant of the effort to shift the focus of economic growth toward domestic consumption.[36] In the meantime, the PBoC's currency proposal was a shot across the bows of the new administration and a sign that Beijing was running out of patience with America.

China's assertive proposal attracted more attention than Gordon Brown's wistful reminders of the 1940s, and rightly so. Not since the days of Mao had China made such a bold proposal on a fundamental issue of global governance. And the Chinese proposal chimed with statements made by both France and Russia, who were also questioning the dollar standard. It also aligned with plans that were being developed at the UN and spearheaded by the Nobel Prize–winning economist Joseph Stiglitz that advanced the idea of an SDR-based global currency.[37] Washington was taken aback. When pressed by journalists, President Obama remarked that he didn't think the world needed a global currency.[38] His new Treasury secretary, Tim Geithner, was less circumspect. Seeking to placate the Chinese, Geithner casually remarked that he was "quite open" to the idea of an "evolution" toward a greater use of SDRs as a global reserve asset.[39] The currency markets were shocked. The dollar lost 1.3 cents against the euro. It was red meat for the Republican right wing and Fox News commentators,

who scandalized their audience by claiming that the Obama administration was scheming to replace the greenback with a global currency.[40] Geithner learned a hard lesson in PR. Rowing back urgently, he took to the TV networks to affirm that, in fact, he agreed with his boss. A strong dollar should remain as the anchor of the world economy.

Perhaps not surprisingly, China's vision of a Bretton Woods 2 did not make it onto Gordon Brown's G20 agenda. Nor, however, would the reality of the situation since the autumn of 2008 be up for discussion. Far from weakening the dollar's grip on global finance, the crisis had in fact strengthened it.[41] In currency markets the demand for US Treasurys as a safe-haven investment had driven the dollar upward. The Fed, through the swap line system, was backstopping the liquidity of the entire global banking system. If the London G20 was truly to have been a second Bretton Woods, the dollar-based banking system, the swap lines and the Fed's new role as global liquidity provider would have been at the center of the discussion. That would certainly have wrong-footed the Europeans, whose banks were among the chief beneficiaries. But no one had any interest in publicizing those fragile arrangements. It was better to leave the broader issues of global currency architecture off the agenda altogether.

IV

It was a delicate balancing act. Washington knew that it wanted cooperation, but it had no interest in trumpeting the central role played by the Fed and the US Treasury since the previous year. The British wanted to bandwagon their own underpowered version of a G2, a reheated special relationship, on the new president. But that was painfully out of touch with reality. On the morning of April 1, 2009, after Brown and Obama had breakfasted together in Downing Street, the president spoke to the press. Complimenting Brown on his diplomacy in bringing the meeting together, Obama remarked: "Well, if there's just Roosevelt and Churchill sitting in a room with a brandy, that's a—that's an easier negotiation. . . . But that's not the world we live in, and it shouldn't be the world that we live in."[42] Across London that very morning, Merkel and Sarkozy were underlining the point. They

had arrived early in London to stage their own breakfast meeting and joint announcement. In Sarkozy's words, "France and Germany will speak with a single voice."[43] What was needed was not fiscal stimulus but a real crackdown on global financial markets. Sarkozy threatened to walk out unless the conference seriously addressed the issue of tax havens. "This has nothing to do with ego, this has nothing to do with temper tantrums," he claimed, preempting the spin that the British were bound to put on any French criticism. "This has to do with whether we're going to be up to the challenges ahead or not." Merkel, characteristically, delivered a morality lesson: "The tendency is not to deal with the roots of the evil. We need to learn something from this crisis."[44]

As the G20 leaders assembled that afternoon in Buckingham Palace, it was a freak show of outsized personalities. When he was not grandstanding, Sarkozy was ostentatiously busy on his cell phone. Argentina's Cristina Fernández de Kirchner reprised her anticapitalist posturing from Washington. Italy's Silvio Berlusconi was noisily desperate to attract Obama's attention. Otherwise, he was prone to nodding off. Merkel was unflappable and hard to budge. The Chinese dug in hard on their negotiating position. Several heads of government were unable to communicate fluently in English and most had little technical command of the material. Over the entire assembly glowered Gordon Brown, sleep deprived and running on a manic high from which he would soon suffer a shattering rebound. As chair in closed session, Brown delivered what was, by all accounts, a domineering, high-energy performance that struck several witnesses as bordering on the inappropriate. Brown was lucky to have Obama as his gracious and engaged second. At several points the negotiations threatened to break down. But though the sausage making was unsightly and at times bizarre, by the end of the main conference day on April 2, the second G20 had produced results.

The communiqué would begin and end with general statements about the scale of the crisis and commitments to work cooperatively to avoid protectionism and to bear in mind the interests of the wider population, the least developed countries, etc. This was the boilerplate. The real politics of the communiqué began in earnest with the section on financial reform. There would be a new global Financial Stability Board, which would devise

improved regulations and discipline the ineffectual private credit-rating agencies. The G20 thus confirmed its role as the de facto lead body, setting the agenda for the Basel Committee, the IMF and other agencies of global governance. As the Germans and the French were determined to block talk of coordinated fiscal stimulus and there was something akin to a conspiracy of silence around the role that the Fed was playing in providing global liquidity, it was by way of the IMF that Brown and Obama would deliver their expansive impulse. The IMF's ambitious director, Dominique Strauss-Kahn, was more than happy for the Fund to play a lead role. But given the loan portfolio it had taken on since the previous autumn and the scale of its commitments in Eastern Europe, the fund urgently needed to replenish its resources. An internal memo drafted in January 2009 suggested that in a worst-case scenario, with the IMF increasing its client list from two to sixteen it would need at least $300 billion in new resources.[45] Treasury Secretary Geithner, true to his "overwhelming force" doctrine, was pushing for a far larger figure than that. The sticking point was that Asian and Latin American agreement to any expansion of IMF resources depended on a redistribution of voting rights. By April 2008, as a result of two rounds of reform, voting rights within the IMF had already been shifted by 5.4 percent, with Korea, Singapore, Turkey and China seeing the biggest increases. But this still left China with only 3.81 percent of the votes and India with 2.34 percent. In London there was an agreement to a further 5 percent shift, largely at the expense of the Europeans. This bought enough support for a truly headline-grabbing increase in IMF resources. The IMF would receive $250 billion in immediate new financing from members. There would be up to $500 billion in new Arrangements to Borrow, which provided the IMF with credits from member states on demand. And finally there would be an issue of $250 billion in SDRs to all the IMF members.[46] This gave Brown the "plump, round headline figure of $1 trillion" that he so craved.[47] It wasn't a conventional Keynesian stimulus, but it represented the conclusion of the lessons learned since the major cycle of international crises that began in 1994 in Mexico. The IMF was equipped with the firepower necessary to deal with the fallout from a transnational, twenty-first-century banking crisis.

But the G20 was not yet home and dry. The sticking point on the final

afternoon was tax havens. Both Sarkozy and Merkel insisted that there must be action to curb the *paradis fiscaux*. Obama had campaigned on the same issue. Gordon Brown, sensitive to the interests of the City of London, was less keen. But it was the Chinese who were most adamant. Macao and Hong Kong functioned as conduits for flight capital from mainland China. But for Beijing to close that door would cause major ructions within the Chinese oligarchy. Furthermore, given its championing of anti-imperialist nationalism, China was not going to allow former colonial possessions to be placed under a new regime of international supervision dominated by Westerners. Sovereignty was a nonnegotiable issue. With only minutes to go before the heads of government dispersed, Brown's G20 threatened to derail over the clash between the French and the Chinese. Brown himself was fully taken up with his chairing duties and could not break away to broker a side deal. It wasn't likely that either France or China would be browbeaten by Downing Street underlings, even of the shouty variety. So it was Obama who swung into action, coaxing the two sides to accept a face-saving compromise under which the G20 would "take note" of a blacklist of tax havens issued by the Organisation for Economic Co-operation and Development (OECD), an organization descended from the Marshall Plan era to which China did not belong and which it could feel free to ignore.

Satisfied with the deal, Sarkozy promptly tried to reclaim the agenda he had launched at the UN the previous September. Ahead of his host, he bounded out of the final session to be first before the cameras. At least for a few moments, the French president posed as the front man of a unified G20. Warming up his Gaullist act, he announced that a "page had been turned" on the history of "Anglo-Saxon capitalism." The age of deregulation was over. It was a token of Brown's success that Sarkozy was so keen to steal his limelight. Disagreement and breakdown had been avoided. Speaking to a global TV audience that he optimistically reckoned at 1 billion, an exhausted Brown delivered the news that the world's leading powers had pulled together. They had agreed to act in a concerted fashion. Obama was happy to declare that "[b]y any measure, the London summit was historic."[48] The decisions they had taken were "bolder than any other response to a crisis in living memory . . . whether they are sufficient, we've got to wait and see." Angela Merkel was more grudging. It was, she admitted, a "very, very

good, almost historic compromise. This time the world does not react as in the thirties. This is a victory for global co-operation."[49]

The London G20 was not mere theater. The incorporation of a key group of emerging markets into global economic policy was a genuine innovation. The ratification of the IMF deal was to prove particularly important. In the years to come it would prove to be a vital resource, ironically enough, for Europe. But if this was the future of global governance, perhaps the gibes about the Congress of Vienna were not entirely wide of the mark. It was exciting for London to be hosting America's glamorous new president, and the faded fixtures of 1990s Cool Britannia were out in force. The message of confidence issuing from the meeting, the huge boost to IMF resources, was good news, above all, for financial markets in London, New York, Tokyo, Shanghai, the media that served them and the audience of investors around the world, large and small. But when talking IMF quotas or tax havens, public participation was not welcomed by the British or the Americans, let alone the Chinese or the Saudis. As a political event the summit was an airtight cabal of executive power, housed in the cavernous bunkers of the ExCeL conference center, shielded from tens of thousands of protesters by a gigantic police mobilization.[50] In the course of the confrontations in the City of London, a homeless newspaper vendor was fatally injured by the police, adding fuel to indignant protests about repressive police tactics. Inside the conference hall, Gordon Brown proved that he was perfectly suited to the role of Treasury secretary to the world. But his position as prime minister of Britain seemed ever more precarious. Indeed, Brown's advisers worried that their boss, having become used to thinking in terms of trillions, might be losing touch with the humdrum reality of a medium-sized country heading into a deep recession.

Though he advocated stimulus at a global level, at home Brown was boxed in. A week before the summit, on March 24, 2009, Mervyn King, governor of the Bank of England, had given evidence to the Treasury Select Committee of the House of Commons and added his voice to those of the Germans, French and Chinese arguing against any substantial fiscal stimulus. "Given how big those deficits are, I think it would be sensible to be cautious about going further in using discretionary measures to expand the size of those deficits," he opined.[51] King thus flatly contradicted the prime

minister, who that same day was addressing the European Parliament in Strasbourg and calling for governments to do "whatever it takes to create growth and the jobs we need." It was an extraordinarily high-stakes political intervention by the governor of the Bank of England, straying beyond monetary policy into the realm of fiscal policy, and it rattled the markets. The following day, the Treasury suffered the first failed gilt bond auction since 1995.[52] An offering of £1.75 billion of thirty-year UK Treasury bonds attracted only £1.67 billion in orders. At 0.93, the cover ratio was believed to be the worst in history. The Opposition could barely contain their Schadenfreude. Tory spokesman Michael Gove quipped that King had "cut up the Prime Minister's credit card."[53] Vince Cable, for Britain's third party, the Liberal Democrats, spoke rather melodramatically of a "very British coup d'état." The governor of the Bank of England had sent "his tanks down the Mall" to "put the Government under house arrest."[54] With the budget deficit yawning to £118 billion, and financial markets jittery, Prime Minister Brown needed the expansive vision offered by the G20 to hide his own limited room for maneuver.

IV

Given that resistance from France and Germany had kept any firm fiscal policy commitments off the G20 agenda at London, it was something of a surprise that the final communiqué spoke in grandiose terms of $5 trillion in fiscal expansion that would save millions of jobs and "accelerate the transition to a green economy."[55] Where that enormous figure came from is something of a mystery. Over the weeks that followed it was left to outside agencies such as the IMF to do the work of compiling data about the emergency spending programs that had been launched around the world. The results were striking.

In total, between 2008 and 2010, crisis-fighting expenditure would come to $1.87 trillion, or $2.4 trillion in PPP-adjusted terms—counting only discretionary spending and emergency tax-cutting measures. It was not $5 trillion, but it was nevertheless historically unprecedented. What was even more striking was the distribution of this spending. Whichever way one

Global Stimulus: The Discretionary Fiscal Response of the G20

	stimulus % GDP			stimulus in PPP $ billions			stimulus in $ billions		
	2008	2009	2010	2008	2009	2010	2008	2009	2010
Argentina	0	1.5	0	0.0	10.6	0.0	0.0	5.7	0.0
Australia	0.7	2.1	1.7	6.1	18.6	15.6	7.4	20.9	21.2
Brazil	0	0.6	0.8	0.0	15.5	22.4	0.0	10.0	17.7
Canada	0	1.9	1.7	0.0	24.6	23.0	0.0	26.0	27.4
China	0.4	3.1	2.7	39.3	335.2	326.3	18.2	158.3	160.6
France	0	0.7	0.8	0.0	15.9	18.7	0.0	18.9	21.2
Germany	0	1.6	2	0.0	49.8	65.5	0.0	54.7	68.4
India	0.6	0.6	0.6	26.4	28.9	32.2	7.3	8.2	10.3
Indonesia	0	1.3	0.6	0.0	24.2	12.0	0.0	7.5	4.5
Italy	0	0.2	0.1	0.0	4.0	2.1	0.0	4.4	2.1
Japan	0.3	2.4	1.8	12.8	97.8	77.7	14.5	120.8	98.9
Korea	1.1	3.9	1.2	14.8	53.3	17.7	11.0	35.2	13.1
Mexico	0	1.5	0	0.0	25.2	0.0	0.0	13.4	0.0
Russia	0	4.1	1.3	0.0	117.5	39.4	0.0	50.1	19.8
Saudi Arabia	2.4	3.3	3.5	26.9	37.9	42.6	12.5	14.2	18.4
South Africa	1.7	1.8	-0.6	9.9	10.4	-3.6	4.9	5.3	-2.3
Turkey	0	0.8	0.3	0.0	8.6	3.6	0.0	4.9	2.2
UK	0.2	1.4	-0.1	4.5	30.3	-2.2	5.6	32.5	-2.4
US	1.1	2	1.8	161.9	288.4	269.4	161.9	288.4	269.4
Regional shares				302.6	1196.7	962.4	243.4	879.5	750.7
China				13.0	28.0	33.9	7.5	18.0	21.4
Other Asia				17.9	17.1	14.5	13.5	19.5	16.9
Europe				1.5	8.4	8.7	2.3	12.6	11.9
US				53.5	24.1	28.0	66.5	32.8	35.9
ROW				14.1	22.5	14.9	10.2	17.1	13.9
				100	100	100	100	100	100

Sources: Author's calculations from IMF, "Update on Fiscal Stimulus and Financial Sector Measures," April 26, 2009, combined with PPP GDP data from Maddison Project, http://www.ggdc.net/maddison/maddison-project/home.htm.

measured it, in 2009 and 2010, Asia and the emerging markets produced the most dramatic response to the crisis. Russia, Indonesia, Korea, Turkey, Brazil and Argentina were now in a position to launch truly substantial fiscal responses.[56] According to the IMF's figures, in 2009 Russia's discretionary crisis response more or less matched that of Germany or exceeded it in PPP terms.[57] And these figures were a serious understatement of China's effort. They did not include the huge lending boom. By comparison, despite the size of the EU's economy, Europe's fiscal response to the crisis was derisory, barely more than 10 percent on the most generous measure. It was a sign of things to come. The only Western fiscal stimulus that weighed seriously in the balance was that launched by the United States.

Chapter 12

STIMULUS

Down a "road to hell" was where the United States was headed.[1] Those were the words of Mirek Topolánek, the lame duck prime minister of the Czech Republic, addressing the European Parliament on March 25, 2009. The embarrassment was that he was not just another Central European conservative. He was speaking in his capacity as president of the European Council just days ahead of the London G20. The economic policies of the Obama administration would destroy confidence, the Czech pressed on. Surging deficits and giant bond sales would "undermine the liquidity of the global financial market."[2] They were fighting words. Everyone knew that conservatives on both sides of the Atlantic were suspicious of Obama's administration, but a "road to hell"? Some wondered whether the translators could possibly have got it right. The *New York Times* reached for history. Perhaps as a survivor of decades of Communist tyranny, Topolánek had a particular allergy to state intervention. President Sarkozy didn't care. He was furious. How could a jumped-up East European minnow be talking about America that way, and on behalf of Europe, to boot? In London Sarkozy upbraided the Czech about his inappropriate tone. On the back foot Topolánek offered a rather less trite and more disarming explanation. Far from being inspired by the horrors of Stalinism, the phrase had popped into his head after an evening spent listening to the heavy metal classic Meat Loaf's "Bat Out of Hell."[3]

Whatever the idiom they expressed it with, what stirred conservatives

on both sides of the Atlantic in early 2009 was outrage at the first major leg-
islative initiative of the Obama administration: what would become known
as the "Obama stimulus," the American Recovery and Reinvestment Act.
Pushed with urgency by the Democrats, it passed the House already on Jan-
uary 28, 2009. At the new president's insistence it was debated in the Senate
in a special weekend session and voted through on February 10. A week later,
on February 17, Obama signed the spending package into law. It was the
largest measure of fiscal stimulus undertaken in the West in the wake of the
crisis and the largest in American history. By the same token, it instantly
polarized the economic policy arena on both sides of the Atlantic.

I

Obama's team never doubted the need to act. Over the winter of 2008–
2009 America's economic situation was deteriorating fast. Jobs were hem-
orrhaging. Detroit was on its knees. There was a pervasive sense of crisis
and a need for renewal. The political stakes were obvious. It was the drama
of the financial crisis in September and October 2008 that had broken
McCain's campaign and handed a huge electoral victory to Obama. The
atmosphere of hope and expectation that surrounded his inauguration was
electrifying. Many projected onto the new president expectations of almost
revolutionary change. Not only had Obama brought the advancement of
African Americans to a new stage, evoking memories of Martin Luther
King Jr. Coming into office in the midst of the financial crisis, he could not
escape comparisons to FDR and his famous first "hundred days." And as if
King and FDR were not enough, the newly elected president invoked an-
other era of Democratic Party optimism. He wanted to offer the new gen-
eration a Kennedy-style moon-shot mission.

Whatever the Obama administration did, it would have to be huge for
the simple reason that the twenty-first-century American economy is huge.
GDP in 2008 was c. $14.7 trillion. To have a meaningful impact the stimu-
lus would, therefore, need to be enormous. The problem was that Congress
had a hard time dealing with this elementary fact. As the controversy over
TARP indicated, a proposal that the federal government should spend a

trillion dollars on work creation was likely to cause indignation, panic or both. So the approach the transition team devised was cautious. They would propose $775 billion to the Democratic Party leadership and hope that the notorious log-rolling tendencies of Congress would take the final total close to $1 trillion.[4] If Republican support could be bought with further tax cuts or more spending, the more the better.

Despite the radical expectations projected onto him, Obama was by inclination a bipartisan centrist. What he had not reckoned with was the sheer violence of the conservative hostility toward him. There was no possibility of bipartisanship. Whereas at least a minority of Republicans had voted with the majority of the Democrats to pass the Fannie Mae and Freddie Mac bailouts and TARP, in January 2009 in the House of Representatives not a single Republican voted for the American Recovery and Reinvestment Act, despite the tax cuts with which it was festooned.[5] In the Senate only three did. It was a warning of the depth of partisan hostility the Obama administration would face. From the outset of his presidency, a large section of Republican opinion effectively denied the legitimacy of Obama's leadership. At the grassroots this expressed itself in the "birther" conspiracy, doubting Obama's status as a natural-born citizen. In Congress it manifested itself in a stance of absolute opposition. America's right-wing think tanks mobilized in force to denounce the bailouts and to discredit the stimulus and the financial regulations to come. By the spring the wave of antigovernment indignation that dubbed itself the "Tea Party movement" would roil the base of the Republican Party and hog the television news cycle. In the background, billionaire "dark money" donors, led by the Koch brothers, stirred the pot.

In 2009 the Republicans were in a minority in both the House and the Senate. But their relentless guerrilla war and the drumbeat of their media outlets had real and immediate effects.[6] Above all they shifted the balance within the broad-church coalition of the Democratic Party. The fact that the administration needed the Democrats to vote en bloc in favor of the stimulus gave leverage to so-called moderates—the Blue Dog Coalition and the New Democrat Coalition—free-market, antispending Democrats who were anxious to preserve their hard-won probusiness credentials.[7] As a result, rather than bidding the stimulus up from $775 billion, the congressio-

nal "moderates" tended to whittle it down. The result was less substantial than the Obama team had hoped for and less than the US economy needed. The headline for the American Recovery and Reinvestment Act was $820 billion. In actuality it was more like $725 billion in new money, $50 billion less than where the Obama team had started.

Politics dictated not just its size but its shape. The president wanted big-ticket items of innovation. But Obama's chief of staff, Rahm Emanuel, and his political team were always skeptical that the president's infatuation with the environmental agenda and green growth would sell. What Capitol Hill wanted were tax cuts and spending programs targeted to please key constituencies. Ultimately, $212 billion of the stimulus went into tax cuts and $296 billion toward improving mandatory programs such as Medicaid (health coverage for lower-income groups) and unemployment relief. This left $279 billion for discretionary spending, of which the president's priorities of green energy and improvements to broadband received $27 billion and $7 billion, respectively.[8] Altogether, the stimulus would patch up or replace 42,000 miles of road and 2,700 bridges. But unlike in the era of the New Deal, there would be no eye-catching logos, no charismatic monuments like those left by the Works Progress Administration.[9]

Nevertheless, it was substantial. In absolute terms it was on a par with the spending of the New Deal. Though it was smaller in relation to a much larger national economy, the Obama stimulus was concentrated over a shorter space of time.[10] In 2009 it placed America alongside the Asian states in the league of activists, outstripping any discretionary fiscal measures taken in Europe. And it worked. Despite the protestations of "freshwater" free-market economists and the complex economic arguments directed against "naïve" Keynesian "pump priming," every reputable econometric study found that the Obama stimulus had a substantial positive impact on the US economy.[11] Estimates by Obama's Council of Economic Advisers put the number of jobs created at 1.6 million per year for four years, for a total of 6 million job-years.[12] The multiplier was positive and above 1. This implies that the effect of government spending on the economy was not just positive. More private economic activity was stimulated than the government originally contributed. So the impact of the government's spending was to shrink the government's share in overall economic activity.

But if this was the case, if the stimulus worked, why didn't the Obama administration ask for more?[13] There were political risks in asking for a figure bigger than $1 trillion. But there were risks to undershooting as well. By 2010, America's unemployment was still stuck above 10 percent. Foreclosures and forced sales were destroying entire communities. Millions of young people left schools and colleges without jobs. Men and women in the prime of life were shut out of the workforce. Many would not return. In the elections of 2010 and 2012 the Democrats fought on the back foot against the backdrop of a limping economy and resurgent Republican activism. They retained the presidency but lost control of Congress. Obama's administration never built the constituency of Democrats-for-life that was shaped by Roosevelt's New Deal. Given that they commanded majorities in both the House and the Senate in 2009, why did the Obama team not set the bar higher and pitch for an even larger number? If maximum force was the best approach to financial stabilization, why, when it came to fiscal policy, was the approach so penny-pinching?

Part of the answer is that the transition team did not fully grasp the scale of the tsunami that was descending on the US economy. From preparatory documents circulated within the transition team in early January 2009, we know that the worst-case scenario envisioned by Obama's staff was for unemployment to reach 9 percent with no stimulus.[14] In fact, even with the largest government-spending program in American history, unemployment topped 10.5 percent. But despite this underestimate, it is clear that the top macroeconomists in the Obama transition team did, in fact, realize that the stimulus ought to be bigger. On December 16, 2008, Christina Romer submitted a report intended for the president-elect arguing that to close the "output gap" by the first quarter of 2011 would require a discretionary stimulus of $1.7–1.8 trillion. Romer's modeling was conventional. Her figures were sound. Her proposal was a trillion dollars larger than the figure the Obama team ultimately pushed through Congress. What decided the issue was politics, or rather the self-censorship of the economics team in the name of politics. Second-guessing the attitude of Chief of Staff Rahm Emanuel and his political operatives, Larry Summers, as head of the National Economic Council, was convinced that he and Romer would lose all credibility if they suggested anything even close to the figure she thought

necessary. The results of Romer's calculation were, Summers quipped, "nonplanetary." He did not want to jeopardize the influence of the economics team by appearing naïve and "unsavvy." The effect was to skew the argument from the start. No figure in excess of $900 billion, half of Romer's baseline, was ever proposed. A similar deflationary calculus ruled out any dramatic and direct action on home-owner debt.

The great political might-have-been of the early Obama administration is why, alongside TARP and the fiscal stimulus, the White House did not start by pushing a comprehensive relief program for home owners.[15] While the banks and lenders were bailed out, 9.3 million American families lost their homes to foreclosure, surrendered their home to a lender or were forced to resort to a distress sale.[16] The measures that the administration did develop to offer mortgage rescheduling were derisory in their impact. In response to criticism, Larry Summers has subsequently insisted that the question of home-owner relief was a constant subject of debate within the administration.[17] He convened regular monthly meetings with the Treasury and the other key agencies to challenge them to come up with better options. No mechanism that was effective, efficient and politically feasible emerged. There were basic obstacles. A program to help millions of distressed borrowers would have had to have been gigantic in scale. Forgiving loans on a substantial scale would have implied losses for the banking system at a time of financial uncertainty. And it would have caused a huge uproar in Congress, where the administration needed to husband its political capital, not so much with Republicans, from whom nothing was to be expected, but with the moderate congressional Democrats. It was a price that Summers, Emanuel and Treasury Secretary Geithner were not willing to pay.

What became evident in the spring of 2009 was that the historical memory that was most alive in the Obama administration was not that of FDR or JFK but that of the last Democratic administration, under Bill Clinton in the 1990s. It was the Hamilton Project's vision that prevailed in the Obama camp. In the face of the crisis the Democrats would prove themselves not as bold or imaginative but as sound managers of the economy whose task it was to put right another era of Republican misrule. Though in 2009 no one dissented from the need for an immediate stimulus, the

Obama team was profoundly committed to the legacy of their mentor, Robert Rubin.[18] Summers, Geithner and Peter Orszag, Obama's director of the Office of Management and Budget, were all veterans of the 1990s Treasury. Orszag and Rubin had argued in 2004 that government deficits would not only squeeze private investment but could set up a negative spiral of confidence and expectations and might trigger a sudden panic in financial markets.[19] Faced with the huge deficits produced by the financial crisis of 2008, there was, thus, no contradiction between the maximum-force approach to bank stabilization and the cautious approach to fiscal policy. Concern for confidence in the financial markets was their common denominator.

II

Despite its notable scale, its effectiveness and the political controversy it stirred up, the Obama stimulus was hedged around by political compromise. Furthermore, despite the urgency with which Congress acted, the stimulus was bound to come too late. Spending programs take months, if not years, to be put to work. The discretionary spending component of the Obama stimulus did not begin in earnest until June 2009, at which point the labor market was close to bottoming out.[20] The less commonly noted corollary is that the open-handed fiscal stance of the first year of the Obama administration was in large part an inheritance of decisions and nondecisions made in 2008, while the future president was still in the Senate.

In January 2009, as a result of the standoff between the Bush administration and congressional Democrats, the federal government was operating without a regular budget and was headed toward an unprecedented deficit in excess of $1.3 trillion. It was a political mess and a daunting fiscal hole, but, as far as the economy was concerned, it was precisely what was needed.[21] Part of the reason why Congress had refused to approve the budget presented to it by the Bush administration a year earlier was because it thought it was based on hopelessly unrealistic economic forecasts. Even as the real estate crisis began to make itself felt, the White House projected a deficit of only $407 billion for 2009. The administration called for $3.1 trillion in spending, and at prevailing tax rates assumed that revenue would

come to $2.7 trillion. Congress doubted both figures and was proven correct. Thanks to the recession, revenue between September 2008 and September 2009 slumped to $2.1 trillion. Meanwhile, spending soared to $3.5 trillion, including a $151 billion installment for TARP and a first tranche of $225 billion on the Obama stimulus. Fighting over TARP and the Obama stimulus made good political theater for all sides. The programs were significant in their economic impact. But the largest part of the fiscal stimulus of 2009 came as a result of the budget standoff of the preceding year and the collapse in tax revenue due to the recession.

Automatic stabilizers are the unsung heroes of modern fiscal policy. In the United States, no more than one third of federal government spending is discretionary. The rest is made up of mandatory expenditures required by existing "entitlements," social programs such as unemployment and disability benefits, or retirement pensions. These tend to increase during a recession. Likewise, tax revenue flows into Treasury coffers at preexisting rates of taxation and contribution levels, driven not by political decisions but by the fluctuating fortunes of the economy. Dominated by these nondiscretionary flows, modern state budgets have a powerful stabilizing effect on the economy. As economic activity declines and the economy calls for stimulus, tax revenue falls, entitlement spending increases and the government deficit automatically expands.

Viewed in these terms, the effect of the crisis of 2007–2009 on the budgets of rich countries was spectacular. Whatever the politics of stimulus spending in Congress, the Bundestag or the House of Commons, the automatic stabilizers delivered a huge and timely stimulus. According to calculations by the IMF, if the US economy had been at full employment in 2009, the crisis-fighting policies adopted by the Bush and Obama administrations would have been enough to produce a deficit of 6.2 percent of GDP—this was the discretionary deficit. The actual general government deficit was 12.5 percent of GDP.[22] More than half the support provided to aggregate demand was automatic or quasi-automatic. And this was typical of all advanced economies. According to the IMF's calculations, of the vast increase in public debt in the developed world over the course of the crisis, just under half was due simply to the reduction in revenue produced by the contraction of the tax base. As profits, wages and spending all declined, this

automatically generated a deficit and thus an offsetting public stimulus. This puts a rather different perspective on the fiscal policy battles at the G20. Though Germany, France and Italy steered clear of the kind of stimulus package launched by the Obama administration, let alone that trumpeted by Beijing, their deficits were widening too. As the private sector deleveraged and cut its spending, they too saw huge nondiscretionary deficits. Indeed, it would have taken a heroic and truly perverse act of austerity to prevent these automatic stabilizers from coming into effect. The net result was dramatic. Between 2007 and 2011, demand in the world economy was stabilized by the largest surge in public debt since World War II.

For macroeconomists this was a cause to celebrate the stabilizing properties of the modern tax and welfare state. For fiscal hawks it was a cause of deep concern. In the long run those debts would require higher taxes to service and repay them. This would pose major political challenges. And how would capital markets react? According to the script set out by conventional fiscal conservatism, one might have expected serious and immediate repercussions. Would the debt shock trigger the loss of confidence that Orszag and Rubin and so many others had warned about? How would savers be induced to hold trillions of dollars in government bonds? Would interest rates have to rise? Would this crowd out private investment? Would bondholders get jumpy? Would the bond vigilantes of the 1990s swing into the saddle, selling government bonds, driving Treasury prices down and yields up? In the spring of 2009, as the scale of the deficit became clear, business media reported that markets were up in arms. In light of "Washington's astonishing bet on fiscal and monetary reflation," the *Wall Street Journal* looked forward to a stern response from bond markets.[23]

So serious were the rumblings and so painful were the memories of the Clinton era that in May 2009 Obama asked budget director Orszag to prepare a contingency plan.[24] The budget director's response was drastic. In the case of a bond market panic, the administration should severely hike taxes. The report was intended to be for the eyes of the president only. When Rahm Emanuel leaked it to Summers it provoked a towering fury. Summers threatened to resign and demanded that in the future he must have complete control of all economic policy input to the president. For all his rumpled, academic persona, Summers had a keen eye for power and

could sense a new agenda of fiscal consolidation forming within the administration. This was a threat to his personal position. But it also violated his instincts as a "new Keynesian" economist. Summers might have censored Romer's stimulus proposal, but he did not believe in the power of the "confidence fairies."[25] To be talking about budget cuts in the early summer of 2009, when the United States was about to hit the trough of the most severe recession since the early 1930s, was wildly premature. If confidence was the issue, the best way to restore it was to engineer a solid recovery.

In the event, Summers and the other skeptics were proven right. There was no run against Treasurys. The bond vigilantes were a spook. America's households were rebuilding their savings. Mutual funds were shifting out of risky mortgage bonds. Everyone wanted Treasurys. These were the kinds of systemic macroeconomic and financial mechanics that all too often escape fiscal hawks, who view the public budget like that of a private household. When the private sector is undergoing a shock episode of deleveraging, when the savings rate is surging as it was in 2009, what is needed to preserve the overall financial balance of the national economy is not for the state to cut its deficit too. Everyone cannot save at once without provoking a recession. As the proponents of "functional finance" have argued since the 1940s, the state must act as a borrower of last resort.[26] In so doing it preserves aggregate demand and provides a flow of safe long-term bonds to financial markets. After the shock of 2008 the entire world was keener than ever to hold safe assets. A huge class of AAA-rated private label securities had shown itself to be far from safe, so the demand for Treasurys was huge. It wasn't only Americans who wanted US government debt. As Treasury debt held by the public increased by $2.9 trillion between the summer of 2007 and the end of 2009, foreign buyers took more than half. Chinese holdings of Treasurys increased by $418 billion.

Among those who were selling were some of the hardest-pressed banks. They needed to shrink their balance sheets. But that adjustment was cushioned by the central banks. In the first phase of what became known as QE1, on March 18, 2009, the Fed announced that it would purchase $750 billion in agency MBS and agency debt, as well as $300 billion in Treasury securities. The Bank of England made a similar announcement on March 9, committing to purchasing first £150 billion and then £200 billion of British

government bonds, or gilts. So, far from swamping the markets with their debt, in 2009 yields on top-rated government bonds actually fell.

In the eurozone things were more complicated. There too the automatic stabilizers kicked in and deficits ballooned. Debt issuance surged. But unlike in the UK or the United States, the ECB is barred from buying newly issued government securities. After Lehman, however, Trichet was in no mood to take risks. Though the ECB did not purchase newly issued government debt, what it did do was to repo sovereign euro bonds.[27] As the eurozone deficits ballooned, the ECB operated what was known informally as the "grand bargain."[28] It supplied hundreds of billions of euros in cheap liquidity to Europe's banks in the form of the so-called Long-Term Refinancing Operation initiated in May 2009.[29] The banks then bought sovereign bonds. On average, the rate Europe's banks paid to the ECB on the CTRO funding was only a third of the yield they earned on their bond holdings. All told, in the eurozone in 2009 the banks loaded up on 400 billion euros' worth of sovereign debt.[30] It was easy and apparently safe profit, and it was Europe's most stressed banks, including Germany's bankrupt Hypo Real Estate and Franco-Belgian Dexia, that were keenest to take advantage. Seeking to maximize their return, they put the ECB's funds into the riskier peripheral bonds from Portugal and Greece that were offering a marginally higher yield. As in the UK and the United States, this helped to stabilize the government debt market, but there was a crucial difference. In the United States and the UK the central banks were pushing liquidity into the banking system. By contrast, in the eurozone, it was the balance sheets of the banks that absorbed the sovereign debt.

III

Fiscal stimulus was clearly necessary over the winter of 2008–2009. The automatic stabilizers were a welcome complement. Together they helped to revive the advanced economies in the worst crisis they had experienced since the 1930s. Thanks to general macroeconomic conditions and the intervention of the central banks, there was no run in the bond markets in either Europe or the United States. Nevertheless, already in the spring of

2009, anxieties about excessive deficits and the need for consolidation were to be heard on both sides of the Atlantic, and nowhere more so than in Germany.

At the G20 in London, Merkel and Sarkozy had taken a public stance on the need for financial consolidation. In large measure this was political theater. Given the shock to Germany's export sector, Merkel's government could not ignore calls for a stimulus package. Unemployment was surging, and in the coming autumn the CDU and SPD had an election to fight. Early in 2009 Angela Merkel's grand coalition brokered a deal. Finance Minister Steinbrück reluctantly agreed to a modest emergency package of extra spending and tax cuts.[31] Automatic stabilizers would take care of the rest. But the question of fiscal consolidation that had preoccupied Merkel's grand coalition since 2005 could no longer be dodged. The SPD and CDU agreed that even as they administered the stimulus, budget balance at both the national and regional levels of government would be enshrined in a constitutional amendment.

This was not a resolution forced on Germany by panic in the bond markets or immediate financial necessity. German government bonds (Bunds) were for the eurozone what US Treasurys were for the dollar world, the safe asset of choice.[32] Despite its gaping deficit in 2009, Germany had no difficulty selling debt. It was not markets but the cross-party consensus on fiscal consolidation that had emerged before the crisis that dictated a decisive and irrevocable turn toward austerity. It was a decision driven by a long-term vision of competitiveness and retrenchment, the lobbying of taxpayer and business advocates and the regional interests of the rich states of western Germany.[33] It was a choice that would change the politics not just of Germany but of the eurozone as a whole.

On Thursday, February 5, 2009, at a spartan Bundeswehr barracks in the precincts of Tegel Airport in the northern suburbs of Berlin, Chancellor Merkel personally brokered the deal.[34] Under pressure from ultraconservative Bavaria, the fiefdom of the CSU, the Länder collectively committed themselves to a constitutional amendment that would end all borrowing by 2020. Until 2019, the stragglers—Bremen, Saarland, Berlin, Sachsen-Anhalt and Schleswig-Holstein—would receive annual subsidies of 800 million euros. In exchange they would submit to the external review of their fiscal policy

by a so-called Stability Council (Stabilitätsrat). Länder that refused to re-
spond to the council's advice would lose federal support. Germany's federal
government, for its part, agreed to bind itself by constitutional amendment
to borrow no more than 0.35 percent of GDP under normal circumstances.[35]
There would be exceptions in case of cyclical shocks, but the cap was se-
vere. It applied to investment as well as to current expenditure.

No heed was given to the consequences that this draconian new rule
would have for one of the largest bond markets in the world. Government
bonds were seen only as a liability, not as a safe asset for savers. Austerity
rhetoric ruled. Prime Minister Seehofer of Bavaria was jubilant. Chancellor
Merkel declared a *Weichenstellung* (a change in the setting of the points).
The debt brake was a demonstration that German federalism worked.[36]
On March 27, 2009, in the Bundestag, Steinbrück made a typically vigorous
defense of the constitutional amendment. It was a matter not of macroeco-
nomics but of democratic autonomy, of "fiscal room for maneuver." Since
the 1970s, despite notional debt limits, annual deficits had resulted in a
budget in which 85 percent of federal spending was consumed by debt ser-
vice and nondiscretionary spending. Fiscal politics were "petrified and de-
void of life" (*"versteinert und verkarstet"*).[37] Restraint on debt would give
back to voters and parliament the freedom to choose their fiscal priorities.
The antidebt consensus did not go entirely unopposed. Peter Bofinger, the
maverick Keynesian member of the Wirtschaftsweisen, the official expert
advisory committee on the German economy, was scathing in his criticism.
If the German federal government was issuing no new bunds, where were
German savers to invest the 120 billion euros that they sought to put aside
every year? Because the German corporate sector was also generating a fi-
nancial surplus, they could not on balance invest their funds in German
businesses. Rather than funding investment at home, Germany's savings
would out of necessity flow into investments abroad.[38] This was the finan-
cial counterpart to Germany's chronic current account surplus, a symptom
as much of repressed domestic consumption and investment as it was of
export success. When it came to the Bundestag vote on May 29, 2009, the
majority was wafer thin—68.6 percent as compared with the two-thirds
required—but the amendment passed. It would take another two-thirds
majority to undo it.

It was a domestic matter first and foremost. But even before it had been carried in the Bundestag, the debt brake was being touted in Berlin as a major element in Germany's foreign economic policy. The strong Deutschmark and the independent Bundesbank had made West Germany a model of conservative economic policy. The tough Hartz IV measures set a standard for "labor market reform" in Europe. Now the *Schuldenbremse* would become Germany's latest instrument of conservative economic governance for export.[39] For a politician of Merkel's ilk, the problem of public debt, like the problem of inflation, was a problem affecting all advanced societies. It went back to the 1960s. It had built up over decades. Now was the time to make a stand. As Merkel headed to the G20 meeting in London she hailed Germany's debt brake as a great achievement. As she told an audience at the German Chamber of Commerce: "We are going to have to try to transfer this to the whole world."[40]

IV

At the London G20, the clash between Merkel, Brown and Obama had enacted familiar transatlantic stereotypes. The Germans were frugal and skeptical about Anglo-Saxon free-market finance. The Americans and the British were freewheeling advocates of whatever it took to keep the capitalist engine spinning. But this was a distortion on both sides. The Germans had plenty of fiscal problems of their own and bankrupt banks to match. Meanwhile, the Obamians were never the full-blooded high spenders that others painted them as. If Treasury Secretary Geithner urged the rest of the G20 to do more, it was in large part in the hope that America might do less. There were Democrats in Congress who wanted to make a major second effort and to push for another round of stimulus. But they got no help from the White House.[41] Inside the administration, Christina Romer cut an increasingly lonely figure in her demand for a bigger fiscal effort. On occasion she would get the backing of Larry Summers. But when she became outspoken in favor of a second round of stimulus, as she did over the winter of 2009–2010, Romer was brutally silenced by Obama himself.[42]

What began to prevail in Washington, DC, as in Europe from the late

summer of 2009, were the fiscal politics of the precrisis period. The aim of fiscal "sustainability" returned to the fore. Geithner at the Treasury targeted a deficit of 3 percent by 2012, a huge tightening relative to the deficit of 10 percent of GDP in 2009. Even more aggressive was Orszag at the OMB, who ran in-house competitions for the best cost-saving ideas.[43] All the Obama administration's medium-term priorities tended to point toward streamlining government and trimming spending. The top political priority was health-care reform. Though this was tarred by Republicans as European-style socialism, given the bloated inefficiency of America's publicly subsidized, profit-making health-industrial complex—which at 17 percent accounted for twice the share of GDP attributable to the financial services industry—the priority of the Affordable Care Act was to cut costs. Likewise, the thrust of Obama's foreign policy was retrenchment. In 2009 the White House was persuaded to put more troops into Afghanistan, but only because it was simultaneously running down its Iraq commitment. America's soldiers didn't like it, but the age of major spending increases was over. Though the Obama stimulus crested in the second year of his presidency, this was offset in 2010 by cuts to other areas of federal spending and a crushing contraction in state and local spending. Though it suited no one to acknowledge the fact, between 2009 and 2010 Germany's deficit was actually increasing more rapidly than that of the United States.[44] Though the arguments were apparently more transparent, the politics of fiscal policy in the wake of the crisis were in their own way no less opaque than those that framed monetary policy.

Chapter 13

FIXING FINANCE

"**C**onfidence" is one of the most quicksilver concepts in economics. In 2007–2008 it had been the collapse in confidence in mortgage securitization, money markets and the banks that brought down the house and necessitated the bailouts. By 2009 confidence was still the problem. But now it was government deficits and the supposed threat of bond vigilantes that seized the headlines. Given actually prevailing conditions in bond markets at the time, the constraints this anxiety placed on fiscal policy were a triumph of precrisis centrist orthodoxy over the facts of the postcrisis situation. While the bond vigilantes never appeared, millons of jobless would pay the price for the failure to sustain fiscal stimulus. And the effects went beyond the labor market. The purpose of restraining fiscal policy was supposedly to maintain confidence and to create space for a private sector recovery. But where was that to come from? The real estate market was still collapsing. Households needed to pay down their debts and restore their overstretched finances. Uplift would have to come from business investment. For that there needed to be financial stability and easy credit, and from there the trail led back to the institutions that had actually been the source of the collapse of confidence in 2008, the banks and their dangerous balance sheets. Having excluded a full-scale fiscal response on grounds of protecting confidence, faute de mieux resurrecting the banks came to seem like the most promising path to recovery.

Though the acute general panic of September 2008 had passed, the

banks were still very fragile. As the full scale of the losses began to sink in—by May 2009 the IMF was estimating $1.5 trillion in write-downs around the world—default insurance premiums on bank debt surged to 300 basis points in the eurozone and 400 basis points in the United States.[1] At those kinds of rates raising new bank funding was prohibitively expensive. And in the spring of 2009 Bank of America and Citigroup, two of America's largest commercial banks, were still in danger.[2] Bank of America was digesting the horrors of the Merrill Lynch balance sheet. At Citigroup the situation was even worse. Despite the double capital injection by the Treasury and the ring-fence around $300 billion of its most toxic assets, by May 2009 Citi's shares were trading at 97 cents.[3] The New York Fed was preparing plans for an all-out rescue effort that would involve guaranteeing all its debt and $500 billion in foreign deposits. Meanwhile, rather than recognizing the political trauma caused by the 2008 bailouts, the bankers in their self-satisfied insulation continued to help themselves to the lion's share of whatever revenue they generated.

In Britain, the most egregious case was RBS, a now majority state-owned bank that announced in February 2009 that it intended to honor £1 billion in bonus contracts.[4] In the United States the figures were far larger. In the 2008 bonus season, after suffering tens of billions in losses, Wall Street paid out $18.4 billion to its top staff. That was two and a half times the amount that Congress approved for the president's priority of modernizing America's broadband infrastructure. Alternatively, if it had been retained by the banks, it would have made a substantial contribution toward their recapitalization.[5] But the investment banks weren't conventional public companies. They were partnerships run primarily for the benefit of their managerial elite and they expected to be paid, whatever happened. In the 2008 bonus season Merrill Lynch alone was responsible for $4–5 billion in payments. And it made sure to pay out earlier than normal in December 2008, just after the firm revealed a fourth quarter loss of $21.5 billion and days before it collapsed into the reluctant embrace of Bank of America.[6] But of all the bonus scandals, the one that really caught the public's attention was AIG. It closed its fourth quarter of 2008 with a loss of $61.7 billion, the largest in US corporate history. Nevertheless, on March 16, 2009, the company announced that its Financial Products division, which had been at the

heart of the toxic spill, would be awarding $165 million in bonuses, a figure that might rise to as much as $450 million. Even President Obama expressed his "outrage" and demanded redress for America's taxpayers.[7] What was to be done?

I

One option was nationalization. That is what the British had been forced to do to Lloyds-HBOS and RBS. Germany's Commerz and Hypo banks were in state hands. Economists pointed out the positive example of Sweden, which when faced with a major banking crisis in the 1990s had taken radical action. After nationalizing and restructuring its banks the economy had bounced back fast. By contrast, Japan had put off restructuring and recapitalizing its banks and had languished ever since. Perhaps the solution was to follow the Swedish example, to break up America's megabanks, restructure, recapitalize and then return them to the market. What would once have been dismissed as Luddite was now merely common sense. In February 2009, former Fed chair Alan Greenspan, who as a young man had sat at the feet of free-market goddess Ayn Rand, told the *Financial Times*: "It may be necessary to temporarily nationalise some banks in order to facilitate a swift and orderly restructuring. . . . I understand that once in a hundred years this is what you do."[8] On network TV news, the Republican senator for South Carolina Lindsey Graham opined that "[t]his idea of nationalizing banks is not comfortable . . . [b]ut I think we've got so many toxic assets spread throughout the banking and financial community throughout the world, that we're going to have to do something that no one ever envisioned a year ago, no one likes."[9]

The intensity of feeling running against the banks in early 2009 was such that President Obama had to take a stance. At a press conference on February 10, 2009, he took up the international examples that everyone was talking about. He acknowledged the off-putting experience of Japan in the 1990s with its botched bailout and recognized that Sweden had done far better after nationalizing its banks. "So," Obama continued, "you'd think looking at it, Sweden looks like a good model." But the president was never

comfortable with the comparison: "Here's the problem," Obama remarked. "Sweden had like five banks [laughs]. We've got thousands of banks. You know, the scale of the US economy and the capital markets are so vast. . . . Our assessment was that it wouldn't make sense. And we also have different traditions in this country. . . . Obviously, Sweden has a different set of cultures in terms of how the government relates to markets and America's different. And we want to retain a strong sense of that private capital fulfilling the core—core investment needs of this country. And so, what we've tried to do is to apply some of the tough love that's going to be necessary, but do it in a way that's also recognizing we've got big private capital markets and ultimately that's going to be the key to getting credit flowing again."[10]

It was not Obama at his most articulate. But it was a clear statement of basic principles. The "core investment needs of the country" were a matter for "private capital." Government stimulus spending, whether on infrastructure or on education, was incidental. What was crucial was getting the banks back on their feet. It was music to the ears of the man who would deliver the "tough love" that Obama promised—Tim Geithner, his Treasury secretary. For Geithner nationalization was never an option. In 2008 at the New York Fed he had seen the depth of the market panic. He had witnessed the ructions over Bear and Fannie Mae and Freddie Mac. He had been in the room on the afternoon of Monday, October 13, alongside Paulson, Bernanke and Bair when they forced the bankers to take TARP capital. That was enough. As far as Geithner was concerned, to have pushed for further nationalizations in 2009 would have been a "deeply transforming policy mistake."[11]

Despite the united front against the Swedish option that Obama and Geithner presented, given boiling public resentment and the drip of scandalous revelations about the bailouts, the way ahead was far from obvious. Larry Summers and Christina Romer, the leading economists in the administration, were compelled by the Swedish example, as was Paul Volcker. Perhaps a short, sharp restructuring under state ownership was what America's financial system needed. So intense did the debate become that on the afternoon of March 15, 2008, a summit was convened in the White House to clear the air.[12] With the president looking on, the argument

swayed back and forth for several hours before Obama impatiently declared that he had other business to attend to and he expected a conclusion by the end of the night. After the president left the room the issue was decided by his foul-mouthed chief of staff, Rahm Emanuel. If bank restructuring and comprehensive recapitalization along Swedish lines would cost upward of $700 billion, it was not going to "f***ing happen." After TARP and the stimulus, with health reform in the pipeline, Emanuel could not ask the centrist Democrats in the House to back more spending. The economists would have to come up with another plan.

By 2009 the problem was no longer the investment banks. They were back in profit. The problem was the ailing commercial banks. Citi was the worst. So rather than a comprehensive restructuring of the entire American banking system, the meeting agreed that the remaining TARP funds should be concentrated on backstopping a "resolution" of Citigroup. This gigantic, oversized monolith should be broken up, downsized, restructured and the worst assets hived off to a bad bank. Without alerting Sheila Bair of the FDIC to the intensity of the debate going on inside the administration, Summers had sounded out with her the possibility of creating an $800 billion bad bank for Citi's worst assets and bailing in its shareholders.[13] The Citi plan was approved by Obama later that evening. The Treasury was charged with working out the details. It ought to have been momentous. Citigroup was huge. Back in 1998 its merger with Travelers Group had sounded the death knell of the old days of "boring" high street banking. By way of Rubin, it was tightly politically connected to the Democratic Party. And the pressure for action was only increased the following day, when the scandal erupted over bonuses paid to AIG's senior staff. The president was furious. He wanted action. The nation's top thirteen bank bosses were summoned to a meeting in the White House.[14]

At this moment there was a real fear on Wall Street that the Obama administration was about to go to war. Given how unpopular the banks were, it would have made good politics. But it didn't happen. Despite the decision endorsed by the president on March 15, Geithner never agreed with restructuring Citigroup. No one had ever unraveled a bank of Citigroup's complexity. It was not clear that the Treasury had the resources and legal authority to carry it through. A protracted restructuring would spook

the markets. In the words of a later postmortem compiled by one of Obama's closest advisers, the Treasury "slow walked" the Citigroup proposal.[15] Though this delaying action bordered on insubordination, Obama showed little inclination to impose his will. As his remarks about the "Swedish case" had suggested, he was far from being a radical on banking issues. When Obama confronted the bank CEOs on March 27 the atmosphere was frosty. But he had summoned them to Washington not to punish them but to remonstrate with them. He appealed to the bankers to show restraint in their compensation and bonuses. "Help me help you," the president pleaded. When several of the CEOs offered the customary justifications for their exorbitant compensation—their businesses were large and risky; they were competing in an international talent pool—the president interrupted in exasperation: "Be careful how you make those statements, gentlemen. The public isn't buying that. . . . My administration is the only thing between you and the pitchforks."[16]

In the spring of 2009, rather than going over to the offensive, Obama and Geithner positioned themselves as the last line of defense for America's financial system. It was their self-appointed mission to calm "the mob." Of course, playing the good cop is a tried-and-tested negotiating tactic. But it is usually combined with stiff demands. Someone has to play bad cop. What was remarkable in 2009 was how little the Obama administration asked in return for the protection it offered. To the amazement of the hardened Wall Street deal makers, the only item on the table on March 27 was voluntary restraint on compensation. That was even less than Paulson had asked for six months earlier when he foisted TARP on them. In truth, if there were pitchforks being wielded by anyone in the spring of 2009, it was not by the Left against the banks but by the right-wing populists. With the lavish attention of Fox News and subsidies from friendly oligarchs, they were organizing themselves in the Tea Party movement. The target of their anger was not Wall Street but the liberals in the White House. The uncomfortable truth was that the Obamians lacked pitchforks of their own. Reviled by the Right and suspected by the Left of being in the pocket of Wall Street, as Geithner himself admitted, the administration would find itself in political "no-man's land."[17]

In his early days as Treasury secretary, Geithner was quite commonly

described as being formerly of Goldman Sachs.[18] Given the precedent set by Paulson and Rubin, it was only to be expected. Geithner looked the part. He had the precocious youthfulness and pugnacity of a hotshot investment banker. The diary log of the New York Fed revealed that during his time there, Geithner regularly socialized with Citigroup executives, where his mentor Robert Rubin held court.[19] And as Treasury secretary, Geithner continued those habits.[20] But for all his cultivation of Wall Street, Geithner was until 2013 a career public servant, and a proud one at that. In his self-portrayal Geithner was not a banker but a soldier, a man of fortitude, serving in the interest of the national economy and the American people, willing to take upon himself the moral burden of dirty hands, to do what was necessary in the public interest. But how did Geithner define that public interest? First and foremost his commitment was to upholding the stability of "the financial system," because without that, the entire economy was bound to fail.[21] That was his key article of faith. The interests of America and the financial system were aligned. To explain his actions we do not need to imagine that he was in the pocket of any particular bank. It was his commitment to the system that dictated that Citigroup should not be broken up. Even more important, the key institutions of financial regulation and government must be protected too. When Geithner resisted bank nationalization it was to shield the monetary authorities as much as any individual bank. A comprehensive attack on Wall Street could all too easily spill over into an attack on the agencies that oversaw its business. In 2009 "audit the Fed" was a battle cry on both left and right.

With Geithner at the helm, the Treasury's response to the crisis was not to tackle "too big to fail" by breaking up the biggest banks. Nor was it to bring the interests of wider society to bear by way of politicized oversight. Instead, the Treasury's solution was to increase the oversight and managerial capacities of the state's regulatory agencies—the Treasury itself, the key regulators and the Fed. If capitalist finance was a given, then one would have to accept the necessity of dealing with gigantic banks and complex, fast-moving markets. One had to accept also that this system was crisis prone. Crises, indeed, were inevitable. All one could hope to do was to build a crisis-fighting capacity at the national and international levels that was adequate to cope. In 2008 the Fed and the Treasury had acted on a

spectacular scale with effects well beyond the boundaries of the American national economy. At the London G20 the IMF had been given the fire-power it needed. What the Treasury aimed to do in 2009 was to continue the consolidation at the national level. As it had done since October 2008, this would revolve around recapitalization. As they recovered from the shock the banks were champing at the bit to repay the TARP funds. To further force the pace the Fed and the Treasury cooperated to introduce a new regime of regulation and oversight known as stress testing. This would be followed by a major political effort to get legislation through Congress that would legitimize and regularize the business of overseeing financial stability. As the acute crisis of 2008 passed into memory, a new relationship between the big banks and the authorities would be given permanent shape.

II

Purely for internal purposes, the New York Fed had for some time been in the habit of conducting crisis simulations with the main banks on Wall Street.[22] In February 2009, in his first major speech as Treasury secretary, Geithner announced that these so-called stress tests would be turned into a comprehensive exercise of public policy. The Fed and the Treasury would inspect and certify the soundness of every major bank operating in Amer-ica. To do so, all the largest US banks would submit their accounts for inspection. Fed and Treasury officials would then apply to that data a hy-pothetical scenario of financial disaster, estimating the losses the banks would suffer and the resources they would be able to mobilize to withstand the shock. Effectively, the Treasury and the Fed would make themselves into the credit-rating agencies in chief—the "United States of Moody's"— official arbiters of private creditworthiness and guardians of confidence in America's financial system.[23] Those banks that were shown to be at risk would be mandated to raise additional capital. Those that could not do so in the private capital market would be required to take money from the TARP fund.

In rejecting the Swedish option, President Obama had gestured to America's "thousands of banks." At the time the president spoke there were,

in fact, 6,978 commercial banks operating in the United States. But those never mattered to Geithner or Bernanke. They were the province of the FDIC. What mattered for systemic stability were the nineteen major banks with assets in excess of $100 billion, c. $10 trillion in total. Subjecting those massively complex institutions to thorough scrutiny would have been a labor of Hercules. The stress tests were something more tactical and fast moving. In a crash effort, a scratch team of two hundred bank examiners, supervisors and analysts ran through the books.[24] The disaster scenario they applied was far from apocalyptic. They assumed that GDP would fall by only 2–3 percent, unemployment would rise to 8.5 percent and house prices would fall by between 14 and 22 percent. That turned out to be optimistic. But even starting from those numbers and the default probabilities they implied was enough to generate sobering conclusions. On top of the losses of $350 billion already recognized by the spring of 2009, under the stress test scenario the banks might expect to suffer a further $600 billion in write-downs and charge-offs by the end of 2010. This, then, posed the truly critical question: How much capital would be required to make the banks safe and restore market confidence? This was a matter of judgment. The Treasury and the Fed weighed a range of options from as little as $35 billion to as much as $175 billion. The risk, if they announced a huge capital shortfall, was that it might shake confidence irreversibly. On the other hand, if they announced a figure that was too low, it would undermine confidence in the stress-testing exercise.[25]

According to inside reports, the original estimates caused consternation in banking circles. Bank of America faced a call for $50 billion in extra capital. Citigroup was called on to raise $35 billion. Wells Fargo was so dismayed at the initial ask of $17 billion that it threatened a lawsuit. In the end they settled on a bargained compromise. By far the biggest burden was imposed on Bank of America, which was required to raise $33.9 billion to exit the emergency ward. Wells Fargo's quota was set at $13.7 billion. As its senior financial officer commented: "In the end we agreed with the number. We didn't necessarily like the number."[26] Ailing Citigroup had more reason to be satisfied. By allowing for future revenue streams, its capital requirement was massaged down to a modest $5.5 billion, a seventh of the original figure.[27] It was barely more than the bank would pay out in bonuses that

year. After weeks of haggling, on May 7, 2009, the public was informed that America's big banks needed to raise a manageable total of $75 billion.

The stress tests were a balancing act that began with an exercise in accounting precision and ended in a game of bargaining and confidence.[28] Whether they were taken in or simply delighted to discover how helpful the Treasury and the Fed were being, the markets responded well. The spread between very safe AA corporate bonds and the price that banks paid to borrow on their Baa bond rating fell from 6 percent to 3 percent, reducing funding costs. The week following the release saw a sustained 10 percent rally in bank stocks, a high tide on which the strongest banks immediately raised $20 billion in additional capital. On June 19 the first nine banks repaid and exited the TARP program. Over the months that followed, the eight banks still in the program, including the giants Bank of America and Citigroup, used every trick in the accounting book and all the help the highly cooperative IRS, Fed and Treasury could provide to exit TARP.[29] In an extraordinary two-week period in December 2009, Citigroup, Bank of America and Wells Fargo raced one another to raise a total of $49 billion in common equity. Bank of America's offering of $19.3 billion was the largest offering of common stock in US history.[30] They crowded the market and could probably have raised more capital at lower cost if they had stretched the issuance over several months. But the authorities were in a hurry to wind up TARP, and for the banks time was of the essence. The sooner they could repay the Treasury, the sooner they could escape the limits on compensation imposed on all TARP recipients, thus allowing them to retain and compete for talent. It was, as Bair ruefully remarked, "all about compensation."[31]

This was the script that the administration liked. A light-touch government intervention had enabled private business to take the lead. Nationalization had been avoided. As President Obama had promised, "[P]rivate capital" would be "fulfilling the core—core investment needs of this country." But what this celebratory narrative glossed over were the more ambiguous implications of the exercise. The stress tests subjected the accounts of the commanding heights of American finance to intrusive scrutiny not by the public and the markets but by select teams of government bank supervisors. By the same token, they placed a seal of official approval on

profit-driven private business activity. They were the model of a new regime of comprehensive, anticipatory oversight but also of entanglement between the American state apparatus and the big banks. This might be obtrusive and expensive in bureaucratic terms. It was onerous for those banks subjected to it. But it also conferred privileges, specifically the implicit promise that a bank that passed the stress test was deemed safe by the Fed and the Treasury. If it came to a crisis, a bank that had passed the test could hardly be denied assistance. Among this group of tightly regulated and closely supported entities, there could be no sudden and unforeseen failures. With that risk removed, it was significantly cheaper for such banks to issue shares and borrow money. One study estimated that in the wake of the crisis the advantage in funding costs enjoyed by the larger banks relative to their smaller peers had more than doubled, from 0.29 to 0.78 percent. For the largest eighteen US banks, this implied an annual subsidy of at least $34 billion.[32]

III

It was no surprise, therefore, that the markets liked the news. The banks were clearly in safe hands. With the implicit backing of the authorities, the banks finally stabilized. This bought time to think of longer-term solutions. The Obama administration could embark on the huge challenge of financial reform.

The political stakes were high. By the summer of 2009 the White House badly needed a "win." The stimulus was a dud in political terms. Health-care reform was facing relentless opposition. Financial reform as a political project was defined by the imperative to "get something done." This forged an unholy alliance between Geithner's Treasury and the West Wing's political operatives headed by Rahm Emanuel. Apart from a pugilistic style and a shared fondness for the f-word, Emanuel's and Geithner's intensity and single-mindedness bent in opposite, but complementary, directions. For the political fixer Emanuel, all that mattered was getting "points on the board." The content of financial reform was someone else's problem. Conversely, for Geithner, with his suspicion of Congress, all that mattered was

passing a piece of legislation that gave as little new power as possible to "populist" politicians and maximized the discretion and firepower of the expert regulators. To achieve this goal, however, the Treasury had to work through Congress, and in particular the two key committee chairs, Barney Frank in the House and Chris Dodd in the Senate. They also had to contend with key regulators like Sheila Bair of the FDIC. They had to channel the energy of campaigners, most notably Elizabeth Warren, the Harvard law professor and consumer rights activist, and fend off the ever present banking lobby.[33]

The result was a sprawling piece of legislation running to 849 pages.[34] Rather than offering a single coherent thesis, the Wall Street Reform and Consumer Protection Act, commonly known as Dodd-Frank, embodied a compendium of crisis diagnoses. Was the crisis due to mass predation of poorly informed borrowers? In which case what was needed was Elizabeth Warren's Bureau of Consumer Financial Protection (Title X). Was it opaque over-the-counter derivatives that had blown up the system? In which case the fix was transparent, market-based trading of derivatives (Title VII— Wall Street Transparency and Accountability). Was it the breakdown of responsibility in the extended chains of mortgage securitization that poisoned the well? In which case securitizers should be required to have skin in the game (Title IX—Investor Protections). Was the sheer size of banks at the root of all the problems? Were they simply too big to fail? In which case the answer was to restrict bailouts and to make the industry pay for them (Title II—Orderly Liquidation Authority) and to cap banks' further growth (Title VI, sections 622 and 623). Had investment banks used client money to gamble? If so, the thing to do was to reinstate 1930s-style divisions between commercial and investment banking by way of the so-called Volcker rule banning "proprietary trading" (Title VI, Volcker rule). All of these theories about the crisis of 2007–2009 had major political resonance. All of them made their way into the meandering text of Dodd-Frank. Many of them were sensible and worthwhile measures that redressed some of the grosser imbalances in the financial services industry. But in general they had little to do with the implosion of the wholesale-funded shadow banking system that actually brought down the house in 2008.

The Treasury had a clearer view of the mechanics of the crisis. It wanted

more capital, less leverage, more liquidity. And it wanted centralized powers in the Treasury and the Fed to deal with the next disaster. It spelled out this vision in a blueprint, which it issued in the summer of 2009.[35] This was in many ways quite different from what emerged as Dodd-Frank. But that was not by accident. Many of the omissions were strategic. As Geithner unabashedly remarked, "[W]e didn't want Congress designing the new capital ratios or leverage restrictions or liquidity requirements. Whatever their flaws, regulators were much better equipped" to decide those technical issues. "History suggested that Capitol Hill would be too easily swayed by the clout of the financial industry and the politics of the moment; we didn't think that was the place for the intricate work of calibrating the financial system's shock absorbers."[36] In other words, what the Treasury and the Fed knew to be the main drivers of the crisis were kept off the legislative agenda. What the Treasury did want Congress to provide were the legal powers that Geithner believed to have been lacking at the crucial moment in September 2008. If the challenge was to structure a more sustainable symbiosis between Washington and Wall Street, that was better done, in the Treasury's view, by way of the administrative and regulatory state, rather than by way of congressional pitch battles.

Though the Treasury sought to orchestrate a chorus of regulators behind its proposals over the summer of 2009, it soon realized that it would face dogged resistance from the FDIC and from within Congress. They shared a deep suspicion of the complicity of the Fed and the Treasury with Wall Street and the enhanced powers that Geithner was looking for. To ensure collective responsibility, Bair and Frank insisted that oversight over the entire system should be exercised not by the Treasury and the Fed alone but by a Financial Stability Oversight Council chaired by the Treasury but gathering together all the key regulators. The idea of crisis management by committee appalled Geithner. But the council, in fact, was given many of the powers that he wanted. It would have the right to designate systematically important institutions. Those could be placed under a regime of heightened supervision and regulation including regular stress testing. If a large bank was on the point of causing a systemic crisis, the council's rights of managerial intervention were extensive. Ahead of time, all systemically important institutions would be required to prepare living wills mapping

out how they should be resolved in case of bankruptcy. And this oversight and control could be extended to foreign banks operating in the United States.

The Fed was pivotal to Geithner's vision of future control. But in political terms it was a liability. To say that the crisis dented the Fed's public standing would be an understatement. It polarized and in due course flipped the politics of the institution.[37] In 2008 Bernanke, like his predecessor, Alan Greenspan, had been significantly more popular with Republicans than with Democrats. By 2010 he was almost equally unpopular with both, and on the right wing the drumbeat of the Tea Party was mounting. Meanwhile, for Obama, Bernanke was a token of the bipartisanship he craved. In August the president announced his nomination for a second term as Fed chair. *Time* magazine ended 2009 by naming Bernanke its man of the year.[38] But that did nothing to endear him to either the right wing of the Republicans or the left wing of the Democratic Party.[39] December 2009 and January 2010 saw fierce clashes in the Senate over Bernanke's reappointment. Desperate to rally support, the White House mobilized influential figures such as Warren Buffett to lobby on Bernanke's behalf. To make matters worse, at the same time Bernanke himself was working the phones, struggling to stop Dodd's Senate draft of the financial reform legislation from stripping the Fed of oversight over the largest banks.[40]

In their effort to retain the Fed's role at the heart of financial governance, Bernanke and Geithner were forced to make a pawn sacrifice. They conceded the formation of a separate consumer finance agency—Warren's Consumer Financial Protection Bureau.[41] It allowed the reform campaign to claim a major win. It drew the fire of lobbyists. And it was largely irrelevant to the vision of systemic stabilization that Geithner and Bernanke were pursuing. They could concede regulation of credit cards and consumer loans as long as they retained oversight over the banks with balance sheets greater than $50 billion. Indeed, consumer protection and macroprudential regulation might very well be at odds. As Larry Summers remarked to the president, the "airline safety board shouldn't be in charge of protecting the financial viability of the airlines."[42] That was fair but it begged a further observation. Whereas there are plenty of safety agencies, there are, in fact, no agencies responsible for ensuring the financial viability of

airlines or any industry other than banks. Airlines are expected to take care of their own finances. But Geithner and Summers preferred to sidestep the ramifications of that thought.

In the wake of Lehman what preoccupied the Treasury most was the question of how a failing megabank could be safely contained. For Geithner there was no substitute for the combination that had finally stabilized the situation in October 2008—wide-ranging guarantee powers by the FDIC ideally in combination with general liquidity support from the Fed and re-capitalization and ring fencing of losses orchestrated by the Fed and the Treasury. The crisis had shown the need to add well-resourced resolution authority for those banks that were beyond saving. But the mood in Congress was ugly and Sheila Bair was on the warpath. In the end Dodd-Frank embodied a severe rejection of the practices of 2008. There would be no more taxpayer-funded bailouts. The Fed could offer general liquidity support but was barred from offering facilities tailor-made for specific banks. In consultation with the president and the Fed, the Treasury was required to place failing institutions under the control of the FDIC. It would operate the bank as a going concern with a view to breaking it up and selling off the component parts. The one element of control that the Treasury preserved was that it would be responsible for funding the FDIC's resolution, with the costs to be recouped after the crisis had passed by a levy on the financial industry. Bernanke and the Fed thought they could live with the deal. The Fed chair had always been unhappy with the ad hoc interventions he had had to make under the terms of section 13(3) emergencies. From Geithner's point of view it was an alarming restriction. As ever, he turned to his favorite analogy between financial crises and national security: "The president is entrusted with extraordinary powers to protect the country from threats to our national security. These powers come with carefully designed constraints, but they allow the president to act quickly in extremis. Congress should give the president and the financial first responders the powers necessary to protect the country from the devastation of financial crises."[43]

For Geithner the "populist fury" of the "atonement agenda" was a dangerous distraction from the tough-minded technical business of addressing a crisis.[44] But the grief and distress caused by the crisis were forces to be reckoned with. They ran through American society in waves, and early

2010, as Dodd-Frank reached a critical point in its labored passage through Congress, was one such moment. Three years since the real estate bubble burst, the full effects of the credit crunch and mass unemployment were making themselves felt. Between 2007 and 2009, 2.5 million homes had been foreclosed and the crest had not yet been reached. As 2010 began, 3.7 million families were more than ninety days past due on their mortgage payments. Millions more were struggling to make ends meet, one or two months behind on their payments. Over the next twelve months 1.178 million homes would slide into foreclosure, the worst year of the crisis. With prices still falling, ever more properties were sinking into negative equity. As one analyst remarked in early 2010: "We're now at the point of maximum vulnerability. People's emotional attachment to their property is melting into air."[45] In the worst-hit areas, such as Florida, fully 12 percent of properties were given up by their owners or seized by banks for foreclosure. Foreclosure proceedings were operating at such a pace that they were given over to quasi-automated legal processes that turned out to be ruinously flawed. In a nightmarish administrative and legal tangle, ever more victims were sucked into the crisis.

The contrast in fortunes between Wall Street and Main Street was increasingly intolerable. The big banks had been bailed out. Some of the most unscrupulous bosses might face legal action, but they were not facing personal ruin. They retired to lifestyles of wealth and comfort.[46] None had gone to jail. And those at the top of the tree on Wall Street were bouncing back apparently without shame or second thought. The bonus season in 2009 was better than ever, netting $145 billion for the executives at the top investment banks, asset managers and hedge funds, as compared with $117 billion in 2008.[47] Goldman made $13.4 billion in profit for its shareholders and paid its own staff $16.2 billion in compensation and bonuses.[48] Astonishingly, even Citigroup, which had a loss of $1.6 billion in 2009 and survived the year only due to government action, paid out $5 billion in bonuses. The bankers were happy to leave the past behind, but the American public was not. In the spring of 2010 Wall Street's approval rating with the general public stood at 6 percent.[49] And the regulators and their lawyers were finally catching up with the events of the last three years. On April 16, 2010, the SEC announced that it would be bringing charges against Goldman

Sachs for misleading the investors to whom it had sold inferior quality mortgage-backed securities. The announcement unleashed a firestorm of indignation. Finally a really big name was going to have to face the music. To the embarrassment of the administration, Dodd-Frank was carried across the finish line not by the energy of the Treasury or the White House but by a new wave of popular fury.

Emotions ran so high in the spring of 2010 that it took a coalition of Treasury, centrist Democrats and business lobbyists to block a last-minute effort to ban any banks enjoying an FDIC guarantee from engaging in derivatives trading of any kind. For the biggest banks this would have been truly costly. The resulting compromise "pushed out" only 10 percent of the least dangerous derivatives. Similarly, a last-minute proposal to address "too big to fail" by putting a cap on the total size of bank balance sheets was blocked in the banking committee by Chris Dodd and other "moderate" allies. One vital late amendment that did make it into the final law was the Collins Amendment of May 2010.[50] Drafted behind the scenes by the FDIC, it demanded that whatever capital standards the Fed and the regulators set for the biggest banks should at least match the level required of the smaller FDIC-regulated banks. Bair wanted to roll back the favoritism shown to the big banks under the Basel II regime. She also wanted to ensure that capital standards applied to holding companies as well as commercial banking subsidiaries. The Fed and the Treasury resisted. They insisted that setting capital requirements was their regulatory prerogative. The banks screamed that the demanding new capital standards would force them to cut credit by $1.5 trillion. It came down to a struggle in the House and Senate reconciliation process, in which Senator Susan Collins and Bair prevailed with the backing of Dodd.

IV

The Dodd-Frank legislation that Obama signed into law on July 21, 2010, was hailed as the most significant act of regulation since the 1930s. Critics scoffed that it did not set a very high bar. It is easy to be cynical about a messy piece of legislation riddled with compromises and defined as much

by what it left out as what it covered. And the incoherence became worse after the passage of the law. While the legislation was in Congress the bank lobbyists—conscious of how high emotions were running—had held back. As they well understood, passing the act was only the first round. Once the law was on the statute books and the argument over implementation began behind closed doors, they swarmed all over the legislation. Amid the inherent complexity of the subject matter, the rivalry between the regulators and the vociferous clamor of the lobbyists, implementing Dodd-Frank became a quagmire.

All told, Dodd-Frank called on regulators and agencies to formulate 398 new rules for the financial sector. Each one became the target for no-holds-barred lobbying by interested parties, who could now operate outside the limelight of congressional debate. By July 2013, three years on from the passage of the law, barely 155 of the 398 required rules had been finalized.[51] The highly controversial Volcker rule was a case in point.[52] How to draw internal divisions inside banks to insulate client money from proprietary trading was a hugely technical and contentious business. Even with the best will in the world it was nearly impossible to draw a line between the actions of a bank in making a market for a client and trading on its own behalf. What emerged was less a "bright" regulatory line than a Rorschach blot. It took until December 2013 for the five agencies involved to agree on a wording of the basic Volcker rule, 1,238 days after Dodd-Frank was passed.[53] The result was a 71-page document with an explanatory addendum that ran to a modest 900 pages. Banks were not so much told what to do as they were invited to demonstrate that they were not in violation of the rule. What exactly would constitute proof of compliance was a matter for further negotiation.[54] The best advice the lawyers could offer was that it was up to banks to decide the level of "regulatory risk tolerance" they were comfortable with. After passing the law in July 2010 and issuing the "final" formulation of the Volcker rule in December 2013, 2014 began with a new round of discussions about the "guidance" that would be issued to explain those regulatory risks. The only thing that was clear was that it would generate enormous demand for compliance officers and corporate lawyers. As Jamie Dimon of J.P. Morgan famously griped, to negotiate the new "system," a banker needed the services not only of a lawyer but of a psychiatrist too.[55]

It wasn't only the bankers to whom Dodd-Frank caused anxiety. Geithner was worried about how it would work in a crisis. He feared that the formalized process of resolution centered on the FDIC would hobble the crisis response. But that put a premium on crisis prevention, and that points to the truly significant change brought about by Dodd-Frank. It perpetuated and institutionalized the stress-testing regime begun in the spring of 2009, and as such it was one of the pioneers of a new type of governance known as macroprudential regulation.[56] This required banks to be assessed not simply in terms of their business models but with regard to their impact on macroeconomic stability. Conversely, macroeconomic scenarios were evaluated in terms of their impact on the key banks. Henceforth, the risk of financial crisis was no longer a matter for ad hoc intervention in emerging market economies, as it had been in the 1990s. It was to be a permanent preoccupation of governments across the G20. The Financial Stability Council created by Dodd-Frank gave the Fed and the Treasury and the other regulators a standing platform from which to develop this new form of oversight and control. As the government regulators became ever more sophisticated in their understanding of modern finance, the banks built gigantic compliance teams to interact on a daily basis with the regulatory authorities. It was in the interaction between the two that the truly crucial work was done of defining the rules for the three parameters that mattered most for financial stability: capital, leverage and liquidity. It was a deeply incestuous relationship rife with conflicts of interest. For American conservatives it was the moment in which high-minded corporate liberalism shaded into a self-dealing of liberal corporatism.[57] And this went beyond the sociology of bureaucratic interaction and the revolving door that connected regulators, law firms and banks. To see how tightly this logic of entanglement worked, one needed only to go back to the original stress tests of May 2009.

It was clear that accrediting the stability of a core group of systemically important banks conferred a privilege on them. It would reduce their funding costs and that was indeed the point. But this takes the focus of the exercise on capital raising at face value and pays insufficient attention to the details of the tests. If the aim was to restore the financial health of the banks, issuing new shares was not the only option. In fact, of the estimated losses of $600 billion predicted in the 2009 stress-test scenario, 60 percent

would be covered by "resources other than capital." An explanatory note attached to the relevant table explained that the main source of these additional "resources" would be "pre-provision net revenue."[58] Pre-provision net revenue (PPNR) is defined as net income from interest and noninterest sources minus noninterest expenses. It is not the same as profit because it does not make allowance for loss provisions, but it is a close relation. For the foreseeable future one of the main concerns of Fed and Treasury policy was to ensure that America's top nineteen banks would earn a sufficiently ample portion of PPNR. The stakes were high. The banks that did not generate enough PPNR would not survive a stress test and would need to go to market or make calls on the TARP fund.

Through the stress tests the Treasury had sidestepped calls for nationalization and the "resolution" of Citigroup. Instead, in the interests of financial stability and minimizing the drain on the TARP fund, the Treasury and the Fed were in effect making it a government objective to restore bank revenue to healthy levels. The logic was inescapable. If financial stability, along with inflation control and employment, was now a key objective of economic policy, then bank profits were one of the key intermediate variables. More profit meant more strength on bank balance sheets and more stability. As part of the stress-testing regime, the Fed compiled statistics on PPNR and developed models with which to predict its likely development according to various macroeconomic scenarios.[59]

But the entanglement did not stop there. It was only logical, having targeted banks' profits, that the regulators should also have a say in what the banks did with them.[60] As a Fed press release spelled out two years later in November 2011 as part of its Comprehensive Capital Analysis and Review:

"[T]he Federal Reserve annually will evaluate institutions' capital adequacy, internal capital adequacy assessment processes, and their plans to make capital distributions, such as dividend payments or stock repurchases. The Federal Reserve will approve dividend increases or other capital distributions only for companies whose capital plans are approved by supervisors and are able to demonstrate sufficient financial strength to operate as successful financial intermediaries under stressed macroeconomic and financial market scenarios, even after making the desired capital distributions."[61]

Obama and Geithner might have blocked the push toward nationalization, but in a truly ironic historical twist, less than twenty years after the defeat of communism, in the wake of the deepest crisis global capitalism had experienced since the 1930s, the bastions of American finance would be required to negotiate government-approved "capital plans" before paying dividends to shareholders. The imperative of guarding systemic stability required nothing less. It was a dramatic act of intrusive regulation in a sector that had once prided itself as the bulldozer of market freedom. And it was clear from the outset that whatever changes America adopted could not stop at its borders. They would have to be flanked by global measures: first, to ensure that America did not suffer competitive disadvantage; and second, to ensure that dangerous practices were not simply offshored. The G20 finance ministers had resolved during their critical meetings in October 2008 that no systemically important institutions would be allowed to fail. Now the question was how they would be regulated. The Americans had made a start. The wider frame would be set by the Basel Committee.

V

The urgency with which change was begun was striking. To get from the banking crises of the early 1970s to the first Basel regulations in 1988 had taken fourteen years of lackluster negotiations. The formal process of revision that turned Basel I into Basel II began in 1999. Eight years later, as the crisis struck, the new standards had still not been fully implemented. Basel III started off at an altogether different pace. The first call to action came from the G20 in November 2008. A new global Financial Stability Board chaired by the head of the Italian central bank, Mario Draghi, convened in the summer. Draghi had trained alongside Bernanke at MIT in the 1970s and was a fluent exponent of the new hybrid of finance and macroeconomics. By September 2009 technical discussions were ongoing. Within weeks, rumors began to circulate that the Basel Committee, in the manner of the US stress tests, had identified thirty financial groups as "systemically important" at a global level.[62] They would be subject to tougher capital

Global Systemically Important Financial Institutions: Assets and Tier 1 Capital (end of 2012)

Capitalization in relation to Basel III Standard

☐ Larger than or equal (8) ■ Less than 50% (5)

■ Between 50% and 100% (16) ◇ Tier 1 Capital ($bn)

Source: A. Rostom and M. J. Kim, "Watch Out for SIFIs—One Size Won't Fit All," World Bank (blog), July 1, 2013, http://blogs.worldbank.org/psd/watch-out-sifis-one-size-wont-fit-all. Data: *The Banker*, July 2012, and bank annual reports.

standards and required to draft living wills that would map out in advance how they would be wound up should it come to the worst. The G20 gave the new regulations its imprimatur at the November 2010 Seoul meeting. The first list of the twenty-nine systemically important financial institutions subject to the full Basel III regime was published in November 2011.

In the wake of the crisis, these twenty-nine institutions, with their headquarters in the United States, Europe, Japan and China, held total assets of $46 trillion. They thus accounted for roughly 22 percent of all financial assets worldwide. Henceforth, they would be subject to a special regime of oversight, not just at the national level through stress tests but at a global level too. Given the mechanics of the 2008 crisis, Basel III focused on new areas of regulation. To give them resilience in the face of a "run on repo," all SIFI would be required to hold sufficient high-quality liquid assets that could be

sold or repoed to cover thirty days of net outflows from their businesses. In addition, to constrain maturity mismatch, banks had to demonstrate that they had sufficient stable long-term funding to match their book of long-term loans. What the Basel III regulations aimed to ensure was that banks could not find themselves in the situation of a Northern Rock, with a giant balance sheet of long-term mortgages funded by unstable short-term wholesale funding. In due course these would emerge as the controversial cutting-edge regulations of Basel III. But in the first phase of the battle over the new regulations it would be the classic issue of capital that was to the fore.

In the aftermath of the crisis, many reform-minded economists were calling for a huge step up in capital.[63] Economists Anat Admati and Martin Hellwig spearheaded a call for banks to be required to hold capital up to 20–30 percent of their balance sheet, the kind of capital ratio that was typical of other businesses and hedge funds. This would have given them huge solidity. And it would have justified much lower rates of return. For the same reason, it was vigorously resisted by the global banks, which had no desire to be turned into boring providers of financial utilities. Leading the charge was the Institute of International Finance. Its members included the entire global banking world, American, European and Asian. Its managing director, Charles Dallara, was a veteran sovereign debt negotiator who had overseen the early steps in Tim Geithner's career at the US Treasury in the 1980s. The assertive chairman of the group was Josef Ackermann, the Swiss CEO of Deutsche Bank. They argued that aggressive recapitalization would slow down lending and thus economic growth. According to the IIF's in-house econometric models, a 2 percent increase in capital requirements for the G-SIFI would cut GDP in the United States, Japan and Europe by 3 percent and would reduce annual growth by as much as 0.6 percent. With the recovery struggling to achieve growth of 1 or 2 percent, that was an ominous forecast.[64] It was a tendentious and hypothetical argument that the advocates of capital raising were forced to counter with their own even more elaborate econometrics.

Amid the war of the economic models in Basel, Sheila Bair made herself into the spokesperson for raising capital. The Swiss regulators were pushing in a similar direction. After the near collapse of UBS and the huge losses at Credit Suisse, they clearly understood that they could not afford to have either of their megabanks fail.[65] The rest of the US delegation did not

go so far as Bair. The compromise that resulted was a substantial change but by no means radical. The new rules specified 7 percent as the basic minimum requirement for Tier 1 common equity in relation to risk-weighted assets for all banks. However, systemically important banks were required to hold higher amounts, depending on their size and impact on the world economy. Between November 2014 and January 2019, the twenty-nine selected institutions would be required to raise their capital in relation to risk-weighted assets to between 8 and 12.5 percent, depending on their degree of systemic importance.[66] A further 3.5 percent could be added in the form, for instance, of convertible bonds that at moments of stress transformed from bonds to equity. Crucially, unlike under Basel II, leverage was measured two ways. The basic standard was set with regard to risk-weighted assets, which banks could calculate according to arcane in-house formulae. But as a cruder test of solidity, risk-weighted leverage would be checked against a simple ratio of total bank assets to loss-absorbing capital. This was not to fall below a 3 percent "leverage ratio" of equity to assets. This left Bair and her fellow campaigners indignant. In the United States, by way of the Collins Amendment and the standard set by the FDIC, the bar was raised higher. But if more was not done at Basel, it had less to do with the American delegation than with opposition from Europe.

Since the crisis, Berlin and Paris had been talking tough about Anglo-Saxon finance and the EU Commission had finally woken up to the need to create a financial firefighting capacity. The Larosière committee on financial regulation reported in February 2009.[67] It recommended an entirely new structure of Europe-wide banking supervision that by 2011 would result in the formation of four new agencies: the European Banking Authority (EBA), the European Securities and Markets Authority (ESMA) and the European Insurance and Occupational Pensions Authority (EIOPA), as well as a European Systemic Risk Board to oversee macroprudential regulation. In organizational terms it was far more comprehensive than anything attempted by Dodd-Frank. But though the Larosière group acknowledged that giant cross-border banks posed huge problems for national supervisors and though the committee recognized that the federal structures of the United States gave it a distinct advantage in crisis management, it recommended no more than ad hoc burden-sharing agreements

and rejected the idea of a common deposit insurance scheme. The vision it offered was of the coordination and harmonization of national measures, not a banking union.[68] Meanwhile, for all the effort put into creating new supervisory agencies, on the question of bank business models and recapitalization, Europe's progress was painfully slow.[69]

With the United States setting the pace, in May 2009 the Committee of European Banking Supervisors announced that it would be conducting a scenario-planning exercise with Europe's banks. But the committee insisted that these were "not a stress test to identify individual banks" and that "the outcomes [would remain] confidential."[70] There was reason to fear the results of a more searching investigation. With banks desperate to avoid the stigma of official assistance, the hundreds of billions in public funds that had been allocated across Europe in October 2008 to fund recapitalization had remained largely untapped. Meanwhile, rock-bottom prices for bank shares made it expensive to raise capital through the markets. As a result, already in April 2009, in its first devastating summation of the financial crisis, the IMF estimated that the United States was significantly ahead in the game of bank recapitalization.[71] According to the Fund, Europe's banks faced at least another trillion dollars in write-downs by 2010 on top of the losses they had already recognized. That was twice as much as was still outstanding in the United States. In local reports from across Europe, even more alarming numbers were circulating. In April 2009 *Süddeutsche Zeitung* got hold of a leaked paper from Germany's bank regulator BaFin that seemed to suggest that there were 816 billion euros of assets on the books of Germany's banks that were either toxic or unsellable under current conditions.[72] In the summer of 2009 Germany introduced new legislation to launch bad banks to absorb this toxic debt. But once again the funds were not taken up. European actions were facilitative, not mandatory. All told, the IMF estimated that to restore something like stability, the European banks would need between $500 billion and $1.25 trillion, either in new capital or in accumulated and retained profits. But far from actively pursuing new funds, over the years that followed, the European banks lagged far behind their American peers.

This striking graph, which shows how aggressively America's banks raised capital relative to their European peers, serves as a fitting conclusion

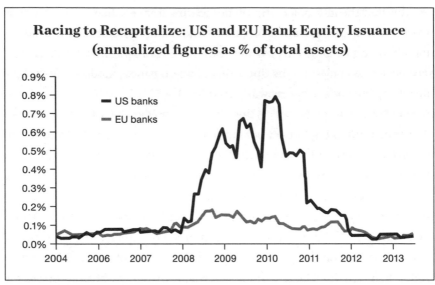

Source: D. Schoenmaker and T. Peek, "The State of the Banking Sector in Europe," OECD Economics Department Working Papers 1102 (2014), figure 8, http://dx.doi.org/10.1787/5k3ttg7n 4r32-en.

to the first phase of the crisis. TARP, followed by the stress tests, the Dodd-Frank regime and capital planning, put the American banking system on a forced road to recovery. It foreclosed more radical options. The banks remained too big to fail. Far from downsizing or breaking them up, by 2013, J.P. Morgan, Goldman Sachs, Bank of America, Citigroup, Wells Fargo and Morgan Stanley were 37 percent larger than they were in 2008.[73] The resources of the state were put one-sidedly at the service of management and shareholders. But if the aim was to get America's banks out of the emergency ward, it worked. As Geithner insisted, the ultimate test of his policy of stabilization was the financial health of the banks, and on that score the record was pretty unambiguous. Between 2009 and 2012 the eighteen largest US banks increased their common capital from $400 billion to $800 billion. They reduced their ratio of risky wholesale funding from $1.38 per dollar of FDIC-insured retail deposits to $0.64. At the same time, they raised the share of their assets in cash, Treasurys and highly liquid instruments from 14 to 23 percent.[74] The elite closure and cooperation that the Treasury and the Fed had finally managed to orchestrate in October 2008 was doing its job.

By contrast, the lack of comprehensive recapitalization of Europe's wounded banking system was an omission that marks one of the fundamental turning points in the crisis. With the help of low-interest loans from Trichet's ECB, many banks resorted to the makeshift of pumping up their profits by buying higher-yielding government debt. But the failure to build new capital would leave the European banks in no position to absorb any further shocks. While the United States began to stabilize, in Europe the banking crisis of 2008 would merge a year later with a new crisis: a panic in the eurozone public debt market. The connecting thread between the crisis of subprime and the crisis of the eurozone was the fragility of Europe's bank balance sheets. Back to back, the combination of the two crises would mark one of the most significant inflections in European economic history since 1945. It would shake Europe's politics to its foundations. It would open a stark divide within the Atlantic economy between Europe and America, and it would pose a profound challenge to transatlantic relations.

Part III

EUROZONE

Chapter 14

GREECE 2010:
EXTEND AND PRETEND

In the summer of 2009, with the acute crisis in the banking sector having been cauterized, both the European and the American economies began to recover. But aftershocks continued. With the insulation provided by the Fed and the Treasury, in the United States these aftershocks no longer manifested as acute stress in the financial system, but in misery spread across millions of households struggling with unaffordable mortgage payments and houses that were no longer worth the debt secured on them. The wave of foreclosures of American homes did not reach high tide until early 2010. Debtors continued to default, in other words, but their disaster did not pose systemic risks. They were the powerless ones who received precious little support from the Obama administration or anyone else. The main props to the economy other than the open-handed liquidity provision of the Fed were the automatic stabilizers of the fiscal apparatus. They left a deep dent in public finances, not just in the United States but across the advanced economies. In 2010 this would trigger a global backlash demanding fiscal consolidation and a return to the agenda of fiscal sustainability that had been so widely touted before the crisis. Controlling the debt-to-GDP ratio would become a mantra. After the largesse of the 2008 bank bailouts came austerity, though not for the same people, of course. But money is fungible. Ultimately, health care, education and local government services were all entries in the same budget that had to accommodate the costs of the crisis.

In the eurozone the switchback from the largesse of the banking crisis to the austerity that followed would take on a particularly dramatic form, because in three of its smaller member states the fiscal impact of the crisis was overwhelming. In the wake of the 2008 crisis, Greece, Ireland and Portugal slid into an increasingly untenable budgetary situation. Of the three, the situations of Greece and Ireland were the most severe. Greece's public debts were simply too large and needed to be restructured. Ireland was overwhelmed by the consequences of its panic-stricken announcement on September 30, 2008, that it was guaranteeing 440 billion euros of bank liabilities. Given the burdens that Greece and Ireland were under by 2009, the only reasonable way forward was to carry out a debt restructuring, also known as haircutting bondholders, or, more euphemistically, as private sector involvement (PSI). In Greece this would have to involve lenders to the state. In Ireland it was the banks' creditors whose claims could not reasonably be met. As in any bankruptcy, this involved an infringement of property rights and would create uncertainty. The risk of contagion was serious. If Greece or Ireland restructured, who would be next? Given the weakened state of Europe's banks, it might be dangerous to inflict further losses on them. And given the degree of their interconnection with the US financial system, that concern would not remain confined to Europe. It is not surprising, therefore, that the Greek and the Irish situations, followed by Portugal's, should have caused political and financial stress and that this should have spread to both sides of the Atlantic. But what happened in the eurozone from 2010 was extraordinary.

The denial, lack of initiative and coordination that had characterized Europe's first response to the banking crisis in September and early October 2008 was a harbinger of things to come. In the first phase of the crisis in the autumn of 2008, the stresses could still be contained at the national level. In 2010 they spilled over into a general struggle for the future of Europe. Europe's single currency almost came apart. Greece, Portugal, Ireland and Spain were driven into depressions the likes of which had not been seen since the 1930s. Italy became collateral damage. France's sovereign credit was put in jeopardy. Prime ministers were ousted. Political parties collapsed. Nationalist passions were stirred to the boiling point. The Obama administration faced the prospect that Europe's new crisis might spill back

on the United States. In the spring of 2009 France and Germany had lec-
tured the UK and the United States about financial stability. A year later
they were reduced to calling on the IMF to help not just Greece but the
eurozone as a whole. And it was not enough. Two years later the eurozone
crisis was still menacing global financial stability.

I

Viewed against the wider canvas of the global crisis stretching from Wall
Street to Seoul, the troubles of Greece and Ireland were not unusual and we
do not need to refer to idiosyncratic features of eurozone governance to
explain them.[1] Ireland was an overgrown offshore banking hub. The costs
of the bailout that Dublin saddled itself with were enough to have put even
the most fiscally sound state in danger. It was Lagarde's nightmare of Oc-
tober 2008 made real: a crisis in Europe's highly integrated financial system
too big for a host country to resolve alone. The politicians in Dublin were
driven by panic and their intimate ties to the local banking community, but
Merkel's veto on any collective European solution made Ireland's situation
untenable. When on January 15, 2009, Dublin was forced to nationalize
Anglo Irish Bank there were already rumors of an IMF intervention. Ire-
land's sovereign bonds sold off and its default risk soared even above that of
Greece's.[2]

 If Greece had been in Hungary's situation in 2008, a member of the EU
but outside the eurozone, it would in all likelihood have joined the East
Europeans in the first round of IMF crisis programs.[3] It was not that Greece
was directly caught up in the transatlantic financial crisis. Its banks had
regional interests at most. The crisis reached Greece by way of its export
and tourism sectors. Then automatic fiscal stabilizers kicked in. Tax reve-
nues slumped. None of this was unusual in 2008–2009. What set Greece
apart was the precariousness of its fiscal position when the crisis struck. It
bears repeating that Greece had not used eurozone membership to go on
an outsized borrowing binge. The bulk of its debts were piled up in the
1980s and 1990s as its two main parties, PASOK (social democrat) and New
Democracy (Christian democratic), lured voters with the promise of West

European modernity and affluence.[4] In 2006 Greece's debt level relative to GDP was lower than it had been when it joined the eurozone in 2001. But it was not reduced by much and would have been worse but for fiddling. Athens's failure was not to have used the exceptional period of rapid growth and low interest rates to substantially reduce its debt burden. Any sudden surge in the deficit, any upward hike in interest rates, was likely to topple it from just about managing to insolvency. That is precisely what happened in 2008. In response to the crisis, the conservative New Democracy government abandoned all fiscal restraint, and at the same time, interest rates for Greece as a weaker sovereign borrower surged.

In July 2009 Athens alerted the Eurogroup to the fact that its deficit might be heading toward 10 percent of GDP or more. But at that point neither side thought it convenient to go public. The break came on October 4, when the Greek electorate turfed out the center-right New Democracy party and gave a large majority to a reform-minded PASOK government. Two weeks later George Papandreou's administration broke the silence.[5] Athens announced to Eurostat, the European statistical agency, that its deficit would exceed 12.7 percent. At a stroke the budget revisions for 2009 took Greece's debt burden from 99 to 115 percent of GDP. Deficits running into the tens of billions adding continuously to the existing stock of debt, combined with surging interest rates, would soon make the problem impossible to contain. In 2010 alone Greece was due to make repayments totaling a massive 53 billion euros. That would have placed a strain on any borrower. But Greece's problems were not due to illiquidity. It was insolvent. To actually stabilize its debts it would, according to one calculation, need to raise tax revenues by 14 percent of GDP and cut expenditure by the same amount. That was politically impossible. What Greece needed to do was to restructure, to agree with its creditors to reduce their claims. To do anything else, to add new loans to an already insupportable debt burden, would postpone the problem but at the price of increasing its scale.

Of course, restructuring was an unpopular option with the creditors. As recently as 2007 Greece's bonds had traded at virtually the same yield as Germany's. They were widely held. At the end of 2009, of Greece's 293 billion euros in public debt outstanding, 206 billion were foreign owned, 90 billion were held by European banks and roughly the same amount by

pension and insurance funds. For those claims to be written down would relieve the burden on Greece. But it would also tumble Greece out of the club of respectable European borrowers. At an earlier moment in its history PASOK might have turned a national bankruptcy into a liberating rupture.[6] By 2009 it was no longer that kind of political party. Restructuring would involve Athens in humiliating negotiations with its creditors. It would most likely involve the IMF. Indeed, restructuring was not just unpopular, it was unspeakable. If you hoped somehow to postpone the inevitable and muddle through, the crucial thing was to preserve confidence. Even mentioning the possibility of restructuring was likely to precipitate a panic, shut off short-term funding and make immediate default inevitable. In due course, however, whatever tactic you adopted, the math was inexorable. Greece's debts were too heavy and growing ever more so. Restructuring was inescapable. But rather than a clean cut, what transpired was a prolonged and agonizing rearguard action clouded by obfuscation and the endlessly repeated tactic of "extend and pretend."

Where did this twisted path begin? As good a place to start as any is in the spring of 2010, when Greek prime minister Papandreou visited Paris for meetings with President Sarkozy and his government. The French made clear that they did not want a crisis. Nor did they want to hear talk of restructuring. They wanted to mobilize funds to bail out the Greeks. Since the turmoil of the fall of 2008, when Budapest had been driven into the arms of the IMF, a secret committee of the larger European states had been meeting to discuss how the eurozone would respond if one of its members was sucked into a Hungarian-style crisis.[7] Paris and the European Commission were united in wanting a Europe-wide solution. To the Greeks this was no doubt reassuring. As would be true throughout the eurozone crisis, there was little or no anti-bailout hysteria in France.[8] Though the French would contribute almost as much in per capita terms to every eurozone rescue measure as Germany, and only fractionally less in overall terms, the issue was never politicized to the same degree. But that begs the question, why was Paris so willing to consider throwing good money after bad in Greece?

President Sarkozy never missed an opportunity to score points at the expense of Anglo-Saxon finance. All the more embarrassing that in Greece

it was France's banks that were most exposed. Paribas was the largest foreign holder of Greek debt. Credit Agricole had a large exposure through a Greek subsidiary. And the most fragile bank of all was Dexia.[9] But why, we have to ask, was Paris so acutely concerned? The balance sheet of BNP Paribas was solid enough to absorb losses in Greece. Dexia's direct exposure to Greece came to only 3 billion euros. Under normal conditions, that was hardly a life-threatening amount. The fact that it was a matter of concern was due, first of all, to the dire state of Dexia's balance sheet. It was truly a weak link and no one in 2010 wanted to fix it. The public would not stand for another bank bailout. And the concerns went far beyond Dexia and its ilk. The entire business model of Europe's biggest banks, even French national champions like BNP Paribas, was a cause for concern. They continued to rely on wholesale finance. If their credit began to fail, they were at the mercy of commercial paper and repo markets. Confidence in funding markets had not recovered from the shocks they had suffered since 2007. A shock to confidence in the eurozone might lead to a general withdrawal of funding. What was at stake was not just Greece, but the far larger network of cross-border debt, in which France's stake, like that of other rich country lenders, was truly enormous.

Altogether, foreign bank lending to what became known as the eurozone periphery—Greece, Ireland, Portugal and Spain—topped $2.5 trillion. Of that total, France's banks had c. $500 billion at stake and Germany's banks had roughly the same. Most of that lending and borrowing was not to governments. Spain and Ireland had been swept up in the gigantic real estate inflation that was now painfully deflating. In Spain, in particular, there was reason to fear for the stability not of the government's finances but of local mortgage lenders. Beyond the periphery, what was even more worrying was Italy's public debt. Italy's budgetary situation was far more tightly controlled than that of Greece's. Indeed, prior to the crisis, it had been running primary surpluses (ahead of debt interest payments). But its debt level was worryingly high, and in May 2008 the Italian premiership had been taken by Silvio Berlusconi, who, despite his business credentials and his conservative coalition partners, was regarded as a dangerous opportunist. No one wanted the flames of panic to leap to Italy. Beyond Italy was Belgium and then France itself. It was this three-tiered structure of

The Eurozone Debt Pyramid (in $ billions)

Exposure to	Type of exposure	1st quarter 2010 exposure of global banks to eurozone debt							
		Germany	Spain	France	Italy	Other eurozone	UK	US	World total
Greece	Public sector	23.1	0.9	27	3.3	22.9	3.6	5.4	92.5
	Banks	10.5	0	3.9	1.2	2.6	2.2	3.1	26.1
	Non bank private	10	0.2	40.2	2.2	14.5	6	5.2	83.2
	Total foreign claims	43.6	1.1	71.1	6.8	40.1	11.8	13.6	20.2
	Other exposure	7.4	0.5	40.5	2	7.8	4.7	27.5	95.2
	Total exposure	51	1.6	111.6	8.8	47.9	16.5	41.2	297.2
Ireland	Public sector	3.4	0.2	8.7	0.9	3.8	7.3	1.9	29.7
	Banks	46	2.5	21.1	3.6	14	42.3	24.6	168.6
	Non bank private	118.1	9.6	20.5	12	66.8	114.4	34.1	421.7
	Total foreign claims	167.5	12.3	50.3	16.5	84.9	164	60.6	621.1
	Other exposure	38.3	3.9	35.4	12.1	7.6	58.4	53.2	222.7
	Total exposure	205.8	16.2	85.7	28.6	92.5	222.4	113.9	843.8
Portugal	Public sector	9.9	10.6	20.4	2.2	11.5	2.6	1.6	62.9
	Banks	20.3	7.4	7.3	3.1	7	6.6	2	55.4
	Non bank private	8.2	66.7	14.4	1.1	8.2	15.8	1.6	118.4
	Total foreign claims	38.4	84.7	42.1	6.5	267	25	5.2	236.7
	Other exposure	8.1	23.3	7.6	2.9	2.4	7.4	32.1	85.6
	Total exposure	46.6	108.8	49.7	9.4	29.1	32.4	37.3	322.4
Spain	Public sector	30		46.9	2.3	19.1	7.6	4.9	127.6
	Banks	95		69.7	11.1	68.7	27.6	28.6	317.4
	Non bank private	55.2		83.1	16.4	98.3	75	28.7	378.2
	Total foreign claims	180.2		199.8	29.9	186.1	110.2	62.2	824.1
	Other exposure	37.7		44.4	12.6	14.4	31.5	124.1	278.5
	Total exposure	217.9		244.2	42.5	200.6	141.7	186.4	1102.6
Italy	Public sector	55.6	11.8	119.4		na	12.2	21.3	371.3
	Banks	54.5	3.1	51.2		na	13.4	13.6	171.4
	Non bank private	66.1	24.2	309.9		na	43	17.8	445.5
	Total foreign claims	176.2	39.3	480.1		143.6	68.6	52.7	988.2
	Other exposure	58.2	20.3	97.6		na	28.8	237.3	487.1
	Total exposure	234.4	59.6	577.7		na	97.4	290	1475.3

Note:
(1) other exposure includes derivative contracts, guarantees and credit commitments
(2) figures for sectoral exposure for Italy for 1st quarter 2010 calculated by applying proportions reported for Q4 2010
(3) figures for other exposure to Italy for Germany, Spain and France calculated by applying proportions relative to total foreign claims for Q4 2010

Sources: BIS Consolidated Banking Statistics and *BIS Quarterly Review*, September 2010, http://www.bis.org/publ/qtrpdf/r_qt1009.pdf.

debt that drove the politics of the eurozone crisis from the French point of view: the small bankrupt sovereign debtors—Greece and Portugal—at the bottom; then the victims of the real estate boom with big liabilities from the banking crisis—Ireland and later Spain; and finally the really big public debtors, led by Italy. As far as Paris was concerned, the long-term sustainability of Greece's debt was less important than holding this giant pyramid in place.

It was no doubt reassuring to Athens to receive such a sympathetic welcome in Paris. But it should have set off alarm bells. Should Greece wish to be the place where France fought its battle for the eurozone's financial stability? Was a bailout designed to minimize the risk to Europe's over-expanded banks and to avoid embarrassment for politicians likely to be in the best interests of Greek taxpayers? The risks to Greece were obvious. On the French side too one might wonder whether, if the aim was to solidify the eurozone, the best tactic was to delay a straightforward and thorough resolution of Greece's huge debt burden. If it was a question of picking a line of defense, was Greece really where one would choose to make one's stand? To use the ugly metaphor that would soon circulate widely in the eurozone, might it not have been better to amputate the gangrenous limb, to push Greece aggressively toward restructuring?[10] There were risks on both sides. Paris opted for extend-and-pretend.

On the German side it looked, at first, as though a similar attitude might prevail. Germany's banks, like France's, were heavily exposed to the weaker eurozone borrowers. The logic of systemic stability was not lost on Berlin.[11] In February 2009, when pressure first built against Greece and Ireland, Finance Minister Peer Steinbrück had calmed markets by announcing: "If one country of the eurozone gets into trouble, then collectively we will have to be helpful. The euro-region treaties don't foresee any help for insolvent countries, but in reality the other states would have to rescue those running into difficulty."[12] A year later, when Papandreou's government was looking for help, Josef Ackermann, the energetic CEO of Deutsche Bank and president of the IIF, was to hand. He traveled to Athens in early 2010 to offer a public-private loan of 30 billion euros.[13] It is conceivable that with both Berlin and Paris on board, applying a sticking plaster might have calmed markets and reduced yields to the point where Greece

could limp on. But the debt was piling up inexorably. And what would have happened when the eurozone was hit by the next shock, from Ireland or Portugal? For an insolvent borrower new debt is a makeshift, not a solution.

In any case, by the spring of 2010 the counterfactual was moot. When Germans went to the polls on September 27, 2009, after a bitterly fought campaign, they threw Steinbrück and the SPD out of office. Angela Merkel continued as chancellor, but now in coalition with the free-market, tax-cutting FDP.[14] They were more to the chancellor's ideological taste, but she was now operating from a far narrower political base and would have to pay even more attention to the home front. To the satisfaction of conservatives, Steinbrück was replaced as finance minister by Wolfgang Schäuble. Schäuble was a committed European integrationist of the 1980s Helmut Kohl generation. As a Christian conservative of the cold war era he had a capacious strategic vision for the EU as an upholder of Western civilization in an age of globalization.[15] For Schäuble, the Rechtsstaat, the legally bound state, was the anchor of his conception of the West, and as finance minister the debt brake anchored in the constitution was his particular legal preoccupation. The CDU's new coalition partner, the FDP, was a probusiness, tax-cutting party, so that constrained Schäuble on the revenue side. What Germany and Europe needed was fiscal discipline. If Greece could not make the grade, then Schäuble since the 1990s had been an unapologetic advocate of a vision of a multispeed Europe, in which a core group set the pace while less competitive and disciplined nations brought up the rear. On February 11, 2010, the Merkel government shocked markets by agreeing with its partners to take emergency measures to support the euro as such, but vetoing any specific offer of help for Greece. As one EU official told journalists, "Germany is stepping totally on the brakes on financial assistance. On legal grounds, on constitutional grounds and on principle."[16]

Berlin's refusal to stick to the bailout script was worrying for the French and shocking for the Greeks. But it should have been no surprise. Article 125 of the Maastricht Treaty banned mutual bailouts. The Lisbon Treaty that finally came into operation in December 2009, just as the Greek crisis exploded, had reinforced the primacy of nation-state responsibility. It also barred the route to the mutualization of debt, which might have allowed a European consortium to share the burden of backstopping some portion of

Greece's liabilities. In a crucial judgment on the Lisbon Treaty delivered on June 30, 2009, the German constitutional court had put a further obstacle in the way of any further moves toward EU integration.[17] Karlsruhe insisted on a stiff test of democratic accountability before any further competences could be transferred to Brussels. What Berlin would agree to on February 11, 2010, was last resort, ultima ratio support for the euro as such. What that meant for a "bad apple" like Greece was unclear. Certainly, Greece should slash its deficits and engage in labor market reform to boost growth. But Germany was in no mood for a bailout. The vast majority of German politicians and public opinion appeared to be willing to let the markets have their way with both Greece and its creditors. If a debt write-down was necessary, so be it. If Athens was unable to pay, then there was support in Germany across the entire political spectrum for the debts to be restructured at the expense of the banks.[18] Polls showed that two thirds of those who supported assistance for Greece also demanded that banks must contribute to the package.[19] These calls were reinforced by lobby groups such as the league of German taxpayers that demanded private sector involvement.[20] It was a harsh and high-risk approach, whose appeal to the German public was consistent with the fact that they tended to blame "other people's" banks and to underestimate the exposure of their own country's financial institutions.

This was the basic dilemma of the eurozone debt crisis. Greece needed a write-off. The Germans were not opposed and favored haircutting the creditors. But Greece's PASOK government did not want to pay the price for a problem in large part created by its predecessor. It wasn't just the state's debts that would have to be restructured but the Greek banking system too. The entire Greek social and political fabric was at stake. The French opposed a write-off and Paris had backing not just from other European debtor nations but from the ECB as well. The ECB was aghast at the prospect of a sovereign default in the eurozone. What about the risks of contagion? Surely what Greece needed was a healthy dose of financial discipline. That was a popular answer. Austerity was the medicine forced down Greek throats for years to come. But the budget adjustment required was unrealistic and its impact on the Greek economy was devastating. As

restructuring was, in the end, inevitable, the question ought to have been how to make it safe, how to build a framework within which debts could be written down and losses inflicted on creditors without unleashing a general panic. The problem was that to even say this out loud was to risk triggering a run before the safety net was ready. While engaging in extend-and-pretend and denying the need for restructuring, it was hard to generate momentum for any collective European effort at institution building. And it could not be done without Germany, which, though it did not shrink from restructuring Greece and its creditors, was anything but enthusiastic about putting in place the mechanisms necessary to make restructuring safe.

The German reluctance was shortsighted but understandable. Already by the spring of 2010 it was clear that a comprehensive solution to the problem of the sovereign debt crisis required (1) an aggressive recapitalization of Europe's banks to allow them to survive the losses, an undertaking on which Europe was lagging behind the United States already in 2009; (2) a European fund to back this bank recapitalization because otherwise the effort might destabilize the fragile finances of smaller states, a proposal already vetoed by Berlin in October 2008; (3) the ECB would need to stabilize bond markets either by providing liquidity to Europe's banks or by active purchases along the lines of the Fed's programs, though outright monetization of debt was barred by the ECB treaty and conservative opinion in Germany abhorred any such intervention; (4) a European TARP, backstopped by the budgets of national governments to buy the sovereign debts of the weakest European states, a proposal blocked by the Lisbon Treaty's ban on mutualization. It was to make all of this somewhat less inconceivable in political terms that one arrived back at financial discipline (5). Taxpayers in solvent northern counties such as the Netherlands and Finland, but above all Germany, would need to know that they were not being taken advantage of. Before there could be any mutualization of liabilities, there would need to be an agreement on fiscal rules. The bar had been set in May 2009 by Germany's debt brake constitutional amendment. Anything less was a compromise as far as Berlin was concerned. It was the working through of these interlocking problems that would make the road

to containment, let alone resolution of the Greek debt crisis, such an agonizing one. All the while the financial markets looked on with a mixture of anxiety, impatience and an eye to the speculative profits to be made by trading on uncertainty.

II

The search for a solution began in early 2010 in Schäuble's finance ministry. Apparently without prior coordination with Angela Merkel's chancellery, Schäuble proposed that the EU should establish a European Monetary Fund (EMF), able to conduct within the eurozone the kind of restructuring, stabilizing and disciplining role that the IMF played on the global stage.[21] One version of the EMF idea, pushed among others by Deutsche Bank's chief economist, Thomas Mayer, was for the fund to backstop debts up to a limit of 60 percent of a country's GDP. Above that level debts would undergo restructuring, with bondholders taking a proportional and uniform haircut.[22]

It was a strikingly ambitious proposal that reflected Schäuble's deeply held federalist European commitments. He was keen to use the crisis to push forward the agenda of European integration left unfinished at Maastricht in 1992. If Berlin had thrown its full weight behind the idea of an EMF and if its budget had been set to an appropriate size—what were needed were hundreds of billions of euros—the crisis might have taken another course. If Berlin had risen to the challenge it is hard to see how the rest of the eurozone governments could have resisted. Something very much like this is what they would eagerly settle for in 2012. But this opportunity for German leadership on the crisis went begging. In the spring of 2010, Schäuble's scheme was shot down, by friendly fire.[23] Chancellor Merkel was no European federalist. She had no desire to reopen the terms of the Lisbon Treaty for which she had fought so hard and which was only just coming into operation. She was not about to endow Brussels with its own monetary fund. She was far too skeptical of Europe's capacity for self-discipline and she had the German constitutional court's Lisbon ruling to think about. She understood that radical measures were necessary, but her own

proposal, rather than creating an EMF, was simply to involve the IMF in disciplining the eurozone.

Forcing Greece to go to the IMF appealed to German conservatives.[24] The Fund, with its ambitious French managing director, Dominique Strauss-Kahn, was keen to be involved. But there was also hesitation. The IMF had already put tens of billions of euros into Eastern Europe. The eurozone would take even more. In a new age of globalization, was a deep engagement in Europe the right direction for the IMF to be headed? And in dealing with European countries with powerful representation on the Fund's own board, could the Fund's economists be certain that their expertise would prevail? Specifically, would the Europeans take the IMF's advice on the question of restructuring? Did they even understand the policy that the IMF was duty bound to pursue? Following its disastrous experience in Argentina's financial crisis in 2001, the IMF had established new rules.[25] The Fund would lend only to solvent borrowers, otherwise there must be restructuring. And if it was to lend, it would insist on lending early, before panic set in. Given the scale of speculative firepower that could be mobilized in leveraged financial markets, to lend once a run had started was likely to be both expensive and ineffectual. Given how far the Greek crisis had already progressed by the early months of 2010, it was hard to argue that it met either of these criteria.

Here again one can glimpse the possibility of an alternative path: Could Berlin have backed an IMF demand for immediate Greek restructuring? Certainly the Fund's own retrospective analysis suggests that this would have been the better path.[26] But Merkel's veto on the European Monetary Fund idea suggests the main obstacle to any such strategy. She was not willing to contemplate the additional flanking measures that would be necessary to make a restructuring safe. And the proposal to involve the IMF rallied the rest of Europe against her. Indeed, Merkel's own finance minister, Schäuble, let it be known that he would regard IMF involvement as a "humiliation" for Europe.[27] For Sarkozy it was unthinkable that the IMF should be involved at all: "Forget the IMF. The IMF is not for Europe. It's for Africa—it's for Burkina Faso!" he told the Greek government in early March.[28] The ECB, likewise, was absolutely opposed both to anything that entailed debt restructuring and to IMF involvement. It was bad enough for

American mortgage-backed bonds to have unleashed the banking crisis. For Trichet it was simply unthinkable that the sovereign signature on euro-zone public debt would not be honored in full. And to involve the IMF in Europe's internal affairs was to add insult to injury. Trichet's objection was not that the IMF was for Africa, but that it was "American."[29]

Trichet had reason to be worried about the outside world, because when it came to the eurozone, it was to the ECB that all eyes turned. If the ECB was a central bank, like the Fed or the Bank of England, there was no need for there to be a sovereign debt crisis at all. Greece had not borrowed in dollars. It had borrowed in euros and had delegated the sovereign power to print its own currency to the ECB. Its fate and that of the entire rest of the eurozone was in Trichet's hands. All the ECB had to do to stop the destabilizing surge in Greek interest rates was to do what central banks do all over the world: buy sovereign bonds. Of course, bond buying was no long-term solution. Greece needed restructuring, fiscal discipline and economic growth. But at stake was the financial stability of a vast economic area. The Greek public debt was a tiny part of Europe's financial system. The treaties that founded the ECB limited its right to buy newly issued Greek debt. But it could buy outstanding bonds as part of a market stabilization effort. If the ECB did not intervene it was a matter not of economics but of politics and over the winter of 2009–2010 it seemed that Europe's central bankers were determined to take a tough line. Rather than continuing the generous liquidity provision it had offered in 2009, the ECB allowed the LTRO scheme to expire.[30] Then in April 2010 it began to discuss a new regime under which it would apply graduated repo haircuts to lower-rated sovereign bonds, limiting their attractiveness to banks.[31] Trichet was engaged in the high-risk gamble of substituting pressure in the bond markets for the euro-zone's missing federal structures of fiscal and economic governance. With the ECB looking on, surging bond yields would force the Greeks to get serious about fiscal discipline and economic reform. In taking this line, Trichet was not only satisfying his own agenda. He was also appeasing the Bundesbank and its hawkish, monetarist head, Professor Axel Weber. Any kind of bond purchases by the ECB were seen in Germany as an inflationary menace. Furthermore, and more pertinently, they were understood to be a form of debt mutualization by stealth. By way of the balance sheet of

the ECB, German taxpayers would end up as creditors to the rest of the eurozone.[32] So too, of course, would all the other shareholders in the ECB. But it was Germany's portion that German Eurosceptics worried about.

Throughout the early months of 2010 the argument was deadlocked. Market pressure on Greece intensified. Foreign investors were unloading what Greek debt they could sell. Hard-liners in Europe might see this as a legitimate way of imposing discipline, but for investors the lack of resolution was unsettling. Who might be next? Ireland? Italy? For the Greek government it was, frankly, terrifying. On May 19, 2010, Athens was due to make payments of 8.9 billion euros. It was not obvious where they would find the cash. Desperate for a way out, the PASOK government looked for help from across the Atlantic.

In the spring of 2010 visitors from Europe bearing bad news were not welcome in the White House. The Obama administration had been closely following the developing Greek debt crisis and had appealed to the Europeans to act fast.[33] But it was itself mired in domestic political mud. Thanks to the botched Massachusetts special election in January following the death of Teddy Kennedy, the Democrats had lost their filibuster-proof majority in the Senate. The passage of health-care reform had become a grueling war of attrition. Dodd-Frank seemed stranded. The last thing the Treasury and the Fed needed was a new crisis. But by the spring of 2010 it was clear that the failure of the Europeans to deal with Greece was threatening precisely that.

Once before, sixty-three years earlier, a political crisis in Greece had triggered a transformation in US policy. On March 12, 1947, after the British had declared their inability to defeat the Communist insurgency in the Greek civil war, President Truman announced the doctrine of containment, one of the opening moves in the cold war. That summer, Truman's secretary of state, General George Marshall, would back up containment with his legendary promise of economic aid for Europe. In 2010 there was no antagonist like the Soviet Union to force the Obama administration's hand. What made Greece into America's problem was not a global clash of ideologies, but the money coursing through the circulatory system of transatlantic finance. America's mutual funds had hundreds of billions of dollars at stake in Europe's banks, above all French banks. It was those same banks

that were exposed in Greece. And the US branches of those same European banks were also major lenders to US households and firms. Any eurozone financial crisis would blow back on America.

On March 9, 2010, a month after Germany blocked the push for a quick Greek rescue, President Obama and his top economic advisers, Larry Summers and Tim Geithner, took time to meet with the Greek prime minister and his delegation. Obama's message was encouraging. Washington would vote its 17 percent share for IMF assistance and would throw its weight behind an approach to Merkel requesting aid from the EU.[34] Opposition to IMF involvement from France and the ECB would be overridden. But the White House made one thing clear. There could be no talk of debt restructuring. "We cannot have another Lehman," Obama emphasized. Whether Greece's debts were sustainable was not America's concern. Washington's priority was containing financial contagion. Restructuring could not be contemplated until the Europeans had found a way to stabilize bond markets and were ready to push through wholesale recapitalization of Europe's banks. And given the Franco-German deadlock, no such agreement seemed likely.

It was from this force field of interests that the first iteration of extend-and-pretend emerged. Europe entered an emergency regime defined not by a single sovereign author, but by the absence of any such authority.[35] At an EU summit on March 25, 2010, overriding objections from both the French and the ECB, and with Washington on her side, Merkel forced through the involvement of the IMF.[36] It would be a joint EU-IMF action, as in the Baltics the previous year. But this time the ECB would be fully engaged. A committee of the EU, the ECB and the IMF would make up the soon to be infamous "troika," dictating policy to Greece and the other "program countries." What was ruled out was restructuring. On that Washington sided with the French and the ECB. Existing Greek debt would be paid off with new loans from the troika, whether or not the result was sustainable. The IMF would have to bend its operating procedures to the occasion. To satisfy Merkel's insistence on the Lisbon rules, the "European" component would not consist of measures taken collectively via the central institutions in Brussels or jointly funded by the member states. That would require treaty change and might violate the line drawn by the German constitutional

court. Instead, it would consist of individual national credits for Athens on a bilateral and voluntary basis coordinated through the Eurogroup, the powerful but informal meeting of the eurozone finance ministers. To avoid the appearance of a bailout—banned by Maastricht—the loans would not be on concessionary terms. Interest rates would be stiff and there would be a processing fee to compensate the lenders for their trouble. Finally, and most important, the support would not be provided preemptively to forestall a loss of market confidence. It would be offered only as an ultima ratio, if and when Greece lost access to the markets. It would be up to Greece, by means of austerity, to forestall that moment for as long as possible.

For ordinary Greeks this meant pay cuts across the public sector. Contract workers were not renewed. The cap on dismissals from the private sector was lifted. The pension age was raised. VAT and other consumption taxes were hiked. An economy already under pressure was subjected to a further contractionary squeeze. A population that already had one of the lower standards of living in Europe was pushed further down the scale. The Greek labor movement mobilized in furious protest. But it was enough at least to satisfy the bond markets. In the last days of March 2010, Athens was able to issue a final tranche of long-term debt: 5 billion euros for seven years at just under 6 percent. Perhaps not surprisingly, investor demand was lukewarm.[37] Europe was preparing a safety net. The only question was when Greece would tumble off the ledge.

III

On March 30 the markets were rocked by news not from Greece but from Ireland. The bill for recapitalizing Ireland's bankrupt banks was soaring. For Anglo Irish Bank alone, Dublin was now budgeting 34 billion euros, more than Ireland's tax revenue in 2010. Soon Ireland's deficit would be worse than that of Greece's.[38] In Ireland it was the banks pulling the sovereign down. In Greece the mechanism worked the other way around. Canny depositors in Greek banks were aware that their savings were invested in the government bonds that Athens was struggling to service. In the early months of 2010, 14 billion euros were withdrawn from Greek banks and

shifted elsewhere in the eurozone. The first to move were the oligarchs moving huge sums by way of Cyprus, but they were soon followed by middle-class depositors pulling out a few thousand euros at a time.[39] Bereft of sources of funding, the Greek banks turned to the Greek central bank, their local branch of the ECB, where Trichet continued to allow them to repo downgraded Greek government bonds. This was a vital life support system and it gave the central bank a whip hand not just over the Greek government but over Greek society and the economy at large. Without approval from Frankfurt there would be no money in the ATMs, but nor would there be any restructuring of Greece's insupportable debt.

In April, as the troika argued over who would contribute what and how large the Greek bailout package would be, time ran out.[40] A downgrade by the Fitch credit-rating agency sent Greek government debt yields surging to 7.4 percent. On the morning of April 22, Eurostat announced that its estimate of the Greek deficit in 2009 had now risen to 13.6 percent of GDP. Ireland's was even larger, at 14.3 percent. Spreads on Greek bonds surged to 600 basis points, raising the borrowing rate to 9 percent, effectively shutting Greece out of the market. The moment had come to reach for the last resort. Urged on by both Schäuble and Geithner, the Greek government triggered the emergency mechanism. Greece needed a lot of money and there was no time to lose.

It was a coincidence but a symbolic one. On the evening of April 22, hours after the Eurostat release had rocked the markets, the world's financial elite were gathered in Washington, DC, for the spring IMF meeting. The evening's entertainment was at the Canadian embassy and it was time for some frank talk. The crisis had moved beyond the European arena. The eurozone now posed a threat to global financial stability. Since March China had been demanding action to defend the value of global investments in euro-denominated assets.[41] As Alistair Darling, Britain's Chancellor of the Exchequer, recalled, the mood was urgent: "You can't overstate the fact that America, with increasing incredulity and anxiety, was watching Europe's inability to act. . . . The message was, 'Why can't you take action? You know you've got to do something.'"[42] As the *Financial Times* put it, the failure of the eurozone to restore stability on its own terms meant that by April 2010, the "rescue" of the euro, "the ultimate expression of

European integration, depended on outsiders in international institutions and the US administration."

But no deal emerged from Washington. The troika was only beginning to haggle with Athens over the terms of a rescue loan. Markets were left hanging. On April 28, 2010, the bottom fell out. The official chronicle of the German finance ministry is, as one might imagine, a sober document. This is how it describes events in Europe's sovereign bond and interbank money markets that day:

"The crisis becomes dramatically acute. Risk premiums for government bonds in some Eurozone member states such as Portugal, Ireland and Spain increase rapidly and reach levels equal to that which prevented Greece from accessing the financial markets in April. In an echo of the final dramatic phases of the financial crisis [of 2008], there is virtually no interbank lending between European banks. Within a very short period, there are overall signs of an acute pending systemic crisis."[43]

What this official narrative disguises is Berlin's own role in precipitating the "acute pending systemic crisis." Ahead of vital regional elections in early May the public agitation in Germany against assistance for Greece was ferocious. The FDP, Merkel's coalition partner, which saw its popularity among its free-market nationalist supporters plunging, played the anti-Greek card uninhibitedly, narrowing the chancellor's room for maneuver. To remind Merkel of the global stakes, on April 28 Dominique Strauss-Kahn and Jean-Claude Trichet both flew into Berlin.[44] But despite the increasing panic, there was no deviation from the minimalist script that Berlin had laid down on March 25. Indeed, Merkel stirred the fires of speculation by reminding the press that admitting Greece to the euro had been a mistake and that Germany's contribution to whatever relief effort emerged would be a voluntary decision taken on terms decided in Berlin.[45] It was not the kind of talk to calm markets. Greek spreads surged to 1,000 basis points, and by the end of the day Washington was sufficiently alarmed for Obama to place a personal call to the chancellery.[46] Nor was Merkel's the only phone ringing in Europe. The logs for Geithner and his staff recall almost daily contact between Washington and Berlin, Frankfurt and Paris.[47] Governments from around the world were pressing the EU to act.

Finally, in the first days of May, the deal was done. Greece agreed with

the troika not only to slash its deficit but to aim for a surplus. It promised to deliver a turnaround in its budget balance of a staggering 18 percent of GDP.[48] In 2010 alone the reduction of its deficit would be 7.5 percent of GDP. Every area of Greek public life would be touched, from ministerial contract cleaners to privatization of state assets. Everything was up for grabs. In exchange, Greece would receive a bailout far larger than previously conceived: 110 billion euros, of which 80 billion would come from the EU and 30 billion from the IMF, payable in quarterly installments over three years. The loans were at tough rates and it was clear that servicing them would create a repayment shock in 2013. But it was the best that the lending countries were willing to offer. Merkel promised an affirmative Bundestag vote for May 7. The question was whether the markets would give Europe that long.

Merkel presented the rescue package to the German Bundestag on Wednesday, May 5. It was, she declared, *"alternativlos"*—without alternative.[49] Merkel's rewording of Margaret Thatcher's famous pronouncement—there is no alternative (TINA)—was to become notorious. Meanwhile, that same day Greece was rocked by a general strike that mobilized both main wings of the Greek labor movement and shut down transport and public services. In Athens protesters fought running battles with riot police. As the parliamentarians debated the austerity program in committee, a firebomb crashed through the window of a branch of Marfin Bank, setting the building alight and killing three staff members. Karolos Papoulias, the grizzled president of the Hellenic Republic and veteran of the Greek resistance in World War II, declared: "Our country has reached the edge of the abyss."[50] On May 6, the Greek parliament convened to vote through what was the most draconian austerity program ever proposed to a modern democracy. That morning, the ECB board was meeting in Lisbon and reporters e-mailed the news that the imperious Jean-Claude Trichet had refused even to discuss the possibility of stepping in to buy Greek bonds. Earlier in the week, on the back of the new fiscal program, the ECB had reluctantly agreed to continue repoing Greek debt, but actively buying bonds was a step too far.[51] It was not what markets needed to hear.

When US trading opened—in the afternoon by European time—prices plunged. By one p.m. the market was down 4 percent. With the ECB

refusing support, there was heavy trading in credit default swaps on Greek government debt. In a single day the Volatility Index (VIX), a measure of market uncertainty, surged by 31.7 percent. The euro plunged, losing 2.5 cents by early afternoon.[52] What was going on between terminals on both sides of the Atlantic that afternoon would later become a matter of dispute in American courtrooms. But at 2:32 p.m. the market went into spasm.[53] Half an hour later, by 3:05 p.m., the main American stock markets had given up 6 percent of their value, erasing $1 trillion from portfolios. As panicked traders fled to quality, demand for US Treasurys surged, driving yields down from 3.6 to 3.25 percent in a matter of minutes.

Thanks to the transatlantic time difference, news of the "flash crash" hit the BlackBerrys of the ECB board as they sat down to dinner in Lisbon. Eighteen months on from the Lehman crisis, it seemed that the delay in bailing out Greece was about to precipitate a second financial catastrophe. Even the head of the Bundesbank, the tough-talking Axel Weber, realized that the ECB could not maintain the hard line that Trichet had taken that morning. The "ECB must buy government bonds," he exclaimed across the dinner table.[54] For the conservative team at the head of the ECB, it was a dramatic moment. They understood that they needed to act. The world was watching. Athens was literally burning. Soon it might be Rome. But the ECB did not want to be the only buyer in the market. It was determined not to let Europe's governments off the hook. It wanted austerity across the board. Furthermore, though the ECB might buy bonds to provide temporary support, what was needed, sooner rather than later, was a giant state-backed fund to provide confidence to the bond markets. Making European governments and taxpayers responsible for each other's debts would create a nightmarish political entanglement, but it would at least reinstate the clear line between fiscal and monetary policy, on which the ECB founded its precious claim to independence.

The next day, on May 7, 2010, the tone at the meeting of the European Council was apocalyptic. Commissioner Rehn and President Trichet delivered dire warnings. "It's Europe. It's global. It's a situation that is deteriorating with extreme rapidity and intensity," Trichet insisted. As the *Financial Times* reported, it came as a shock to the sometimes provincial European Council: "Leaders of smaller eurozone countries not fully plugged into

world financial markets had, until this moment, not appreciated the gravity of the crisis. But even more experienced leaders appeared stunned." "[Nicolas] Sarkozy was white with shock," reported one ambassador. "I've never seen him so pale."[55] But despite the sense of crisis, and despite the deal on Greece, there was no agreement on creating a general security umbrella for the eurozone as a whole. Sarkozy pointed the finger back at the ECB. How could Europe's central bank stand by while the credit of Europe's governments was ruined? Why was the ECB not acting like the Fed or the Bank of England? "Sarkozy was screaming: 'Come on, come on, stop hesitating!'" recalled one EU policy maker. Sarkozy was backed by Italy's Silvio Berlusconi and Portugal's José Sócrates, both of whom had reason to fear a general sovereign debt crisis. But Merkel, the Dutch and the Finns all pushed back. The ECB was independent. It must be free to act as it saw fit. Friday, May 7, ended without agreement. But after events on Wall Street, it was clear that something big had to be done before trading resumed in Asia on Monday, May 10. The Europeans were going to have to move from the national bailout for Greece toward providing a more comprehensive financial backstop for their entire currency zone. They could not expect to handle their problems state by state through bilateral agreements with the IMF. Whereas a few weeks earlier they had balked at coming up with a few tens of billions of euros, now they were going to have to contemplate far larger numbers.

Under huge pressure from governments around the world, Europe's leaders reconvened on the afternoon of Sunday, May 9.[56] Obama had worked the phones to Merkel and all the other key European leaders. Ben Bernanke called an impromptu conference call of the FOMC to approve the renewal of the swap lines to the ECB, the Bank of England, the Swiss National Bank and the Bank of Canada.[57] Likewise, the G7 convened a conference call to coincide with the meeting of the European finance ministers. Japan, Canada and the United States were on the line. At this crucial moment Schäuble was hospitalized by an allergic reaction to a medication. So Spain took the chair, and France's finance minister, Christine Lagarde, found herself as the liaison between the two groups. With two phones on the go at once, she had the EU 27 in one ear and the G7 in the other. The scale of the bailout fund agreed was enormous: 60 billion euros came from the EU Commission

funds, 440 billion from the European governments. Dominique Strauss-Kahn offered to use the IMF's resources to back the fund at the same ratio that had been employed in Latvia the previous summer. But whereas tiny Latvia had needed only a few billion euros, now the IMF pledged 250 billion. It was by far the largest commitment the IMF had ever made to any program. The $1 trillion pledged to the IMF at the London G20 that was supposed to mark the advent of a new age of global firefighting would be deployed to rescue Europe. The figures were impressive, but the all-important question was how the rescue fund would be constituted and financed. Was this a first step toward the mutualization of sovereign debts, and thus a radical step beyond Lisbon? Berlin was not going to concede anything of the sort.[58] The entire deal hung in the balance until a Dutch participant with expertise in shadow banking suggested that the European Financial Stability Facility (EFSF) be incorporated as a private special purpose vehicle registered in the tax haven of Luxembourg. Eurozone governments would contribute capital on a country-by-country basis without assuming any overarching intergovernmental "European" commitment.

Even in this makeshift form, the EFSF would take months to put in place. What was needed when trading resumed on Monday morning was immediate support for Europe's bond markets. That could come only from the ECB. The EFSF agreement satisfied Trichet. The governments were now serious. The question was whether he could carry the board of the ECB, and specifically whether he could win over the Bundesbank. After coming around to bond buying at the moment of panic on May 6, Axel Weber had subsequently had a change of heart. He did not want to risk breaking ranks with German public opinion and his German colleague on the ECB board, chief economist Jürgen Stark. On his way back to Frankfurt from Portugal, Weber retracted his agreement. Nevertheless, on Sunday, May 9, Trichet put the proposal to the vote and won majority approval. He then waited to make any public announcement until the early morning of May 10, when Europe's governments were finally ready to present their ramshackle bailout fund.[59] The ECB would not move first.

Over the days that followed, the markets calmed. Despite the opposition from Germany, the ECB's promise to buy helped. There was less rush to sell if there was a purchaser of last resort. But to make this commitment

manageable for the ECB, there was one further, unpublicized facet to the deal. Even if there was no immediate restructuring of Greek debt, the banks should not be permitted to offload their entire holdings of distressed debt. A concomitant of the ECB's bond buying, insisted on with particular force by Merkel and Schäuble, was that all the eurozone finance ministries would pressure their leading banks to refrain from selling their holdings of Greek and other troubled bonds. The bargain was never complete. In Germany, Deutsche Bank led a group that agreed to hold on to the debt for three years.[60] But many smaller banks refused to take the pledge. And rumors quickly spread that of the first 25 billion euros in bonds bought by the ECB, the vast majority had come from France.

The IMF put its imprimatur on the deal at a meeting of the board on Sunday, May 9, 2010. With Strauss-Kahn on the ground in Europe, the chair in Washington was taken by John Lipsky, a Bush appointee who had alternated time at the IMF with stints at J.P. Morgan. No one around the table at the IMF's headquarters was pleased with the situation.[61] It was an enormous engagement. It was profoundly disturbing that it was being undertaken to manage a crisis in Greece, a comparatively rich European country, at the behest of the EU. The Greeks were being lent vastly more than their quota, the capital contribution that normally limited a country's IMF borrowing rights. The Fund was required to share control over the program with the other members of the troika, and its own experts were far from persuaded that Greece's debts were sustainable. As they put it cagily: It was undeniable that "significant uncertainties around" the program made it "difficult to state categorically" that Greece would ever be able to pay back its debts. Normally this would be a red flag. Who, after all, would benefit from Greece taking on new loans from official lenders to pay off existing private debts it could not service? The outspoken Brazilian board member insisted that the program not be referred to as "a rescue of Greece, which will have to undergo a wrenching adjustment, but as a bailout of Greece's private debt holders, mainly European financial institutions."[62]

One could hardly ask for a clearer statement of the "bait and switch" substitution, by which a problem of excessive bank lending was turned into a crisis of public borrowing.[63] But this substitution resulted less from a skillful ideological conjuring trick than from a lowest common denominator

compromise between the main players in the Greek debt drama—Germany, France, the ECB, the IMF and the Obama administration. Certainly at the IMF there was little illusion about the compromises they were entering into. On May 9 the tone in the room at the IMF board meeting was so negative that Lipsky felt it necessary to put the opposite case. Lipsky was fully committed to the White House line. He was a devotee of Geithner's logic of maximum force.[64] Indeed, Lipsky liked to embarrass his cosmopolitan IMF colleagues by calling for the Fund to adopt not the Powell Doctrine but "shock and awe," the title the US military gave to their devastating aerial assault on Baghdad in 2003.[65] From the chair at the crucial meeting in Washington on May 9, Lipsky recognized the concerns and criticism of his colleagues, but pronounced himself "a little disturbed by the suggestion that the Fund program should obviously have involved debt restructuring or even default." Restructuring "would have had immediate and devastating implications for the Greek banking system, not to mention broader spillover effects." This was what was ultimately decisive.

The IMF board approved the disproportionate and risky Greek bailout not because it made sense in its own terms, or was good for Greece, but because on the track record to date, Europe's inability to contain the Greek crisis meant that there was "high risk of international systemic spillover effects."[66] Instead of restructuring Greek's unsustainable debts, what would be restructured were its entire public sector and its creaky economy. Heroic assumptions about cost cutting and efficiency gains were the ways in which the IMF squared the Greek program with its conscience. Perhaps if it were shaken thoroughly enough, "sclerotic" and "clientelistic" Greece could be jolted onto a higher growth path that would make its debts sustainable after all. Austerity and "reform" were the only items on the agenda that the otherwise divided parties to the deal could agree on. Whether this was economically effective or politically sustainable and what it would mean for the democratic politics of Europe was another matter altogether.

Chapter 15

A TIME OF DEBT

"Well, my message, Glenn, is that PI[I]GS are us. . . . [W]e very quickly could find ourselves in a similar situation to Greece."[1] These were the words of historian Niall Ferguson, then at Harvard, on Glenn Beck's Fox News TV show on February 11, 2010. The "we" Ferguson invoked were the citizens and taxpayers of the United States. The PIIGS were the eurozone problem cases—Portugal, Ireland, Italy, Greece and Spain. Beck and his guests regaled their audience with scenes of disorder, strikes, riots in the streets, cars burning. As Greece demonstrated, once markets lost confidence there was no easy way out. As Ferguson put it in drastic terms: "You either have to default on a large part of the debt or you have to inflate it away. There really aren't many other options open to our country that has debts this size. And none of these processes is really much fun." If interest rates spiked it could happen in the United States within the year. As Ferguson explained: "[T]he lesson of what's going on in Europe today and what happened to Russia 20 years ago is that collapse can sneak up on you and strike very sudden [sic] indeed." Given this prospect, Ferguson hailed the populist backlash that was going on in America against big government. That was a healthy sign. But it needed something else: "[U]ntil there's a political leader that has the courage to spell out to Americans, 'We need to do this, we need to reform our system, root and branch,' then I'm afraid we're going to slide downhill in the direction not just of European economics but of Latin American economics."

Ferguson was the Ivy League academic. Beck was one of the most excitable drummer boys of American conservatism. But fear of debt and its potentially disastrous implications was everywhere in 2010. It had been there before the crisis, in the Rubinite calls for consolidation and in the campaign for a debt brake in Germany. It was now massively amplified by the shock of 2008–2009. This dealt the most serious blow to government finances that any of the major developed countries had suffered since World War II. The fate of Greece in 2010 seemed to spell out what lay in store for any state that slid over the edge into insolvency. Warnings ranged from outrageous rants and scaremongering from the likes of Beck to ultrarespectable academic research, most notably by two former IMF economists, Carmen Reinhart and Kenneth Rogoff.

Following their surprise bestseller *This Time Is Different: Eight Centuries of Financial Folly*, in January 2010 Reinhart and Rogoff launched a research paper with the title "Growth in a Time of Debt."[2] This purported to show that as public debts passed the threshold of 90 percent of GDP, economic growth slowed down sharply. It was a slippery slope that ended in a cliff. Excessive debt weighed on growth, which made the debt even less sustainable, further slowing growth. To avoid this fate, it was crucial to take action sooner rather than later. On closer inspection, Reinhart and Rogoff's analysis turned out to be riddled with errors. Once their Excel spreadsheet was properly edited, there was no sharp discontinuity at the 90 percent mark and the case for emergency action was far weaker than they made out.[3] But in early 2010 their arguments ruled the roost. In the *Financial Times* they opined: "[T]he sooner politicians reconcile themselves to accepting adjustment, the lower the risks of truly paralysing debt problems. . . . Although most governments still enjoy strong access to financial markets at very low interest rates, market discipline can come without warning." Once bond markets realized the full measure of the "fiscal tsunami" unleashed by the banking crisis, their judgment would be merciless. "Countries that have not laid the groundwork for adjustment will regret it."[4] No one was safe. As Rogoff told Germany's right-wing *Welt am Sonntag*, a newspaper that hardly needed encouragement: "Germany's public finances are not on a sustainable path. . . . There will come a time when Germany will have its own Greece problem. . . . [I]t won't be as bad as in Greece, but it will be painful."[5]

As commentators as knowledgeable as Ferguson, Reinhart and Rogoff must have been aware, the market discipline on display in the eurozone had not "come without warning." The ECB and the German government were deliberately courting the bond vigilantes who swarmed over Greece. If they wanted to ease the pressure, all the ECB needed to do was what the Fed, the Bank of England or the Bank of Japan did as a matter of course—buy Greek bonds. But the ECB had no intention of doing that, not, at least, until the very last minute. The ECB meant to send a message: Austerity or else! They must have been delighted by the global reaction. The year 2010 would become a turning point in the recovery. Using Greece as its exemplum, an alliance of convenience among right-wing fearmongers, conservative political entrepreneurs and centrist fiscal hawks shifted the political balance. Though unemployment remained high, though output was limping back, stimulus was abandoned. Earlier and more sharply than in any other recession in recent history, the fiscal screw was turned. On both sides of the Atlantic the result was to stunt the recovery.

I

The most remarkable instance of austerity contagion was the UK. The hotly contested election that would bring an end to the long reign of New Labour concluded on May 6, 2010, the same day that banks burned in Athens and the flash crash sent US financial markets plunging. Fiscal politics were key to both the election and the coalition negotiations that followed. Britain had been among those hardest hit by 2007–2008. Though the Bank of England, unlike the ECB, never let there be any question of official support for UK Treasury debt, and though the UK maintained its credit rating, sterling plummeted against the dollar and the euro. As long as the Bank of England stabilized the bond market, it was not an immediate cause for concern. But it made Governor Mervyn King into a pivotal figure and, as he had demonstrated in the spring of 2009 ahead of the G20 meeting in London, he was not afraid to bring his influence to bear.[6]

On December 21, 2009, "shadow" Chancellor George Osborne opened

the electoral campaign for the opposition Tory party by claiming that unless Britain put together a credible program of fiscal consolidation, it would soon go the way of Greece. "By testing the patience of international investors," Osborne declared, "Labour are playing with economic fire." Countries that wished to retain a AAA rating did "not have the luxury of waiting for the recovery to be secured before announcing credible fiscal consolidation plans."[7] Osborne bolstered his case with quotes from analysts at Paribas, Deutsche and Barclays. Bill Gross, the star fund manager at bond market giant PIMCO, chimed in to tell the *Financial Times* that he had now placed UK bonds in the category of "must avoid." In his characteristically flamboyant style, Gross declared that UK public debt was "resting on a bed of nitroglycerine" and should be placed in a "ring of fire" that included not just the UK, Greece and Ireland, but Spain, France, Italy, Japan and the United States.[8] On February 14, 2010, twenty senior economists, including Ken Rogoff, wrote to the *Sunday Times* repeating Osborne's charge that the Labour government was not doing enough to bring the budget under control.[9] They were answered by a letter to the *Financial Times* from a much longer and no less distinguished list who opposed the call for fiscal retrenchment as premature and pointed out the irony that "[i]n urging a faster pace of deficit reduction to reassure the financial markets, the signatories of the *Sunday Times* letter implicitly accept as binding the views of the same financial markets whose mistakes precipitated the crisis in the first place!"[10]

The result of the May 6 election was a defeat for Labour, but the conservatives failed to win a majority and were left needing the support of the Liberal Democrats. The coalition negotiations became a high-stakes struggle over the future of fiscal policy.[11] "The deficit," wrote David Laws, a Liberal negotiator, "was the spectre which loomed over our talks."[12] The conservatives made spending cuts the central issue of the negotiations. And the Tory debt hawks knew that they could count on both the Treasury and the Bank of England. On May 12, 2010, Mervyn King instructed the new government that "[t]he most important thing now is . . . to deal with the challenge of the fiscal deficit. . . . I think we've seen in the last two weeks, particularly, but in the case of Greece, over the last three months, that it doesn't make sense to run the risk of an adverse market reaction."[13]

In what was dubbed an "emergency budget" in June 2010, Chancellor Osborne slashed spending and raised VAT. The aim was to calm markets by committing to close the deficit by 2015.[14] The argument in 2010 was "necessity." But, as Neil Irwin later commented: "Britain . . . was embarking on something that has rarely been attempted . . . cutting spending and raising taxes in a preemptive strike against the risk of a future debt crisis."[15] As Paul Krugman remarked from New York: "It's one thing to be intimidated by bond market vigilantes. It's another to be intimidated by the fear that bond market vigilantes might show up one of these days."[16] As the squeeze continued, other motives revealed themselves. Shrinking the state, it turned out, was an aim in itself. The ultimate goal, as David Cameron would put it in his speech to the Lord Mayor's Banquet three years later, was "something more profound": to make the state "leaner . . . not just now, but permanently."[17]

By 2015 Chancellor Osborne would claim to have slashed £98 billion in annual spending from the UK budget. From a maximum of 6.44 million public sector employees in September 2009, the UK public sector workforce would be reduced to 5.43 million in July 2016.[18] One million jobs were cut, privatized or outsourced. It was a reduction larger than that imposed by the Thatcher or Major governments of the 1980s and 1990s. Translated to the US public sector payroll, it would be the equivalent of the elimination of 3.3 million positions. Because pension and health spending were ringfenced, the pain was concentrated above all in local government. As the minister in charge roundly declared: "[L]ocal government is a massive part of public expenditure. It has lived for years on unsustainable growth, unsustainable public finance. . . . People blame the bankers, but I think big government is just as much to blame as the big banks."[19] Between 2010 and 2016 spending by local councils on everything from elderly day-care centers to bus services, public parks and library facilities fell by more than a third. Britain became a darker, dirtier, more dangerous and less civilized place. Hundreds of thousands of people who were barely coping on disability and unemployment benefits were tipped into true desperation.[20] According to the OECD, only Greece, Ireland and Spain were put through worse contractions than those inflicted on the UK.[21]

The reason why American liberals followed the politics of the UK so

Sources: Congressional Budget Office, "Understanding the Long-Term Budget Outlook" (July 2015), and Congressional Budget Office, "Historical Data on Federal Debt Held by the Public" (July 2010), www.cbo.gov/publication/21728.

closely was not just their partisanship for the defeated Gordon Brown. They feared that events in Britain in 2010 might foreshadow a similar turn at home. Nor did the pressure come only from alarmist experts and the alternate reality of Fox News. It came from inside the Obama administration. As early as February 2009 the president had hosted a Fiscal Responsibility Summit at the White House. A year later, the administration was under pressure from Democratic Party centrists anxious about their fiscal credentials. The administration needed their support in raising the ceiling that limits debt issuance by the federal government.[22] To the horror of Keynesian commentators, on January 27, 2010, in Obama's second State of the Union address, it was deficit reduction, not jobs, that took priority.[23] Obama promised that as of 2011, all nonmilitary discretionary spending would be frozen at its current levels. "[F]amilies across the country are tightening their belts and making tough decisions," Obama declared. "The federal government should do the same."[24] It was the simplistic householder analogy that drove economists to despair.[25] And it was fully in tune with the talk of "fiscal responsibility" that now dominated Washington. As one conservative commentator remarked, "[I]f the arguments in the coming years are between spending freezes and spending cuts, then we've already won."[26] On

February 18, 2010, by executive order, the president appointed the National Commission on Fiscal Responsibility and Reform, also known as the Simpson-Bowles Commission. It was to make recommendations designed to achieve primary budget balance by 2015. Simpson-Bowles would not report until December, after the congressional midterms. In the meantime, damaging divisions opened within the Obama administration over the fiscal issue.[27] Hawks like Orszag were pushing for tax hikes even for those earning below $250,000. This would violate a basic Obama campaign pledge, and it was bitterly resisted on political grounds by Emanuel as chief of staff, but also on economic grounds by Larry Summers. Meanwhile, the alternative to debt alarmism was spelled out most cogently by Ben Bernanke, who had recently been reappointed as Fed chair. Bernanke did not deny the scale of the deficits or the serious implications in the long run of a much larger debt burden. But he cautioned against drastic austerity efforts. America's nascent economic recovery might not withstand a sharp fiscal shock. The crucial thing was to separate the short and medium term. Continued short-term stimulus should be accompanied by a realistic plan as to how to end deficits in the medium term.[28] The combination would provide both an immediate prop to the economy and a comforting lift to investor confidence.

It was not enough for budget hawks like Orszag, who left the administration in the summer of 2010.[29] The judgment of the electorate on Obama's first two years would be even more devastating. With unemployment stuck just shy of 10 percent, four out of five Americans rated the economic situation as bad or fairly bad. The Tea Party was rallying conservative nationalist opinion against the Washington elite.[30] Even among Democrats, a plurality attributed the bailouts of 2008 to their own side.[31] They were wrong about the president, but given who had supported the measure in Congress, the association was not entirely far-fetched. On November 2 the angry electorate handed a historic victory to the Republicans. The GOP gained sixty-three seats in the House of Representatives, the largest swing since 1948. It was a shift that would redefine American politics.

Desperate not to allow the recovery to grind to a halt, the Obama administration worked feverishly to pass a second round of stimulus in the lame duck session of the old Congress. The Tax Relief, Unemployment

Insurance Reauthorization, and Job Creation Act of December 2010 provided, by some estimates, a demand boost of as much as $858 billion.[32] But it was a measure of their political predicament that the stimulus now consisted entirely of tax cuts, including the prolongation of the grossly inequitable giveaways for top income earners inherited from the Bush era. Two years into eight years in office, it would be the last major economic policy bill that the Obama administration would pass. In the New Year, with the new Republican Congress, they would be on the defensive. Because they included modest increases on the revenue side, the centrist recommendations of the Simpson-Bowles committee were dead on arrival, even though they were heavily slanted toward cuts in entitlements. Led by Eric Cantor, the forceful House majority leader, the so-called "Young Gun" Republicans would countenance no tax increases.[33] Their target was immediate spending cuts of $100 billion, which, when concentrated in discretionary spending, would cause havoc across a range of federal programs, including food safety, disaster relief and air traffic control. By "starving the beast," they would lift the curse of big government and revive the American dream.

II

Both the United States and the UK had suffered severe fiscal damage from the financial crisis. It was not, therefore, surprising that they faced calls for retrenchment. Were there other economies that might take up the slack? Apart from Japan and the emerging market economies, the obvious candidate to serve as a global counterweight was Germany. As Angela Merkel admitted in the summer of 2010, "[O]ther EU members, and the US administration, have urged Germany to spend more to maintain the current economic recovery, and reduce its export surplus."[34] But that was not how Germany saw its role. The crisis, so the prevalent German interpretation went, was a result of excessive debt. What the world needed to guide its recovery was for Germany not to act as an expansionary counterweight but to lead the way in offering a model of austerity.

Given the prevailing mood, it was easy enough to make the case. Germany's deficit was running at 50 billion euros per annum. Its debt had

surged beyond 80 percent of GDP. The Reinhart and Rogoff meme had reached Europe. Finance Minister Schäuble invoked the menacing 90 percent threshold to argue for the need for immediate countermeasures.[35] Announcing the largest budget cuts in the history of the Federal Republic, on Monday, June 7, Chancellor Merkel declared that restoring Germany's budget balance would constitute a "unique show of strength. . . . Germany as the largest economy has a duty to set a good example."[36,37] In 2011, 11.2 billion euros ($13.4 billion) were to be cut, and a total of 80 billion euros by 2014. In Germany too this required choices to be made about the future shape of the state. Tellingly, the heaviest cuts proposed by the Merkel government fell on the defense ministry, which was asked to cut by 25 percent by 2014. The strength of the Bundeswehr was to be sliced and conscription to be phased out. For Berlin it was more important to achieve the 3 percent deficit rule specified by the eurozone's Stability and Growth Pact than it was to honor its commitment to NATO to spend at least 2 percent of GDP on defense.[38]

At the G20 in Toronto in June 2010 the scene was set for another round in the transatlantic argument over fiscal policy. Ahead of the meeting Obama published an open letter calling for fiscal consolidation to be staggered so as to avoid jeopardizing recovery.[39] Schäuble took to the pages of the *Financial Times* to defend his country's distinctive long-term approach to economic policy against US short-termism. He championed the debt brake as a stability anchor for Europe.[40] He had the backing of Prime Minister Cameron as well as that of the Canadian hosts. At the insistence of the Obama administration the final text of the G20 communiqué referred to the need to sequence fiscal consolidation so that "the momentum of private sector recovery" was not jeopardized.[41] But this was trumped by demands for fiscal consolidation.[42] After the worst economic crisis since the 1930s, at a time when, according to the OECD, 47 million people were unemployed across the rich world, and the total figure for underemployed and discouraged workers was closer to 80 million, the members of the G20 committed themselves to simultaneously halving their deficits over the next three years.[43] It was the householder fallacy expanded to the global scale. It was a recipe for an agonizingly protracted and incomplete recovery.

Note: Eurostat for Europe, downloaded November 29, 2014. Eurozone Government Expenditures are for the 18 countries that make up the current membership in the eurozone.

Sources: BEA for US, downloaded November 29, 2014.

For Germany even that was not enough. The lesson that Berlin drew from the Greek crisis was that the eurozone's Stability and Growth Pact had failed. Germany, or rather the Red-Green coalition that had ruled Germany back in 2003, had to accept a measure of responsibility. Now, with Merkel and Schäuble at the helm, Berlin would take the lead in rededicating the eurozone to self-discipline. This was vital not only to restore economic health. It was essential for the politics of the eurozone. The Greek crisis had shown that Europe's governments would have to work together. Federalists like Schäuble still insisted that the ultimate answer to the crisis would be "more Europe." But for that to be acceptable to the taxpayers of Northern Europe, they had to be reassured that everyone was playing by the same rules.

As the crisis in the eurozone gathered in intensity and Germany's pivotal role became ever more pronounced, the rhetoric became more heated. Protesters waved placards showing Merkel's face graffitied with a Hitler mustache. This was not only offensive and grotesquely unfair. It also represented a fundamental misunderstanding of Germany's position. When it

was accused of imperialism, the German political class could honestly reply that it did not harbor ambitions for continental domination. But Berlin did have a vision of economic and fiscal discipline, which had to be generally accepted before Germany would consent to any further steps toward integration.[44] For reasons of global competitiveness it was essential that government spending and debt be brought under control. Europe's demographic pressures made the case only more urgent. As for labor markets and unemployment, the rest of Europe had to learn the lessons of Germany's Hartz IV reforms. When Keynesians worried about domestic demand, the German answer was exports. An aging continent should be exporting to the world and building up a nest egg of financial claims on the fast-growing emerging markets. On this, Merkel's new coalition with her probusiness FDP partners was clearer than ever. Germany had passed a constitutional amendment in the form of the debt brake. If Germany was to agree to pool financial liabilities with the rest of the eurozone, it must insist on nothing less from its partners. Prosperous as they were and as much as they benefited from European integration, taxpayers and voters in the CDU heartlands would simply not accept the transformation of the EU into a continental "transfer union." It was only if the rest of Europe could guarantee conformity to a common set of rules that Berlin could contemplate pooling sovereignty. The problem was that those rules had to be decided, upheld and imposed. And that is where things got uncomfortable.

Over the summer of 2010, rival plans for a new regime of European economic governance were being prepared by teams working separately for President Barroso of the EU Commission and Herman Van Rompuy, the first permanent head of the European Council, a position created by the Lisbon Treaty and designed to reinforce the intergovernmental character of EU decision making.[45] Berlin's ultimate goal was to have constitutional debt brake provisions like the one it had passed in 2009 written into law for all the eurozone members. Those deviating from the rules would be subject to an automatic system of sanctions, including the suspension of voting rights. For those in real financial trouble the sanctions would be even more severe. As Trichet put it, "[W]hen you activate a support mechanism, a country loses de jure or de facto its fiscal autonomy."[46] France, for its part, resisted automatic sanctions. Not surprisingly, smaller countries that had

reason to fear that the rules might be applied more strictly to them opposed any talk of the suspension of voting rights.

These were weighty issues for Europe's future. But how did they relate to the short-term question of financial stabilization? By the summer it was already clear that the fix devised to contain the Greek crisis in May 2010 was not sustainable. The worst fears of the more pessimistic IMF analysts were rapidly being confirmed. Not only was the PASOK government slow to push through the changes the troika demanded, but when it did, the results were counterproductive. In a classic Keynesian downward spiral, demand fell and unemployment surged further, reducing incomes. In 2010 Greek GDP would fall by 4.5 percent. Worse would follow in 2011.[47] The tax revenues flowing to Athens, which even at the best of times were hardly ample, slowed to a trickle as wages, profits and consumer spending contracted. The May 2010 program had been premised on the assumption that Greece would be able to return to capital markets within two years. But with the deficit expanding and its debt burden rising, there was little chance of that. By the end of August 2010 the yield spread of the Greek ten-year bond relative to Bunds had surged to 937 points, higher than it had been even at the height of the spring crisis.[48] And yet in the face of failure, the troika remained committed to holding Greece to the May 2010 program.

If there was any justification for the protracted torture of Greece, it was the fear that an immediate debt restructuring would unleash contagion to other sovereign debtors across the eurozone and destabilize Europe's banks, thus causing a far wider crisis. So the immediate priority for European economic policy ought to have been to use the time bought by extend-and-pretend to strengthen the resilience of the eurozone financial system and the health of the banks. If one were to follow the American example, the obvious next step was to conduct a stress test to estimate likely losses, and then to carry out an energetic recapitalization with either public or private funds.

Both in 2009 and 2010 the Europeans conducted stress tests of a sort. The 2010 exercise went further than that in 2009 in naming individual banks. But it too was a farce. The results published on July 23, 2010, proclaimed that of ninety-one leading European banks, only seven would see their primary Tier 1 capital reduced to dangerous levels by a sovereign

bond crisis.[49] In total the Committee of European Banking Supervisors estimated that Europe's banks needed to raise no more than 3.5 billion euros in new capital. But, as was pointed out by skeptical analysts, this optimistic result depended on assuming that the vast majority of the sovereign debt held by banks, had zero risk of default, or was fully protected by the EU's financial stability facility.[50] According to the reckoning of the OECD, on less rosy assumptions the potential loss to Europe's banks from a peripheral bond crisis was not the 26.4 billion euros allowed for by the official results, but 165 billion euros. These losses would be concentrated in the national banking systems of the vulnerable countries—Greece, Ireland, Portugal and Spain. They would suffer catastrophic damage. If the crisis were to spread to Spain or Italy, that would put both the German and the French banking systems in jeopardy. As always, the most serious risks were concentrated in the balance sheets of a few dangerous banks. Dexia and Fortis were at the top of the list, as was Germany's troubled Hypo Real Estate. According to the OECD, Hypo's capitalization was so inadequate that a sovereign debt crisis in any one of Italy, Spain, Ireland or Greece would put its survival in question.

The European institutions did not have the authority to intervene in national banking policy. The funds for recapitalization that had been created in 2008–2009 were spotty and facultative rather than mandatory in their application.[51] National governments were too complacent and unwilling to disturb the comfortable status quo. Instead, Europe engaged in a double pretense. The troika went on pretending that Greek debt was sustainable, if only Athens adopted enough austerity. This was not true, as was becoming evident month by month: Greece was simply being driven into the ground. Meanwhile, the stress tests purported to show that Europe's banks were robust, which they clearly were not. Indeed, their weakness ought to have been the best argument for refusing to risk Greek restructuring. This, however, was not an argument that the ECB could make out loud, for fear of triggering panic. Furthermore, it would have necessitated serious action on the recapitalization front, which both the banks and the national governments resisted. Caught in this double bind, the troika was reduced to pretending that all was well on every front. Meanwhile, in Greece unemployment

rose from a low of 8 percent in the summer of 2008 to more than 12 percent in 2010. For young people it was already more than 30 percent.

If the Greeks were the victims of extend-and-pretend, who were the beneficiaries? Billions of euros from the first tranche of the May 2010 program were disbursed to Athens, which in turn paid them to its creditors. Those who were lucky enough to hold debt expiring in 2010 or 2011 were paid on time and in full. Those banks that decided to cut their losses and sell out could find buyers among the hedge funds who picked up debt for as little as 36 cents on the euro, gambling that things could only get better and that in the worst case they would get some cut of a final settlement.[52] French and Dutch banks seem to have been most active in breaching the informal embargo on Greek bond sales. French bank holdings of Greek debt fell between March and December 2010 from $27 billion to $15 billion, Dutch from $22.9 billion to $7.7 billion.[53] But the flight out of Greek bonds did not extend to the entire periphery. As they sold off Greek and Irish bonds, Europe's banks chased yield by rotating their money into Spanish and Italian bonds.[54] In general one might have expected European banks with an interest in their own survival and prosperity to be energetically recapitalizing and reorienting their businesses for a future beyond the crisis. But there was little sign of that. Whereas America's big banks operated under the discipline of annual "capital plans" and were required to retain whatever profit they didn't distribute as bonuses so as to rebuild reserves, Europe's banks were free to do as they saw fit. In a desperate effort to keep their shareholders happy, they paid out what little profit they earned in dividends in the hope that at some point in the future they would be able to raise new capital.[55] But that moment was not now.

III

In the Greek case the question of restructuring debt and forcing the banks to recognize losses had been kept off the agenda. But Ireland forced it back into play. Astonishingly, in the summer of 2010 all of Ireland's banks were

passed as fit by the European stress tests, even Anglo Irish Bank, the most notorious basket case of 2008. At that point Irish bank borrowing from special ECB facilities already came to 60 billion euros and the entire Irish banking system was only weeks away from a "funding cliff," when the government guarantee issued in September 2008 would expire and they would lose all access to funding markets. Thereafter they would be entirely dependent on the Irish central bank and the ECB. On September 30 the Irish government announced that, given its obligation to backstop the banks, in 2010 Ireland's public borrowing requirement would surge from 14 percent to a jaw-dropping 32 percent of GDP. This would take Ireland's public debt from a modest 25 percent of GDP in 2007 to 98.6 percent in 2010. The Irish government, once a paragon of austere public finance, was forced to withdraw from the bond market.[56]

If Ireland were to continue to honor the entire debt burden of its banks, owed in large part to foreign investors, the impact would be harrowing. Since the onset of the crisis in 2008, Irish incomes had been subject to emergency levies, young people's job-seeker allowances had been slashed, health benefits for those over seventy were means-tested, public sector pay was cut between 5 and 10 percent, welfare recipients saw cuts of 4 percent and child benefits were reduced.[57] The bank bailout costs announced in September implied further cuts and tax increases. Informally, with the assistance of the IMF, Dublin began exploring its options.[58] A vocal faction within the IMF had never reconciled themselves to their retreat over Greek debt restructuring. Ireland presented an opportunity to bail in the investors who had profited from Ireland's financial boom. If only the creditors of the most troubled Anglo Irish Bank took a haircut, the savings were estimated at 2.4 billion euros. If investors in all four of the protected banks were haircut, the budgetary relief might amount to as much as 12.5 billion euros. In relation to total tax revenue of 32 billion euros, these were huge savings. The position of the ECB was well known by this point. It would fight restructuring to the last ditch. But what would be the position of the rest of the eurozone? German public opinion was running ever hotter against any further eurozone programs that did not require the banks and their investors to contribute.[59]

On October 18, 2010, Sarkozy and Merkel were hosting President Medvedev of Russia at the Norman seaside resort town of Deauville. Somewhat to the alarm of Washington, the announced agenda of their meeting was to discuss future areas of cooperation for foreign policy, notably in the Middle East.[60] The news from Deauville would make headlines. But it was not the Atlantic alliance that was at stake. It was the eurozone. Without consulting with their eurozone partners, the ECB or the United States, Merkel and Sarkozy—soon to be dubbed "Merkozy"—hammered out a new agenda. It consisted of a blend of French and German ideas. The Stability and Growth Pact first agreed in 1997 would be reinforced with German-style constitutional debt brake rules. But the French got Germany to agree that when it came to disciplinary measures there must be an element of political discretion. Sanctions would be triggered only by a qualified majority vote in cases where governments ran deficits greater than 3 percent of GDP or debts in excess of 60 percent of GDP. Sanctions would be tough—up to and including deprivation of voting rights. But discipline was not all. There would also be an institutionalized version of the European Financial Stability Facility, which would be put on a solid legal footing by 2013 at the latest, by way of treaty change. It would provide emergency loans to any eurozone member in trouble. But there would be no repeat of the Greek deal. Merkel and Sarkozy agreed that as of 2013, in any future crisis, creditors would be bailed in. It would not just be taxpayers who put up new funds. Haircutting the creditors would help to bring debts down. It was equitable. And it would serve a useful disciplining function. Creditors would take their responsibilities more seriously if they knew that they had skin in the game. The package was announced without forewarning in a press release late in the afternoon of October 18, 2010.

To say that Deauville came as a shock would be an understatement. France and Germany had acted alone. It smacked of the old days, of the Europe of the Six, not the new Europe of the post–cold war era. Not only had they acted alone but they had addressed what everyone knew was the hot-button issue of the crisis—PSI and debt restructuring—unilaterally and without preparing either the markets or their partners. For Trichet it was a disaster. The unspeakable contingency of restructuring had been blurted

out in public. When the news of Merkel and Sarkozy's deal reached Luxembourg, where the finance ministers were meeting, the president of the ECB was incandescent. "You're going to destroy the euro," Trichet shouted across the conference table at the French delegation. Ten days later Trichet confronted Sarkozy face-to-face. "You don't realize how serious the situation is," he belabored the French president, only for Sarkozy to snap back: "Maybe you're talking to bankers. . . . We are responsible to citizens."[61] Trichet might have prioritized confidence in financial markets, but Merkel and Sarkozy had to consider the indignation of European voters. In the Bundestag Merkel knew that majorities for her European policy would be fragile, at best, if haircuts were not part of the deal.[62] As Mario Draghi, Trichet's successor, would later acknowledge, talk of PSI might be premature from the point of view of the markets, but "to be fair again, one has to address another side of this. The lack of fiscal discipline by certain countries was perceived by other countries [i.e., Germany] as a breach of the trust that should underlie the euro. And so PSI was a political answer given with a view to regaining the trust of these countries' citizens."[63]

How much damage did the Deauville announcement really cause? Advocates of extend-and-pretend would insist forever after that it was Merkel and Sarkozy who tipped Ireland over the edge, that Trichet was right, that this was Europe's "Lehman moment": an unforced, politically motivated error. But, as in the case of Lehman, political and technical judgments were mingled. Given its gigantic budget deficit and the expiry of the 2008 guarantee for its banks, Ireland was heading into rough waters in any case, with or without Deauville. Spreads on Irish government debt were already surging before Merkel and Sarkozy's surprise announcement. Deauville did not help. But it did not cause a market panic. The markets were already reckoning with the risk of a bail-in.[64] The main impact of Deauville was to harden the attitude of the ECB. Trichet was determined that Dublin should not use Merkel and Sarkozy's announcement as cover to burn the banks' bondholders. Instead, Ireland must accept a program like that imposed on Greece. And, as in Greece, with Irish banks wholly dependent for their day-to-day survival on ECB funding, Trichet had the whip hand.[65]

Dublin did not surrender without a fight. To find itself pushed into the financial emergency ward alongside Greece was a humiliating shock. So the

ECB applied main force. On November 12 the ECB Governing Council threatened to withdraw support from the Irish banking system while leaking to the media that Ireland was about to apply for a bailout. On November 18 the Irish central bank chairman, Patrick Honohan, fresh from an ECB meeting in Frankfurt, contacted Irish broadcaster RTÉ to say that a national bailout was only days away.[66] On November 19 Trichet spelled out to the Irish prime minister in a confidential letter the conditions under which the ECB would be willing to extend its assistance to the Irish banks.[67] Dublin must immediately apply for aid and submit to the instructions of the troika. It must agree to an urgent program of further fiscal consolidation, structural reforms and financial sector reorganization. The banks must be fully recapitalized and the repayment of the ECB's short-term financing for the Irish banking system must be fully guaranteed.

Despite the exorbitant quality of the ECB's demands, on November 21 Dublin had no option but to comply. The *Irish Times* responded with a remarkable editorial that captured the mood of national humiliation. It was emblazoned with a line from Yeats's elegy to romantic Irish nationalism, "September 1913"—"Was it for this?" Was it for this, the paper asked, that Irish nationalists had fought their centuries-long struggle: "a bailout from the German chancellor with a few shillings of sympathy from the British chancellor on the side. There is the shame of it all. Having obtained our political independence from Britain to be the masters of our own affairs, we have now surrendered our sovereignty to the European Commission, the European Central Bank, and the International Monetary Fund." But rather than lapsing into self-pity, the *Irish Times* went on: "The true ignominy of our current situation is not that our sovereignty has been taken away from us, it is that we ourselves have squandered it. Let us not seek to assuage our sense of shame in the comforting illusion that powerful nations in Europe are conspiring to become our masters. We are, after all, no great prize for any would-be overlord now. No rational European would willingly take on the task of cleaning up the mess we have made. It is the incompetence of the governments we ourselves elected that has so deeply compromised our capacity to make our own decisions."[68]

For all its brilliance, not the least remarkable thing about this editorial is where it put the blame. "The governments we ourselves elected" bore the

historic guilt, not Ireland's bankers, investors and their business partners across Europe and the wider world, not financial experts, economists and regulators. The loss of political sovereignty was no doubt painful. But who would really pay the price for "cleaning up the mess"? Would it be voters and taxpayers, or those who had profited from inflating the credit bubble? In the Greek case, at least, the debts were public. In Ireland taxpayers were being asked to pay for huge losses incurred by deeply irresponsible banks and their investors all over Europe. On December 7 Dublin announced a budget with a new round of 6 billion euros in cuts, half of what would have been saved if the bank bondholders had been haircut across the board. Instead taxes were raised on low-paid workers. Child-care allowances were cut and college fees were increased. Benefits for the unemployed, caregivers and the disabled were slashed.

Setting aside the gross inequity of the troika's demands, was it even plausible that Ireland posed risks of contagion comparable to Lehman? As Martin Sandbu of the *Financial Times* put it with rare force: "Lehman was a global bank." Its business "was at the heart of the world's financial plumbing." Not rescuing it proved to be a disaster. The Irish banks, by contrast, were "a small racket in Europe's financial periphery, busily and exuberantly losing . . . investors' money in the time-honoured way of lending more for houses than they were worth." Nothing "systemic" depended on their creditors being repaid in full.[69] Of course there was some risk of spillovers. But if French and German banks suffered collateral damage, that was because they had participated so enthusiastically and profitably in the Irish boom. Given that responsibility was so widely spread, was it reasonable to impose the entire cost of containing the fallout on Ireland's taxpayers alone? As Ajai Chopra of the IMF later remarked: "Yes, there would have been spillovers. But . . . the ECB could have stepped in. . . . That's what a central bank is for, to deal with these sorts of spillovers."[70]

But that was not the kind of central bank the ECB thought itself to be. On November 26 its representatives in Dublin made clear that if haircutting was involved, there would be no bailout. A day later the IMF team in Dublin received direct instructions from Washington to drop any further efforts to enroll the banks. The finance ministers of the G7 had let Dominique Strauss-Kahn know that none of them welcomed talk of haircuts, and

this was particularly true of the United States. As Tim Geithner later put it: "I was on the Cape [Cod] for Thanksgiving, and I remember doing a G7 call . . . in my little hotel room. . . . I said, 'If you guys do that [haircuts], all you will do is accelerate the run from Europe. . . . [U]ntil you have the ability to in effect protect or guarantee the rest of Europe from the ensuing contagion, this is just [a] metaphor for our fall of '08.'"[71] With the IMF heretics silenced, the Irish were left with no alternative. Prime Minister Lenihan admitted resignedly: "I can't go against the whole of the G7." For Ireland to haircut unilaterally would be "politically, internationally, politically inconceivable."[72] On November 28 Ireland agreed to accept 85 billion euros in emergency loans: 63.5 billion euros from the troika; the rest came in the form of bilateral support from other EU members, notably the UK, whose own financial markets had contributed so much to the debacle.

Another deal was sewed up. Debts would be honored. The population of Ireland paid the price. A "Lehman moment" was avoided. But the result was not to restore confidence to the markets. The European financial crisis could not be contained by transferring the costs to taxpayers on a nation-by-nation basis. The resulting bailouts preserved the form of stability,

Source: William A. Allen and Richhild Moessner, "The Liquidity Consequences of the Euro Area Sovereign Debt Crisis," *World Economics* 14, no.1 (2013): 103–126, graph 2.3.

but were not credible in their substance. In two surges, first in the spring and then in the fall of 2010, spreads on European bank credit default swaps—the price of insurance against default on bank bonds—surged above those charged to American banks. The first trigger was Greece, the second was Ireland. Europe's financial crisis was simply too big and too interconnected to be handled on a national basis. The losses needed either to be pushed down to the investors all across Europe who had profited from the banks' unsustainable business models or to be raised to the level of a coordinated European bailout. Extend-and-pretend on a national basis merely turned banking crises into fiscal crises, which widened uncertainty while deflecting attention from the real issue.

IV

In their defense, legalists at the ECB would argue that the central bank's mandate gave it only one objective, price stability. They could derive from that an obligation to maintain the functioning of Europe's financial markets and Europe's banks. And Trichet would thus justify his interference in Greek and Irish affairs and more to come. What the ECB did not have was a mandate to concern itself with the economic welfare of the eurozone or its member states in any broader sense. It was a willfully simplistic and conservative interpretation.[73] It was ruinous for the eurozone. The crisis would begin to be overcome only when the ECB began to step beyond it.

The Fed never took such a narrow view. It had a mandate both to preserve price stability and to maximize employment. This was a legacy bequeathed by the more broad-gauge economic policy debate of the 1970s. But it was anchored deep in the Fed's organizational DNA by the memory of the Great Depression. The deflationary misery of the 1930s was the defining event in the Fed's history. That was the history that Bernanke had pledged not to repeat. In 2010 the United States had survived the worst of its crisis. But it was far from fully recovered. The housing market was still in shock. The percentage of outstanding mortgages in foreclosure proceedings was heading toward a grim record over the winter of 2010–2011 at 4.64 percent—more than 2 million homes. Since early in 2010 Bernanke had

been sounding the alarm about an excessive tightening of fiscal policy. On the afternoon of November 3, the day after the dramatic midterm congressional elections, the Fed announced its response. After an intense internal debate, the Federal Open Market Committee resolved to begin purchasing securities at the rate of $75 billion per month for the next eight months. QE2 had arrived.

How exactly quantitative easing works remains a subject of controversy.[74] Large-scale purchasing of mainly short-term bonds drives up bond prices and thus reduces yields. Reduced short-term rates may help to lever down long-term rates and thus to stimulate investment. But that depends on there being businesses willing to invest, which cannot be taken for granted at a time of crisis. The most direct effect of QE comes via financial markets. As the central bank hoovers up bonds, it drives down yields, forcing asset managers to go in search of yields in other classes of assets. Switching out of bonds into stocks inflates the stock market, increasing the wealth of those with stock portfolios, tending to make them more willing to both invest and consume. This, to say the least, is an uncertain and indirect method of stimulating the economy. By boosting the wealth of already wealthy households, it is predestined to increase inequality. Low-income households have no way of participating in capital gains.

QE was never anything other than an emergency expedient adopted by the Fed in light of the fiscal policy logjam in Congress. But the Fed itself was not insulated from the polarization of American politics.[75] The FOMC vote on QE2 was split three ways. A vocal minority argued that the stimulus should have been much larger. The markets had already priced in a QE2 announcement at $75 billion. To have a substantial impact the Fed needed to deliver a surprise. Bernanke demurred. He did not want to stray too far beyond the sense of "normality" because to do so might in fact stoke a mood of anxiety and thus be counterproductive.[76] As Bernanke put it at the meeting to critics on the board: "There is no safe thing to do. . . . I'd like to frame our decision today as a very conservative, middle-road approach, namely, we recognize that doing nothing carries serious risks of further disinflation and of a failure of the recovery to meet escape velocity."[77] On the FOMC there were also two votes objecting to QE2 not on the grounds that it was inadequate but because it was too expansionary.

Beyond the Fed's walls the reactions were more intemperate. In the superheated political climate of the Republican election triumph of November 2010, what hogged the headlines was the news that the Fed was embarking on a plan to "print" tens of billions of dollars every month. On the part of the conspiratorial right wing, Bernanke's intervention reinforced the conviction that dark forces were at work. Glenn Beck warned his millions of Republican viewers on Fox that they should not be deceived by their congressional victory; the actual reins of power were held by liberal inflationists. What threatened America was a hyperinflationary "Weimar moment."[78] Meanwhile, a prominent list of conservative intellectuals, including—once again—historian Niall Ferguson and Amity Schlaes of the Council on Foreign Relations, joined Sarah Palin in calling on the Fed to "cease and desist."[79] Significantly, they pointed out that "[t]he Fed's purchase program has also met broad opposition from other central banks" across the world. This was no exaggeration. After eighteen months of wrangling at the G20 over fiscal policy, QE2 produced an open rift over monetary policy.

This was predictable, but it was not necessary. The two agenda-setting innovations of October and November of 2010—the Merkozy PSI agenda of Deauville and Bernanke's QE2—could have been complementary. As Chopra of the IMF had laid out, the ideal accompaniment for aggressive debt restructuring in Ireland would have been an ECB bond-purchasing program designed to insulate the other fragile members of the eurozone from the fallout. The push for PSI and bond market intervention were both responses to the inadequacy of the course embarked upon in Greece in May 2010. But in the eurozone the two never joined hands. Instead, rather than seeing QE as the necessary accompaniment to a more sustainable resolution of the eurozone debt crisis, Berlin's conservatives led the international front against monetary experiments.

The Fed announced QE_2 only days before President Obama and his team departed for the latest G20 summit, this time in Seoul. There they met unprecedented criticism. In the words of one of the US Treasury officials who ran the gauntlet, Seoul was a "**** show." The Brazilians, as the putative leaders of the left wing of the emerging markets, inveighed against the risks

of hot money and accused Bernanke of a beggar-thy-neighbor devaluation of the dollar. They warned of a "currency war."[80] For the Chinese, the Fed's action was a sign that "[t]he United States does not recognize . . . its obligation to stabilize capital markets," as Zhu Guangyao, China's vice finance minister, put it. "Nor does it take into consideration the impact of this excessive fluidity on the financial markets of emerging countries."[81] Wolfgang Schäuble went furthest. Once more America had revealed itself as an agent of global economic disorder. First it had created the fiasco of Lehman. Then it had championed stimulus. Now the Fed was monetizing public debt. As the G20 convened, the German finance minister denounced American economic policy as "clueless" and as likely to "increase the insecurity of the world economy."[82] The Fed's policies made "a reasonable balance between industrial and developing countries more difficult and they undermine the credibility of the US in finance policymaking." Whereas Germany had stuck with its model of export success that did not need "exchange rate tricks," the "American growth model" was, according to Schäuble, "in a deep crisis. The Americans have lived for too long on credit, overblown their financial sector and neglected their industrial base."[83]

The Americans did not go down without a fight. Tim Geithner countered that the real source of imbalances in the world economy was not US monetary policy but the mercantilist trade policies of China and Germany. The Fed was not deliberately depreciating the dollar. It was targeting domestic conditions, not the exchange rate.[84] If others wanted to prevent their currencies from appreciating, all they had to do was to match the Fed's low interest rate policy with an expansion of their own. What the critics dubbed a "currency war" could thus have been turned into a comprehensive program of monetary expansion, countering the slide into a double-dip recession not just in the United States but in Europe as well. If they didn't choose to join the stimulus, then all they had to do was to allow their currencies to appreciate, which, as Washington had been preaching since the early 2000s, would restore balance naturally. It was Germany's export dependence and China's determination to peg its currency that put the United States in charge. If they wanted to free ride on American aggregate demand, they should at least have the grace to do so quietly. If there were grievances,

Cash of Small/Large Domestic and Foreign Banks Versus Fed Bank Reserves (in $ millions)

- Cash assets of large domestic banks
- Cash assets of small domestic banks
- Cash assets of foreign banks
- Reserve balances (RH axis)

Source: Federal Reserve, "Assets and Liabilities of Commercial Banks in the United States—H.8," https://www.federalreserve.gov/releases/h8/current/default.htm. Accessed 1 March 2018.

Geithner suggested, why not agree to allow the IMF to resume the project begun before the crisis, of monitoring and overseeing international imbalances, not only America's deficit, but China's and Germany's surpluses as well.[85] But that was a nonstarter. Germany would never admit that its trade surplus was anything other than a reward for its competitiveness and productive virtue. The back-and-forth had the effect only of producing a dizzying moment of unreality. While tens of millions were without work and the European welfare state was hollowed out at the behest of the troika, Fox News terrorized its viewers with images of Ben Bernanke as a sorcerer's apprentice unleashing Weimar-style hyperinflation and Germany's finance minister denounced a proposal by the US Treasury secretary as reminiscent of the bad old days of Soviet-style "economic planning."[86]

While Berlin denounced QE as a source of instability, Europe's banks took a very different view. For every billion dollars' worth of securities the Fed purchased, it credited an account with a corresponding amount of

dollars. But who was it that held those dollar accounts with the Fed and thus "funded" QE? As the Fed's statistics show, it was not America's banks that took advantage of QE to unload large portfolios of bonds or to hold cash, though some American pension funds and mutual funds did sell bonds to the Fed. The banks most actively involved in QE2 were not American but European, running down their US securities portfolios and building up Fed cash balances.[87] From November 2010 there is a near one-for-one identity between the expansion of the Federal Reserve balance sheet and the expansion of dollar cash balances held by non-US banks with the Fed. This would suggest that, far from the Fed increasing the "insecurity of the world economy," it was, in effect, acting as the world's piggybank. As the eurozone stumbled back toward crisis, Europe's banks abandoned the standstill agreement of May 2010. They shifted money out of Europe, shrank their US operations, deleveraged their balance sheets and built up a huge pile of cash. Thanks to QE2 they held that liquidity reserve not with the ECB but with the ultimate guarantor of the global financial system, the Fed. It was not a recipe for economic expansion. But in the absence of any solution to the eurozone crisis, it did at least promise a cushion of stability.

Chapter 16

G-ZERO WORLD

The commitment to austerity in 2010 drove critical economists to impatient fury. Why was the world embarked on a course that was so self-evidently counterproductive and so damaging to the prospects of tens of millions of unemployed around the world? Whose interests were being served by preserving this reserve army? Paul Krugman asked in the *New York Times*.[1] Whose interests were served by a lopsided deficit debate in which minor tax increases were traded for huge cuts in entitlements? What kind of shock would it take to break this impasse? Historical experience was not encouraging. FDR's New Deal had not been enough. It had been hobbled by its own timidity and by relentless opposition from the Right.[2] To unleash the full capacities of the American state it had taken the national emergency of a war. "The fact is," Krugman insisted, "the Great Depression ended largely thanks to a guy named Adolf Hitler. He created a human catastrophe, which also led to a lot of government spending."[3] That didn't mean that Krugman was hoping for World War III. But he couldn't resist telling *Playboy* magazine that "[i]f it were announced that we faced a threat from space aliens and needed to build up to defend ourselves, we'd have full employment in a year and a half." In light of events in 2011, one can't help wondering whether Krugman assumed too much coherence in twenty-first-century politics.

The year, in fact, began with a geopolitical earthquake: the Arab Spring. And true to Krugman's script, this triggered military intervention and calls

for a Marshall Plan for the Middle East.[4] But after Afghanistan and Iraq there was no appetite anywhere in the West for nation building in foreign lands. Among conservative commentators, alarm at the overthrow of friendly Arab dictators mixed with the dismayed reaction to Bernanke QE's to form a heady cocktail. A *Wall Street Journal* op-ed drew comparisons to the 1970s, when global inflation had helped to trigger the fall of the shah and Khomeini's revolution in Iran.[5] Now, by "printing money" and driving up commodity prices, it was the Fed's QE program that was destabilizing the world. As the Tunisian and Egyptian dictatorships toppled, conservative social media activists urged their followers to tweet "Bernanke has blood on his hands."[6] Meanwhile, the liberal press fired back: It wasn't monetary policy that was responsible for high commodity prices and food riots, it was global warming. That riposte allowed Paul Krugman to equate conservative opposition to quantitative easing to climate change denial.[7] It wasn't so much a serious debate about the Arab Spring as indicative of the increasingly unhinged quality of American political discourse.

Europe was closer to the North African drama, but its reaction was hardly more coherent. France, Britain and Germany fell out over the NATO intervention in Libya, with Germany siding, as it had done at the Seoul G20, with China and Russia. Merkel's government refused to give its vote in the UN Security Council for the aerial campaign against Gaddafi. Meanwhile, the EU squabbled disgracefully about who should accommodate the desperate refugees and migrants who poured through Libya into Italy. It was a dispiriting accompaniment to the rolling crisis in the eurozone. In the summer of 2011 it was not only the stability of Middle Eastern regimes but the creditworthiness of Italy and the United States that would be placed in doubt. Little wonder, perhaps, that two acute observers of the contemporary scene should refer to the world in 2011 as being governed not so much by the G20, G8 or G2 but by G-Zero.[8]

I

By the spring of 2011 austerity was biting deep into the social fabric of Europe. Spending cuts and tax increases were slashing demand and squeezing

economic activity. Across the eurozone, 10 percent of the workforce were unemployed. But unemployment for those between the ages of fifteen and twenty-four was 20 percent. And on the troubled periphery, the numbers were numbing in scale. In Ireland general unemployment reached 15 percent and youth unemployment 30 percent, in Greece 14 percent and 37 percent, respectively. In Spain 20 percent of all adults and 44 percent of young people were unemployed by the summer of 2011. Half a generation had their launch out of education and into working life aborted. Nevertheless, the demand for further austerity was unrelenting. After Ireland and Greece had subordinated themselves to troika programs, on March 23, 2011, Portugal's prime minster, José Sócrates, resigned after failing to gain support for budget cuts. A week later, on April 2, Spain's social democratic prime minister, José Luis Rodríguez Zapatero, announced that he would not run for reelection and would prioritize stabilizing Spain's finances. On April 7 Portugal became the third country to place itself under a troika program.[9]

The sense that Europe's welfare state was being subjected to a relentless program of rollback driven by the demands of bankers and bond markets provoked outrage. Stéphane Hessel, former French resistance fighter and ecological activist, survivor of Buchenwald, Dora and Bergen-Belsen, became an unlikely bestselling author with his well-timed manifesto *Indignez-Vous! (Time for Outrage!)*.[10] To oppose the demands of global finance Hessel summoned the spirit of resistance martyr Jean Moulin, who died in 1943 at the hands of the Gestapo. Taking up Hessel's slogan on May 15, 2011, ahead of local elections, a crowd of twenty thousand Spanish protesters occupied the most symbolic square in Madrid, the Puerta del Sol. The *indignados* would remain there for a month, defying efforts by the police and courts to evict them.[11] Building a tent city, they declared that "we are not goods in the hands of politicians and bankers."[12] And the M15 movement continued long after their original camp was dispersed. June 19, 2011, witnessed the largest wave of demonstrations in Spain's tumultuous modern history, bringing perhaps as many as 3 million people—7 percent of the Spanish population—onto the streets.[13] Scaled to the size of the United States, the equivalent demonstration would have involved 19 million protesters. Among the more humorous Spanish chants was one directed at

Greece, their partners in austerity: "Hush! The Greeks are sleeping." In 2010 Greece had been rocked by massive protests. But since the fall, resistance in Greece had ebbed. On May 28, 2011, Athens answered the Spanish challenge and the latest round of cuts demanded by the troika with the occupation of Syntagma Square. A week later, June 5 saw a gigantic rally, with between 200,000 and 300,000 participants in the capital city. Syntagma would be cleared only after violent clashes on June 28–29 pitting revolutionary militants against riot police, many of whom made no secret of their sympathy for Greece's neofascist Golden Dawn movement.

A resurgent nationalism, defending sovereignty against the impositions of the crisis, would be one of the most powerful political responses to the crisis. This had both left- and right-wing variants. Both were at their most vocal in Greece, where the diktat of the troika awakened memories of occupation, civil war and dictatorship. On the Left it was commonplace in the demonstrations of 2010 and 2011 to associate Germany's veto over eurozone economic policy with Nazi imperialism. Meanwhile, Greece's own fascists paraded openly in the streets.[14] The membership of the Golden Dawn party reveled in torch-lit processions, adorned with runic flags and shielded by heavily muscled storm troopers. Golden Dawners harassed and attacked leftists and non-European immigrants, while laying on soup kitchens, reserved, of course, only for hungry Greeks. In a textbook rerun of the 1930s, a comprehensive social and economic crisis provided the setting for a program of national racial community.

The modes of resistance produced by the crisis were significant in their own right. Marches, demonstrations and strikes were combined with encampments, claiming territory. Public spaces manicured and modernized beyond recognition during the boom years were reclaimed for an alternative mode of life.[15] In Greece, defiance of the troika took the form of the nonpayment of taxes and fines. In Spain, with 500,000 families facing eviction and a life crushed under unpayable debts—there is no bankruptcy protection for mortgage debtors under Spanish law—protesters specialized in new forms of nonviolent, direct confrontation.[16] So-called *escraches* brought flash mobs together, organized via social media, to "get in the faces of politicians," forcing the unresponsive elite to acknowledge the scale and intensity of the emergency.[17] If markets were entitled to panic, why should

citizens be expected to preserve a proper demeanor? Why was it only the "confidence" of investors that mattered?[18]

The new Left that began to take shape in response to the eurozone crisis would in due course shake up European politics.[19] In Greece, the coalition of the radical Left, known as Syriza, a combination of antiglobalization movements and breakaway elements of the Communist Party that had first formed ten years earlier, positioned itself under its charismatic young leader, Alexis Tsipras, as the radical alternative to PASOK, as the party willing to lead the Greek people in their struggle against oligarchs at home and the troika in Brussels.[20] In Spain the ranks of the protesters of 2011 included the articulate professor of political sociology and left-wing talk show host Pablo Iglesias, who would go on to be the main mover behind the Podemos party that was founded in 2014.[21] Like Syriza, Podemos activists freely invoked the language of "the people" to bind together a broad-based coalition against the government's austerity line.[22] Podemos championed the cause of "*la gente*" against "*la casta*"—the corrupt clique bent on stealing "democracy from the people."[23]

Greek and Spanish politics would never be the same again. The crisis had leaped from the financial to the political sphere. But in the spring of 2011 the protests were held at arm's length by the incumbent governments. What forced a change in policy was not protest, however passionate and imaginative, but the inescapable realization that extend-and-pretend, the "fix" cobbled together in 2010, simply did not work.

II

Greece's situation was deteriorating. It was implementing austerity but the debt to GDP burden was rising, not falling. Cutting government expenditure did not have the energizing effect on private business activity that the advocates of expansionary austerity imagined, but rather the reverse.[24] Consumer spending and investment plummeted. As demand collapsed, this led to further job losses and declining tax revenues. By the early summer of 2011 it was clear that Greece would not be able to access capital markets in 2012, as had been assumed. This meant that the Europeans

would have to come up with further loans or find some way of reducing Greece's obligations ahead of the 2013 deadline. The IMF would not continue to disburse money into a program that was not fully funded. One year on from the crisis of the spring of 2010, patience was running out in Berlin too. At a G7 meeting on April 14, after Strauss-Kahn had set out the IMF's terms, Schäuble weighed in. "We cannot just buy out the private investors with public money," he admonished.[25] Merkel's coalition was fragile. The FDP was, frankly, Eurosceptic. The SPD, if it was to vote with Merkel on Europe, demanded that the bondholders must be burned. But the EU Commission and the French government demurred, and Trichet would stop at nothing to keep restructuring off the agenda. When on April 6 the Greeks formally requested a discussion of reprofiling—restructuring the debt not by reducing the amounts owed but by extending the period of payment and the interest owed—Trichet forced them back into line by threatening to cut off the Greek banks.[26]

The ECB's position was not purely negative. What Trichet wanted was for the national governments to take over the task of bond market stabilization that the ECB had undertaken since May 2010. The European Financial Stability Facility agreed among the European governments on May 10, 2010, had begun operating. It was the vehicle for the bailout loans to Ireland and Portugal. But its legal status was fragile. Its funding was on a voluntary and bilateral basis. And it was to be used only in emergencies to buy up new debt issued by states shut out of the capital markets. It was not authorized to do the job that had been offloaded on the ECB, buying bonds in the secondary market to stabilize prices and yields. For Merkel to designate a common European fund for bond market stabilization was political poison because it smacked of debt mutualization, with all the political and legal ramifications that entailed. The Bundesbank might not like the ECB's bond buying, but it could be justified as routine central bank intervention. To let Trichet carry the can was the lesser of two evils as far as Merkel was concerned.

This was the basic inconsistency in the German position. Berlin was not just the relentless advocate of austerity. It was also the most consistent and clearheaded on restructuring and PSI. But when it came to its necessary concomitants, starting with backstopping the rest of the bond market,

Berlin was inconsistent and incoherent. Nor did Berlin show any particular energy in recapitalizing its banks, allowing Hypo Real Estate and the weaker Landesbanken to become millstones around its neck. Bailing in creditors without backstopping the bond market and strengthening the banks was not so much responsible policy as a high-wire act that the ECB, the French and the Americans all regarded with horror. And this is the most charitable interpretation of Berlin's motivations. The less charitable reading was that Germany was engaged in a strategy of tension, deliberately fostering market uncertainty to bully the rest of the eurozone into submission.[27] Meanwhile, Germany enjoyed the privileges of a safe haven. While the PIIGS groaned under rising yields, Germany's interest rates were sliding inexorably toward the zero lower bound. The uncertainty in the eurozone was not good for export business. But Germany's exports to the rest of the world were booming. Labor markets were tightening. It was a long way from the affluence and complacency of Munich or Frankfurt to the turbulent streets of Madrid and Athens. Berlin could afford to wait it out.

It was Trichet and his colleagues at the ECB who found the status quo unacceptable. As a result of months of bond buying, by the spring of 2011 they found themselves as proud owners of 15 percent of Greece's junk-rated public debt. When further negotiations about the European Stability Mechanism, the permanent replacement for the EFSF, did not provide for the purchasing of bonds in the secondary market, the ECB's patience ran out. It was time for Frankfurt to draw the line. The public side of the ECB's new harder stance was interest rate policy. As the eurozone crisis heated up again in April and July 2011, the ECB, in one of the most misguided decisions in the history of monetary policy, raised rates.[28] In the ECB's defense, it was true that inflation in Germany and other hotspots of the eurozone economy was picking up. The asymmetry between the relative prosperity of Northern Europe and the rest of Europe was all too real. But the ECB's move was clearly intended as a political signal. The ECB was asserting its independence. It was putting Europe's governments on notice. It would be up to them to take responsibility for the debt markets.[29] Nor were interest rates the only way to send the message. Without fanfare, indeed, without public announcement of any kind, in mid-March the European Central

Bank stopped purchases of eurozone sovereign bonds and introduced differentiated haircuts on repos for lower-rated bonds.[30]

It took a few weeks for the markets to register the serious tightening of credit conditions. Then they sold off. The yield spread between the safest and riskiest eurozone bonds surged. The Greek spread reached 1,200 points and this time the fear was different. In 2010 the markets had moved against individual countries, first Greece, then Ireland. Now a wall of money was moving against the eurozone as a whole. One key indicator was American money market funds, key contributors to the cash pools from which European banks sourced their funding, huge sources of liquidity managed by giant asset managers like BlackRock. Whereas in early 2011 they were still providing as much as $600 billion in funding to European banks, from the spring they drastically curtailed their exposure.[31] Over the course of the year they would reduce their commitment to European banks by 45 percent. French banks were particularly hard-hit. Even giants like BNP were not exempt. On Wall Street large bets were now being placed not just on the default of the weakest borrowers—by the spring S&P was reckoning with a 50–70 percent haircut on Greek debt and a 1-in-3 chance of outright disorderly default—increasingly, investors were betting on the collapse of the euro itself. The most aggressive hedge fund managers swung their money first one way then the other, betting against the dollar on the back of the ECB's interest rate increase and then the other way, taking huge positions against European sovereigns, banks and other vulnerable stock.[32] Big Wall Street names like bond king Bill Gross at PIMCO and John Paulson, the hedge fund hero of 2008, let it be known that they were bearish on Europe. They had always been skeptical about the eurozone, admittedly, but with the ECB and the national governments at odds, the Europeans seemed bent on self-destruction, and there was money to be made on that too.

Nor was it only American money that was signaling its lack of confidence. A huge internal movement of funds within the eurozone was afoot. This was registered in a previously obscure but soon to be notorious appendage of the Eurosystem known as the TARGET2 balances.[33] As money flowed out of bank accounts in Greece, Ireland, Spain and Portugal in search of safety, it moved to Germany and elsewhere in the core eurozone.

If funding markets had been functioning normally, the stressed peripheral banks would have found replacement funding in interbank markets without troubling their central banks. The recipient banks in the north were, after all, flush with flight money, and their Greek counterparts were willing to offer good rates. But interbank lending in Europe had never recovered from the shocks of 2007 and 2008 and had been dealt a further blow in the panic of April 2010. So instead, peripheral banks drew their funding from their national central banks, which, because they were no longer sovereign issuers of domestic currency, drew their euros from the ECB headquarters in Frankfurt, while at the same time the Bundesbank and other recipients of flight money piled up credits. Suddenly, in the spring of 2011, thanks largely to the journalistic entrepreneurship of the economist professor Hans-Werner Sinn, the German public was alerted to the shocking and quite misleading news that they were secretly providing a huge "credit" to the periphery.[34] Hundreds of billions of euros would be "forfeited" if the currency system collapsed.

This alarmist interpretation of the accounting data should be seen less as a piece of economic analysis than as a symptom of the increasing loss of legitimacy on the part of the euro system. What the TARGET2 balances

Source: Bruegel, National Central Banks.

registered was not a "loan" by Germany to the rest of the system. The TAR-
GET2 balances were the offsetting official counterpart to an enormous
movement of private funds *into* German bank accounts from the eurozone
periphery. Some of those moving funds were rich Greek or Spanish busi-
nesses. But in large part it was Germany's own investors bringing their
euros home. They were able to do so without risk of currency losses or a
massive Deutschmark appreciation, which would have hurt Germany's ex-
porters, thanks to the monetary union and the ECB's clearing system. Sinn
liked to inflame his readers with dark scenarios in which a breakup of the
euro resulted in a loss of Germany's bookkeeping claims on the ECB. It was
a grim and uncertain prospect. But one thing was certain: The funds that
anxious investors had already moved to safety in Germany were very un-
likely to leave. What Germany was benefiting from was something akin to
the exorbitant privilege enjoyed by the United States in the global economy.
At times of stress, global money moved into dollars. In the eurozone, money
moved to Germany.[35] It was a privilege measured by the yield spread. As the
yields on crisis-country bonds soared, those on Bunds eased. It was one of
the factors that helped to feed Germany's prosperity bubble. That a flow of
funds into Germany should come to be seen as a burden was symptomatic
of the feverish discourse of the crisis.

III

By May 2011, confidence was so shaky that a secret Eurogroup meeting was
hurriedly convened in Luxembourg. Scheduled for Friday, May 6, it was
meant to restore unity and coherence. Instead it turned into a PR disaster.
When Schäuble insisted that they must start by discussing restructuring
and PSI, Trichet stormed out. He wouldn't countenance such talk. On the
other hand, to proceed without him was impractical, as the only thing
keeping the Greek banks alive was ECB support.[36] No one fancied the idea
of having to restructure them too. When *Der Spiegel* got wind of the meet-
ing and markets in the United States began to react, the spokesman for
Jean-Claude Juncker, the veteran prime minister of Luxembourg and Euro-
group chair, flatly denied that any meeting was taking place.[37] Hours later

the same spokesman was forced to admit that the leaders had indeed met. "There was a very good reason to deny that the meeting was taking place," he told the assembled journalists. "We had Wall Street open at that point in time." The euro was plunging. Lying was a matter of "self-preservation." When the *Wall Street Journal* asked whether such deception might undermine the "market's confidence in future euro-zone pronouncements," Juncker's spokesman retorted that the market already appeared to discount any comments by ECB president Trichet and France's finance minister, Lagarde. Whatever they said on the subject of Greece's debt, "nobody seems to believe it." So what further harm could be done by a convenient lie? Juncker himself had come to similarly stark conclusions: "Monetary policy is a serious issue," the Eurogroup chair told an audience in April. "We should discuss this in secret, in the Eurogroup. . . . If we indicate possible decisions, we are fueling speculations on the financial markets and we are throwing in misery mainly the people we are trying to safeguard from this. . . . I am for secret, dark debates. . . . I'm ready to be insulted as being insufficiently democratic, but I want to be serious. . . . When it becomes serious, you have to lie."[38] By May 2011 the effort to defend the indefensible, to uphold extend-and-pretend, had resulted in a complete breakdown of credible and coherent communication about the eurozone's economic policy. Juncker was unusual only for feeling that he didn't need to dress it up, which, as far as a tiny bourgeois tax haven like Luxembourg was concerned, might have been true. Projected onto a larger stage of the EU, the implications of Juncker's "realism" were rather more disconcerting.

With Europe's credibility draining away, what was needed was a "reset," a clarifying intervention that would restore credibility and stop the crisis of confidence from widening. That is what Dominique Strauss-Kahn, as head of the IMF, seems to have had in mind when he scheduled meetings, first with Angela Merkel and then with the Eurogroup, for mid-May 2011. Strauss-Kahn "was going to push for a big firewall," recalled one senior US official. "We were putting a considerable amount of expectation on the outcome of those meetings."[39] Inside the IMF, a new head of steam of opposition to extend-and-pretend was building. The Fund's Ireland team had never been satisfied with the inequitable deal forced on Dublin by the ECB and the G7 in November 2010. Ireland's problems, Ajai Chopra insisted,

were not merely Irish in scope, "they are a shared European problem" that required joint European action.[40] What was needed was to beef up the EFSF, giving it more resources and wider authority to intervene. Furthermore, as Ireland showed, Europe's banks were too big to bail by any but the largest states. So Chopra insisted that if banks could not raise enough capital from private sources, there should be coordinated recapitalization across the EU.[41] Already a year earlier, in March 2010, Strauss-Kahn had challenged the Europeans to establish a jointly funded bank resolution authority.[42] Without that, any steps toward major debt restructuring were dangerous to contemplate.

By May 2011 the IMF had clearly formulated the basic logic of a eurozone fix that went beyond extend-and-pretend, and Strauss-Kahn seems to have been bent on delivering it. But minutes before his departure from JFK on May 14, the managing director of the IMF was hauled off his flight by officers of the NYPD to face charges of sexual assault and unlawful imprisonment. It was a bewildering turn of events. Much of European opinion was in uproar at the spectacle of such a prominent figure being reduced to the indignity of a New York perp walk. Did the presumption of innocence not hold in America?[43] In France those who did not blame the Americans blamed Sarkozy, who was widely suspected of plotting to eliminate Strauss-Kahn as a rival for the presidency.[44]

Meanwhile, the hope that the IMF might shake the eurozone out of its paralysis evaporated and the Fund was left without a managing director. The question of succession opened a sore wound. In 2007 the emerging markets had been promised that the next head of the IMF would be one of theirs. Now, faced with the eurozone crisis, it was argued that because the IMF was so deeply engaged in Europe, it was crucial to have a European at the helm. Had Latin Americans, Asians or Africans ever had the temerity to make the analogous case, one can only imagine the reaction. The Europeans didn't even blink. Their candidate for the job was Christine Lagarde, who had proven both her loyalty and her competence as Sarkozy's finance minister. She had the backing of Europe, the United States and China. Meanwhile, as the eurozone spiraled toward crisis, the IMF's push for decisive action was aborted. While Lagarde readied herself for her new role, the helm was taken by John Lipsky, the IMF's American number two.

Lipsky was all for large-scale support actions in the interest of systemic stability. If there were to be private sector involvement, on the other hand, it would have to be voluntary, and modest in scale. The priority of systemic stability and preventing contagion reasserted itself. This was no time for dangerous talk about debt restructuring or bank recapitalization. What mattered was containing the crisis and preventing uncertainty spreading from Europe.

IV

Strauss-Kahn never made it to his discussion with Merkel. But on June 5 the German chancellor headed to Washington.[45] By inclination, Merkel was an Atlanticist. But not since 2003 had relations been so strained. On economic policy Germany and America had been out of step since the crisis began. The storm over QE2 had been embarrassing. And where had Germany been in Libya? What was Berlin's plan for Europe? The discussions with Obama were intense. Merkel returned home on June 8 with a Presidential Medal of Freedom and a new tune. There would be no more talk of Greek default or Grexit. In exchange for further austerity from Greece, there would be another aid package. Private sector involvement, i.e., debt restructuring, would be part of the bargain, as Germany had wanted from the start. But it would be voluntary. It would be a creditor-led restructuring, with the banks exercising a veto over the manner and scale of the debt write-down. What was still missing from Berlin's pronouncements was any bold plan for a European bond fund or recapitalization. The net effect, therefore, was to heighten the tension. What the markets heard was that there would be PSI but without an adequate safety net.

On June 29 the battered Greek government pushed the fourth round of austerity through parliament, including privatization, tax increases and pension cuts. It did so in the wake of the violent clearance of Syntagma Square occupation and a two-day general strike. It did so in the face of IMF calculations that suggested that to achieve debt sustainability Greece needed to sell off public assets to the tune of 50 billion euros. Indeed,

according to a further IMF assessment released on July 4, even that would not be enough.[46] It would take not only austerity and privatization but a truly heavy bondholder haircut to get Greece to sustainability. The tone of the talks with the International Institute of Finance (IIF), which had begun on June 27, suggested that there was little prospect of that. The banks and other bondholders were making only modest concessions. That suited the ECB, which was desperate that there should be no "default event," but it stood in jarring contrast to the tens of billions of euros in cuts that Athens was imposing on its citizens. For Greece, the new Merkel-Obama dispensation was revealing itself to be extend-and-pretend in a new guise.

By June, as the S&P ratings agency downgraded Greece to CCC—the lowest score awarded to any sovereign borrower—and spreads surged to 1,300 points, the markets were asking a new question. If the eurozone couldn't handle Greece, what if it faced more serious trouble? What if it had to deal with a crisis in Spain, or in Italy? Twenty years earlier, in the early 1990s, Italy had been on the rocks. Since then Italy's debt had stabilized. Rome managed primary surpluses. But its debt was still dangerously high in relation to GDP. And given the size of the Italian economy—the eighth largest in the world by nominal GDP—its debts were enormous: 1.8 trillion euros. Alarmingly, in the last days of June 2011, following the decision to implement PSI in Greece, 100 billion euros of Italian debt had been sold off. European banks were pulling back, with French banks leading the way. The share of foreign holding of Italian debt fell from 50 to 45 percent in a matter of weeks.[47] That was enough to send Italy's borrowing costs up from 4.25 to 5.54 percent between June and August of 2011. That might not seem like a large number. But given Italy's huge refinancing needs, it spelled disaster. Between the second half of 2011 and the end of 2014 Rome calculated that it would need to borrow 813 billion euros in refinancing and new loans. A 25 percent increase in the cost of servicing such a huge volume of debt was a serious matter indeed. If a run began on Italy, it might well be game over for the eurozone.

Contrary to North European prejudice, the Italian political class was by no means oblivious to the seriousness of the situation. Italian economists, notably the "Bocconi boys," named after the preeminent business school in Milan, had contributed as much as anyone to the new consensus

of spending cuts and "expansionary austerity."[48] Faced with the emergency of 2008–2010, Italy had permitted itself virtually no stimulus. The question was whether Rome had the will and capacity to respond to the new panic in the bond market. And, in particular, how Prime Minister Berlusconi would react.

Berlusconi was a figure wreathed in scandal.[49] He had faced allegations for crimes including racketeering, large-scale tax evasion and corruption. But on February 15, 2011, in the most embarrassing charge of all, he had been indicted for paying for sex with a minor and abuse of office in his efforts to cover up his liaison with an exotic dancer and call girl known as "Ruby the Heartstealer." Rather than resigning, Berlusconi clung to his office. On April 6, 2011, as financial markets watched anxiously, Italy's prime minister went on trial. The proceedings were immediately adjourned, but hearings would resume at the end of May. Meanwhile, a dark cloud of uncertainty and disrepute hung over the Italian government. Further doubts were raised at the end of May, when Berlusconi's political alliance between Forza Italia and the Lega Nord lost control of Milan, his personal fiefdom.[50] Even at the best of times, Berlusconi's instincts were those of a crowd pleaser. Now that he was fighting for his political life, could he be counted on to push through the kind of austerity that his finance minister, Giulio Tremonti, was demanding?

Over the weekend of July 9–10 Merkel intervened personally with Berlusconi to urge on him the seriousness of the situation. Europe's future hung on Italy. But was it Italy, or was it, in fact, Germany that was the weak link? To many in Europe it was unclear whether Merkel herself was truly committed to holding the euro together. Ugly whispers began to circulate that Germany's veteran chancellor, Helmut Kohl, father of the euro and German reunification, was questioning whether his European legacy was safe in Merkel's hands. "This girl [Merkel] is destroying my Europe," Kohl was reported to have told one journalist.[51] Only reluctantly were Merkel and Schäuble persuaded to defer summer travel plans and call an emergency meeting of the European Council on July 21 to discuss eurozone stabilization. The issues were predictable: fiscal adjustment and austerity, PSI, restructuring and debt sustainability, ECB bond buying. Only Europe-wide bank recapitalization, the final element in a coherent crisis-containment

strategy, was not yet on the table. But what was Berlin's game? Were Merkel and Schäuble engaged in truly hair-raising brinksmanship? Or, cocooned in their relative prosperity, did the German political class simply not understand the pressures the rest of the eurozone was under?

On July 14, 2011, in response to market pressure, the Italian parliament adopted a severe 70 billion euro austerity program, on a par with Germany's 2010 effort.[52] But doubts remained as long as Berlusconi was at the helm. And the issue of PSI in Greece remained unresolved. Trichet was sticking to his guns. If there was anything approaching full-blown restructuring of Greek debt, the ECB would disallow Greek bonds as eligible collateral. Panic was again spreading through eurozone debt markets. What had originally been a problem of small fry, like Greece and Ireland, was rapidly becoming a comprehensive crisis of Southern Europe, including large economies like Spain and Italy. Whereas in 2007 eurozone bond investors had regarded Greek debt as equivalent to that offered by Germany, by September 2011 the CDS spreads on Italy and Spain were higher than those of Egypt in the throes of revolution.[53] The three countries in the world judged most likely to default were all in the eurozone—Greece, Ireland and Portugal—well ahead of Belarus, Venezuela and Pakistan.[54] The revolutionary mood seemed to have jumped the Mediterranean. The violent scenes in Athens fed fantasies of social disorder spreading across Europe. Supposedly serious financial analysts were talking of "hyperinflation, military coups and possible civil war."[55] But it wasn't any longer a matter of individual predatory hedge funds, or one or two overexcited analysts talking the euro down; commercial banks and pension funds from across Europe and the United States were pulling tens of billions of euros out of Italy and the program countries.[56] Once eurozone sovereigns lost their standing as issuers of safe assets, institutional investors had no option but to reallocate their portfolios. And that affected the European banks too. In the summer of 2011 wholesale funding was drying up.[57]

With only days to go until the July 21 summit, the possibility dawned on Paris that Merkel might be willing to let the upcoming talks fail.[58] The debt reduction so far agreed with the bank lobbyists was too low to satisfy Berlin. The resources and mandate for the EFSF were insufficient to reassure the French, calm the markets or persuade Trichet to resume bond

buying. If the talks failed, no one would be safe, including France. To break the deadlock Sarkozy realized that he would have to deal with Merkel one-on-one. The French president arrived in Berlin on July 20 at 5:30 p.m. and immediately hit a roadblock over the EFSF. It soon became clear that Berlin and Paris could not settle the matter without involving Trichet. He was summoned from Frankfurt, arriving on the last plane into Berlin at 10:00 p.m. The deal had to be done not between Germany and France but between Germany, France and the ECB. In the early hours of July 21 Sarkozy and Merkel took turns on a single cell phone to read out to Van Rompuy, the president of the European Council, the terms of their agreement. That afternoon in Brussels the package was formally presented to and voted on by the other governments.

Greece would receive an additional 109 billion euros, meeting its financing needs through 2014 and enabling the IMF to continue as part of the troika. The interest it paid on its loans would be lowered to 3.5 percent. Maturities would be extended and, through a menu of PSI options, Greece's creditors would make a contribution, though the precise amount remained to be determined. The ECB would be indemnified for any losses it suffered. If the Greek banks suffered irreparable damage they would be recapitalized out of troika funds.[59] Most important, the governments stated emphatically that PSI applied only to Greece. It was the only insolvent eurozone sovereign. All others would honor their obligations without fail. To contain contagion the EFSF would be beefed up and at the behest of the ECB it would be empowered to enter the secondary market and to establish credit lines for nonprogram countries, such as Spain and Italy. The EFSF would no longer act only as an ultima ratio, as Merkel had insisted since March 2010, but as a preemptive agency, helping to stabilize markets to forestall any threat arising. These, finally, were the elements of a workable solution—buy-in by the Greeks, debt restructuring, further loans, cooperation with the ECB and backstopping by a newly empowered EFSF. There was even partial recognition of the need for bank recapitalization. The general structure was fine. But did the sums add up? And who was to pay?

One neuralgic point was the scale of PSI. The initial figure that had emerged from the polite negotiations with the IIF was only 20 percent. The bankers were not permitted in the intergovernmental meetings on July 21.

But they gathered in the corridors outside. When the governments let it be known that 20 percent was insufficient, the IIF offered 21 percent. With this symbolic concession there was general satisfaction that a deal had been done. No one did the math. It was a matter of gestures, not arithmetic. When the IMF's representative queried Greece's sustainability under the assumption of such a modest restructuring, the meeting was treated to a "furious denunciation" by Charles Dallara of the IIF.[60] The indignation too was for show. In private Dallara was only too happy to boast of the astonishingly generous deal that his lobbying had secured for his clients, the big banks.[61]

The result of this compromise was that Greece would pay the reputational price for having restructured its debts, but it would gain precious little financial relief. It would be left carrying a debt burden of 143 percent of GDP, which was clearly unsustainable. As one Goldman Sachs analyst commented: "This tendency to 'under-size' otherwise good policy initiatives has been a recurrent feature of European policies." A member of the UBS economics team was less polite: "This is fiddling around at the margins. . . . The debt needs to halve." As to the new support facilities provided by the EFSF, Willem Buiter, chief economist at Citigroup, told Bloomberg Television, "The European Financial Stability Facility has gone from being a single-barreled gun to a Gatling gun, but with the same amount of ammo. . . . It needs to be increased in size urgently."[62] If Italy went critical, the EFSF would need not 200–400 billion but 1–2 trillion euros. Otherwise, only the ECB, with its bottomless supply of euros, could backstop the system.

In the meantime, investors were on edge. At the end of July it emerged that Deutsche Bank had cut its holdings of Italian debt by 88 percent since the beginning of the year.[63] For Italians in Berlusconi's camp it was a clear case of blackmail. In the circles around Finance Minister Tremonti there was talk of a stab in the back.[64] Earlier in the year Rome had had the temerity to suggest that any joint European bailout fund ought to be funded in proportion not to GDP but to the size of bank claims that were being rescued. Not surprisingly, this was not a popular idea in Berlin. Tremonti was convinced that the precipitate sales by Deutsche were a message from Merkel and Schäuble. Whatever the truth of the matter, the suspicion was symptomatic. Trust was breaking down.

V

If money was fleeing out of Europe, where was it to go? The answer since the onset of the financial crisis had been, paradoxically, the United States. As US subprime went bad, there had not been the panicked dollar sell-off that many had feared. Instead, investors shifted into US Treasurys, the very top of the global monetary pyramid. In 2008 the dollar surged and US interest rates fell. Successive waves of QE reversed that trend. The dollar slid against its major trading partners. This imposed losses on investors and made US bonds marginally less attractive. By the summer of 2011, however, something far more ominous was on the horizon.

At the start of the year, as the new Republican majority in Congress flexed its muscles, the effort to craft a bipartisan, long-term approach to fiscal consolidation broke down.[65] For want of a budget, in April 2011 the US federal government already came close to a shutdown. On May 16 the permissible ceiling of federal debt was reached, at $14.3 trillion. With tax revenue covering only 60 percent of current spending, Washington had hit the limit of its legal right to borrow. The Treasury was forced to adopt "extraordinary measures," including borrowing from government cash reserves and selling assets from the civil service retirement fund.[66] This would see the Treasury through until August 2. After that, the US federal government would face a choice between paying salaries or paying its creditors. America was sliding toward something even worse than concerted austerity, a chaotic shutdown risking default on its obligations to both domestic and foreign creditors.

In late July 2011, as Sarkozy, Merkel and Trichet diced with the future of the eurozone, the United States was perilously close to the edge. There was no longer any disagreement in Washington about the need for urgent fiscal consolidation.[67] But there was a huge divide between Democrats insisting on a balanced approach to deficit reduction, involving tax increases as well as entitlement cuts, and Republicans focused exclusively on spending reductions. The Speaker of the House, John Boehner, was looking to assert his control over the Tea Party faction by striking a deal with the White House to achieve deficit cuts of $4 trillion over ten years. But on

July 22 the talks between Boehner and the Obama administration broke down over Republican demands for slashing reductions in medical spending and the White House insistence on a $1.2 trillion increase in taxes.[68] Journalists began compiling calendars as to which bills due in August the American government should pay first. Constitutional specialists were debating the pros and cons of executive prerogative, or coining trillion-dollar platinum coins with which to repay the national debt.[69] If Greece was a problem, and Italy was too big to fail, there was simply no reckoning what a US default might do. In August alone, the Treasury had to roll over almost $500 billion in debt.[70] With the eurozone wobbling, the American money market funds that were pulling out of European bank bonds continued to shift into US Treasurys. But appearances were deceptive. Investor demand for US government debt held up, but above all in lower-risk, short maturities. The average maturity of US Treasurys held by the MMFs declined from ninety-five days in January 2010 to only seventy days at the end of July 2011.[71] Meanwhile, financial engineers began to contemplate the need for something no one had contemplated before—credit default swaps against US Treasurys.[72]

Prior to 2008 the market for US Treasury CDS had not existed. What would have been the point of insuring the risk-free asset class on which the entire global financial system rested? In the wildly improbable event of a US default, the general destabilization would be such that it was unclear whether any private financial entity would still be in a position to act as a reliable counterparty. Who would be left standing to pay out on insurance against the end of the world? Nevertheless, having first come into existence during the turmoil of 2008, when it seemed that Fannie Mae and Freddie Mac might fail, in the course of 2011 the niche market for CDS on US Treasurys sprang back into life. In the last days of July just over a thousand contracts were outstanding, with spreads running to 82 basis points. It was a fraction of what investors in Greek debt paid, but it was astonishing that the market existed at all.

On July 31, 2011, Washington pulled back from the abyss. A budget compromise was reached that would impose automatic austerity if the two warring parties could not agree on cuts by the end of the year. Reluctantly, sufficient Tea Party radicals were won over to the Republican leadership's position for the deal to go through. It took heavy lobbying and hours of

alarmist lectures by credit-rating experts and former officials from the Bush administration to convince the Republican insurgents of the dramatic consequences of a default. But the damage was done. As Mitch McConnell, the Republicans' leader in the Senate, blithely informed the media: "I think some of our members may have thought the default issue was a hostage you might take a chance at shooting. Most of us didn't think that. What we did learn is this—it's a hostage worth ransoming."[73] As Jason Chaffetz, one of the hard-line Tea Party newcomers, remarked, the threat had been real. "We weren't kidding around. . . . We would have taken it down."[74]

On August 3 China's Dagong ratings agency was the first to draw the obvious conclusion. It downgraded the United States from A+ to A. As Dagong remarked: "[A]t this crucial juncture, neither the Democratic Party nor Republican Party has shown any consideration for the general interest in order to argue for their own partisan interest; they had a hard time making the correct choice in a timely manner leaving the world in terror, which highlights the negative role of the US political system on an economic basis."[75] The US political system, the Chinese analysts concluded, "cannot resolve the fundamental influence of low economic growth, high deficit and increasingly higher debt to the debt service capability through increasing real wealth creation, with the declining national solvency irreversible. It is natural that QE3 monetary policy will be enabled for the next step, which will throw the world economy into an overall crisis; the status of [the] US dollar will be essentially shaken in this process." This was the judgment of the G20 at Seoul turned into the language of credit rating. The year ended with a big sell-off of US government debt by Beijing. But there was no rout. The long buildup of Chinese claims on the US taxpayer had ended. But the portfolio stabilized at between $1.2 trillion and $1.3 trillion.

Criticism from China was only to be expected. More surprising was the fallout at home. On August 5 the unthinkable happened. One of America's own ratings agencies, Standard & Poor's, downgraded the United States from AAA to AA+. S&P cited the "political brinkmanship of recent months" and the mounting evidence that "America's governance and policymaking" was "becoming less stable, less effective, and less predictable."[76] It also pointed to the supposedly unsustainable level of US debt and the

speed of its accumulation, which would take it well over 90 percent of GDP by 2021—the notorious Reinhart and Rogoff threshold. But when the US Treasury was handed the explanation for S&P's decision, it became clear that the ratings agency had committed an elementary mistake. By applying the figures for debt growth to the wrong benchmark scenario, it had wildly overstated the deficit to be expected over the next ten years. Even more surprisingly, when this error was pointed out, S&P did not retreat. It left the downgrade in place as well as the explanatory text—minus the modeling error. This led the Treasury to fire off an official denunciation. "S&P still chose to proceed with their flawed judgment by simply changing their principal rationale for their credit rating decision from an economic one to a political one. . . . The magnitude of this mistake—and the haste with which S&P changed its principal rationale for action . . . raise fundamental questions about the credibility and integrity of S&P's ratings action."[77] No one doubted the weakness of the US political system. But S&P had delivered just one more demonstration of how broken the ratings agencies were. It was their AAA certifications, handed out to hundreds of billions of subprime MBS, that had helped to precipitate the crisis in 2008. It was their serial downgrades that were setting the pace of the crisis in the eurozone. But it turned out that they could not even get their sums right on the US budget.

VI

Trillions of dollars of debt were losing their status as safe assets. The US Treasury was accused by the German finance minister of interventionist tendencies akin to communism. NATO was squabbling over Libya. The loose monetary policy of the Federal Reserve was blamed for fomenting revolt in the Middle East. The EU was locked into a self-deceptive nonsolution to the Greek debt crisis, and when it was not engaged in extend-and-pretend it was openly and unabashedly lying. Both Italy's prime minister and the managing director of the IMF were up on sex charges. Washington was willfully toying with bankruptcy. The ratings agencies could not do

their arithmetic. Millions of people were in the streets, protesting, demanding a "rupture," unable or unwilling to pay debts they had contracted or that had been contracted in their name.

Over the weekend of August 6–7, as the world digested the downgrade of America's sovereign debt, heads of government, central bankers and Treasury officials interrupted their summer vacations for a frantic round of telephone conferences. But all that emerged were lame communiqués, which did nothing to inspire confidence. On Monday, August 8, rocked by bad news from both sides of the Atlantic, stock markets sold off sharply. President Obama was left to remark: "We now live in a global economy where everything is interconnected, and that means that when you have problems in Europe and in Spain and in Italy and in Greece, those problems wash over into our shores."[78]

In the general crisis of legitimacy in 2010–2011 there was no Archimedean point. There was no place to stand above the fray. Bringing this home was the point of the protesters "getting in the face" of government officials in Spain and Italy. They wanted to break through the invincible authority and distance that separated decision makers from those their decisions impinged upon, to force them to come face-to-face with a different reality. And over the summer of 2011 a small band of US activists determined to do the same at the hub of the world financial economy in New York.

On August 19, 2011, representatives of the New York Stock Exchange met with agents of the FBI for an unusual conference.[79] Trawling the Internet for suspicious activity, the FBI had got wind of an "anarchist" network dubbed "Occupy Wall Street." Its aim was to spread the protest movement that had gained such scale in Europe to the United States. The occupation of Zuccotti Park right next to Wall Street was scheduled for September 17. The US media at first ignored the story. The first to cover it were Agence France-Presse and the *Guardian*.[80] But within weeks the tiny encampment that lodged itself within hailing distance of Wall Street would become headline news around the world.[81]

Given the scale of the social media storm it unleashed, it is important to put Occupy Wall Street in perspective. It was tiny compared with the gigantic antiausterity mobilizations in Europe. The global Occupy demonstrations that took place on October 15, 2011, attracted perhaps as many

as a million demonstrators in Spain, 200,000 to 400,000 in Rome, tens of thousands in Portugal. In New York between 35,000 and 50,000 protesters marched. But the New York occupation had a symbolic significance far in excess of its modest scale. It articulated radical opposition at the very heart of US capitalism. Imitation camps sprang up across the United States, in Philadelphia, Oakland, Boston, Seattle, Atlanta, L.A., Denver, Tucson, New Orleans, Salt Lake City and many other cities. Further afield there were notable solidarity camps in London, Seoul, Rome, Manila, Berlin, Mumbai, Amsterdam, Paris and Hong Kong. Estimates vary, but protesters in at least nine hundred cities around the world staged sympathy demonstrations.[82] Across the United States, wherever they sprouted, the Occupy camps could expect the watchful presence of the FBI and even US counterterrorism authorities. But despite their tiny size and ramshackle appearance, the obvious and unsettling fact was that the anger of the radical minority was shared by a wide swath of US public opinion.

In October 2011 a poll conducted for the *New York Times* and CBS News found that almost half those questioned felt that the FBI's "anarchist camp" reflected the views of most Americans.[83] Two-thirds thought wealth should be distributed more evenly—nine out of ten Democrats, two thirds of Independents and even one third of Republicans agreeing with that sentiment. But only 11 percent of Americans trusted their government to do the right thing, 84 percent disapproved of the Congress that had threatened to bring the US federal government to its knees and 74 percent thought their country was on the wrong track. Since January 2009 the Obama administration had been straining every muscle to put the lid on popular discontent. Rather than seeking to mobilize the indignation simmering in American society, it had found one technocratic fix after another. Two years later the result was a spectacular delegitimization from both the Left and the Right.

Chapter 17

DOOM LOOP

On September 1, 2011, Pedro Passos Coelho, Portugal's new prime minister, made his first visit to Berlin. His host, Chancellor Merkel, began the joint press conference by announcing how pleased she was to hear that the troika had just submitted its first report on Portugal's structural adjustment program and had declared itself satisfied with the progress being made. She was delighted also to hear that Coelho saw no obstacle to incorporating a German-style debt brake into Portugal's constitution. Then, in the question-and-answer session that followed, it seemed that Chancellor Merkel let the cat out of the bag. Asked about the question of parliamentary control over the European Financial Stability Facility, recently mandated by the German constitutional court, Merkel deadpanned: "We do live in a democracy and we are pleased about that. It is a parliamentary democracy. That means that the budget is a key prerogative of parliament. Thus we will find ways to organize parliamentary codetermination in such a way that it is nevertheless market conforming, so that the appropriate signals appear in the markets. I hear from our budget specialists that they are conscious of this responsibility."[1]

Market-conforming codetermination—was this what European democracy had been reduced to by the autumn of 2011? Was this the hidden agenda of the troika programs, imposed not only on the parliaments of Greece, Ireland and Portugal but on the Bundestag as well—to make them market conforming? For many who joined the protests of 2011, Merkel's

words confirmed their jaundiced view of the EU as little more than a container for the rule of the markets, or that new buzzword of the crisis, "neoliberalism."[2] Merkel did little to clarify the situation. On September 22, a few days ahead of the IMF meeting in Washington, she welcomed the first German pope, Benedict XVI, to the chancellery. Quizzed by curious journalists, Merkel volunteered that the European crisis had been at the heart of their conversation: "We spoke about the financial markets and the fact that politicians should have the power to make policy for the people, and not be driven by the markets. . . . This is a very, very big task in today's time of globalization."[3]

In their flailing generality, these statements are symptomatic of the depth of the crisis by the autumn of 2011. In the space of barely three weeks, the German chancellor managed to tell the press that politicians should be responsible to markets and to tell the pope that politicians should make policy for "the people" regardless of those markets. Was it a contradiction? Or was she implying some kind of synthesis? If so, was it a matter of finding the market-conforming mode of expression that would allow politicians to slyly exert their power or, more ominously, a matter of hammering democracy into such conformity that no market ever need fear the policy parliament might make? Did anyone in Berlin know? No surprise that Gregor Gysi, the sharp-tongued spokesman of Die Linke, should lash Merkel's handling of the eurozone crisis as an engine of chaos and confusion.[4]

The very least one can deduce is that the optimistic dogma under which democracy and markets were seen as natural and necessary complements—the mantra of the aftermath of the cold war—was dead.[5] In its place the crisis had put a more realistic awareness of the potential tension between the two. But this generalization too has its risks, particularly when it is assumed that it is financial markets, not politics, that force the tension. Certainly in the course of the eurozone crisis that had not been the case. The pressure the more fragile members of the eurozone were under depended not on some inescapable clash of peoples and markets, or global capitalism and democracy.[6] It was dictated, first and foremost, by the willingness, or not, of the ECB to buy bonds. In the markets many banks and traders were not just crying out for the EU to undertake a stabilization effort but betting billions that it ultimately would. What delayed the stabilization and

escalated the conflict between democracy and markets to an extraordinary pitch was the struggle among Germany, France and the ECB over the future governance of the eurozone, a question in which politics and economics were inseparably intertwined. Ironically, the result, as in 2010, was to escalate the crisis to the point that European affairs could no longer be safely left to the Europeans.

I

The compromise of July 21 on a new Greek aid package was supposed to be flanked by a new round of bond buying by the ECB. Ireland and Portugal, at least, were judged to be making sufficient progress under their IMF-supervised programs. So on August 4, 2011, the ECB let it be known that it was once again in the market for their bonds. Prices and yields promptly stabilized. This was the cheery backdrop to Coelho's visit to Berlin. But as far as Italy and Spain were concerned, Trichet did not want to let them off the hook so easily. The ECB needed further proof of conformity. To make the point, on August 5 Trichet dispatched a confidential memo to prime ministers Zapatero and Berlusconi, spelling out what would be necessary for the protection of the ECB's bond purchases to be extended to them.[7] In the case of Italy, weight was added to the missive by the signature of Mario Draghi, head of the Italian central bank and Trichet's anointed successor at the ECB.

Neither Spain nor Italy had applied for a troika program, but that did not stop the ECB from demanding huge cuts to government spending and increased taxation. In the Italian case, Trichet and Draghi called for the privatization of local public services, a proposal that had recently been decisively rejected in a nationwide referendum.[8] The ECB also called for dramatic changes to labor market policy, infringing on rights of Italian and Spanish trade unions. Such changes were necessary, the ECB insisted, to cut unemployment and increase growth. It was a blatant attempt to shift the balance of social and political power by means of monetary policy, poorly disguised by the ECB's proviso that care should be taken to ensure

that the social safety net remained intact. In case these unpopular measures encountered opposition, Trichet and Draghi suggested that the Italian government should invoke the decree powers of Article 77 of the Italian constitution, which allowed executive action "in cases of extraordinary need and urgency." Originally designed to counter the specter of Communist insurrection during the cold war, Article 77 was a legal fig leaf that had been repeatedly invoked since the 1970s to cover "emergency measures."[9] Its overuse had been criticized by the Italian courts. If Berlusconi was worried about the legality of these proceedings, Trichet and Draghi advised that he should apply retrospectively for parliamentary sanction. Perhaps not surprisingly, legally minded members of Berlusconi's cabinet wondered whether it was their malodorous prime minister or Draghi and Trichet who posed the greater risk to the rule of law.

The Spanish government chose to keep the ECB's letter secret. If it was to be humiliated it preferred not to have the fact made public. As a sign of their compliance, Spain's two largest political parties agreed to amend the Spanish constitution, unchanged in thirty-three years, to provide for a balanced budget amendment.[10] By contrast, Berlusconi accepted Trichet's terms but under public protest. He would later say that the ECB's instructions "made us look like an occupied government."[11] But rather than embarrassing the ECB, the expostulation from Rome served only to enhance Trichet's reputation as a hard-liner, which, in an ironic twist, freed him to act. On August 7 the ECB began buying Italian and Spanish bonds under the Securities Markets Programme (SMP).[12]

This was enough to calm the markets and stave off the immediate risk of a disaster. But Berlusconi's government was evasive about the full scale of the austerity measures it was willing to adopt. The Italian economy was perched on the edge of a severe recession. Markets remained jumpy. And as everyone realized, things were going to get worse before they got better. The compromise on Greece hammered out on the weekend of July 20–21 had been inadequate from the start. Rather than achieving sustainability, Greece's consolidation program was falling consistently behind schedule. To escape insolvency Greece needed a haircut far larger than that squeezed out of the bankers over the summer: not 21 percent but something closer to

50 percent. If this was not to cause panic, it would need to be framed by a solid Franco-German agreement on the future governance of the eurozone. France was truly the last line of defense. If the crisis spread by way of Rome to Paris, the game would be up. Ominously, in the fall of 2011, as the ECB intervened to prop up Italian public debt, the spread of the ten-year French bonds relative to bunds nudged upward to 89 basis points.[13] In reaction, Merkel and Sarkozy tightened their alliance. What Sarkozy desperately needed was a wall of money. With the ECB pursuing a strategy of tension, the only way to really calm markets would be to expand the EFSF or to agree to a wholesale mutualization of eurozone public debt. It was Berlin's agonizingly slow acceptance of these basic facts that set the pace of the crisis.

On September 29 the Bundestag finally voted on the puny expansion of the EFSF bond market stabilization fund agreed on July 21. It was widely seen as a decisive vote for the future of Merkel's coalition.[14] Though the EFSF was supported by the majority of the Bundestag, on the German right wing the bond buying of the ECB had triggered a furious reaction. At the crucial ECB board meeting in August, Merkel's hard-line new appointee as head of the German Bundesbank, Jens Weidmann, once a star pupil of Axel Weber and Merkel's personal economic adviser, not only voted against bond buying but made his opposition public.[15] On September 9 Jürgen Stark, the German member of the ECB board and the bank's chief economist—the man widely thought to be behind the ECB's interest rate hikes earlier in the year—resigned in protest. To stop the momentum of the conservative rebellion Merkel needed to win the EFSF vote in the Bundestag, not with the votes of the pro-European SPD opposition but on the basis of her own *Kanzlermehrheit*—with the votes of her coalition partners. In the event, on September 29 Merkel got the votes, but by a painfully narrow margin. Out of the 330 members of the government coalition, only 315 voted for the motion, 4 more than the 311 needed. Merkel was on top, but she had little room for maneuver.

In any case, as soon as the Bundestag had voted it was clear that it had been overtaken by events. As everyone in the markets realized, the EFSF fund that had been agreed over the summer was too small. The Bundestag vote on September 29 was simply the occasion to start talking about how the fund might be leveraged, something that had been explicitly ruled out

by Schäuble ahead of the vote.[16] Unless the markets suddenly calmed, Merkel's government would soon be rolling the parliamentary dice again.

II

In the summer it had finally been acknowledged that any Greek debt restructuring would require a full-scale bailout of Greece's own banks. They held so much Greek public debt that their balance sheets would not survive the debt write-down. What the European governments were still struggling to accept was that the problem was far wider than that. The politics of extend-and-pretend might have the benefit of deflecting attention from the creditor banks to the bankrupt government borrowers. It was the citizens of the troika-supervised countries who paid the price. But it also allowed European policy makers to avoid getting to grips with the underlying problems of financial stability. The assumption, presumably, was that given time the banks would take care of themselves. But despite the fairy-tale numbers produced by the European stress tests, it was clear that this was wishful thinking. In fact, Europe's banks were sliding back toward the cliff edge in the fall of 2011. They were struggling to cope with pressure from six directions at once. The legacy losses from 2007–2008 were still on their books. Their holdings of European sovereign debt were increasingly impaired. The troubles of the eurozone economy were bad for new business. The new capital and liquidity requirements of Basel III required painful balance sheet adjustment. In their most profitable niche markets in the United States, Europe and Asia, the European banks faced fierce competition from the resurgent American and Asian banks. And in light of all this, wholesale money markets were increasingly leery about offering funding. A slow contraction of balance sheets was one thing. If funding markets shut down, Europe would face a repeat of 2008. Given that acute threat it was not without risk to openly address the long-term issues of the sector. But if the problem of recapitalization was not squarely faced, how would the banks ever be made safe?

In August 2011, as she established herself as managing director of the IMF, Christine Lagarde took up the baton that Strauss-Kahn had dropped

when he was carted off to Rikers Island jail. Already in 2009 IMF analysts had highlighted the inadequacy of European bank recapitalization.[17] Now, two years later, in light of the escalation of the eurozone sovereign debt crisis, the IMF estimated that the minimum the European banks needed was $267 billion in new capital.[18] It was a daunting challenge, but without it, all other crisis-fighting measures on the side of fiscal and monetary policy would lack a solid foundation. European political obfuscations were obscuring the basic lesson of 2008: Questions of macroeconomic policy and systemic stability could not be hygienically separated from the workings of megabanks, now more politely known as systemically important financial institutions.

The banks, of course, defended what they took to be their own interests. Never one to shrink from alarmism where bank regulations were concerned, the Institute of International Finance estimated that Basel III plus national regulations would force banks worldwide to raise their capital by $1.3 trillion by 2015.[19] It was a huge ask and many banks might simply prefer to shrink their balance sheets, flattening the fragile recovery. At the meeting of the Financial Stability Board on September 23 in Washington, Jamie Dimon of J.P. Morgan counterattacked. He condemned the new capital rules and challenged Mark Carney, the chairman of the Bank of Canada and head of the SFB, so violently that Lloyd Blankfein of Goldman Sachs felt it necessary to personally intercede.[20] Bizarrely, Dimon denounced the Basel III rules as anti-American, whereas, in fact, the pressure they placed on the Europeans was far more severe. Rather than raising capital, like their American counterparts, Europe's main lenders were deleveraging en masse, cutting the size of their loan business. On the basis of plans published by the banks themselves, analysts predicted a contraction of between 480 billion and 2 trillion euros. From the point of view of the regulators, this was exactly what was intended. The banks needed to "derisk." But it wasn't only a matter of corporate strategy. What was driving the contraction as much as anything else was the collapse in demand for loans. That spelled trouble ahead for the eurozone economy and it threatened a vicious circle in which a widening depression forced banks to make ever larger provisions for a new wave of nonperforming loans, further tightening pressure on their balance sheets.

Europe's Banks Under Pressure: Fall 2011 (in billions of euros)

	2008 legacy assets	PIIGS debt	Expected deleveraging
RBS	79.6	10.4	93–121
HSBC	54.3	14.6	83
Deutsche Bank	51.9	12.8	30–90
Crédit Agricole	28.2	16.7	17–50
Sociéte Générale	27.5	18.3	70–95
Commerzbank	23.8	19.8	31–188
Barclays	20.7	20.3	20
BNP Paribas	12.5	41.1	50–81

Note: PIIGS debt refers to holdings of Portuguese, Italian, Irish, Greek and Spanish sovereign debt.

Sources: Bank of England, *Financial Stability Report* 30 (December 2011), and http://www.fore castsandtrends.com/article.php/770/.

It was not the misery of youth unemployment in Spain and Greece that made the eurozone crisis into an object of global concern. The world would wake up late to what would be dubbed the "populist danger." In 2011 it was the prospect of European banking crisis that seized the attention of policy makers around the world. If the trillion-dollar balance sheets of the French, German, Swiss, Italian and Spanish banks were shaking, then the City of London and Wall Street would not be safe. And, as in 2008, the influence ran both ways. If the withdrawal of funding from American sources put the European banks under excessive pressure, they would drastically curtail their business in the United States. As William Dudley of the New York Fed later explained to Congress: "Money market mutual funds which were providing dollar funding to the European banks during the summer and fall [of 2011] were pulling back. Other lenders, large asset managers, were also pulling back from the European banks. And this was causing those banks to start to get out of their dollar book of business. . . . [T]his was going on at a pretty feverish pitch through the late fall and in through the early winter."[21] The panic was spreading to the American banks themselves. In the fall of 2011 the premium on American bank credit default swaps began to rise ominously.[22]

III

On the morning of September 16, 2011, Treasury Secretary Geithner flew to Warsaw to attend, for the first time, the monthly meeting of European finance ministers and central bankers. In his widely leaked remarks he apparently began on a humble note.[23] "Our politics are terrible, maybe worse than they are in many parts of Europe," he said. The debt ceiling battle had ended in Congress only six weeks earlier. "Given the damage we caused the world in the early stages of the financial crisis and given the challenges we have, we are not in a particularly strong position to provide advice to all of you, so I come with humility." But he then went on to insist that the "ongoing conflict" between Europe's governments and the ECB was "very damaging." "You have to, governments and the central banks have to, take out the catastrophic risk from markets." Austria's outspoken finance minister, Maria Fekter, later commented that the American Treasury secretary's tone had indeed been "very dramatic."[24] What Geithner proposed was standard American maximum-force firefighting doctrine. "The firewall you build has to be perceived as larger than the scale of the problem. You can't succeed by shrinking the problem to fit your current level of financial commitments. . . . It's more dangerous to escalate gradually and incrementally than with massive preemptive force." According to the Treasury's own estimates, the eurozone needed a fund of at least 1 trillion euros and preferably 1.5 trillion.[25] Picking up an idea launched by Mark Carney of the Bank of Canada and Philipp Hildebrand of the Swiss Central Bank, Geithner argued that the European Financial Stability Fund should be leveraged to give it sufficient firepower to act as a firewall.[26] The EFSF could borrow against the capital invested in it by Europe's governments. It was a neat solution, but controversial in Europe, particularly in Germany, because as it increased the fund's firepower, it also increased the liability for losses.

It was the Europeans who invited Geithner to Warsaw. But in the wake of the Wall Street crash of 2008 and the congressional budget crisis of July 2011, there was probably no moment in living memory in which Europe was less willing to listen to financial advice from America. Jean-Claude Juncker refused point-blank to discuss Geithner's bailout fund proposal

with a nonmember of the eurozone. Geithner stalked out of the encounter refusing comments to the press. As one New York analyst commented: "I'm not sure it's productive for Secretary Geithner to have gone to Poland given the European resentment towards the U.S. . . . I fear that it may cause Europeans to cut off their nose to spite their face."[27] That trivializing diagnosis was telling in its own right. But the rebuff to the United States was undeniable. On Geithner's return, the *New York Times* ran an unflattering piece contrasting the reception he had received with the triumphalism of the 1990s, when *Time* magazine had hailed his mentors—Greenspan, Summers and Rubin—as "The Committee to Save the World." In September 2011 Sheila C. Bair, Geithner's longtime nemesis as the chair of the FDIC, commented that the Treasury's advice might have been more compelling if it had come jointly from the United States and China, a point that the Chinese would make at the next G20 meeting.[28]

As the leaders of world finance convened in Washington for the annual IMF meeting at the end of September 2011, the mood was grim. The world's financial institutions were staring into "the abyss," they declared.[29] From the sidelines Larry Summers, recently retired from the White House, declared: "Now, when these problems have the potential to disrupt growth around the world, all nations have an obligation to insist that Europe find a viable way forward."[30] The Europeans could not go on pretending that all that was at stake were matters of eurozone governance. The G20 premeeting issued a communiqué stressing that, in the face of the ongoing eurozone crisis, "[w]e commit to take all necessary actions to preserve the stability of banking systems and financial markets as required." Geithner and his British counterpart George Osborne combined to demand an end to Europe's "political crisis." The emphasis on politics was telling. Canada's finance minister expressed incredulity that the global gatherings had been talking about Greece since January 2010.[31] Geithner warned of a "cascading default, bank runs and catastrophic risk" if Europe failed to build a big enough firewall. Lagarde, from her new vantage point in Washington, insisted that there was still "a path to recovery," but "much narrower than before, and getting narrower."[32] And yet a week *after* the IMF meeting, the EFSF plan that Merkel would squeeze through the Bundestag was undersized, and Finance Minister Schäuble publicly denied any plan to increase

it by means of leverage. The Europeans, and the Germans in particular, still did not "get it."

In the first week of October, as if to demonstrate that the dark talk in Washington was not merely alarmism, a run began on the Franco-Belgian bank Dexia, one of the casualties of 2008 that was most exposed to peripheral eurozone debt.[33] Once again the European Banking Authority had embarrassed itself. Over the summer Dexia had passed the third European stress test with flying colors. A postmortem revealed that the stress tests had failed to account adequately for losses resulting from a restructuring of Greek debt. Furthermore, they had ignored altogether the issue of liquidity. In 2008 it had been collateral calls that triggered the disaster at Lehman and AIG. In 2011 they did the same to Dexia.[34] The bank had contracted a huge portfolio of interest rate swaps on which it now faced demands for tens of billions of euros in collateral. The Belgian and French governments were forced into an expensive bailout at the worst possible moment. Given the potential impact on French public debt, the governor of the Banque de France, Christian Noyer, was forced to deny claims that France's credit rating might be in jeopardy.[35]

Meanwhile, from the other side of the Atlantic came news of trouble at the high-profile brokerage firm MF Global. American regulators had ordered MF Global to boost its net capital to cover against the multibillion-dollar position it had built in Irish, Spanish, Italian and Portuguese sovereign bonds. Inverting the legendary big short position that speculators had built against mortgage-backed securities in 2007, MF Global had taken a "big long" in eurozone sovereign debt. It was gambling that other investors were underrating the stability of the eurozone and the value of peripheral bonds. As institutional investors like pension and insurance funds and banks offloaded their eurozone securities, it was MF Global that bought them up. As had been true in the case of the big short, there was a race between market sentiment and the ability of the contrarian investor to stay liquid. In October 2011 time ran out on MF Global. The regulator's call for more capital triggered inquiries into its balance sheets and revealed that to tide it over in the face of huge market pressure it had been dipping into client funds. By the end of October one of the most high-profile investors betting that the eurozone did indeed have a future collapsed.[36]

It was a bitter irony that it was precisely as MF Global filed for protection that the eurozone finally began to take steps toward a more decisive resolution of the crisis. On October 23 the European leaders held a gathering to sketch the outlines of yet another stabilization plan. It involved deep debt restructuring, new loans for Greece, an expansion of the EFSF, bank recapitalization— finally, all the elements of a solution were on the table. Indeed, the issues were beginning to be monotonously familiar. That, however, did not mean that the way forward was obvious or politically easy. On October 26 Merkel addressed the Bundestag to tell them that the expansion of the EFSF they had voted to approve a month earlier had not been enough and that the fund might, after all, need to be leveraged.[37] On the promise that under all circumstances Germany's liability would remain capped at 211 billion euros, Merkel again got the majority she needed. With Germany at least formally on board, European leaders assembled for a second time in Brussels on the afternoon of October 26 to finalize the third rescue package for Greece.

Composition and Estimated Bond Holdings of Creditor Committee (in billions of euros)

Steering Committee Members		Further Members of the Creditor Committee			
Allianz (Germany)	1.3	Ageas (Belgium)	1.2	MACSF (France)	na
Alpha Eurobank (Greece)	3.7	Bank of Cyprus	1.8	Marathon (US)	na
Axa (France)	1.9	Bayern LB (Germany)	na	Marfin (Greece)	2.3
BNP Paribas (France)	5.0	BBVA (Spain)	na	MetLife (US)	na
CNP Assurances (France)	2.0	BPCE (France)	1.2	Piraeus (Greece)	9.4
Commerzbank (Germany)	2.9	Crédit Agricole (France)	0.6	RBS (UK)	1.1
Deutsche Bank (Germany)	1.6	DekaBank (Germany)	na	Société Gén. (France)	2.9
Greylock Capital (US)	na	Dexia (Belg/Lux/Fra)	3.5	UniCredit (Italy)	0.9
Intesa San Paolo (Italy)	0.8	Emporiki (Greece)	na		
LBB BW (Germany)	1.4	Generali (Italy)	3.0		
ING (France)	1.4	Groupama (France)	2.0		
National Bank of Greece	13.7	HSBC (UK)	0.8		

Notes: Estimates of bond holdings refer to June 2011, creditor committee composition to December 2011.

Source: Jeromin Zettelmeyer, Christoph Trebesch and Mitu Gulati, "The Greek Debt Restructuring: An Autopsy," *Economic Policy* 28, no. 75 (2013): 513–563.

This time PSI would be the cornerstone of the entire deal. The haircut would be deep. Banks and their shareholders would have to recognize tens of billions of euros in losses. Rumor had it that the Germans were pushing for 60 percent. The creditors, negotiating from offices in the basement of the EU's Justus Lipsius building, held out for less, and they were a powerful group. Despite the ongoing sell-off of peripheral bond assets, in 2011 all the major banks of France, Germany and Italy still held Greek bonds. So too did Greece's own banks, major insurance funds and American hedge funds.

To shift this weighty coalition of financial interests it took not only financial inducements but also a forceful personal intervention by Merkel and Sarkozy. At 4:04 a.m. on the morning of October 27, a deal on "voluntary bond exchange" at 50 percent was announced.[38] The plan promised to reduce Greece's debt below 120 percent of GDP. To tide it over Greece was to receive another 130 billion euros in funding, bringing the total in emergency loans it had received since 2010 to 240 billion euros, or more than 100 percent of Greek GDP. To contain the fallout from this momentous decision, all other euro area member states solemnly reaffirmed "their inflexible determination to honour fully their own individual sovereign signature." The EFSF was to be boosted to close to 1.2 trillion euros by means of leverage or by using its resources not to make loans directly but as an insurance fund to cover losses on private securities. And Europe's banks were expected to recapitalize to the tune of 106 billion euros, though it was left up to them how they raised the funds. At last, Europe had produced a package that at least in outline recognized the fundamentals of the problem. Debt reduction, recapitalization and backstopping were the keys. The questions of who would pay and how exactly the EFSF would be equipped still had to be settled, but before those essential technical issues could be broached, Europe had to deal with the political fallout.

IV

By the end of October 2011, after two years of economic disaster and financial panic, the Greek political system was coming apart. Unemployment now stood at 19.7 percent, up from 8 percent in 2008. The public mood was

ugly. Since the onset of the crisis the Greek opposition—on both the left and right—had consistently refused to join with the government in facing the demand of the foreign creditors. The entire disastrous austerity program had been conducted on the strength of the majority that PASOK had won in October 2009. The party was paying the price. In the third week of October giant demonstrations across Greece challenged the latest round of cuts. The strikes were unprecedentedly wide-ranging. "[T]rash collectors, teachers, retired army officers, lawyers and even judges walked off the job."[39] A member of the Communist party was killed in clashes with the police. On October 28, the day of commemoration of national resistance, the venerable president of the republic Karolos Papoulias, himself a partisan veteran, was howled down by protesters in Thessaloniki. Seeking to regain the initiative, on the evening of October 31 Prime Minister Papandreou convened a meeting of his party and announced that it was time to call the majority of the Greek people into action and to shame the opposition into supporting the measures dictated by the troika.[40] There would be a referendum— yes/no on the EU's latest debt restructuring and austerity program.

It was a reasonable political move on Papandreou's part, but did Greece still have the kind of freedom of maneuver a referendum implied? The complex deal that had been announced in the early hours of October 27 was the result of months of agonizing discussion between Paris and Berlin, Brussels, the ECB and the IIF representing creditors from around the world. Merkel had twice whipped the Bundestag. The July 21 plan had been ratified by every parliament in Europe. Now, without prior warning, the Greek premier was adding a further democratic hurdle. Markets aside, how were the other parliaments to react? What if the Greek voters rejected the proposal? Merkel, at least, had been given some prior intimation of Papandreou's gamble. But October 31 was the first that Paris had heard of it and Sarkozy was incandescent. The Greeks were putting the entire stabilization package in doubt and France knew that it was no longer safe. On November 2 Papandreou was summoned to the G20 meeting in Cannes, not a forum to which Greece was normally invited, to explain himself.[41]

At a press conference in Cannes Sarkozy and Merkel laid down the law: If there was to be a referendum there could be only one question: "in or out" of the eurozone. "Our Greek friends must decide whether they want to

continue the journey with us. . . . We want them to stay inside the euro, but they must obey the rules." Otherwise, they would receive "not a single cent" from French and German taxpayers. In fact, the majority of the Greek political class and Barroso as commission president judged the proposition of a monthlong referendum campaign far too risky. On November 3–4, in side meetings at Cannes, Merkel and Sarkozy maneuvered with the Greek opposition and Papandreou's ambitious finance minister, Evangelos Venizelos, to abort the referendum proposal and end Papandreou's premiership. Papandreou was replaced by a safe technocratic pair of hands, Lucas Papademos. The new Greek prime minister was an American-trained economist and central banker, a former vice president at the ECB.[42]

But the real stuff of the Cannes meeting, once the Greeks were hammered into line, was the search for a fix for Italy. If the worst came to the worst Greece could be let go. Italy had to be stabilized. In a preemptive move to restore confidence, the IMF had proposed an 80-billion-euro precautionary program that would come with such tight financial provisions that it would rob Berlusconi of any wiggle room.[43] Berlusconi refused the role assigned to him. The only public result that emerged from Cannes was an agreement by Rome to accept IMF monitoring on a voluntary basis, as a matter of pride and self-vindication, but not as the condition on a loan. Indeed, Berlusconi let it be known that he had rejected an offer of IMF money. Italy thus got the worst of all worlds: the stigma of having been considered for an IMF program and the duress of oversight, without access to new money.

This, at the time, appeared to be the dispiriting upshot of the Cannes conference: the removal of the Greek prime minister, deadlocked negotiations, no aid for Italy and a further faux pas by Berlusconi. Three years later it emerged that something far more dramatic had transpired. Lagarde's Italian proposal was a sideshow. The real news was that Paris and Berlin were maneuvering to unseat the Italian prime minister. As Geithner put it in transcripts compiled for his memoirs: "The Europeans actually approach us softly, indirectly before the thing [Cannes meeting] saying: 'we basically want you to join us in forcing Berlusconi out.' They wanted us to basically say that we wouldn't support IMF money or any further escalation for Italy, if they needed it, if Berlusconi was prime minister. It was cool,

interesting."[44] Geithner could not hide his approval of the basic idea: "I really actually felt, I thought what Sarkozy and Merkel were doing was basically right which is: this wasn't going to work. Germany, the German public were not going to support, like, a bigger financial firewall, more money for Europe, if Berlusconi was presiding over that country." Unfortunately, a further page of Geithner's candid observations was redacted. In his memoirs, Geithner says that he informed the president of this "surprising invitation" from Europe, but concluded, "[W]e couldn't get involved in a scheme like that. 'We can't have [Berlusconi's] blood on our hands,'" Geithner told the president.[45]

But whether the White House accepted the "suprising invitation" or not, Berlusconi's days in office were numbered. His government was disintegrating from within. The Northern League was refusing to cooperate in the changes to the pension system demanded by the rest of Europe and the IMF. Finance Minister Tremonti was pushing for Berlusconi to resign.[46] Already in mid-October, Angela Merkel had made phone calls directly to the Italian president, Giorgio Napolitano, to explore alternatives.[47] Napolitano, a longtime PCI apparatchik—Henry Kissinger's favorite Eurocommunist—had agreed that it was "his duty . . . to verify the conditions" of Italy's "social and political forces." By November 12, with his coalition crumbling, Berlusconi lost a vote of confidence in parliament and resigned. What the "condition" of Italy's "social and political forces" apparently demanded was rule by technocrat. The man who recommended himself was Professor Mario Monti.[48] Like the new Greek prime minister, he had a background as an academic economist with exposure to the United States. As European commissioner for internal market and then for competition between 1995 and 2004, he acquired the nickname "the Italian Prussian." After leaving the commission, Monti served as international adviser to Coca-Cola and Goldman Sachs and founded Bruegel, Europe's most influential think tank.[49] In 2011 he was summoned from his position as president of Bocconi University to become Italy's prime minister. To make this elevation to the head of government possible, Monti, who held no elected office, received from Napolitano the honorary position of "life senator."

In mid-November the governments of two eurozone members were taken over by men without democratic credentials whose main qualification

was that they were undeniably market conforming.[50] Critics pounced on the web of connections that tied key eurozone decision makers to Goldman Sachs and its bond market dealings in Europe.[51] It was surely more than coincidence that Monti, Draghi and Otmar Issing, Merkel's favorite economic adviser, had all worked for Goldman. But to describe this simply as a defeat of democracy at the hands of global markets would be misleading, to say the least. There have been many governments felled by market pressure. But Geithner was right. The driving force in the eurozone in the fall of 2011 was political, not economic. Berlusconi had to go because otherwise there would be no agreement from the "German public," at least as represented by Merkel's government, to a bigger European firewall. The gutting of Greek and Italian democracy in 2011 was the result of a toxic combination of massive financial integration with Berlin's dogged insistence on intergovernmentalism. The lack of overarching structures with which to compensate for the asymmetric effects of the crisis enforced conformity to Berlin's vision of financial probity, one state at a time. Around the chancellery in Berlin, in the wake of the changes in Greece and Italy they were not bemoaning the oppressive force of markets. Senior officials could be heard boasting: "We do regime change better than the Americans."[52]

But the twisted logic of the crisis was far from fully played out. Installing "Prussians" at the head of two of the most dangerously indebted eurozone countries no doubt made Merkel and Schäuble more comfortable. But as far as the markets were concerned, the character of the national governments in Italy and Greece was a secondary concern. What the markets and the rest of the G20 were waiting for was the next step: a decisive move toward a higher level of European integration. What was needed was a decision on the EFSF, and that depended not on Greece or Italy but on overcoming Germany's objections to a larger stabilization fund.

No eurozone member could risk a direct showdown with Berlin, and Merkel knew it. So it came as a nasty surprise for the German delegation at Cannes when at 9:30 in the evening on November 4 Sarkozy called the heads of government back for a conference on the Italian question, and it was not the French president but President Obama who was in the chair. As one member of the German delegation commented to the *Financial Times*: "It was strange. . . . It was . . . a signal that Europe was not able to do that; it

was a sign of weakness."[53] It would have been closer to the truth to say that it was a sign of Germany's strength and stubbornness. Sarkozy ceded the chairmanship to Obama in the hope that America's weight and influence would be enough to overcome Germany's political and legal objections to the solution the eurozone desperately needed. As Obama put it: "Our preference in the US is that the ECB should act a bit like the Federal Reserve." In other words, the ECB should calm the markets by buying bonds. If that was vetoed by the Bundesbank because it blurred the line between fiscal and monetary policy, what Europe needed was a truly massive government-backed bond-buying fund with in excess of 1 trillion euros in effective purchasing power, ideally in excess of 1.5 trillion. Given the limitations of the existing EFSF, the Americans and the French proposed an improvisation that would involve topping up the fund with SDRs issued by the IMF and then leveraging the enlarged pot. It was a neat technical fix, but the subterfuge was too obvious. The Bundesbank would not agree to a plan that transferred huge influence to the EFSF by way of the IMF, entities over which it had no direct influence.[54] Even Obama's pressure was not enough. Merkel offered that if Italy agreed to be disciplined by the IMF, she could go back to the Bundestag to get authorization to approve an increase in the eurozone rescue fund. But she could not agree to the leveraged SDR fix. Even if all nineteen other members of the G20 backed by every financial authority in the world insisted that this was the best way forward, if the Bundesbank was against it, Merkel would rather let markets rip.

At the time, the G20 did no more than record the negative result of the meeting. A discreet veil was drawn over the details of the discussions. No one doubted where the obstacle lay. It was only several years later that investigative reporting established how close Merkel had come to a physical collapse under the pressure exerted on her by Obama and Sarkozy. On the verge of tears she blurted out, "That is not fair. I cannot decide in lieu of the Bundesbank: *Ich will mich nicht selbst umbringen* [I do not want to kill myself]. I am not going to take such a big risk without getting anything from Italy."[55] Behind closed doors there was no more talk of globalization, democracy and markets, the abstractions that Merkel had bandied about with the pope. What defined the parameters of an acceptable solution to the eurozone crisis was the constitution of the Federal Republic, the autonomy

of its central bank and the political interests of the German center-right. If the Americans found this frustrating, Merkel expostulated, they had no one to blame but themselves. It was they who had created the embryo of the Bundesbank in 1948 as the founding institution of West Germany. At Cannes in November 2011, it was as if the entire transatlantic settlement since World War II were being put in play.

Merkel was not playacting. She knew how narrow her coalition's majority was. If she had returned to Berlin with the Franco-American proposal, she might well have faced a major mutiny on the Right and the need for early elections. Given the opinion polls at the time, that was not an attractive option for Merkel. With support for her FDP coalition partners collapsing, a German election at the end of 2011 might well have yielded a majority for Red-Green.[56] That was not the outcome to the eurozone crisis that Sarkozy wanted. Given the pressure that France was coming under, Paris was in no mood to take risks. The French and Americans backed off.

V

The showdown in Cannes in November 2011 was an indication of how serious the stresses on Europe had become. But it left the eurozone stuck on the German roadblock and divided over its future direction. At the ECB, which the hard-line Bundesbankers had abandoned in protest, the German seat was taken by Jörg Asmussen, a market-orientated but pragmatic civil servant with social democratic leanings, very much in the Rubin-Summers-Orszag mode, one of the architects of German financial globalization under Germany's Red-Green coalition in the early 2000s. Having witnessed the workings of the ECB and the G20 up close, he commented on the cruel dilemma he faced: "Either you do what is right for Europe and they crucify you in Germany or you are the hero of the FAZ [the conservative *Frankfurter Allgemeine Zeitung* newspaper] and you ruin Europe."[57]

The tension could be felt even inside such a major financial actor as Deutsche Bank. Among the financial blogging community a PowerPoint deck was circulating that showed Deutsche's Anglophone and London-based research department worrying that the eurozone had reached a dangerous

tipping point, from which only urgent action by the ECB could save it. Without such intervention, Europe might face a doom loop of public and private insolvency and illiquidity.[58] As in Greece, bad sovereign debts would pull down the banks. Or as in Ireland, failed banks would pull down the state's credit. Only the ECB could break this loop. It was the "missing ingredient" in all European crisis management efforts to date. Meanwhile, from Deutsche Bank's head office in Frankfurt, *Der Spiegel* quoted CEO Josef Ackermann toeing the Bundesbank line.[59] "If we start developing the ECB into a bank that performs completely different tasks beyond maintaining price stability," Deutsche's boss opined, "we will lose people's confidence." He was at odds with his own analysts and those of every other major bank in the Anglosphere, but in Germany it was Ackermann's line that was the mainstream. The chief economist of insurance giant Allianz advised "strongly against unlimited purchases of government bonds." If a country was unable to sort out its finances, he said, "we should let the markets speak." The chief economist of Commerzbank, Jörg Krämer, warned that if "the virus of mistrust spreads to the ECB, it will have serious consequences." ECB bond purchases permanently transferred wealth from Northern to Southern Europe, "without democratic legitimization and without the debt problems being solved." Meanwhile, even Germany was no longer immune to the virus of insecurity. On November 23, 2011, the Bund suffered a bond auction that was described by market watchers as a "complete and utter disaster," with only 3.644 billion out of 6 billion euros' worth of German ten-year bonds finding buyers.[60]

Some direction was clearly needed in the eurozone. And it could only come from Berlin. The point was made with historic force by Poland's foreign minister, Radek Sikorski, an Oxford-educated former journalist. Speaking on November 28, 2011, choosing as his platform the German Council on Foreign Relations in Berlin, Sikorski demanded "that Germany—read Merkel—step up and lead. If she did so, Poland would be at her side."[61] In his view the greatest threat to the security and prosperity of Poland today was "not terrorism, it's not the Taliban, and it's certainly not German tanks. It's not even Russian missiles," which Moscow had just threatened to deploy along the EU's eastern border. In Sikorski's view the most ominous scenario was a collapse of the eurozone, which would no doubt take the

weaker states on the eurozone's periphery with it. And Sikorski went on: "I demand of Germany that, for your own sake and for ours, you help it survive and prosper. You know full well that nobody else can do it. I will probably be the first Polish foreign minister in history to say so, but here it is: I fear German power less than I am beginning to fear German inactivity. You have become Europe's indispensable nation. You may not fail to lead."

A month on from Cannes, in the first week of December 2011, two visions of Europe's future were circulating in Brussels.[62] What Merkel and Sarkozy subscribed to was an updated version of the agenda first agreed at Deauville in 2010: fiscal discipline written into domestic law and international agreements. For France it offered the safety of association with Germany. Merkel, for her part, needed Sarkozy to counter allegations of German unilateralism. But in light of the widening and escalation of the crisis in 2011 it could not but appear a minimal and essentially negative agenda. In their joint letter to the European Council in early December, Merkel and Sarkozy made no commitments on bank recapitalization and no mention of the simmering crisis in the sovereign bond market. On the most optimistic reading, the Merkel-Sarkozy fiscal compact was the essential political precondition for Germany to take further steps. But in Brussels the push was now on to actually take those steps. On December 7 Van Rompuy, the president of the European Council, published his "interim report." Though the European Council was supposed to be the guardian of the minimal intergovernmental vision of the Lisbon Treaty, under the pressure of the crisis Van Rompuy was now calling for bold moves. He proposed a major increase in the financial firepower of the EFSF/ESM. It should be available, in extreme cases, to recapitalize Europe's ailing banks, thus breaking the doom loop. And to back it up, in a "longer term perspective," Van Rompuy called for the EU to face the need for debt mutualization. Limited by strict criteria and all necessary European oversight, there should be some pooling of European credit, shielding the weaker members behind the creditworthiness of the stronger borrowers, thus eliminating the element of market panic that was making the situation of Italy untenable. Some version of these steps was what the entire G20 was calling for. It was what progressive voices in Europe were advocating. Indeed, the idea of eurobonds was attracting the cautious backing of the German opposition, the SPD. But for

Merkel, and in particular for her coalition partners, the FDP, they were anathema. And to add further to German indignation, whereas Sarkozy and Merkel's fiscal compact was to be instituted by solemn amendment of EU treaties, Van Rompuy proposed that his more far-reaching measures could be put through by so-called secondary legislation and limited agreement among the eurozone members. For Berlin it was clear. Brussels was up to its usual "tricks."

At this critical juncture another force came into play to compound the impasse. Aside from Poland, the other major EU member not in the eurozone was the UK. London had watched the eurozone crisis unfold with a mixture of Schadenfreude and frustration.[63] On every possible occasion Prime Minister Cameron lectured the eurozone members on the need for deeper integration, while at the same time exempting London from any commitments. For the good of Europe, Britain and the wider world economy, London demanded that the eurozone move toward full economic union. Meanwhile, for Cameron, struggling to contain an upsurge of Euroscepticism in the Tory party, Europe's crisis was an opportunity to haggle. By exploiting the divisions within the eurozone, Cameron thought he could obtain explicit opt-outs for the City of London, especially from demands for a tax on financial transactions. But any such concessions were violently opposed by Sarkozy, and Merkel needed France far more than she needed the UK. When he realized that he was isolated, Cameron announced that he would not only veto a collective deal among the twenty-seven EU members.[64] He would exercise his right to block any steps toward deeper integration by the eurozone members within the framework of the EU.

For Britain's relationship to the EU it was a parting of the ways. It was clear that at least as far as Britain's conservatives were concerned, a decision would soon be necessary on whether they could continue as cooperative members of the union. For the eurozone what emerged from the clashes of early December 2011 was the lowest common denominator of both options on offer. Germany got its fiscal compact, although it was cast not in the form of the treaty change that Merkel had wanted but in the minimal legal form of an intergovernmental agreement outside the framework of the Lisbon Treaty.[65] The terms of the fiscal compact were draconian. In the future, Europe's budgets were to be balanced or in surplus. By constitutional

amendment or its equivalent, deficits were to be restricted to 0.5 percent of GDP. The European Court of Justice was to oversee the transposition of these rules at a national level. States that had a deficit in excess of 3 percent of GDP would be subject to automatic sanctions unless a qualified majority of states were opposed. Countries with debt levels in excess of 60 percent of GDP were required to embark on debt reduction. It was the German debt brake vision transposed to the European level. On the broader issue of completing the eurozone's architecture, Merkel conceded nothing. There would be no shared liability for European borrowing, no eurobonds, no bank recapitalization and no increase in the size of the EFSF/ESM. The only concession from Berlin was that as of July 2012 the improvised EFSF would be replaced by a permanent European Stability Mechanism with the power to intervene in secondary bond markets and the adequacy of the EU's firewall would be reassessed as soon as March 2012. Berlin also agreed to lay the ghosts of Deauville to rest by limiting any future PSI to standards set by the IMF. Despite the intensity of the Italian crisis and the drama at Cannes, it was still Germany that set the pace.

With intergovernmentalism resulting in such minimal and essentially negative solutions, would the one powerful federal agency of the eurozone, the ECB, rise to the challenge? All eyes were on Mario Draghi, who had taken over as president of the ECB on November 1, 2011. At the Treasury in Rome in the 1990s, he had been a crucial member of the team that carried Italy into the euro. Since 2006 he had been in the spotlight as governor of the Bank of Italy. Before that he had served as a vice chairman at Goldman Sachs, following a stint at the World Bank. He had earned his Ph.D. in economics in the cradle of American macroeconomics, MIT, in the 1970s at the same time as Ben Bernanke and Lucas Papademos, who was now serving as Greek prime minister. At MIT, Mervyn King of the Bank of England and Bernanke had been office mates. Between them the central banking fraternity at least had an immediate answer to the problems facing Europe's financial system. The banks were under enormous pressure from the withdrawal of wholesale funding, and the shortage of dollar funding was particularly acute. It was horribly reminiscent of 2008. To relieve the funding pressures caused by the withdrawal of the American money market funds, the Bank of France, among others, had resorted to

emergency measures to make dollars available to French banks.[66] Now, on November 30, all the major central banks of the world—the Fed, the ECB, the Bank of England, the Bank of Japan, the Swiss National Bank and the Bank of Canada—reopened the swap lines put in place in 2008 and reduced the interest rate paid. The global reach of the deal was "theatre"; Japanese and Canadian banks were not under any pressure. It was, once more, the eurozone that needed the dollars.[67]

In the summer of 2012 Mario Draghi would emerge as the "savior of the euro." As such he would be demonized as an Italian inflationist by the German right wing and celebrated by the Anglophone world as a competent central banker. But what this narrative ignores is that Draghi's ability to change the conversation in the summer of 2012 had one essential precondition: backing from Berlin. Commonly the strength of Draghi's relationship with Merkel is put down to Draghi's finesses as a politician.[68] But this passes over the fact that though German hard-liners opposed all activism by Europe's central bank, for Merkel the ECB had been a useful tool from the start. She had done it quietly, but on several occasions she had effectively distanced herself from the Bundesbank, recognizing that ECB intervention was the necessary complement to the decade-long process of transferring Germany's vision of "reform" to the rest of Europe. Despite the howls of protest from the German right wing, Merkel knew she could count on Europe's central bankers. She had nothing to fear from a fiscal and monetary conservative like Trichet. Draghi was suitable as a partner precisely because he showed every sign of agreeing with Germany's vision of how to revise the European welfare state.[69] Indeed, that was as much part of Draghi's identity as an American-trained economist and Goldman Sachs alumnus, as was his expansive view of central bank policy.

As Draghi reminded the readers of the *Financial Times* shortly after taking over at the ECB, he was a veteran of Italy's tough stabilization efforts of the 1990s.[70] In August 2011 Draghi cosigned Trichet's ultimatum to Berlusconi demanding changes to Italy's public services and labor markets. Draghi shared with his predecessor both the frustration over Rome's evasiveness and the foot dragging of the rest of Europe's governments. On December 1, 2011, Draghi marked the beginning of his ECB presidency by appearing before the European Parliament to throw his weight behind the

Merkel-Sarkozy plan for fiscal discipline.[71] And his sympathy with German demands for "reform" was unfeigned. As Draghi told the *Wall Street Journal* in February 2012, Europe's social model that prioritized job security and social welfare was "already gone." What, after all, did talk of a social model mean when 50 percent of Spanish youth were unemployed?[72] Europe's labor markets would have to be reinvented, presumably along the lines of Germany's Hartz IV agenda. In his grad student days at MIT in the 1970s, Draghi recalled, his American professors had marveled at Europe's willingness to "pay everybody for not working. That's gone." For the new head of the ECB there was "no feasible trade-off" between labor market reform and fiscal austerity. "Backtracking on fiscal targets would elicit an immediate reaction by the market," and Draghi made clear that he had no intention of softening that discipline. In December 2011 in conversation with the *Financial Times*, he refused to discuss putting the ECB behind the EFSF as the ultimate guarantor of the EU's firewall. Nor would he countenance talk of QE for Europe. He started his term in office by insisting that Trichet's bond-buying program, the securities market program, was neither "eternal nor infinite."[73] Indeed, given Draghi's subsequent reputation, it bears repeating that as of 2012, his first year in office, bond buying by the ECB ceased. His priority was to restore a "system where the citizens will go back to trusting each other and where governments are trusted on fiscal discipline and structural reforms."

What Draghi was willing to do immediately was to prop up the banks.[74] The swap lines were one mechanism. Another was to revive the ECB's familiar device of cheap bank funding. With credit markets spooked, in 2009 and 2010 Europe's banks had been forced to resort to increasingly short-term funding sources, which now needed to be rolled over. If they could not find new funding the eurozone was threatened by a major credit crunch.[75] Already in October 2011 the ECB had announced that it would be offering liquidity to the European banking system in the form of the long-term refinancing operation (LTRO)—long-term loans at highly favorable interest rates.[76] Draghi opened the spigot, offering financing at favorable rates over the unprecedentedly long term of three years and taking much lower grades of collateral.[77] On December 21, 2011, 523 banks took 489 billion euros in funding. In February there were 800 takers for another 500 billion. Of

the first tranche of the LTRO, 65 percent went to banks in the stressed periphery—Italy, Spain, Ireland and Greece.

Though Draghi hastened to explain that this was "obviously not at all an equivalent to the ECB stepping-up bond buying," in due course the trillion euros in LTRO loans would feed back into bank purchases of sovereign debt.[78] This raised demand in bond markets and lowered yields. It supported the sovereign debt market. It allowed banks to earn easy profits on the spread between the 1 percent charged by the ECB and the 5 percent on offer for those willing to hold Italian government bonds.[79] But as in 2009, it came at a price. Rather than allowing Europe's fragile banks to unload dubious assets in exchange for safe cash, as QE did in the United States, the ECB's program added to their holdings of peripheral government debt.[80] Spanish and Italian banks were particularly proactive. Banks and sovereigns were thus tied ever more closely together. And neither side was safe. On January 14 S&P conducted a review of its European sovereign ratings and downgraded seven of them. France and Austria lost their prized AAA rating. Portugal was reduced to "junk." Within the eurozone only Germany, the Netherlands, Finland and Luxembourg retained their coveted AAA rating. Even the eurozone's own bailout fund, the EFSF/ESM, was at risk of a downgrade. The Europeans protested, as had Washington following its downgrade by S&P, but this time the ratings agency was firm in its judgment. Months of negotiations had "not produced a breakthrough of sufficient size" to warrant optimism about the eurozone's future.[81] Despite the Sturm und Drang of the fall of 2011, the political impasse had not been broken. Control of the timeline was everything, and Berlin set the pace. At the G20, outside the Cannes Palais des Festivals on November 5, Merkel had opined: "The debt crisis will not be solved all in one go, [and] it is certain that it will take us a decade to get back to a better position."[82] That was revealing as to Germany's time horizon, but the question was, did the rest of Europe have that long?

Chapter 18

WHATEVER IT TAKES

In the first half of 2012 the rotating presidency of the G20 fell to Mexico. On Friday, January 20, 2012, a week after the S&P downgrade of eurozone sovereigns, finance officials from around the world assembled in Mexico City. On their agenda was a remarkable request. The eurozone members of the G20 were calling on the rest of the world to contribute $300–400 billion in additional funding to enable the IMF to backstop crisis fighting, not in an emerging market or in one of the less-developed countries of sub-Saharan Africa but in Europe. The non-European members of the G20, led by the United States, China and Brazil, considered the European request and turned it down. As Mexico's deputy finance minister remarked to the press: "There is a recognition of the measures Europe has taken. But it's also clear that more needs to be done."[1]

Amid the din of world events, the incident barely warranted a headline. But the location of the meeting, the nature of the request and the response by the rest of the G20 add up to a remarkable historical denouement. It was also indicative of the precarious state in which the eurozone was left hanging by the bruising battles of 2011. The G20 and S&P concurred: The Europeans had not done enough. They had not squarely addressed the basic instabilities with regard to the sovereign bond market and bank recapitalization, which had sucked the IMF into its engagement in Europe back in 2010. They had eventually recognized Greece's insolvency and were on the point of pushing through a debt restructuring. That was essential, but

haircutting Greece's creditors served only to increase pressure in bond markets. In political terms, Europe had satisfied the German insistence on austerity, which Berlin promised would open the door to further steps toward integration. But December 2011 revealed how reluctant Berlin was to actually make the next move. Meanwhile, the consensus that had been built around austerity policies in 2010 was beginning to crumble.

The European fiscal compact of December 2011 was imposed by force of Franco-German cooperation. But Sarkozy was up for reelection in May 2012, and his main rivals for the presidency, the Socialists, were campaigning against the agreement. That was predictable. What was less so was that the IMF itself would be calling for a rethink. In its briefing for the full meeting of finance ministers and central bank governors that would convene in Mexico City on February 25–26, 2012, the IMF's headline was stark. The "overarching risk" to the world economy was of an intensified global "paradox of thrift." As households, firms and governments around the world all tried to cut their deficits at once, there was an acute risk of global recession. "This risk is further exacerbated," the IMF went on, "by fragile financial systems, high public deficits and debt, and already-low interest rates, making the current environment fertile ground for multiple equilibria—self-perpetuating outcomes resulting from pessimism or optimism, notably in the euro area."[2] The place where the paradoxes of thrift were most visible was Greece.

I

In the protracted struggle to get to the October 2011 debt deal for Greece, the entire discussion had revolved around the Greek budget and concessions to be made by its creditors. The 50 percent haircut had been forced through in the hope of getting Greece to a debt level of 120 percent of GDP. From there, according to the mandatory fiscal adjustment procedure specified in Sarkozy and Merkel's fiscal compact, it would be possible to get Greece down to a debt ratio of 60 percent of GDP, the target originally specified in the Maastricht Treaty. The fiscal arithmetic was pleasing, but what it ignored were the feedback loops highlighted by the IMF. The problem in

achieving debt sustainability was Greece's collapsing GDP as much as it was its elevated debt level. By the time of the discussions in Mexico in early 2012, it was clear that the deal hammered out three months earlier was no longer viable, not because the Greek government or the creditors were reneging but because the Greek economy was contracting too fast.[3]

For many European governments, at this point enough was enough. They could not ask their parliaments to consider yet another Greek rescue. It was time to consider more radical options. Rather than trying to manage a negotiated restructuring, perhaps it would be better to leave Greece to its fate. An outright default might result in Greece tumbling out of the eurozone. But Greece would at least be free of its debts. And if new borrowing was shut off, Athens would be forced to adopt fiscal discipline as a matter of sheer survival. It was in early 2012 that top-secret planning began for the eventuality of a Grexit.[4] Work on the so-called Plan Z would continue until August 2012, when it was finally stopped by Berlin. It was stopped because the upshot of the planning exercises was always the same. It would likely be ruinous for Greece, and the ramifications of Grexit for the rest of Europe were entirely unpredictable. They were unpredictable because Europe still had not built an adequate shield to protect the other fragile eurozone members from the fallout from a Greek bankruptcy. It was to reinforce and extend that inadequate safety net that the Europeans were applying to the G20 to support an expanded IMF facility. But the G20's answer was clear. The rest of the world would regard Grexit as a failure not just of Greece, but also on the part of the larger European states that pretended to global standing as members of the G20. On February 19, 2012, Japan and China, in a rare show of unity, declared that they were willing to back the appeal for increased IMF funding, but only if the Europeans raised the cap on the ESM stability mechanism, to which the Bundestag was clinging.[5] The Europeans must help themselves first.

The ESM expansion would come at the end of March.[6] Berlin blocked any truly dramatic move. But by counting the money already disbursed to Greece, allowing the EFSF facilities to continue and raising the combined lending limit of EFSF and ESM to 700 billion euros, Europe could claim that it was mobilizing a firewall of 800 billion euros or "more than USD 1 trillion." It was a fudge that allowed the IMF board to sign off on continued

support for Europe's stabilization efforts. But what no one in Europe wanted to do in early 2012 was to renegotiate the Greek deal of October 2011.[7] The governments had committed 130 billion euros and that was the limit. If Greece was sliding further away from sustainability, it was up to the Greek government to make further savings, and up to the creditors to make further concessions. A new round of negotiations with the IIF began in February, which yielded an increase in the haircut from 50 to 53.5 percent. What was left of the Greek debt would be exchanged for two-year notes backed by the EFSF and long-dated, low-coupon bonds. For this modest advance on the October program to offer any hope of fiscal sustainability, it would take extreme discipline on the part of Athens, and that begged the next question. Having ousted Papandreou as prime minister in a backroom coup after aborting his referendum proposal, the troika had fashioned for themselves a cooperative government in Athens. But by the same token, Papademos, the central banker turned prime minister, lacked legitimacy. Elections were scheduled for April 2012 and he would surely lose. The main opposition party, New Democracy, had presided over the onset of the crisis and had consistently refused to support Papandreou's government in the negotiations since 2010. So that placed any new agreement with Athens in question from the start. How were the Greeks to be nailed down? With typical forthrightness, German finance minister Wolfgang Schäuble suggested that perhaps it would be better for the Greeks not to hold elections.[8] Suspending Greek democracy would allow the key measures to be put through before the voters were given a chance to have their say. But that suggestion provoked outrage in Athens. So, instead, what the troika managed to extract was a promise from the hitherto evasive leader of New Democracy, Antonis Samaras, that if he were to take office he would abide by any deal negotiated by his predecessors. Whatever happened in the elections, the fiscal program would have priority. On that basis Greece and its creditors engaged in the latest round of extend-and-pretend.

To describe the debt restructuring of 2012 in these terms—as no more than a continuation of the makeshift measures that had characterized the Greek debt crisis from the beginning—may seem unduly dismissive. The restructuring that was forced on the creditors of Greece between February and April of 2012 was the largest and most severe in history, larger in

Greek Public Debt Before and After 2012 Restructuring

	Dec '09	Feb '12 bn euros	Dec '12	Feb '12 % of debt	Dec '12
Bonds held by private creditors		205.6	35.1	58.7	12.2
Treasury bills held by private creditors		15	23.9	4.3	8.3
EU/EFSF		52.9	161.1	15.1	56.0
ECB/National Central Banks		56.7	45.3	16.2	15.8
IMF		20.1	22.1	5.7	7.7
Total debt	**301**	**350.3**	**287.5**	**100.0**	**100.0**

Source: Jeromin Zettelmeyer, Christoph Trebesch and Mitu Gulati, "The Greek Debt Restructuring: An Autopsy," *Economic Policy* 28, no. 75 (2013): 513–563.

inflation-adjusted terms than the Russian revolutionary default or Germany's default of the 1930s.[9] By April 26, 2012, 199.2 billion euros in Greek government bonds were converted in exchange for 29.7 billion in short-term cash equivalent notes drawn on the EFSF and 62.4 billion in new long-term bonds at concessionary rates. All told, Greece's private creditors had conceded a reduction of 107 billion euros. Allowing for the much later repayment of the new long-term bonds, the net present value of claims on Greece was cut by 65 percent. In December 2012 the claims of private creditors were further reduced by a buyback of the recently issued long-dated bonds.

The problem was that the funds to sweeten the deal and induce the creditors to engage in the "voluntary" write-down did not come out of thin air. Nor did the money to pay for recapitalizing the Greek banks in the wake of the restructuring, or to pay for the December 2012 buyback. All this was funded by new borrowing from the troika. Furthermore, the 56 billion euros in Greek bonds held by the ECB were exempt from the 2012 restructuring. So the overall reduction in Greece's debt burden was far less than advertised. As a result of the debt restructuring of 2012, Greece's public debt was reduced from 350 billion to 285 billion euros, a 19 percent reduction. The really dramatic transformation was not in the quantity of debt but in who it was owed to: 80 percent was now owed to public creditors—the EFSF, the ECB or the IMF. In effect, Greece swapped a reduction of its

obligations to private creditors of 161.6 billion euros for an increase in obligations to public creditors of 98.8 billion euros.

This substitution was the one constant in the endlessly shifting politics of Greek debt: public claims replaced private debts. And this is revealed even more starkly if we look not at stocks of debt but at flows of funds.[10] Of the 226.7 billion euros that Greece was to receive in financing from European sources and the IMF between May 2010 and the summer of 2014, the vast majority flowed straight back out of Greece in debt service and repayment. Creditors in Greece and elsewhere received 81.3 billion euros in repayment of principal. Those creditors lucky enough to have debt maturing before the date of the restructuring were paid in full. It was precisely the arbitrariness of this outcome that led the IMF, under normal circumstances, to oppose emergency lending to insolvent debtors. For Greece they had made an exception on "systemic" grounds. On top of that, 40.6 billion euros were used to make regular interest payments, again to creditors in both Greece and the rest of the world. To sweeten the debt exchange of 2012, 34.6 billion euros were used to provide some incentive to those who had clung to their bonds. Recapitalizing the Greek banks, whose balance sheets were destroyed by the restructuring, took 48.2 billion euros. This meant that altogether, of the 226.7 billion euros in assistance loans received by Greece, only 11 percent went toward meeting the needs of the Greek government deficit and directly to the benefit of the Greek taxpayer.

The bond market was no longer the principal arbiter of Greece's financial fate. But for that it substituted the full weight of the troika, the IMF, the EU, the ECB and the national governments of Europe. It was now with them that Athens would have to negotiate its financial future. This had two sides.[11] On the one hand, as nonmarket lenders, the Greek Loan Facility and the EFSF could decide on loan terms by political fiat. In 2010 the terms had been punitive. By the spring of 2012 the EFSF was offering Athens long-dated loans on concessionary terms. Though the headline debt figure remained exorbitant, annual debt servicing charges were more modest. On the other hand, without the "private cushion," the politics of Greek debt were now stark. Concessions to Greece came directly at the expense of the troika, and that meant, above all, the taxpayers of the rest of Europe. Negotiations would be tough and overtly political. And they could not be avoided.

The 2012 restructuring had not answered the question of Greece's solvency. The question of restructuring would return.

In 2009 when the crisis began, Greece's public debt had stood at c. 299 billion euros.[12] As a result of the crisis it had surged to 350 billion euros. The 2012 deal cut it back to 285 billion euros. But in the interim, as a result of the recession, the eurozone crisis and the policies demanded by the creditors, the Greek economy had crash-landed. Whereas in 2009 Greece's GDP had stood at roughly 240 billion euros, in the course of 2012 it would slump to 191.1 billion euros.[13] If Greece's debts had been unsustainable in 2009, in 2012, even allowing for the concessions granted by the official creditors, it clearly still was. In the interim, Greek society had been battered beyond recognition.

In 2008 Greek unemployment had been 8 percent. Four years later it was rising inexorably toward 25 percent. Half of young Greeks were without jobs. In a nation of ten million, a quarter of a million people were fed daily at church-run food banks and soup kitchens. Meanwhile, the Greek parliament had been reduced to a factory for decrees demanded by the troika. In the eighteen months following the May 2010 bailout, the Athens parliament had whipped through 248 laws, one every three days. By 2012 it wasn't only the trade unionists and the Greek Left who were up in arms. Judges, military officials and civil servants were mounting resistance to the subordination of the Greek state. And there were other ways of expressing dissatisfaction and distrust. In the spring of 2012 the draining of funds from Greek banks accelerated at an alarming rate. As the election now scheduled for May 2012 approached, the euro system was discreetly sluicing billions in cash into Greece to preserve a veneer of normality. In total, 28.5 billion euros were quietly airlifted into Greece to disguise the size of the bank run.[14]

On May 6 the population was finally given its say. The result was a spectacular demonstration of quite how deep disillusionment went.[15] PASOK, the party that since the 1970s had been identified more than any other with Greece's democratic transformation and which had had the misfortune of governing during the worst of the crisis, saw its vote share fall from 43.9 to 13.2 percent. The new left-wing movement, Syriza, together with the Communist KKE, garnered almost twice as many votes as

PASOK. On the Right, New Democracy plunged from 34 to 18 percent, while the fascist Golden Dawn scored 7 percent. Even with the fifty-seat parliamentary bonus awarded to New Democracy as the leading party in the polls, no government could be formed. New elections were called for June 17. In the meantime, Greece hung in midair. There was no mandate for a government that was willing to accept responsibility for the measures that the Eurogroup insisted were essential for it to remain in the eurozone. As Schäuble and numerous other European politicians made clear, the Greek vote in June would be a referendum on its continued euro membership.[16]

II

The Greeks were not the only voters to deliver their verdict on the track record of Europe on May 6, 2012. That same day, in the second round of the French presidential elections, the voters rejected Sarkozy in favor of the Socialist, François Hollande.[17] Sarkozy's promise to hold France in line with Germany was not what the voters wanted. Hollande had campaigned on an antiprivilege, antibank platform, proposing taxes on higher earners and on financial transactions.[18] He promised that he would renegotiate Merkozy's fiscal compact of December 2011. The key to sound finances, as the new French government saw it, was not self-defeating austerity but growth. Crucially, Hollande gained not only the French presidency. The Socialists also won the National Assembly elections in June.[19] There was a solid majority in France, it seemed, not for conformity to the Merkozy vision but for change.

And the mood was shared on the Left in Germany. Though they had coauthored Germany's own debt brake, the SPD was alarmed by the disastrous development in the eurozone. They were soaring in the polls, and what the SPD demanded in 2012 was a new focus not on debt and fiscal sustainability but on growth. And this appeal received support from an unexpected corner: the IMF. The emphasis on the paradox of thrift in the G20 briefing for Mexico City was the first sign of a major shift in Fund thinking on fiscal policy.[20] In the summer of 2012 its staff revisited the forecasts they had made in the spring of 2010 as the eurozone crisis began

and discovered that they had systematically underestimated the negative impact of budget cuts. Whereas they had started the crisis believing that the multiplier was on average around 0.5, they now concluded that from 2010 forward it had been in excess of 1.[21] This meant that cutting government spending by 1 euro, as the austerity programs demanded, would reduce economic activity by more than 1 euro. So the share of the state in economic activity actually increased rather than decreased, as the programs presupposed. It was a staggering admission. Bad economics and faulty empirical assumptions had led the IMF to advocate a policy that destroyed the economic prospects for a generation of young people in Southern Europe.

The conservative coalition in Berlin was losing its grip. In the French presidential election Merkel's engagement on the side of Sarkozy had been unabashed. She refused to make even a token appearance with Hollande, who was publicly challenging the fiscal compact. It was probably to Hollande's benefit. Now Berlin would have to hold the line without its major European partner.[22] Nor were Merkel's problems only across the Rhine. At home, the popularity of the CDU-FDP government was sagging. The coalition had been built on the extraordinary surge in support garnered by the market-liberal Eurosceptic FDP in 2009 in the wake of the first phase of the crisis and the unpopular bank bailouts. By 2012 that support was fading. On May 13 the CDU faced important regional elections in Nordrhein-Westfalen (NRW).[23] With a population of 17 million and a GDP almost three times that of Greece, NRW was the largest state of the Federal Republic. Home to the Ruhr, it was a former heavy industrial area struggling to find a place for itself in a world in which China, not Germany, made the steel. Tellingly, the polls in NRW were triggered early because of the inability of its regional government to draft a budget in conformity with the debt brake that the grand coalition had imposed on Germany in 2009.[24] For Merkel, the result was devastating. The SPD surged. A new protest party, the Pirates, entered the regional parliament, and Merkel's CDU slumped to 26 percent. It was by far the worst result for her party in this crucial state since the founding of the Federal Republic.[25]

And then, as if to compound the political upheavals of May, the last aftershock of the real estate crisis struck, in Spain. Along with Ireland,

Spain had the distinction of experiencing one of the most extreme housing bubbles in the world. When that burst, the effect, as in Ireland, was devastating. The difference is that Spain is big—with a population of more than 45 million, compared with Ireland's 4.5 million. Before the crisis, Spain's economy was comparable in size to that of the state of Texas. So the bursting of the Spanish bubble was an event of macroscopic proportions. As the housing market collapsed, Spain's unemployment rate shot up. Of the 6.6 million increase in unemployment in the eurozone between 2007 and 2012, 3.9 million was accounted for by Spain—60 percent of that grim total. As bad as Greece's situation was, it was small by comparison and accounted for only 12 percent of the increase in eurozone unemployment. Most catastrophic of all was Spain's youth unemployment rate, which by the summer of 2012 had surged to 55 percent.[26] Even allowing for an extensive black economy, it was a deeply dismaying statistic.

Unlike Dublin, Spain's social democratic government managed to keep the travails of its mortgage banks—the regional *cajas*—out of the headlines in the first phase of the global crisis.[27] A bailout fund took many of the worst loans off their books. In 2010 the weakest *cajas*, many of them entangled with Spain's two leading political parties, were aggregated in a bad bank, Bankia/BFA. The number of *cajas* was cut from 45 to 17, but at the price of creating a larger and more dangerous entity. At 328 billion euros, Bankia's balance sheet ran to 30 percent of Spanish GDP. Not surprisingly, despite endorsement by global investment banks, the attempt to sell Bankia shares to global investors was an embarrassing flop. In November 2011, as the crisis reached its height, the socialists called a snap election, which handed power to a new conservative government headed by the People's Party of Mariano Rajoy. It is unclear whether Rajoy's cabinet grasped the severity of the situation. Perhaps Spain's Christian Democrats hoped for solidarity from Berlin. If so they were disappointed and Madrid's tone toward the EU became more belligerent.[28] New loss provisions called for from the Spanish banks were inadequate to calm the markets. By the spring of 2012 only huge injections of liquidity from the ECB were keeping Spain's financial system afloat. But maintaining liquidity was not the same as restoring solvency. On May 9, 2012, Bankia declared that it was on the point of bankruptcy and urgently needed recapitalization. By May 25, with

Bankia under new management, the figure had risen to 19 billion euros in new capital.[29] With its economy already depressed, the last thing Spain needed was a new round of banking crises, and it would be even worse if a bank bailout spiraled, Irish style, into a bank-sovereign doom loop. Following the Bankia announcement, yields on Spanish public debt surged to 6 percent and then began to inch up toward 7 percent, above which Spain's debt burden would begin to snowball as rising debt service costs further inflated the deficit.

By May 2012 it was clear that Europe was once again sliding toward the edge. Bond market yields were rising around the periphery. It was a dire outlook. According to IMF figures, in the course of 2012 alone, Europe's governments and banks needed to roll over and refinance debts amounting to an impressive 23 percent of GDP.[30] They simply could not afford interest rates to surge out of control as a result of a panic in Spain.

III

It was the looming crisis in Spain that forced the question of comprehensive eurozone reform, which had been blocked by Merkel over the winter of 2011–2012, back onto the agenda. At the end of April, speaking to the European parliament, Draghi called for a political road map to frame further moves toward fiscal union. Meanwhile, France's new president and Mario Monti's embattled government in Rome were coordinating their positions. With Italy's yields inching ominously upward, Monti needed a Europe-wide fix. Would the Spanish crisis result in a basic change in position or simply another iteration of German delaying tactics? If Merkel continued to veto any talk of sovereign debt pooling, would she be more flexible on the issue of bank recapitalization? Would a banking union with collective responsibility for banking supervision and bailouts finally unlock the door to a eurozone solution?

On June 9, 2012, eurozone finance ministers agreed that the situation in Spain was so urgent that Madrid should be provided with 100 billion euros from EU resources to fund recapitalization.[31] To stop the doom loop, however, what was required was a separate Europe-wide bank bailout fund

that had the resources to intervene in and recapitalize banks directly. If instead the funds injected into the Spanish banks were booked to the Spanish government's accounts, it risked amplifying the crisis. As if to prove the point, on June 14, 2012, Moody's downgraded Spain to a rating of Baa3, one notch above junk. The future of the European Union, Spain's foreign minister declared, would be played out in the next few days. And, as he reminded Berlin, when the *Titanic* sinks "it takes everyone with it, even those travelling in first class."[32] Indeed, the casualties list might stretch beyond Europe. Spain was not in Italy's league. But from Spain the crisis could easily spread outward. As had repeatedly been the case since 2010, the eurozone's failure to resolve its internal problems made Europe into the world's problem.

In May 2012 the telephone log of Tim Geithner at the US Treasury shows an ominous spike, with dozens of calls to Brussels, the IMF and eurozone finance ministers.[33] At the Camp David meeting of the G8 on May 18–19 Obama took Merkel and Monti aside for an eyebrow-raising two-and-a-half-hour side meeting. In November 2011, at the G20 in Cannes, the eurozone had dominated the talks. Nine months later, as the G20 summit convened in the glaring sunlight of the gated Mexican resort of Los Cabos, Europe was still at the top of the agenda. The world's policy experts, politicians and media had to come to terms with the fact that the eurozone's problems were not only not fixed but getting worse by the day. The impatience was palpable. At a press conference on June 19 the questions put to commission president Barroso were so aggressive that he lost his cool. In response to a Canadian journalist asking about the risks to North America emanating from the eurozone, Barroso snapped back: "Frankly, we are not here to receive lessons in terms of democracy or in terms of how to handle the economy. . . . This crisis was not originated in Europe. . . . [S]eeing as you mention North America, this crisis originated in North America and much of our financial sector was contaminated by, how can I put it, unorthodox practices, from some sectors of the financial market."[34] And continuing in this self-righteous vein, Barroso added that Europe was a community of democracies. Finding the right strategy took time. Several of the G20 were not even democracies. What did Europe have to learn from them?

Clearly, old hierarchies died hard. But, equally clearly, Europe needed

help. At Cannes, Obama had tried to work through Sarkozy to shift the German position. That had failed. Sarkozy would not risk a breach with Merkel. By the summer of 2012, Washington had more levers to bring to bear. Italy's premier, Mario Monti, had visited the White House early in 2012 and was hailed by *Time* magazine as a potential savior of Europe.[35] Though he was the godfather of the Bocconi school of neoclassical economics and a classic Italian free-market liberal, Monti had become convinced that the eurozone bond markets could no longer be trusted. Speculators were pricing into their assessment of Italian and Spanish bonds not the particular fiscal situation in those countries but the probability of a systematic breakdown. The talk was of "redenomination" risk and for that there could only be a collective solution. But to shift the eurozone into action, Monti needed allies. Washington was supportive. But it was the break in the Merkozy front in May 2012 that was decisive. Not only was the newly elected Hollande pressing for a new emphasis on stimulus and growth but officials in the French Treasury were coming around to the idea of a banking union. The speculative pressure they had seen unleashed in the autumn of 2011 when Dexia failed and France's own credit rating was in doubt had convinced them that without risk pooling no one was safe.[36] As a third, Monti and Hollande could count on Mariano Rajoy, Spain's Christian democratic prime minister. Rajoy was no visionary. Indeed, he often gave the impression that he barely grasped the extremity of Spain's situation. But there was no doubt that Madrid desperately needed the talk of a eurozone breakup to end.

On the second day at Los Cabos, Obama and Monti sprang a trap. In a one-on-one meeting with Merkel, the American president presented the German chancellor with a plan that had been drafted by the Italians.[37] The scheme proposed that for states that were running suitably responsible fiscal policies, the ECB or the ESM should put a cap on bond market yields. If yields rose above the threshold of sustainability, this would trigger intervention to restore a more normal level of interest rates. It would be a quasi-automatic mechanism that did not require intrusive inspection or supervision of the troika variety. Merkel indignantly refused even to discuss the idea on the procedural grounds that it had not been cleared in advance with her staff. She would accept no proposal that blurred the line between monetary

and fiscal policy from whatever source it came. For the Germans the "autonomy" of the ECB remained sacrosanct. The tone was tense and it was thought that it would be best to cancel the after-dinner plenary that had been scheduled at Obama's request. Enough had been said in private conversations. No one wanted to repeat the scenes at Cannes.

Once more Merkel had stopped a transatlantic push for emergency action. But pressure was now building on both sides of the Atlantic. On June 17, to general relief, the Greek election had clarified the political scene to the point at which a new government could be formed. PASOK was wiped out. Voters now clustered around New Democracy on the Right and Syriza on the Left.[38] For those opposed to the troika Syriza was now the main choice. Samaras formed a government on June 20. A government was better than no government, but given Samaras's track record during the crisis to date, it was hard to know what to expect. Would he stick to his commitment to honor the agreements of the Papademos government? The answer was far from obvious, and planning for the possibility of Grexit continued. In any case, by June 2012 Greece was no longer the main concern. If some concerted collective action plan was not put in place, Spain was in mortal danger and Italy would soon follow.

Scrambling for leverage, Monti and Hollande convened a meeting in Rome on June 22 to agree on a Growth Pact for Europe, notionally to be worth 130 billion euros in investments and tax breaks. They knew that Merkel was vulnerable because her FDP coalition partners were trying to save their skins by rallying the Eurosceptic vote and opting out of the chancellor's European policy. This left Merkel dependent on the opposition SPD, who were coordinating their position with the French Socialists.[39] The SPD demanded German backing for a growth agenda as the price for their votes in the Bundestag. Further multiplying the fronts on which Merkel had to fight, on June 26 the so-called quadriga—European Council president Herman Van Rompuy, European Central Bank head Mario Draghi, European Commission president José Manuel Barroso and Eurogroup chair Jean-Claude Juncker—returned to the vision that Berlin had vetoed in December. They proposed a banking union backed by eurozone-wide deposit insurance and a joint crisis fund. Nor did they shrink from suggesting the need for shared debt issuance.[40] Merkel's response was not long in coming.

Within twenty-four hours she used a meeting of her coalition partners, the FDP, to announce: "There will be no collectivization of debt in the European Union for as long as I live."[41] In Germany the drumroll against additional eurozone bailouts was mounting. Merkel's room for maneuver was further tightened on June 21 when the Federal Constitutional Court ruled that in agreeing with France's demand to bring forward the creation of the ESM to the summer of 2012, the government had violated the Bundestag's right to prior consultation. The message was clear. There must be no backdoor bailouts.

On June 28, 2012, the European Council convened in Brussels in an atmosphere of "deep crisis."[42] Spain was clearly sliding toward the abyss. Three days earlier Madrid had formally applied for 100 billion euros in external assistance to recapitalize and restructure its banks. To stop the impending disaster, there was no alternative but for the council to approve the creation of a banking union. This would provide for the direct recapitalization of banks, independent of their home country governments, once an effective overall supervisory regime was established. Finally, a structural solution adequate to the crisis was coming into view. In the short term Germany agreed to an immediate bailout for the Spanish banks, provided a strict stress test was applied. This was a step of enormous significance. Four years on from 2008, what Europe was finally acknowledging was that even more than a fiscal union, what the eurozone needed was joint responsibility for its financial sector.

What this did not resolve, however, was the boiling uncertainty in government debt markets. For Italy and Spain, facing interest rates rising toward 7 percent and beyond, this was a life-or-death issue. They could not hope to stabilize their public finances unless bond markets were calmed. On the evening of June 28 Monti and Rajoy forced a showdown.[43] Just as council president Van Rompuy was about to announce Europe's crowd-pleasing new Growth Pact to the press, they declared that they would veto the pact unless there was an agreement also to address the new crisis in sovereign bond markets. It was an ambush. For Merkel to have lost the Growth Pact would have left her vulnerable in the Bundestag. But she had also promised to hold the line on bank bailouts and bond buying and now she was at risk of capitulating on both. It took until 4:20 in the morning on

June 29 for the chancellor to finally give way. After a negotiating session lasting a total of fifteen hours, Barroso and Van Rompuy went before the press to announce agreement not only on the Growth Pact but also on a plan that would permit support by the ESM for the government debt of all countries that were in compliance with the rules of fiscal governance agreed in December. It would be the entitlement of all eurozone members, not emergency assistance granted by way of a humiliating application to the troika. As he left the meeting, a jubilant Monti exclaimed, Europe's "mental block" has been broken![44]

It was indeed a breakthrough. But in both political and financial terms, in July 2012 the eurozone was still in flux. Merkel's retreat did not pacify the German conservatives. The new Greek government was still regarded as a liability. Meanwhile, Spain was spiraling toward disaster. To trigger the bond market support mechanism, a eurozone member had to conform to the 3 percent deficit rule. Spain was a long way from that. In the summer of 2012 it was struggling to slash its budget deficit from 11.2 to 5.4 percent of GDP. The Eurogroup was still working out the details of the Spanish bank recapitalization. As the Spanish banking system suffered a silent bank run and the interbank lending market shut down, Spain's banks drew a massive 376 billion euros in funding from the ECB.[45] The regional governments across Spain were in trouble. In July Valencia applied to Madrid for aid. Catalonia might be next. On July 23 the Spanish ten-year bond surged to 7.5 percent and its CDS shot up to 633 basis points. That same day the Spanish minister for economic affairs, Luis de Guindos, jetted to Berlin in the hope of obtaining an endorsement from Schäuble that might reassure markets and open the door to ECB bond buying. Spain was facing, De Guindos warned, "an imminent financial collapse."[46] But Schäuble was grudging in the support he was willing to give his fellow Christian Democrat. For Germany to approve immediate bond buying, Madrid would need to make changes to its pension system and demonstrate its commitment to budget balance. Conformity to Germany's idea of the European social bargain was the price for backing from Berlin. The eurozone still hung in the balance.

Three days later, on Thursday, July 26, Mario Draghi flew to London ahead of the opening of the Olympic Games to attend a Global Investment Conference designed to promote the UK as a business center. The mood in

London was not friendly.[47] Mervyn King, speaking ahead of Draghi on the panel, let it be known that he did not regard European political union as a possible solution. As Draghi later confided to a friend: "I really got fed up! All those stories about the dissolution of the euro really suck." The expression he used in Italian was apparently rather more colorful.[48] So Draghi decided to change the script. The markets needed to understand the qualitative change that Europe was undergoing. The eurozone might have started life as an ill-shapen construction, but under the pressure of the crisis it was developing fast. Global markets needed to appreciate the fundamental changes that were reshaping Europe. Following the December 2011 fiscal pact, the summit of June 2012 was a turning point because for the first time since 2008 all the leaders had restated with a powerful voice that the "only way out of this present crisis is to have more Europe, not less Europe."[49] The forward motion of the EU's integration machine was resumed. The point that Draghi wanted to drive home to global markets was political. "When people talk about the fragility of the euro and the increasing fragility of the euro, and perhaps the crisis of the euro," he told the skeptical City of London crowd, "very often non-euro area member states or leaders underestimate the amount of political capital that is being invested in the euro." These were not empty words because "actions have been made, are being made to make it irreversible." And there was "another message" that Draghi wanted investors to hear: "Within our mandate, the ECB is ready to do whatever it takes to preserve the euro." Then, pausing for effect, he added: "And believe me, it will be enough."

IV

In retrospect, Draghi's "whatever it takes" speech has come to be seen as the turning point of the eurozone crisis. In the aftermath, markets immediately calmed. Yields for the most vulnerable borrowers came down. There was no more talk of a eurozone breakup. It is an explanation with deep appeal. The ECB had held the key to stability all along. Draghi, finally, was the one to turn it. But this is a retrospective construction. The more or less open struggle over the direction of ECB policy that had begun back in 2010

Source: Thomson Reuters, from Marcus Miller and Lei Zhang, "Saving the Euro: Self-Fulfilling Crisis and the 'Draghi Put,'" in *Life After Debt* (Basingstoken, UK: Palgrave Macmillan, 2014), 227–241.

was not ended by Draghi's speech on July 26. His initial intervention was extremely fragile. It could easily have been undone. It took a lot of help to make Draghi's speech into a historic turning point, and even then it was painfully incomplete.

In the hours that followed Draghi's address, as its import sank in, there was confusion at ECB headquarters in Frankfurt. As one senior ECB official commented to Reuters: "Nobody knew this was going to happen. Nobody."[50] The ECB's media department and the editors of the bank's Web page did not have an advance copy of the speech to make available to the press. Draghi had vaguely discussed his plan with a few of his fellow executive board members. But given its likely impact, he had clearly felt it was better to hold the decision close and to present the world with a fait accompli. Significantly, Jens Weidmann, president of the Bundesbank, was among those who learned about Draghi's message through the news. None of Europe's capitals had received advance warning, nor had Klaus Regling, the head of the EFSF, whose agency would play a key role in Draghi's plan. Draghi had had "nothing precise in mind," said an official at the ECB's headquarters in Frankfurt. "It was a rash remark." As Reuters put it: Draghi's "words were a gamble. . . . [T]he speech was just the beginning."

If Draghi's speech was a rallying call, what mattered was who followed. Over the weekend, Eurogroup chief Jean-Claude Juncker threw himself behind Draghi: "The world is talking about whether the eurozone will still exist in a few months," he declaimed. Europe had "arrived at a decisive point."[51] Juncker warned the German government about allowing itself the luxury of "getting caught up in domestic politics in euro questions." Meanwhile, Merkel, Monti and Hollande issued joint statements insisting on their determination to hold the euro together. To complete the eurozone quadrilateral, Monti announced that he would shuttle to Madrid to meet with Rajoy.

Washington was quick to jump on Draghi's bandwagon. On the morning of Monday, July 30, Treasury Secretary Geithner flew to Europe to visit Schäuble at his vacation residence on Sylt. The media were divided over what transpired. Some reported agreement, others a dogged refusal by the German to compromise.[52] Geithner was concerned that Germany was still toying with dumping Greece out of the eurozone. As he wrote in his memoirs: "The argument was that letting Greece burn would make it easier to build a stronger Europe with a more credible firewall. I found the argument terrifying." Letting Greece go could create "a spectacular crisis of confidence." The flight from Europe "might be impossible to reverse." It wasn't clear to Geithner either "why a German electorate would feel much better about rescuing Spain or Portugal or anyone else."[53] After seeing Schäuble, Geithner dropped in on Draghi in Frankfurt. As Geithner later recalled, the upshot was far from reassuring. Draghi told Geithner that his remarks in London had been prompted on the spot by the deep skepticism he had sensed in his audience of hedge fund managers. He realized that he would need to shake the markets. As Geithner put it, "[H]e was just, he was alarmed by that and decided to add to his remarks, and off-the-cuff basically made a bunch of statements like 'we'll do whatever it takes.' Ridiculous . . . totally impromptu . . . Draghi at that point, he had no plan. He had made this sort of naked statement."[54] On his return to Washington Geithner was pessimistic: "I told the President that I was deeply worried and he was, too. . . . [A] European implosion could have knocked us back into recession, or even another financial crisis. As countless pundits noted, we didn't want that to

happen in an election year, but we wouldn't have wanted that to happen in any year."[55]

In fact, German opposition to Draghi's initiative was fierce.[56] Some insiders are convinced that it was not until the German government's joint meeting with its Chinese counterparts on August 30 that Merkel and Schäuble were finally committed to backing the ECB's initiative and holding Greece in the currency zone.[57] Chinese prime minister Wen Jiabao certainly made clear that he held the major European countries, Germany and France, responsible for the destiny of the eurozone and that continued Chinese purchases of European bonds depended on their taking effective action.[58] Perhaps the position of the Obama administration was too familiar by this point and the battle lines too clearly drawn to carry much additional weight. As usual, the inflation hawks at the Bundesbank were aghast at the idea of ECB bond buying. But for Merkel it was the better of two bad options. For Spain to have been supported out of the funds of the ESM would have raised far more serious political and legal issues.[59] On September 6 the Bundesbank made its displeasure known by casting the lone vote against Draghi's plan. Indeed, Weidmann was so indignant that he demanded an interview with Draghi to impress upon him that the Bundesbank should not be regarded as just another vote on the ECB's council. It must have a veto.[60] But with backing from both Merkel and Schäuble the die was cast. The ECB formalized its new role as a conditional lender of last resort, under the title of Outright Monetary Transactions (OMT).[61] But this was a strictly conditional promise. The ECB would go into action only if the country in question had agreed on an austerity and aid program approved by the ESM. It was hedged with far more conditions than the unconditional bond buying in which the ECB had engaged under Trichet.

Even after Draghi's "whatever it takes" speech, the ECB's monetary policy was profoundly constrained. The same was not true to the same degree for its counterpart in the United States. In 2012 the pace of the US recovery was flagging. The conservative stampede that had opposed any further expansion of monetary activism in 2011 had run its course. On September 13, 2012, the FOMC voted for QE3.[62] It would be the biggest Fed expansion yet. Initially, the Fed committed to purchasing $40 billion per month in Fannie

Mae and Freddie Mac agency bonds. What was different was that it under-took to do so until the Fed saw "substantial improvement in the outlook for the labour market." Additionally, the FOMC announced that it would likely maintain the federal funds rate near zero as long as unemployment remained above 6.5 percent and the Fed's inflation forecast did not exceed 2.5 percent. On December 12, 2012, the FOMC announced an increase in the amount of purchases from $40 billion to $85 billion per month. Be-cause of its open-ended nature, QE3 would earn the popular nickname "QE Infinity."

In his memoirs, Bernanke commented: "Like Mario Draghi, we were declaring we would do whatever it takes."[63] But this was far too kind to the Europeans. Draghi's OMT as it emerged by September 2012 was a condi-tional confidence-building measure. It worked by calming markets and stopping the panic. But beyond that it provided no stimulus to the eurozone economy. In truth, the ECB's possibilities were limited. QE for Europe with Germany's conservatives on the warpath was unthinkable.[64] As the euro-zone economy stagnated and its banks deleveraged, the LTRO facilities were progressively paid back. Unlike the Fed, whose balance sheet Ber-nanke was actively expanding, the ECB's balance sheet contracted back to

Fed and ECB Balance Sheets, 2004–2015

Source: Fed, ECB.

where it had been in the crisis-ridden fall of 2011. Europe was sliding ever deeper into its second recession.

V

If one asks how the acute phase of the eurozone crisis was finally halted, Draghi's July 26 speech offers two answers. One was that given by Draghi himself. The eurozone crisis was halted because of the enormous investment of political capital made by Europe's governments. It was halted by the construction of a new apparatus of government: the Greek restructuring, the fiscal compact, banking union, ESM, the ECB's OMT facility. Those who bet against the eurozone's future misjudged the scale of the investment being made by Europe's governments. That was the message that Draghi wanted to ram home. As Draghi said, it was a political message about the seriousness of European state building. The delays might come at a huge cost to its citizens. But in its usual crablike fashion, Europe was moving once more toward "ever closer union."

But the answer extracted from the speech by most of those who heard Draghi that day in the City of London was rather different. They remained skeptical of the EU and uninterested in the details of its politics. What they took from Draghi's speech was not its specific content or the sea change in eurozone politics that made it possible. They heard one single and simple message. Here was a powerful central banker and he was saying that he would do "whatever it takes." Finally, a European policy maker had realized what was needed. He was speaking the language of the financial Powell Doctrine, in the City of London, to an audience of investors, in English. What Draghi was signaling was that Europe, finally, "got it."

Implicit in this rendition of what happened in the summer of 2012 is another narrative, at odds with Draghi's intended meaning. "Whatever it takes" was, in fact, a form of surrender. The eurozone was finally giving in to what Anglophone economic commentators had been calling for all along. If only the ECB had moved to the Fed model earlier, as Obama had spelled out at Cannes, the worst of the eurozone crisis might have been avoided. What Draghi now promised was what Geithner, Bernanke and

Obama had been preaching to the Europeans since 2010: "Do it our way." Nor was it a coincidence that it was Draghi—an American-trained economist; a Goldman Sachs associate; a paid-up member of the global financial community; a "friend of Ben"; an internationalized, urbane Italian, not a provincial German—who delivered this conclusion to the agonizing story of the eurozone crisis. The Draghi formula—America's formula—was self-fulfilling. He spoke the magic words. The markets stabilized. The eurozone was saved by its belated Americanization.

Looking back over the course of events since 2007, if one stopped the historical clock in the autumn of 2012, the story of the North Atlantic financial crisis could thus be twisted back into a familiar shape. Faced with a crisis of historic proportions, after its own fashion, the Obama administration had delivered a twenty-first-century demonstration of hegemonic leadership. It lacked the urgency and razzmatazz of the Marshall Plan era, but the upshot was decisive. Not only had America led the way through its own domestic stimulus and monetary policy programs. Through discreet diplomacy and the Fed's massive liquidity programs, it had helped Europe across its worst crisis since the end of World War II. Americanization was the answer. Nor were the exponents of US economic policy shy about trumpeting their achievements. *The Courage to Act* would be the title of Bernanke's memoir. The melodrama caused his more bashful European colleagues to wince. It was not the kind of language one associates with the recollections of an academic economist turned central banker. Other, more academic titles in the wake of the 2012 stabilization echoed the general mood of optimism. In the end, it had turned out to be a *Status Quo Crisis*.[65] *The System Worked*.[66] The global economy had survived and America had reasserted a new version of liberal hegemony. Europe resumed the forward march to a United States of Europe it had begun under American guidance in 1947. Among academic commentators, a cottage industry grew up on both sides of the Atlantic benchmarking Europe's new efforts at integration against American history. Was Europe still at the Philadelphia stage, or was a Hamilton moment on the horizon?[67]

It was, one should add, a reasonable assessment, certainly if one stopped the clock in November 2012 and if one skated over America's unfortunate role in 2010 in endorsing the first round of extend-and-pretend. This

narrative was also, in the American context, a thoroughly political one. As Geithner acknowledged, 2012 was an election year. And if the financial crisis and its European aftermath had finally been contained, the Democrats deserved whatever credit was due. Since 2008 the congressional Republicans had been obstructive if not downright dangerous. Campaigning for a second term as president in 2012, Obama cashed in. Gone was the modesty that characterized his speeches in 2008–2009 in the wake of the embarrassment of the Bush presidency. Now Obama trumpeted American exceptionalism without reserve: "I see it everywhere I go, from London and Prague, to Tokyo and Seoul, to Rio and Jakarta," he declared to a group of air force cadets in the summer of 2012. "There is a new confidence in our leadership. . . . [America remains] the one indispensable nation in world affairs. . . . I see an American century because no other nation seeks the role that we play in global affairs, and no other nation can play the role that we play in global affairs."[68] As far as international economic policy was concerned, Obama's victory in November 2012, Bernanke's QE3 and Draghi's speech combined to put the seal on the narrative. Centrist liberal crisis management had prevailed. In America's new century, diversity, world openness and technocratic pragmatism would go hand in hand.

But this reconciled narrative of crisis resolution obscures deep tensions on both sides of the Atlantic. In Europe, the eurozone had survived. Draghi was right. An important phase of state building had emerged from the crisis. But it was at an appalling economic and political cost. The governments of Italy and Greece had been overturned. Ireland and Portugal had been put on troika tutelage and Spain had escaped by the skin of its teeth. And though the acute sovereign bond crisis was over, after two years of nail-biting anxiety, consumer and business confidence were shot. Unemployment took a huge toll on eurozone demand. Fiscal policy was constrained by the German drive to balance budgets. Perversely, Germany's trade surplus was surging at a time of plunging aggregate demand across the continent. It was a time, if there ever was one, for an active monetary policy. But stopping the bond market panic was one thing, reviving the eurozone economy another. Unlike the Fed, Draghi had no mandate. As social misery deepened, as the sense of humiliation set in, what would be the reaction across Europe? Nor was it only the "victims" who were unsatisfied. German

conservatives were indignant at Merkel's litany of compromises. In the German media, Draghi, the savior of the eurozone, faced hostility and doubt. Unless this German Euroscepticism could be overcome, there was little prospect of actually realizing the agenda of ambitious integration and institution building that Draghi had trumpeted in his London speech.

In the United States, Obama's reelection might energize his followers. But what exactly did his new American century consist of? What would be its priorities? In his first term Obama had been preoccupied with overcoming the legacy of Bush's mistakes and coping with the crisis. But was the crisis really over? And even if it was, did that mean that America could face the future unencumbered? Or, having survived the crisis, did America now face the same challenges that had brought Obama as a junior senator to the launch of the Hamilton Project in 2006—challenges that had only amplified and intensified since? In foreign policy circles the beginning of Obama's second term saw an impassioned argument over American retrenchment and the foundations of its international power.[69] And in economic policy too there were skeptics. Had enough really changed to make another crisis less likely? Had the tensions within the financial system really been resolved, or merely contained? If another Great Depression had been avoided, did that have the perverse effect of removing the spur to truly profound reform?[70] It was not without irony that among the Cassandras one of the loudest and most compelling voices was none other than Larry Summers, Treasury secretary to Clinton and chief economic adviser to Obama until December 2010. Twelve months on from Obama's second election victory, at an IMF event in November 2013, Summers warned: "[M]y lesson from this crisis, and my overarching lesson, which I have to say I think the world has under-internalized, is that it is not over until it is over, and that time is surely not right now."[71] He could not have known how right he would turn out to be.

Part IV

AFTERSHOCKS

Chapter 19

AMERICAN GOTHIC

Amid the banking crisis of 2008, the American motor industry had been collateral damage. With sales collapsing, GM and Chrysler were knocked to their knees. In December 2008 a truculent Congress voted down an emergency aid package, but neither Bush nor Obama thought they could let GM and Chrysler fail. These once great powerhouses of American industrialism were rescued by diverting funds originally allocated to the bank bailout. By 2013 both GM and Chrysler were back in profit. Like the rest of American big business, they weathered the storm and Chrysler celebrated its recovery in the way that corporate America does, by booking a slot to run a headline-grabbing commercial during the Super Bowl in February 2014. They wanted something that would make a splash and they commissioned the man to do it. The spot was written, directed and acted in person by Bob Dylan, the wizened bard of offbeat Americana. Against a backdrop of Hopperesque noir, Dylan delivered a striking piece of high-caliber nationalist kitsch:

Is there anything more American than America? 'Cause you can't import original. You can't fake true cool.

You can't duplicate legacy. Because what Detroit created was a first and became an inspiration to the . . . rest of the world.

Yeah . . . Detroit made cars. And cars made America. Making the best, making the finest, takes conviction.

And you can't import the heart and soul, of every man and woman working on the line.

You can search the world over for the finer things, but you won't find a match for the American road and the creatures that live on it.

Because we believe in the zoom, and the roar, and the thrust. And when it's made here, it's made with the one thing you can't import from anywhere else. American pride. So let Germany brew your beer, let Switzerland make your watch, let Asia assemble your phone.

We . . . will build . . . your car.[1]

His lines were all the more resonant because of what the audience could be expected to know about the place where the spot was filmed, Detroit. If the American motor industry was back from the dead, the same could not be said for Motor City.

Since its heyday in the postwar era, Detroit had long been a city in decline. At its peak it had a population of 1.8 million, of whom 500,000 were African American. Hit by deindustrialization and white flight following the 1967 riots, by 2013 the population of the urban core of Detroit had shrunk to 688,000, of whom 550,000 were African American. They were left behind in a city that was literally falling into ruin, burdened with debts running into the tens of billions of dollars. With most of the major factories that had made it one of the industrial heartlands of the world closed down, Detroit was caught in a death spiral of unemployment, racial disadvantage and unsafe and predatory financing.[2] By 2013, 36 percent of Detroit's population were classed as living below Michigan's far from generous poverty line. The unemployment rate was 18 percent. The city was an extreme example of the doom loop in which public and private financial distress compounded each other. In 2005, of all the mortgages in Detroit, 68 percent were subprime.[3] As the crisis cut a swath across America, 65,000 homes in Detroit were foreclosed. Of those, 36,400 were considered of so little value that they were simply abandoned, joining a total stock of 140,000 blighted properties. Trying to contain the contamination effect, the city demolished entire tracts. Though it received state and federal subsidies for the house-razing program, it cost Detroit $195 million. That came on top of lost tax revenues of $300 million.[4] None of this could the city afford. Detroit

appointed an emergency manager who in June 2013 filed for bankruptcy, with debts owing between $18 billion and $20 billion. It was the biggest city bankruptcy in American history.[5]

As viewers of Dylan's Chrysler spot knew, Detroit was an extreme case, but it was not alone. Former industrial cities and towns across America were struggling. A few went bankrupt. In 2011 Jefferson County, Alabama, which included the steel city of Birmingham, had filed. In 2012 it was the turn of Stockton and San Bernardino, California. These were poorly governed places, burdened with the side effects of America's ramshackle welfare state, with economies struggling against long-term decline or the immediate impact of the real estate bust. They were far from being carbon copies of northern postindustrial Detroit. But taken together they symbolized the bewildering turn from American Dream to American nightmare.

It wasn't new news. Already in the late 1970s, Bruce Springsteen had offered a mournful soundtrack for postindustrial America.[6] In 2006 Obama had reminded the bigwigs of the Hamilton Project of the harsh realities of "people in places like Decatur, Illinois, or Galesburg, Illinois. . . . This is not a bloodless process," he had said. But for most of Obama's first term it wasn't the worries of such places that preoccupied economic policy. It was the fight to save Wall Street and global finance. The protests of 2011 and their politicization of inequality had begun to change the conversation, but it was in the eighteen months following Obama's reelection in November 2012 that the sense of American malaise reached a new pitch.[7] With the crisis no longer dominating the horizon, the concerns about America's long-term trajectory that had worried liberal centrists already in the early 2000s, the sense that things weren't "normal," came roaring back.

I

One unexpected but symptomatic manifestation was Larry Summers's minatory speech at the IMF in November 2013.[8] His subject was the recovery and its deeply disappointing pace. American policy makers might congratulate themselves that they were leading the Europeans out of the recession and they were right to do so. Since 2010 Europe's economic record had

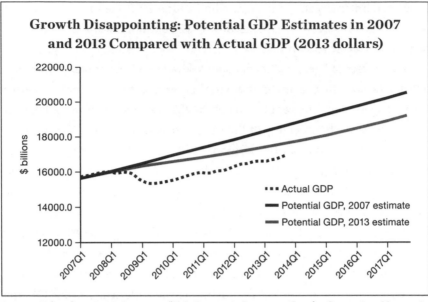

Growth Disappointing: Potential GDP Estimates in 2007 and 2013 Compared with Actual GDP (2013 dollars)

Source: Taken from L. H. Summers, "U.S. Economic Prospects: Secular Stagnation, Hysteresis, and the Zero Lower Bound," *Business Economics* 49, no. 2 (2014): 65–74. Data: CBO.

been even worse. But America's own recovery was the slowest on record. On the "plucking model" of business cycles, after a downward shock as severe as that in 2008, one might have expected the rebound to be vigorous. In 2009–2010 the recovery had started strongly, but since then economic growth had relapsed to a depressing extent. Where was the "bounce"? What was wrong?

The conventional view was that the United States was suffering from the aftereffects of an exceptionally severe financial crisis. This was no ordinary business cycle. It would take time for markets and balance sheets to recover.[9] It was precisely to avoid such hangovers that economists like Reinhart and Rogoff argued for financial restraint. If you avoided the credit bubble and the excessive upswing, you might avoid the bust. Keynesians like Krugman insisted that this was all very well, but the recovery had been needlessly slowed by the premature shift to austerity. As Krugman put it punchily, "[I]t all went wrong in 2010."[10] The global shift to austerity for which Reinhart and Rogoff had been the cheerleaders reduced the recovery to an agonizing crawl. Bernanke's QE could compensate to some degree, but it could not make up for the shortfall in aggregate demand.

These were the parameters of the economic policy debate familiar since 2009 and long before. What they did not capture was the sense that a deeper and more serious problem was afflicting America's economy and the society built on it. The hypothesis that Summers suggested to his audience at the IMF in November 2013 was disconcerting and unfamiliar; so jarring, in fact, that Summers, who is not given to either modesty or self-doubt, acknowledged, "[T]his may all be madness, and I may not have this right at all." But in light of the data, the question had to be put: What if the inadequate recovery was not simply down to policy failure? What if there was a deeper problem, a chronic shortfall in the demand for investment relative to the supply of savings, resulting in a sustained condition of "secular stagnation"?

To see the force of this argument, Summers invited his surprised audience to look back to the period before the crash. In retrospect, everyone agreed that monetary policy before 2008 had been "too easy.... [T]here was a vast amount of imprudent lending going on. Almost everybody believes that wealth, as it was experienced by households, was in excess of its reality. Too easy money, too much borrowing, too much wealth." But if that were the case, one would have expected the American economy to have been on a dramatic bull run. It was not. Despite the excesses of the housing boom, growth up to 2008 had been average. Indeed, when compared with the 1950s and 1960s it had been slow, which is why places like Detroit were in such a precarious position. "Unemployment wasn't under any remarkably low level. Inflation was entirely quiescent. So somehow, even a great bubble wasn't enough to produce any excess in aggregate demand." So imagine, Summers continued the train of thought, "how satisfactory" the perfor mance of the US economy would have been in the early 2000s "in the absence of a housing bubble, and with the maintenance of strong credit standards." It would have been just as disappointing as the current recovery was turning out to be. It might have been worse.

In an astonishing makeover of America's recent economic history Summers proposed that for at least two decades American economic growth had been on weak foundations. To achieve no more than a "normal" rate of growth it had depended on "abnormal" financial bubbles. Looking back over recent decades, Summers asked in a subsequent speech, "[C]an we identify

any sustained stretch during which the economy grew satisfactorily with conditions that were financially sustainable? Perhaps one can find some such period, but it is very much the minority, rather than the majority, of the historical experience."[11] It was a remarkable indictment of the policy consensus of which Summers himself had been a defining figure.[12] It had dramatic implications for current policy. If America simply waited, the long-awaited rebound from the crisis of 2008 might never arrive.

To address the chronic shortfall in investment, what Summers advocated was a new era of government activism. The United States would not match China, of course. Nor was that appropriate. But the conditions were right for a big burst of public investment. This would rebuild America's infrastructure, and in so doing it would address the more fundamental questions posed by Detroit. Physical reconstruction would be a means to restore a sense of national coherence and national pride. As Summers remarked on another occasion: "Look at Kennedy airport. It is an embarrassment as an entry point to the leading city in the leading country in the world. The wealthiest, by flying privately, largely escape its depredations. Fixing it would employ substantial numbers of people who work with their hands and provide a significant stimulus to employment and growth. . . . If a moment when the United States can borrow at lower than 3 percent in a currency we print ourselves, and when the unemployment rate for construction workers hovers above 10 percent, is not the right moment to do it, when will that moment come?"[13]

Belatedly, what Summers was calling for was what Obama's administration had failed to deliver, a concerted drive to unify American society around a sustained program of investment-driven growth and comprehensive modernization. The efforts at stimulus in 2009 and 2010 had not been negligible. But they had been hedged around by the anxieties of the moment, resistance from Congress, a spectacular and aggressive mobilization of right-wing opinion and Larry Summers's own nervousness about losing standing with the savvy political operatives. The result was a recovery that was not just slow but deeply inequitable. If the shocking images of dilapidation in Detroit and other postindustrial cities around America were not enough, devastating statistical data completed the picture.

In October 2013 two French economists, one working in California,

the other back in Paris, published the latest release of a long-running proj-
ect on American inequality.[14] Emmanuel Saez and Thomas Piketty were at
this point not unknown. An earlier paper in which they mapped top in-
comes in the United States over the long run had yielded the "We are the
99 percent" slogan that the Occupy movement had used to such good ef-
fect.[15] Nevertheless, the data they released in October 2013 were astonish-
ing. From the latest round of tax releases they calculated that of the growth
generated by the economic recovery since 2009, 95 percent had been mo-
nopolized by the top 1 percent. That tiny fraction of the population saw
their incomes rebound from the trough of the recession by 31.4 percent.[16]
Meanwhile, 99 percent of Americans had experienced virtually no gain in
income since the crisis. The data were subsequently revised to show a less
extreme disproportion.[17] But in 2013 the numbers were a sensation. The
slow growth in GDP that worried Summers, in fact, hid two radically diver-
gent realities. Whereas a tiny elite were doing extremely well, for average
Americans the secular stagnation thesis that Summers advanced as a ten-
tative academic hypothesis was simply the lived reality of the last forty

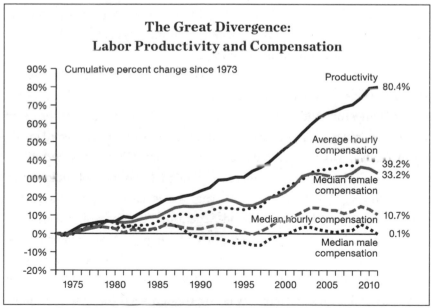

Source: Lawrence Mishel, "The Wedges Between Productivity and Median Compensation Growth,"
EPI Issue Brief 330 (2012): 1–7, http://www.epi.org/publication/ib330-productivity-vs-compen
sation/.

years. Since America's bicentennial in 1976, productivity growth, which drove overall economic growth, and the returns to labor in the form of household incomes had starkly diverged. The average American shared only to a small degree in national economic growth as measured by GDP statistics. Almost all the benefits of growth were being monopolized by the highest paid and those wealthy enough to own significant portfolios of financial assets. The financial crisis of 2008 had revealed how in extremis national economic policy was subordinated to the needs of a cluster of giant transnational banks. Now, in the face of a dismal recovery, the correspondence between economic growth and the progress of a national society was being challenged from the bottom up. Could the national economy any longer be plausibly presented as a project common to all Americans?

II

The decay of the American Dream had been a staple of Barack Obama's political discourse since his days as a junior senator. It was a common thread in the Hamilton Project agenda. In December 2013, a year into his second term as president, Obama visited a community center in Ward 8, an African American section of Washington, DC, to make a major speech about America's ongoing social crisis.[18] He described the "daily battles" of ordinary Americans struggling against the "relentless decades-long trend" toward "dangerous and growing inequality." The "basic bargain at the heart of our economy has frayed," he declared. Of course, the trend toward growing inequality was not confined to America. But, Obama insisted, there must be no more evasion, "this increasing inequality is most pronounced in our country. . . . [S]tatistics show . . . that our levels of income inequality rank near countries like Jamaica and Argentina." Comparable "wealthy allies, countries like Canada or Germany or France . . . have greater mobility than we do, not less." Half of all Americans would experience poverty during at least one period of their lives. "The combined trends of increased inequality and decreasing mobility pose a fundamental threat to the American Dream, our way of life and what we stand for around the globe." Inequality was, the president declared, the "defining challenge of our time."

The racialized distress of cities like Detroit was clearly shocking. But, as Obama emphasized, America's crisis was not confined to predominantly African American communities. Across the country, class, not race, was the most important determinant of an American's life chances, and the big story of his second term as president was rural white working-class despair. It was Appalachia—West Virginia and Kentucky—held back by structural change, educational failure and immobility, that lurched into the headlines. At its most extreme, this lethal cocktail came to be symbolized by an epidemic of drug addiction, fed by cheap heroin from Mexico and rampant opioid abuse.[19] Already in 2007 deaths from drug overdose had overtaken road accidents as a major cause of death in the United States.[20] Among white Americans, deaths from overdose increased by 297 percent between 2010 and 2014 alone. Unlike in any other developed society, life expectancy among working-class white Americans had been decreasing since the early 2000s. In modern history the only obvious parallel was with Russia in the desperate aftermath of the fall of the Soviet Union. One journalistic essay and academic research paper after another confirmed the disaster, until the narrative was capped in 2015 by Anne Case and Angus Deaton's famous account of "deaths of despair."[21]

The crisis was undeniable. The question was what to do about it. When the left wing of the Democratic Party had taken up the issue of inequality in the 1990s at the time of the Clinton administration, the standard diagnosis had been technical and economic.[22] Globalization had pushed top incomes up and lower incomes down. Since the 1990s, the impact of these factors had only increased. Imports of cheap manufacturers opened up by NAFTA and Chinese accession to the WTO benefited consumers, but depressed wages and robbed blue-collar Americans of secure manufacturing jobs and the health and retirement benefits that went with them. By 2013, experts close to the American labor movement estimated that the trade deficit with China had cost 3.2 million jobs and the competition of low-wage foreign labor had depressed the wages of the 100 million American workers without college education by $180 billion.[23] These were substantial effects, but in an economy with a workforce of more than 150 million and a wage bill of more than $7 trillion, they were nowhere near large enough to explain the huge surge in inequality. So globalization was supplemented

by the thesis of skills-biased technological change.[24] This postulated that, independent of globalization and foreign trade, the trend in technological development had offered disproportionate benefits to those with higher skills in every walk of life and across the entire American economy, whether exposed to trade or not.

The standard reformist response was to advocate for a role for federal and state government in improving education, providing affordable access to community colleges and offering trade adjustment assistance. Hence, the focus of the Hamilton Project in 2006 on making sure that underprivileged kids made good use of their summer vacations. But after twenty years, given the mounting inequality and declining mobility, these measures could hardly be deemed a success. Disillusionment with conventional reformist solutions was a hallmark of the "new" inequality debate that sprang to life after 2011. Though there had been many well-intentioned efforts by government agencies to modify and improve the condition of average Americans, on balance their net effect had been modest, to say the least. Between 1977 and 2014 the share of national income going to the top 1 percent before taxes and benefits had risen by 88.8 percent. After fiscal redistribution their share increased by 81.4 percent. Nor did the tax and welfare state prevent the share of the bottom 50 percent from declining from 25.6 to 19.4 percent.[25] Nor was this by accident. Every conceivable source of leverage and influence had been exploited by those with money to maximize their advantage. As billionaire investor Warren Buffett famously put it: "Actually, there's been class warfare going on for the last 20 years, and my class has won."[26] Buffett was so appalled at the consequences that in 2011 he made himself into a spokesman for proposals to impose a minimum 35 percent tax on America's highest earners, a proposal that Obama had backed but that had been blocked by the Republicans in Congress.[27] It was a sign of both Buffett's personal decency and the utter lopsidedness of the balance of power in twenty-first-century America that a program of social improvement should consist of well-meaning billionaires volunteering to pay a bit more for the greater good of American society.

For those at the bottom of the pile, none of this was news. Opinion polls, especially those commissioned by the right wing, had for a long time

been recording the profound resentment among the American population at the way that both the economy and the political system seemed to be engineered to their disadvantage.[28] These views were often dismissed as conspiracy theory, and often deservedly so. Online news sources like Breitbart, which rode to prominence on the back of the Tea Party movement, provided a platform for toxic racial and anti-Semitic rhetoric.[29] But if one stepped back from the poisonous language and crude logic, the assumptions that inequality was "systemic" and that "the system" was rigged against ordinary working-class Americans were not paranoid but simply realistic. From a radically different perspective and with completely different intent, the American Left had always made the case. Indeed, it was this radical skepticism that set them apart from the liberal centrists who dominated the Democratic Party. The Left did not trust the institutions. They did not believe that electing well-intentioned products of elite colleges to steer a machine designed to favor the wealthy offered any hope of fundamental change. As the Occupy slogan of 2011 put it, "The system isn't broken, it's rigged."[30] In many ways the liberal centrists were the last to know. They, of all the segments of political opinion, had the most invested in the idea that America's social ills were amenable to technocratic remedy and that the state was a suitable instrument for making such change. It was precisely the conversion of commentators of this ilk to a more radical view that marked how serious the sense of crisis had become.[31]

In a remarkable series of articles following the 2012 election, Paul Krugman at the New York Times adopted a profoundly dark view of American society, economy and politics. "What do the pre- and postcrisis consensuses have in common?" Krugman asked in December 2013.[32] "Both were economically destructive: Deregulation helped make the crisis possible, and the premature turn to fiscal austerity has done more than anything else to hobble recovery. Both consensuses, however, corresponded to the interests and prejudices of an economic elite whose political influence had surged along with its wealth. . . . Some pundits [might wish to] depoliticize our economic discourse, to make it technocratic and nonpartisan. But that's a pipe dream. Even on what may look like purely technocratic issues, class and inequality end up shaping—and distorting—the debate." This

from a Nobel Prize–winning economist who in the 1980s and 1990s had counted squarely in the mainstream.

Robert Reich, a former Clinton-era Labor secretary, underwent a similar disillusionment at exactly the same historical moment. "For a quarter century," he now admitted, "I've offered in books and lectures an explanation for why average working people in advanced nations like the United States have failed to gain ground and are under increasing economic stress." He had pitted an interventionist state against the forces of globalization and technological change. What Reich now recognized was that much of this was "insufficient," if not "beside the point," because it overlooked a "critically important phenomenon: the increasing concentration of political power in a corporate and financial elite that has been able to influence the rules by which the economy runs. . . . The problem is not the size of government but whom the government is for."[33]

After the events of 2008–2009 and the spectacularly lopsided bailouts, could anyone seriously doubt whom government was for? At the level of personnel, the revolving door that connected the Treasury, the Fed and the top banks continued to spin at a steady pace. By 2014 both Bernanke and Geithner were on their way from public service to well-upholstered positions in finance. Geithner went to the well-connected investment bank Warburg Pincus. Bernanke advises the Citadel hedge fund and chaired an advisory board for the giant PIMCO bond fund, owned by Allianz of Germany, which also included as its members Jean-Claude Trichet and Gordon Brown as well as Anne-Marie Slaughter of the Obama foreign policy team.[34] It was like a mini reunion of 2008 crisis fighters. And they had plenty to celebrate. Share values were recovering to their precrisis levels and beyond. The banks were rebuilding their balance sheets. As they piled up capital and reserves, rates of return in the financial sector were down. But, as the stress tests had always intended, pre-provision net revenue was bouncing back and the extra capital made the banks safer. America's financial giants were expanding their businesses, pushing into markets vacated by their ailing European competitors.[35]

Clearly, Wall Street enjoyed a privileged connection to government. After 2008 no one could doubt that. But what was striking in the aftermath

of the crisis was how critical commentary on America's political economy widened its scope beyond the banks. In so doing it followed the evolving contours of the economy itself. With the advent of the smartphone and social media boom in 2007, tech had regained the luster it had lost in the dot-com crash. Silicon Valley was the new cutting edge of American capitalism. Big Pharma continued to rake in profits. As oil prices resurged from their lows in 2009, big oil and the new technology of fracking were back. As the recession of 2008–2009 receded, what came ever more to the fore was a tendency toward concentration and oligopoly that went far beyond Wall Street. One of the side effects of Bernanke's QE policy of low interest rates was that it made it hugely attractive for companies to borrow to buy out their competitors. In three giant merger waves, cresting in 2000, 2006 and 2015, with the antitrust authorities looking on, American capitalism remade itself in a more concentrated and monopolistic mode.[36] By 2013 profits were booming to an almost embarrassing extent.[37] Even chronic loss makers, like the airlines, were now making money. But the really big returns were elsewhere. As Peter Orszag, Obama's former director of management and budget, now at Citigroup, and Jason Furman, serving as chair of the Council of Economic Advisers, reported in a research paper, two thirds of the nonfinancial firms that had managed to achieve a return on invested capital of 45 percent or more between 2010 and 2014 "were in either the health care or information technology sectors."[38] What allowed such gigantic profits and enormous salaries to be concentrated in these sectors were market power, IP protection and government-licensed pricing.[39]

Silicon Valley saw no need to apologize. Theirs was the great technological and entrepreneurial success story of the late twentieth and early twenty-first centuries. Antitrust, data protection and intrusive tax investigations were, as far as Tim Cook of Apple was concerned, nothing more than "political crap," antiquated road bumps on the highway to the future.[40] As tech oligarch Peter Thiel told audiences and readers: "Creating value isn't enough—you also need to capture some of the value you create." That depended on market power. "Americans mythologize competition and credit it with saving us from socialist bread lines," but Thiel knew better. As far as he was concerned, "[C]apitalism and competition are opposites.

Capitalism is premised on the accumulation of capital, but under perfect competition, all profits get competed away. The lesson for entrepreneurs is clear . . . [c]ompetition is for losers."[41]

One could hardly ask for a more crass statement of robber baron hubris. The implications were bleak. America's massively skewed distribution of income and wealth was the product of inherited assets, amplified by pervasive technological and economic change and Warren Buffett's "class war," which extended to every facet of the political regulation and deregulation of the economy. If this was so, what would it take to counteract the imbalance and to redress the astonishingly one-sided outcomes? A polite European social democrat like Thomas Piketty inferred from his inequality data that what the world needed was a global wealth tax. This was the message of his remarkable global bestseller, *Capital in the Twenty-First Century*, which redefined the public debate about inequality in 2014.[42] That would certainly help to offset the tendency toward massive inequality. But in a system as starkly polarized and lopsided as that of the United States, what relevance did such well-meaning suggestions have? The tax proposal wasn't wrong. It just sidestepped the reason it was needed in the first place, the brutal struggle for privilege and power, which for decades had enabled those at the top to accumulate huge wealth, untroubled by any serious effort at redistribution. The answer, if there was one, was clearly not technical. It was political in the most comprehensive sense. Power had to be met with power.

In January 2014 Reich went to Congress to testify. "I've served in Washington, and know how difficult it is to get anything done unless the broad public understands what's at stake and actively pushes for reform. That's why we need a movement against economic inequality and in favor of shared growth—a movement on a scale similar to the Progressive movement at the turn of the last century that fueled the first progressive income tax and antitrust laws, the women's suffrage movement that got women the vote, the labor movement that helped animate the New Deal of the 1930s and fueled the great prosperity of the first three decades after World War II, the Civil Rights movement that achieved the landmark Civil Rights and Voting Rights Acts, and the environmental movement that spawned the Environmental Protection Act and other critical legislation."[43]

Reich's call to arms was powerful and compelling. To fix a rigged system, what was needed was a comprehensive mobilization. But as Reich was only too well aware, the progressive Left were not the only ones who could draw this conclusion. In fact, the American right wing got there first. Unlike liberal progressives, the libertarian right wing in the United States had never doubted that government was a problem. Indeed, they had always vociferously argued that it was the entire problem. America's downward slide, the long-running trends toward inequality and oligarchy, the disaster of 2008, the lopsided recovery from it, were all symptoms of the profound corruption brought about by big government meddling and its capture by interest groups. Obama's crisis politics were simply the latest phase. In response to Obama's December 2013 inequality speech, Fox News speakers did not hesitate to mobilize the extraordinary Piketty and Saez data on the lopsidedness of the recovery, but only to turn them against the president: "He's saying he wants to take out inequality and his policies from the beginning have been to equalize." But what had happened to inequality under the Obama administration, the Fox anchors demanded to know. "[T]he top 1 percent—their income rose by 31.4 percent between 2009 and 2012. Income for everyone else, you know how much that grew? 0.4 percent. These are just facts here. 95 percent of income gains have gone to the top 1 percent. So this system that he's talking about, he is the system. It's his system!"[44]

Of course the low top tax rates that had helped to create that outcome of extreme disparity were set by a Republican Congress and kept there by them. But the polemic was telling. A large part of the American Right agreed with Obama that the American Dream was in trouble, but for them, he was the personification of everything that was wrong. His defeat of Mitt Romney in 2012 only vindicated them in their belief that existing Republican politics were hopelessly inadequate. The Republicans would never achieve the transformation they craved with a candidate like Romney, an upper-class banker. In 2013, while the Democrats were still lulled by the sweet scent of Obama's second victory, the Right counterattacked. Their target was the great social policy initiative of Obama's first term, the Affordable Care Act. The hostage they would take was the budget.

III

In 2011 the Tea Party caucus had come close to forcing the United States into fiscal crisis. That had been avoided at the last minute by a compromise under which a bipartisan "super committee" would make recommendations on deficit reduction. When that failed to reach agreement in January 2012, it meant that automatic sequester cuts would be triggered in January 2013, affecting the entire government machine, including defense.[45] This nondiscretionary mechanism was popular with the Rubinite fiscal reform crowd.[46] Among the loudest and most influential voices for budget cuts was the coalition of business interests and Washington insiders gathered by Peter G. Peterson in the Fix the Debt campaign.[47] They had a strong preference for entitlement cuts and, given their suspicion of the kind of "political crap" that frustrated businessmen and policy experts alike, automatic sequester was far from being the worst of all possible worlds. As Obama's ex–budget director Peter Orszag put the argument in October 2011 in the wake of the first budget showdown with the Tea Party: "To solve the serious problems facing our country, we need to minimize the harm from legislative inertia by relying more on automatic policies and depoliticized commissions for certain policy decisions. In other words, radical as it sounds, we need to counter the gridlock of our political institutions by making them a bit less democratic. . . . We need to jettison the Civics 101 fairy tale about pure representative democracy and instead begin to build a new set of rules and institutions that would make legislative inertia less detrimental to our nation's long-term health."[48]

Unless something was done, the automatic cuts coming down the road in 2013 were huge—$563 billion in a single year, a contractionary antistimulus that might well trigger a new recession. To avoid this disaster, tense negotiations began in the hope of reaching a deal. The so-called grand bargain worked out between Obama and Boehner in 2011 was a lopsided demonstration of Washington's rigged politics in action. It traded deep cuts in entitlements for some carefully chosen increases in taxes that would hit higher-income households but cushion "job-creating" and "growth-generating" businesses. To the Left it was outrageous.[49] The mainstream deficit-reduction campaign

was riddled with conflicts of interest. Many of the most active exponents of entitlement cuts were lobbyists for targeted tax exemptions. As one cynical observer put it, "It's easier to get face time in Washington as a deficit hawk than as a corporate hack."[50] Meanwhile, the effort by Peterson lobbyists to present the austerity movement as a grassroots and youth-driven movement was exposed as a risible joke. The campaign included a bus tour of college campuses called "The Can Kicks Back," a bizarre YouTube clip in which the venerable Senator Alan Simpson was persuaded to dance Gangnam style, and a cack-handed effort to deluge Congress with scripted letters from indignant teens protesting the debt burden their grandparents were threatening to pass down to them. It wasn't so much grassroots as "Astroturf."[51]

Countering the posttruth of the mainstream austerity campaign made for good journalistic exposés. It also made sense for the Left to focus its fire on the likes of Peterson, Orszag, Simpson and Bowles, who were assumed to be the real power brokers in Washington. What no one reckoned with was the astonishing aggression and energy of the Far Right, which was not interested in reducing government so much as stopping it altogether. The Tea Party caucus inside the Republican Party was a small, determined and well-funded group. As far as deficit reduction was concerned, they would accept only spending cuts. And the spending they wanted to stop, in particular, was Obamacare, which they regarded as a lethal "socialist" threat to America's future. The Republican leadership might worry about losing centrist votes. They knew that the budget crisis of 2011 had not played well with the electorate. But the most hard-core Tea Party advocates did not listen. To the Taliban of the Right, it was clear that Romney had lost because he was a moderate, compromising on immigration and health care. The only way to win back the electorate, at least the electorate in their gerrymandered Republican congressional districts, was to take the hardest line possible.

By January 2013 no cross-party agreement had been reached. The automatic sequester was put off for two months by stopgap legislation. Meanwhile, the debt limit was raised sufficiently to cover spending until May. With a substantial section of the Republicans agreeing to modest tax increases on the highest earners and on large inheritances, it seemed as though a crisis might be avoided. But the timeline was now pressing. On

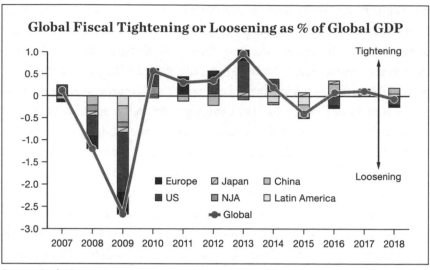

Source: Credit Suisse.

March 1 the sequester cuts came into full effect, hitting the budgets of the military, FEMA, the FBI, the FDA and the SEC. America's apparatus of government began to go into hibernation.[52] In 2013 the sluggish economic recovery in the United States would be further slowed down by a fiscal tightening equivalent to almost 1 percent of global GDP. The United States moved from being significantly more expansive than the EU in 2008–2009 to being far more contractionary.

Meanwhile, to keep basic government functions going, ad hoc spending authorizations were approved to cover the federal government through September. Crafting a proper budget for 2014 was more than Congress could manage. On March 21, March 23 and April 10, first the House, then the Senate, and finally the White House released separate budget proposals. The Senate and the White House were close together in terms of both the deficit reduction ($1.8–1.9 trillion over ten years) and the balance of spending cuts and tax increases they proposed.[53] The Republicans in the House were in a different world. They called for much bigger cuts ($4.6 trillion over ten years) to be achieved entirely by slashing spending. The House would not consider the Senate budget, and neither the Senate nor the House would vote on the White House proposal. The incoherence of US

fiscal policy was reaching a new pitch. On May 19 the debt ceiling was reinstated at a level that covered borrowing since suspension in February but without provision for any new debt. The Treasury was, therefore, forced back on the expedients it had resorted to in 2011, raiding government cash tills and running down reserve funds. By mid-October the Treasury would run out of money and be forced to prioritize bill payments. It would be tantamount to a selective default. To prepare for this contingency, mainstream Republicans in May 2013 proposed a bill to ensure that at least the government's bondholders were paid.[54] To John Boehner, the conventionally minded Republican leader in the House, this seemed like a sensible first step to order the federal government's affairs in case of bankruptcy. But the Democrats had no interest in making the unthinkable more manageable, and the proposal that Chinese creditors should be paid ahead of serving military and social security recipients made easy political meat. The Full Faith and Credit Act was soon dubbed the "Pay China First Act" and voted down by the Democrats. Obama announced that he would veto the bill if it passed.

With the summer having gone by without any movement toward a deal, on September 25 the Treasury announced that it would run out of cash on October 17, 2013. Nancy Pelosi appealed to Boehner to remember the sacrifice that the Democrats had made to pass the TARP program for President Bush.[55] But that cut no ice with a Republican majority that did not remember the Bush years fondly and was terrified of being outflanked on their right wing by the Tea Party caucus, for whom TARP and the bailouts were anathema. With the Republicans demanding swinging cuts and privatization of Medicare, no deal could be reached, and on October 1, 2013, at 12:01 a.m. Eastern Time, the government went into partial shutdown, with up to 850,000 federal employees put on temporary unpaid leave.[56] The White House was forced to suspend the president's foreign travel. At a meeting of APEC in Indonesia, the American president would not make his rendezvous with his Chinese counterpart. It was not until October 16, hours before the Treasury's final deadline, that the Senate passed a continuing resolution to fund the government through February 2014, a temporary expedient with which the Republican leadership fell into line once they realized the political damage they were suffering from the standoff.

IV

Though a disaster was avoided, it is important not to normalize what had happened. The radical right wing of the Republican Party, xenophobic nationalists, many of them evangelical zealots, motivated by a worldview fashioned by the alt-right, or Pat Buchanan's extreme America-first nationalism, a group whose hard core accounted for 10 percent of the House of Representatives, had threatened to paralyze the most important nation-state in the global system. As Steve Bannon, the editor of the Breitbart news site, a cheerleader of the Tea Party and a rising star of the alt-right, gushed to a *Daily Beast* journalist in November 2013: "I'm a Leninist. Lenin wanted to destroy the state, and that's my goal too. I want to bring everything crashing down, and destroy all of today's establishment."[57] For the likes of Bannon, the crisis of 2008 and the bailout had marked a fundamental caesura in American history. The morning of September 18, 2008, when Bernanke and Paulson's alarmism had scared President Bush into approving the TARP plan, was a fundamental turning point. It was a moment, according to Bannon, at which the threat of systemic collapse revealed the true power structure: "We are upside down; the industrial democracies today have a problem we have never had before; we are over-leveraged . . . and we have built a welfare state which is completely and totally unsupportable."[58] Only a no-holds-barred struggle against the liberal elite and the state they had constructed in their image could save America. If this discomforted the failed Republican establishment as well, all the better.

To challenge the power structure, Robert Reich had called for a new progressive age, a new civil rights movement, a movement unafraid to question the status quo at all levels. That challenge had arrived, but it came from the Right, not the Left. The world was aghast. In Japan, *Newsweek* appeared on newsstands declaring "Ruined America—a Superpower Destroys Itself." The *Wall Street Journal* reported on "Shutdownfreude" spreading across Europe, as for once it was America, not the eurozone, that was in the dock of global public opinion.[59] *Der Spiegel* commented bleakly: "The United States had embarrassed itself on the global stage. . . . Is this how a superpower behaves?"[60] One might respond that only a superpower could possibly

afford to behave like this. But how long would the United States be able to uphold that position if it was internally so at odds that it was unable to decide whether to honor its debts or pay its soldiers? Predictably, Xinhua, China's official news agency, took a dim view. Editorialist Liu Chang wrote: "As US politicians of both political parties are still shuffling back and forth between the White House and the Capitol Hill without striking a viable deal to bring normality to the body politic they brag about, it is perhaps a good time for the befuddled world to start considering building a de-Americanized world."[61] On a lighter note, a Canadian comic living in China commented: "Chinese must be wondering: When will America embrace real reform? How long can this system survive? Where is America's Gorbachev?"[62]

Nor was it only foreigners who were worried. If the Tea Party would turn the Republican Party into a vehicle for an attack on the creditworthiness of US government, what was safe? So far the Tea Party had made Obamacare its main target. What would be next? By 2014 the Republican Right would block immigration reform and refuse to fund the Export-Import Bank, both priorities of American business. At the G20 the Americans were embarrassed to report that funding for the IMF was being held hostage by Republican opponents of abortion who wanted contraception excluded from Obamacare.[63] What if the Republican zealots targeted Fed independence or trade policy next?

Of course, there were business interests aligned with the Tea Party on tax and welfare issues. The coal lobby wanted environmental regulation stripped away. A clique of right-wing oligarchs saw the movement as the vehicle for a cultural and socioeconomic counterrevolution.[64] But with the 2013 budget fight, the mainstream of the American business leadership could no longer ignore the problem. Over the winter of 2013–2014, the Chamber of Commerce mobilized not to fight organized labor but to resist the Republican insurgency. "No fools on our ticket" was the Chamber's slogan for the 2014 midterms, a euphemism for excluding the Tea Party.[65] A spokesman for the Chamber put it this way: "The crowd that wants to come to Washington and blow the place up and shut the place down, that's a threshold issue for us. . . . We care about governing."[66]

By 2014 the signs of realignment were undeniable. While the Tea Party inveigled against "special interests" that had "come to dominate our political

culture," "self-serving politicians" and "the interfering strong hand of a powerful elite," it was Democratic candidates who advertised themselves as "business friendly."[67] As Senator Chuck Schumer of New York put it, "Democrats and business are on the same side on a range of issues. . . . The Tea Party has dragged the Republican Party so far to the right that business is now closer to mainstream Democrats than Republicans."[68] The alignment that had first become clear during the bank bailout of 2008 was becoming something more entrenched. In the name of nationalism and the American Dream, the right wing claimed the cause of systemic change, while the Democratic Party establishment filled the middle ground the Republicans vacated. The question of the comprehensive progressive campaign to fight for greater equality was left begging.

Chapter 20

TAPER TANTRUM

That the astonishing events in Congress in 2013 did not lead to an immediate crisis in the bond market pointed to the resilience of the US Treasurys as the global safe asset of choice. Though the Chinese and Germans might complain and the market blipped, demand for US Treasurys quickly recovered. Ultimately, the market for IOUs drawn on the American taxpayer was underwritten by the Fed. Unlike the ECB, America's central bank left no doubt that it backed its government's debt. QE3 bond purchases provided immediate support, keeping prices up and rates down. This provided at least one point of stability for global investors. But after the events of 2013 questions could no longer be avoided. Was one of the unintended side effects of the stability generated by the Fed to free politics from market constraints and thus enable Republican extremism? Did America's ability to ride out short-term budget crises like those of 2011 and 2013 lead contemporaries to underestimate the future dangers that the degeneration of American democracy might bring with it? And how long would the Fed's technocratic interventions compensate for America's lackluster economic recovery and the shambles in the legislative branch? How long could the Fed continue with QE3? When would the Fed begin tapering? Compared with the chaos in fiscal policy, these were, on the face of it, "normal" monetary policy questions, except that since 2008 there was no longer any such thing as normal monetary policy. The enormous expansion

of the Fed balance sheet underpinned not just the US banking system but the entire global dollar system. Furthermore, the Fed had not just expanded its balance sheet, it had changed its composition. Buying up long-term securities in exchange for cash reserves, the Fed had absorbed onto its books the maturity mismatch that had undone the shadow banking system. After successive phases of QE, it was the Fed that held long-term securities that were matched against short-term liabilities such as cash and deposits by American and European banks.

Despite some nail biting by inflation hawks, this posed no immediate stability risk. The banks were happy to hold their cash reserves with the Fed. If interest rates went up, the Fed, as one of the largest holders of bonds, would suffer a capital loss. But this was more than made up for by the $350 billion in profits that the Fed paid to the Treasury between 2008 and 2013.[1] The real question was the likely fallout in the financial markets and money markets when the Fed changed its stance. Any move to moderate the Fed's bond purchases, let alone to unwind its position, implied a comprehensive adjustment in the willingness of the markets to absorb not only a greater volume of bonds but also some of the maturity mismatch that the Fed was carrying. And that would have to happen at the same time as short-term interest rates were nudging up. If, on the other hand, the Fed continued QE3, its balance sheet would further inflate, bond prices would remain elevated, interest rates would remain stuck near zero and imbalances would further accumulate. In 2008 the Fed had embarked on a vertiginous tightrope walk from which there was no way back to the certainties of the great moderation.

I

Both at home and abroad, the Fed's low interest rate policy created a superheated investment climate. By its bond-purchasing program, which pushed up bond prices and depressed yields, the Fed incentivized investors to shift out of bonds and to place their funds in higher-risk, higher-return assets. How far this impulse actually went to explain the stock market boom is debatable. The econometric evidence is strongest for the impact of QE1 in

Propping Up the Markets? The Association (Possibly Spurious) of the S&P 500 and the Fed's Balance Sheet

Source: Federal Reserve Economic Database (FRED).

launching the first phase of the stock market recovery in 2009.[2] But for the average Wall Street booster, the visual association between the Fed's balance sheet and the surging value of the S&P 500 was plenty to be going along with. As a strategist for Citigroup told the *Financial Times*, "Everything revolves around monetary policy. It's not the underlying economics that's driving things, it's central bank liquidity."[3] In 2008 the Fed had intervened to stop the market from imploding. It had pumped trillions into the financial system. Now the markets hung on its every word.

Investors looked for higher yields not just in US equities but further afield. Dollars were cheap for everyone. Any investor who was willing to take a gamble on exchange rate movements could borrow cheaply in dollars and invest in high-yielding emerging markets. Assuming the dollar did not sharply appreciate before the debt was due, it would be a profitable carry trade.[4] By the middle of 2015, governments and businesses outside America would pile up $9.8 trillion of debts denominated in dollars.[5] Much of this went to rich, developed world economies. But $3.3 trillion was owed by

emerging market borrowers, both government and private. From the point of view of the yield-chasing investor, the more exotic the securities the better. In September 2012 Zambia issued its first dollar-denominated bond. With a modest 5.6 percent coupon, a $750 million offering attracted more than $11 billion in bids.[6] A year later a state-backed tuna-fishing venture in Mozambique raised $850 million. Altogether, African sovereign borrowers garnered $17 billion in bond funding in 2012–2013.[7] In May 2013 the boom reached its peak, with the $11 billion ten-year bond issued by Petrobas, Brazil's state-owned oil company. It was the largest bond issue ever by an emerging market corporation. Demand was so great that the yield on the Petrobas issue fell to as little as 4.35 percent, less than many sovereign borrowers.[8]

This global interest in emerging market debt was exciting from the point of view of the borrowers. But it also exposed them to serious risks. Huge, aggressively managed funds crowded into tight markets. As the IMF pointed out, given that the largest five hundred asset management companies had more than $70 trillion in their portfolios, a 1 percent reallocation implied a flow in or out of an asset class of $700 billion. This was enough either to swamp or to starve the emerging markets. The withdrawal of funds that had caused such stress in 2008 around the periphery of the world economy had amounted to only $246 billion. The unprecedented inflow that transformed the outlook of those same economies in 2012 was $368 billion.[9] This disproportion created risk for the borrowers. But it was potentially bad news for the investors as well. If there was to be a sudden wave of withdrawals, the small size of emerging financial markets would amplify the stampede effect.[10] If the Fed reversed its policy and money flooded back to the United States, who would be the first to sell? Who would get out without fatal losses?

According to BIS data, professionally managed funds increased their stake in emerging market equity and bonds from $900 billion to $1.4 trillion between 2008 and 2014.[11] Set against global totals running into the tens of trillions, those were not huge numbers. But they were comparable to the stock of toxic subprime assets, which had caused such havoc in 2007–2008, and to the debts of Greece, Spain and Ireland, which had destabilized the eurozone in 2010–2012. After subprime and after eurozone

sovereign debt, were emerging markets to be the next volume in the "trilogy" of debt crises?[12]

Not for nothing the financial officials of booming emerging markets like Brazil complained about the influx of hot money from the United States. At the G20 in Seoul in November 2010 they had lambasted Bernanke for adopting QE2, dropping US interest rates and allowing the dollar to slide. By 2013 many emerging markets had gone beyond the war of words to adopt capital controls. Brazil, South Korea, Thailand, Indonesia all took steps to slow the inflow of funds and curb the appreciation of their currencies. Fifteen years earlier in the heyday of the "Washington consensus" this would have put them beyond the pale. Restraining international capital movement was a retreat from the most fundamental liberalizing policy of the 1970s and 1980s. But the advocates of the market revolution had foreseen neither the emerging market crises of the 1990s nor monetary policy on the scale of QE. Faced with the giant flux of the global credit cycle, amplified by spillover effects from the Fed's crisis fighting, controls on capital inflows were grudgingly accepted as a pragmatic necessity, even by the IMF.[13] It was, the *Economist* magazine commented, "as if the Vatican had given its blessing to birth control."[14]

II

As far as the markets were concerned, everything depended on when and how the Fed changed course. Back in September 2013 Bernanke had made the giant bond-buying program of QE3 that was soaking the world in dollar liquidity conditional on America's labor market. He had promised that interest rates would stay at rock bottom until unemployment fell below 6.5 percent. In the spring of 2013, with the US economy beginning to edge toward that threshold, the Fed began to drop hints. The moment was approaching at which it would consider slowing the pace of asset purchases. It was a delicate game. The Fed didn't want to "taper" too abruptly. The labor market was not yet fully recovered. The sluggish recovery that was troubling Larry Summers might not withstand a sudden spike in interest rates. For the investors, on the other hand, it was crucial to be ahead of the

game. If they knew that the Fed was going to raise rates in the foreseeable future and that bond prices would fall, they wanted to be the first to sell. Of course, no one could know for sure whether the Fed would indeed begin to taper or precisely when. So another reason to sell was to test the Fed's resolve. As Richard Fisher, chair of the Dallas Fed and himself a former hedge fund manager, put it to the *Financial Times* in characteristically colorful terms: "Markets tend to test things. . . . We haven't forgotten what happened to the Bank of England [when George Soros broke the pounds peg in the ESM in September 1992]. I don't think anyone can break the Fed . . . but I do believe that big money does organize itself somewhat like feral hogs. If they detect a weakness or a bad scent, they'll go after it."[15] For Fisher, given this tendency to herding, it "made sense" for the Fed "to socialise the idea that quantitative easing is not a one-way street." But given the likely impact on the fragile recovery of a large step up in interest rates, Fisher did not expect Bernanke to go from "Wild Turkey to 'cold turkey' overnight." The feral hogs should beware of getting ahead of themselves.

On May 22, 2013, Bernanke took the plunge. He told Congress, "If we see continued improvement and we have confidence that that is going to be sustained, then in the next few meetings, we could take a step down in our pace of purchases."[16] The markets skipped a beat. Then, at 2:15 p.m. on June 19, 2013, Bernanke made a more specific announcement. Conditional on continued positive economic data, the FOMC would vote on scaling back its monthly bond purchases from $85 billion to $65 billion at the upcoming September 2013 policy meeting. The bond-buying program might wrap up entirely by mid-2014. Despite weeks of preparation, Bernanke's statement triggered a full-scale "taper tantrum." In a matter of seconds yields surged from 2.17 to 2.3 percent. Two days later they had risen to 2.55 percent and would peak at 2.66 percent. These were small changes in absolute terms, but amounted to an increase in interest costs of almost 25 percent and inflicted a correspondingly serious capital loss on bondholders. US equity markets reacted in sympathy, losing 4.3 percent in a matter of days.

In the emerging markets Bernanke's May announcement had already been enough to provoke a violent reaction. If the Fed reduced its purchases, bond prices began to ease and yields nudged upward, the emerging markets would come under a double pressure. Not only would their rates have to

adjust by at least the same amount as the United States, but they would face an amplification effect through the exchange rate. As the *Economist* explained, a "stock of dollar debt is like a short position," i.e., a speculative position assuming that the dollar exchange rate will either remain level or fall.[17] A Fed interest rate increase signaled not only higher borrowing costs but a likely upward movement in the dollar. Exposed emerging market borrowers would run to cover their dollar exposure, amplifying the currency adjustment and increasing the pressure on other dollar borrowers. Already in the spring of 2013, as markets began to worry about Bernanke's next move, the emerging markets felt the pressure. For the emerging markets the funding boom was over. The exchange rates of what Morgan Stanley dubbed the "Fragile Five"—Turkey, Brazil, India, South Africa and Indonesia—declined precipitously. Western investors pulled their money.[18] Interest rates went up to counter the "vacuum cleaner" effect of Fed policy.[19] Capital controls put in place to curb excessive inflows did not prevent foreign money from leaving. But they limited the scale of the damage. As one Brazilian central banker remarked: "We knew this was going to come, and we prepared ourselves."[20]

Stern American observers noted that the global credit cycle was not fate.[21] Countries that had allowed their currencies to appreciate had been subject to a smaller inflow of funds. Nor, when the global credit cycle reversed, did everyone lose funding at the same pace. Among the emerging markets the hardest hit were those with less than fully sound financial positions. The Fed tightening was going to be tough for everyone, but if they did not put their budgets in order, they had only themselves to blame.[22] That made sense as a moral message and it conveniently deflected responsibility from the United States. It was up to the emerging markets to look after themselves. But it did not turn out to be well supported by the evidence. The biggest losers among the emerging markets, in fact, tended to be those that had attracted the largest foreign inflows, which also tended to be those with the most solid financial records.[23] In any case, home truths about fiscal discipline came late for those now facing a funding squeeze. Some buckled down. Raghuram Rajan, the onetime critic of financial market euphoria and former chief economist of the IMF, now earned his spurs as India's central bank governor by raising rates and stabilizing the rupee.[24] But the

taper tantrum was a test of political as well as financial resilience. Not all governments responded with equanimity to such abrupt external pressure.

When QE taper talk hit the Turkish currency in May 2013, President Erdoğan was struggling with a dramatic domestic challenge as protesters clashed with riot police in Istanbul's Gezi Park.[25] Erdoğan had no doubt about how to interpret this coincidence. It was no coincidence at all. The internal political and external financial pressures on his government were part of a "conspiracy by unspecified foreign forces, bankers, and international and local media outlets" to push for regime change.[26] For Erdoğan, the pressure was being applied to all the countries that dared to claim a new place for themselves on the world stage—countries like Brazil and Turkey. "[T]he symbols are the same, the posters are the same, Twitter, Facebook are the same, the international media is the same. They are being led from the same center . . . the same game, the same trap, the same aim." The masters of social media in Silicon Valley, the crusading liberals at the State Department and the Fed were all in on it. In an inflammatory speech he denounced the connections between Turkish private banks, international capital groups and, according to at least one report, Israel. "Who won from these three-week long [sic] demonstrations?" President Erdoğan asked. "The interest lobby won. The enemies of Turkey won."[27] Foreign experts might insist that Turkey had simply to put its economic house in order, but Erdoğan had other ideas. Frustrated with the EU's failure to proceed with Turkish accession negotiations and the Obama administration's failure to act in Syria, he lurched toward Moscow. Turkey, Ankara let it be known, would welcome membership in the Economic Cooperation Organization founded by Russia and China in Shanghai.[28] Compared with the capricious West, the Russia-China axis seemed to promise stability.

At the G20 in Saint Petersburg on September 5–6, 2013, as the world waited to see how the Fed's Open Market Committee would vote, the tone was more measured than that from Ankara, but the message was loud and clear. The Fed needed to acknowledge that everyone, including the United States, was living in an "interdependent world." The finance ministers of both Brazil and Indonesia demanded more clarity from Bernanke. China, which was exposed to the United States not just through trade but also through its giant dollar bond holding, was no less vociferous. As one official

spokesman put it: "Given that U.S. monetary policy has a huge influence on emerging markets and the global economy, we hope that U.S. monetary policy authorities, whether exiting or scaling down stimulus, will not only consider the U.S.'s own economic needs but also think about economic circumstances in emerging markets."[29] Rajan was the emerging market spokesman with the highest personal profile in the United States. During the crisis of 2008, he reminded America, the emerging markets had undertaken "huge fiscal and monetary stimulus" in support of global growth. The industrialized countries could not now "wash their hands . . . and say we'll do what we need to and you do the adjustment. . . . We need better cooperation and unfortunately that has not been forthcoming so far."[30]

"Interdependence" was one of the nostrums of the age of globalization. And it was all very well to call for greater cooperation. But why should the Fed listen to such demands? In 2008 it had provided liquidity to the entire world economy. Now it was doing its best to sustain the revival. But its mandate was national. It was responsible for the American economy, not the wider world. As far as the Fed was concerned, the really compelling argument was that of blowback. This was what had clinched the case for the massive swap line action in 2008. And this was the point made in the fall of 2013 by IMF managing director Christine Lagarde. The reverberations from the Fed's huge monetary shocks, she warned Washington, "may well feed back to where they began," i.e., back on the United States.[31] But it was one thing for the Fed to acknowledge that Europe's megabanks might bring the house down. It was quite another to make the same claim for the emerging markets. Looking at the numbers, no one could seriously argue that the business cycles of Indonesia or India had much impact on US financial stability.[32] The interdependence of the global age was all pervasive, but it was emphatically not symmetrical. Some received shocks, others dealt them out.

In any case, given that Republican insurgents were in the process of shutting down the federal government, and were eyeing the IMF's budget as a potential hostage, it would have been politically disastrous for the Fed to acknowledge that it was conditioning its latest policy move on business conditions in Indonesia. Instead, the protests from the emerging markets provided a convenient occasion for the Fed to make a stout show of

American patriotism. As Dennis Lockhart, president of the Atlanta Fed, reassured Bloomberg TV in August 2013: "You have to remember that we are a legal creature of Congress and that we only have a mandate to concern ourselves with the interest of the United States. . . . Other countries simply have to take that as a reality and adjust to us if that's something important for their economies." James Bullard of the Saint Louis Fed emphasized the same point: "We're not going to make policy based on emerging-market volatility alone."[33]

III

Then, on September 18, came the Fed's long-awaited decision. After the buildup since May, the FOMC announced that it would leave interest rates where they were and continue bond buying at the current rate, pending "more evidence that progress will be sustained."[34] The taper, the prospect of which had been giving the markets jitters since May, was off.

The decision to change nothing unleashed a frenzy of interpretation not about the likelihood of tapering but about why it had not happened. Were the doves on the Fed board resisting an interest rate shock? Had Bernanke got cold feet? Was he kicking the can down the road for his successor to deal with?[35] Or was the Fed consistent in its policy, but bad at forecasting? Between the spring of 2013, when it began to think about tapering, and September, when it decided to postpone it, the Fed had adjusted its forecast for economic growth sharply downward.[36] If the economy was recovering less strongly than expected, this would rescue the Fed's reputation as a consistent policy maker, but at the price of undermining confidence in its forecasts and highlighting the downturn in expectations. Or was the Fed neither cowardly nor a bad forecaster? Was it playing a subtle tactical game? If it was committed to ensuring that the US economy completed its slow recovery without interruption from a premature and violent increase in rates, it needed to know how severely bond markets would react to a reduction in monetary stimulus. The evidence of the taper tantrum in June 2013 was clear. The markets were impatient. Investors would rapidly tighten credit conditions on any hint of movement by the Fed. If the Fed believed

that what was necessary was something more gradual, then after the initial tapering announcements in May and June, it needed to shock markets a third time in the opposite direction, letting them know that though tapering was coming, it was not a one-way bet.[37]

Four different interpretations: Fed politics, Fed weakness, Fed forecasting error, Fed game playing. Which was it? How were markets to know, and without knowing, how were they to react? Given the Fed's hesitancy, one might have expected the bond vigilantes to take up the fight. There was profound hostility to Bernanke among the more militant investor crowd. In October 2013 Larry Fink, the CEO of BlackRock, the largest asset manager, accused the Fed of feeding "bubble-like" market conditions.[38] His chief investment officer for fixed income complained that there were "tremendous distortions" building in interest rates.[39] But there was no unanimity in the market. Bill Gross at Allianz-PIMCO argued that investors should accept the inevitable. If the aim of the Fed was to engineer a gradual exit from the gigantic debt bubble of the boom years—what Ray Dalio at the Bridgewater hedge fund called "beautiful deleveraging"—bond investors would have to accept that this came at their expense.[40] They should abandon their expectation of an imminent increase in rates. "Right now the market (and the Fed forecasts) expects fed funds to be 1 percent higher by late 2015 and 1 percent higher still by December 2016. Bet against that. . . . In betting on a lower policy rate than now priced into markets, a bond investor should expect a certain pastoral quietude in future years, much like that grazing cow, I suppose. Not that exciting, but what the hay, it's an existence! . . . Mother Nature nor Mother Market cares not a whit for your losses nor your hoped for double-digit return from an equity/bond portfolio that is priced for much less. Be a contented cow, not a voracious crow, and graze wisely with increasing certainty that the Fed and its forward guidance is your best bet for survival."[41]

With trillions of dollars at stake and markets feverishly trying to second-guess the Fed's policy, was Bill Gross's pastoral image not wishful thinking? Rather than a herd grazing contentedly, to the *Financial Times* it seemed that relations between the markets and the Fed were increasingly coming to resemble the contorted psychodrama of a rocky marriage. Investors might take Gross's advice and "practice believing that central banks

love me." But the refrain hid deep tensions and uncertainties. For the past five years, under the influence of massive Fed stimulus, investor strategies had come to resemble one another, leaving them to second-guess themselves, one another and the central bank: "What are you thinking? What are you feeling? What have we done to each other? What will we do?—a refrain equally applicable to a concerned policy maker as a nervous husband.... The whole thing reeks of a marriage built on shaky foundations."[42] At any given moment the balance might be upset by a shift in policy or a market mood swing. The consequences for the entire global economy would be "deeply unpredictable."[43]

IV

"I will practice believing that the Fed loves me" was also the prescription that foreign central bankers would have to follow. The decision not to halt QE3 eased pressure on emerging markets. India's rupee, which had been hardest hit by the taper tantrum, rebounded from 68 to the dollar to 61.9 to the dollar in early October.[44] Indonesia's currency stopped its precipitous slide. This was a relief. But Rajan and his colleagues would have to believe that the Fed bore them in mind despite the fact that Congress jealously watched over the Fed's exclusively American mandate and despite the fact that the Fed had made its decision while ostentatiously flaunting its indifference to the rest of the world. All the more significant was what the Fed did behind the scenes. On October 31, 2013, in the weeks following the September taper pullback and the congressional budget standoff, the Fed, the ECB, the Bank of Japan, the Bank of England, the Bank of Canada and the Swiss National Bank made a low-key, joint announcement:

"[T]heir existing temporary bilateral liquidity swap arrangements are being converted to standing arrangements, that is, arrangements that will remain in place until further notice. The standing arrangements will constitute a network of bilateral swap lines among the six central banks. These arrangements allow for the provision of liquidity in each jurisdiction in any of the five currencies foreign to that jurisdiction, should the two central banks in a particular bilateral swap arrangement judge that market

conditions warrant such action in one of their currencies. The existing temporary swap arrangements have helped to ease strains in financial markets and mitigate their effects on economic conditions. The standing arrangements will continue to serve as a prudent liquidity backstop."[45]

The swap lines that had been so crucial to stabilizing global financial markets and which had been uncapped in October 2008 were now being established on a permanent basis.[46] As in 2008, this network had limits. None of the most fragile emerging markets were included in the inner core of the Fed's swap network. But they were not left out in the cold either. What began to take shape were regional subnetworks. These were uneven. There was nothing of note around the core European central banks. But in Asia the central banks were more active. In September 2013, as anxiety about the Fed's tapering rose to a crescendo, India negotiated an increase in its existing swap line arrangement with Japan from $10 billion to $50 billion. In December Japan doubled the swap line facilities it offered to Indonesia and the Philippines and announced that it would be looking to negotiate similar bargains with Singapore, Thailand and Malaysia.[47] Japan's enormous reserve holdings of dollar assets, second only to those of China's, gave it the means to offer such facilities. And in the event of a crisis, the Bank of Japan could always draw on the Fed. Thus dollar liquidity would percolate out through the entire system.

As in 2008–2009, in 2013 the public bluster about the need for a new monetary order and a "de-Americanized world" distracted from the reality that a powerful new network of liquidity provision was being rolled out across the world economy. The swap-lines story stayed buried on the interior pages of the *Financial Times* and the *Wall Street Journal*.[48] There was no fanfare, no new Bretton Woods Conference. There was also no congressional or parliamentary approval. These were administrative measures. But they were also far more than that. Five years on from the crisis, while markets remained unsettled and the American political system was racked by dissension, the global dollar system was being given a new and unprecedentedly expansive foundation.

About the technical efficacy of the swap lines there was little doubt. Their political legitimacy was a different matter. And in the autumn of 2013 one couldn't help thinking of another of America's technical systems of

power that had been revealed earlier that year: the NSA's electronic surveillance network.[49] The network that Edward Snowden exposed in early June also centered on US power and technological capacity. It too was no American monolith. Like the Fed, the NSA worked through local agencies. It too promised to provide a blanket of security for the United States and its allies. Of course spying and exchanging currencies were not the same things. But they did have in common that their functional power and administrative efficacy were not matched by anything resembling public political authorization. They were testimony, at one and the same time, to the continuing significance of US global power and the difficulty in justifying that power in public either in the United States or in the countries whose governments and business interests were enrolled in America's network.

Chapter 21

"F*** THE EU": THE UKRAINE CRISIS

Before 2008 the driver of crisis was expected to be the balance of financial terror between the United States and China. A huge unwinding of the global disequilibrium centered on China and America and driven by profound domestic imbalances in each of them would, it was feared, rock American power to its foundations. In 2008 the expansion of the EU and NATO in the face of Russian opposition had added another dimension of risk. Georgia and Russia had clashed and Moscow had approached Beijing to mount a joint attack on America's fragile finances. Beijing had held back. There was no great dollar selloff. The geoeconomic course of the crisis took an unexpected and innovative direction. The Fed's liquidity swap lines stabilized the dollar-based financial system. In November 2008 the upgrading of the G20 had added a global leadership forum and this had been important in legitimizing the dramatic expansion of IMF resources in 2009. This backstopped the IMF's urgent engagement in Eastern Europe. A year later, remarkably, the IMF would find itself committing hundreds of billions of dollars to rescuing the eurozone. At the same time, the United States was aggressively pushing a new system of regulation for global banking through the normally slow-moving Basel Committee.

In 2008 and 2009 Washington kept ahead of the geoeconomic challenges unleashed by the crisis. Could it stay on pace? In May 2010 the Obama administration and the IMF were crucial to forcing the Europeans

toward the first fix for the eurozone. But then things began to get sticky. November 2010 was a turning point. The Democrats lost control of Congress. The recovery was so lame and the fiscal impasse so threatening that the Fed launched its cautious second wave of QE, to be met with violent opposition at the G20 meeting in Seoul. But carping at the G20 was one thing. When it came to chaperoning the Europeans through the near disaster of 2011 and 2012 it was obvious that only the Obama administration could serve as a counterbalance to Germany. Obama was right. At least as far as Europe was concerned, the United States as an "inside outside" arbiter was indispensable. But with the stabilization of Europe and the beginning of the second Obama administration, the questions of the Bush era returned.[1] Should Washington maintain its massive global footprint? Could it safely withdraw? Would either internal constraints or external pressures allow this to be decided as a matter of deliberate choice? Would it be an orderly retreat, leaving a legacy of stability, or would it be a disorderly rout?

I

Impelled as she was by the energy and sense of mission that descended from the 1990s as well as her own ambitions for the presidency, Hillary Clinton, as secretary of state, was in the proactive camp. In the autumn of 2011, as it finalized the pullout from Iraq, Clinton's State Department tried to get back on the front foot. The "pivot to Asia" was its new initiative.[2] In military terms this consisted of the redeployment of a carrier battle group to the Pacific. In economic terms it axed on the Trans-Pacific Partnership (TPP). As Europe slid deeper into crisis in 2011, the US Treasury and trade representative pressured Canada and Mexico to join them in a wide-ranging trade and investment treaty with the leading economies of Asia, not including China. The aim was not to face China down, let alone to stop its economic growth. Everyone had too much to gain. The aim was to establish a bloc strong enough to offer a counterweight to China's rising strength. It was, as one of Hillary Clinton's indiscreet correspondents dubbed it, a "de facto China containment alliance."[3]

Back to 1947 containment was the glue that held together the powerful

alliance network that the United States had constructed in Western Europe and East Asia. That alliance system massively extended America's reach. It was the grounds on which committed liberal internationalists defended the idea that America remained a hegemonic force.[4] But it also exposed the United States to risk. Containment could be given different shadings, and those depended as much on America's allies as on any decision in Washington. The allies had their own politics and their own economic problems. Their enrollment in America's sphere, whether through finance, trade or security policy, excited those interests further. From Beijing's point of view, America's Asian pivot took on a distinctly darker coloration with the election in December 2012 of the nationalist politician Shinzo Abe as the Japanese prime minister. Abe was deeply concerned about China's power. He was unabashed in his support for a stronger and more independent Japanese military. And he was also willing to override domestic economic interests for the sake of strategic cooperation with the United States. He was even willing to sacrifice Japan's rice farmers to make his country into a key pillar of TPP.[5] If he was willing to do that, what else might he do? By 2014 there was talk of a war scare between Japan and China.

Corralling South Korea, Australia, Japan and Vietnam into the American geoeconomic alliance system was, if anything, too easy. Their interest in containing China was obvious. The risk was that America's new engagement with Asia would harden positions and trigger regional clashes, which were not in America's interests. That was not the case with the Europeans. But by the same token, their enrollment in the project of containing China was less reliable. The EU was deeply interested in Chinese trade and investment. Germany wanted to sell cars and engineering equipment. When they tired of the endless battles in the eurozone, Berlin's policy elite liked to fantasize about a global future in partnership with Beijing.[6] The City of London was angling for a special position in the internationalization of the RMB.[7] Nor were the Americans the only ones pursuing an expansive geoeconomic strategy.

In October 2013, on his way to the APEC meeting in Bali, President Xi Jinping announced China's new investment bank proposal. It was a bold multilateral initiative to upgrade Asia's infrastructure. Everyone was invited to join. It was a leaf straight out of America's own playbook, and

Washington did not like it. The Obama administration let it be known that it did not approve the Chinese initiative, and South Korea, Japan and Australia promptly fell into line.[8] But the UK, which was doing everything possible to court Chinese business, took up the offer from Beijing to become a founding member of the Asian Infrastructure Investment Bank.[9] Washington was furious.[10] London had made its decision, a State Department official let it be known, without prior consultation. America did not approve the "trend toward constant accommodation of China, which is not the best way to engage a rising power."[11] But London wasn't listening, nor were the other Europeans who promptly signed up too. Asked about US opposition, one British official commented wryly that it must be difficult for the Obama administration to conduct international economic policy under current political conditions. If Congress wouldn't approve a tiny increase in China's IMF quota, what was to be expected on trade and investment? "They couldn't have got congressional approval to join the AIIB, even if they wanted to."[12] Indeed, thanks to the congressional shutdown, Obama was prevented from attending APEC's Bali meeting. America's domestic political problems were spilling over into the conduct of global strategy and the world was not going to wait.

Given the stresses that the United States was evidently under, it might have made sense to invert Kissinger's famous move in the 1970s and to seek a closer relationship with Russia as part of the effort to contain China. It is unclear whether Washington was ever willing to take Russia seriously as a strategic partner, at the level even of Japan or Saudi Arabia.[13] In 2009 the Obama administration did set out to build better relations. With Medvedev as president, the "reset" seemed promising. To promote his modernizing agenda, Medvedev was invited to tour Silicon Valley in the company of Governor Schwarzenegger.[14] Russian business eagerly seized the opportunities offered by cheap dollar funding. In 2011 Medvedev was compliant over NATO's intervention in Libya, so much so that it provoked a counterreaction in Moscow. Putin, biding his time in the number two position as prime minister watching footage of Gaddafi's horrible fate, became morbidly preoccupied. The same Western powers that had shamelessly courted the Libyan dictator had turned on him, bombing his military and delivering him to the vengeful mob. One would be a fool to trust them. Medvedev's

appeasement would only invite further aggression. Putin would have to take back control. This decision was only confirmed when Moscow erupted in protests over the winter of 2011–2012 following rigged parliamentary elections. Clinton barely disguised her enthusiasm for regime change. Instead of reset and détente, Putin returned to the presidency in 2012 with new determination. In opposition to the liberalism of the Obama administration, the Kremlin donned the garb of conservative cultural nationalism. Gay rights, feminist pop provocateurs and the Greek yogurt rations for America's Olympic athletes all got sucked into a postmodern rerun of the cold war.[15]

It was certainly not the balancing against China that one might have expected. But nor was it the Americans who brought about the open crisis in relations between Russia and the West. It was America's most important ally, the Europeans. The EU would later claim that it "sleepwalked" into the Ukraine crisis. This was part of a piece with its guileless insistence that "the EU does not do geopolitics."[16] That perhaps described the naïveté of some officials in Brussels, but it never really rang true. It would be fairer to say that European nation-states did not agree on the geopolitics they were pursuing by way of the EU. France and Berlin loved the détente with Moscow. Poland and Sweden did not. With active support from NATO, the "new Europeans" championed the EU's Eastern Partnership with the post-Soviet states. It was no secret in Warsaw or Riga that this, like TPP, was a "de facto containment" policy. As far as Poland was concerned, the priority was clear. In the words of President Bronislaw Komorowski: "Never again do we want to have a common border with Russia."[17]

The instruments of the EU's Eastern Partnership were EU Association Agreements. These were complex documents harmonizing regulations, liberalizing trade and the movement of workers. The agreement with Ukraine, initialed in 2012, was hailed as the most extensive agreement ever completed with a non-EU member. It ran to 1,200 pages of technical detail, subdivided into the twenty-eight separate subsections of the *acquis communautaire*.[18] Trade and business regulations were the main focus of the Association Agreements, but they were not innocent with regard to security policy. Article 4 of the Ukraine Association Agreement called for "political dialogue in all areas of mutual interest. . . . This will promote gradual

convergence on foreign and security matters with the aim of Ukraine's ever-deeper involvement in the European security area."[19] Article 7 provided for "EU-Ukrainian convergence in foreign affairs, security and defence." Under Article 10 on "Conflict prevention, crisis management and military–technological cooperation," Ukraine and the EU were to "explore the potential of military and technological cooperation. Ukraine and the European Defence Agency (EDA) will establish close contacts to discuss military capability improvement, including technological issues."[20]

By 2013 talks with Ukraine were the most advanced. But the EU's Eastern Partnership negotiations proceeded on a broad front. At a summit conference in Vilnius on November 29–30, 2013, Brussels was hoping not only to sign the Association Agreement with Ukraine but to initial agreements with Moldova, Georgia and Armenia. Brussels had also been negotiating with Belarus.[21] After incorporating the Baltics and the East European Warsaw Pact in the early 2000s, Brussels was now seeking to deepen and transform its relations with the rest of what had once been the western Soviet Union. It was undeniably a major shift in international relations and it was all the more significant for the fact that it clashed directly with Russia's ambitions for the region. Since 2011 Russia had been developing its Eurasian Customs Union into a more comprehensive Eurasian Economic Union. It was clearly intended as an alternative to the EU's Eastern Partnership. The details of its agreements were far less onerous than those demanded by the EU. But they meant entering into a lopsided relationship with Russia, and the customs union included setting a common external tariff. This was incompatible with the EU Association Agreement.

With goodwill a compromise between the EU's Association Agreements and the Eurasian Customs Union could no doubt have been worked out. But that was not the mood on either side. The technical and economic issues of harmonizing two different economic blocs were overlaid by geopolitical tension whether Brussels acknowledged it or not. There was a choice to be made: Did the East European governments want to face west or east? Brussels let it be known that membership in Putin's Eurasian Union was incompatible with an EU Association Agreement. Commission president Barroso refused the Kremlin's invitation for negotiations between the two blocs.[22] Brussels did not accept their equivalence. In the absence of any

agreement between the two, Moscow informed Ukraine and Armenia that if they proceeded with the EU, they should expect sanctions from Russia. Signing an Association Agreement would be a "suicidal step."[23] Under the anodyne labels of association, cooperation and convergence, a heavy geopolitical weight was being imposed on a fragile region under considerable economic and political stress.

II

Across the post-Soviet world, the economic and political recovery from the shock of 2008 was uneven. On the northern flank, the Baltics continued on their course toward the West. Estonia joined the euro on January 1, 2011. Latvia, the pivotal crisis country of 2009, adopted the common currency on January 1, 2014, followed a year later by Lithuania. The rest of Eastern Europe was supposed, under the terms of their 2004 accession, to join the euro in due course too. But progress in that direction was set back severely by the eurozone crisis. Polish foreign minister Sikorski announced in December 2011 that he looked forward to Poland joining the euro by 2016, but only if the currency union was reformed and it was clearly in Poland's national interest to do so.[24] Donald Tusk, as prime minister, promised to launch a national debate on euro membership. But the main opposition, the nationalist Law and Justice party, promptly responded by denouncing any further steps toward European integration as "subordination to Germany."[25]

In Poland the nationalists were in opposition. In Hungary they were the government. In the April 2010 election, the ruling Socialist Party paid the price for its corrupt and duplicitous handling of economic policy and the financial disaster of 2008. Promising to protect the Hungarian nation and Hungarian pensioners from the depredations of the IMF, a coalition headed by the nationalist Fidesz party and the Christian Democrats won 53 percent of the vote. Even more startlingly, the Jobbik movement, which toyed openly with neofascism, scored 17 percent, bringing the total nationalist vote to 70 percent. Among Fidesz's heresies was its refusal to separate the questions of political sovereignty and financial dependence. Ignoring protests from the IMF and the EU, it justified its taxes on foreign banks and a

raid on private pension funds in terms of harsh historical necessity.[26] Since freeing itself from the Soviet yoke, over the past twenty years Hungary "had to bitterly experience the validity and truth of the old wisdom that a nation can be subjugated in two ways—with the sword or with debt."[27] As Greece was submitting itself to the troika in April 2010, a defiant Prime Minister Orban told a news conference: "In my view, neither the IMF nor the EU's financial bodies are our bosses. We are not subordinate to them." Hungary would negotiate but it would not accept "diktats."[28]

Orban's aggressive nationalism and Fidesz's campaign to curtail civil liberties and political pluralism reversed the liberalization of Hungarian political culture since the end of communism. But, after their own fashion, Orban's aggressive revenue-raising measures and nationalist austerity worked. Inflation came down to below 2 percent. In December 2011 an agreement was reached with the foreign banks on a deal to share the cost of restructuring household debts. With Hungary having met the 3 percent budget deficit target, the EU lifted the humiliating Excess Deficit Procedures under which the country had labored since its accession to the union. In the context of the emerging market boom, foreign lenders looked leniently on Orban's nationalist experiment. With ample funding, in the summer of 2013 Hungary paid off the IMF and asked the Fund to shut its office in Budapest.[29] To further bolster his position, in early 2013 Orban embarked on a new détente with Moscow. An alliance with Russia was by no means an obvious choice for a Hungarian nationalist. But Orban was given a warm welcome in the Kremlin. Putin cheered his experiment in illiberal democracy and offered material assistance in the form of nuclear reactor technology and subsidized gas supplies, which were popular with Fidesz voters.[30]

Securely embedded in both the EU and NATO, Hungary could afford to take the risk of balancing between East and West. A tiny candidate country for an EU Association Agreement, like Armenia, menaced by sanctions from Russia, was not in the same position. Faced with a clear threat from Moscow, in September 2013 Yerevan pulled back. It declared its intention of joining Putin's Eurasian Customs Union, prompting Brussels to close the door on the Association Agreement.[31] This setback for the EU's Eastern policy made Ukraine all the more important. Given its size and geopolitical significance, it was Kiev's posture that would decide the balance of influence

in the region. The EU was convinced of its own legitimacy. It offered the rule of law and prosperity. Its promise was the future. Ignoring the evident risk that Ukraine was too weak economically, too fragile politically and too exposed in geopolitical terms to stand the pressure generated between Russia and the West, Brussels pushed forward.

That Ukraine needed a change was undeniable. Even after the losses of 2008–2009 were made good, according to official figures average incomes in 2013 were barely higher than in 1989. Unlike in its neighbors to the west, the post-Communist transition in Ukraine had produced a generation of stagnation. While a tiny minority grew fabulously rich, the standard of living for the least well-off was kept at a tolerable level only by a system of pensions and energy subsidies that consumed 17 percent of GDP. In 2008 the IMF had provided emergency assistance. But the program came with demands for changes in taxes and benefits that made it impossible for a government to sustain legitimacy. By the time of the February 2010 election, much of the population was deeply disillusioned. Ukraine was falling further and further behind not only its Western neighbors but Putin's Russia too. President Yushchenko effectively withdrew from the electoral race, leaving Prime Minister Tymoshenko to go head-to-head with Yanukovych, whose fraudulent election had triggered the revolution of 2004. With the electorate split between East and West, in 2010 it was Yanukovych who won a narrow majority fair and square.

Yanukovych was a corrupt manipulator who tacked back and forth between the West and Russia. He took funds from the IMF. He continued negotiations with the EU.[32] He imprisoned Tymoshenko on corruption charges and used her as a pawn. At the same time, he dallied with Putin and his Eurasian bloc. As his clan enriched itself, his popularity drained and foreign exchange reserves dwindled. On the occasion of the next elections, which he had little hope of winning, it seems that he was preparing the security forces for a showdown.[33] But the 2014 election was not the only deadline. Already in 2013, negotiations with the EU and the Russians had reached a point that forced Kiev to a decision that would depend, among other things, on the shifting international financial climate.

Up to the spring of 2013, under the impulse of the Fed's quantitative easing, dollars flowed even to Ukraine. On April 10, 2013, Kiev turned

Source: Benn Steil and Dinah Walker, "Was Ukraine Tapered?," February 25, 2014, Geo-Graphics Blog CFR, https://www.cfr.org/blog/was-ukraine-tapered.

down the latest offer from the IMF to help finance its gaping current account deficit and instead launched a 1.25 billion eurodollar bond issue, which was eagerly taken up by the markets at the comparatively modest interest rate of 7.5 percent.[34] But then Bernanke's taper pronouncement of May 22 hit the markets. Interest rates surged to 10 percent. Searching for alternative sources of funding and personal enrichment, Yanukovych canvassed the world for options. He explored shale-gas development with Shell and Chevron. In the fall of 2013 a deal was on the books to lease to China an enormous holding of 7.5 million acres of prime farmland—5 percent of the entire land mass of Ukraine, 10 percent of its arable land, an area the size of Belgium. China was not just after Lebensraum. It was also offering to put $10 billion into port facilities in Crimea.[35] But it was the talks with the EU that were pivotal. The promise that Yanukovych had made to the Ukrainian population was the promise of Europe. Ukraine's officially sponsored media were talking up the Association Agreement as a prelude to full membership. The EU gave no indication that that was likely, but it did nothing to deflate expectations. Western press sources billed the Vilnius summit

quite openly as the climax of a "six-year campaign to lure Ukraine into integration with the EU and out of the Kremlin's orbit."[36]

The threat was not lost on Russia, and its threats of sanctions mattered: 25 percent of Ukraine's exports went to the EU, but 26 percent went to Russia, and much of the rest went to CIS states within Putin's reach. In early September Yanukovych was still browbeating reluctant pro-Russian members of his party to accept the Western deal.[37] What was not clear, until Kiev received the IMF's letter of November 20, 2013, was quite how unattractive the Western terms would be. The IMF offered Ukraine only $5 billion and noted that it would be expected to use $3.7 billion of it to repay the 2008 loan due in 2014. No one in Kiev had reason to expect generosity from the IMF. But the EU's offer came as a real shock. A committee of German experts had estimated that Ukraine would stand to lose at least $3 billion per annum in trade with Russia due to sanctions. In Kiev the estimated loss had been inflated to something closer to $50 billion. Brussels swept all these figures aside.[38] In conjunction with the Association Agreement, all that the EU was willing to offer was 610 million euros. In exchange the IMF demanded big budget cuts, a 40 percent increase in natural gas bills and a 25 percent devaluation.[39] It was anything but the pot of gold that Yanukovych had promised. There were Ukrainian oligarchs with personal fortunes larger than this. Even without considering the sanctions to be expected from Russia, to have accepted such a deal would have been a political disaster.[40] In Kiev there was outrage. "We could not contain our emotions, it was unacceptable," Ukraine's permanent representative for NATO told Reuters. When his country turned to Europe for help, they "spat on us. . . . [W]e are apparently not Poland, apparently we are not on a level with Poland. . . . [T]hey are not letting us in really, we will be standing at the doors. We're nice but we're not Poles."[41] Fortunately for Kiev, or so it seemed, Moscow had an alternative plan. On November 21, 2013, Putin offered, and Yanukovych accepted, a gas contract on concessionary terms and a $15 billion loan. The condition was that Ukraine, like Armenia, would join the Eurasian Customs Union.

In light of subsequent events, Yanukovych's decision would come to be seen as the Pavlovian response of a pro-Moscow stooge. It was quite

possible that he was subject to Russian blackmail. But setting such rumors aside, his choice was hardly inexplicable. As Ukraine's prime minister, Mykola Azarov, explained, "[T]he extremely harsh conditions" of the EU-IMF package had decided the issue.[42] Nor was this logic hidden from the Europeans in the immediate aftermath of the debacle. On November 28, 2013, speaking to *Der Spiegel*, European Parliament president Martin Schulz admitted that EU officials made mistakes in their negotiations with Ukraine. "I think we underestimated the drama of the domestic political situation in Ukraine."[43] Ukraine, he said, "had been in a deep economic and financial crisis" since the introduction of democracy. "They desperately need money and they desperately need a reliable gas supply." Schulz said he understood why Ukraine moved toward Russia. "It is not especially popular in Europe to help states which are in a crisis . . . and if you look at Moscow's proposals, they would offer Ukraine short-term assistance that we, as Europeans, cannot and do not want to afford."

What no one reckoned with—not Yanukovych, the Russians or the EU—was the reaction of a vocal and bold minority among the Ukrainian population. The opinion poll evidence does not suggest that there was an overwhelming majority for a decisive shift toward the EU. According to Kiev's International Institute of Sociology, in November 2013 only 39 percent of respondents favored association with the EU, barely 2 percent more than the 37 percent who favored a Russian-led customs union.[44] And those numbers were based on a hypothetical, not the stern terms offered by the IMF and the EU. But events in Ukraine in 2013 were not decided by a referendum on the basis of clearly costed alternatives. They were driven by enthusiastic, fired-up minorities inspired by hopes and fears of Russia and Western Europe and an eclectic range of political imagery drawn from every part of the political spectrum.

In November and December hundreds of thousands of people rallied to Kiev's freezing streets to protest Yanukovych's abrupt decision to reject the Association Agreement. But they made no overthrow attempt and Yanukovych might have ridden out the storm but for the ill-advised decision, encouraged by Moscow, to crack down. By using his majority in parliament to ram through constitutional changes, on January 16 he triggered a second wave of mass protests and the occupation of government buildings across

Ukraine. At this point, the involvement of the EU and the United States became overt. Quite how deeply Washington was engaged was revealed by the infamous bugged conversation between Victoria Nuland, assistant secretary of state for European and Eurasian affairs, and the US ambassador to Ukraine, which is as illuminating in its characterization of US-EU relations at this point as it was in its blunt instrumentalization of Ukraine's politicians. On January 28, 2014, as Nuland discussed options with Ambassador Pyatt, she casually remarked: "That would be great I think to help glue this thing and have the UN glue it and you know, fuck the EU." For Nuland's taste, the EU was too slow moving and too willing to compromise with President Yanukovych, with whom it had been eagerly pursuing a comprehensive Association Agreement only a few months earlier. Without flinching, Ambassador Pyatt replied: "We've got to do something to make it stick together, because you can be pretty sure that if it does start to gain altitude the Russians will be working behind the scenes to try to torpedo it."[45]

Two weeks later, a desperate last stand in the streets of Kiev brought an end to Yanukovych's presidency. On February 21, in talks that were brokered by the foreign ministers of Germany, France and Poland and witnessed by Putin's representative on the spot, Yanukovych was offered the protection of his office until new presidential elections were held at the end of 2014. But as support from within his party and the security forces melted away, he thought better of taking the risk.[46] He too remembered Gaddafi's fate. Early in the morning on February 22 he fled, leaving a vacuum. Short-circuiting constitutional procedures, a new provisional government took office pending elections scheduled for May 25. What the EU had intended as a protracted transition had become a revolutionary overthrow. And rather than waiting for the outcome of the election, the provisional government, dominated by Tymoshenko's Fatherland Party and a sprinkling of Maidan activists, moved rapidly to consolidate the new dispensation. It would reverse Yanukovych's abrupt decision of November. It would draw a clean line with Russia, sign the European Association Agreement and conclude new financial agreements not with Russia but with the IMF and the European Union.

How was Moscow to react? The choice at Vilnius in November 2013 had been pitched by both sides as a strategic turning point. Thanks to the

niggardliness of the IMF-EU offer, Moscow had won a significant victory, only for that to be overturned by popular protest and regime change, which, even if it had the support of a considerable fraction of the Ukrainian people, was of dubious legality and was undeniably Western inspired. For Russia to have meekly accepted this outcome would have been worse than if Yanukovych had signed the Association Agreement in the first place. On the night of February 22–23 the Kremlin decided to act. Taking advantage of local protests and activating plans prepared in 2008 to counter a fast-track NATO application, on February 27, 2014, Russian troops in perfunctory disguises seized control of the Crimean peninsula.[47] A few days later, to further ramp up the pressure on Kiev, Russia put its muscle behind a separatist uprising in the eastern region of Donetsk.

III

The comprehensive economic, political and diplomatic clash between the West and Russia that had been foreshadowed in the proxy war in Georgia in 2008 was now unleashed on an altogether more significant stage. With Ukraine's territorial integrity at stake, on April 13, 2014, the provisional government in Kiev launched an "antiterrorist" operation to take back control of the Donbass. In Washington and at NATO headquarters there were those calling for immediate military aid for Kiev and a full-throated return to the cold war. McCain and other Republican hawks would have loved to have rallied a war party. Doing so perhaps might have contributed to restoring coherence to their troubled party. But as he had done in Syria in 2013, Obama refused the call to escalate.[48] In Europe there was no support for military action. It was not that Ukraine would be denied weapons. But, as in Syria, the arms would be supplied through covert channels. The public front of the West's reaction was economic sanctions.

Putin's line had always been that geoeconomics were geopolitics. In Ukraine, struggles over trade negotiations and customs treaties had escalated into an undeclared war. Now the economy itself would be weaponized. Or would it? To pressurize Iran, the United States had developed a ferociously effective regimen of sanctions. Russia as a globally integrated

economy was far more vulnerable. Not only did Russian businesses need to export but they had supped deeply at the trough of cheap dollar credit. By early 2014 they owed $728 billion.[49] But by the same token, large vested interests in the West were at stake. Apart from anything else, Russia was the number two supplier of oil and gas exports to world markets. At a time of extreme fragility in the emerging market economies, the United States did not want to precipitate further tension in commodity markets. To the frustration of the hard-liners, the United States stayed its hands and never applied the full force of its sanctions weapon. Instead it targeted individual members of the clique close to Putin, the most prominent of whom was Igor Sechin, the boss of oil giant Rosneft.[50] Furthermore, Washington limited access to capital markets for key corporations—Rosneft, Novatek, Gazprombank and VEB.[51] This was painful, but given the limited volume of US-Russian economic relations, it was far from decisive.

The crucial question was whether Europe would throw its weight behind America's sanctions. Russia-EU trade was ten times larger than Russia-US trade. The EU received 41 percent of all Russia's exports. This gave the EU considerable leverage, but also meant it had more to lose. German corporate leaders and senior politicians, such as ex-chancellor Gerhard Schröder, continued to cultivate friendly relations with Putin even as Russia's troops made incursions into Ukraine. France had two big aircraft carriers on order from Russia. Italy's energy corporations were deeply entangled in Black Sea projects. London, the playground of the oligarchs, was the place to make sanctions tell. The Cameron government talked a good game, but was less quick to act. Nor was it merely economic interests that were at stake. In Germany there was deep skepticism about any overhasty alignment with the United States.[52] Since the summer of 2013 the NSA spying scandal had cast a deep shadow over German-US relations. A year later, the percentage of Germans who saw the United States as a "trustworthy partner" was down to 38 percent, numbers last seen in the Bush era.[53] Whereas 68 percent of Americans favored extending NATO to Ukraine, 67 percent of Germans were against it. Likewise, 63 percent of Germans rejected EU membership for Ukraine.

To the indignation of right-wingers in Congress, all that the EU could agree to were individualized sanctions against eighteen leading Russian figures. Senator John McCain was moved to declare, "If the Europeans decide

that the economic considerations are too important to impose severe sanctions on Vladimir Putin . . . then they are ignoring the lessons of history."[54] Appeasement had failed against Hitler in 1938. It would fail against Mr. Putin. In May transatlantic tensions were mounting to such a pitch that Merkel and Obama hastily convened talks in the White House. Merkel had no doubt about the need for action, but she could not ignore European public opinion, and McCain's outbursts were not helpful. The two agreed that Obama would restrain the American hawks while Merkel moved to build a consensus in Europe around tougher measures.

In the meantime, if no military aid was forthcoming and only minimal sanctions were applied to Russia, would the West at least provide generous financial support to Ukraine? Just to meet its outstanding obligations, the new government in Kiev estimated that it needed $35 billion over two years. That was not far off the estimates presented by Yanukovych's regime six months earlier, which had been rejected out of hand. In March 2014 Kiev put in a request for $15 billion from the IMF. The Obama administration backed the appeal and sought to leverage it to break the deadlock in Congress over IMF reform. The administration linked a $1 billion loan guarantee for Ukraine that was popular with the Republican right wing to a proposal to unblock IMF funding.[55] The Ukraine crisis was a clear demonstration, the White House insisted, of the IMF's strategic importance to the United States. Globalist critics of the IMF pounced on the pronouncement.[56] The subservience of the IMF as a tool of US policy stood starkly revealed. Except that the Republicans in Congress did not agree. They cut out the IMF funding proposal.

Lagarde and the IMF soldiered on without America's full backing.[57] For a well-run country, at peace and with the institutions to make the most of its ample endowments, Ukraine's debt burden would have been far from excessive. But Ukraine was none of those things. Given the huge political uncertainty, the insecurity produced by Russian intervention and its weak institutions, there was, in fact, a strong case to be made that Ukraine's debts were insupportable. Ukraine was insolvent and its debt should be written down. That would have been IMF protocol. But Ukraine was no ordinary case. In 2010 Greece had been funded under the "systemic exemption." The risk of financial contagion justified an unsustainable bailout. In

April 2014 in Ukraine, systemic risk was recast in geopolitical terms. The IMF's main shareholders did not want to see the embattled pro-Western regime in Kiev declared bankrupt within weeks of an anti-Putin revolution. So despite the obvious risks and despite Ukraine's appalling track record of program compliance, the IMF plunged in once again. Out of enthusiastic talk of reform and overoptimistic assumptions about economic recovery, the IMF concocted a scenario that allowed it to lend Ukraine $17 billion over two years. A further 11 billion euros would come from the EU and $1 billion in loan guarantees from the United States. Japan chipped in too. In addition, the EU agreed to take 98 percent of Ukraine's exports tariff free. Visa-free travel was envisioned for 2015. For the winter, the EU promised to backstop Ukraine's energy supplies by providing a flow of gas through Slovakia, Poland and Hungary.

It was a substantial commitment. But it fell well short of what Ukraine needed. The aid from Europe would be stretched over seven years. The IMF loan, as always, came with tough conditions. Gas prices were to be raised by 56 percent and the government payroll cut by 10 percent.[58] The foreign exchanges were to be liberalized to allow the exchange rate to adjust to a competitive level, a high-risk operation that was likely to put huge pressure on Ukraine's banks. The largest risk of all were the military operations in eastern Ukraine. The IMF had never previously lent to a country at war. So in putting together the April 2014 package, the Fund simply ignored the evidence of the escalating conflict. As Lagarde admitted in a press statement, this put the entire program in jeopardy from the start.[59] Within days of the conclusion of the financial package it became clear that Ukraine did indeed face the worst-case scenario. Rather than calming, the conflict in eastern Ukraine intensified.[60] In early May, scrambling to raise an army, Kiev was forced to reintroduce conscription. As the oligarch Petro Poroshenko took office as Ukraine's president in the last week of May 2014, he faced the impossible challenge of implementing an IMF austerity program while fighting a war; a war, moreover, that Russia would not let Ukraine win. Kiev's only hope was that while military escalation placed ever greater stress on Ukraine's fragile economy, it would also clarify the political stakes of the conflict and suck in the West.

In July a vigorous offensive by Ukraine's forces was on the point of

overwhelming the Donbass rebels. Moscow's response was to resupply the breakaway militia with heavy weapons. A conflict of small-scale skirmishes was escalating into a more or less openly declared war involving the mobilization of tens of thousands of men, mass displacement and thousands of casualties. On July 17 a rebel antiaircraft battery armed with new Russian missiles jubilantly reported that they had shot down a heavy transport plane. It turned out to be Malaysian Airlines flight MH17, with 298 passengers and crew on board. It was the moral indignation in the aftermath of that outrage that enabled Merkel to push through a much stronger sanctions regime. The EU blocked the export to Russia of any military equipment, oil industry equipment and the issuance of long-term debt in the EU by Russia's state-owned banks and energy corporations. The United States doubled down by restricting access to capital markets for Sberbank and pressuring ExxonMobil and BP to drop their collaborations with Russian energy partners. But the real thrust of twenty-first-century sanctions was financial. By September 2014 Rosneft, Transneft, Gazprom, Novatek, Sberbank, VTB, Gazprombank and Bank of Moscow, along with arms makers United Aircraft Corporation and Kalashnikov, were all locked out of Western financial markets. Two of the banks most closely linked to Putin and his entourage had hundreds of millions of dollars frozen in US accounts.[61]

Moscow, for its part, resorted to more classic retaliation. It did not cut off gas supplies. But it issued a blanket ban against agricultural imports from Europe while increasing its military support for the Donbass rebels, who mounted a bloody counteroffensive on August 23–24. With the front line frozen, Kiev was forced to accept a ceasefire brokered in Minsk by Germany and France on September 5. With the new cold war between Russia and the West having escalated into a comprehensive and violent confrontation, it now came down to a trial of strength.

III

Since the shock of 2008, Russia's official financial position had been rebuilt. In early 2014 Moscow's foreign currency reserves stood at $510 billion. As

in 2008, it was not the state but Russia's globalized private sector that was vulnerable. Though the oligarchs of course toed Putin's line, the markets did not lie. The escalation of tensions over Ukraine caused an immediate capital outflow. When the Russian Federation Council, on Saturday, March 1, 2014, gave a patriotic vote of approval for the deployment of Russian troops on Ukrainian territory, it was followed on "Black Monday," March 3, by a spectacular 11–12 percent market slump.[62] For internationalized Russian banks like Sberbank—a giant that controlled 28 percent of Russian bank assets—sanctions created a truly schizophrenic situation. As its CEO, Herman Gref, mused, 50 percent of Sberbank's freely marketable shares were held by US and British investors, but the bank was now barred from raising funds in the West.[63] Perforce, over the course of 2014, Russian companies paid down their foreign debt from $729 billion to $599 billion, with the central bank deploying its reserves to enable the repayment.[64] Tension was building, but it was not until autumn that the crisis broke.

The third round of sanctions in the wake of the downing of MH17 bit deep. At the same moment, Janet Yellen's Fed finally ended QE3, tightening credit conditions around the world. And then cooperation in OPEC broke down. Saudi Arabia ended its production restraint and oil prices collapsed. With or without sanctions, by the autumn of 2014 Russia would have been in serious financial difficulty. The combination of sanctions, Fed monetary tightening and a plunge in commodity prices was devastating. So devastating, in fact, that it has raised the question of whether this conjunction was entirely coincidental, or whether the United States and the Saudis were collaborating to launch a strike against Russia.[65]

Oil politics are a rich field for conspiracy theory. There certainly are back channels between Washington and Riyadh. Secretary of State Kerry was in the gulf in the fall of 2014. The Saudis had every reason to act, if not over Ukraine then over Syria.[66] Along with Iran, Russia was the main backer of Assad's die-hard regime. Saudi Arabia was its sworn enemy. There is no conclusive proof. Nor is a conspiracy necessary to explain these concurrent events. The oil market was under stress. America's new fracking technology had opened up a new source of supply that was cheap and highly elastic. From the point of view of the Russian economy, in any case, the ultimate motivation was irrelevant. Oil prices plunged from $112 per barrel in June

Ruble-Dollar Exchange Rate and Oil Prices

Russian troops seize Crimean Parliament

Malaysian Airlines Flight MH17
shot down over Ukraine

US and EU
sanctions announced

Additional US, EU, and Japanese
sanctions announced

G7 countries extend
sanctions another six months

EU extends sanctions
another six months

EU and Canada
toughen sanctions

EU extends sanctions
until July 2016

Brent oil price per barrel (left axis) Russian ruble (right axis)

Source: Bloomberg, Global Investors.

to around $60 per barrel by December 2014 and kept on falling. On top of sanctions and tightening credit conditions, it was a body blow.

In October the Russian central bank intervened heavily to prevent an immediate ruble collapse. But it needed to husband its reserves, and in November it exited the market. Starting at 33 to the dollar before the Ukraine crisis began, by December 1, 2014, the ruble had fallen to 49 against the dollar. This was terrifying for Russian corporate borrowers, who owed $35 billion in debt repayments by the end of the year. There was a scramble for survival. Rosneft, which had $10 billion to pay, was in the market hoovering up euros and dollars.[67] The strain on weaker Russian businesses was unbearable. In December, Trust Bank, a high street lender, and UTair, Russia's third-largest airline, failed, and the central bank was forced to offer guarantees for the entire banking sector.[68] On the morning of Monday, December 15, the ruble began to plunge, ending the day down by 8 percent. That night, after a long evening of debate involving Putin himself, the central bank decided that it would hike interest rates from 6.5 percent to 17 percent. The announcement was made at one a.m. It was intended to reas-

sure investors and punish speculators. It didn't work. It was read not as reassurance but as a sign of panic. As markets opened on the morning of Russia's "Black Tuesday," December 16, the foreign exchange market went into free fall. By the end of the day the ruble had fallen to 80 against the dollar. The following day Sberbank came under concerted attack. A million of its customers received text messages from addresses outside Russia warning that the bank was about to be cut off altogether from external liquidity. On December 18, $6 billion were withdrawn. Over the following week the total came to $20 billion.[69,70] It was a spectacular bank run even by the standards of 2007–2008.

The oligarchs were once again exposed. Estimates vary, but the combination of the Ukraine imbroglio, the oil price shock and the December 2014 turmoil cost the twenty richest Russians between $62 billion and $73.4 billion.[71] Once again Putin called in favors and demanded action. Measures were passed calling for the end to the offshore hoarding of wealth. An amnesty was offered to those who would bring their cash home. Meanwhile, the central bank attempted to get a grip on the situation with an increase in deposit insurance and the recapitalization of ailing banks. President Putin called for the authorities to abandon general principles of policy. They would need to be in "manual override" to see the country through. But there was one general principle that would not be abandoned. Russia did not want to ruin its reputation in the eyes of foreign investors by resorting to capital controls. Instead, to provide the necessary foreign exchange, the central bank ran down its reserves, which dipped as low as $388.5 billion on December 26. This cushioned the collapse of the ruble, but the pressure continued. The Western ratings agencies started by downgrading Gazprom. In January they lowered the rating of Rosneft, Transneft and Lukoil. Then the ruble slumped by 7 percent, giving up much of the ground it had recovered since the end of 2014.[72] That, in turn, posed the question of the central bank's reserves. What Russia was struggling to contain was something akin to the bank-sovereign doom loop that had menaced the eurozone until 2012. But what was now at stake was not just financial solvency but victory in a geopolitical tug of war.

In his first period as president, Putin's legitimacy had been based in large part on a sustained recovery in living standards. That easy narrative

was broken by the crisis of 2008. From 2014 onward economic expectations were further diminished. Over the winter of 2014–2015 GDP was falling by more than 10 percent per annum. It would not stabilize until the second half of 2015. For ordinary Russians the crisis of 2014–2015 was considerably worse than that of 2008–2009. Real wages fell more sharply and rebounded less vigorously. The Russia that emerged from the Ukraine clash was above all a nationalist regime whose citizens were called upon to pay whatever price was necessary for their nation's reemergence on the global stage. It was tough, but it was a role that came easily. And, indeed, in some respects one might even say it was convenient.[73] As prime minister during the 2008 crisis Putin had thrown himself into hands-on domestic crisis fighting.[74] Since his return to the presidency in 2012, the Kremlin had been inciting nationalism to offset disappointing economic growth and disappointing poll ratings. Given the collapse in oil prices in 2014–2015, some campaign of nationalist incitement was only to be expected. The crisis in Ukraine was perfectly timed. Even with the economy languishing, Putin's personal popularity surged from a low in 2013 in the mid-40s to a record 89 percent approval in June 2015.[75]

Russia suffered, but if the economy was a weapon, it cut both ways. You could not damage Russia without damaging its neigbors. The much-feared emerging market crisis hit the post-Soviet world with a vengeance.[76] Between the end of 2013 and early 2015 the currencies of Kazakhstan, Azerbaijan and Belarus devalued by 50 percent against the dollar. The Kyrgyz, Moldovan and Tajik currencies lost between 30 and 35 percent of their value. Across Central Asia, the effect was to force sudden and sharp increases in interest rates and to place enormous pressure on the balance sheets of those banks and businesses that had globalized and borrowed abroad.[77] Meanwhile, family incomes were squeezed as remittances from migrant workers in Russia plunged.[78] In Tajikistan, the most remittance-dependent country of the world, where approximately one half of its working-age males earned their living in Russia, it threatened a catastrophic fall in household income and foreign exchange earnings. Kyrgyzstan, the world's second-most remittance-dependent country, was also badly affected.[79]

But if the crisis took its toll on the entire region, the epicenter of the

shock was Ukraine. In the emergency bailout of April 2014, the IMF had started its estimate of Ukraine's economic situation from an exchange rate of 12.5 hryvnia to the dollar. The IMF had called on Kiev to impose currency controls to prevent capital flight, while letting its currency float and allowing domestic prices to adjust to whatever level would ensure the viability of government-owned gas firms. If this program had been adopted, it would have squeezed both ordinary Ukrainians and wealthy Ukrainians, who would see their funds trapped in a depreciating currency. Instead, the Ukrainian central bank did the reverse.[80] It permitted billions of dollars to flee the Ukrainian banking system while using its precious exchange reserves to stem the decline in the exchange rate. While prices surged by 50 percent, the result was to favor the most wealthy Ukrainians, who swapped their assets into dollars at favorable exchange rates. All told $8 billion drained from the currency reserves. Whatever money was pumped into Ukraine simply bled out. With exchange reserves depleted to as little as $4.7 billion by February 2015, the central bank finally abandoned the exchange rate. As the European powers struggled to make diplomacy work and the hawks in Washington and at NATO headquarters were urging ramped-up military support, between February 5 and February 6 the currency plunged by 50 percent in twenty-four hours.[81] Prices were adjusted on a daily basis, and to combat hoarding, a system of de facto rationing was introduced, which limited each consumer to buying fixed quantities of flour, oil, rice and buckwheat. Meanwhile, GDP fell by almost 18 percent year on year, making Ukraine's debts progressively less and less sustainable.

With the battle in the Donbass ongoing, the government of the revolution of 2014, like its predecessor in 2004, was seeing its legitimacy evaporate in the face of insurmountable economic problems. To enable the new Ukrainian regime to survive, in the spring of 2015 there was no alternative to further foreign assistance. On March 11, 2015, the IMF recommitted itself to Ukraine, relaunching the agreement of the previous year, this time rated at $17.5 billion. It would be the cornerstone of a $40 billion four-year deal, supported by the EU. But this time, at last, the IMF acknowledged that there would have to be debt restructuring.

IV

In 2014, the comprehensive crisis, both geopolitical and financial, that had threatened the post-Soviet sphere in 2008 had arrived and the verdict it delivered on the hegemony of the United States and its alliance system was ambiguous, to say the least. A popular upheaval had swung Ukraine forcibly toward Europe. The Association Agreement eagerly signed by President Poroshenko in June 2014 was finally ratified in July 2017. The West had not let Ukraine sink. But neither had it saved it from crisis. Ukraine's financial position remained precarious. The debt restructuring deal that was eventually done in August 2015 satisfied the IMF's demand for private sector involvement in formal terms. But, in fact, it imposed minimal losses on the hedge funds that had gobbled up Ukraine's distressed debt. It bought Ukraine only the slightest amount of debt relief, cutting its debts from $71 billion to $67 billion, while Ukraine's GDP continued to plunge.[82] The viability of the package would depend on the unpredictable course of domestic reform and the intensity of the confrontation with Russia, which neither the United States nor Europe had mustered the resources or political will to decisively repel. As far as Russia was concerned, even in combination with the oil price shock, the sanctions were painful but not decisive. By the spring of 2015 Putin's regime had regained its grip. If and when oil prices began to stabilize, Moscow's position would recover. Sanctions would soon prove deeply unpopular within the EU. To general amazement, Russia would find prominent sympathizers even in the United States. While it bided its time, Moscow could cause trouble in the Middle East, it could fish in troubled waters in the United States and it could look for new strategic partners farther afield.

In the cold war the interplay among Washington, Beijing and Moscow had been crucial in shifting the balance of power. In principle, a resurgent China could pick and choose. It had no particular reason to prefer Putin. But in the spring of 2014 in the East Asian arena, tensions between Japan and China were rising to a dangerous level. Washington gave notice that it meant to stand behind its strategic pivot. It would not countenance China's assertion of rights in the South China Sea. But for America to take a strong

line in Asia while at the same time confronting Russia in Europe had its price. It offered Russia an opportunity and Putin seized it. In the spring of 2014, as the seriousness of Russia's confrontation with the West became clear, the Moscow leadership resolved on a strategic approach to China.[83] China would provide Russia with support against the West. If the United States and the EU were determined to oppose Russia in economic terms, it would find markets in China and sources of capital in Shanghai and Hong Kong. China, for its part facing resistance in the South China Sea, could build a Eurasian land route via Russia and Central Europe. The EU had shown no interest in joining America's "de facto containment alliance" in Asia. Russia would provide the bridge. A start was made in May 2014 with the signing of a $400 billion, thirty-year Sino-Russian gas deal.[84]

Though the strategic logic was strong, in practice, Moscow found that doing business with China was fraught with difficulty. The Chinese were tough negotiators. Russia's hard-pressed oligarchs were reluctant to commit to long-term deals when they were not negotiating from a position of strength. Laying the necessary infrastructure eastward was monumentally expensive and Russia's elite were leery of opening up Siberia to ever greater Chinese influence. Gas diplomacy in an age in which prices for fossil fuels were gyrating was a volatile business. But for both Moscow and Beijing, the point went beyond economics. It was about redefining the balance of power and affirming multipolarity. It would not be the incumbent hegemon that would shape the twenty-first-century order but the rising power of Asia and its allies. In so doing, Moscow and Beijing were also giving a new ending to the twentieth century.[85] The symbolism of guest lists at the anniversary celebrations for victory in World War II in 2015 was hard to ignore. Seventy years after that struggle, in which China, Russia, the United States, Britain and France had been united against the Axis, a new relationship was being constructed between China and Russia, a relationship that had the potential to reshape Eurasia. In Moscow on May 9 and Beijing on September 3, Xi Jinping and Vladimir Putin were each other's guests of honor at spectacular commemorative ceremonies. Obama, Cameron, Hollande and Merkel gave their excuses.[86] In the spring of 2015 the one Western leader who would look to the former allies of World War II for support would be the embattled left-wing prime minister of Greece.

Chapter 22

#THISISACOUP

In the Maidan demonstrations of the winter of 2013–2014 Ukrainians enthusiastically waved the blue banner of the EU. After the grinding battles of the eurozone it was something of a relief for Europe to be celebrated by anyone anywhere. The pro-EU demonstrators in Kiev hailed Europe as the future. To them it offered the promise of democracy, freedom, prosperity, the rule of law, the "good Europe." It was an image that stemmed from the era of the 1990s and early 2000s, when Europe had celebrated the end of the cold war, economic growth and the prospect of "ever closer union." For some pundits, in both Europe and the United States, the clash with Putin was an occasion to reaffirm that vision against outside threat.[1] But the question in the wake of the eurozone crises of 2008–2012 was whether the main threat to the good Europe, in fact, came from without or from within. Anxiously watched by the rest of the world, the 2012 stabilization of the eurozone had been based on a compromise among Germany, Italy, Spain, France and the rest. It was driven by the fear of an escalation that would take down first Spain and then Italy. A year later the acute phase of the crisis had passed. But as the second recession to hit Europe in short succession began to make itself fully felt, the EU entered a new season of discontent.

I

The eurozone's stabilization in 2012 was conditioned on the expectation of further forward movement. That was the program with which the European Council of June 28–29 had addressed the Spanish crisis. It was the message that Draghi had delivered in London. The fiscal compact, the banking union, the development of the ESM and the ECB's OMT were major steps toward the consolidation of the eurozone. The question, as ever, was whether they were sufficient and whether the EU had the will to move at the requisite speed. On the banking union everything remained to be done, and Berlin was in no hurry to sign up to a common resolution fund until the full extent of the damage in Southern Europe was uncovered.[2] Germany and France were bitterly divided over the banking crisis that exploded in Cyprus in 2013.[3] Meanwhile, Merkel had her own reform agenda. Not satisfied with having transferred the Schuldenbremse to Europe, she wanted to push the German vision of labor market reform to the European level as well.[4] In 2013 her mantra was competitiveness and unit labor costs. For this too, as for budget discipline, Germany wanted contracts and rules.

Merkel's authority in the wake of the eurozone crisis was remarkable and Germany was the most comfortably situated of Europe's economies. Labor markets were tight and global demand for Germany's exports was booming.[5] Even if exports to the rest of Europe were flat, Germans had little reason to doubt the narrative of their own national success. But even in this cocoon of prosperity, German politics were not immune to stress. The weak link was the FDP, Merkel's chosen coalition partner since 2009.[6] The FDP's probusiness, tax-cutting agenda had no more than niche appeal in Germany at the best of times. Its national sovereignist position came increasingly under pressure in the course of the eurozone crisis. It would have made a good basis for opposition. Inside a government constantly forced to make compromises to hold the eurozone together, the FDP was playing a losing hand. The indignation aroused in Germany in 2012 by talk of eurobonds, the further round of assistance for Greece and Draghi's activism heightened the party's political difficulties. And these became acute in the spring of 2013 with the emergence of the first overtly Eurosceptic party

in modern German politics, the Alternative für Deutschland.[7] Though in 2015 it would go on to lead the campaign against Merkel's refugee policy, gathering a nativist electorate around it, the AfD was originally founded by a group of conservative professors opposed to Merkel's compromising policy on the eurozone. In the German general election of September 2013, to the relief of the mainstream, the AfD failed to break through the 5 percent hurdle required to enter the Bundestag. But it took enough of the FDP's votes to drop them out of parliament for the first time since 1949. On the back of a much-increased vote for the CDU, Merkel would become chancellor for a third time, once more in coalition with the SPD. Despite coming in second, the SPD drove a hard bargain and claimed a remarkable share of the key cabinet portfolios. But the grand coalition gave Merkel a broad parliamentary base, and the most vital element of continuity was provided by Wolfgang Schäuble, who continued as finance minister. In September 2014 Schäuble announced to the Bundestag the joyous news that for the first time since 1969 he would be budgeting for zero new debt. In a world shaken by the violence in Ukraine, Syria and Iraq and terrified by the Ebola epidemic, he declared, Germany's robust financial position would send a message of confidence.[8] The program of the debt brake on which Germany had embarked in 2009 was being realized ahead of time.

The rest of the eurozone had more immediate worries. In both economic and political terms the pressure was relentless. The crisis fighting of 2012 had stopped the immediate catastrophe. But the shocks to confidence delivered between 2011 and 2012 sucked the eurozone economy down and the straitjacket of fiscal consolidation squeezed tightly. The deep recession did not begin to ease until the second half of 2013. By that point unemployment in Greece and Spain had peaked at 26–27 percent. When it came, recovery was agonizingly slow and was overshadowed by the increasingly worrying news from the emerging markets. In 2014, with prices falling all around the world economy, the EU was stalked by the fear of deflation. Was the EU sliding toward the economic quicksand that had trapped Japan since the 1990s, with bad debts weighing on recovery and inadequate demand feeding on itself?[9] How could Europe respond? The fiscal compact constrained government spending even on much-needed investment. In Spain, which was undergoing one of the most severe adjustments, public

spending both on infrastructure and education was slashed.[10] But net of depreciation it was Germany that had some of the lowest levels of public investment in Europe. Would the ECB finally make good on its promise to do "whatever it takes"? Draghi cut rates, but would the ECB go a step further and embark on QE?[11] As inflation slid toward zero and expectations moved into negative territory, the economic case for action by the ECB was serious. But with nationalist resentment on the rise in Germany and the Bundesbank still smarting from its defeat in 2012, so too were the political risks.

While economists and politicians argued over policy options, a large segment of Europe's population had simply had enough. Across Europe, opinion polls showed a sharp decline in support for the EU even in states that had historically been overwhelmingly favorable.[12] And then came the EU's parliamentary elections of May 2014. The results rocked the European political establishment. Eurosceptic nationalist parties made dramatic gains. UKIP won in Britain. More significantly, the National Front (FN) won in France, taking 25 percent of the vote, as compared with the middle-of-the-road conservative UMP with 20 percent and the ruling Parti Socialiste with 14.7 percent. The FN drew on France's deep strain of nationalism, anti-Semitism and postcolonial racism. But since January 2011 Marine Le Pen had run a campaign to de-demonize the party, refashioning it as a vehicle for popular nationalism pitched against globalization and the EU. To its petit bourgeois base the FN added a large part of what would once have been thought of as the constituency of the Left—blue-collar and unemployed voters.[13] When the FN's voters were asked ahead of the May 2014 election what mattered to them they mentioned three things. For 63 percent immigration was a top priority. A similar number raised economic issues. But hostility to the EU came top of the list: 83 percent of FN voters were persuaded that belonging to the EU had aggravated the effects of the economic crisis on France; 81 percent thought that the economic policy of the current government conforming to the demands of austerity would likely fail. Given the experience of Europe since 2008, one could hardly say that these were unreasonable opinions. Two thirds of FN voters drew the conclusion that France should leave the euro.

The pool of right-wing nationalist resentment on the margin of European

politics was not new, though it gained new adherents and far greater cred-
ibility in light of the disastrous mishandling of the crisis. What was new
was the mobilization on the Left. By contrast with the FN's furious, lower-
class, poorly educated base, the new parties of the Left were updated and
energized iterations of the kind of progressive social movement that Europe
had repeatedly seen since the late 1960s. In Spain, Podemos was an off-
spring of M15, an imaginative broad-based social movement, headed by a
university teacher, with an electorate that had a larger percentage of univer-
sity graduates than any other political force in Spain.[14] Syriza had the most
balanced representation of upper-, middle- and lower-class groups of any
party in Greece. What drove the surge in support for the Left from 2008 was
not fundamentalist opposition so much as the sense that the EU was betray-
ing Europe's own promise.

The immediate reaction of mainstream media to the May 2014 result
was to dismiss both left- and right-wing critics of the status quo as "popu-
list."[15] The impatience and irrationality of the parties of protest would undo
the good work of fiscal consolidation done since 2010. They were splitting
Europe at a moment when it needed to stand united against the new threats
on its borders.[16] There were dark rumors of Russian infiltration. That was
alarming, no doubt. But in 2014 a new cold war was among the more reas-
suring scenarios on offer. What if Europe was marching back not to the
1950s but to the 1930s? Was the script not hauntingly familiar? A financial
crisis met with obstinate austerity led to mass unemployment and political
radicalization. When melded with fears of Putin's meddling and terror at-
tacks by radical Islamists, memories of Europe's dark history could easily
be stewed into a terrifying image of a new Dark Continent. In perhaps the
most dramatic manifestation of this apocalyptic brand of Euroscepticism,
in March 2015 the widely read American monthly *Atlantic* posed the ques-
tion: "Is It Time for the Jews to Leave Europe?"[17] Influential journalist Jef-
frey Goldberg constructed for his American audience a narrative in which
disaffected unemployed Islamic youth, festering in Europe's rundown hous-
ing projects and inner cities, were entangled with the continent's deep-
rooted anti-Semitic history and the rise of the new Right. When asked in
the accompanying video what the last European Jew should do on depart-
ing the "Old World," Leon Wieseltier commented simply: "Spit!" The fear

and vitriol this expressed fed off memories that went back to the Holocaust and long before. What is striking is that this alarmist narrative should have gained traction when it did.

After the apparent escape from crisis in 2012, two years later Europe found itself again at an impasse. To secure its functional viability, the eurozone needed to make bold steps toward further integration. But in light of the mounting popular backlash and the ongoing economic uncertainty, where was the political momentum to come from? After the verdict delivered by Europe's voters in May 2014, who would want to risk a wave of referenda to ratify treaty change? Meanwhile, most of Europe outside the prosperous northern core was struggling to return to something like normal economic growth. Given time, would the German formula of austerity and reform work? Spain and Ireland were crawling their way back. But across much of Southern Europe the unemployment crisis was still acute. In 2014 the questions were getting ever louder. Would the mounting political backlash against the EU outrun Europe's halting economic recovery? Would that recovery even continue? By 2014 the risk of deflation was undeniable. The emerging markets on which Germany relied for its growth were faltering. If stagnation threatened, the political pressures would further escalate. Would the ECB be forced out of its defensive position into a more activist policy? As ever, the place where the tensions within the eurozone were most acute was Greece.

II

After six years of recession, the social crisis in Greece was manifest. In 2014 unemployment reached close to 27 percent. More than half of Greece's young people were out of work, and whereas they might once have drawn on their families for support, the main breadwinner all too often had lost his or her source of income too. By 2015 half of the population was relying on the pension income of a senior citizen to get by, an alarming statistic given that half the pensions paid to senior citizens were below the poverty level. According to Eurostat, if the standard of poverty was anchored at the precrisis level, then almost half of the Greek population was at risk by

2015.[18] The OECD reported that one in six was going hungry on a daily basis.[19] In Athens the homeless were everywhere. For those lucky enough to keep their jobs, real wages were down by 25 percent. At the same time, taxes had risen steeply. A nation of small-property owners was furious at new land taxes. VAT that bore most heavily on the poorest was up from 13 to 24 percent. Contrary to popular belief, in Northern Europe the Greece welfare safety net was far from luxurious and the health system was collapsing under the pressure of cuts. To escape the labor market crisis, since 2008, 400,000 Greeks had emigrated, out of a population of 10 million. Those who left were predominantly well-educated young people, including tens of thousands of doctors.[20]

Not only was Greece experiencing a social crisis but it was doing so at the behest of the troika. Given that the majority of Greeks wanted very much to preserve their standing in Europe, first PASOK and then New Democracy had seen no option but to comply with the demands of the troika creditors. But, not surprisingly, the crisis produced a broad-based mood of protest that was fueled by the desire for social solidarity and national self-assertion. On the Right the beneficiary was the racist Golden Dawn, a true neofascist movement. But by far the more popular response was Syriza, the party of the radical Left, which in the May 2014 European elections easily overtook the governing party, New Democracy.

Realizing that its support was dwindling, Samaras's coalition government appealed to the EU and Berlin for concessions. If Greece could emulate Ireland and Portugal in making an early exit from its troika program, it would be a great win for Europe and might give the Eurogroup's collaborators a chance at the polls. But Berlin waved the suggestion away. They had never trusted Samaras and they were not about to make concessions. Hoping for a new mandate, Samaras called for elections. As was now commonplace, proausterity governments around Europe as well as the IMF chimed in. The Greek voters were left in no doubt that as far as "Europe" was concerned, New Democracy, PASOK and the centrist To Potami party were the acceptable choices. Rajoy, Spain's conservative prime minister, campaigned for Samaras in Athens. Given the rise of Podemos, Spanish conservatives were desperate to avoid a left-wing victory. But on January 25, 2015, that is what the Greek voters delivered. Syriza, led by the youthful activist Alexis

Tsipras, formed a government and, refuting the expectations of moderate social democrats in Berlin and Brussels, picked as its coalition partner not the centrist pro-European To Potami but the ultranationalist ANEL. Their views on religion and cultural values might not mesh, but ANEL could be relied upon to go all the way in a confrontation with the EU.[21]

The confrontation would be tough. The challenge for Syriza was to force open the painful and unresolved question of Greek solvency. By buying out the private bondholders, the 2012 debt restructuring had removed market pressure from Athens. But given its declining economy, the Greek debt burden was still excessive. And by substituting public loans from the EU and the IMF for private debt, the 2012 deal had, if anything, raised the political stakes. It was one thing to burn private creditors who had gambled on high-yield Greek debt. It was quite another to suggest to conservative Northern Europe taxpayers that they should make further deep concessions to Greece's rebellious left-wing government. The result in 2015 was a renewed political confrontation, but one in which the fronts were dizzyingly inverted, or at least so they appeared in the rendering of the Greek situation offered by its new finance minister, Yanis Varoufakis.[22]

An unorthodox leftist who had spent much of his career outside Greece in the Anglophone academy, Varoufakis was never a Syriza insider. He had no stake in its old Left politics or in orthodox Marxism. As Greece's debts were no longer market loans but debts owed to the troika, his tactic was to mobilize the pragmatism of the market against the financial orthodoxy of the eurozone. He courted the support of the City of London, the *Financial Times* and authorities like Larry Summers, as well as a coterie of American economic advisers that included both confirmed leftists such as Jamie K. Galbraith and Jeffrey Sachs, onetime exponent of "shock therapy" for the post-Communist world. Varoufakis argued that the ideologues on the Greek debt question were not those who insisted that unpayable debts were unpayable. The ideologues were the conservative disciplinarians in the Eurogroup who insisted that debts must be paid as a matter of principle regardless of the cost. The "system" that Varoufakis attacked was not capitalism but Europe's moribund and dysfunctional austerity fixation and its collaborators in Greece and beyond.

Juxtaposing rational economics against conservative ideology was an

effective political argument on Varoufakis's part. It would win him a considerable international following. But it underestimated his opponents. The project of fiscal consolidation imposed on Europe under German leadership was certainly political. But it was not only that. It was a vision of a long-term reordering of Europe's society and economy. Merkel was fond of shocking unsuspecting visitors with the remark that unless Europe reformed it would go the way of Inca civilization.[23] In pursuit of its goal, to be realized over the course of a decade, Berlin did not flinch from imposing heavy short-term costs. That is what reform of a failing social and economic model entailed. That was the lesson of the collapse of communism, the economic project of German unification and the incorporation of Eastern Europe into the EU. In pursuing that project one could make concessions neither to the short-term time horizons of markets nor to Syriza-style protest politics. To ensure that Europe stayed the course, it was essential to contain "political contagion." It would be disastrous to make concessions to the Far Left government in Greece, concessions that during the crisis had been denied to the governments of Eastern Europe, Ireland, Spain and Portugal. Whatever the misery of the Greek population, it hardly mattered in the wider economic balance of the eurozone. The battle was about the wider questions of political discipline and authority, which, as the conservative globalists in Berlin saw it, were the foundations for long-term economic success.

The fight was all the more bitter because the austerity hawks in the Eurogroup knew that the centrist governments of France and Italy were susceptible. In 2012 Hollande's government in France had wanted to push a more expansive policy. The growth agenda, which had been so crucial to the political maneuvering following Hollande's election, had made precious little headway. Now the new government in Rome headed by the popular centrist Matteo Renzi was tempted in a similar direction.[24] That made it all the more important to hold the line against Syriza. Germany was the anchor, but in the most crucial negotiations, Finance Minister Schäuble barely needed to speak. The Dutchman Jeroen Dijsselbloem chaired the Eurogroup session, and the argument against Syriza would be carried by austerian stalwarts like Spain's Luis de Guindos and Portugal's Maria Luís Albuquerque. They knew that in stopping Syriza they were fighting for their

own political lives and the project they had dedicated their countries to when they signed up to the austerity agenda in 2011.

The irony was that in expressing their preference for the established parties in Greece, the Eurogroup and the IMF were aligning themselves precisely with those political forces and social interests that had created Greece's deplorable fiscal situation. Nor were these entanglements limited to politics. At the heart of the business oligarchy and its media network were Greek banks. They had been recapitalized in 2012 as part of the restructuring deal at the expense of the Greek taxpayer. But they continued to depend heavily on funding from the Greek central bank and the ECB. Since June 2014 the Greek central bank had been headed by Yannis Stournaras, another of Greece's persuasive economics professors, one of the architects of Greece's admission to the original eurozone and finance minister in the outgoing Samaras government.[25] When it became clear in December 2014 that Syriza was ahead in the polls and that it might soon come to power, Stournaras did nothing to staunch a slow-bleeding bank run. Ahead of the election, better-off Greeks had already withdrawn 16 billion euros from the banks. When Tsipras took office, a further 8 billion euros were pulled out in a matter of only three weeks.[26] The effect of this capital flight was to push the banks ever deeper into dependence on the ECB.

If the Syriza government refused to cooperate with the troika, the ECB, as it had done in Ireland and Greece before, could threaten to curtail emergency lending to the banks. It would be a devastating blow. But did the troika really want to risk a renewed crisis in the eurozone? This threat of financial contagion was the major bargaining counter of the Greek government. If Brussels, Frankfurt and Berlin pushed Greece over the edge, it might take others with it. But in this regard, three days before Syriza took office the game was decisively changed. On January 22, 2015, Mario Draghi announced that the ECB was finally adopting full-scale QE. Two and a half years after Draghi's "whatever it takes," it was not a move that the ECB undertook with any enthusiasm. Between 2012 and 2014 Draghi had allowed the balance sheet of the ECB to contract. What forced his hand in 2015 was the acute threat of deflation. To counter slumping prices, Draghi had tried every alternative. A new installment of the Long-Term Refinancing operations this time found no takers. The European banks were intent

on deleveraging. It was not until September 2014 that Draghi commenced "QE lite" by buying private asset-backed securities.[27] Predictably, there was immediate indignation in Germany. The trigger for bolder action was a preliminary opinion issued on January 14, 2015, by the European Court of Justice, which decided in a case referred to it by the German supreme court that Draghi's bond-buying scheme of 2012 had not constituted a prima facie breach of the ban on monetary financing.[28] Without waiting for a final ruling, the ECB acted. On January 22, 2015, Draghi announced that until eurozone inflation stabilized safely in the positive range, the ECB would buy sovereign bonds at the rate of 60 billion euros per month.[29]

In the coincidence of the ECB's turn to monetary activism with Syriza's election victory in January 2015, the economic and political consequences of the eurozone crisis finally caught up with each other. The conjuncture would have fateful consequences. Ironically, it was the ECB's bond-buying program, long opposed by Europe's conservatives, that freed them to fight the battle for political containment by any means necessary. With the ECB in the market there was no risk that the Greek drama would spill over into financial contagion. As the ECB's purchases kicked in and drained sovereign bonds from the markets, yields on Spanish, Portuguese and Italian debt fell. In 2010 the IMF had advocated precisely this course so as to allow the Irish banking crisis to be resolved in an equitable fashion—through PSI and not entirely at the expense of taxpayers. Then, Trichet had blocked the way. Now Draghi's deployment of QE enabled the conservative majority of the Eurogroup to lay siege to Greece's left-wing government without fear of precipitating a general crisis.

Did this mean that the outcome was foreordained? Did Syriza even comprehend the depth of the predicament it was in? From contemporary sources and publicly available information it was unclear. But Varoufakis's memoirs reveal that at least some within Tsipras's cabinet understood the scale of the challenge. As an economic theorist, Varoufakis's specialty was game theory. He knew that Draghi's turn to QE boxed Athens in. If the Syriza government wanted to gain purchase on the debt negotiations, it needed a threat of its own that would restore the risk of financial contagion. Varoufakis believed that a wrinkle in the bailout agreement of 2012 combined with the mounting wave of nationalist resentment in Germany gave

Greece the leverage it needed.[30] On the books of the ECB were 30 billion euros in bonds purchased under Trichet's SMP program. These were left untouched by the 2012 restructuring and they were under Greek law. If Greece unilaterally defaulted on those bonds, it would inflict severe losses on the ECB, highlighting the dangers involved in bond buying and more or less forcing the German right wing to reopen the question of the legality of QE. With QE's legal foundation in question, confidence would crumble. The firewall would be down. The entire eurozone periphery would be in peril once more and the Eurogroup would have to take Greece's demands seriously for fear of panic spreading through the markets.

Given Greece's weakness, it is melodramatic to describe this as the nuclear option. But what Varoufakis was preparing was certainly a dirty bomb. To force the Eurogroup to negotiate in earnest, Greece would threaten to unhinge the fragile political balance on which Draghi's stabilization of the entire eurozone depended. It would deliberately unleash civil war in the eurozone. Due to legal technicalities, it was in fact unclear whether a Greek default would hit the ECB directly or simply Greece's own central bank. But the threat certainly caused alarm in Frankfurt and Brussels. Varoufakis had the legal order for a default drafted and kept on hand in his ministry. The question was whether the Tsipras government would have the nerve to deploy its deterrent at the crucial moment.

III

The first round of meetings between Greece's new government and its creditors in Brussels went so badly that they came close to precipitating an immediate "rupture." Merkel, her foreign minister, Frank-Walter Steinmeier, and their French counterparts jetted into Brussels on February 12, 2015, for a European Council meeting fresh from grueling negotiations with Putin over the Minsk II ceasefire in Donbass. Ukraine, not Greece, was top of the agenda, and the new Greek foreign minister did not endear himself to his colleagues by threatening to veto further sanctions against Putin.[31] In his first Eurogroup meeting on February 11, Varoufakis struck a more conciliatory tone, insisting on Syriza's European credentials and its commitment

to work in good faith. He insisted that they were not "populists, promising all things to all people." But Schäuble's response was blunt. Syriza had not been part of the 2012 deal with the Greek political parties. But Varoufakis needed to understand, as far as the fundamentals of the eurozone were concerned, that "elections cannot be allowed to change economic policy."[32] It was an astonishing statement on its face, but one that encapsulated the dilemma in which the eurozone found itself. As a result of the crisis, national economic policy was increasingly a matter of international agreements. As far as the Eurogroup was concerned, the Greek debt memorandum was the road map. Whatever the complexion of its national government, Greece was expected to stick to it. Though form was preserved, tempers frayed and there were rumors that Varoufakis and Dijsselbloem had almost come to blows.[33] Schäuble would no doubt have been happy to see Greece thrown out there and then. But a personal intervention by Merkel on February 20 secured a stay of execution, allowing the new Greek government, with the approval of the creditors, to offer its own list of reform proposals to replace the memorandum.[34] The release of the outstanding 7.2 billion euros was postponed until agreement was reached and the reforms were implemented.

What followed were months of agonizing back-and-forth over achingly familiar ground. Would Athens be able to satisfy the creditors with its austerity proposals? Would the creditors be willing to discuss Syriza's demand for a second round of debt restructuring? It was attritional. As the negotiations dragged on, Greece's banks drained reserves, becoming ever more dependent on the ECB, while the Syriza government lost steam. For many on the left wing of Syriza, the February 20 compromise that kept Greece in the euro would come to seem a mistake. Tsipras's government had wasted the political momentum of its victory, missed its chance to carry out a popular rupture with Brussels and henceforth negotiated from a weakening position. But Tsipras did not want to provoke a break before negotiations had even begun. Varoufakis wanted to see whether leverage would work. He knew that every time he mentioned the possibility of default on the SMP bonds, it made the ECB blanch.[35]

Was there any possibility that a compromise would be worked out? As far as the debt was concerned, Greece's insolvency was manifest. But there

was no evidence that the creditors were ever willing to budge. Pursuing an Atlanticist strategy, the group around Varoufakis hoped that the swing factor in the negotiations might be the IMF. Most analysts at the Fund regretted that Dominique Strauss-Kahn had enrolled the IMF in the first iteration of extend-and-pretend. Five years on from 2010, Greece's debts were still unsustainable. Restructuring was essential. But Lagarde was loath to break with her European partners. Given her own political background, she had little sympathy for Syriza. And the IMF team on the ground was embedded with the troika and committed to implementing its tough program. As if to reinforce the Fund's commitment, the former head of its delegation to Greece, Poul Thomsen, was promoted to head the IMF's entire European operation.[36] Off the record Thomsen agreed with the majority of his IMF colleagues that the Greek debt was unsustainable. But as Athens would discover, harping on the issue of sustainability was a double-edged sword. Sustainability depended not just on the debt level but on the future course of Greek growth. Though on issues like the fiscal multiplier the IMF had come around to a more "liberal" view, when it came to long-run economic growth the Fund cleaved to the old religion. To raise its growth rate Greece must undo labor market regulation and free restrictive business licensing. This required detailed and highly intrusive "supply side reform."[37] Furthermore, the Greek government could always raise money through privatization sales. To implement such measures was painful for any government. For a Left coalition like Syriza it was political suicide.

If the IMF was of two minds, would its key shareholder, the United States, swing the balance? Five years earlier, when the crisis began, Papandreou's embattled PASOK government had found comfort in Washington. In the immediate aftermath of Syriza's victory Obama again sounded encouraging.[38] Too much should not be asked of a people that were already on their knees, the president opined. "You cannot keep on squeezing countries that are in the midst of depression."[39] Meanwhile, America's celebrity economists of the center-left, headed by Paul Krugman and Joseph Stiglitz, threw their weight behind Varoufakis's call for a "rational" debt program for Greece. But none of this went down well in Berlin. Nor did Athens get much sympathy from Obama's new Treasury secretary, Jack Lew. A lawyer, hedge fund manager and Citigroup alumnus, Lew came from the hawkish

side of the Obama administration. A new Greek crisis "would not be a good thing in a world economy just recovering from a deep recession," Lew pointed out. It was up to the Greek government to do its best to win its creditors' trust.[40] As tension escalated in April, Jason Furman, the latest chairman of Barack Obama's Council of Economic Advisers, weighed in to comment that a Greek crisis was not "an experiment we want to run." But when he was asked to rank a disorderly Greek exit on a "scale of one to 10, where the collapse of Lehman is a 10," Furman opined that "a Greek default would likely register as a six; that is down from eight in 2012."[41] When the stakes had been high, Washington had not hesitated to meddle in the politics of the euro area. For a crisis that registered only 6 out of 10, Washington was not about to jeopardize its relationship with Berlin. As one American official told Varoufakis: "For us you belong to the sphere of influence of Berlin, which we will not question."[42]

If no help could be expected from Washington, what about China, the new power in the global economy? Beijing saw the Eastern Mediterranean as a natural extension of its Eurasian One Belt, One Road logistical network. China had already taken a high-profile and controversial stake in Piraeus port.[43] Varoufakis eagerly explored the possibility of attracting additional Chinese capital and even Chinese intervention in the market for Greek Treasury debt. Beijing seemed interested. But the bond buying Beijing promised never materialized. When Varoufakis inquired why, the answer he received from Beijing was stark. Beijing had pulled back because Berlin had let the Chinese know that it did not welcome their intervention in the Greek crisis.[44]

China and America as partners appealed to those Greeks like Varoufakis who thought of themselves as "modernizers" and did not have deep roots in the Greek Communist milieu. For the Old Guard of Syriza, Russia was the obvious option.[45] In 2015 Merkel and Hollande were still struggling to contain the Ukraine crisis. Putin was making increasingly interventionist moves in Syria. Could Greece exploit its strategic location in the Eastern Mediterranean to gain leverage? On April 8 Tsipras traveled to Moscow to meet with Putin. But in the Kremlin he heard the same thing that the Greeks were hearing from Washington and Beijing. Putin's message was simple: "You must strike a deal with the Germans."[46]

But who in Germany was Greece to deal with? The authority in financial policy was held by Finance Minister Schäuble, but, as he made increasingly clear, he did not believe that Greece had a future in the euro area.[47] Did Merkel share the same view? She was a more pragmatic politician than Schäuble; surely she would not want to see the breakup of the euro. Tsipras thought he could prevail upon her through personal diplomacy. Varoufakis, on the other hand, thought that what Merkel needed to understand was the threat that Greece could pose to Draghi's stabilization efforts. Merkel exploited the gap between them. Seeking to split the Greek prime minister from his more left-wing cabinet members, she favored him with a series of personal meetings that convinced Tsipras that she would eventually deliver a compromise. The question was when and on what terms. The longer Merkel waited, the more desperate Greece became.

In April, amid talk of Greek default, the yield on the few outstanding Greek bonds still traded on open markets soared to 26.2 percent.[48] Back in 2012 this might have triggered anxiety in Rome, Madrid and Lisbon. But now there was no contagion. The ECB was unfazed. As Draghi remarked: "We have enough instruments at this point in time…which although they have been designed for other purposes would certainly be used at a crisis time if needed. . . . We are better equipped than we were in 2012, 2011 and 2010."[49] With the ECB's bond purchasing not only soaking up all newly issued government debt in the eurozone but reducing the total stock of sovereign debt available for private investors by 265 billion euros, there was little reason to fear bond vigilantes. The deliberate default on the ECB's bond holdings planned by Varoufakis was supposed to puncture this complacency. But, as was becoming clear, Tsipras shrank from using the threat.

If no compromise could be reached and if Tsipras was unwilling to use Greece's only real weapon, was there any way out of the impasse? For the creditors, it would have been easiest if Tsipras and his eccentric crew simply disappeared from the scene. But so soon after their handsome electoral victory that was too much to hope for. The EU was haunted by the ghosts of 2011. As the *Financial Times* noted, Brussels was "sensitive to accusations" that "the EU was complicit in ending the tenure of George Papandreou, Greece's prime minister . . . and Silvio Berlusconi."[50] But the Eurogroup made no secret of the fact that they wanted Tsipras to ditch

Impact of ECB Bond Purchases, 2015

	2015 Gross bond issuance	Redemption	2015 Net bond issuance	QE purchase for 2015	Net supply less QE
Germany	159	155	4	113	−109
France	187	118	69	89	-20
Italy	185	196	−11	77	-88
Spain	142	92	50	56	-6
Netherlands	48	37	12	25	−14
Belgium	33	21	11	16	-5
Austria	17	13	4	12	-8
Finland	10	5	5	8	-3
Ireland	14	2	11	7	4
Portugal	13	6	7	11	-4
Greece	7	7	0	13	-13
Total	**814**	**651**	**162**	**427**	**-266**

Source: Morgan Stanley Research, National Treasuries.

Varoufakis and the left wing of his party.[51] Historical precedents were readily to hand. Europe had a track record of curbing radical left-wing governments. After a few "wild months" in the autumn of 1998, Germany's Red-Green government under Gerhard Schroeder had jettisoned Oskar Lafontaine as finance minister.[52] In 1983 Mitterrand's turn to a hard currency policy had presaged the ouster of the Communists from his coalition government. Looking further back, the *Financial Times* helpfully suggested as a precedent "Britain's 1931 National Government."[53] Would Tsipras be Greece's Ramsay MacDonald? After another round of bullying by the Eurogroup at the Riga summit on April 25, with Merkel's active encouragement, Tsipras moved Varoufakis aside. He remained as finance minister, but Euclid Tsakalotos, the minister for international economic relations, would be the lead debt negotiator. Another opportunity to deploy the Greek deterrent went begging.

Athens was bending. But months of siege warfare were taking their toll on both sides. Merkel and Schäuble might sleep easily, but Brussels had more invested in the idea of the good Europe. In May it seemed that

the troika might be wavering. The commission was warming to the plucky Tsipras. The French government did not want to see Greece humiliated. The IMF was skeptical about the sustainability of the creditors' demands. It took a meeting on June 1 in Berlin to harden the resolve of the troika and to force Syriza finally into the corner.[54] The IMF and the eurozone "bridged their differences." The Fund's worries about sustainability were soothed by requiring Athens to force through tough reforms of its labor markets and business regulations. That would allow the creditors to make optimistic assumptions about future growth and relieve them of the need to make any immediate commitment to future debt forgiveness.[55] As far as Athens was concerned, it was the worst possible outcome.[56] Economists in the City of London estimated that under the creditors' plan, the Greek economy would plunge by a further 12.6 percent by 2019 and the Greek debt ratio would soar to a staggering 200 percent. As Wolfgang Munchau put it in the *Financial Times*, Greece had nothing to lose by saying no. "[A]cceptance of the troika's programme would constitute a dual suicide—for the Greek economy, and for the political career of the Greek prime minister."[57]

Was it suicide or assassination? When Athens refused to yield, European efforts to delegitimize the Syriza government in the eyes of its own population were overt. Jean-Claude Juncker and Slovak finance minister Peter Kažimír publicly declared that their disagreements were only with Mr. Tsipras's government and not with the Greek people.[58] Taking the hint, on June 18 a rally of pro-Euro anti-Syriza Greeks was called on Facebook. The riot police were pulled back; the government avoided any public confrontation with the pro-EU crowd. But Syriza's confidence was rattled. The demonstration made clear that the Left were not the only ones who could mobilize extraparliamentary forces. After the demoralizing slog of Syriza's first months in office, it was no longer obvious which side could count on more active popular support.[59] In early June Tsipras and Tsakalotos once more sought a compromise. Athens would meet the creditors' austerity target by a combination of increased retirement age and heavy increases in tax and social security contributions. For forty-eight hours this raised hopes of a deal. But there were sticking points. While agreeing to run a huge primary budget surplus, Syriza was still insisting on "political essentials,"

weighting the adjustment less toward welfare cuts and more toward tax increases on wealthy Greeks. This satisfied the demand for social equity, but creditors insisted that it "could end up strangling the economy."[60] Furthermore, what Syriza wanted in return was a precommitment to debt restructuring. On that Germany would not budge.

Without access to the last tranche of the 2012 program, Athens was days away from defaulting. In a desperate bid to rally support, Tsipras sprang a new surprise.[61] At one a.m. on the morning of June 27 he went on television to announce that he was calling a referendum. It would be up to the Greek people to decide either to accept or to reject the creditors' memorandum. Tsipras, for his part, declared that he would campaign against acceptance, calling on the Greek population to reject the "blackmail ultimatum."[62] The Eurogroup was horrified. As Merkel made clear, with the Athens government campaigning against agreement there could be no further compromise.[63] The following day, Sunday, June 28, the ECB pulled the trigger. It froze its emergency liquidity support for Greece's banks at its current level. The next day this would unleash a disastrous bank run. The ECB could have gone further. It could have terminated emergency liquidity assistance altogether and demanded repayment. At the crisis meeting of the ECB's board, there were certainly votes to be had for such a drastic course of action. But the ECB's overwhelming power put Draghi in a delicate position.[64] As a member of the troika and chief provider of financial life support to the Greek banking system, the ECB was "judge, jury and executioner."[65] Draghi did not want to appear as though he were further escalating the tension or "deliberately worsening Greece's financial plight."[66] Capping Greek access to liquidity assistance was drastic enough. To avoid an immediate collapse, the Greek banks were preemptively closed, cash withdrawals were limited to 60 euros per day and capital controls limited capital flight. Middle-class depositors formed impatient queues to withdraw their cash. Greece's privately owned media were in an uproar. The irresponsible radicals of Syriza, they told their audience, had taken the country over the edge.

With the creditors refusing either to negotiate or to make concessions until the results of the referendum were known, on June 30 Athens announced that it was delaying payment on money owed to the IMF. This was

no mere administrative matter. The IMF is acknowledged as the super-senior creditor in international lending. Being in arrears to the IMF put Greece on a short list that included Sudan, Somalia, Zimbabwe, Afghanistan and Cambodia under the Khmer Rouge.[67] And the size of its debts was unprecedented. Greece owed repayment on $26 billion to the IMF over the next ten years.

But at this crucial moment the IMF did not respond as one might have expected. In the summer of 2015, the dissatisfaction inside the Fund over the European approach to the Greek debt crisis finally broke into the open. Between a first blog post by its chief economist, Olivier Blanchard, in mid-June and the formal issuance of a paper on Greek debt sustainability in mid-July, the world's leading financial authority declared the policy of extend-and-pretend practiced since 2010 both economically and politically unsustainable. Greece would have to make further tough decisions, no doubt, but the troika and the Eurogroup needed to stop pretending that that would be enough. Debt restructuring had to be on the table.[68] With the backing of the US board members, overriding resistance from the European representatives, on July 2 the IMF published a preliminary report outlining the full absurdity of the programs so far. Instead of the 50 billion euros in privatization receipts scheduled in 2012, Greece had received 3.2 billion. The current program and all the variants haggled over since Syriza took office were unrealistic. No one who was serious would proceed on the basis that primary surpluses of 4 percent, massive structural changes and 2 percent GDP growth per annum were a realistic scenario.[69] After what their country had been through since 2010, no political party in Greece could be expected to "own" such a drastic policy mix. Without ownership, one could not expect fulfillment. The IMF now called for at least 50 billion euros in debt relief, a doubling of repayment times and 36 billion euros in short-term financing to allow Greece to survive until 2018.[70]

It was a nasty surprise to the Europeans that the Americans would have let this happen. As late as early June, at the convivial G7 meeting in Bavaria, Obama had acted the part of a loyal ally. But it was a measure of the stability that Europe had now attained that the clash should have come out into the open. The only consideration that had justified the IMF's

involvement in the Greek bailout in May 2010 was the risk of systemic contagion. Thanks to Mario Draghi's bond-buying, there was no longer any risk of that. The IMF could afford to voice principled opposition without fear of practical consequences. It would make no new commitments to the eurozone's exercise in self-delusion. But it did not do the one thing that would have placed Berlin under serious pressure: It did not withdraw from the troika.

For the Greek population the choices were starker. Did they dare to challenge the creditors? Would a no vote mean the end of Greek membership in the euro or even the EU? Despite overt and massive intimidation, on July 5 a remarkable 61.31 percent voted against accepting the troika proposal. Given that the plan had by that point been repudiated as unsustainable by the IMF, the vote was not so much a wild act of political desperation as a brave and much-needed assertion of common sense. But the response from the creditor side was unyielding. Athens had until July 12 to come up with an even more austere and even less sustainable proposal or face expulsion from the eurozone. On July 9, with help from the French Treasury, the Syriza government cobbled together a new scheme, taking up a compromise on welfare cuts and tax increases proposed by the commission and coupling it to an appeal for modest debt write-offs and new credits of 53 billion euros. For the left wing of Syriza it was shameful surrender. Varoufakis, who resigned following the referendum, joined the internal party opposition. Meanwhile, Tsipras set off to Strasbourg in the hope of rallying support across Europe. On July 10 he made an appearance in the European Parliament, where he was greeted by a storm of approving whistles not only from the Left but also from the Far Right. Boos and catcalls came from the center.[71] European politics were dividing between upholders of the status quo and a motley crew denouncing the eurozone as a German prison.

On Saturday, July 11, with the principals scheduled to meet the following day, the finance ministers of Europe gathered in Brussels for a premeeting. It soon became clear that, far from softening, Berlin's position had hardened. If Greece wanted to stay in the eurozone, Schäuble insisted that it must demonstrate its credibility by agreeing to a 50-billion-euro collateral fund made up of Greek national assets placed under direct creditor control. With that in place there could be further loans and another effort

to make a go of extend-and-pretend. Alternatively, if Greece preferred the path of sovereignty, Schäuble offered a five-year "time-out" from the eurozone, which might be accompanied by debt restructuring and "humanitarian" relief.[72] There was talk of emergency supplies of medicines to Greek hospitals. What was not on the table was a repeat of 2012, deep debt restructuring with Greece remaining in the eurozone. Haircutting banks was one thing, haircutting the German taxpayer quite another. Greece would have to exit. But what if it did? What if Greece took the time-out option? It would mean that eurozone membership was reduced to a conditional status. How long would it be before Schäuble was offering a time-out to Italy or Spain? For the French it was unacceptable.[73] The Germans posed as the paymasters of Europe, but France too would bear a heavy burden in the event of any Greek rupture. The French had worked closely with Athens to draft its latest compromise proposal. Schäuble had simply swept it aside.

To clear the air, Michel Sapin, the French finance minister, proposed that they just "get it all out and tell one another the truth to blow off steam."[74] The group therapy didn't go well. The ensuing conversation was described by one participant as "extremely hard, violent even." Significantly, the battle went beyond national interest. In the words of France's youthful economy minister, Emmanuel Macron, Greece was provoking a veritable European civil war, a "war of religion," with the Nordics, the East Europeans, Germany and the Netherlands in one camp, and France, Italy, Spain and the rest in the other.[75] A painful climax was reached when Schauble and Draghi locked horns and the German finance minister ended up fuming that he was "not an idiot." At that point Dijsselbloem thought it best to call a halt to proceedings. The deal would have to be done by the heads of government the following day.

When the climactic summit began on the afternoon of Sunday, July 12, 2015, despite the presence of the entire union, the negotiations involved only four actors: Merkel; Tsipras, who was advised by his new finance minister; Donald Tusk, as president of the European Council; and Hollande, effectively representing the wider interests of the other member states. The negotiations were laborious and painful. Merkel abandoned Schäuble's alarming time-out proposal but clung to the guarantee fund. Tsipras conceded the fund, but could not accept that it should be run out of Brussels or Luxembourg. It

would control Greek assets. It must be headquartered in Athens. As Hollande insisted, "[I]t was a question of 'sovereignty.'"[76] Merkel conceded. The fund would be sited in Greece and could be used, if necessary, to recapitalize Greece's banks and for other domestic investment purposes. But even with that compromise agreed, by early in the morning of Monday, July 13, there was still no deal. At seven a.m., after a full night of talks, Merkel and Tsipras were 2.5 billion euros apart. Both, it seemed, wanted to walk away in exhausted frustration. At this fateful moment Tusk intervened. The two parties could abandon the talks, but if they did, he would not hesitate to tell the world that they had allowed "Europe to fail" over what was in the final analysis a trivial amount of money. It wasn't the prospect of economic disaster that brought Merkel to her senses, but the likely political fallout from letting Greece go. When it came to the moment of decision she did not feel bound by financial logic. She did not want to be the chancellor who "broke Europe." That was more important than finally resolving the question of Greek debt. She split the difference. Germany would agree to yet another bailout. Greece would receive new loans from Europe totaling 86 billion euros. In exchange, Athens accepted severe intrusions on its sovereignty. It was required to whip through yet more cuts within forty-eight hours. Parliamentary sovereignty was reduced to a rubber stamp.

There was no rupture. Greece was still in the eurozone. Europe had regained its capacity for a rather brutal form of collective action. The ECB had demonstrated the pacifying power of central bank intervention. Greece was held on the path of "reform" demanded by the troika. But as the IMF's démarche had made clear, this was a matter of politics as much as financial crisis management. The European creditors had doggedly refused to discuss the only issue that mattered—debt restructuring. What was at stake was not macroeconomic performance but the imposition of discipline on a wayward eurozone member. Shielded from financial contagion, a conservative financial settlement had been demonstratively imposed on a left-wing government with a strong democratic mandate. The perverse effect of the ECB's "liberating" move to QE was that it allowed extend-and-pretend and its concomitant, relentless austerity, to continue.

IV

Launched by Syriza sympathizers in Barcelona on the night of July 12–13, #Thisisacoup went viral on Twitter, being taken up by 377,000 users world-wide in a matter of hours and generating a billion impressions in a matter of days.[77] Closer to home, in Athens, members of the Left Platform, led by Panagiotis Lafazanis, the former energy and environment minister, met at the Oscar Hotel on the night of July 14 to discuss how they might go through with the Grexit that Schäuble had offered, but Merkel, Tusk, Hollande and Tsipras had done everything to avoid. It had been a mistake not to make the break with Brussels already in February. Now, before the prison door closed once more, they should effect a rupture, if necessary by radical means. Their target was the national mint, where they believed 22 billion euros were held in reserves, enough to cover pensions and other essential government bills until they had rolled out a new national currency. If the central bank governor, Yannis Stournaras, resisted, as they expected he would, they would have him arrested. The meeting was far from clandestine. There were journalists swarming outside the hotel. It is hard to know how seriously to take such talk. But as one participant recalled: "Obviously it was a moment of high tension. . . . [Y]ou were . . . aware of a real revolutionary spirit in the room."[78] It didn't come to that. Tsipras and the mainstream of Syriza whipped the necessary measures through parliament. The left wing split from Syriza, only to be humiliated in the September general election, which vindicated Tsipras's leadership, returning him with a virtually unchanged majority and the new loan deal in place. A majority of Greeks, it turned out, wanted eurozone membership, even at the price of continued troika oversight.

Across Europe, what shocked centrists was the violence of the July clashes. Donald Tusk, who had seen the final round of negotiations up close, agreed with the Greek radicals. There was a real mood of revolutionary impatience in the air. As far as Tusk, a cold war liberal and veteran of Solidarność, was concerned, it was all very alarming. "[T]oo much Rousseau not enough Montesquieu," he told a bemused audience of financial journalists.[79]

Jürgen Habermas, the closest equivalent to those Enlightenment thinkers twenty-first-century Europe has to offer, was aghast. Merkel had "carried out an act of punishment" against Greece's left-wing government, he told the *Guardian*. "I fear that the German government, including its social democratic faction, have gambled away in one night all the political capital that a better Germany had accumulated in half a century." Germany had "unashamedly revealed itself as Europe's chief disciplinarian and for the first time openly made a claim for German hegemony in Europe."[80]

There was no doubt, of course, that Merkel and Schäuble had played a strong hand. But what exactly did they have to show for it? What upset German right-wingers was not the bruising nature of the encounters with Greece but how little Germany had gained. Who, after all, was the victor in the decisive encounters of July 12–13, 2015? Certainly not Schäuble, who had been cut loose by his own chancellor. What had prevailed was the determination to "preserve Europe" at the price of another unsustainable bailout deal. For the German Right, Merkel's sellout in the Greek crisis was a fitting prelude to her disastrous betrayal of the German nation in the Syrian refugee crisis that autumn. The beneficiary was the AfD—the right-wing, promarket party that had first come into existence in April 2013 to protest against Berlin's endless concessions in the eurozone crisis. As Schäuble would snark, the AfD's rise was 50 percent down to Draghi; the other half, presumably, was down to his boss and her liberal posturing over the Syrians.[81] Schäuble was no xenophobe. The historic stakes were high. What Merkel was jeopardizing with her dithering concessions was the historic mission of the CDU: to tame German nationalism and to bind it to Europe.

The German right wing saw some things clearly. They understood that, as powerful as it was, Germany's dominance was incomplete at best. What had stabilized the eurozone in 2012 was a halfhearted lurch toward deeper integration covered by the markets' perception that Draghi was finally "Americanizing" the ECB. In 2015 once more, it was not simply German conservatism that triumphed. The necessary complement to the containment of Syriza was QE. As it had been in the United States, it was a perversely complementary package. Austerity without QE would have been paralyzing in economic terms. QE without austerity would have been impossible politically for conservatives to bear.[82] How tightly the two were

coupled would become clear in the second half of 2015 as the tensions left by the eurozone crisis continued to rack European politics. The anti-Syriza front in the Eurogroup had reason to worry. First in Portugal in October 2015, and then in Spain in December 2015, elections delivered serious blows to the conservative and centrist parties that had toed the line of austerity since 2010.

In the Spanish general election of December 2015, the two-party system based on the conservatives and the Socialists that had shaped the transition to democracy since General Franco's death in 1975 imploded. With the conservatives crashing to 28 percent and the Socialists to 22 percent, they commanded the loyalty of only half the electorate.[83] The majority of the rest was shared between two entirely new parties, Podemos and the Citizens party. Podemos scored 20.7 percent, which was disappointing only when compared with the 30 percent plus it had commanded in the polls shortly after its formation in 2014. It lost support in 2015 in part because of the beating being dealt out to Syriza, but also because of the rise of the even newer Citizens party, which described itself as a "progressive" party espousing a program of social, cultural and economic liberalism. Both Podemos and the Citizens party promised a new set of clean hands to overcome corruption. Both did remarkably well. But the outcome of the election was inconclusive. No side had a clear majority to govern. The divide between the Socialists and Podemos was too deep to enable a left-wing government. In 2016, after a second round of voting, the dogged conservative prime minster, Rajoy, clung on. With its economy limping back from the dead, Spain, like Ireland, would be celebrated as the poster child for austerity adjustment policies.

In Portugal the economic recovery was slower. Unlike Spain, it had borne the brunt of a full-blown troika program. In 2015 its youth unemployment rate was just shy of 60 percent and long-term unemployment hovered around 40 percent. The PàF center-right coalition headed by Pedro Passos Coelho, who had taken office in June 2011, had fought the long fight for eurozone stabilization. When the election campaign began it had seemed as though PàF would be roundly defeated. But the turmoil in Greece and the protection offered by the ECB's QE contributed to swinging the result. On October 4, 2015, Coelho and the PàF saw their vote plunge

relative to their 2011 result by 12 percent. But at 38.6 percent they still came in far ahead of the Socialists at 32.3 percent. With relief, President Cavaco Silva, a conservative financial economist, turned to Coelho to make the first attempt to form a new government. But though PàF had won a plurality, it was a long way short of a viable majority. The Socialists, though their electoral performance had been disappointing, had other options. If they were willing to form an alliance with the radical Left Bloc, Portugal's equivalent of Syriza, and the ex-Communist Unitary Democratic Coalition, they had a majority. Pulling off this alignment would require a break with the taboos of the cold war and the conventions of Portuguese democracy since the end of dictatorship in the 1970s. As was true in Germany for the SPD and Die Linke, the Portuguese Socialists had hitherto refused to deal with the ex-Communists. But after years of austerity, PS leader António Costa took the plunge and entered talks to form a three-party left-wing government.[84]

How would President Silva respond? It was for him a profound dilemma. As he stated with remarkable frankness: "In 40 years of democracy," the Portuguese governments had never depended on the radical Left parties, which questioned the Lisbon Treaty, the EU's budgetary treaty, the banking union, the Stability and Growth Pact, the euro and NATO membership.[85] As the president made clear, as far as he was concerned, the right to govern in Portugal depended on a commitment to those institutions and the values they embodied. And in 2015 there was a further correlate. Portugal must qualify for inclusion in the ECB's quantitative easing program. It was Draghi's bond buying that had given Portugal shelter from the Greek storm. Eligibility for inclusion in the ECB program, in turn, depended, by fiat of the ECB, on the rating of the international credit agencies. The best-known ratings agencies—Fitch, Moody's and Standard & Poor's—had all downgraded Portugal to junk in 2011. The only exception was DBRS, the least well known of the international ratings agencies. It was on DBRS's bond rating that Portugal's membership in the "respectable club" of Europe depended.[86] If it were to drop out of the ECB program, the financial consequences would be catastrophic, and as far as President Silva was concerned, that had clear implications. "This," Silva opined, "is the worst moment for a radical change to the foundations of our democracy. . . . After we carried

out an onerous programme of financial assistance, entailing heavy sacrifices, it is my duty, within my constitutional powers, to do everything possible to prevent false signals being sent to financial institutions, investors and markets."[87] To allow the left-wing majority to take power would be a false signal.

Unsurprisingly after the events in Greece, Angela Merkel was not shy about letting it be known that she agreed. The prospect of a left-wing anti-austerity coalition in Lisbon was "very negative."[88] But what option did President Silva have? He couldn't very well call new elections with an alternative government ready and waiting. On November 24, Silva faced the inevitable and named Costa as Portuguese prime minister. But he did not simply allow the majority principle to prevail either. Instead, in a constitutionally dubious arrangement, Silva made Costa's appointment conditional on promises.[89] The government must respect Portugal's commitments to the European Union's stability pact, whereby all eurozone members were required to reduce budget deficits to below 3 percent of GDP. It must remain committed to NATO. It must continue with the restructuring of Portugal's ailing banking system as previously planned. It must limit the role of trade unions in deciding government policy and respect the existing balance between employers and labor. Schäuble had announced that elections should not change economic policy. Portugal's president clearly agreed. Watched over by the president, the creditor governments of the EU, the ECB, the bond-rating agencies and the bond markets, the Left coalition took office. What it could do with political power, whether Portuguese democracy within the frame of the eurozone was more than a matter of extend-and-pretend, would depend on its ability to bend the constraints imposed upon it. At least, unlike Greece, the arithmetic of Portugal's debts did not condemn it from the start.

V

Against left-wing governments, in weak and dependent members of the eurozone, the tactics of financial pressure worked. The Eurogroup's project of political and economic discipline prevailed. For all their bravado and the

genuine excitement they awakened both at home and abroad, the governments of Tsipras and Costa did not promise revolution. They promised national autonomy and self-respect, and, above all, social improvement. This made them vulnerable to the threat of immediate economic suffocation. After all, what good was a small increment to your pension or shorter waiting lists for social housing if a cap on ECB liquidity assistance left you unable to get cash out of the bank?

But the challenge to the status quo in the EU did not come only from the Left. Overshadowed by the struggles with Greece, the nationalist wave that had made itself felt in the European parliamentary election of May 2014 was gathering force. In 2014 it was the FN, UKIP and the Danish People's Party that made the headlines. The following year, the British Conservative Party unexpectedly won an outright majority in the May 2015 general election. The British Conservatives were a broad church. David Cameron had led the party out of the wilderness of Opposition along the path of cultural modernization. But the right wing of the party belonged squarely in the nationalist camp—preoccupied with sovereignty, immigration and flag-waving traditionalism.[90] Further to the right lurked the mavericks of the anti-EU UKIP, excluded from Westminster, but the winners of the European elections in 2014. A few weeks after the British Conservatives' victory, the Law and Justice party won the Polish presidency on a ticket of overt nationalism and cultural conservatism.[91] They too were nationalists hostile to the intrusions of Brussels and the threat of German "domination." Over the summer and autumn of 2015, the drama of the Syrian refugee crisis and Angela Merkel's well-intentioned but cack-handed response fed the nationalist flames. Germany was not just imperious. It was opening the doors of an alien invasion. It was a double gift for nationalist demagogues. By the autumn of 2015, Law and Justice had captured the Polish parliament and government as well as the presidency.

Together, Poland and the UK accounted for 100 million citizens of the EU, 20 percent of the total, with governments pandering to the most skeptical Europhobic elements. It was unsettling to Brussels, but it had wider ramifications too. Historically, the UK was America's preeminent ally in Europe, both in NATO and as the anchor of the transatlantic eurodollar system. Since the early 2000s Poland had been in the van of Donald Rums-

feld's "new Europe." It was the East European state most closely aligned with America's geopolitical project. Earlier in the year, Syriza had tried in vain to gain leverage in Europe by interesting global actors in its predicament. The United States, China and Russia had all declined. They would not meddle in Germany's sphere of interest. Poland and the UK posed challenges to the EU status quo that were far harder to contain.

Chapter 23

THE FEAR PROJECTS

T he year 2016 began with the nationalist government in Warsaw picking fights with Brussels over the freedom of the press, the independence of the judiciary and abortion rights. In their challenge to the EU they could count on applause from Viktor Orbán's self-proclaimed "illiberal democracy" in Hungary. Meanwhile, the British government was demanding negotiations over opt-outs from the European future. The British prime minister let Brussels know that he would be happy to take a pro-European position. But from the outset, Cameron's approach was disconcertingly transactional. If he did not get the concessions he demanded, his threat was that he would lead the campaign against EU membership in a referendum scheduled for the summer of 2016.

Nationalism and xenophobia were the common denominators of the challengers from the Right. But, unlike the leadership of Law and Justice, Cameron was in an awkward position. He was struggling to square a groundswell of popular sentiment fanned by the propagandists of his own party with a broader agenda of business-driven globalism. Since the 1970s EU membership had shaped the competitive modernization of the UK economy. The Tories, as much as any party, had participated in that drive. The City of London in its twenty-first-century form had emerged as one of the most important strands of the UK-EU relationship. Its offshore relationship to the eurozone had defined both Britain's and Europe's places in the networks of financial globalization and their relationship to the United States.

Now, in an extraordinarily high-risk bid to channel and manage the politics of popular nationalism, the Tory government was putting London's position as a crucial node in the network of the global economy in play.

I

Less than ten years earlier, the City of London had been riding high. It was the prized jewel in New Labour's economic crown. It was Britain's ticket to global significance. It was the standard the deregulators of Wall Street aspired to, the location of choice for fast-moving, high-end global finance. All the more shattering was the shock of 2008. The City became a site of crisis and failure.[1] Tens of thousands lost their jobs. The two most resilient UK banks—Barclays and HSBC—sidestepped Brown's ballyhooed program of recapitalization. This left the government to nationalize not just Northern Rock but Lloyds-HBOS and RBS as well. In the wake of the crisis "rebalancing" was an agenda shared by both Labour and the coalition government that replaced it.[2] British banking legislation went well beyond Dodd-Frank. The once widely touted FSA was abolished. Banking supervision was reincorporated into the Bank of England. The new conception of macroprudentialism did not allow for a neat distinction between regulation and economic policy functions. The Banking Reform Act of 2013 would divide up bank functions and ring-fence retail activity. Financial services were no longer part of Britain's narrative of national success.

But unlike in the case of Wall Street, tightening the regulation of British banks is not the same as curbing the City of London. The City is not first and foremost a national financial center. Its main business is global. The conference in London on July 26, 2012, at which Draghi made his famous speech was an event for global investors designed to showcase the City. Ahead of the Olympic Games, Bank of England governor Mervyn King had sport on his mind. The City of London, he remarked, was like the All England Lawn Tennis and Croquet Club, the hosts of Wimbledon.[3] The setting is quintessentially English. But it is a global tournament. Though King didn't elaborate, the further implication of his remarks was that Britain's banks stood to the City as Britain's eternally struggling national tennis

program stood to Wimbledon. They were a national preoccupation. They might produce the occasional champion, but neither they nor the rest of the British economy were the main attraction.

The modern City of London had been built on the eurodollar system. Thanks to the Fed, that had survived the crisis. But the American regulators understood London's role as the platform for some of the most extreme risks that the American banks had built up. As it was put to a congressional committee in 2012 by a senior US regulator, the United States had allowed its risks to migrate to London only for them to "come right back here, crashing to our shores."[4] Within the capacious framework of Dodd-Frank, US regulators were now sharply tightening the regulations of foreign banks in the United States and of US bank operations overseas.[5] The European banks that had epitomized the connection between the City of London and Wall Street, the likes of Barclays and Deutsche, UBS and Credit Suisse, were under huge pressure. By 2015, of all the European banks that had once challenged for top rankings on Wall Street, only Deutsche Bank was still competing for a top spot in global investment banking, and that was widely seen as a sign of its desperation.[6] Deutsche had no other secure business line to fall back on. The traffic on the whole was from the United States to Europe. All the big American banks still maintained a major presence in London. But it was a sign of the times that in 2014, Wall Street was for the first time ranked above the City as a global banking location in Z/Yen Group's widely watched report.[7]

How could London regain its edge? In the wake of the crisis, the major competitors of America's global banks were not European but Asian. The "British" bank that had done best out of the crisis was HSBC. Driven by competitive pressure, London embarked on a remarkable twenty-first-century gamble. As it had done for the United States, the City of London would remake itself as China's financial gateway to the world.[8] Side-stepping the geopolitics of Sino-American competition, a special relationship to China would restore London's competitive edge. In the spring of 2012, the City of London Corporation initiated a project to make the City into a key center for renminbi trading. The result was a series of spectacular firsts. Already in 2012, HSBC had issued the first RMB-denominated bond and London claimed 62 percent of all RMB payments business outside China. In June

2013, to backstop the expanding RMB business, the Bank of England entered into a swap arrangement with the PBoC. Beijing conferred on London-based asset managers the privilege of being the first Western firms to be allowed to invest directly in RMB-denominated shares. In October 2014 the UK Treasury itself issued a RMB 3 billion bond.[9] The United States had long borrowed from China. Now the UK would borrow in the Chinese currency.

In making these moves the Bank of England explicitly cited the model of the eurodollar markets of the 1970s. The difference, of course, was that in facilitating the emergence of the eurodollar market, London had enabled global finance to escape government regulation. By contrast, in facilitating the internationalization of the renminbi, the City of London and the UK government were working hand in glove with the authorities in Beijing. London insisted on normalizing this relationship. China was a crucial emerging market. Liberalization would follow internationalization. What this turned a blind eye to was the fact that both the United States and China were playing for geoeconomic position. China's proposal for the Asian Infrastructure Investment Bank brought this out into the open. Washington's furious reaction to London's eagerness to join the Chinese-led bank was telling.

The boldness of London's move becomes even more remarkable when we consider the wider field it had to be situated in. In the 1980s Britain had positioned itself similarly as an entrepôt for Japanese investment—by both Japanese banks and manufacturers. Britain as a gateway for global FDI was a voice for market liberalization inside the EU. In the twenty-first century, playing off the Americans and the Chinese in financial services might be thought of as analogous to Germany's position as a global exporter of high-tech manufactures. On his visit to Beijing in 2013 this seemed to be Cameron's vision. He offered Britain as a partner "uniquely placed to make the case for deepening the EU's trade and investment relationship with China" and held out the vision of an "ambitious and comprehensive EU-China Free Trade Agreement."[10] But that made the question all the more pressing. How secure was the UK's place in the EU?

The 2008 crisis marked a break in Britain's relations with the EU. As the UK economy went into recession, the popular mood toward Europe soured. Nor did the Tories in Opposition do anything to dampen that resentment.

The huge surge in Eastern European migration welcomed by the Blair and Brown governments made an excellent stick to beat Labour with. Once the Tory-led coalition began to force through its austerity agenda, the strain that immigration allegedly imposed on the NHS and social services provided a lightning rod. Britain's lopsided growth added further to the sense of frustration. Whereas the production sectors of the UK economy—manufacturing, construction, etc.—stagnated, between 2010 and 2014 financial services surged ahead by 12.4 percent.[11] Driven by the wealth of the City, in London and its environs, house prices rocketed by 50 percent between 2013 and 2016, spectacularly outstripping growth in the rest of the country. London was the cosmopolitan global city par excellence, the preferred home of oligarchs. In economic terms "rebalancing" was a myth. In political terms it was not. Across much of the UK, London's cosmopolitan affluence aroused a deep antipathy. For conservative commentators friendly to UKIP, "'London' has become shorthand for faraway people with no grasp of the nation's problems."[12] London was one capital of this elite, Brussels another. The populist tabloid *Daily Express* began campaigning for Brexit in November 2010 and became the first newspaper to align itself with UKIP.[13] In October 2011, as the eurozone crisis reached its height, eighty Tory backbench MPs broke with government demanding a referendum on the Lisbon Treaty and further EU constitutional change.[14] Polls in the fall of 2011 showed barely one-third of the British electorate approving of continued EU membership, with over 50 percent against.[15]

If the modernizing, big-business wing of the Tory party wanted to maintain its grip, it clearly needed to resolve the European issue once and for all. And the pressure came from two sides—from outside as well as inside Britain.[16] The reaction to the crisis visible in Europe was ominous for London. As usual the French were the enemy. Sarkozy and Trichet seemed bent on displacing the City of London, which they regarded as a source of financial instability, from the center of euro-denominated finance. With the governments of Europe struggling to contain the eurozone crisis, it could not help but seem anomalous that most trading in euros and most transactions in euro-denominated derivatives took place in London. Many member states liked the idea of a financial transactions tax. From the opposition benches, both the French Socialists and the German SPD were

pushing the idea. Given the political weakness of her coalition partners, Merkel could not afford to ignore them. A study by the commission came to the inevitable conclusion that any such tax would generate 62 percent or more of its revenue in the City of London.

It was these tensions that unloaded in December 2011 in the disastrous clash between the UK and the rest of the EU over the fiscal compact. Tellingly, Cameron came to the do-or-die eurozone talks in Brussels with one key agenda item, to protect the City of London.[17] The plans being touted by Van Rompuy for deep integration, up to and including eurobonds, were unacceptable to both Berlin and London. So Cameron believed that he had the basis for a deal. In exchange for his support in blocking the federalist agenda, Merkel would promise Cameron to exempt the City from any onerous regulations. That proved to be a misunderstanding. To navigate the eurozone crisis, Merkel needed Sarkozy and the SPD in the Bundestag far more than she needed Cameron. Feeling betrayed, Cameron vetoed the deal, leaving him looking like a narrow-minded lobbyist for the City of London.[18] Meanwhile, Merkel and Sarkozy's grand fiscal compact was reduced to an intergovernmental bargain.

The clash was appallingly badly handled by Cameron, but it was not without logic. To get a grip on the eurozone crisis, Berlin and Paris clearly did need to move toward deeper fiscal and financial integration. At every meeting of the European Council, at the G20, at the G8, in public and in private, the British government urged this logic on the eurozone.[19] To Anglophone economists, the functional necessity was simply inescapable. Draghi's "whatever it takes" came as a profound relief. But though eurozone consolidation was a necessity, for the leaders of the Tory party it had serious political implications. The banking union and a fiscal union were unacceptable to a broad swath of opinion in Britain, not just the Europhobes. If deeper eurozone integration was a matter not of whether but of when, London would have to force Brussels to openly embrace the model of a multispeed and multitiered Europe.

It is easy to forget in retrospect, but the Brexit referendum was not conceived as an in-out choice on UK membership in the EU "as is." Nor was it merely a means to extract minor concessions. London operated from the hubristic assumption that Britain could change the EU's course. While the

euro countries continued on their path toward deeper integration, Britain would force Brussels to formally recognize not just a multispeed but a multidirectional model. The UK was not heading more slowly to ever closer union. If the Tories had their way, it was not heading there at all. Brussels needed to be brought to accept that fact as well as its implications for the political economy of Europe. The "offshore" status of the City of London as an inside-outside financial hub had to be permanently recognized. Not only was this confrontation inescapable, but now was the moment for London to force the issue. To move forward from the crisis of 2010–2012, to consolidate the institutional structures of the eurozone, its members would have to face the difficult business of treaty change. Those complex negotiations would have to start in 2013 once the eurozone had stabilized. They would culminate in 2016 at the latest. It was during those delicate negotiations that Britain would have maximum leverage. The eurozone's agonizing efforts at consolidation would open the window of strategic opportunity for Cameron to negotiate a new dispensation.

It was this triple calculation—the effort by the metropolitan leadership of the Tory party to assert control over its party base; the hubristic assumption that London had enough clout to force the structural questions on the EU; and the judgment that now was the time to do it—that culminated in Cameron's fateful speech at the new headquarters of the Bloomberg news corporation in the City of London on January 23, 2013.[20] It was not an overtly anti-European speech, but Cameron insisted on the need to redefine the purpose of the EU beyond the eurozone. He had promised that he would curb immigration to the UK. To do so he wanted to limit the rights of EU citizens to claim benefits in the UK. He wanted safeguards for the noneurozone members of the EU against further decisions on integration by the Eurogroup core. He wanted, at least as far as the UK was concerned, to draw a line under the basic European promise of ever closer union. He called for negotiations and on that basis promised that there would be a referendum by 2017 at the latest.

It was a coherent strategy but a risky one. As spring turned to summer in 2013, it became obvious that the British were overoptimistic in imagining that the eurozone would move from the crisis of 2010–2012 to full-scale renegotiation of the treaties. That might make sense from the point of view

of economic governance, but Berlin, Paris and Brussels understood all too well how vulnerable treaty talks would make them. After the shocking result delivered by the May 2014 European elections, treaty renegotiation was postponed for the foreseeable future. Cameron's window of opportunity never opened. The idea of a grand bargain between Britain, the Dutch and the Germans to negotiate a new liberal vision of the common market was stillborn.[21] In the summer of 2014 the choice of Juncker as the new commission president, in the face of a bitter campaign of British opposition, was a sign that London's leverage was dwindling fast.[22] In 2014–2015, Europe was struck by the Ukraine crisis, the struggle over Greece and the refugee crisis, all of which made the EU look bad, the UK look grossly uncooperative and Cameron's reform agenda look trivial. Cameron spoke grandly of his new vision of the European future. But didn't it all come down to irresponsible xenophobic pandering and the selfish interests of the City of London?[23]

But Cameron could not pull back, all the less when in May 2015 the Tories unexpectedly won an outright majority. The countdown to the promised referendum was ticking. Even without treaty talks, could Cameron negotiate any significant concessions from Brussels? Berlin wanted to help. Merkel was keen to avoid the lurching upset to the balance of power in Europe that would result from Brexit. But after the December 2011 debacle and London's tasteless campaign against Juncker, Britain's brand was toxic.[24] Even the nationalists in Warsaw were hard to win over to the demand to limit the freedom of movement. It was, after all, directed against Poles. There wasn't very much that Tusk, as president of the European Council, could offer Cameron. The EU couldn't allow the UK to dictate the future course of integration. Freedom of movement and the equal treatment of EU citizens were nonnegotiable. Desperate to be able to present the British voters with some sort of deal, on February 20, 2016, Cameron settled for an "emergency brake" that would allow the UK to limit benefit payments to migrants for a "one-off" seven-year period.[25] In addition, Tusk agreed that the EU should recognize "that the United Kingdom . . . is not committed to further political integration in the European Union. . . . References to ever-closer union do not apply to the United Kingdom." As one experienced British member of the European Parliament commented: "Left as they are,

the words mean little of substance. Indeed, nothing might change. All Treaty articles could just continue to apply to the UK."[26] It would be up to London to assert itself. It was a far cry from Cameron's promise of January 2013 that Britain could initiate a fundamental rethink of the EU's purpose. It was much less than the British prime minister needed to hold the Tory party together. Immediately, two Tory heavyweights—mayor of London Boris Johnson and education minister Michael Gove—broke away to launch the "mainstream" Tory wing of the Brexit campaign in the referendum that was now set for June 23, 2016.

II

When confronting Syriza the year before, German finance minister Schäuble had declared that as far as he was concerned, elections could not be allowed to interfere with the fundamentals of economic policy. Greece's economy accounted for 1 percent of the EU's GDP. In the Brexit referendum a simple majority would decide over the future of a country whose economy accounted for 17 percent of the whole. For the UK the stakes were enormous. Half of Britain's trade, or c. $200 billion, went to the EU. Of Britain's stock of $1.2 trillion in FDI, half was from the EU. Both European and non-European investors favored Britain because of its membership in the union. The Japanese car industry had made the UK into its main base for exports to the rest of Europe. By 2015, 3.2 million EU citizens were living in the UK, of whom 2.3 million had jobs, 7 percent of the workforce; 1.2 million UK citizens lived permanently in the EU. Of course trade, investment and migration would have happened between the UK and Europe whether or not the UK was a member of the EU. But how much? According to the best guesses of the economists, trade with other EU members was 55 percent greater than one would have expected without EU membership.[27] For the City the questions were even more acute. Tens of thousands of jobs and billions of pounds in business depended on the so-called passporting arrangements, which allowed banks in London to operate as though they were inside the eurozone. It was a convenient fiction for European, British,

American and Asian financial firms. It was not a concession that London could hope to maintain if it was no longer even a member of the EU.

Popular support for the EU was uncertain. Brussels was a red rag to the nationalist Right. The bankers and the London "elite" were unpopular. The answer of the Remain campaign was to double down. It set up its base camp in the City. Its strategy was never to win voters to the EU. The EU, the strategists decided, was unsellable. Europe's politicians were asked not to make appearances in Britain. They would only make matters worse. Headed by the top PR team of the conservative party, backed up by Liberals and Labour, the Remain campaign had one message: "British voters will never love the European Union. But maybe they can be terrified into voting not to leave it."[28] It was a strategy aptly dubbed "Project Fear"—a term first coined in the context of the Scottish independence referendum in 2014. Its architects were the Australian PR guru Lynton Crosby and Jim Messina, who had been hired from Obama's White House. Messina made clear what he thought the stakes were: "Given these challenging economic times, the very last thing we should do is risk the U.K. and EU economies with this risky [Brexit] move."[29] What Messina and his cohorts meant by "the economy" was business. So their campaign set itself to winning a popular majority for the simple and unapologetic proposition that if the EU was good for UK business, then Remain was good for Britain.

Fifty of Britain's leading firms were persuaded to sign a statement that Britain will be "stronger, safer and better off" in a "reformed EU."[30] Behind the scenes there was an effort by the Confederation of British Industry to persuade its leading members to put warnings about Brexit in their annual reports.[31] The City of London Corporation overrode objections from Brexit voices to openly support Remain.[32] Some business leaders worried, somewhat squeamishly, that to spell out the job losses and the cancellation of investment projects that would likely follow on Brexit might have the air of blackmail. At least as far as the trade unions were concerned, they need not have worried. Labour MP Pat McFadden, a former government minister and cochair of the Labour Party's Remain campaign, insisted, "I think business has a legitimate voice in the debate and if they want to make their views known they have every right to do so."[33] Unite, Britain's biggest trade

union and principal donor to the Labour party, with around 500,000 members, sent a clear message: "The message to our members in BMW, Airbus, etc., is very straightforward—it's jobs, rights, remain."[34]

The same message was echoed from around the world. On April 12 the IMF announced that "severe regional and global damage" might follow if Britain voted to leave. According to the IMF, the mere fact of holding the referendum was so damaging to investor confidence that the Fund was forced to lower its forecast for UK growth by 15 percent, from 2.2 to 1.9 percent. The consequences of an actual Brexit, Lagarde warned, ranged from "pretty bad to very, very bad."[35] The G7 meeting in Tokyo let it be known that a "UK exit from the EU would reverse the trend towards greater global trade and investment, and the jobs they create and is a further serious risk to growth." As Angela Merkel put it, the G7 intended to send "the signal that all who sat here want Britain to stay part of the EU."[36] Back in Britain the UK Treasury came out with a lengthy report claiming that the damage would be between £2,600 and £5,200 per annum per household. By 2030 GDP might be lower by as much as 6 percent, costing the government between £20 billion and £45 billion in tax revenue, doing severe damage to public services, or forcing a substantial increase in tax rates.[37]

The Remain campaign was the legendary Clinton-era slogan "It's the economy, stupid" transposed in the most literal and massive form. It echoed the determinism of Thatcher and Merkel's "There Is No Alternative." The total alignment of interests and expertise that it presented could not but appear uncanny. Characteristically, Chancellor Osborne gave voice to the unease that many felt but most did not openly express. The total unanimity of authoritative opinion behind Remain, he told journalists, was "not a conspiracy. It's called a consensus. . . . [T]he economic argument is beyond doubt."[38]

It was never, however, quite as monolithic so the Remain campaign would have liked. Given that the outcome was uncertain and a large part of the population clearly preferred Brexit, there were risks for companies identifying too openly with Remain.[39] The City of London was not unanimous. A libertarian wing was attracted to the idea of breaking with Brussels. All the more telling was the stance of the major foreign investors in the City. The loudest of all and the most committed to the Remain cause were

America's investment banks. Given their role in the City of London, they had a huge stake in Britain's position in the EU and they were not afraid to say so. London was their gateway to the European economy and to eurozone business. As economists from Goldman Sachs pointed out, BIS statistics showed that US banks held $424 billion in claims (assets) on UK borrowers at the end of 2015, including $46 billion in loans to UK banks. Derivatives, guarantees and credit commitments brought the total to $919 billion. UK bank exposure to the United States was even larger, at $1.4 trillion of financial claims.[40] Given these investments, it was hardly surprising that Goldman Sachs, J.P. Morgan and Morgan Stanley all made substantial and early donations to the Remain campaign.[41] Jamie Dimon of J.P. Morgan campaigned openly alongside Osborne in favor of Remain.[42]

That the United States was not indifferent to Britain's position in Europe was the message that President Obama came to London to deliver in person on April 22, 2016. He made his visit at Cameron's personal request. Obama was hugely popular with the UK public and he did not hold back. In the BBC's words, the American president delivered a "full on, no-holds-barred effort to persuade Britain to stay in the EU." The special relationship, World War II and the challenges of the present all demanded that the UK remain an integral part of Europe.[43] Obama understood that it might be sensitive for an outsider to address Britain at such a delicate moment, but "I will say, with the candor of a friend, that the outcome of your decision is a matter of deep interest to the United States." Furthermore, the British public needed to know that the Brexit campaign's hope that it would be able, rapidly, to strike a new trade treaty between an "independent" Britain and the United States was based on false premises. America's focus in trade negotiations was on the big blocs. The Transatlantic Trade and Investment Partnership between the United States and the EU—the Atlantic counterpart to the TPP in Asia—was the key to the future. "Maybe some point down the line there might be a U.K.-U.S. trade agreement," but "it's not going to happen any time soon. . . . The U.K. is going to be in the back of the queue."[44]

American power and money were clearly signaling where it wanted Britain to line up. The extension of Wall Street to Europe by way of the City of London, which had defined international finance since the 1970s, was on

the line. Little wonder that the leading intellectual journal of the Left put the choice as follows: "[A] vote to remain, whatever its motivation, will function in this context as a vote for a British establishment that has long channeled Washington's demands into the Brussels negotiating chambers, scotching hopes for a 'social Europe' since the Single European Act of 1986."[45]

III

The monolithic focus of the Remain campaign aimed not only to "own the economy, own business, and own the fact that you'll be better off [by voting to stay]"; in so doing they set out to draw a line between reasonable and unreasonable politics. Without economic arguments, the Brexiteers would be driven onto more marginal terrain, above all immigration and "isolating Britain from the world."[46] This, the Remain team hoped, would bring the more eccentric and troubling elements of the Brexit camp to the fore, notably Nigel Farage and the UKIP. Their inflammatory rhetoric would drive away undecided middle-of-the-road voters. As a tactic it had the intended effect. The Brexit campaign did indeed bring immigration to the fore. What the Remainers underestimated was the risk they were running. They did not appreciate that along with the desire to put two fingers up to the establishment, immigration and xenophobia were, in fact, winning cards.

The racial politics did not stop even at the person of the president of the United States. What right, Boris Johnson demanded to know, did Obama have to suggest to Britain concessions of sovereignty that the United States would never accept? Why should Britain trust a president who had removed the bust of Churchill from the Oval Office? "Some said it was a snub to Britain. Some said it was a symbol of the part-Kenyan President's ancestral dislike of the British empire—of which Churchill had been such a fervent defender. Some said that perhaps Churchill was seen as less important than he once was. Perhaps his ideas were old-fashioned and out of date." Johnson's artfully placed dog whistle about the "part-Kenyan President" did the job. Johnson whistled and Farage came. Where Johnson prevaricated, Farage's racist growl was unambiguous. As far as the leader of the UKIP

was concerned, it was obvious that "Obama, because of his grandfather and Kenya and colonialization, bears a grudge against this country."[47]

In May, as the Brexit campaign gathered pace, it was immigration that came ever more to the fore. Cameron himself had given hostages to fortune. Five years earlier he had promised that the figure would be cut to "tens of thousands."[48] In late May 2016 the Office for National Statistics reported that net migration in the previous year had, in fact, reached 333,000, the second highest figure on record. On June 16 the Farage wing of the Brexit campaign unveiled its most dramatic poster. Entitled "Breaking Point," it featured a bedraggled column of Syrian refugees marching toward what was, in fact, the Slovenian border. It had little to do with Brexit as such, but it gave new meaning to the slogan of taking back control. European disorder was what Britain must be defended against.[49] Later that same day a crazed neo-Nazi advocate of Brexit murdered the popular Remain MP Jo Cox in broad daylight. Remain's Project Fear had met its match.

Referendum day began with Remain in a relatively confident mood. By the early hours of June 24 it was clear that Brexit had won a narrow victory. In retrospect, the polls had been indicating the likely outcome for some time. Brexit won in the same areas that the UKIP had triumphed in in 2014. And it won with the same kind of people. Core Tory voters, the elderly, provincial middle class, voted en masse for Brexit. They probably always would have. But they were joined by a large cohort of lower-income, less-well-educated voters who had been drifting to the right since the 1990s. According to one polling group, 60 percent of people in the upper-middle- and middle-class socioeconomic groups—those in professional and managerial jobs—backed Britain's EU membership, whereas among the unemployed and unskilled workers the percentage was reversed.[50] Sixty percent of Labour voters turned out for Remain. But that went only to show that in much of the country, the Labour Party was largely divorced from poorer and less-well-educated voters. Apart from education, the other socioeconomic variable that weighed heavily in the balance was the pain inflicted by austerity since 2010, and that hurt worst where decline was a long-term phenomenon.[51] But even more than low education and low income, Brexit voting was correlated with authoritarianism. On the kind of cultural maps drawn by

marketing experts, Brexit voting sat in close proximity to values like security, support for the death penalty and a preference for the public flogging of sex offenders.[52]

A Brexit vote, whatever its motivation, added fuel to the nationalist fire. What is far less clear is that a Brexit vote was a vote against globalization. That was the assumption of commentators around the world.[53] And it was a reasonable thing to imagine on the basis of a conventional understanding of Brexit's likely impact. But it was to misunderstand the mind-set of the Brexiteers. They, in fact, imagined that leaving Europe was a way to restore Britain's greatness and freedom. As a nationalist vote against Europe, Brexit was not a vote for Britain to play a smaller role in the world. Rather on the contrary, it was a demand that Britain should play a role in the world independent of Europe, not submerged within it. As Tory party Home secretary and future prime minister Theresa May would put it, what Britain had voted for on June 23 was "to leave the European Union and embrace the world. . . . It was the moment we chose to build a truly Global Britain."[54] Brexit was a vote for autonomy. Or to put it less politely and more truly in the spirit of the vote, it was a vote for national adventurism. And an adventure is certainly what the UK got.

IV

As the referendum result was announced, sterling suffered its biggest one-day loss in history.[55] There was a brief moment of panic in real estate investment funds. Would a collapsing pound unravel international investments in London? On Friday, June 24, global stock markets saw $2 trillion wiped off share values.[56] By the following Monday losses had risen to $3 trillion. Whereas investors had been expecting interest rates to keep edging up as the Fed moved away from quantitative easing and were thus rebalancing their portfolios away from fixed-income bonds, funds now flooded into safe assets like Treasurys, driving yields down.[57] Was this a prelude to another 2008?

Diagnosing the economic data was itself a political issue. Remain had predicted that Brexit would be a disaster. They had laid out an apocalyptic

scenario. And in the aftermath, governor of the Bank of England Mark Carney stuck to the script. The economy was suffering, he told journalists in July, from "economic post-traumatic stress disorder amongst households and businesses, as well as in financial markets."[58] The swap lines were readied for reactivation. Despite sterling's plunge there would be no shortage of dollar liquidity. On August 4 Carney ramrodded an emergency stimulus package of bond buying through the Bank of England board. Viewed from the bleak perspective of a defeated advocate of Remain, this made perfect sense. Carney was doing his best to forestall the worst. But it was the advocates of Brexit who now set the terms and Carney's actions infuriated them. For the Bank of England to be activating swap lines and lurching into another round of QE was to signal a crisis, of which the most die-hard Brexiteers denied the reality. In their view, far from calming the markets, the Bank of England's overreaction was feeding uncertainty, inducing the panic that Remain had predicted but which had failed to arrive.[59] For Ashoka Mody, a nonconformist ex-IMF economist who had seen the Irish crisis in 2010 close up, the drill was all too familiar. Though Carney's instruments were different—implementing QE rather than refusing it—it was a strategy of tension like that pursued by the ECB during the eurozone crisis. If the Bank of England kept its cool, allowing the pound to slide and the British economy to rebalance, there was no reason to expect a crisis. Ruth Lea, a pro-Brexit economist, declared, "The BOE's package on Aug. 4 was premature and may well turn out to be, if not unnecessary, actually counterproductive. . . . I'd have much preferred if he had kept quiet and just waited until he had some hard data."[60] Once the initial shock had worn off, far from collapsing, consumer demand surged on a wave of cheap credit as households sought to get ahead of whatever price increases might be coming their way.[61] The handful of economists who had supported Brexit demanded that their Remain colleagues apologize for misleading the public about the likely fallout.[62]

It was true. There had been no implosion. But there had not been any Brexit either. Brexit, it turned out, was a process, not a single moment of decision. It was an unfathomably complex and protracted process. The Brexiteers had promised freedom and control. They had promised regime change. And as Adam Posen, president of the influential think tank the

Peterson Institute in DC, and formerly of the Bank of England Monetary Policy Committee, put it: "Regime changes are not neutral. Constitutions reflect the interests of those dominant at the time."[63] But who was dominant in post-Brexit Britain? That precisely was the question.

It is hard to think of any moment in Britain's recent history in which the locus of power was less obvious than in the aftermath of Brexit. The Remain coalition had included the leadership of both main political parties and what most people think of as the establishment. They lost a crucial referendum by a slender margin and surrendered authority to their opponents, who revealed themselves to be utterly unprepared for their own victory. How often had the Left fantasized about such a moment of disempowerment? But this was no new dawn. After a few weeks of chaos in the conservative camp, Theresa May emerged as the new prime minister. It was a logical fit. May had made her reputation as a stern Home secretary pushing a protective agenda of immigration restriction.[64] Though she had cautiously campaigned for Remain, she was well suited to represent the insular majority. And she put a brave face on things. The population had voted for Brexit and that is what she would deliver.

For the City of London and British big business, the vote was a breathtaking shock. And for some commentators it was precisely this body blow that offered the prospect of a grand rebalancing. Was this a moment at which the structures of power and money that had consolidated around the City of London since the 1970s might be cracked open? Mody hailed the result because it shattered the "nexus between an ever larger financial sector and a strong pound. . . . The only people who truly lose from the pound's depreciation are those who borrowed short-term dollars to invest in long-term property assets. This 'elite' group continues to hold the microphones of policymaking and its words reverberate through the financial press."[65] London's wealth had long crowded out the rest of the British economy; perhaps now, with a devalued pound, UK manufacturing might recover its competitiveness.[66] In fact, of course, Britain's largest manufacturing exporters had thrown their weight solidly behind the Remain campaign and with good reason. Given the ferocity of global competition, the last thing they needed was years of uncertainty about market access. Industries like the large motor vehicle industry were foreign owned—mainly German and

Japanese. Those investors might well see Brexit as a signal to withdraw. The devaluation benefited them only marginally because most exports from the UK have low price elasticity and the gains in competitiveness were substantially offset by the increase in the cost of imported materials.[67]

That the status quo had suffered a blow was undeniable. Whether it would give way to something better balanced and more prosperous in the foreseeable future was a different question. The groundswell of anti-EU sentiment had been building for decades. But it was a politics of resentment and protest. It had not formulated a positive alternative vision. Now May and her personal advisers had to come up with an agenda. To the astonishment of many, it seemed that they were determined to carry out a radical pivot. Overnight they would replace David Cameron's agenda of upper-class modernization with national welfarism with an admixture of soft authoritarianism.[68] As May put it in a defining speech to the Tory party conference in October 2016: "Today, too many people in positions of power behave as though they have more in common with international elites than with the people down the road. . . . But if you believe you are a citizen of the world, you are a citizen of nowhere. You don't understand what citizenship means."[69] Skipping over the Tory party's own policies since 2010, May returned to the crisis of 2008. "It wasn't the wealthy who made the biggest sacrifices after the financial crash, but ordinary, working-class families. And if you're one of those people who lost their job, who stayed in work but on reduced hours, took a pay cut as household bills rocketed, or someone who finds themselves out of work or on lower wages because of low-skilled immigration, life simply doesn't seem fair." Though May spoke about the victims of 2008 and Tory austerity in the third person, the Lehman moment served as retrospective justification for a fundamental reorientation. Henceforth she would put "the power of government squarely at the service of ordinary working-class people." She pilloried uncaring bosses, tax-avoiding international companies, Internet companies that refused to cooperate in the fight against terrorism and corporate directors who took out "massive dividends while knowing the company pension is about to go bust." Using language more to be expected from Putin or a Latin American demagogue, she warned: "I'm putting you on warning: this can't go on any more."[70]

Control, restricting immigration and equity would have priority over

absolute growth. It was not a liberal vision. It implied an entirely new apparatus of regulation and control. As one critic noted, May's effort to exclude foreigners from the workforce would require putting "in place a degree of government interference in the labour market that would make even the most die-hard socialist blush. Margaret Thatcher must be turning in her grave."[71] It was a small price to pay for someone with May's background in the Home Office—what might politely be described as the "protective branch" of government. But it begged the following question: How far was May really willing to go in curbing the excesses of big business? It was one thing to erect barriers against foreign workers and unwanted refugees, quite another to deal with a major foreign investor. When Nissan threatened to rethink its investment in Sunderland, the "muscular state" was quick to invite the car company to Downing Street for talks.[72] The government would later deny that it had promised to indemnify Nissan for the costs of a bad Brexit deal. But Nissan was an early sign that "taking back control" might not turn out to be the bold act of autonomy that some imagined. It might very well turn out to be a rather expensive and humiliating process of negotiation.

And what about the City of London? After Brexit, could it continue to function as the hub between global finance and the eurozone? Could it continue as the main center for euro clearing and euro derivatives? The bankers were not about to give up without a fight. The City lobbied hard for the government to prioritize the existing passporting agreements, under which banks operating in London were de facto recognized as operating inside the eurozone.[73] If no such deal was forthcoming, research commissioned by the City threatened that the collapse in business with the euro area might result in losses as large as £32 billion to £38 billion in revenues, 65,000 to 75,000 jobs and perhaps as much as £10 billion in tax receipts per annum.[74] These, of course, were precisely the kinds of estimates mobilized by the Remain campaign, to little effect. What influence would they have now?

In the immediate aftermath of the referendum it seemed that Downing Street might be amenable to a compromise deal. But by January 2017 the mood had hardened. The UK would insist on the right to restrict the freedom of movement and judicial sovereignty, and this meant that London could expect no concessions from Brussels. Not only did Brexit mean Brexit,

but Brexit meant "hard Brexit." This was the message that May delivered in speech after speech and also in direct talks with leading finance bosses. When asked by Lloyd Blankfein of Goldman Sachs, one of the largest corporate donors to the Remain campaign, to rank the City of London in her list of priorities, May dodged the question.[75] The bankers realized with incredulity that they were no longer top of the list. The City's passporting arrangements were less important than regaining "control" over Polish plumbers.[76]

But who, in fact, would determine the outcome of Brexit? Over the winter of 2016–2017 the realization began to dawn that the freedom and control one claimed for oneself also applied to those one detached oneself from. What freedom the UK gained at what price would depend on the kind of bargain that the EU was willing to offer now that it was free of the troublesome British. The advocates of Brexit insisted that Germany and others would be forced to offer Britain a good deal on account of their export interests. Britain's gaping trade deficit would be its chief bargaining card. But this simplistic logic was a poor guide to the functioning of a complex organization like the EU, in which an entire mesh of interests and concerns would be brought to bear on the Brexit question.[77]

With remarkable speed and with clear leadership from Berlin, the other states of the EU agreed on a tough bargaining position, which insisted that there would be no trade talks before the terms of the divorce were settled. Britain would have to agree to meet its financial obligations to the EU, running into the tens of billions of euros. There could be no access to the common market without freedom of movement. The writ of the European Court of Justice would continue to run as far as citizens of the EU were concerned. Once Britain triggered Article 50, setting Brexit in motion, there would be a two-year clock. No deal would mean that Britain would crash out of the EU into limbo. It would even have to renegotiate its position in the World Trade Organization. As Juncker explained to May over dinner in London in May 2017, the British were kidding themselves if they imagined there was a "good outcome" to Brexit.[78]

Characteristically, as the true complexity and difficulty of the situation began to dawn on London, May's government reacted with drastic, crude and contradictory threats. In her October 2016 speech to the Tory party conference, May had linked the demand for sovereignty to a vision of

national solidarity. But as the negotiating positions hardened, it became clear that there was also another option. As May put it to the EU's ambassadors in mid-January at a set-piece meeting in Lancaster House: If Britain could not get an acceptable trade deal from the EU, it would walk away without agreement. If the EU took a "punitive" stance, Britain would respond by abandoning the "European model" and setting "the competitive tax rates and the policies that would attract the world's best companies and biggest investors." Britain would reconfigure itself, journalists reported, as a "low-tax Singapore of the west."[79] Days later Chancellor Philip Hammond repeated the threat. He personally hoped that the UK would be "able to remain in the mainstream of European economic and social thinking. But if we are forced to be something different, then we will have to become something different." To regain competitiveness Britain might be forced to reconsider its "economic model. . . . And you can be sure we will do whatever we have to do."[80] The Remain campaign had always insisted that the Brexit decision put the entire economy in play. With the threats they made as they approached negotiations with the EU in January 2017, Hammond and May effectively acknowledged the force of the Remain position. Far from taming British capitalism, the muscular state would turn the City of London and Britain's offshore position into a battering ram.

This kind of bravado might help to warm the hearts of Brexiteers. But it left serious players in global business nonplussed. The City of London had not asked for Britain to abandon the "mainstream of European economic and social thinking." The European mainstream suited the bankers just fine. They had had a large hand in defining it. The proposals that had worried the Tories in 2011, notably the financial transactions tax, had evaporated. There might well be challenges from the ECB or the French over euro-denominated business. But that was not a reason for leaving. It was a reason to fight one's corner. The transnational business community in London was networked in the EU at the highest level. The president of the ECB was one of their own.[81] In the summer of 2016, when former commission president Barroso looked around for a new job, it turned out that his idea of the "European model" was to join Goldman Sachs's London operation.[82] The idea that Europe was in some way inimical to the operation of British-based global

business belonged to the realm of late-Thatcherite fantasy. On the other hand, the "freedom" of Brexit meant radical uncertainty. None of the leading American banks wanted to be preparing contingency plans to move their euro business out of London, but what was the alternative? Though London had huge attractions, its national politics had become unresponsive. The subordinate nodes in the transatlantic financial network—Paris, Dublin, Frankfurt—beckoned. And if not, perhaps the days of the transatlantic, offshore dollar were numbered. The City had sensed the way the wind was blowing. Asia was the new frontier.

V

Faced with the Brexit vote, the EU concerted its position with daunting speed. Negotiating complex treaties was what Brussels was good at. But there was no denying the shock. The EU had suffered many crises in its history. "Europe advances in disguise," Jacques Delors, the legendary father of the single market and the euro, was fond of saying. But Brexit capped a prolonged succession of setbacks that challenged this optimistic teleology. Was this, Alex Stubb, finance minister of Finland, wondered, Europe's "Lehman Brothers moment"?[83] In containing Syriza, the chief worry of the conservatives in the Eurogroup had been political contagion. Brexit revived that fear. As a spokeswoman for Moody's commented: "The downside risks to global growth stem not from the possibility of a recession in the UK, but from the possibility that developments in the UK may give rise to increased political risk elsewhere in the EU."[84] Marine Le Pen hailed the Brexit referendum as a "dazzling lesson in democracy."[85] The right-wing nationalist Geert Wilders in the Netherlands called for a "Nexit" vote. Would a nationalist, Europhobic wave spread from Britain, Poland and Hungary to the rest of Europe? For almost a year after Brexit, that risk seemed all too real. And the stakes were high. Europe's economic stabilization depended on calm in the bond markets. As one analyst commented: "There is no guarantee that investors' emotions will not turn wild again if signs of political contagion from the UK into mainland Europe become more visible."[86]

The elections came thick and fast. In December 2016 a constitutional amendment in Italy was voted down, leading to the resignation of left-of-center prime minister Renzi. In Austria the presidential election was bitterly contested by the Far Right. In the Netherlands Geert Wilders and his right-wing party were on the march. Theresa May announced an election in Britain with a view to securing a large Brexit majority. But the real question surrounded France. Given the electoral base she had accumulated and the Front's performance in the May 2014 European elections, there was little doubt that in the upcoming presidential election in May 2017 Marine Le Pen would make it into the final runoff. The question was who would run against her: a traditional conservative, a centrist modernizer in the form of Emmanuel Macron or the real terror of the establishment, the left-wing Mélenchon? A Le Pen versus Mélenchon runoff was the nightmare of the markets.[87] Whatever else divided these two, they had in common their antipathy toward Germany.

In the spring of 2017 the world held its breath. The euro gyrated. European political uncertainty was the key "tail risk" for fund managers. The ECB's bond buying was the one major source of stability. However unlikely the scenario, if Le Pen were to break through in France, it was hard to see how even the ECB's largest program could have avoided another sovereign debt crisis. As it turned out, the center held. In every case the electorate opted against the populist right wing. In France, the charismatic former minister in Hollande's government Emmanuel Macron, taking votes from both the center-right and the center-left, won first the presidency and then the National Assembly elections. This put a cap on the populist spook.[88] To their council meeting in June 2017, Europe's leaders showed up in a bullish mood. The EU had survived. It had tamed the Left in Greece and Portugal. It had seen off the right-wing surge. The negotiations with Britain would be painful but one-sided. Europe was back. But by the summer of 2017 it faced a new challenge to its identity and to its role in world affairs, a challenge that came not from inside but from without. The challenge had announced itself a year earlier, from a golf course in Scotland on the day after the Brexit referendum.

That sunny Friday morning outside the clubhouse in Turnberry Ayrshire, the cameras were trained on an American businessman holding forth en-

thusiastically about the referendum result[89]: "Basically they took back their country," he declared to the skeptical Scottish audience. Obama should never have meddled. "It's not his country, it's not his part of the world, he shouldn't have done it, and I actually think that his recommendation perhaps caused it to fail." The speaker identified unreservedly with Brexit. "People want to take their country back, they want to have independence in a sense, and you see it with Europe, all over Europe. . . . You're going to have many other cases where people want to take their borders back, they want to take their monetary [sic] back, they want to take a lot of things back, they want to be able to have a country again. . . . People are angry, all over the world people, they're angry. . . . They're angry over borders, they're angry over people coming into the country and taking over, nobody even knows who they are. They're angry about many, many things."

The speaker was inarticulate. He was not well informed. He did not seem to appreciate that his Scottish audience had voted overwhelmingly to remain. The day after the shock result, the EU certainly had other things to worry about. But what demanded attention, what made the sound bites newsworthy, was the fact that the man in question was the presumptive nominee of the Republican Party to replace Barack Obama as president of the United States.

Chapter 24

TRUMP

On July 21, 2016, a burly figure strode across a podium dressed seemingly to inspire memories of Captain America, Citizen Kane or a 1930s fascist rally. The man in the spotlight was there to deliver a speech with which he meant to change American history.[1] It was a flaming denunciation of the Obama administration. He evoked an alarming image of America harried by terrorism, violence and chaos. He told his audience 180,000 illegal immigrants with criminal records were that very night "roaming free," terrorizing and murdering innocent Americans. Meanwhile, lives were getting tougher. "Household incomes are down more than $4,000 since the year 2000. Our manufacturing trade deficit has reached an all-time high—nearly $800 billion in a single year. The budget is no better. President Obama has doubled our national debt. . . . Yet, what do we have to show for it? Our roads and bridges are falling apart, our airports are in Third World condition, and forty-three million Americans are on food stamps." Why were things this bad? Because "big business, elite media and major donors" had all conspired for decades to rig the system. Now those same forces were lined up behind his opponent. "She is their puppet, and they pull the strings." At this point the crowd reacted with chants for her to be thrown in jail. Against this elite conspiracy the man in the spotlight promised to fight for the "neglected, ignored, and abandoned . . . the laid-off factory workers, and the communities crushed by our horrible and unfair

trade deals . . . the forgotten men and women of our country. People who work hard but no longer have a voice. . . . History is watching us," he declared, "waiting to see if we will rise to the occasion, and if we will show the whole world that America is still free and independent and strong." His answer boomed around the hall. He promised one thing: "to put America First. Americanism, not globalism, will be our credo."

If someone had written a script as to how an economic crisis and democratic decay would lead to a nationalist backlash in the United States, this denouement might have seemed a little cartoonish. But this was no script. It was real, or at least it was "reality." The man giving the speech was the same property tycoon and TV personality who had helicoptered onto the Turnberry golf course in Scotland to revel in Brexit a month before. Donald Trump was running for election as president of the United States on the Republican ticket against Hillary Clinton. Trump's closest confidante was his daughter Ivanka. And if you liked her convention outfit, Macy's department store was promoting her clothing line on Twitter.[2]

The following day, during a press conference in the Rose Garden, President Obama attempted to restore a sense of normality. "[T]his idea that America is somehow on the verge of collapse, this vision of violence and chaos everywhere," the president told the press, "doesn't really jibe with the experience of most people. I hope people the next morning walked outside and birds were chirping and the sun was out, and this afternoon, people will be watching their kids play in sports teams and go to the swimming pool and folks are going to work and getting ready for the weekend. And in particular, I think it is important, just to be absolutely clear here, that some of the fears that were expressed throughout the week just don't jive with the facts."[3]

In July 2016 Obama's riposte seemed to many like a welcome dose of common sense. With hindsight, the president's lines talk about "chirping" birds and kids enjoying a long, hot American summer read differently. They remind us of the complacency that would cost the Democrats the election. The Clinton team did not take seriously the view of modern America summoned up by their opponent. On November 8 Trump imposed his reality on theirs. Though Clinton ran up huge numbers in New York State and

California and won the popular vote, it was Trump who gained a slender majority of the electoral college and would become the forty-fifth president of the United States.

It was the most disorienting event experienced by the American political class in generations. The unthinkable had happened. The Democratic establishment had been confident about 2016. Admittedly, since 2008 congressional elections had not gone well. But 2012 entrenched the Democrats' belief that the presidency was theirs for the taking.[4] Under their stewardship America had weathered the crisis. As Americans returned to postcrisis normality, the inevitable dominance of the more modern and diverse Democratic Party would make itself felt. American society had deep problems, no doubt. The economy was not running at the speed they would have liked. But once Clinton and the latest generation of Democratic Party technocrats got back on track, there was nothing that could not be fixed. Obama's Affordable Care Act and Dodd-Frank were starters. What America needed was more of the same. Against this, what did the Republicans have to offer? Not only was Trump personally unfit for high office but his dark vision of American crisis was out of touch with reality.

As it turned out, 2012 had been misleading. Obama ran as a moderately popular incumbent, and his Republican opponent, Mitt Romney, a Mormon governor of Massachusetts with a much-trumpeted track record in venture capital, could hardly have been less well suited to harnessing popular discontent. Four years later Obama was out of the picture and the Republican field was wide open. As a result, the presidential race of 2016 turned out to be more about the financial crisis of 2008 than 2012 had been. The upshot was explosive and unpredictable.

I

The most obvious mark of the financial crisis of 2008 on the election of 2016 was the fact that Bernie Sanders was a serious contender for the Democratic Party nomination. Sanders wasn't even a member of the party. He was a self-declared democratic socialist. He was a confirmed foe of Wall Street. In 2008 he had voted against TARP. He called for the big banks to

be broken up. He wanted bankers jailed and a return to New Deal–era banking regulations. The spirit of Occupy energized his troops. With Independents and young voters he was wildly popular.[5] The fact that Sanders was viable as a candidate reflected the finding of opinion pollsters that among American voters under the age of thirty, more had a positive view of socialism than of capitalism.[6] The anger of 2008 was still very much alive and Sanders fanned it. Hardly a rally went by without crowds shouting their indignation at the bailout. Regular Americans were still struggling back from the recession. As Sanders pointed out in a typical flourish in September 2015, applauding the Fed's decision not to raise interest rates: "At a time when real unemployment is over 10 percent, we need to do everything possible to create millions of good-paying jobs and raise the wages of the American people. It is now time for the Fed to act with the same sense of urgency to rebuild the disappearing middle class as it did to bail out Wall Street banks seven years ago."[7]

Harping on the historic injustice of 2008 not only played to "Bernie's" base. It was an excellent weapon with which to beat the front-runner, Hillary Clinton. Clinton was the consummate insider. She was a former secretary of state and senator for New York, and as such irredeemably entangled with Wall Street.[8] By the spring of 2016 Clinton and Sanders were dueling over Dodd-Frank. Sanders wanted to go back to the decisive moment in 2009 and do it right, to break up the banks. Clinton's answer was that Dodd-Frank should be rigorously enforced. This teed up Sanders to ask whether Clinton's reticence had anything with the $600,000 in fees she had collected giving speeches for Goldman Sachs. Would she release the transcripts?[9]

For the Left, Clinton's Goldman Sachs speeches were what her Libya e-mails were for her opponents on the Right: a further sign of her untrustworthiness. How deeply was Clinton entangled with the bank now better known as the "vampire squid"?[10] Even the New York Times called for Clinton to release the text of the speeches. Weighing the issue, her campaign managers decided that Clinton's words were not, in fact, fit for public consumption. She would look too friendly to the banks.[11] We know this because starting in July, as she closed in on winning the nomination, internal memos from the Clinton campaign began to be dumped en masse in WikiLeaks

folders. Who, in fact, compromised the security of the Democratic Party machine was to become a matter of complex technical and legal dispute.[12] But at the time the conviction rapidly took hold that it was down to hackers with ties to Russia.[13] Was the mounting confrontation with Putin, which had reached a new pitch in intensity over Ukraine and Syria, blowing back on the United States, and on Clinton in particular? Behind the scenes America's intelligence agencies scrambled to uncover the extent of Russian interference in America's presidential election. On the basis of sources inside the Kremlin they were forced to conclude that given Clinton's well-known hostility to Putin's regime, Moscow was doing what it could to derail her campaign. Even if the Russians could not change the outcome, they would do their best to undermine the legitimacy of America's already fragile political system. Moscow was serving notice that two could play at the game of regime change. By the fall Obama was seriously weighing his options, including sanctions that would, in the words of an anonymous administration source, amount to "cratering" the Russian economy.[14] That scenario did not unfold, because Putin pulled back. But it was clear that this would be no ordinary election. Quite how unusual it would be was becoming clear on the Republican side.

Whereas the battles within the Democratic Party had a clear-cut, Left-versus-Right logic, and the establishment maintained its grip, what was happening to the Republicans was more disorientating. The GOP was out of control. In truth, the party had never recovered from the shipwreck of the late Bush presidency, the shock of 2008 and the Tea Party mobilization triggered by the financial crisis. The splits within the party that had precipitated the congressional budget crises of 2011 and 2013 were wider than ever. In 2013 the shutdown was called off as default loomed, but the Right had had their taste of blood. First, in June 2014 they unseated the leader of the House, Eric Cantor, in a primary. Then, in October 2015, the ill-fated John Boehner was ousted as House Speaker by a mobilization of the right-wing Freedom Caucus.[15] With the party in turmoil, the establishment candidates who had been expected to dominate the presidential primaries—figures like Jeb Bush—rapidly faded. It was the darlings of the Right who surged to the fore. The "dark money" of the billionaire donors, led by the Koch brothers,

swung behind Texas senator Ted Cruz.[16] But it was Trump who took the votes of the Republican base by a majority of almost two to one.[17]

If Jamie Dimon quipped that to make sense of Dodd-Frank one needed the services of a lawyer and a psychiatrist, the same is no doubt true of the business of deciphering Donald Trump. But historians can contribute too.[18] Trump offered to a bewildered present a throwback to an earlier era. Born in 1946, the same year as Bill Clinton, Trump would take office at seventy years of age, recycling a rancid version of the baby boomer narrative, which in the 1990s had still seemed fresh. Trump's racial attitudes reflected the animosities of the era of civil rights, desegregation and New York in the 1970s. His boorish manners and sexism echoed the Manhattan party scene of the 1980s, when bond traders toasted one another as "big swinging dicks." The sense of national crisis that drove his campaign was a reflux not so much of the recent past as of the first moment when modern Americans felt the world changing around them—the late 1970s and early 1980s. The trauma of defeat in Vietnam, America's urban crisis and angry Japan bashing—thirty years on Trump was still harping on those fears, but now transposed onto new enemies: China, Islam and undocumented Latino immigrants.

His main shtick was that he was a businessman, a deal maker. And because his business was real estate, Trump lived the American business cycle close up. As Hyman Minsky, the legendary analyst of financial crises, observed already in 1990, Donald Trump was the very epitome of a Ponzi scheme capitalist, living hand to mouth by borrowing against the expected appreciation of his assets.[19] As a result, crises punctuated Trump's career. He was hit hard by the early 1990s recession, almost losing his business. By 2008 he was less vulnerable, having diversified into media and branding. But his real estate exposure was still significant. Indeed, he was seeking to increase it. In 2006 he started a mortgage brokerage and announced plans to open a mortgage lending business. Luckily for Trump, neither got off the ground. By 2008 his casino business was failing again and would ultimately close. But Trump's real vulnerability was a gigantic condo development in Chicago.[20] It was a spectacular project, the tallest building to be built in the United States since the Sears Tower, and sales had originally gone well. But in 2008 Chicago condo sales stopped dead. By the fall it was clear that

Trump and his business partners were in trouble. Since his bankruptcies of the 1990s, Trump was no longer on good terms with the major American banks, so the Chicago project got its funding mainly from Deutsche Bank's North American real estate arm. In the first week of November 2008, as Barack Obama celebrated his election victory with his adoring Chicago base, Deutsche and Trump went to war. Deutsche sued for $40 million, for which Trump was personally liable. Trump responded with an astonishingly audacious legal broadside. He claimed that the greatest financial crisis since 1929 constituted force majeure, akin to a natural disaster. He therefore demanded more time for the project to pay off. Deutsche's own suit was typical of a predatory and dangerous lender that had helped to bring on the crisis. Trump's countersuit claimed $3 billion in compensation for the damage it was causing to his reputation. It was pure legal swordplay, but it bought him the time he needed.

In a tight spot Trump is nothing if not pragmatic, and he was certainly not one to be squeamish about the maxims of free-market economics. Faced with the 2008 crisis he knew that American business needed all the help it could get. He had decades of experience working the subsidies available from American government. He liked the cut of Obama's jib; 2009 was not his moment to get on the anti-Obama bandwagon. As he remarked to a bemused Fox News host, commenting on an early Obama appearance: "I thought he [Obama] did a terrific job. . . . This is a strong guy knows what he wants, and this is what we need. . . . [I]t looks like we have somebody that knows what he is doing finally in office, and he did inherit a tremendous problem. He really stepped into a mess." On Obama's stimulus Trump was equally unabashed: "Well, something had to be done. And whether it's perfect or not, nothing is perfect. And it's a whole trial-and-error thing. . . . It's a very, very tough—we are having . . . we're having the worst year, the worst couple of years, since the Great Depression. And you mentioned the early '80s. I mean, the early '80s get blown away by this deal. . . . [W]hen you look at the banks, had trillions of dollars not been poured into the banks, you would have an insolvent banking system, and then you would absolutely have 1929. They did the right thing."[21] Whereas Trump was reluctantly willing to support the bank bailout, he was positively enthusiastic when it came to helping Detroit: "I think the government should stand behind

them 100 percent. You cannot lose the auto companies. They're great. They make wonderful products." When conservative interviewers tried to deflect Trump toward the cause of tax cutting, it was an easy sell. Trump doesn't like paying tax. But he stuck to his guns on stimulus spending. "[B]uilding infrastructure, building great projects, putting people to work" was the right thing to be doing.[22]

Six years on from the crisis, Trump's enthusiasm for an activist, engaged, "strong" presidency remained. What had changed was his attitude to Obama, which had curdled from admiration to vituperative animosity. It was this that formed the bridge to the Right: not programmatic or intellectual affinity but the tabloid absurdity of the *National Enquirer* and the "birther" conspiracy. Despite having cultivated minority audiences early in his television career, Trump now played the race card.[23] In 2013, after Romney's defeat radicalized the right wing, Trump positioned himself ever more aggressively as a spokesman of the anti-immigration wing of the Republican Party. By 2014 he had branded the idea of building a "Wall" and had literally trademarked the slogan "Make America Great Again." Xenophobia, nationalism and an apocalyptic diagnosis of America's situation formed the bridge. The right wing loved Trump's slogan, as much for what it acknowledged about the present as for what it promised for the future: America, their America, was in trouble.

If in the Republican primaries it was above all Trump's unabashed appeal to white male voters that swung the decision, what made this worrying for the party establishment was the way this correlated with his appeal to economic nationalism. Since the 1980s the party leadership had nailed itself to the mast of globalization. The idea of NAFTA was launched by the Reagan administration. It had been crafted by Bush senior only to be carried across the line in 1993 by Clinton. In the 1990s "globalization" was a bipartisan project of the Republicans and the Rubinite wing of the Democratic Party. Their push extended not only to goods and capital. It extended to labor too. The business lobby favored immigration reform, which would give residence rights to the large and cheap workforce of undocumented migrants. Opposition to regulation of all kinds, "freedom" for labor, goods and capital were the ideological bracket that joined American business interests in a single block, from small contractors to the Davos set. There

were sectors, perhaps most notably in coal mining, where this alignment did not hold. In polluting industries such as fossil fuels, opposition to globalism, the rejection of the politics of climate change and the blue-collar appeal of American nationalism fit together all too neatly.[24] But those were exceptional cases. On the whole, the Republican Party preserved an uneasy truce between the nationalist base and the globalist leadership. In the 1990s the right-wing nationalist campaigner Pat Buchanan had twice threatened to undo that fragile balance. But it was the progressive breakdown of party coherence after 2008 that really tore it apart. In 2015 Trump exploded onto the scene with the alt-right squarely behind him and transformed the debate. Untouched by concern for economic doctrine, his updated version of 1970s Japan bashing energized the party, promising to keep "illegals" out and to bring blue-collar jobs back to America. Following their new tribal leader, Republicans abandoned free trade en masse. The percentage saying that free trade agreements were bad for America surged from 36 percent in 2014 to 68 percent two years later. By that point only 24 percent of Republicans were still willing to fly the flag for free trade.[25]

For the Republican elite, as Trump stormed to the nomination, it was bewildering. "The pillars of the Republican economic agenda have completely collapsed into dust," a member of the American Enterprise Institute acknowledged. "They're gone, at least for this election."[26] The US Chamber of Commerce did not go down without a fight, openly challenging the Republican nominee on the issue of trade. But to no avail.[27] Trump and the protectionist agenda triumphed.

The result by the summer of 2016 was a remarkable inversion. Though behind the scenes oligarchic megadonors were hard at work stoking the flames of right-wing radicalism, America's name-brand corporations no longer wanted to be associated with the Republicans. When Romney won the party's nomination in 2012, the money men had flocked to the party. Corporate America lined up to sponsor the Republican convention in Tampa. In 2016 no big names in American finance wanted to be associated with the platform from which Trump would give his apocalyptic acceptance speech. Even if some of the Wall Street top brass felt loyalty to the GOP, they could not stomach Trump and did not want to risk insulting their clients or their workforce. It was a matter of business culture. As one

PR adviser commented: "Any corporation will look at this from the perspective of whether or not they would want their CEO sharing a stage at Davos, Aspen or Sun Valley with the Republican nominee. If the answer is no, they won't be going to Cleveland." Remarkably, the consultant felt necessary to explain: "The risk of violence in the convention," between pro- and anti-Trump protesters, "is secondary as security will be strong inside the perimeter." America's incipient civil war atmosphere was less of a concern than the question of "whether Mr. Trump and the ideas he . . . represents are homogenous with a company's brand and business plan."[28] No one wanted images of "Confederate flags waving over corporate brands."[29]

And the 2008 financial crisis was on the mind not only of Sanders supporters. In the pages of the *Washington Post*, former Treasury secretary Hank Paulson put the question: "What would have happened if a divisive character such as Trump were president during the 2008 financial crisis? . . . The only reason we avoided another Great Depression was because Republicans and Democrats joined together to vote for the Troubled Asset Relief Program."[30] In fact, as Paulson knew firsthand, the bipartisanship of 2008 had not come easily. Divisions within the GOP had almost derailed the Bush administration's efforts to contain the global bank run. It was the Bush White House and the Democrats, not their Republican counterparts in Congress, who carried the unpopular crisis-fighting measures. Now, Paulson warned: "we are witnessing a populist hijacking of one of the United States' great political parties. The GOP, in putting Trump at the top of the ticket, is endorsing a brand of populism rooted in ignorance, prejudice, fear and isolationism."[31] This derailment of one of America's ruling political parties posed a threat that was no less than systemic. For Paulson this left only one choice. He called on his fellow Americans to back Clinton.

In fairness, Trump might have countered by pointing to his track record. In 2008 he had vigorously applauded the bailout. But Trump in 2016 had no desire to remind his supporters of that. "Candidate Trump" was no longer the high-rolling New York wheeler-dealer of 2008. He had morphed into something altogether darker. The man running his presidential campaign was Steve Bannon, the sulfurous impresario of Breitbart and self-proclaimed "Leninist" of the 2013 shutdown. He was only too happy to take up Paulson's challenge. In Bannon's dark vision of American history, the

moment on the morning of September 18, 2008, when Paulson and Bernanke confronted President Bush with the need for a massive bailout marked a new epoch, what Bannon called the "fourth turning," the opening of an apocalyptic phase of struggle.[32] On the morning of September 18, 2008, the United States had come close to losing its soul. For Bannon, the mission of the Trump presidency was to seize back control from the globalist elite. As the extraordinary final TV spot of the Trump campaign declared: "It's a global power structure that is responsible for the economic decisions that have robbed our working class, stripped our country of its wealth and put that money into the pockets of a handful of large corporations and political entities."[33] The images accompanying the voiceover put faces to that global power structure: George Soros, Fed chair Janet Yellen and Lloyd Blankfein of Goldman Sachs. From the richest businessman ever to run for president, it was a remarkable antibusiness message. It was also the most transparently anti-Semitic campaign spot in recent history. Whether one agreed with Bannon or not, there was no denying that in the decade since the crisis began, American politics had traveled a long way.

Back in 2007, former Fed chair Alan Greenspan had been asked by the Zürich daily *Tages-Anzeiger* which candidate he was supporting in the upcoming presidential election. His response was striking. How he voted did not matter, Greenspan declared, because "(we) are fortunate that, thanks to globalization, policy decisions in the US have been largely replaced by global market forces. National security aside, it hardly makes any difference who will be the next president. The world is governed by market forces."[34] This was the mantra of an age of globalization without alternatives. Of course, Greenspan didn't simply approve of a world governed by market forces, he had done as much as anyone to create it. As Fed chair he had made the markets into the ultimate arbiter of American economic policy. In the early years of the Clinton presidency, he had helped to shepherd the Democrats into a new partnership with Wall Street, thus further limiting the political alternatives on offer. Globalization was not a natural process, opposed to politics. It had been shaped since the 1940s by an alliance of America's politicians, business elites and policy experts like Greenspan. The election of 2016 revealed how severely the crisis of 2008 had shaken that alliance and the world it had fostered. Most fundamentally, the crisis

had exposed the deep unreality of Greenspan's conception of a world governed by markets. As the crisis revealed, government by market forces was at best a fragile condition. As the global financial system imploded it was the markets themselves that needed governing, by state action on a gigantic scale. And that meant that who governed and where they obtained their political support was not incidental. Elections and party politics did matter. Indeed, faced with the choices in 2016 even Alan Greenspan was no longer indifferent. Unlike Paulson he could not bring himself to endorse Clinton. But he did warn journalists that the "economic and political environment" was the worst he had "ever been remotely related to." He was deeply concerned that "crazies" risked undermining America. And contrary to his confidence ten years earlier he now admitted that "politically, I haven't a clue how this comes out."[35]

The Trump campaign may have seemed crazy, but it was not asleep at the wheel. Online media immediately hit back. "Who's Greenspan calling crazy?" pro-Trump websites demanded to know. And then they turned the tables on the former Fed chair and his successors. Were Trump's policy positions "[c]razier than negative interest rates? Crazier than paying banks to keep loanable funds in sterile depository accounts at the Fed? Crazier than having the Fed buy up trillions in government debt, remit the interest payments back to treasury, and then count that as revenue to the federal budget?"[36] If all of this now passed for normal monetary policy, was their candidate crazy for denouncing the Fed for fueling a "false economy" and an "artificial stock market"? With the Fed balance sheet expanded to $4.4 trillion in pursuit of a full employment target mandated by legislation passed in the days of Jimmy Carter, could one seriously deny that the economy was politicized?[37] Were the Trump and Sanders campaigns crazy or simply stating what should have been obvious: the fiasco of the project of Greenspan's generation. Financial globalization that Greenspan and his ilk had worked so hard to institutionalize as a quasi-natural process had been exposed as just that, an institution, an artifact of deliberate political and legal construction with stark consequences for the distribution of wealth and power.

II

Disturbing as they were to the status quo, in the summer of 2016 the most common response to the Trump and Sanders campaigns was to dismiss them as a passing spook. Once Clinton had knocked Sanders out, she would beat Trump by a landslide. While the alt-right continued to fly the flag, Republican donors shifted their money from the presidential campaign toward House and Senate races with a view to ensuring that as president, Hillary Clinton would face a solidly hostile Congress. Only the inner core of Trump's campaign and the audience of Fox News, swaddled in what the mainstream denounced as "alternative reality," continued to believe in victory. On election night, even as the results swung Trump's way the mainstream media could barely hide their disbelief and dismay.[38] Within hours the recrimination and finger pointing began. It was the white working class and the racists who had rallied to Trump. Women and minorities had failed to turn out for Clinton. Or, it was down to Russian meddling. There was a global alignment of forces against liberalism. President Obama himself weighed in to declare that Trump, like Brexit, was an expression of protest against globalization.[39]

In fact, a deep dive into the poll data showed that Trump's voters were better off than the average American.[40] The voters with the lowest incomes—overwhelmingly minorities—continued to vote Democratic. But a detailed accounting of the electoral statistics did show a significant shift to the Republicans among white male voters with less than a college education. It was less immediate misery than anxiety about the future that drove the Trump vote, fears that in the white population were associated with hostility to Latinos and black Americans, and among men with hostility to upwardly mobile women.[41] Trump improved on Romney's miserable tally in the Rust Belt states. Dog-whistle racism and nationalism solidified this constituency. Even an issue such as trade was saturated with racial markers.[42] In one advertising spot after another, the face of the American worker displaced by foreign imports was that of a burly white man in a hard hat. And campaigning mattered. Concentrating their effort where it counted,

the Republicans put in relentless legwork and media time in key midwestern states that the Democrats considered theirs by right. The complacency, the refusal to countenance the reality of Trump's appeal went deep. The Democrats offered nothing to counter Trump's manufacturing "cargo cult."[43] In answer to Trump's crude appeals to white male nationalism, Clinton offered anodyne conformity to the polite conventions of corporate globalism. That did not play with the 7 million Americans who had voted for Obama and now shifted to Trump. They were looking for a candidate who did not appear to represent the establishment. Though they constituted only 4 percent of the electorate their votes were enough to hand Michigan, Pennsylvania and Wisconsin to the Republicans, rendering Clinton's huge tallies in New York and California irrelevant. What the Democratic operatives failed to understand was that the race was theirs to win, not to lose.[44] Clinton was running to succeed a two-term Democratic presidency. A change was in order. The economy might not be the disaster that Trump suggested, but it was not booming. To overcome these handicaps, Clinton needed to energize the Democratic base. That she utterly failed to do.

In the aftermath, the shock of Trump's election produced a state of confusion and stunned puzzlement reminiscent of Brexit. If Donald Trump had been elected president, who actually ruled America? Surely some branch of the establishment would intervene to constrain or redirect this aberrant popular choice.[45] The idea of the "deep state" no longer belonged to the realms of marginalized conspiracy theory or radical critique; it was mainstream media discourse and it influenced the Trump team themselves, who circulated memoranda on which bits of the deep state they would have to do battle with first.[46] With the FBI and the CIA sitting through the evidence of Russian interference and with Trump seemingly bent on picking a fight, it was from the security apparatus and law enforcement that the pushback was expected. But in truth the entire establishment of the United States had lined up against the president-elect. In August 2016 the *Wall Street Journal* contacted every single surviving member of the president's Council of Economic Advisers back to the days of Richard Nixon—all forty-five of them. Though twenty-three were Republican appointees, none would endorse Trump.[47]

Trump did not back down. If there was one thing he had been elected to do, it was to stir things up. This meant conflict, the more and the noisier the better. He was set on his agenda of economic nationalism. It wasn't even a choice. He simply did not know any different. In December 2016 he intervened at Carrier, an Indianapolis manufacturer of furnaces and air conditioners, to persuade them to keep one thousand jobs in the United States. The state of Indiana, where Trump's vice president, Mike Pence, was governor, stumped up millions in tax rebates. Company spokesmen helpfully announced that they had confidence in Trump's promise to reform the corporate tax code and to improve business conditions in the United States. Then the president-elect jetted in to Indianapolis to hail his first economic policy achievement and to reveal another reason why United Technologies, Carrier's parent, might have wished to cooperate. "Companies are not going to leave the United States any more without consequences," Trump declared menacingly. "Not going to happen. . . . [L]eaving the country is going to be very, very difficult."[48] Or as he tweeted later that weekend: "Any business that leaves our country for another country, fires its employees, builds a new factory or plant in the other country, and then thinks it will sell its product back into the U.S. without retribution or consequence, is WRONG!"

For conventional commentators it was jaw-dropping. Did the president-elect not understand that the success of American business depended precisely on their ability to deploy labor and capital globally? As several commentators remarked, his threatening tone was "more like the populism of Hugo Chavez than even something Bernie Sanders would say. It's the kind of threat that would find its ultimate expression in currency controls— that favored instrument of economic dictators around the world."[49] Had a left-winger engaged in such provocation, barring intervention by the Treasury and the Fed, the markets would surely have plummeted. But nothing of the sort happened in the wake of Trump's election. Trump was a challenger, but not all challengers are alike. Among Democratic voters deep political grief went together with economic gloom. But what was no less remarkable was the reaction on the other side. Republican supporters of all kinds—from regular voters to small businesses and traders in the financial markets—exploded with new optimism.[50] It was somewhat embarrassing to bigwigs on Wall Street who thought the new president was incompatible

with their "brand values," but bank shares were among those making the biggest gains. Trump liked to bang on about abolishing Dodd-Frank. If that happened it would be good for the banks, at least in the short run. Health-care stocks surged as markets anticipated a rollback of Obamacare and its cost cutting. There was also a bump in infrastructure stocks. Meanwhile, bonds sold off as the prospect of Trumpflation made it all the more likely that the Fed would raise rates.[51]

And this "Trump bump" was only confirmed when the president set about recruiting a team. He kept loyalists and ideologues around him. He made no concessions on substance of policy, but he widened his coalition by stocking his cabinet with wealthy corporate managers and generals. The most astonishing thing, given the menacing rhetoric of his final attack ad, was the return of Wall Street. Trump supposedly canvassed Jamie Dimon of J.P. Morgan for Treasury secretary before plumping for the obvious alter-native, Goldman Sachs. Both the number one and number two positions at the Treasury were to be filled by men—Steve Mnuchin and Jim Donovan—with Goldman Sachs pedigree. Dina Powell, who moved to the influen-tial assistant position at the White House, had formerly headed the bank's philanthropic efforts. National Economic Council director Gary Cohn was formerly Goldman's president. Meanwhile, to head the Securities and Ex-change Commission, Trump's team proposed a partner from Goldman's main law firm, Sullivan & Cromwell. There was some anxiety from the White House chief of staff about the optics, but that was assuaged when Donovan withdrew.[52]

To a conventional programmatic political mind this was a flagrant con-tradiction and suggested that the establishment was reasserting control. But it was not clear whether Trump understood programmatic policy de-bate in the conventional sense. What Trump did understand, or at least what he inhabited, was a rawer world of power, a world dominated by a single logic: bully or be bullied. As one commentator put it, Trump viewed the world as a "kind of Manhattan real estate market writ large, a vicious snake pit where the strong and hungry eat the weak and soft."[53] From this point of view, the fact that Trump had criticized the leaders of Wall Street then hired them as his subordinates was not a sign of contradiction or self-subversion. It was a sign of his triumph. Trump's populism revolved not so

much around policy as around the pure realization of power. He, Trump, was not only a successful businessman, he was also famous and had great TV ratings. He could challenge the establishment in his electoral campaign, pillory the chair of the Fed and demonize the CEO of Goldman Sachs and win. Having won, he could then audition Jamie Dimon of J.P. Morgan for Treasury secretary and reject him in favor of a minor Goldman Sachs alumnus who was more to his liking. If you could do all these things, you clearly were king of the hill, all the better for being king by popular acclamation. That is all Trump needed and it was a story to which he returned obsessively.

The revolving door that feeds government in America regularly rotates between public service and the corporate world. In firms like Goldman Sachs, the rotation is de rigueur for senior figures. It is not easy for a patriotic American to turn down an invitation from the White House to serve. But why, one has to ask, would a senior business figure be willing to be associated with such an administration? To which the simple answer is that Trump's victory changed everything. His objectionable personality and outlandish policy proposals now had to be weighed against the more basic political question of who would do what for whom.

III

When it came to governing, it was not easy to fashion a coherent program out of such a mixed coalition. But there was one thing on which the Trump administration and the Republicans in Congress could agree: overturning the Obama legacy. In this sense, after a campaign shaped by the aftereffects of 2008, the first phase of the Trump administration was also molded by the legacy of 2008, but in negative. The first twelve months of the Trump presidency offered an audit on the robustness of the state-building project pursued by the Democrats since the crisis. How much of it would stand up in the face of the onslaught of a Republican president and a Republican Congress? In 2008, pondering the fiscal track record of the George W. Bush administration, Brad DeLong had wondered what was the right strategic

and tactical course for the Democrats, "when there is no guarantee that any Republican successors will ever be 'normal' again."[54] Nine years on the question was more pressing than ever. Since 2009 the congressional Republicans had been waging relentless political war, first against the stimulus, then the Affordable Care Act, also known as Obamacare. Twice in 2011 and 2013 they had taken the debt ceiling hostage. Now, with control of both the presidency and Congress, what would they do?

Obamacare was the scalp they wanted most and it ought to have been easy. As it had emerged from its congressional ordeal in March 2010, the Affordable Care Act was mangled and flawed. But for all their grim determination, in the critical first six months of the Trump presidency the Republicans could neither replace nor repeal it. What stood in their way was the inherent complexity of the subject matter and deep divisions within their party. But their failure also reflected the fact that the ACA, like any truly major piece of social or economic legislation, had created its own social constituency. Even an institution as deeply disappointing as the ACA was hard to budge once tens of millions of people came to depend on it and hundreds of billions of dollars began to flow through its channels. Indeed, among the states that benefited most from the extension of health coverage under Obamacare were Kentucky and West Virginia, diehard Trump country.[55] As Trump took office, support for the ACA among the most important group of voters, Independents, had risen from 36 percent in 2010 to 53 percent.[56] By the summer, when the desperate Republican congressional leadership made a last bid simply to repeal Obamacare without replacement, they had the support of only 13 percent of Americans.[57] Not surprisingly, sufficient Republican moderates refused to go along.

If they couldn't repeal and replace Obamacare, what could they do? By the summer of 2017 it seemed that the incoherence of the Republicans, when faced with the complex reality of modern government, might prevent them from taking any effective action.[58] The ACA fight had left little room on the legislative agenda. Trump's promised infrastructure program was a will-o'-the-wisp. Tax reform was much discussed with no apparent action. Meanwhile, basic financial questions could not be dodged. The debt ceiling remained in place, and when the Treasury hit its borrowing limit in the

spring of 2017, it was forced to resort to the familiar makeshifts.[59] Treasury Secretary Mnuchin vainly called on Congress to raise the ceiling. But in the summer the House went into recess without a vote. In the meantime, the new director of the Office of Management and Budget was Mick Mulvaney, a founding member of the Freedom Caucus, which had diced with default in 2011 and 2013.[60] He did not want to make concessions to the centrists or the Democrats. The extreme spending cuts demanded by his old friends in the Freedom Caucus had no majority. For Trump's budget director a shutdown was not the worst option. If the United States was to crash into the debt ceiling and be forced to prioritize claims, a default in all but name, so be it.[61] Astonishingly, the president seemed to agree. In May 2017 Trump tweeted blithely about a "good shutdown."[62]

As the summer came to an end, despite their control of both the White House and Congress, it seemed as though the Republicans would fail to resolve the budget issue. The real question was whether the Democrats would allow them to drive the United States off the fiscal cliff. When Obama was in the White House, the Democrats had pilloried the Republicans for failing to carry their share of the burden of government. Could they refuse to back the president, even if the president was Trump? Before this dilemma could really bite, natural disaster intervened. With Hurricane Harvey having devastated a large part of Texas and another hurricane roaring into Florida, neither Trump nor the Democrats wanted to look inactive.[63] At a meeting in the Oval Office on September 6 the president did an about-face. He not only abandoned the Republican congressional leadership but also cut off his own Treasury secretary in midsentence to strike a deal with the Democrats. It was a dizzying inversion that sent pundits scrambling for historical examples of "independent" presidents who had risen above the American party system.[64] The realities were more hard edged than that. With Chuck Schumer and Nancy Pelosi having saved the administration from a shutdown, Trump was only too happy to cheer on the Republicans as they returned to the attack.[65] Scrapping Obamacare might not sell as a political proposition, but cutting taxes surely would. The Republicans in the House and Senate began urgent work on "tax reform."

The resulting tax bill that passed both houses of Congress in December

2017 was hugely controversial. The sugar coating, such as it was, consisted of across-the-board reductions in personal income taxation and cuts to exemptions that principally hit high-income local taxpayers in states that voted Democratic. But these were time limited. Within a few years many lower-income Americans would be paying higher taxes. Of more lasting benefit to the very wealthy was raising the estate tax threshold to $11 million. And what really mattered was a 40 percent cut in the rate of business taxation, which meant that profits could either be retained for growth or paid out to shareholders. Given the vast inequality in wealth holding and particularly in the holding of equity—the top quintile of the American income distribution owns 90 percent of corporate equity—the benefits go to the better off. Then for good measure, the Senate added the removal of the single-payer mandate that required all Americans to take out health insurance. Without this mandate, by most estimates, 13 million Americans would drop out of coverage. As many low-risk individuals left the insurance plans, the premiums for those who did remain would surge. DeLong's fears were amply confirmed. In its redistributive impact and the scale of the giveaway, 2017 stood in comparison with the huge Reagan tax cut of 1981 and those of Bush in 2001 and 2003.[66]

To ease the passage of their tax measures through Congress and to calm the nerves of fiscally conservative Republicans, the Treasury and fellow traveling Republican economists talked down the deficit implications.[67] They resorted to the old Reagan-era arguments that lower tax rates would boost growth and thus raise government revenues. Even the notorious Laffer curve, purporting to show a positive relationship between lower tax rates and government revenue, made a comeback.[68] But the vast majority of economists were scornful of these evasions. The tax cuts would clearly add to the deficit. Simpson and Bowles, who had headed Obama's national commission on fiscal responsibility and reform, denounced the tax plan as a return to the era of "deficit denial."[69] In fact, it was not so much denial as hard-nosed political calculation. There was no way to cut the corporate tax rate to as little as 21 percent without incurring deficits.[70] Nor did this scare the activist Republicans. As they saw it, the larger the deficits, the more urgent the need to move on to stage two of their program.[71] With the tax

cuts threatening to add a trillion and a half dollars to the national debt, spending cuts would be mandatory. Medicaid would be pared back as far as the law permitted and the rest of the federal government would be cut to the bone. These were the Republican tactics not of the 1980s but the 1990s. The congressional Republicans were starving the beast.

Liberals were understandably indignant about the gross inequity of the tax proposal. The UN's special rapporteur on extreme poverty, who happened to be touring the United States visiting some of the 40 million Americans who lived in conditions of deep deprivation, denounced the tax plan as "a bid to make the US the world champion of extreme inequality."[72] But even setting equity concerns aside, starving the beast was a failed fiscal strategy. Historically, the spending cuts that were supposed to follow on the tax cuts did not arrive. It was easier to rail against tax breaks than it was to get them repealed. Key areas of welfare spending had supporters even in the Republican ranks. At the same time the Republican plans to expand the army by 10 percent and raise the navy to 355 fighting ships would increase military spending, the largest element of discretionary spending, by $683 billion, or 12 percent, over the decade to 2027.[73] Rather than shrinking big government, the main effect of Republican fiscal tactics was likely to be a further reduction in America's already deeply inadequate tax base. Following the tax cuts, the federal government's take of GDP would fall to 17 percent, a figure befitting an emerging market state rather than the government of an advanced economy.[74]

In 2009, when a Democrat was in the White House appealing for Congress to provide a stimulus to the American economy as it plunged into the worst crisis since the 1930s, the Republicans had voted, to a man and a woman, against a stimulus. They denounced Obama's Recovery and Reinvestment Act as a ruinous demonstration of fiscal irresponsibility. Now, with unemployment at lows not seen since the boom time of 2007 but with Trump in the White House, they were working hard to deliver a ten-year $1.4 trillion stimulus. In their defense it might be said that given the sluggishness of the recovery and the large number of people who had retreated from the workforce during the crisis, there was a case to be made for running the economy hot.[75] But even those who advocated such an adventurous

policy found it hard to justify the Republican tax plan.[76] America's wealthiest did not need further benefits. Investment was certainly depressed, but it was not for lack of funds. America's corporations had trillions of dollars in cash on hand. What was clearly long overdue was a public investment program, to make good the embarrassing deficits in America's infrastructure. But there was little enthusiasm for that from Congress. The Republicans needed to end Trump's first year in office on a high. They needed to deliver for their donors.[77] The 2017 "tax reform" did both.

When budget hawks inside the Clinton and Obama administrations had worried about deficits, what was on their minds was market confidence. How would the markets react to the latest round of spendthrift Republican policy? Increasing the debt by perhaps as much as $1.5 trillion over ten years ought surely to produce a reaction. Following the surprising election outcome, bond markets had been twitchy.[78] Anticipating that the Trump administration would launch a major infrastructure drive and add further stimulus with tax reform, the markets expected the Fed to bring interest rate increases forward. Over the winter of 2016–2017 this prompted bonds to sell off and yields to rise. With the ECB and the Bank of Japan both engaged in QE, the dollar appreciated sharply, sending a ripple of uncertainty around the world of dollar borrowers. Their debt-servicing costs were going up. But then, as the reality of the shambolic Trump administration and the continuing self-paralysis of the Republicans in Congress became clear, the fever broke. Driven by tech euphoria, the stock market continued to boom. The Fed insisted that it would continue its stepwise increase in interest rates. But there were few signs of panic in the bond market.[79] The tax cuts with which the Republicans ended the year produced a shrug from the bond markets. As one analyst commented: "Whatever grade you assign to the end result, the bond market and economists are adding an extra 'minus' to the grade. So, if you think it's a 'B' effort, the market's grade is a 'B minus.'"[80] The markets weren't cheering but neither did the Trump administration have vigilantes on its tail.

The congressional infighting over Obamacare and the Republican tax cuts was bare-knuckle American politics. But a clue to the relative calm in the Treasury market could be found in the same set of influences that had

also preserved calm in the face of the Bush-era deficits of the early 2000s—the global demand and supply of safe assets. In the fall of 2017 the IMF published a remarkable table that showed the issuance of debt since 2010.[81] As this data revealed, austerity and QE had led to a major reshuffling of security portfolios. Given the budget-control measures adopted in Europe, the active bond buying by the ECB and the even greater activism of the Bank of Japan, they were, for the foreseeable future, not significant suppliers of safe assets to global investors. Not only was the ECB hoovering up eurozone bonds, but Germany, the chief supplier of European safe assets, was running a budget surplus. On a global scale over the next five years, the United States would be the only source of safe, Treasury-grade assets for investors worldwide. Whatever you might think of the Trump administration, if you needed to park a large volume of funds in safe government debt, there was no alternative to US Treasurys.

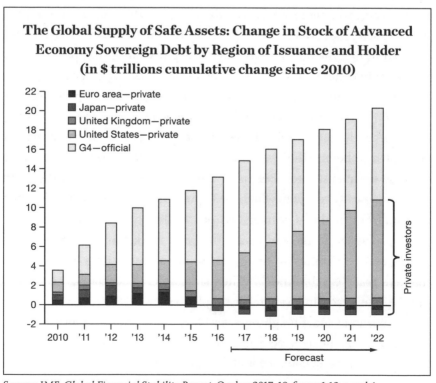

Source: IMF, *Global Financial Stability Report*, Ocober 2017, 19, figure 1.13, panel 4.

IV

The Republican campaigns to roll back Obamacare and cut taxes were of long standing. Trump's targeting of Wall Street in his election campaign was more novel. But it made electoral sense. Almost a decade on from the financial crisis, the banks were still deeply unpopular. A poll in the summer of 2017 revealed that 60 percent of Americans still regarded Wall Street as a "danger to our economy," and only 27 percent thought regulation had gone far enough or posed "a threat to innovation or economic growth." Fully 47 percent of Trump's voters wanted to "keep or expand" Dodd-Frank, as opposed to only 27 percent favoring repeal or scaling back. When it came to financial products and services, 87 percent of Republicans and 90 percent of Independents favored regulation.[82] Wall Street lobbyists might wail against Dodd-Frank, but as the Obama administration insiders knew, it was they who had held back the popular tide running against the banks. And Trump, it turned out, was no different.

His campaign attacks were politics pure and simple. The leaders of Wall Street had never liked Trump. They clearly preferred the Clinton brand. He had paid them back in kind and he had won. The question of who was boss had been answered. Trump's about-face once in office was utterly unabashed. He would do as befitted a boss-president. There would be a bonfire of regulations and in particular those of his predecessor. The thought of doing a "big number" on Dodd-Frank pleased POTUS. And it pleased him also to bestow favors on and receive applause from powerful interests, even those he had previously made a show of attacking. As he told a meeting of CEOs in April 2017: "For the bankers in the room, they'll be very happy."[83] To have favors lavished on them by the man who had pilloried them on the stump might seem topsy-turvy. But the bankers were not complaining. As the *Financial Times* commented: "Imagine going to the races, betting 98 per cent of your stake on the favourite [Clinton], which loses in the final stretch, and going home with huge winnings."[84] As far as Wall Street was concerned it turned out that the game of politics was heads I win, tails you lose. Neither the politicians nor Wall Street gave a second thought to the angry voters who had actually put Trump in the White House.

To help with the gutting of Dodd-Frank it was only too easy to find bank lobbyists and business-friendly economists. And enthusiasm also came from the Republicans in the House. Led by Jeb Hensarling, who back in 2008 had spearheaded opposition to the bailouts and was now chairman of the Financial Services Committee, the House rapidly passed the so-called Financial CHOICE Act—where CHOICE stands for Creating Hope and Opportunity for Investors, Consumers and Entrepreneurs. It not only defanged Dodd-Frank. It was libertarian purism. It would scrap the Volcker rule and make stress tests a biannual rather than an annual affair. It eliminated the Orderly Liquidation Authority, insisting that failing banks should simply be referred to the bankruptcy courts.[85] Astonishingly, in the name of the freedom to choose, the CHOICE act even promised to gut Elizabeth Warren's Consumer Financial Protection Bureau.[86]

For an administration habitually decried as populist, the remarkable thing was how spectacularly unpopular such legislation would have been. Like ACA repeal, the CHOICE Act had little or no chance of passing the blocking position the Democrats held in the Senate. As in the battle against Obamacare, the struggle was best waged outside the spotlight. Even if Dodd-Frank remained in place, the regulatory regime was fair game. This was a legacy of the discretionary conception of financial governance that framed Dodd-Frank. Pursuing maximum freedom from congressional interference, Geithner's Treasury had pushed for the agencies to have the widest possible latitude in their regulatory efforts. Now that discretion could be used to fundamentally change the regime of bank supervision without the need for legislation. Mnuchin's Treasury began preparing a series of reports on its approach to financial regulation, opening the door to the bank lobby.[87] By one count fully 75 percent of the bankers' recommendations were incorporated into the Treasury's new regulatory blueprint.[88,89] Unpicking the Volcker rule, which had taken almost four years to assemble, began by asking the banks how they would like it changed.[90] In November 2017 rather than scrapping the Orderly Liquidation Authority and restoring the role of the bankruptcy courts as the CHOICE Act had proposed, the Treasury decided that it preferred to retain control over the liquidation of a megabank in crisis.[91] Even if there were to be no more bailouts, the prospect of another Lehman was not attractive. The Trump administration exposed

the basic weakness of Geithner's regulatory design. It depended on those operating the law to have a programmatic commitment to systemic stability. Without that, the legislation per se was largely empty.

Arguably the most radical section of the CHOICE Act was the provisions pertaining to the Fed. They constituted an all-out assault on central bank activism as practiced by Ben Bernanke. In the future the CHOICE Act demanded near total transparency of all Fed meetings. The act called for the FOMC to declare a mathematical policy rule to justify its interest rate choices. As its default the act specified the so-called Taylor rule, named after John B. Taylor of Stanford University, a favorite of the Right and a longtime academic rival of Ben Bernanke. His rule called for interest rates to be set as the sum of:

The rate of inflation over the previous 4 quarters;

One-half of the difference between the real GDP and an estimate of potential GDP;

One-half of the difference between the rate of inflation over the previous 4 quarters and 2 percent;

and an assumed real interest rate of 2 percent.

It was a mechanical formula that required interest rates to be adjusted upward if inflation was high and unemployment low, or downward if the reverse was the case. If the Fed preferred a different rule, the CHOICE Act stipulated that it must spell out its own formula in similarly mechanical terms and demonstrate econometrically that its rule was preferable to the Taylor model.

As the authors of the bill were well aware, enshrining this formula in law implied an entire alternate history of American monetary policy back to the crisis and before. Taylor and his disciples blamed the crash on the fact that in the early 2000s, under Greenspan, rates had been too low.[92] During the crisis, on the other hand, if one applied the Taylor formula, interest rates should have been pushed into negative territory. A strict application of the Taylor rule in the autumn of 2008 would have called for rates

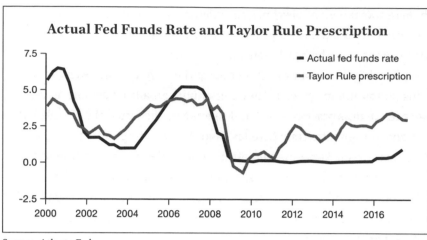

Source: Atlanta Fed.

of below zero, effectively a tax on savings deposits. It was because he judged that impracticable that Bernanke had adopted quantitative easing. The CHOICE Act would ban any such improvisation. Once the acute crisis had passed, instead of QE2 and QE3, Taylor's formula would have called for rate increases. There would have been no worrying about taper tantrums, whether at home or abroad. Indeed, no regard would be paid to conditions anywhere in the world other than the United States, unless, of course, the Fed dared to include its wider global concerns as a variable in its own interest rate equation.

The CHOICE Act was first and foremost a political gesture. Promising to curb the discretion of the Fed played well on the Republican side. But on the substance of policy there was, in fact, no disagreement. Taylor rule or not, 2017 was clearly a time to tighten, to raise rates and to start, tentatively, unwinding the gigantic balance sheet built up during the era of QE.[93] After ending security purchases under QE3 in October 2014, the Fed had made the first move to raise rates in December 2015. It had then paused before inching them up again in December 2016, March 2017 and June 2017. The FOMC ended 2017 by laying a path of at least three further increases in 2018.

As always, a subtle game was played out between the FOMC and the markets. Janet Yellen proved herself a master of this game, managing to socialize the idea of rate increase without triggering panic. But there was never much chance of her tenure being extended into the Trump presidency.[94]

There was talk that John B. Taylor himself might be in line to take Yellen's place. Trump liked the look of Kevin Warsh, an underqualified New York princeling who had been parachuted onto the Fed board by the Bush White House in 2006. But in the end he settled on Jerome Powell. It was a strikingly conventional choice. Powell was a Republican investment banker in the Mitt Romney–Hank Paulson vein. He had earned the trust of the Obama administration by campaigning within the Republican Party against the shutdown of 2011.[95] That had led to his nomination to the Fed board in December 2011, where he had distinguished himself by his loyalty to both Bernanke and Yellen. He was also thought to be supportive of the Dodd-Frank framework.[96] But what recommended Powell to Trump were most likely his personal attributes. He was not an academic economist. He was a rich businessman. With a personal net worth estimated in excess of $100 million Powell was by far the wealthiest person to take the position of Fed chair since the 1930s. Unlike Professor Taylor, Powell was nondoctrinaire when it came to policy. Under his stewardship the White House would not have to fear unduly painful increases in interest rates.

V

Building a new administration and setting a domestic policy agenda was a protracted and complex business, for which Trump and his coterie were ill prepared. All the more forceful was their approach to foreign relations, where the White House and the executive branch had far more leeway. Within forty-eight hours of his inauguration on Friday, January 20, 2017, Trump announced his intention to renegotiate NAFTA. The next day, Monday, January 23, he withdrew the United States from the Trans-Pacific Partnership. TTIP, the object of years of laborious negotiation with the EU, was also left for dead.

It was a spectacular overturning of a centerpiece of Obama-era foreign economic policy. TPP was a showpiece of American grand strategy in a multipolar age. It was a shock to America's allies. Committing to TPP had cost many Asian countries, most notably Japan, serious political capital. And it begged the question: If there was no grand regional alliance, where

did that leave Obama and Clinton's pivot to Asia and the de facto policy of containing China? Indeed, abandoning TPP and TTIP was not just a break with the Obama era, it was a reversal of America's sponsorship of multilateral trade policy dating back to the 1940s.[97] At the first G20 meeting attended by Treasury Secretary Mnuchin in Baden-Baden in March 2008, it was impossible to reach agreement even on a simple pledge "to resist all forms of protectionism."[98] As Wolfgang Schäuble noted in his usual uncompromising fashion, the meeting had reached an "impasse."[99] All Mnuchin had to offer by way of clarification was that the new administration had a "different view on trade." Philip Hammond, the UK chancellor, advised his colleagues that it was better to give the Trump administration more time: "If we demand a hard answer now, I'm pretty sure we won't like the answer we get."[100]

Meanwhile, in Washington a battle was raging over NAFTA. As far as Trump was concerned it was "one of the worst deals ever."[101] As he told journalists after three months in office, he "was really ready and psyched to terminate" it.[102] The relish was obvious. Bannon and economic adviser Peter Navarro, a nationalist trade economist, urged him to follow his instincts. For the announcement they had earmarked a rally in Harrisburg, Pennsylvania, on April 29, 2017, to celebrate his first hundred days in office. For Mexico and Canada it would have been a brutal blow. Realizing the seriousness of the situation, they rapidly coordinated their positions. Desperate to prevent a precipitate break, hundreds of American business leaders lobbied the White House. The secretary for agriculture, the commerce secretary and the secretary of state all pleaded for a stay of execution. In the end the decisive argument appears to have been a map showing quite how much of "Trump country" would be hurt by withdrawal. Did the president really want to put Texas in play? The map "shows that I do have a very big farmer base, which is good," Trump later told journalists. "They like Trump, but I like them, and I'm going to help them."[103] That meant not canceling NAFTA. Instead, Washington would renegotiate. But it would do so from a weakened position. The Obama administration had spent years haggling for improved access to Canadian agricultural markets, cross-border licensing of financial services and improved labor standards with Mexico. To do so it had used not raw threats but the lure of the even bigger trade deal, TPP, a project into which the United States had inveigled Mexico and Canada at

the Los Cabos G20 summit in 2012. With TPP gone, all the concessions on NAFTA already agreed were consigned to the dustbin of history.[104] Trump's renegotiation would start from scratch with little but threats to offer.

NAFTA, TPP, TTIP were regional treaties. The truly global forum for trade policy was the WTO. It was an original creation of the founding moment of American globalism in the 1940s.[105] The United States had long been its most powerful backer. President Trump did not attend the party to celebrate the seventieth anniversary of its founding in November 2017 at the Ronald Reagan building in Washington, DC, but he sent his ill wishes by way of Fox News. "The WTO was set up for the benefit [of] everybody but us. . . . They have taken advantage of this country like you wouldn't believe," he told the news channel.[106] As his trade representative, Trump appointed the veteran trade warrior Robert Lighthizer, who in the 1980s had been responsible for extracting the agreements by America's major competitors to voluntarily restrain their steel exports to the United States. Lighthizer blasted the WTO with a broadside. He objected to the judicial activism of the WTO's trade arbitration panel, its pandering to the special pleading of large developing countries like India, its failure to address areas of chronic industrial overcapacity such as steel and above all its inability to get to grips with the unprecedented challenge to economic liberalism posed by the rise of Chinese state capitalism.[107] In Washington's view, the WTO should confine itself to providing a forum for bargaining between the major trading powers. The United States should throw off any restraint on its ability to retaliate against economies that it considered to be discriminating against it. But rather than translating this vision into positive proposals for the WTO, the Trump administration adopted the tactics the Republicans had used to such effect in Congress. The United States refused to permit the appointment of new arbitrators to WTO panels, threatening to hollow out the institution, making it increasingly dysfunctional and illegitimate. If there was no actual éclat at the WTO meeting in December 2017, the lack of progress on any area of trade liberalization was dismal.[108] Lighthizer did not even deign to stay until the end of the conference.

The shock delivered by the new administration to global economic institutions was severe. There had been nothing like this since the 1930s and nowhere was this felt more acutely than in Europe. In the early days it was

unclear whether the Trump team actually acknowledged the EU as a counterparty or understood that the United States no longer maintained bilateral trade relations with individual European countries. In an interview given just days before he took office, Trump dismissed the EU as a "vehicle for Germany." According to inside sources, members of his entourage were placing phone calls to European leaders to ascertain which countries might be "leaving next."[109] Trump's people believed the Brexit hype. There was a fear in Europe that Trumpery would spread. London was about to trigger Article 50 and formal exit proceedings. The Austrian, Dutch and French elections were all in play. There were forces in the White House that openly supported not only Brexit but Marine Le Pen and the Front.[110]

Once the initial shock wore off, international forces began to concert themselves. Mexico and Canada worked together closely to do what was possible to save NAFTA. The other parties to TPP decided to go ahead without the United States. By late May, when Trump made his first visit to Europe, the "populist" spook had passed. Macron was in the saddle in Paris. When the American president refused publicly to underline America's commitment to Article 5 of the NATO treaty and gave notice of his intention to withdraw from the Paris climate change agreement, Merkel had seen enough. Germany was in general election mode and the spectacular swing in European public opinion against Trump gave Merkel every reason to act. On May 28, 2017, the day after Trump's departure, speaking to an enthusiastic crowd in Munich, the German chancellor announced that Europe had to adjust to a new reality.[111] After Trump and Brexit, it was clear that Europe could no longer rely completely on its long-standing American and British allies. "The times in which we can fully count on others are somewhat over, as I have experienced in the past few days. We Europeans must really take our destiny in our own hands. Of course we need to have friendly relations with the US and with the UK and with other neighbours, including Russia. But we have to fight for our own future ourselves."[112]

It was no doubt a remarkable moment. As Richard Haass, president of the Council on Foreign Relations, tweeted: "Merkel saying Europe cannot rely on others & needs to take matters into its own hands is a watershed—& what US has sought to avoid since WW2."[113] But what did it actually amount to? Europe's own process of consolidation in the wake of the crisis seemed

stalled. President Macron of France offered a bold vision of Europe's future in a major speech at the Sorbonne.[114] But who was it addressed to? After the inconclusive elections in Germany in September 2017, there was only a caretaker government in Berlin. Italy was creaking under the weight of years of recession. Spain was thrown into chaos by Catalonia's bid for independence. Furthermore, any moves toward further integration and self-determination for the Continent were bound to arouse resistance. If Britain was leaving, the difficult Eastern Europeans remained. In July 2017, on his second trip to Europe for the G20 meeting in Hamburg, Trump made a point of stopping in Poland. In front of a crowd of supporters of the Law and Justice government, Trump found a European audience that loved him. The flags waved as he proclaimed America's commitment to NATO as a bulwark of civilization and a bastion for the people of the West who "still cry out 'We want God.'"[115] Trump had segued from "America first" to a "clash of civilizations," but neither one nor the other would go down well with the multicultural crowd that was awaiting America at the G20 meeting. As Hammond, the British chancellor, had pointed out, sometimes it was better not to push the Trump administration too hard for a clarification of its position. There was reason to fear that one might not like the answer.

Clearly, Merkel's vision of a united Europe fighting for its own future would have to tackle deep internal divisions. Nor was the rise of right-wing nationalism Europe's only point of difference. Trump's protectionism was directed not just against Asian competitors. Germany too was in the crosshairs. As ever, Finance Minister Schäuble was quick to respond. He would no more take criticism from Trump and Mnuchin than he had from Obama, Geithner, the IMF or fellow Europeans.[116] In the German view a trade surplus was first and foremost a reward for export competitiveness. But the kind of gigantic deficit run by the United States also pointed to deeper macroeconomic imbalances. It was hardly surprising that given Germany's budget surplus and America's large and growing government deficit there should be a difference in their trade accounts. This was the familiar repertoire of arguments about transatlantic trade. But this time Schäuble added a twist. It was true, he admitted, that German exports enjoyed a competitive advantage. The euro was undervalued. But it was not Germany that set interest rates or the value of the euro. It was the ECB. To the horror of

German savers, Mario Draghi's expansive policy of QE was driving European bond yields into negative territory and depressing the value of the euro. Visiting Washington in April 2017 Schäuble told American audiences that he had warned Draghi about the tendency of the ECB's expansive monetary policy to inflate Germany's trade surplus.[117] That it was causing tension with the United States was predictable. The ECB stood firm, and the IMF backed the continuation of QE in Europe. But Schäuble had served notice of how Trump's attacks might be instrumentalized in the long-running argument over eurozone economic policy. The furor around Trump should not cause one to forget how bitterly Europeans and Americans had squabbled over economic policy in the "good" Obama years.

The ECB's belated monetary expansion at a time of Fed tightening was a real source of transatlantic imbalance and it was a reminder of the disharmony over monetary policy that had marked the world economy since the onset of the crisis, a disharmony to which conservative voices in Germany had contributed as much as anyone.[118] Nor were the chronic surpluses of Germany, the Netherlands and China figments of the Trumpian imagination. They pointed to real and persistent imbalances in the world economy. In global trade policy as in so many other areas, the outrage caused by the uncouth belligerence of the Trump administration too easily obscured the reality of the problems it was gesturing toward. At the G20, the atmosphere was self-congratulatory. The WTO earned applause for seeing the world economy through the financial crisis of 2008 far better than it had fared during the Great Depression of the 1930s. There had been no catastrophic lurch toward high tariffs and protectionism.[119] There had been no repeat of the Smoot-Hawley tariff of 1930. The twenty-first-century system of global governance might not be popular, but it had worked, or so the story went. Ten years on from the crisis, it was, therefore, the height of populist irresponsibility to indulge in backbiting economic nationalism. For the defenders of the status quo, Trump made a perfect caricature enemy against whom to reassert the nostrums of liberalism. But this deflected attention from a more complex and ambiguous reality. The idea that Trump constituted a sudden and shocking break with a prevailing liberal success story depends on an unduly sanguine view of the global backdrop. This was as true with regard to trade as it was with regard to monetary policy. In fact,

the last major effort to negotiate a global trade deal, the Doha round, had come to a crashing halt in the summer of 2008. World trade had recovered from the disaster of 2008–2009. But since 2010 trade volumes had stagnated. In 2015 they had declined.[120] This was driven in part by the business cycle. The taper tantrum and the setback to commodity prices had rocked the emerging markets. But it also reflected a wave of protectionist measures adopted by countries across the world, concentrated not on tariffs but on a variety of nontariff barriers.[121] No one imagined that Trump's personal views on trade reflected arcane knowledge of new types of protectionism. He was regurgitating opinions first formed in the 1970s and 1980s. But if the expert staff around Lighthizer was looking for ammunition to demonstrate the reality of discrimination against US exports, it was ready to hand. Through tax breaks, subsidies and export credit systems, not to mention China's state capitalism, world trade was increasingly shaped not only by corporate value chains, but also by state intervention. A large part of America's huge trade deficit was accounted for not only by Chinese trade discrimination, but also by lost export earnings siphoned through offshore tax havens, located not only in the Caribbean but also in the EU.[122] In this respect too the once-robust assumption that globalization was an inevitable, natural process was losing its power to convince. Trump's trade hawks did not advocate a return to the 1930s, but neither were they willing to continue the pretense that the naïve triumphalism of 1989 with its easy assumptions about the inevitable victory of democratic capitalism any longer "jived with the facts." As the national security strategy issued in December 2017 darkly declared: "There is no arc of history that ensures that America's free political and economic system will automatically prevail."[123]

V

Such talk was no doubt supposed to suggest a profound realist wisdom. But it was in fact symptomatic less of a bold or coherent new worldview than of the rather desperate mood in Washington. It was particularly rich coming from an administration whose supporters in Congress had in the name of god-given American values repeatedly tried to sabotage crisis-fighting

efforts and who now demanded that the Fed should ensure the best of all possible worlds by following a nondiscretionary, automatic policy rule. The "arc of history" sonorously rejected by Trump's security hawks had, of course, been invoked by President Obama.[124] But in using that figure of speech he had referenced not deterministic neoconservative philosophies of history, but the prophetic voice of one of America's greatest freedom struggles. There was indeed no determinacy. The question was how the arc might be beat. Even if one accepted some version of the disillusioned narrative of the world economy offered by the Trump camp, the question was how to respond. Was "America first" an adequate answer, even for America? Whatever the answer to that question, the reality that the rest of the world had to deal with was that the American electorate had put in office an erratic, narcissistic nationalist who no longer offered any commitment to upholding an international order unless it directly and immediately connected to American national interests, however those were defined. Given the size and reach of the American nation-state and its economy, this had profound global consequences.

In 2008 the United States had been at the epicenter of the crisis. Both the Bush and Obama administrations had faced the hard fact that there was little or nothing that was automatic about the functioning of the global financial system. It had taken unprecedented efforts, led by the United States and the rest of the G20, to stabilize both "America's free political and economic system" and the world economy. In 2017 the United States was once again at the center of global concern, but this time it was uncertainty emanating from America's erratic new government that was the key.[125] And once it was framed that way, the question that Paulson had put in the summer of 2016 could not be dodged. How might the United States fare in a future financial crisis under President Trump? Would he be able to rally a concerted response? If the haggling over the debt ceiling in 2017 was anything to go by, it would again come down to a bargain between pragmatic centrist Republicans and congressional Democrats.

Of course, we can peer only dimly into the future. So what might we learn by looking to the past? If there is a question that may throw light on our future prospects it is not how Trump might have coped in 2008, or how he may cope with some future contingency, but why in 2017, when he took

office, Trump did not face a global economic implosion. It may seem like a perverse question. In 2017 economic growth in the United States was steady. Unemployment was down to precrisis levels. The markets were booming. In Europe the economy was finally bouncing back. An immediate crisis was not in the cards. The real force of the question becomes apparent if we direct our attention, in conclusion, not to America and Europe, the old hub of transatlantic globalization, but to China and the emerging markets, where the future of the world economy will be decided. There the years prior to 2017 had been anything but calm.

Chapter 25

THE SHAPE OF THINGS TO COME

On January 17, 2017, as the World Economic Forum assembled at Davos to consider the implications of Brexit and Trump, China's President Xi Jinping stepped to the rostrum to deliver the opening plenary. It was a speech widely seen as announcing China's new role as an "anchor of globalization."[1] Eight years earlier the governor of PBoC had made headlines around the world by proposing a new Bretton Woods. That intervention staked China's claim to be a major voice in global economic governance. In 2017 Xi no longer needed to break down the door. All he had to do was to declaim the most basic platitudes of what had once been the global consensus, reinforcing them with a bracing dose of historical materialism, a few ancient proverbs and a reassuring recitation of China's mind-blowing growth record.[2] It was exactly the message that the CEOs, investors and policy experts at Davos wanted to hear, and Xi was exactly the person to deliver it. Unlike Trump, he was clearly a sophisticated individual. He might head a Communist party, but as a "princeling" he had the reassuring air of someone born to power. Unlike Angela Merkel, Xi did not need to convince anyone of his capacity and will to act on a scale commensurate with China's place in global affairs. His evident authority demonstrated China's arrival not just as a major economy but as a superpower. For many across the world, particularly in Europe, China was already *the* economic superpower. Amid the awed sense of a historic transition, memories were short. It was easily forgotten that at Davos only a year earlier, the talk

had been not of Chinese hegemony but of China's economy unleashing a global disaster.

I

The emerging market economies had been in trouble since the taper tantrum of 2013. Two of the great economic success stories of the new millennium, Brazil and South Africa, had crash-landed. The commodity price collapse in the fall of 2014 dealt a heavy blow to exporters of oil, gas, iron ore and other raw materials. Russia and much of Central Asia were struggling under the impact of sanctions and the Ukraine crisis. Given lackluster growth in Europe and the United States, the one sustaining force in the world economy was China's relentless growth, and in 2015 even that suddenly seemed in doubt.

On June 12, 2015, while the West was distracted by events in Greece and Ukraine, China's stock market began to slide. From a high of 5,166, in three weeks the Shanghai Composite Index plunged 30 percent. With the state-directed "national team" of investors—companies and funds—pumping billions of yuan into the market, stock prices temporarily stabilized. But in mid-August, amid fears of a yuan devaluation, the market fell again and reached a new low just above 3,000 in September. From that plateau government intervention temporarily pushed it higher. But on January 4, 2016, the collapse resumed. By February further waves of selling took the index down to 2,737, not much more than half of its level six months earlier.

For the regime it was deeply embarrassing. In 2013 Xi had launched his new administration on the promise of the "China Dream." Unwisely, party propaganda outlets had tied this directly to the fortunes of the stock market.[3] Hundreds of millions of Chinese had entrusted their savings to the market. Those investments were now collapsing, just as the regime was gearing up for massive anniversary commemorations to mark the victory over Japan in 1945. The September 3 Victory Day Parade was to be a monumental event, making good on the incantation "Never forget national humiliation" and answering with the celebration of victory. Putin was the guest of honor. It was fitting that, at the same time, the yuan was gaining

recognition as an international currency. In the fall of 2015, the IMF was on the point of including China's currency in its SDR benchmark. A condition of being included in the IMF basket was that Beijing should allow the yuan to move more freely. For decades, the yuan had been a one-way bet. Against the overvalued dollar the only way was up. But when in early August 2015 Beijing liberalized currency trading, the yuan promptly plunged.

Clearly, something was very wrong, and, unlike in 2008, it was clear that the source of trouble was inside China. In years of explosive growth, supercharged since 2008 by a massive surge in credit, Chinese heavy industry had built up huge overcapacity. The real estate sector was weighed down by overbuilding. The stock market had been pumped up by "irrational exuberance" and a wave of dangerous margin lending. China had an overinflated shadow banking sector horribly reminiscent of that which had come crashing down in Europe and America in 2007–2008.[4] But what worried the observers studying the Chinese scene most acutely was the huge wave of money that was exiting China at the rate of hundreds of billions of

Source: Brad Setser, "Asia Is Adding to Its FX Reserves in 2017 (China Included?)," *Follow the Money* (blog), August 21, 2017, https://www.cfr.org/blog/asia-adding-its-fx-reserves-2017-china -included.

dollars per month in search of safe haven.[5] Did they know something that the rest of the world did not?

For twenty years the undervaluation of the yuan had been a constant in world economic affairs. Now it seemed the tables were turned. Was China about to become just another emerging market boom gone bad, albeit the largest the world had ever seen? It was a terrifying thought and it begged a question. How could a country with a strong trade balance and huge reserves be sliding toward a currency crisis? It was eerily reminiscent of 2008, when champion exporters like South Korea and Russia had found their banks in trouble and struggling desperately for dollar funding. And the explanation was the same in 2015 as it was in 2008. Globalization operated through different channels at different levels. The visible trade channel on which countries like South Korea and China were so dominant was only one, and not the most decisive, channel for a financial crisis. An economy with a strong trade surplus, ample foreign currency reserves and an appreciating currency might well have banks, corporations and private citizens accumulating debts in foreign currencies. The need for dollar funding had been the common denominator of the South Korean, the Russian and the European banks in 2008. It made them acutely vulnerable to a shift in interest-rate differentials or a reversal in the direction of exchange-rate movements. It wasn't the balance of trade but their corporate balance sheets that made them vulnerable. In 2008 China had not yet been fully incorporated into this logic. Its globalization was still "classic"—dominated by its trade account. It was precisely this familiar quality of China's development and its counterpart in America's "twin deficits" that distracted Western analysts from the massive financial tensions building up in North Atlantic balance sheets. But since 2008, as China's breakneck modernization continued, it had become ever more integrated in financial terms.

The commercial logic driving China's financial integration was compelling. Chinese businesses were investing like none had ever invested before. Interest rates in China were low. But thanks to Bernanke's QE they were even lower in the dollar world. The only likely movement in the yuan was upward. Put the two together and you had the ingredients for a profitable "carry trade": borrow in dollars; invest in yuan; repay the dollar loan from the proceeds of the booming Chinese economy at an appreciating

yuan exchange rate.[6] If China's exchange regulations made it difficult to import US dollars directly, one or two further steps were added: borrow in dollars; buy commodities; use the expected receipts from the sale of the commodities as collateral to borrow in yuan; invest the yuan in China. Profit could be made three ways: on the spread between Chinese returns and dollar funding costs; on the depreciation of the dollar against the yuan; and on the likely increase in the value of the commodities, driven upward by booming Chinese demand.

According to BIS estimates, by the end of 2014, while China's official reserves reached $4 trillion at their peak, cross-border claims against Chinese businesses had surged to $1.1 trillion, most of which was denominated in dollars and more than $800 billion of which was owed to large Western banks.[7] All told, 25 percent of China's corporate debts were in dollars, but only 8 percent of its corporate earnings. This mismatch was profitable but risky. If any one of the underlying conditions changed—interest rates, exchange rates or commodity prices—then the position could become loss making. In 2015 all three conditions changed. The Fed's retreat from QE promised that the interest margin would soon be shifting the wrong way. The slowdown in China's own growth and the sudden collapse in oil prices in 2014 reversed the momentum of commodity prices. Xi's drive against corruption in China caused wealthy families to move assets out of the country. The outflow exerted downward pressure on the yuan. For those holding some part of the $1.1 billion in foreign exposure, this combination of factors was very bad news, and due to the fact that this was common knowledge it risked a stampede.[8]

Over the winter of 2015–2016 what threatened the world economy was, in the words of the *Economist,* nothing less than a "calamity."[9] The emerging market boom, which for so long had energized the narrative of globalization, had ground to a shuddering halt. Russia, Central Asia, Brazil and South Africa were already in recession. An implosion of the Chinese economy, with a plunging yuan and investors scrambling for the exit, could easily have pushed the world economy into recession. The *Economist* painted a horror scenario in which the funds flowing out of China and a huge glut of overcapacity amplified a global cycle of deflation, the momentum of which would have been

more unstoppable than in 2008. Industrial and commodity producers would be left insolvent. At the same time, if the yuan peg broke, it would not be the only currency to devalue. Dollar carry trades across the emerging markets would unravel, provoking a general financial crisis. Western banks would not be immune.

The scenario was terrifying. Even the possibility of its unfolding was enough to spread panic. Commodity markets were intensely nervous. After falling off a cliff in November 2014, oil had stabilized in the spring of 2015 at c. $60 per barrel. But China was now the world's largest crude importer. The prospect of a China crisis coupled with the abundant supply of shale oil from the United States and the intransigent stand of the Saudi government sent markets over the edge once more.[10] Between the summer of 2015 and January 2016, prices halved from $60 to $29 per barrel. As the Saudis no doubt intended, this dealt a painful blow to the heavily leveraged US shale industry and sent ripples of anxiety through American financial markets. Even in the advanced economies propped up by quantitative easing, deflationary pressures were looming. In January 2016 the question at Davos was not how China would lead, but how it would cope. Could Beijing prevent a collapse? Would a Chinese implosion turn the jarring reversal of the fortunes in the emerging markets into a comprehensive rout? A year on, this is the global crisis that the Trump administration did not inherit. The question is, why not?

Any answer must start with the actions taken in Beijing. On the basis of its dramatic response to the crisis of 2008, the Chinese regime had a formidable reputation for effective economic policy. But in 2015 China's initial response to the crisis was anything but reassuring. The fumbling efforts to stabilize the Shanghai stock market exposed the myth of Beijing's omnicompetence.[11] QE with Chinese characteristics was not a success. The August 2015 liberalization of foreign exchange trading was mishandled. But Beijing held its nerve. Rather than allowing the yuan to continue its slide, the PBoC stabilized a new peg. Capital controls were stiffened, but otherwise the PBoC allowed the unwinding of exposed dollar positions. If this was an adjustment of balance sheets and not a general panic, it was the right thing to do. From their peak of $4 trillion in the summer of 2014, China's

currency reserves fell by early 2017 to $3 trillion. Watching the monthly drain of tens of billions was nail biting, but eventually at the lower level reserves stabilized. To revive demand in early 2016, Beijing unleashed another credit boom and a fiscal stimulus, while at the same time it set about purging the most overexpanded heavy industrial sectors of overcapacity. Western media ordinarily known for their advocacy of market freedom could not hide their relief that Beijing's grip had been restored. As the *Economist* remarked: "With capital now boxed in, much of it flowed into local property: house prices soared, first in the big cities and then beyond. Sales taxes on small cars were reduced by half. Between them, these controls and stimuli did the trick."[12] In reaction commodity prices rebounded and manufacturing surged across Asia, pulling China's giant manufacturing capacity back from the brink. The threat of global deflation receded.

This is how the triumphalist narrative goes. China is not just another crisis-prone emerging market. Beijing is in control. A threat of crisis spawned in China that threatened to destabilize the world economy was contained by China. So far so good, one might say. But 2015 demonstrated not only that China was neither invulnerable nor omnicompetent. Even more significantly, it demonstrated that it was not autonomous. In 2008 the question had been whether China would dump its dollar holdings and destabilize the United States. Eight years later, thanks to China's deeper financial integration, the question was reversed. As Beijing struggled to gain a grip on its stock market and the drain of foreign exchange, the question was not whether China would dump the dollar but whether the Fed would cooperate with China's efforts to stabilize the yuan.

For Janet Yellen and the Fed board it was a deep dilemma. The year 2015 started with the FOMC expecting to continue the process they had begun when they ended QE in December 2014. They were going to raise rates. The question was how far and how soon. After the taper tantrum of 2013 the Fed was acutely aware of the possible consequences for emerging markets.[13] But with the American economy slowly moving toward full employment, they wanted to move off zero, if for no other reason than to give themselves room for maneuver when the next setback came. More generally, there was an insistent urge to "normalize." Despite all the talk of

secular stagnation, it was hard to accept that zero interest rates or the Fed's massively inflated balance sheet should be a permanent feature of the world economy. But now blocking the path to normalization was the threat of a China crisis. In 2013 the Fed had flaunted its exclusive focus on the state of the US national economy. Could they take the same approach to China?

Over the summer of 2015 the Fed prevaricated, but at the September FOMC meeting the question could no longer be dodged. The majority of analysts expected the Fed to move rates up a notch. But then came the shock devaluation of the yuan and the second slide in the Shanghai Stock Exchange. Whatever the limitations on the Fed's mandates, markets were global. They could not ignore the threat from China. On August 24 America's Dow Jones lost 1,000 points and the Fed pulled back. The normalization of US monetary policy was put on hold and Janet Yellen made no secret of the board's reasoning. Instability in China was the key. In the press conference on September 18, 2015, as she explained the FOMC's decision, journalists counted Yellen making six references to China and ten to "global" factors. Unlike in 2013, when it had been India and Turkey under pressure, the risk of spillback from China to the United States was too important to be ignored. Indeed, the effect of Chinese deflation on the world economy was so powerful that there was no need for the Fed to pile on with its own interest rate increase.[14]

For Beijing the Fed's forbearance came as a relief. The Chinese liked the idea of the Fed acknowledging interdependence. In October 2015 finance minister Lou Jiwei had the temerity to tell a meeting of the IMF that the Fed couldn't raise interest rates because China was on the line. "The United States isn't at the point of raising interest rates yet and under its global responsibilities it can't raise rates," Lou said. The United States, he argued, "should assume global responsibilities" because of the dollar's status as a global currency.[15] In the United States the reaction was more mixed. As troubled American market watchers immediately pointed out, Yellen's conditioning of US policy on China enormously complicated the business of interpreting the Fed's next move. The markets had predicting the Fed down to a science. No one in the West was sure that they knew how to read Beijing.[16]

In December 2015, on the basis of America's own improving jobs market, the FOMC went ahead and raised rates. It was the first rate increase since 2006.[17] Yellen's announcement made clear that the Fed intended to set a signal that the recovery had consolidated. But on both wings of American politics it was hotly contested. Bernie Sanders supporters rallied outside the New York Fed building demanding to know "What Recovery?" Millions of Americans were still a long way from where they were in 2008. On the other hand, conservative opinion, eventually joined by Donald Trump, was irate that Yellen had not moved sooner. The message from the markets was similarly mixed. Initially in December 2015 investors were relieved that the Fed had finally embarked on normalization. Then the uncertainty in China and the emerging markets and the collapse in oil prices came back to the fore. The year 2016 began with a major market sell-off. By mid-February the S&P 500 had fallen by 11 percent. Once more the Fed paused, a decision vindicated over the summer when markets reacted to Brexit with a spectacular sell-off. A fact too often overlooked by those struggling to understand Hillary Clinton's defeat in November 2016 is the sheer nervousness about the US economy. Eight years on from 2008, the Sanders-Clinton-Trump contest was not set against the backdrop of a boom. So uncertain was the mood that the Fed did not consider it safe to raise rates until the end of the year, when the Trump bump was in full swing and the specter of global deflation had finally lifted.

II

In 2015–2016 the world economy dodged a third installment of the global crisis. The emerging market recessions remained confined to individual economies—Russia, Brazil, South Africa—and particular commodities—notably oil. The downturn did not become generalized. It did not spread to the advanced economies. The slow recovery of the eurozone, Britain and the United States continued. Too easily forgotten, this fact should frame our understanding of the extraordinary political and geopolitical turmoil of the years since 2013. In the Ukraine crisis the commodity price collapse even worked to the advantage of the West in multiplying the pressure of sanctions

on Russia. Meanwhile, the Greek drama of 2015, Brexit and Trump's election all took place against the backdrop of a nervous calm. We did not in 2017 face the full force of Paulson's question: How would America and the world have fared if Trump at his inauguration had faced the kind of challenges facing Obama in 2009?

But though crisis was avoided in 2015–2016, the stakes were going up. If we go back to the period before 2008, a "China crisis" had seemed in the cards then. But what worried observers was the possibility of a mass sell-off of dollar-denominated assets by China's reserve managers. As the storm clouds gathered, holding China in place was the first priority of Paulson's Treasury. And Paulson was willing to pay a high political price for doing so. Brad Setser's quip was to the point: Fannie Mae and Freddie Mac were "too Chinese to fail."[18] Nationalizing them helped to prevent a simultaneous Atlantic and Chinese crisis with consequences too awful to contemplate. But Paulson's financial diplomacy also highlights the fact that in 2008, managing Sino-American financial relations was still very much a matter of intergovernmental relations. By contrast, in 2015–2016 not only were the risks on the Chinese side but the people moving the money were private businesses and investors. In less than ten years, Chinese commercial and financial integration had come a staggeringly long way. Given the narrative unfolded in this book, this has daunting implications.

This book has examined the struggle to contain the crisis in three interlocking zones of deep private financial integration: the transatlantic dollar-based financial system, the eurozone and the post-Soviet sphere of Eastern Europe. The challenges were immense. The implosion entangled both public and private finances in a doom loop. Bank failures forced scandalous government intervention to rescue private oligopolists. The Fed acted across borders to provide liquidity to banks in other countries. The crisis spilled over into a question of international relations: Germany and Greece, the UK and the eurozone, the United States and the EU. And those questions were not posed in a power-political vacuum but in a geopolitical force field, graphically illustrated by the clashes with Russia over the destiny of Georgia and Ukraine. The challenges were mind-bogglingly technical and complex. They were vast in scale. They were fast moving. Between 2007 and 2012, the pressure was relentless.

In its own terms, as a capitalist stabilization effort, the response patched together by the US Treasury and the Fed was remarkably successful. Its aim was to restore the viability of the banks. It not only did that but also provided massive liquidity and monetary stimulus to the entire dollar-based financial system, to Europe and the emerging markets beyond. All the more telling was the inability of the Democratic Party that carried the brunt of the effort to capitalize in political terms. In fact, TARP and the bailouts became dirty words and the Fed suffered a spectacular loss of legitimacy. Overshadowed by memories of 2008, the 2016 election delivered a stark verdict. With Trump as president and the Republicans dominating Congress, it is an open question whether the American political system will support even basic institutions of globalization, let alone any adventurous crisis fighting at a national or global level.

Faced with this American abdication, one might once have suggested that the euro area could provide an alternative. But the failure of the ECB, Germany and France to devise a workable crisis-fighting strategy made the euro into a source of danger and instability for the world economy between 2010 and 2015. If it was saved, it was in large part due to outside pressure and assistance. Nor is it reassuring that the necessary measures were for a painfully long time resisted by Germany, the eurozone's most powerful member. Far from seeing Europe as a promising partner for global economic governance, Beijing and the rest of the G20 were repeatedly left wondering what on earth the Europeans were up to.[19] The Germans might reply that they were teaching discipline, forcing Europe to prepare for a future of global competition. But what use was that if not only Greece but Ireland, Portugal, Spain and Italy were overwhelmed by the immediate crisis? Finally, in 2012, what Monti politely referred to as the "mental block" was overcome. The ECB's newfound activism stabilized bond markets. But further progress on the essential financial underpinnings of banking union have been painfully slow and Berlin still blocks the path to the issuance by Europe of a common safe asset, aka eurobonds.[20] As ever, the Franco-German axis is key. In 2017 the vote for Macron was a vote for Europe. Not for Europe as it stands, but for a new course.[21] That depends on Germany. In May 2017, faced with the disaster of Trump's foreign policy, Merkel

declaimed the need for Europe to forge its own path. But whether Berlin will be a partner for such a project after the German elections of 2017 is an open question. The rise of the AfD is ominous. It is now largely known as a racist anti-immigrant and refugee party. But it had its origins in 2013 in furious right-wing reaction to Draghi and the ECB. No less consequential for Europe is the end of the grand coalition. The role of the FDP in Merkel's handling of the eurozone crisis in 2010–2012 was baneful, as was that of the right-wing CSU in Bavaria. At the time of writing, Europe waits for the formation of a new German government.

The transatlantic relationship is not built on money alone, of course. It is meshed with deep cultural, political, diplomatic and military relations. And those extended, or at least so it seemed, to Eastern Europe, which was so eagerly integrated into the EU and NATO in the early 2000s. In East Asia, America's alliance system was always more loosely knit. And the victory of the West in the cold war was far from complete. China's economic triumph is a triumph for the Communist Party. This is still the fundamental reason for doubting the possibility of truly deep cooperation with China in global economic governance. Unlike South Korea, Japan or Europe, China is not a subordinate part of the American global network. When the United States extended swap lines in 2008, it was acting in a zone that is both a depoliticized realm of economic activity and yet framed by a deep power relationship. The politics of Chinese foreign investment and suspicion of the role played by its state-owned enterprises suggest that deeply shared economic interests, of the kind that legitimated the Fed's swap lines for Europe, will be far harder to develop. And experience on the frontier of Western power in Eastern Europe hardly gives grounds for optimism about the ability of either Washington or the Europeans to conduct financial diplomacy in areas of real geopolitical tension. During the height of the crisis in 2008–2009, the West was, frankly, neglectful of Eastern Europe, despite the fact that talk of NATO expansion had led to a war with Russia in Georgia only weeks before the outbreak of the crisis in August 2008. In 2009, significantly, it was veterans of the George H. W. Bush administration who were warning that Eastern and Western Europe were once more at risk of dividing. Then, in 2013, the EU sleepwalked into confrontation with Putin

over Ukraine. And all of this at a moment when the Obama administration was pushing TPP, seen in Beijing as aggressive containment, and Japan and China were confronting each other over rocky islands in the East China Sea. No doubt the Trump administration is unpredictable, but it was on Obama's watch, with Hillary Clinton as secretary of state, that relations with Russia and China escalated to this degree. Russia survived sanctions because of its reserves. China's resources are far larger. Perhaps they are such that one does not need to envision a world of truly close cooperation between the Fed and the PBoC. But those Chinese reserves are the result of the system of financial regulation and exchange control that the West has for so long criticized. China's ability to stop the drain of its foreign exchange reserves involved a renewed tightening of those controls. In economic terms it was only partially successful. And within China itself it involves a power struggle between those parts of the elite whose primary concern is to get their wealth to safety and the regime managers struggling to preserve stability. Huge financial risks remain. As the great economist Abba Lerner once cuttingly remarked, "Economics has gained the title Queen of the Social Sciences by choosing solved political problems as its domain."[22] The future of China's political economy and its relations with the West do not belong to that domain.

III

The events of 2015–2016 in China recall another major theme of this book. Even to a regime as competent and well informed as that of China, the economic setbacks came suddenly and unexpectedly. We have various words for this—panic, crisis, freeze, implosion, run, sudden arrest, sudden stop, radical uncertainty—and all these descriptions of what has happened or has threatened to happen to the global financial system since 2007 point to one thing: the fact that on top of the structural, slow-moving tensions that global integration may generate, it also produces sudden ruptures, events that cannot be fully accounted for or reduced to structural terms, or regulated by law. These crises are hard to predict or define in advance. They are

not anticipated and often deeply complex. And they are urgent. Such mo-
ments demand counteracting intervention. They demand action. It is this
juxtaposition that frames the narrative of this book: large organizations,
structures and processes on the one hand; decision, debate, argument and
action on the other.

One way to think of such moments is in terms of the metaphors of emer-
gency, or of firefighting. Among American crisis fighters, military vocabulary
was commonplace: maximum force, the Powell Doctrine, shock and awe, big
bazooka. But one might also say that what is called for is that intangible and
volatile thing, political leadership and action. This depends on formulating
plans and programs, rallying support and fending off opposition.

When the financial crisis escalated in the waning days of the Bush
administration in 2008, doubts about American leadership were rife. And
as far as the Republican Party was concerned, they were amply justified. At
that critical moment the Republican Party failed as the bracket between its
mass base and the imperatives of systemic stabilization. It was that experi-
ence that Paulson saw reenacted in even more extreme form in 2016, in the
disempowerment of the Republican elite and the selection of Trump as
candidate. In 2008 the systemic interest in a bailout was obvious. It ex-
tended across the Atlantic. But in its political essentials it took a fragile
cross-party coalition assembled by elite Republicans and the Democratic
Party leadership to hold the United States together and provide the under-
pinnings for the global stabilization efforts of the Fed and the Treasury.
America's subsequent political polarization and Trump's election in 2016
throw the historic significance of that coalition once more into stark relief.

This is the American side of the drama. As such it has global significance.
But it has its counterparts everywhere touched by the crisis. In Europe and
in Asia too. The eurozone crisis posed the question over and over again. How
could coalitions be assembled for unpopular but essential actions? Whose
will, stamina, endurance, interests and willingness to compromise would
prevail? It is shocking, perhaps, that this degree of indeterminacy should
characterize one of the most vital pivots of the global order. But building such
ad hoc and lopsided political coalitions is what the governance of capitalism
under democratic conditions entails. In the twentieth century, it was what

made the difference between the Treaty of Versailles and the Marshall Plan, or Herbert Hoover's and FDR's responses to the Great Depression. The political in "political economy" demands to be taken seriously.

Since 2007 the scale of the financial crisis has placed that relationship between democratic politics and the demands of capitalist governance under immense strain. Above all, this strain has manifested itself not in a crisis of popular participation, or the ultimate control of policy by elected leaders, but in a crisis in the political parties that have historically mediated the two. It has tested their programs, their coherence and their ability to mobilize support, and they have been found wanting. In many countries this has swept away the moderate parties of the Left, in Greece and France most notably. They paid the price for their inability to constructively counter the stresses of the eurozone crisis. In the Bundestag election of 2017, both of the two main parties in Germany, widely seen as the country that came through the crisis least affected, slumped to historic lows in popularity. In the United States and Britain it is the mainstream parties of the Right that have suffered the critical fracture, with dramatic consequences in the form of Brexit and potentially even more far-reaching implications from the increasing incoherence of the Republicans in the United States. The GOP commands an impressive vote-winning organization, a take-no-prisoners media machine, deep fund-raising resources. But to judge by the record of the last ten years, it is incapable of legislating or cooperating effectively in government.

Given the once fashionable view that we live in an age of postdemocracy, or even postpolitics, the significance of these strictly political developments comes as something of a surprise. By dint of their massive weight, complex social systems such as the financial markets, and apparatuses like the modern state and the interstate system that it inhabits, create a sense of solidity. They make us doubt whether they could possibly be amenable to political agency, decision or debate. We suspect technocratic preemption and usurpation around every corner and often with good reason. There are ways of describing the operations of these systems that void the presence of politics. But if a history such as this has any purpose, it is to reveal the poverty of such accounts. Political choice, ideology and agency are everywhere across this narrative with highly consequential results, not merely as

disturbing factors but as vital reactions to the huge volatility and contingency generated by the malfunctioning of the giant "systems" and "machines" and apparatuses of financial engineering. Success and failure, stability and crisis, can indeed pivot on particular moments of choice. It is not for nothing that we refer to a "Lehman moment." And there were others: Deauville; Cannes 2011; "whatever it takes"; not to mention the Brexit referendum or the jaw-dropping American election of November 2016.

Back to the 1500s and the conjoined birth of capitalism and the modern state system, such moments of decision, contingency, choice and attendant drama have been constitutive of our sense of modern history. Though that sense of history might temporarily have been in abeyance after 1989, it has returned with a bang. Such moments are the coordinates of memory and commemoration. They motivate action: After September 15, 2008, avoiding another Lehman became an idée fixe of crisis managers around the world. They make up the timeline of narration and history. They define anniversaries, triggering debate and reexamination. Given the turmoil of the early twentieth century, the early twenty-first century is crowded with centennials. In 2014 came the biggest of them all: the centennial of 1914. Commemoration and discussion of the outbreak of World War I was attended with profound interest around the world. Historians recalled the Urtrauma of the twentieth century.[23] And they did so against the backdrop of conflict in Ukraine and East Asia that made the lessons of 1914 seem particularly pertinent. In a less literal way, 1914 may also be a good way for thinking about the kind of historical problem that the financial crisis of 2008 represents.

There is a striking similarity between the questions we ask about 1914 and 2008.[24] How does a great moderation end? How do huge risks build up that are little understood and barely controllable? How do great tectonic shifts in the global order unload in sudden earthquakes? How do the "railway timetables" of giant technical systems combine to create disaster? How do anachronistic and out-of-date frames of reference make it impossible for us to understand what is happening around us? Did we sleepwalk into crisis, or were there dark forces pushing? Who is to blame for the ensuing human-induced, man-made disaster? Is the uneven and combined development of global capitalism the driver of all instability? How do the passions

of popular politics shape elite decision making? How do politicians exploit those passions? Is there any route to international and domestic order? Can we achieve perpetual stability and peace? Does law offer the answer? Or must we rely on the balance of terror and the judgment of technicians and generals?

These are the questions that we have asked about 1914 for the last one hundred years. It is not by accident that their analogues are also the questions we ask about 2008 and its aftermath. They are the questions that haunt the great crises of modernity.

NOTES

INTRODUCTION: THE FIRST CRISIS OF A GLOBAL AGE

1. http://www.un.org/en/ga/63/generaldebate/brazil.shtml.
2. http://www.un.org/en/ga/63/generaldebate/pdf/usa_en.pdf.
3. http://www.un.org/en/ga/63/generaldebate/pdf/philippines_en.pdf.
4. http://www.un.org/en/ga/63/generaldebate/argentina.shtml.
5. http://www.un.org/press/en/2008/080923_Sarkozy.doc.htm.
6. http://www.un.org/en/ga/63/generaldebate/pdf/uk_en.pdf.
7. P. H. Gordon and J. Shapiro, *Allies at War: America, Europe, and the Crisis over Iraq* (New York: McGraw-Hill, 2004).
8. J. Habermas and J. Derrida, "February 15, or What Binds Europe Together: Plea for a Common Foreign Policy, Beginning in Core Europe," *Frankfurter Allgemeine Zeitung*, May 31, 2003, in *Old Europe, New Europe, Core Europe*, ed. D. Levy, M. Pensky, and J. Torpey (London: Verso, 2005).
9. T. Purdum, "It Came from Wasilla," *Vanity Fair* 39 (2009).
10. G. Jarvie, D. Hwang and M. Brennan, *Sport, Revolution, and the Beijing Olympics*, (Oxford: Bloomsbury Academic, 2008); and M. E. Price and D. Dayan, *Owning the Olympics: Narratives of the New China* (Ann Arbor: University of Michigan Press, 2011).
11. G. Toal, *Near Abroad: Putin, the West and the Contest over Ukraine and the Caucasus* (New York: Oxford University Press, 2017).
12. D. Trump, "Remarks of President Donald J. Trump—As Prepared for Delivery, Inaugural Address" (speech, Washington, DC, January 20, 2017), https://www.whitehouse.gov/inaugural-address; and for video, http://www.cnn.com/videos/politics/2017/01/20/trump-speech-america-first-sot.cnn.
13. For an excellent sociopyschological approach to the consequences of the crisis in the United States and Britain, see T. Clark, *Hard Times: Inequality, Recession, Aftermath* (New Haven, CT: Yale University Press, 2014).
14. A. S. Blinder, *After the Music Stopped* (New York: Penguin, 2014), is simultaneously the best economist's account of the crisis and exclusively American. And G. Packer, *The Unwinding: An Inner History of the New America* (New York: Farrar, Straus and Giroux, 2013).

15. In deep agreement with L. Panitchin and S. Gindin, *The Making of Global Capitalism: The Political Economy of American Empire* (London: Verso, 2012); E. S. Prasad, *The Dollar Trap: How the US Dollar Tightened Its Grip on Global Finance* (Princeton, NJ: Princeton University Press, 2014); H. M. Schwartz, *Subprime Nation: American Power, Global Capital, and the Housing Bubble* (Ithaca, NY: Cornell University Press, 2009); and P. Gowan, "Crisis in the Heartland," *New Left Review* 55 (2009), 5–29.

16. I. Bremmer, "The Return of State Capitalism," *Survival* 50 (2008) 55–64; and J. Gyriel, "The Return of Europe's Nation-States: The Upside of the EU's Crisis," *Foreign Affairs* 95 (2016), 94.

17. Attributed to Douglas Adams of *Hitchhiker's Guide to the Galaxy* fame, the notion of a "sudden stop" was introduced into international economics by way of G. A. Calvo, "Capital Flows and Capital-Market Crises: The Simple Economics of Sudden Stops," *Journal of Applied Economics* 1 (November 1998), 35–54.

18. A. Tooze, *Statistics and the German State: The Making of Modern Economic Knowledge* (Cambridge: Cambridge University Press, 2001); and T. Mitchell, *Rule of Experts* (Berkeley: University of California Press, 2001).

19. R. Skidelsky, *Keynes: The Return of the Master* (New York: PublicAffairs, 2010).

20. Paul Krugman has vigorously and convincingly defended the 1930s-era IS-LM as essential to understanding the mechanics of the recession and the sluggish recovery; see P. Krugman, "IS-LMentary" (*Conscience of a Liberal Blog*), *New York Times*, October 9, 2011, and "Economics in the Crisis" (*Conscience of a Liberal Blog*), *New York Times*, March 5, 2012.

21. R. Baldwin, "Global Supply Chains: Why They Emerged, Why They Matter, and Where They Are Going," in *Global Value Chains in a Changing World*, ed. D. K. Elms and P. Low (Geneva: WTO, 2013), 13–60.

22. H. S. Shin, "Globalisation: Real and Financial," BIS 87th Annual General Meeting, https://www.bis.org/speeches/sp170625b_slides.pdf.

23. M. Obstfeld and A. M. Taylor, "International Monetary Relations: Taking Finance Seriously" (*CEPR Discussion Paper No. DP12079*, June 2017), https://ssrn.com/abstract =2980858.

24. Some of the key texts are T. Adrian and H. S. Shin, "Liquidity and Leverage," *Journal of Financial Intermediation* 19 (July 2010), 418–437; C. Borio and P. Disyatat, "Global Imbalances and the Financial Crisis: Link or No Link?" (BIS Working Paper 346, 2011); and S. Avdjiev, R. N. McCauly and H. S. Shin, "Breaking Free of the Triple Coincidence in International Finance," *Economic Policy* 31 (2016), 409–451.

25. Paradigmatically, D. Yergin and J. Stanislaw, *The Commanding Heights: The Battle for the World Economy* (New York: Simon & Schuster, 2002).

26. B. Bernanke, "The Great Moderation," Eastern Economic Association, Washington, DC, February 20, 2004.

27. In place of many, D. Harvey, *A Brief History of Neoliberalism* (New York: Oxford University Press, 2007).

28. Summarizing a complex multistranded literature, G. Ingham, *The Nature of Money* (Cambridge: Polity, 2004).

29. In place of many, A. Roberts, *The Logic of Discipline: Global Capitalism and the Architecture of Government* (New York: Oxford University Press, 2011).

30. "Re-Thinking the Lender of Last Resort" (BIS Working Paper 79, September 2014), available at SSRN: https://ssrn.com/abstract=2504682.

31. Whereas the swap lines involving trillions of dollars receive no more than a series of passing mentions, an entire chapter is devoted to AIG in B. Bernanke, *Courage to Act* (New York: W. W. Norton, 2015), 270–291.

32. D. Coyle, *GDP: A Brief but Affectionate History* (Princeton, NJ: Princeton University Press, 2015); P. Lepenies, *The Power of a Single Number: A Political History of GDP* (New

Royal Borough of Windsor and Maidenhead

Maidenhead Library
St Ives Road
Maidenhead, SL6 1QU
Tel. 01628 796969

Kiosk 1

Self Service Receipt for Check Out

Name: ***********1293

Title: Crashed : how a decade of
financial crises changed the world

Item: 9580000087051

Due Back: Borrow Successful

Total Check Out: 0
18/00/2019 13:16:46

Books and audio-books: 3 week loan
DVDs and magazines: 1 week loan

Thank you for using self service
To renew items go online at
www3.rbwm.gov.uk/libraries
Automated renewal line 0303 123 0035
or phone us on 01628 796969

York: Columbia University Press, 2016); and T. E. Shenk, "Inventing the American Economy," Columbia University Academic Commons (PhD, 2016), https://doi.org/10.7916 /D8NZ87N1.

33. From the French side, this is noted by M. Roche, *Histoire secrète d'un krach qui dure* (Paris: Albin-Michel, 2016). For the German repression of the crisis, see L. Müller, *Bank-Räuber: Wie kriminelle Manager und unfähige Politiker uns in den Ruin treiben* (Berlin: Econ, 2010).

34. See Marco Buti at the European Institute, Columbia, April 2016, see https://www.you tube.com/watch?v=7aGtNbmvmTs.

35. In refusing to accept that either theories of optimum currency or divergent growth regimes doom the euro and in focusing on finance, the interpretation offered here agrees with M. Sandbu, *Europe's Orphan: The Future of the Euro and the Politics of Debt* (Princeton, NJ: Princeton University Press, 2015); E. Jones, "The Forgotten Financial Union: How You Can Have a Euro Crisis Without a Euro," in *The Future of the Euro*, ed. M. Matthijs and M. Blyth (New York: Oxford University Press, 2015); E. Jones, "Getting the Story Right: How You Should Choose Between Different Interpretations of the European Crisis (and Why You Should Care)," *Journal of European Integration* 37.7 (2015), 817–832; and W. Schelkle, *The Political Economy of Monetary Solidarity: Understanding the Euro Experiment* (Oxford: Oxford University Press, 2017).

36. T. Wieser quoted in C. Gammelin and R. Löw, *Europas Strippenzieher: Wer in Brüssel Wirklich Regiert* (Berlin: Econ, 2014), 65.

37. M. Blyth, *Austerity: The History of a Dangerous Idea* (Oxford: Oxford University Press, 2013), 73.

38. As acknowledged with admirable frankness in T. F. Geithner, *Stress Test: Reflections on Financial Crises* (New York: Crown, 2015).

39. For the essential importance of the idea of a "muddle" for Keynesian liberalism, see G. Mann, *In the Long Run We Are All Dead: Keynesianism, Political Economy, and Revolution* (London: Verso, 2017).

40. "From Clout to Rout: Why European Companies Have Become a Fading Force in Global Business," *Economist*, June 30, 2016.

41. M. Fratzscher, *Die Deutschland-Illusion: Warum wir unsere Wirtschaft überschätzen und Europa brauchen* (München: Carl Hanser, 2014); J. Bibow, "The Euro Debt Crisis and Germany's Euro Trilemma," *Levy Economics Institute* (Working Paper 721, May 2012); and S. Dullien, "A German Model for Europe?," *European Council on Foreign Relations*, July 2013.

42. "CSU für Apple, Linke gegen Steuerdeals," *Neues Deutschland*, September 1, 2016.

43. J. B. Stewart, "Deutsche Bank as Next Lehman Brothers: Far-Fetched but Not Unthinkable," *New York Times*, October 6, 2016.

44. C. Goodhart and D. Schoenmaker, "The United States Dominates Global Investment Banking. Does It Matter for Europe?," *Bruegel Policy Contribution* (2016).

45. "Special Report: How Mario Draghi Is Reshaping Europe's Central Bank," *Reuters*, January 9, 2013; and L. Elliott, "Take a Bow Mario Draghi—Has the ECB Chief Saved the Eurozone?," *Guardian*, June 8, 2017.

46. Z. Micah, "The Myth of the Indispensable Nation," *Foreign Policy*, November 6, 2014.

47. D. W. Drexner, *The System Worked: How the World Stopped Another Great Depression* (Oxford: Oxford University Press, 2014).

48. E. Helleiner, *The Status Quo Crisis: Global Financial Governance After the 2008 Meltdown* (Oxford: Oxford University Press, 2014).

49. B. Eichengreen, *Hall of Mirrors: The Great Depression, the Great Recession, and the Uses and Misuses of History* (Oxford: Oxford University Press, 2015).

50. T. Frank, *Listen, Liberal: Or, Whatever Happened to the Party of the People?* (New York: Macmillan, 2016).

51. Among many, two particularly thoughtful pieces are W. Davies, "The Age of Post-Truth Politics," *New York Times*, August 24, 2016; and A. M. Rondón, "Donald Trump's Fictional America," *Politico*, April 2, 2017, https://www.politico.com/magazine/story/2017/04/donald-trumps-fictional-america-post-fact-venezuela-214973.
52. C. Forelle, "Luxembourg Lies on Secret Meeting," *Wall Street Journal*, May 9, 2011.

CHAPTER 1: THE "WRONG CRISIS"

1. Conference moderated by P. Orszag, "Restoring America's Promise of Opportunity, Prosperity and Growth," Brookings Institution, Washington, DC, 2006, http://www.hamiltonproject.org/assets/legacy/files/downloads_and_links/Restoring_Americas_Promise_of_Opportunity_Prosperity_and_Growth_Transcript.pdf.
2. R. Rubin, *In an Uncertain World: Tough Choices from Wall Street to Washington* (New York: Random House, 2003); and N. Prins, *All the Presidents' Bankers: The Hidden Alliances That Drive American Power* (New York: Nation Books, 2014).
3. R. Altman, P. Orszag, J. Bordoff and R. Rubin, "An Economic Strategy to Advance Opportunity, Prosperity, and Growth," The Hamilton Project, April 2006, http://www.hamiltonproject.org/assets/legacy/files/downloads_and_links/An_Economic_Strategy_to_Advance_Opportunity_Prosperity_and_Growth.pdf.
4. For a dissection of video footage of Obama's performance, see https://www.nakedcapitalism.com/2013/04/obama-at-the-hamilton-project-2006-this-is-not-a-bloodless-process.html.
5. Orszag, "Restoring America's Promise."
6. Joint Committee on Taxation Estimated Budget Effects of the Conference Agreement for H.R. 1836, May 26, 2001, JCX-51-01.
7. P. Blustein, "Reagan's Record," *Wall Street Journal*, October 21, 1985.
8. S. M. Kosiak, *Cost of the Wars in Iraq and Afghanistan, and Other Military Operations Through 2008 and Beyond*, CSBA, December 15, 2008; and J. Stiglitz and L. Bilmes, *The Three Trillion Dollar War* (New York: W. W. Norton, 2008).
9. T. Oatley, *A Political Economy of American Hegemony: Buildups, Booms, and Busts* (New York: CUP, 2015).
10. Data from https://www.cbo.gov/about/products/budget-economic-data#2.
11. A. Sinai, P. Orszag and R. Rubin, "Sustained Budget Deficits: Longer-Run US Economic Performance and the Risk of Financial and Fiscal Disarray," Brookings Institution, January 5, 2004.
12. See the highly influential account by B. Woodward, *The Agenda: Inside the Clinton White House* (New York: Simon & Schuster, 1994).
13. D. Wessel and T. T. Vogel Jr., "Arcane World of Bonds Is Guide and Beacon to a Populist President," *Wall Street Journal*, February 25, 1993, A1.
14. "The Long-Term Budget Outlook," CBO, Washington, DC, 2005, 26. For a Republican view see L. Ball and N. G. Mankiw, "What Do Budget Deficits Do?," NBER Working Paper 5263, September 1995.
15. An essential claim common to P. Anderson, *American Foreign Policy and Its Thinkers* (London: Verso, 2015); and A. Negri and M. Hardt, *Empire* (Cambridge, MA: Harvard University Press, 2000).
16. The phrase is Robert Zoellick's, then deputy secretary of state, as found in R. Zoellick, "Whither China? From Membership to Responsibility," New York, September 21, 2005 (New York: NCUSCR, 2005), https://2001-2009.state.gov/s/d/former/zoellick/rem/53682.htm.
17. M. J. Dunne, *American Wheels, Chinese Roads: The Story of General Motors in China* (Singapore: Wiley, 2011).
18. Z. Wang, *Never Forget National Humiliation: Historical Memory in Chinese Politics and Foreign Relations* (New York: Columbia University Press, 2012).

19. M. Mandelbaum, *Mission Failure: America and the World in the Post–Cold War Era* (Oxford: Oxford University Press, 2016).

20. Linking his distinctive approach to the hierarchical nature of money, shadow banking and the "money view" see the presentation by Perry Mehrling, "Shadow Banking, Central Banking, and the Future of Global Finance," City University London, February 2, 2013, https://www.city.ac.uk/__data/assets/pdf_file/0018/163440/Mehrling_Future -Global-Finance-126sn0t.pdf.

21. E. Ilzetkzi, C. M. Reinhart and K. S. Rogoff, "Exchange Arrangements Entering the 21st Century: Which Anchor Will Hold?," (NBER Working Paper 23134, 2017).

22. M. Pettis, *The Volatility Machine: Emerging Economies and the Threat of Financial Collapse* (New York: Oxford University Press, 2001).

23. *Time* (cover), February 1999; and Rubin and Weisberg, *In an Uncertain World*.

24. G. A. Calvo, "Sudden Stop, Financial Factors and Economic Collapse in Latin America" (NBER Working Paper 11153, 2005).

25. "The Argentine Crisis, 2001–2002," Rabobank, August 23, 2013, https://economics .rabobank.com/publications/2013/august/the-argentine-crisis-20012002-/.

26. M. Wolf, *Fixing Global Finance* (Baltimore: Johns Hopkins University Press, 2008).

27. M. P. Dooley, D. Folkerts Landau and P. Garber, "The Revived Bretton Woods System," *International Journal of Finance & Economics* 9 (2004), 307–313.

28. D. A. Steinberg, "Why Has China Accumulated Such Large Foreign Reserves?," in *The Great Wall of Money: Power and Politics in China's International Monetary Relations*, ed. E. Helleiner and J. Kirshner (Ithaca, NY: Cornell University Press, 2014), 71.

29. E. M. Truman, "Sovereign Wealth Funds: The Need for Greater Transparency and Accountability," Peterson Institute for International Economics, August 2007, https://piie .com/publications/pb/pb07-6.pdf.

30. P. G. Peterson, "Riding for a Fall," *Foreign Affairs* (September/October 2004), https:// www.foreignaffairs.com/articles/united-states/2004-09-01/riding-fall.

31. N. Roubini, "The US as a Net Debtor: The Sustainability of the US External Imbalances," November 2004, http://people.stern.nyu.edu/nroubini/papers/Roubini-Setser -US-External-Imbalances.pdf.

32. S. Edwards, "Is the US Current Account Deficit Sustainable? And If Not, How Costly Is Adjustment Likely to Be?" (NBER Working Paper 11541, August 2005).

33. N. Ferguson and M. Schularick, "'Chimerica' and the Global Asset Market Boom," *International Finance* 10 (2007), 215–239, http://onlinelibrary.wiley.com/doi/10.1111/j .1468-2362.2007.00210.x/abstract.

34. Ferguson and Schularick, "'Chimerica.'"

35. L. H. Summers, "The United States and the Global Adjustment Process" (speech, Stavros S. Niarchos Lecture Institute, Washington, DC, 2004).

36. R. Suskind, *The Price of Loyalty: George W. Bush, the White House, and the Education of Paul O'Neill* (New York: Simon & Schuster, 2004), 291–292.

37. B. Delong, "I Belong to No Organized Political Party," *Grasping Reality with Both Hands* (blog), November 2006, http://www.bradford-delong.com/2006/11/index.html.

38. A. Berman, *Herding Donkeys: The Fight to Rebuild the Democratic Party and Reshape American Politics* (New York: Picador, 2010).

39. The quotation is from Matthew Yglesias in B. Delong, "I Belong to No Organized Political Party."

40. "Brad Delong: The Democrats' Line in the Sand," *Economist's View*, June 30, 2008, http://economistsview.typepad.com/economistsview/2008/06/brad-delong-the.html.

41. L. R. Jacobs and D. King, *Fed Power: How Finance Wins* (Oxford: Oxford University Press, 2016).

42. Minutes of the Federal Open Market Committee (FOMC) meeting, June 29–30, 2004, https://www.federalreserve.gov/fomc/minutes/20040630.htm.

43. The so-called Mundell-Fleming model of open economy macroeconomics originated already in the 1960s, see J. M. Boughton, "On the Origins of the Fleming-Mundell Model" (*IMF Staff Papers* 50, 2003), 1–9.
44. B. Bernanke, "The Global Saving Glut and the US Current Account Deficit," No. 77, Board of Governors of the Federal Reserve System (US), 2005.
45. B. Bernanke, "On Milton Friedman's Ninetieth Birthday" (conference to honor Milton Friedman, November 8, 2002).
46. M. Friedman and A. J. Schwartz, *A Monetary History of the United States, 1867–1960* (Princeton, NJ: Princeton University Press, 2008), 407–414.
47. Ben S. Bernanke, "Constrained Discretion and Monetary Policy," remarks before the Money Marketeers of New York (New York: New York University, 2003).
48. B. Applebaum, "Bernanke, as Professor, Tries to Buff Fed's Image," *New York Times*, March 20, 2012, and B. Bernanke, "The Federal Reserve and the Financial Crisis Origins and Mission of the Federal Reserve," Lecture 1, George Washington University School of Business, March 20, 2012.
49. T. Adams, "The US View on IMF Reform" (Conference on IMF reform, September 23, 2005), https://piie.com/commentary/speeches-papers/us-view-imf-reform.
50. P. Blustein, *Off Balance: The Travails of Institutions That Govern the Global Financial System* (Waterloo, Ontario: CIGI, 2013), 51–66.
51. "Paulson May Be Bringing Heft to China Currency Drive," *Taipei Times*, June 1, 2006.
52. One powerful advocate for a G2 approach was the influential Fred Bergsten; see "A Partnership of Equals: How Washington Should Respond to China's Economic Challenge," *Foreign Affairs* 87 (July/August, 2008): 57–69.
53. "Fact Sheet Creation of the US-China Strategic Economic Dialogue," *US Department of the Treasury,* September 20, 2006, https://www.treasury.gov/press-center/press-releases/Pages/hp107.aspx. H. M. Paulson Jr., "A Strategic Economic Engagement: Strengthening US-Chinese Ties," *Foreign Affairs* 87 (September/October 2008), 59–77.
54. For the quotes that follow, see "The Panic About the Dollar," *Economist,* November 29, 2007; G. Steingart, "A Pearl Harbor Without War," *Der Spiegel,* November 13, 2007; "Supermodel 'Rejects Dollar Pay,'" *BBC News,* November 6, 2007; M. Nizza, "Heads Turn over Model's Disputed Dollar," *New York Times,* November 6, 2007; "Gisele Bundchen Doesn't Want to Be Paid in Dollars," *Fox News,* November 5, 2007; C. Giles, "Adjustment or Affliction?," *Financial Times,* December 10, 2007; and D. Usborne, "Rappers Join Models in Insisting on Euros as Greenbacks Fall Further Out of Fashion," *Independent,* November 17, 2007.
55. P. Krugman, "Will There Be a Dollar Crisis?," *Economic Policy* 22 (2007), 436–467.
56. D. W. Drezner, "Bad Debts: Assessing China's Financial Influence in Great Power Politics," *International Security* 34 (Fall 2009), 7–45.
57. J. B. DeLong, "The Wrong Financial Crisis," *Vox,* October 10, 2008.

CHAPTER 2: SUBPRIME

1. Y. Barnes, "Around the World in Dollars and Cents," *Savills World Research,* 2016, http://pdf.euro.savills.co.uk/global-research/around-the-world-in-dollars-and-cents-2016.pdf.
2. Congressional Budget Office, "Housing Wealth and Consumer Spending Report," 110th Cong., January 2007.
3. UNCTAD, *Trade and Development Report 2010,* New York, 44.
4. O. Jordà, M. Schularick and A. M. Taylor, "Betting the House," Federal Reserve Bank of San Francisco, June 2014.
5. O. Jordà, M. Schularick and A. M. Taylor, "The Great Mortgaging: Housing Finance, Crises and Business Cycles," *Economic Policy* 31 (September 2014), 107–152.
6. W. L. Silber, *Volcker: The Triumph of Persistence* (New York: Bloomsbury Press, 2012), 125–215.

7. L. Silk, "The Interest Rate Issue," *New York Times,* July 21, 1981.
8. On the politics of this moment, see S. Eich and A. Tooze, "The Great Inflation," in *Vorgeschichte der Gegenwart: Dimensionen des Strukturbruchs nach dem Boom,* ed. A. Doering-Manteuffel, L. Raphael and T. Schlemmer (Göttingen: Vandenhoek & Ruprecht, 2015).
9. Remarks by Governor Ben S. Bernanke, "The Great Moderation," at the meetings of the Eastern Economic Association, Washington, DC, February 20, 2004. For a review of the literature that Bernanke was drawing on see James H. Stock and Mark W. Watson, "Has the Business Cycle Changed and Why?," *NBER Macroeconomics Annual* 17 (2002), 159–218.
10. R. K. Green and S. M. Wachter, "The American Mortgage in Historical and International Context," *Journal of Economic Perspectives* 19 (2005), 93–114.
11. Simplifying a more complicated story analyzed in W. H. Starbuck and P. N. Pant, "Trying to Help S&Ls: How Organizations with Good Intentions Jointly Enacted Disaster," in *Organizational Decision Making,* ed. Z. Shapira (Cambridge: Cambridge University Press, 1996), 35–60.
12. T. Curry and L. Shibut, "The Costs of the Savings and Loan Crisis: Truth and Consequences," *FDIC Banking Review,* https://www.fdic.gov/bank/analytical/banking/2000dec /brv13n2_2.pdf.
13. Schwartz, *Subprime Nation,* 96–101.
14. R. K. Green and A. B. Schnare, "The Rise and Fall of Fannie Mae and Freddie Mac: Lessons Learned and Options for Reform," No. 8521, USC Lusk Center for Real Estate, 2009.
15. R. Rothstein, *The Color of Law: A Forgotten History of How Our Government Segregated America* (New York: W. W. Norton, 2017).
16. J. B. Judis and R. Teixeira, *The Emerging Democratic Majority* (New York: Macmillan, 2002).
17. The most influential statement of the case is C. W. Calomiris and S. H. Haber, *Fragile by Design: The Political Origins of Banking Crises and Scarce Credit* (Princeton, NJ: Princeton University Press, 2014). For a critical review, see M. Konzcal, "Guest Post: A Review of *Fragile by Design,*" Roosevelt Institute, November 3, 2017.
18. D. Jaffee and J. M. Quigley, "The Future of the Government Sponsored Enterprises: The Role for Government in the US Mortgage Market" (NBER Working Paper 17685, Cambridge, MA, 2011).
19. N. Fligstein and A. Goldstein, "A Long Strange Trip: The State and Mortgage Securitization, 1968–2010," in *The Oxford Handbook of the Sociology of Finance,* ed. A. Preda and K. Knorr-Cetina (Oxford: Oxford University Press, 2012), 339–356.
20. The story is well told in M. Lewis, *Liar's Poker* (New York: W. W. Norton, 2010); and B. McLean and J. Nocera, *All the Devils Are Here: The Hidden History of the Financial Crisis* (New York: Penguin, 2010).
21. K. Dennis, "The Ratings Game," *University of Miami Law Review* 63 (2008–2009); and L. J. White, "The Credit-Rating Agencies and the Subprime Debacle," *Critical Review* 21 (2009), 2–3, 389–399.
22. N. Fligstein and A. Goldstein, "The Anatomy of the Mortgage Securitization Crisis," in *Markets on Trial: The Economic Sociology of the US Financial Crisis, Part A,* ed. M. Lounsbury and P. M. Hirsch (Bingley: Emerald Group, 2010), 29–70.
23. Jaffee and Quigley, "The Future of the Government Sponsored Enterprises."
24. A. B. Ashcraft and T. Schuermann, "Understanding the Securitization of Subprime Mortgage Credit," *Federal Reserve Bank of New York Staff Reports* 318 (March 2008).
25. A. Goldstein and N. Fligstein, "The Transformation of Mortgage Finance and the Industrial Roots of the Mortgage Meltdown," *Mimeo,* 2014.
26. P. Gowan, *The Global Gamble: Washington's Faustian Bid for World Dominance* (London: Verso, 1999).

27. P. Augar, *The Greed Merchants: How the Investment Banks Played the Free Market Game* (London: Penguin, 2005).

28. G. Tett, *Fool's Gold: The Inside Story of J.P. Morgan and How Wall St. Greed Corrupted Its Bold Dream and Created Financial Catastrophe* (New York: Free Press, 2009).

29. G. Krippner, *Capitalizing on Crisis: The Political Origins of the Rise of Finance* (Cambridge, MA: Harvard University Press, 2011).

30. Z. Pozsar, "Institutional Cash Pools and the Triffin Dilemma of the US Banking System" (*IMF Working Paper* 11/109, August 2011).

31. P. Gowan, "Crisis in the Heartland," *New Left Review* 55 (January/February 2009).

32. Augar, *Greed Merchants*, 34.

33. Tobias T. Adrian and H. S. Shin, "Liquidity and Lleverage," *Journal of Financial Intermediation* 19 (2010), 418–437.

34. D. MacKenzie, *An Engine, Not a Camera: How Financial Models Shape Markets* (Cambridge, MA: MIT Press, 2006), 211–242.

35. G. F. Davis and M. S. Mizruchi, "The Money Center Cannot Hold: Commercial Banks in the US System of Corporate Governance," *Administrative Science Quarterly* 44 (June 1999), 215–239.

36. The following is based on Goldstein and Fligstein, "The Transformation of Mortgage Finance."

37. K. Grind, *The Lost Bank: The Story of Washington Mutual—the Biggest Bank Failure in American History* (New York: Simon & Schuster, 2012).

38. A. Blundell-Wignall, P. Atkinson and S. H. Lee, "The Current Financial Crisis: Causes and Policy Issues," *OECD Financial Market Trends* (2008). As the authors stress, "2004 is critical in thinking about causality."

39. W. Poole, "The GSEs: Where Do We Stand?," *Federal Reserve Bank of St. Louis Review* 95 (November/December 2013), 601–611.

40. An outstanding introduction to the economics of structured finance and the crisis generally is A. Milne, *The Fall of the House of Credit: What Went Wrong in Banking and What Can Be Done to Repair the Damage?* (Cambridge: Cambridge University Press, 2009).

41. Summarizing the safe assets shortage literature, R. J. Caballero, E. Farhi and P. Gourinchas, "The Safe Assets Shortage Conundrum," *Journal of Economic Perspectives* 31 (Summer 2017), 29–46.

42. D. Clement, "Interview with Gary Gorton," Federal Reserve Bank of Minneapolis, December 1, 2010.

43. G. Gorton, "The History and Economics of Safe Assets" (NBER Working Paper 22210, April 2016).

44. Goldstein and Fligstein, "Transformation"; V. V. Acharya, P. Schnabl and G. Suarez, "Securitization Without Risk Transfer," *Journal of Financial Economics* 107 (2013), 515–536; and E. Engelen et al., *After the Great Complacence: Financial Crisis and the Politics of Reform* (Oxford: Oxford University Press, 2011), 61.

45. Tett, *Fool's Gold*, 124–143.

46. V. V. Acharya, P. Schnabl and G. Suarez, "Securitization Without Risk Transfer."

47. T. Adrian and H. S. Shin, "Financial Intermediaries and Monetary Economics," *Federal Reserve Bank of New York Staff Reports* 398 (revised May 2010).

48. T. Adrian et al., "Repo and Securities Lending," *Federal Reserve Bank of New York Staff Reports* 529 (revised February 2013).

49. G. B. Gorton and A. Metrick, "Who Ran on Repo?" (NBER Working Paper 18455, October 2012).

50. E. Callan, "Lehman Brothers—Leverage Analysis," Lehman Brothers, April 7, 2008, https://web.stanford.edu/~jbulow/Lehmandocs/docs/DEBTORS/LBEX-DOCID %201401225.pdf.

51. S. Olster, "How the Roof Fell In on Countrywide," *Fortune*, December 23, 2010.

52. Ibid.

53. Engelen et al., *After the Great Complacence*, 56.

54. https://web.archive.org/web/20090226105739/http://oversight.house.gov/documents/20081022112154.pdf.

55. "Ker-ching: The Thorny Issue of Bankers' Bonuses," *Economist*, January 26, 2008.

56. A. Haughwout et al., "'Flip This House': Investor Speculation and the Housing Bubble," *Liberty Street Economics* (blog), Federal Reserve Bank of New York, December 5, 2011.

57. R. G. Rajan, "Has Financial Development Made the World Riskier?" (NBER Working Paper 11728, November 2005).

58. M. D. Knight, "General Discussion: Has Financial Development Made the World Riskier?," Kansas City Federal Reserve, 2005, https://www.kansascityfed.org/publicat/sympos/2005/pdf/GD5_2005.pdf.

59. E. Helleiner, *States and the Reemergence of Global Finance: From Bretton Woods to the 1990s* (Ithaca, NY: Cornell University Press, 1996).

60. D. Rosato, "Confessions of a Former Real Estate Bull," *CNN Money*, January 6, 2009.

61. D. Lereah, Why the Real Estate Boom Will Not Bust (New York: Crown, 2005).

62. L. Kudlow, "The Housing Bears Are Wrong Again," *National Review*, June 20, 2005.

63. Acharya, Schnabl and Suarez, "Securitization Without Risk Transfer."

64. E. R. Morrison and J. Riegel, "Financial Contracts and the New Bankruptcy Code: Insulating Markets from Bankrupt Debtors and Bankruptcy Judges," *American Bankruptcy Institute Law Review* 13 (2005), 641–644.

65. H. M. Schwartz, *Subprime Nation*, 180.

66. "Shorting Home Equity Mezzanine Tranches: A Strategy to Cash In on a Slowing Housing Market," Deutsche Bank, February 2007, http://www.valuewalk.com/wp-content/uploads/2015/05/2007_Subprime_Shorting-Home-Equity-Mezzanine-Tranches-1.pdf.

67. M. Nakomoto and D. Wighton, "Citigroup Chief Stays Bullish on Buy-outs," *Financial Times*, July 9, 2007.

CHAPTER 3: TRANSATLANTIC FINANCE

1. The phrase "Bush's feral capitalism" comes from Robin Cook, Tony Blair's former foreign secretary; see R. Cook, "A Strong Europe—Or Bush's Feral US Capitalism," *Guardian*, October 28, 2004.

2. "Lessons from a Crisis," *Economist*, October 2, 2008.

3. "Le discours de Nicolas Sarkozy à Toulon," *Le Monde*, September 25, 2008.

4. S. Zedda, "Italian Banks' Paths Through the Crisis," *Scientific Research*, March 2016.

5. B. Setser, "Too Chinese (and Russian) to Fail?," *Follow the Money* (blog), Council on Foreign Relations, July 12, 2008; and Schwartz, *Subprime Nation*, 101–104.

6. C. Bertaut, L. P. DeMarco, S. Kamin and R. Tryon, "ABS Inflows to the United States and the Global Financial Crisis," *Journal of International Economics* 99 (2012), 219–234, and B. Bernanke, C. Bertaut, L. DeMarco and S. Kamin, "International Capital Flows and the Returns to Safe Assets in the United States, 2003–2007" (*International Finance Discussion Papers*, 2011).

7. D. O. Beltran, L. Pounder and C. Thomas, "Foreign Exposure to Asset-Backed Securities of US Origin" (*International Finance Discussion Papers* 939, August 2008, table 6, line 6).

8. Bank of England, *Financial Stability Report* (October 22, 2007), table 2.14.

9. M. Lewis, *The Big Short: Inside the Doomsday Machine* (New York: W. W. Norton, 2010); and United States Senate Permanent Subcommittee of Investigations, "Wall Street and the Financial Crisis: Anatomy of a Financial Collapse," April 13, 2011.

10. HSBC, "Fact Sheet," April 2005, http://www.banking.us.hsbc.com/personal/pdf/fact_sheet_4-05.pdf.

11. M. Zaki, *UBS, les dessous d'un scandale: Comment l'empire aux trois clés a perdu son pari* (Lausanne: Favre Sa, 2008), 121.

12. "Deutsche Bank to Acquire MortgageIT Holdings, Inc.," Deutsche Bank, July 12, 2006.

13. V. Acharya and P. Schnabl, "Do Global Banks Spread Global Imbalances? The Case of Asset-Backed Commercial Paper During the Financial Crisis of 2007–09," Jacques Polak Annual Research Conference, November 5–6, 2009.

14. N. Baba, R. N. McCauley and S. Ramaswamy, "US Dollar Money Market Funds and Non-US Banks," *BIS Quarterly Review*, March 2009.

15. H. S. Shin, "Global Banking Glut and Loan Risk Premium," Jacques Polak Annual Research Conference, November 10–11, 2011.

16. Bertaut et al., "ABS Inflows to the United States and the Global Financial Crisis."

17. T. Norfield, *The City: London and the Global Power of Finance* (London: Verso, 2017); D. Kynaston, *City of London: The History*, vol. 4 (London: Penguin, 2002); and N. Shaxson, *Treasure Islands: Uncovering the Damage of Offshore Banking and Tax Havens* (New York: St. Martin's Press, 2012).

18. E. Helleiner, *States and the Reemergence of Global Finance: From Bretton Woods to the 1990s* (Ithaca, NY: Cornell University Press, 1996).

19. J. Green, "Anglo-American Development, the Euromarkets, and the Deeper Origins of Neoliberal Deregulation," *Review of International Studies* 42 (2016), 425–449.

20. P. Augar, *The Death of Gentlemanly Capitalism: The Rise and Fall of London's Investment Banks* (London: Penguin, 2000).

21. The office was inherited by Lehman from Enron in 2001, https://en.wikipedia.org/wiki/25_Bank_Street.

22. "Triennial Central Bank Survey: Report on Global Foreign Exchange Market Activity in 2010," Monetary and Economic Department, Bank for International Settlements, December 2010, http://www.bis.org/publ/rpfxf10t.pdf.

23. L. Jones, "Current Issues Affecting the OTC Derivatives Market and Its Importance to London," City of London, April 2009, https://www.cityoflondon.gov.uk/business/economic-research-and-information/research-publications/Documents/research%202009/Current%20issues%20affecting%20the%20OTC%20derivatives%20market%20and%20its%20importance%20to%20London.pdf.

24. G. Morgan, "Supporting the City: Economic Patriotism in Financial Markets," *Journal of European Public Policy* 19 (2012), 373–387.

25. R. Wade, "Financial Regime Change?," *New Left Review* 53 (September/October 2008).

26. "Financial Regulation: Industry Changes Prompt Need to Reconsider US Regulatory Structure," US Government Accountability Office, GAO-05-61, October 6, 2004.

27. A. Baker, "Restraining Regulatory Capture? Angloamerica, Crisis Politics and Trajectories of Change in Global Financial Governance," *International Affairs* 86 (2010), 647–663.

28. Wade, "Financial Regime Change?"

29. M. Singh and J. Aitken, "The (Sizable) Role of Rehypothecation in the Shadow Banking System" (IMF Working Paper WP/10/172, July 2010).

30. Green, "Anglo-American Development."

31. M. Hirsch, *Capital Offense: How Washington's Wise Men Turned America's Future Over to Wall Street* (Hoboken, NJ: Wiley, 2010), 200.

32. Zaki, *UBS*, 75.

33. L. S. Talani, "The Impact of the Global Financial Crisis on the City of London: Towards the End of Hegemony?," *Competition and Change* 15 (February 2011), 11–30.

34. D. K. Tarullo, "Regulating Large Foreign Banking Organizations," *Harvard Law School Symposium on Building the Financial System of the Twenty-first Century: An Agenda for Europe and the United States*, March 27, 2014.

35. "Rating Action: Moody's Downgrades Depfa Entities to A2, BFSR at D+," Moody's Investors Service, September 30, 2008.

36. G. Robinson, "Hypo to Buy Depfa Bank for €5.7bn," *Financial Times*, July 23, 2007.

37. W. Munchau, *The Meltdown Years* (Munich: McGraw-Hill, 2010), 19–28.

38. D. K. Tarullo, "Banking on Basel," Peterson Institute for International Economics, 2008.

39. R. Abdelal, *Capital Rules: The Construction of Global Finance* (Cambridge, MA: Harvard University Press, 2007), 88.

40. Abdelal, *Capital Rules*, 193–194.

41. A. Blundell-Wignall, P. Atkinson and S. H. Lee, "The Current Financial Crisis: Causes and Policy Issues,"' *OECD Financial Markets Trends* (2008).

42. A. Blundell-Wignall and P. Atkinson, "The Subprime Crisis: Causal Distortions and Regulatory Reform" (2008), in P. Bloxham and C. Kent, *Lessons from the Financial Turmoil of 2007 and 2008*, proceedings of a conference, Reserve Bank of Australia, Sydney.

43. "The AIG Rescue, Its Impact on Markets, and the Government's Exit Strategy," 111th Cong., US Government Printing Office, June 10, 2010; and R. Peston, "How Banks Depend on AIG," *BBC News*, September 16, 2008.

44. "The AIG Rescue, Its Impact on Markets," 111th Cong.

45. A. Baker, "Restraining Regulatory Capture? Anglo-America, Crisis Politics and Trajectories of Change in Global Financial Governance," *International Affairs* 86 (2010), 647–663.

46. M. Thiemann, "In the Shadow of Basel: How Competitive Politics Bred the Crisis," *Review of International Political Economy* (February 5, 2014), 1203–1239.

47. M. Berlin, "New Rules for Foreign Banks: What's at Stake?," *Business Review*, Federal Reserve of Philadelphia, 2015; and "Letter SR 01-1: Application of the Board's Capital Adequacy Guidelines to Bank Holding Companies Owned by Foreign Banking Organizations," Board of Governors of the Federal Reserve System, January 5, 2001, https://www.federalreserve.gov/boarddocs/srletters/2001/sr0101.htm.

48. S. Bair (speech, Risk Management and Allocation Conference, July 25, 2007).

49. S. Bair, *Bull by the Horns: Fighting to Save Main Street from Wall Street and Wall Street from Itself* (New York: Free Press, 2012), 38–39.

50. S. G. Cecchetti, "Five Years in the Tower" (speech, BIS Annual Conference, 2013). In 2008 Deutsche's leverage would soar to 70:1. On UBS, see Zaki, *UBS*, 117.

51. C. Hughes and J. Grant, "City Limits: London Counts the Cost of Six Stormy Months for Banks," *Financial Times*, January 20, 2008.

52. J. R. Dearie and G. J. Vojta, "Reform and Modernization of Financial Supervision in the United States: A Competitive and Prudential Imperative," *Mimeo*, 2007.

53. A. Appadurai, *Banking on Words: The Failure of Language in the Age of Derivative Finance* (Chicago: University of Chicago Press, 2015).

54. P. Blustein, *The Chastening: Inside the Crisis That Rocked the Global Financial System and Humbled the IMF* (New York: PublicAffairs, 2003).

55. Roche, *Histoire secrete d'un krach qui dure*, 99–100; and P. Blustein, *Off Balance*, 113–114.

56. M. Obstfeld, J. C. Shambaugh and A. M. Taylor, "Financial Instability, Reserves, and Central Bank Swap Lines in the Panic of 2008" (NBER Working Paper 14826, 2009).

57. P. McGuire and G. von Peter, "The US Dollar Shortage in Global Banking," *BIS Quarterly Review*, March 2009.

58. For a review of the arguments see J. Aizenman and L. Jaewoo, "Financial Versus Monetary Mercantilism: Long-Run View of Large International Reserves Hoarding," *World Economy* 31 (2008), 593–611.

CHAPTER 4: EUROZONE

1. The most authoritative history is H. James, *Making the European Monetary Union* (Cambridge, MA: Harvard University Press, 2012); a useful economist's introduction is J. Pisani-Ferry, *The Euro Crisis and Its Aftermath* (Oxford: Oxford University Press, 2014). On the politics see D. Marsh, *The Euro: Battle for the New Global Currency* (New Haven, CT: Yale University Press, 2009).

2. R. Abdelal, *Capital Rules: The Construction of Global Finance* (Cambridge, MA: Harvard University Press, 2007).

3. M. E. Sarotte, *1989: The Struggle to Create Post-Cold War Europe* (Princeton, NJ: Princeton University Press, 2009).
4. Among many others, T. Mayer, *Europe's Unfinished Currency: The Political Economics of the Euro* (New York: Anthem Press, 2012). The author was chief economist at Deutsche Bank from 2009–2012.
5. A concern expressed early by D. Gros, "Will EMU Survive 2010?," Center for European Policy Studies, January 17, 2006.
6. T. Bayoumi and B. Eichengreen, "Shocking Aspects of European Monetary Unification" (NBER Working Paper 3949, 1992).
7. M. Feldstein, "The Political Economy of the European Economic and Monetary Union: Political Sources of an Economic Liability," *Journal of Economic Perspectives* 11 (1997), 23–42.
8. U. G. Silveri, "Italy 1990–2014: The Transition That Never Happened," *Journal of Modern Italian Studies* 20 (2015), 171–175.
9. K. Dyson and K. Featherstone, "Italy and EMU as a 'Vincolo Esterno': Empowering the Technocrats, Transforming the State," *South European Society and Politics* 1.2 (1996), 272–299.
10. "The Sick Man of the Euro," *Economist*, June 3, 1999.
11. R. R. G. Heinze, *Blockierte Gesellschaft* (Opladen: VS Verlag, 1998); and K. v. Hammerstein et al., "Die blockierte Republik," *Der Spiegel*, September 21, 2002.
12. A. Hassel and C. Schiller, *Der Fall Hartz IV* (Frankfurt: Campus, 2010); and S. Beck and C. Scherrer, "Der rot-grüne Einstieg in den Abschied vom 'Modell Deutschland': Ein Erklärungsversuch," *Prokla* 35 (2005), 111–130.
13. S. Dullien, "A German Model for Europe?," European Council on Foreign Relations, July 1, 2013.
14. M. Fratzscher, *Verteilungskampf: Warum Deutschland immer ungleicher wird* (Munich: Carl Hanser, 2016); and C. Odendahl, "The Hartz Myth: A Closer Look at Germany's Labour Market Reforms," Center for European Reform, June 2017.
15. H. Geiling, ed., *Die Krise der SPD: autoritäre oder partizipatorische Demokratie* (Münster: LIT, 2010).
16. A. Crawford, *Angela Merkel: A Chancellorship Forged in Crisis* (Sussex: Bloomberg Press, 2013); and M. Qvortrup, *Angela Merkel: Europe's Most Influential Leader* (New York: Overlook Press, 2016).
17. "The Merkel Plan," *Economist*, June 15, 2013.
18. Rede von Bundeskanzlerin, "Dr. Angela Merkel beim Weltwirtschaftsforum am," January 25, 2006 in Davos, https://www.bundesregierung.de/Content/DE/Bulletin/2001 _2007/2006/01/07-1-Merkel.html.
19. C. Egle and R. Zohlnhöfer, eds., *Die zweite Große Koalition: eine Bilanz der Regierung Merkel 2005–2009* (Wiesbaden: VS Verlag für Sozialwissenschaften, 2010).
20. Peer Steinbrück, *Unterm strich* (Hamburg: Hoffmann und Campe, 2010).
21. A term launched by Colin Crouch in 2000 that acquired far more traction in Germany than in the Anglosphere. C. Crouch, "Coping with Post-Democracy," *Fabian Ideas*, no. 598 (2000); C. Crouch, *Post-Democracy* (Cambridge: Polity, 2004); and "Postdemokratie?," *Aus Politik und Zeitgeschichte*, February 1, 2011.
22. S. Lessenich, "Die Kosten der Einheit," Bundeszentrale für politische Bildung, March 30, 2010.
23. "Steinbrück setzt auf schwarze Null," *Der Tagesspiegel*, July 4, 2007.
24. W. Wolfrum, *Rot-Grün an der Macht: Deutschland 1998–2005* (Munich: C. H. Beck, 2013).
25. For an insightful but uncritical portrait, see N. Irwin, *The Alchemists: Three Central Bankers and a World on Fire* (New York: Penguin, 2013).
26. C. Ban, *Ruling Ideas: How Global Neoliberalism Goes Local* (Oxford: Oxford University Press, 2016).

27. D. Gabor and C. Ban, "Banking on Bonds: The New Links Between States and Markets," *Journal of Common Market Studies* 54 (2015), 617–635.

28. S. Cheun, I. von Köppen-Mertes, and B. Weller, "The Collateral Frameworks of the Eurosystem, the Federal Reserve System and the Bank of England and the Financial Market Turmoil," Occasional Paper No. 107, European Central Bank, 2009; and D. Gabor, "The Power of Collateral: The ECB and Bank Funding Strategies in Crisis," (May 18, 2012), available at SSRN: https://ssrn.com/abstract=2062315 or http://dx.doi.org /10.2139/ssrn.2062315.

29. W. Buiter and A. Sibert, "How the Eurosystem's Treatment of Collateral in Its Open Market Operations Weakens Fiscal Discipline in the Eurozone (and What to Do About It)," CEPR Discussion Papers No. 5387, 2005; and the discussion in Schelkle, *Political Economy of Monetary Solidarity*, 145–148.

30. For two instances, Bernanke, *Courage to Act*, 477; and M. Lewis on Greece, the Eurozone and the implicit German guarantee, "How the Financial Crisis Created a 'New Third World,'" *NPR Fresh Air*, September 30, 2011, http://www.npr.org/templates/tran script/transcript.php?storyId=140948138.

31. S. Storm and C. W. Naastepad, "Myths, Mix-ups and Mishandlings: What Caused the Eurozone Crisis?," Institute for New Economic Thinking Annual Conference, April 11, 2015, table 2.

32. P. Lourtie, "Understanding Portugal in the Context of the Euro Crisis," in *Resolving the European Debt Crisis*, ed. W. R. Cline and G. Wolff (Washington, DC: PIIE, 2012).

33. C. Wyplosz and S. Sgherri, "The IMF's Role in Greece in the Context of the 2010 Stand-By Arrangement," Independent Evaluation Office of the IMF, BP/16-02/11, 2016.

34. S. Kalyvas, *Modern Greece: What Everyone Needs to Know* (Oxford: Oxford University Press, 2015); and M. Husson, "The Greek Public Debt Before the Crisis," March 2015, http://hussonet.free.fr/graudite.pdf.

35. Sandbu, *Europe's Orphan*, 24.

36. P. R. Lane, "Capital Flows in the Euro Area," *Economic Papers* 497 (April 2013).

37. G. Gorton and A. Metrick, "Securitization" (2011), in *Handbook of the Economics of Finance*, ed. G. Constantinides, M. Harris and R. Stulz (North Holland: Elsevier, 2012); and T. Santos, "Antes del Diluvio: The Spanish Banking System in the First Decade of the Euro," in *After the Flood: How the Great Recession Changed Economic Thought*, Edward L. Glaeser, Tano Santos and Glenn Weyl, eds. (Chicago: University of Chicago Press, 2017).

38. Schelkle, *Political Economy of Monetary Solidarity*, 180–185.

39. Storm and Naastepad, "Myths, Mix-ups and Mishandlings."

40. P. R. Lane, "The Funding of the Irish Domestic Banking System During the Boom," *Journal of the Statistical and Social Inquiry Society of Ireland* 44 (2014), 40–71.

41. S. Royo, "How Did the Spanish Financial System Survive the First Stage of the Global Crisis?," *Governance* 26 (October 2013), 631–656; Santos, "Antes del Diluvio."

42. A. Cárdenas, "The Spanish Savings Bank Crisis: History, Causes and Responses" (Working Paper 13-003, Universitat Oberta de Catalunya, 2013); and Santos, "Antes del Diluvio."

43. T. Santos, "El Diluvio: The Spanish Banking Crisis, 2008–2012," manuscript, Columbia Business School, Columbia University (2017).

44. Santos, "Antes del Diluvio."

45. I. Jack, "Ireland: The Rise and the Crash," *New York Review of Books*, November 11, 2010, reviewing F. O'Toole, *Ship of Fools: How Stupidity and Corruption Sank the Celtic Tiger* (London: Faber and Faber, 2009).

46. P. De Grauwe, "How to Embed the Eurozone in a Political Union," *Vox*, June 17, 2010. For a devastating review of the blindspots of conventional theories of optimum currency area and their insistence on fiscal integration see Schelkle, *Political Economy of Monetary Solidarity*, 174–179. For a review of discussions about financial stabilization

following the Maastricht Treaty of 1992 see M. Obstfeld, "Finance at Center Stage: Some Lessons of the Euro Crisis," Directorate General Economic and Financial Affairs No. 493 (DG ECFIN), European Commission, 2013.

47. For an alarmingly bland summary of the EU's precautionary arrangements see ECB, "The EU Arrangements for Financial Crisis Management," *ECB Monthly Bulletin*, February 2007. One of the first to highlight the size of the potential problem from the onset of the crisis was N. Veron, "Is Europe Ready for a Major Banking Crisis?," *Bruegel Policy Brief* (August 9, 2007).

48. D. K. Tarullo, "Regulating Large Foreign Banking Organizations" (speech, Harvard Law School Symposium on Building the Financial System of the Twenty-first Century: An Agenda for Europe and the United States, March 27, 2014).

49. A. Milward, *European Rescue of the Nation State* (London: Routledge, 1992).

50. L. H. Summers, "Summers Speaks," *Magazine of International Economic Policy* (Fall 2007), http://www.international-economy.com/TIE_F07_Summers.pdf.

51. G. Majone, *Europe as the Would-Be World Power* (Cambridge: Cambridge University Press, 2009).

52. M. Bernard, *Valéry Giscard d'Estaing: Les ambitions déçues* (Paris: Armand-Colin, 2014).

53. M. O'Neill, *The Struggle for the European Constitution: A Past and Future History* (Basingstoke, UK: Routledge, 2009).

54. M. K. Davis Cross, *The Politics of Crisis in Europe* (Cambridge: Cambridge University Press, 2017).

55. S. Kornelius, *Angela Merkel: The Chancellor and Her World* (London: Alma Books, 2014).

56. For an excellent discussion, see H. Kundnani, *The Paradox of German Power* (Oxford: Oxford University Press, 2015).

57. S. Fabbrini, *Which European Union? Europe After the Euro Crisis* (Cambridge: Cambridge University Press, 2015).

58. R. Kagan, "Americans Are from Mars, Europeans Are from Venus," *Sunday Times*, February 2, 2003, which gave rise to the following book: R. Kagan, *Paradise and Power: America and Europe in the New World Order* (London: Vintage, 2003).

59. Habermas and Derrida, "February 15, or What Binds Europeans Together."

60. In deep agreement with the basic diagnosis common to P. Anderson, *The New Old World* (London: Verso, 2009); and P. Baldwin, *The Narcissism of Minor Differences: How America and Europe Are Alike* (Oxford: Oxford University Press, 2009).

61. J. Herf, *War by Other Means: Soviet Power, West German Resistance, and the Battle of the Euromissiles* (New York: Free Press, 1991); and L. Nuti, F. Bozo, M. Rey and B. Rother, eds., *The Euromissile Crisis and the End of the Cold War* (Washington, DC: Woodrow Wilson Center Press, 2015).

CHAPTER 5: MULTIPOLAR WORLD

1. M. E. Sarotte, *1989: The Struggle to Create Post-Cold War Europe* (Princeton, NJ: Princeton University Press, 2010).

2. G. Soros, "Not Without US Aid," *Wall Street Journal*, December 7, 1989.

3. M. G. Gilman, *No Precedent, No Plan: Inside Russia's 1998 Default* (Boston: MIT Press, 2010).

4. P. Blustein, *The Chastening: Inside the Crisis That Rocked the Global Financial System and Humbled the IMF* (New York: PublicAffairs, 2003), 235–277.

5. J. Johnson, "Forbidden Fruit: Russia's Uneasy Relationship with the US Dollar," *Review of International Political Economy* 15 (2008), 379–398.

6. P. Ther, *Europe Since 1989: A History* (Princeton, NJ: Princeton University Press, 2016).

7. J. M. Goldgeier, *Not Whether but When: The US Decision to Enlarge NATO* (Washington, DC: Brookings, 1999).

8. S. F. Szabo, *Parting Ways: The Crisis in German-American Relations* (Washington, DC: Brookings, 2004).
9. "Outrage at 'Old Europe' Remarks," *BBC News,* January 23, 2003.
10. R. Prodi, "Europe and Peace" (speech, University of Ulster, April 1, 2004).
11. J. Becker, "Europe's Other Periphery," *New Left Review* 99 (May/June 2016).
12. R. Martin, *Constructing Capitalisms: Transforming Business Systems in Central and Eastern Europe* (Oxford: Oxford University Press, 2013).
13. J. Hardy, *Poland's New Capitalism* (London: Pluto Press, 2009).
14. M. Ferry and I. McMaster, "Cohesion Policy and the Evolution of Regional Policy in Central and Eastern Europe," *Europe-Asia Studies* 65 (2013), 1502–1528.
15. K. Wolczuk, "Integration Without Europeanisation: Ukraine and Its Policy Towards the European Union" (EUI working paper 15, Robert Schuman Centre of Advanced Studies, 2004).
16. A. Polese, "Ukraine 2004: Informal Networks, Transformation of Social Capital and Coloured Revolutions," *Journal of Communist Studies and Transition Politics* 25 (2009), 255–277.
17. "Doing Business 2006," World Bank (September 13, 2005), http://www.doingbusiness .org/reports/global-reports/doing-business-2006.
18. "Classification of Exchange Rate Arrangements and Monetary Policy Frameworks," *IMF,* June 30, 2004.
19. For an outstanding treatment of the Romanian case, see D. Gabor, *Central Banking and Financialization: A Romanian Account of How Eastern Europe Became Subprime* (Basingstoke, UK: Routledge, 2010).
20. J. Johnson, *Priests of Prosperity: How Central Bankers Transformed the Postcommunist World* (Ithaca, NY: Cornell University Press, 2016).
21. Blustein, *Off Balance,* 1–12.
22. "Simulating Financial Instability," Conference on Stress Testing and Financial Crisis Simulation Exercises, European Central Bank, July 12–13, 2007, https://www.ecb.eu ropa.eu/pub/pdf/other/simulatingfinancialinstability200809en.pdf?f6427026b cf400e849ff88415b1386ba.
23. Blustein, *Off Balance,* 67–92.
24. "Minister Rinkēvičs: The Foreign Ministry Building Is a Touchstone for the Nation's History," *Ministry of Foreign Affairs of the Republic of Latvia,* November 15, 2013.
25. T. Rostoks, "Latvia's Foreign Policy—Living Through Hard Times," *Diplomaatia* (blog) (April 2010), https://www.diplomaatia.ee/en/article/latvias-foreign-policy-living-through -hard-times/.
26. R. Sakwa, *The Crisis of Russian Democracy: The Dual State, Factionalism and the Medvedev Succession* (Cambridge: Cambridge University Press, 2010); and R. Sakwa, *Putin and the Oligarchs: The Khodorkovsky-Yukos Affair* (London. I. B. Tauris, 2014).
27. P. Hanson, "The Economic Development of Russia: Between State Control and Liberalization" (ISPI Working Paper 32, October 2008).
28. Johnson, "Forbidden Fruit."
29. F. Hill and C. G. Gaddy, *Mr. Putin: Operative in the Kremlin* (Washington, DC: Brookings, 2013), chapter 5.
30. P. Anderson, "Incommensurate Russia," *New Left Review* 94 (July–August 2015).
31. World Bank in Russia, *Russia Economic Report* 17 (November 2008), table 1.9.
32. A. E. Stent, *The Limits of Partnership* (Princeton, NJ: Princeton University Press, 2014); and Hill and Gaddy, *Mr. Putin.*
33. P. Gallis, *NATO and Energy Security,* CRS Report for Congress (August 15, 2007).
34. "Kudrin Has Reservations on Dollar," *Moscow Times,* April 24, 2006.
35. Johnson, "Forbidden Fruit."
36. The text of Putin's speech is at "Putin's Prepared Remarks at 43rd Munich Conference on Security Policy," *Washington Post,* February 12, 2007.

37. "At $US250 a Barrel, We're Headed for Meltdown," *Sydney Morning Herald*, June 21, 2008.
38. A. E. Kramer, "As Gazprom Goes, So Goes Russia," *New York Times*, May 11, 2008.
39. "Putin's Prepared Remarks."
40. D. Trenin, "Russia Leaves the West," *Foreign Affairs* 85 (July/August 2006), 87.
41. "Gates Dismisses Putin Remarks as Blunt Spy Talk," *Reuters*, February 12, 2007.
42. "Migration in Europe: Case Studies: Bulgaria and Romania," CRCE 2010 Colloquium, 2010.
43. "Country report: Lugoj, Romania," Ungersteel, http://www.ungersteel.com/unger/down load/UngerSteelGroup_Lugoj-property_Exposee.pdf.
44. *Europe Real Estate Yearbook* (The Hague: Europe Real Estate Publishers, 2008), 362.
45. "ING Real Estate Buys in Germany and Romania," *PropertyEU* (October 9, 2007).
46. G. Toal, *Near Abroad: Putin, the West and the Contest over Ukraine and the Caucasus* (Oxford: Oxford University Press, 2017).
47. "The President's News Conference with President Viktor Yushchenko of Ukraine in Kiev, Ukraine," *The American Presidency Project* (April 1, 2008), http://www.presidency.ucsb .edu/ws/?pid=76910.
48. S. Erlanger and S. L. Myers, "NATO Allies Oppose Bush on Georgia and Ukraine," *New York Times*, April 3, 2008.
49. Ibid.
50. C. Rice, *No Higher Honor: A Memoir of My Years in Washington* (New York: Broadway Books, 2011), 422.
51. J. Mearsheimer, "How the West Caused the Ukraine Crisis," *Foreign Affairs* (August 2014).
52. R. Youngs, *Europe's Eastern Crisis* (Cambridge: Cambridge University Press, 2017), 50–64.
53. R. Peston, "Russia 'Planned Wall Street Bear Raid,'" *BBC News*, March 17, 2014.
54. T. Vorobyova, "Russia Will Not Dump Fannie, Freddie Debt: FinMin," *Reuters*, August 20, 2008.
55. Peston, "Russia 'Planned Wall Street Bear Raid.'"
56. For this train of events, see the *Independent International Fact-Finding Mission on the Conflict in Georgia Report* (September 2009).
57. Varvara, "President Medvedev: Events in South Ossieta Show That Russia Is a Force to Be Reckoned With," *Voices from Russia* (September 6, 2008), https://02varvara.word press.com/2008/09/06/president-medvedev-events-in-south-ossetia-show-that -russia-is-a-force-to-be-reckoned-with/.
58. "Georgian War Exposes Rift with Russians," *Deutsche Welle*, August 15, 2008.
59. A. Rahr, *Putin nach Putin* (Munich: Universitas-Verlag, 2008), 269.
60. "Press Conference by President of France Nicolas Sarkozy" (United Nations press conference, September 23, 2008), http://www.un.org/press/en/2008/080923_Sarkozy.doc .htm.

CHAPTER 6: "THE WORST FINANCIAL CRISIS IN GLOBAL HISTORY"

1. The mechanism described brilliantly for the United States by A. Mian and A. Sufi, *House of Debt: How They (and You) Caused the Great Recession, and How We Can Prevent It from Happening Again* (Chicago: University of Chicago Press, 2014), applies generally.
2. For a narrative of the main bank failures, see Milne, *Fall of the House of Credit*, 195–256.
3. DealBook, "UBS's Hedge Fund: A Post-Mortem," *New York Times*, June 4, 2007.
4. T. Buck, "National Reputation Hangs on IKB Rescue," *Financial Times*, August 2, 2007.
5. Roche, *Histoire Secrète*.
6. "BNP Paribas Suspends Funds Because of Subprime Problems," *New York Times*, August 9, 2007.
7. Munchau, *The Meltdown Years*, 102.

8. Irwin, *The Alchemists*, 2.
9. L. Elliott, "Credit Crisis—How It All Began," *Guardian*, August 4, 2008.
10. H. S. Scott, *Connectedness and Contagion: Protecting the Financial System from Panics* (Cambridge, MA: MIT Press, 2016).
11. H. S. Shin, "Reflections on Northern Rock: The Bank Run That Heralded the Global Financial Crisis," *Jounal of Economic Perspectives* 23 (2009), 101–119.
12. "Lessons of the Fall," *Economist*, October 18, 2007.
13. United States Financial Crisis Inquiry Commission, *The Financial Crisis Inquiry Report* (New York: PublicAffairs, 2011), 283.
14. The significance of runs in triparty repo, bilateral repo and ABCP markets is debated between G. Gorton and A. Metrick, "Securitized Banking and the Run on Repo," *Journal of Financial Economics* 104, no. 3 (2012), 425–451; G. B. Gorton, *Misunderstanding Financial Crises: Why We Don't See Them Coming* (Oxford: Oxford University Press, 2012), 39–40; and A. Krishnamurthy, S. Nagel and D. Orlov, "Sizing Up Repo," *Journal of Finance* 69, no. 6 (December 2014), 2381–2417.
15. G. B. Gorton and A. Metrick, "Who Ran on Repo?" (NBER Working Paper 18455, 2012); T. Adrian and H. Y. Shin, "The Shadow Banking System: Implications for Financial Regulation," *Federal Reserve Bank of New York Staff Reports* 382 (July 1, 2009).
16. Gordon and Metrick, "Securitized Banking and the Run on Repo."
17. L. Ball, "The Fed and Lehman Brothers: Introduction and Summary" (NBER Working Paper 22410, 2016).
18. "Liquidity Management at Lehman Brothers," Lehman Brothers, July 2008.
19. A. Copeland, A. Martin and M. Walker, "Repo Runs: Evidence from the Tri-Party Repo Market," *Federal Reserve Bank of New York Staff Reports* 506 (July 2011).
20. T. V. Dang, G. Gorton and B. Holmstrom, "Haircuts and Repo Chains," Working Paper, October 17, 2013.
21. Ball, "The Fed and Lehman Brothers," 37.
22. The authoritative account of the AIG disaster is Congressional Oversight Panel, "The AIG Rescue, Its Impact on Markets, and the Government's Exit Strategy," *June Oversight Report* (June 10, 2010).
23. G. Morgenson and L. Story, "Testy Conflict with Goldman Helped Push A.I.G. to Edge," *New York Times*, February 6, 2010.
24. Ibid.; https://fcic-static.law.stanford.edu/cdn_media/fcic-testimony/2010-0701-Goldman-AIG-Collateral-Call-timeline.pdf.
25. P. E. McCabe, "The Cross Section of Money Market Fund Risks and Financial Crises" (FEDS Working Paper 2010-51, September 12, 2010).
26. M. T. Kacperczyk and P. Schnabl, "How Safe Are Money Market Funds?," *Quarterly Journal of Economics* 128 (2013), 1073–1122.
27. Board of Trustees of the Primary Fund-In Liquidation, "Additional Information Regarding Primary Fund-In Liquidation," September 23, 2014.
28. Gorton and Metrick, "Securitized Banking and the Run on Repo."
29. Goldman's self-justificatory official narrative hastens to add that this was an artifact of self-imposed new accounting rules. The next day the pool rebounded to $89 billion, but even this was 20 percent down on the level only days earlier. http://www.goldmansachs.com/media-relations/in-the-news/archive/response-to-fcic-folder/gs-liquidity.pdf.
30. P. Krugman, *End This Depression Now!* (New York: W. W. Norton, 2012), 115.
31. V. Ivashina and E. Scharfstein, "Bank Lending During the Financial Crisis of 2008," *Journal of Financial Economics* 97 (2010), 319–338.
32. P. McGuire and G. von Peter, "The US Dollar Shortage in Global Banking and the International Policy Response" (BIS Working Paper 291, October 2009).
33. Transcript of the FMOC meeting, September 16, 2008.
34. A. R. Sorkin, *Too Big to Fail: The Inside Story of How Wall Street and Washington Fought to Save the Financial System—and Themselves* (New York: Penguin, 2010), 1–2.

35. https://www.juliusbaer.com/files/user_upload/your-private-bank/investment
 -excellence/research/european-wealth-report/documents/Wealth_Report_Europe.pdf.
36. ING Economic and Financial Analysis, "Household Wealth in Europe: Post-Crisis Re-
 covery Leaves Big Differences Between Countries and Households," January 18, 2016.
37. R. Lydon and T. McIndoe-Calder, "The Great Irish (De)Leveraging 2005–14," Irish Eco-
 nomic Analysis Division Central Bank of Ireland, March 2017.
38. P. K. Brooks, "IMF Survey: Households Hit Hard by Wealth Losses," *World Economic
 Outlook*: IMF Research Department, June 24, 2009.
39. US Department of Treasury, "The Financial Crisis Response: In Charts," April 2012.
40. "The Cost of the Crisis: $20 Trillion and Counting," *Better Markets*, July 2015.
41. A. Bangalore, "US Housing Market: Share of Underwater Homes Trending Down,"
 Market Oracle, July 13, 2012, http://www.marketoracle.co.uk/Article35579.html.
42. E. Wolff, "The Asset Price Meltdown and the Wealth of the Middle Class," *US2010:
 Discover America in a New Century*, May 2013.
43. State of Working America, "African Americans," Economic Policy Institute (ND),
 http://www.stateofworkingamerica.org/fact-sheets/african-americans./
44. D. G. Bocian, W. Li and K. Ernst, "Foreclosures by Race and Ethnicity: The Demograph-
 ics of a Crisis," Center for Responsible Lending Research, June 18, 2010.
45. M. Hall, K. Crowder and A. Spring, "Neighborhood Foreclosures, Racial/Ethnic Transi-
 tions, and Residential Segregation," *American Sociological Review* 80.3 (2015), 526–549.
46. Mian and Sufi, *House of Debt*, 38.
47. Brooks, "IMF Survey."
48. "The Bankruptcy of General Motors: A Giant Falls," *Economist,* June 4, 2009.
49. K. Hill, D. Menk, J. Cregger and M. Schultz, *Contribution of the Automotive Industry to
 the Economies of All Fifty States and the United States* (Ann Arbor, MI: Center for
 Automotive Research, 2015).
50. "The Crisis in the Car Industry: No Opel, No Hope," *Economist*, March 5, 2009.
51. B. Deilus, "Economic Performance of Mexico and South Korea After 2008 Crisis"
 (2015), http://www.boeckler.de/pdf/v_2015_10_23_desilus.pdf; M. A. Villarreal, *The
 Mexican Economy After the Global Financial Crisis,* Congressional Research Service,
 September 16, 2010.
52. J. Sidaoui, M. Ramos-Francia and G. Cuadra, "The Global Financial Crisis and Policy
 Response in Mexico," (*BIS Papers* 54, 2010).
53. "75 Years of Toyota," http://www.toyota-global.com/company/history_of_toyota/75years
 /index.html.
54. M. Fackler, "Toyota Expects Its First Loss in 70 Years," *New York Times*, December 22,
 2008.
55. M. Sommer, "Why Has Japan Been Hit So Hard by the Global Recession?," IMF Staff
 Position Note, March 18, 2009.
56. K. Otsuka, "Resurgent Hitachi Goes Global After Painful Reforms," *Japan Times*, May
 28, 2015.
57. "Japan's Electronics Giants: Unplugged," *Economist*, February 5, 2009.
58. R. Baldwin, ed., *The Great Trade Collapse: Causes, Consequences and Prospects*
 (VoxEU, 2009), 58, http://voxeu.org/content/great-trade-collapse-causes-consequences
 -and-prospects.
59. K. Hopkins, "German Economy Suffered Worst Postwar Slump in 2009," *Guardian*,
 January 13, 2010.
60. H. Comert and S. Colak, "The Impacts of the Global Crisis on the Turkish Economy and
 Policy Responses," *Economic Research Center*, December 2014.
61. M. Yalçin, "Evaluation of the 2008 Global Financial Crisis' Effects on Turkish Economy:
 Is It Tangential?," May 15, 2012, https://www.academia.edu/1564330/Effect_of_2008
 _Global_Financial_Crisis_over_Turkey.
62. Baldwin, *Great Trade Collapse.*

63. H. Hakimian and N. Dhillon, "Global Economic Crisis: A Catalyst for Change in Saudi Arabia?," Brookings Institution, February 25, 2009.

64. R. Wigglesworth, "Gulf Bank Chief Quits as Kuwait Crisis Deepens," *Financial Times*, October 28, 2008.

65. A. Hanieh, *Capitalism and Class in the Gulf Arab States* (New York: Palgrave Macmillan, 2011).

66. P. Lewis, "Dubai's Six-Year Building Boom Grinds to Halt as Financial Crisis Takes Hold," *Guardian*, February 13, 2009.

67. International Labour Office, "Global Employment Trends 2011: The Challenge of a Jobs Recovery."

68. Clark, *Hard Times*, 41–67.

69. International Labour Office, "Global Employment Trends 2011."

70. M. Holder, "Unemployment in New York City During the Recession and Early Recovery: Young Black Men Hit the Hardest," Community Service Society, December 2010.

71. F. Cai and K. W. Chan, "The Global Economic Crisis and Unemployment in China," *Eurasian Geography and Economics* 50, no. 5 (2009), 513–531. For a contrasting effort to estimate global unemployment see International Labour Office, "Global Employment Trends 2011" (Geneva: ILO, 2011).

72. P. Krugman, "The Great Recession Versus the Great Depression," *New York Times*, March 20, 2009.

73. B. Eichengreen and K. O'Rourke, "Tale of Two Depressions: What Do the New Data Tell Us?," *CEPR*, March 8, 2010.

74. Sorkin, *Too Big to Fail*, 417.

75. M. Taibbi, "Secrets and Lies of the Bailout," *Rolling Stone*, January 4, 2013.

76. A. Sorkin, D. Henriques, E. Andrews and J. Nocera, "As Credit Crisis Spiraled, Alarm Led to Action," *New York Times*, October 1, 2008.

77. C. Borio, "Capital Flows and the Current Account: Taking Financing (More) Seriously," (*BIS Working Paper* 525, 2015).

78. Bernanke, *The Courage to Act*, 386.

79. M. Egan, "2008: Worse Than the Great Depression?," *CNN Money*, August 27, 2014.

80. Bernanke, *Courage to Act*, 386, 561.

81. Ibid., 561.

82. Geithner, *Stress Test*, 200.

83. "Securitization" rhetorics as strategies of government have been productively analyzed by the so-called Copenhagen school of security studies led by B. Barzun and O. Waeve. For critical reviews see H. Stritzel, "Towards a Theory of Securitization: Copenhagen and Beyond," *European Journal of International Relations* 13.3 (2007), 357–383; and M. McDonald, "Securitization and the Construction of Security," *European Journal of International Relations* 14.4 (2008), 563–587.

84. Sorkin, *Too Big to Fail*, 417.

85. J. Gerth, "Paulson Book: Behind the Scenes, GE's Top Exec Confided Credit Woes," *ProPublica*, February 5, 2010; and B. Condon and N. Vardi, "Harvard: The Inside Story of Its Finance Meltdown," *Forbes*, February 26, 2009.

86. The question put most forcefully by Mian and Sufi, *House of Debt*.

CHAPTER 7: BAILOUTS

1. M. Wolf, "The Rescue of Bear Sterns Marks Liberalisation's Limit," *Financial Times*, March 25, 2008.

2. For contrasting comparisons, see P. Culpepper and R. Raphael, "Structural Power and Bank Bailouts in the United Kingdom and the United States," *Politics and Society* 42 (2014), 427–454; C. Woll, *The Power of Inaction: Bank Bailouts in Comparison* (Ithaca, NY: Cornell University Press, 2014); and the symposium on financial power in *Accounting, Economics and Law* 6, no. 1 (2016).

3. Swiss National Bank, *Financial Stability Report* (2009); and Zaki, *UBS*, 184–190.

4. T. Geithner, "Reflections on the Asian Financial Crises," Trends in Asian Financial Sectors Conference, Federal Reserve Bank of San Francisco, June 20, 2007.

5. J. Schildbach, "Bank Performance in the US and Europe: An Ocean Apart," Deutsche Bank, September 26, 2013.

6. US Department of the Treasury, "The Financial Crisis Response: In Charts," April 2012.

7. On the legitimacy and illegitimacy of adhocracy see P. A. Wallach, *To the Edge: Legality, Legitimacy, and the Responses to the 2008 Financial Crisis* (Washington, DC: Brookings, 2015).

8. Bernanke, *Courage to Act*, 432.

9. F. Norris, "3 Major Banks Offer Plan to Calm Debts in Housing," *New York Times*, October 16, 2007.

10. D. Berman, "A Bailout for Citigroup?," *Deal Journal* (blog), *Wall Street Journal*, October 14, 2007.

11. A. Barr, "HSBC's Bailout Puts Pressure on Citi, 'Superfund,'" *MarketWatch*, November 26, 2007; D. Wilchin, "HSBC Is Not Interested in SIV Bailout Fund," *Reuters*, November 26, 2007; and S. Jones, "SIV Watch: Superfund Not So Super," *Financial Times*, December 6, 2007.

12. I. Fallon, *Black Horse Ride: The Inside Story of Lloyds and the Banking Crisis* (London: Robson Press, 2015).

13. A. Nolting, "German Banking Gets Boost from Mega-Merger," *Der Spiegel*, September 1, 2008.

14. K. Kelly, *Street Fighters: The Last 72 Hours of Bear Stearns, the Toughest Firm on Wall Street* (New York: Portfolio, 2009). For an account from inside Paulson's Treasury, see P. Swagel, "The Financial Crisis: An Inside View," *Brookings Papers on Economic Activity* (Spring 2009), 1–63.

15. On the invocation of 13(3), see Wallach, *To the Edge*, 46–49.

16. P. Coy, "Volcker Shuns the Blame Game," *Bloomberg Businessweek*, April 10, 2008, https://www.bloomberg.com/news/articles/2008-04-10/volcker-shuns-the-blame -gamebusinessweek-business-news-stock-market-and-financial-advice.

17. W. Poole, "Moral Hazard: The Long-Lasting Legacy of Bailouts," *Financial Analysts Journal* 65, no. 6 (2009), 17–23; J. H. Cochrane, "Lessons from the Financial Crisis," Hoover Institution, January 11, 2010; and V. Reinhart, "A Year of Living Dangerously: The Management of the Financial Crisis in 2008," *Journal of Economic Perspectives* 25 (2011), 71–90.

18. W. S. Frame, "The 2008 Federal Intervention to Stabilize Fannie Mae and Freddie Mac" (Federal Reserve Bank of Atlanta Working Paper 2009-13, April 2009); and W. S. Frame, A. Fuster, J. Tracy and J. Vickery, "The Rescue of Fannie Mae and Freddie Mac," *Federal Reserve Bank of New York Staff Reports* 719 (March 2015).

19. B. Setser, "Too Chinese (and Russian) to Fail?"

20. T. Ferguson and R. Johnson, "Too Big to Bail: The 'Paulson Put,' Presidential Politics, and the Global Financial Meltdown: Part 1: From Shadow Financial System to Shadow Bailout," *International Journal of Political Economy* 38 (2009), 3–34.

21. Swagel, "The Financial Crisis."

22. Paulson, *On the Brink*, 151.

23. D. W. Drezner, "Bad Debts: Assessing China's Financial Influence in Great Power Politics," *International Security* 34 (2009), 34.

24. Peston, "Russia 'Planned Wall Street Bear Raid.'"

25. Paulson, *On the Brink*, 152.

26. Ibid., 153.

27. C. Hulse, "Behind a G.O.P. Revolt, Ideology and Politics," *New York Times*, July 26, 2008.

28. G. Farrell, *Crash of the Titans: Greed, Hubris, the Fall of Merrill Lynch, and the Near-Collapse of Bank of America* (New York: Crown Business, 2010).

29. Sorkin, *Too Big to Fail*, 348.

30. Ball, "The Fed and Lehman Brothers."
31. Geithner, *Stress Test*, 190. The best academic defense of the Paulson-Geithner-Bernanke position is W. Cline and J. Gagnon, "Lehman Died, Bagehot Lives: Why Did the Fed and Treasury Let a Major Wall Street Bank Fail?," Peterson Institute for International Economics No. PB13-21, 2013.
32. Bernanke, *Courage to Act*, 288.
33. *Wall Street Journal* staff, "Barney Frank Celebrates Free Market Day," *Wall Street Journal*, September 17, 2008.
34. Swagel, "Financial Crisis," 41.
35. Editorial, "Wall Street Casualties," *New York Times*, September 15, 2008.
36. Editorial, "Wall Street Reckoning," *Wall Street Journal*, September 15, 2008.
37. Geithner, *Stress Test*, 190.
38. T. Ferguson and R. Johnson, "Too Big to Bail," 5–45; and Ball, "The Fed and Lehman Brothers."
39. A. Darling, *Back from the Brink: 1000 Days at Number 11* (London: Atlantic Books, 2011), 121–122.
40. For this and the following, see Congressional Oversight Panel, "The AIG Rescue, Its Impact on the Markets and the Government's Exit Strategy."
41. Swagel, "The Financial Crisis," 1–63.
42. R. Sidel, D. Enrich and D. Fitzpatrick, "WaMu Is Seized, Sold Off to J.P. Morgan, in Largest Failure in US Banking History," *Wall Street Journal*, September 26, 2008.
43. "Text of Draft Proposal for Bailout Plan," *New York Times*, September 20, 2008.
44. For the memo, see N. Kashkari and P. Swagel, "'Break the Glass' Bank Recapitalization Plan," US Treasury Department; and Sorkin, *Too Big to Fail*, chapter 5, http://www.andrewrosssorkin.com/?p=368.
45. Swagel, "The Financial Crisis."
46. P. Mason, *Meltdown: The End of the Age of Greed* (London: Verso, 2009), 22.
47. M. Landler and S. L. Myers, "Buyout Plan for Wall Street Is a Hard Sell on Capitol Hill," *New York Times*, September 23, 2008.
48. C. Isidore, "Bailout Plan Under Fire," *CNN Money*, September 23, 2008.
49. G. Robinson, "Never Underestimate the Power of Populist Scare Mongering," *Financial Times*, September 30, 2008.
50. "Bernanke, Paulson Face Skeptics on the Hill Despite Dire Warnings," *Wall Street Journal*, September 24, 2008.
51. Cited in Wallach, *To the Edge*, 85.
52. W. Buiter, "The Paulson Plan: A Useful First Step but Nowhere Near Enough," *CEPR*, September 25, 2008, http://voxeu.org/article/paulson-plan-useful-first-step-nowhere-near-enough.
53. Mason, *Meltdown*, 33.
54. From contrasting political perspectives this is the common refrain of R. Suskind, *Confidence Men: Wall Street, Washington, and the Education of a President* (New York: HarperPerennial, 2011); C. Gasparino, *Bought and Paid For: The Unholy Alliance Between Barack Obama and Wall Street* (New York: Portfolio, 2010); and R. Kuttner, *A Presidency in Peril* (White River Junction, VT: Chelsea Green Publishing, 2010).
55. C. Hulse, "Conservatives Viewed Bailout Plan as Last Straw," *New York Times*, September 26, 2008.
56. Paulson, *On the Brink*, 288; and Bernanke, *Courage to Act*, 320.
57. M. Langley, "As Economic Crisis Peaked, Tide Turned Against McCain," *Wall Street Journal*, November 5, 2008.
58. H. M. Paulson, "When Mr. McCain Came to Washington," *Wall Street Journal*, February 6, 2010.
59. C. Hulse and D. Herszenhorn, "Defiant House Rejects Huge Bailout; Next Step Is Uncertain," *New York Times*, September 29, 2008.

60. A. Twin, "Stocks Crushed," *CNN Money*, September 29, 2008.
61. L. Elliot, J. Treanor, P. Wintour and S. Goldenberg, "Bradford & Bingley: Another Day, Another Bail-out," *Guardian*, September 28, 2008.
62. Y. Melin and P. Billiet, "Le scandale Fortis, une histoire belge," *La Revue*, January 16, 2009.
63. C. Schömann-Finc, "Skandalbank HRE: Wie Ackermann Merkel in der Rettungsnacht über den Tisch zog," *Focus Money*, September 16, 2013.
64. F. O'Toole, *Ship of Fools: How Stupidity and Corruption Sank the Celtic Tiger* (London: Faber & Faber, 2009).
65. S. Carswell, *Anglo Republic: Inside the Bank That Broke Ireland* (London: Penguin, 2011).
66. Darling, *Back from the Brink*, 143.
67. Ibid., 144.
68. Gammelin and Löw, *Europas Strippenzieher*, 59.
69. L. Phillips, "France and Germany at Odds over EU 'Paulson Plan,'" *EU Observer*, October 2, 2008.
70. E. Cody and K. Sullivan, "European Leaders Split on Rescue Strategy," *Washington Post*, October 3, 2008.
71. Munchau, *Meltdown Years*, 136.
72. DPA, "Banken fordern Hilfe von der EU: Deutsche Banker warnen vor einem europäischen 'Flickenteppich,'" *Zeit Online*, October 2, 2008.
73. D. Gow, "Greece's Deposit Guarantee Deepens EU Financial Rift," *Guardian*, October 2, 2008.
74. G. Brown, *Beyond the Crash* (New York: Free Press, 2010), Kindle location 924.
75. A. Seldon and G. Lodge, *Brown at 10* (London: Biteback Publishing, 2011), footnote 148, Kindle locations 5686–5688
76. C. Bastasin, *Saving Europe: Anatomy of a Dream* (Washington, DC: Brookings, 2015), 15.
77. Gammelin and Löw, *Europas Strippenzieher*.
78. Deutscher Bundestag 16. Wahlperiode, Beschlussempfehlung und Bericht des 2. Untersuchungsausschusses nach Artikel 44 des Grundgesetzes Drucksache 16/14000 (Berlin, 2009).
79. D. Goffart, *Steinbrück—Die Biografie* (Munich: Heyne, 2012), 191.
80. Seldon, *Brown at 10*, Kindle locations 5706–5710.
81. Paulson, *On the Brink*, 332–333.
82. A. Smith and M. Arnold, "Here Is the Big Reason Banks Are Safer Than a Decade Ago," *Financial Times*, August 22, 2017.
83. R. Perman and A. Darling, *Hubris: How HBOS Wrecked the Best Bank in Britain* (Edinburgh: Birlinn, 2012).
84. Seldon, *Brown at 10*, Kindle locations 6856–6861.
85. FSA, "The Failure of the Royal Bank of Scotland," *Financial Services Board Report* (December 2011). The final cash outlays for the RBS rescue of £115 billion (138 billion euros) would make it the largest bailout on record. Schelkle, *The Political Economy of Monetary Solidarity*, 171.
86. D. Lin, "Bank Recapitalizations: A Comparative Perspective," *Harvard Journal on Legislation* 50 (2013), 513–544.
87. C. Binham, "Barclays and Former Executives Charged with Crisis-Era Fraud," *Financial Times*, June 20, 2017.
88. P. Krugman, "Gordon Does Good," *New York Times*, October 12, 2008.
89. D. Wessel, *In Fed We Trust, Ben Bernanke's War on the Great Panic* (New York: Crown, 2009), 235.
90. Darling, *Back from the Brink*, 192 (Kindle edition).
91. Seldon, *Brown at 10*, Kindle location 5946.

92. A. Sutton, K. Lannoo and C. Napoli, *Bank State Aid in the Financial Crisis: Fragmentation or Level Playing Field?* (Brussels: CEPS, 2010).
93. G. Brown, *Beyond the Crash: Overcoming the First Crisis of Globalization* (New York: Free Press, 2010), Kindle locations 1125–1128.
94. N. Clark and D. Jolly, "French Bank Says Rogue Trader Lost $7 Billion," *New York Times*, January 25, 2008.
95. Summarizing the important conclusions of C. Woll, *The Power of Inaction*. See also E. Grossman and C. Woll, "Saving the banks: The political economy of bailouts," *Comparative Political Studies* 47.4 (2014): 574–600.
96. On the politics of the German bailouts, see L. Müller, *Bank-Räuber: Wie kriminelle Manager und unfähige Politiker uns in den Ruin treiben* (Berlin: Econ Verlag, 2010).
97. T. Braithwaite, K. Scannell and M. Mackenzie, "Deutsche Bank Whistleblower Spurns Share of $16.5m SEC Award," *Financial Times*, August 18, 2016.
98. *Spiegel* staff, "Germany's Faltering Bank Bailout Program: The Bottomless Pit—Part II: A Waste of Taxpayers' Money," *Der Spiegel*, December 23, 2008.
99. Taibbi, "Secrets and Lies of the Bailout."
100. Paulson, *On the Brink*, 333.
101. Reuters staff, "Paulson Gave Banks No Choice on Government Stakes: Memos," *Reuters*, May 13, 2009.
102. Wessel, *In Fed We Trust*, 240; and Paulson, *On the Brink*, 365.
103. Kuttner, *Presidency in Peril*, 121.
104. Gammelin and Löw, *Europas Strippenzieher*, 57.
105. In unabashed celebration of Carl Schmitt, see E. Posner and A. Vermeule, *The Executive Unbound: After the Madisonian Republic* (Oxford: Oxford University Press, 2011). For Schmitt on economic emergency see W. E. Scheuerman, "The Economic State of Emergency," *Cardozo Law Review* 21 (1999), 1869.
106. On the difficulty in locating sovereignty even when the exception is declared see J. White, "Emergency Europe," *Political Studies* 63.2 (2015), 300–318.
107. P. Swagel, "The Financial Crisis," 1–78.
108. S. M. Davidoff Solomon, "Uncomfortable Embrace: Federal Corporate Ownership in the Midst of the Financial Crisis," *Minnesota Law Review* 95 (2011), 1733–1778.
109. Even in the UK case, the management of the new, state-owned bank assets was handed off to an unpolitical agency, the UK Financial Investments Ltd, to hold them at arm's length from the Treasury. P. Burnham, "Depoliticisation: Economic Crisis and Political Management," *Policy & Politics* 42.2 (2014), 189–206.
110. P. Veronesi and L. Zingales, "Paulson's Gift" (NBER Working Paper 15458, October 2009).
111. Lin, "Bank Recapitalizations," 513–544.
112. Bair, *Bull by the Horns*, Kindle locations 142–143.
113. Special Inspector General for the Troubled Asset Relief Program, "Extraordinary Financial Assistance Provided to Citigroup, Inc.," Washington, DC: Office of SIGTARP, January 13, 2011.
114. B. Bernanke, "Acquisition of Merrill Lynch by Bank of America," Congressional Committee on Oversight and Government Reform, June 25, 2009. BofA did not in the event activate the ring-fence loss protection agreement. Kuttner, *Presidency in Peril*, 144–146.
115. D. Dayen, "The Most Important WikiLeaks Revelation Isn't About Hillary Clinton," *New Republic*, October 14, 2016. J. Podesta, "Fw: Huffpost: The Obama Test: Personnel Is Policy," WikiLeaks, *Podesta Emails*, October 25, 2008.
116. C. Rampell, "Christina D. Romer," *New York Times*, November 25, 2008.
117. For a devastating report, see M. Taibbi, "Obama's Big Sellout: The President Has Packed His Economic Team with Wall Street Insiders," *Common Dreams*, December 13, 2009.

CHAPTER 8: "THE BIG THING": GLOBAL LIQUIDITY

1. Gillian Tett, "ECB injects €95bn to Help Markets," *Financial Times*, August 9, 2007.
2. Irwin, *The Alchemists*, 43–73.
3. McGuire and von Peter. "The US Dollar Shortage."
4. N. Baba and F. Packer, "From Turmoil to Crisis: Dislocations in the FX Swap Market Before and After the Failure of Lehman Brothers" (*BIS Working Paper* 285, July 2009).
5. Transcript of the FOMC meeting, September 16, 2008.
6. W. A. Allen and R. Moessner, "Central Bank Co-operation and International Liquidity in the Financial Crisis of 2008–9" (*BIS Working Paper* 310, May 2010).
7. M. Obstfeld, J. C. Shambaugh and A. M. Taylor, "Financial Instability, Reserves, and Central Bank Swap Lines in the Panic of 2008" (NBER Working Paper No. 14826, January 2009).
8. R. Marino and U. Volz, "A Critical Review of the IMF's Tools for Crisis Prevention" (DIE Discussion Paper, April 2012).
9. Transcript of the FOMC meeting, October 28–29, 2008.
10. Wessel, *In Fed We Trust*, 140.
11. J. L. Broz, "The Federal Reserve as Global Lender of Last Resort, 2007–2010," International Political Economy Society, University of Virginia, November 9–10, 2012.
12. T. Adrian and H. S. Shin, "Prices and Quantities in the Monetary Policy Transmission Mechanism," *International Journal of Central Banking* 5, no. 4 (2009), 131–142.
13. L. Randall Wray, "Bernanke's Obfuscation Continues: The Fed's $29 Trillion Bail-Out Of Wall Street," *Huffington Post*, December 14, 2011.
14. A useful reference is James Felkerson, "$29,000,000,000,000: A Detailed Look at the Fed's Bailout by Funding Facility and Recipient," Levy Economics Institute (Working Paper 698, December 2011).
15. A. Berger, L. K. Black, C. H. Bouwman and J. Dlugosz, "Bank Loan Supply Responses to Federal Reserve Emergency Liquidity Facilities," *Journal of Financial Intermediation* 32 (October 2017), 1–15.
16. E. Benmelech, "An Empirical Analysis of the Fed's Term Auction Facility" (CATO Papers on Public Policy, Working Paper 18304, 2012): 57–91.
17. T. Adrian, C. R. Burke and J. J. McAndrews, "The Federal Reserve's Primary Dealer Credit Facility," *Current Issues in Economics and Finance* 15, no. 4 (2009), 1.
18. M. D. Bordo, O. F. Humpage and A. J. Schwartz, "The Evolution of the Federal Reserve Swap Lines Since 1962," *IMF Economic Review* 63, no. 2 (2015), 353–372. On the development of the United States as a global lender of last resort since the 1960s see D. McDowell, *Brother Can You Spare a Billion? The United States, the IMF, and the International Lender of Last Resort* (Oxford: Oxford University Press, 2016).
19. FOMC meeting, October 28–29, 2008, https://www.federalreserve.gov/monetarypol icy/files/FOMC20081029meeting.pdf.
20. Perhaps the first outside commentator to realize their significance was P. Mehrling, "Understanding the Fed's Swap Line," *Financial Times*, November 18, 2008, http://blogs.ft.com/economistsforum/2008/11/254/. He was followed by M. Obstfeld, J. C. Shambaugh and A. M. Taylor, "Financial Instability, Reserves, and Central Bank Swap Lines in the Panic of 2008," *American Economic Review* 99 (2009): 480–486; D. McDowell, "The US as 'Sovereign International Last-Resort Lender': The Fed's Currency Swap Programme During the Great Panic of 2007–09," *New Political Economy* 17.2 (2012), 157–178; J. L. Broz, "The Politics of Rescuing the World's Financial System: The Federal Reserve as a Global Lender of Last Resort" (November 20, 2014), *Korean Journal of International Studies* 13 (August 2015), 323–351.
21. For a recent example, see "US Dollar-British pounds swap agreement," January 16, 2014, https://www.newyorkfed.org/medialibrary/media/markets/USD_Pound_swap_agree ment.pdf.

22. Wessel, *In Fed We Trust,* 141.
23. Conference call, FOMC, October 7, 2009, https://www.federalreserve.gov/monetary policy/files/FOMC20081007confcall.pdf.
24. Conference call, FOMC, December 6, 2007, https://www.federalreserve.gov/monetary policy/files/FOMC20071206confcall.pdf.
25. Helleiner, *Status Quo Crisis,* 36.
26. FOMC meeting, October 28–29, 2008.
27. The fourteen were the ECB, SNB, Bank of Japan, Bank of England, Bank of Canada, Reserve Bank of Australia, Sveriges Riksbank, Norges Bank, Danmarks Nationalbank, Reserve Bank of New Zealand, Banco Central do Brasil, Banco de México, Bank of Korea, and Monetary Authority of Singapore. See M. J. Fleming and N. J. Klagge, "The Federal Reserve's Foreign Exchange Swap Lines," *Current Issues in Economics and Finance* 16 no. 4 (2010), 1.
28. Irwin, *The Alchemists,* 169.
29. "No One Telling Who Took $586 Billion in Swaps with Fed Condoning Anonymity," Bloomberg, December 11, 2011; and "Alan Grayson & Ben Bernanke," CSPAN, July 21, 2009, https://www.youtube.com/watch?v=n0NYBTkE1yQ.
30. FOMC meeting, October 28–29, 2008.
31. Irwin, *The Alchemists,* 154.
32. K. Karlson, "Checks and Balances: Using the Freedom of Information Act to Evaluate the Federal Reserve Banks," *American University Law Review* 60 (2010), 213.
33. J. Anderlini, "China Calls for a New Reserve Currency," *Financial Times,* March 23, 2009; and UN, "Report of the Commission of Experts of the President of the United Nations General Assembly on Reforms of the International Monetary and Financial System," New York, 2009.
34. J. Steele, "I'm a Young President, Don't Try to Label Me," *Guardian,* July 2, 2008.
35. B. Benoit, "Germany Sees an End to US Hegemony," *Financial Times,* September 26, 2008.
36. L. Phillips, "US Laissez-Faire to Battle European 'Social Market' at G20," *EUObserver,* November 14, 2008, https://euobserver.com/foreign/27114.
37. Interview with author.

CHAPTER 9: EUROPE'S FORGOTTEN CRISIS: EASTERN EUROPE

1. B. Setser, "Where Is My Swap Line? And Will the Diffusion of Financial Power Balkanize the Global Response to a Broadening Crisis?," October 18, 2008, https://www.cfr.org/blog/where-my-swap-line-and-will-diffusion-financial-power-balkanize-global-response-broadening.
2. FOMC meeting, October 28–29, 2008.
3. M. J. Burrows and J. Harris, "Revisiting the Future: Geopolitical Effects of the Financial Crisis," *Washington Quarterly* 32, no. 2 (2009), 27–38.
4. Conférence de presse, November 14, 2008, http://discours.vie-publique.fr/notices /087003590.html.
5. V. Feklyunina and S. White, "Discourses of 'Krizis': Economic Crisis in Russia and Regime Legitimacy," *Journal of Communist Studies and Transition Politics* 27 (2011), 385–406.
6. N. Robinson, "Russia's Response to Crisis: The Paradox of Success," https://www.academia.edu/2125038/Russia_s_Response_to_Crisis_The_Paradox_of_Success?auto =download.
7. S. Guriev and A. Tsyvinski, "Challenges Facing the Russian Economy After the Crisis," in A. Åslund, S. Guriev and A. Kuchins, eds., *Russia After the Global Economic Crisis* (New York: Columbia University, 2010), 9–38.
8. L. Harding, "Russia's Oligarchs Lose 70% of Their Wealth in a Year," *Guardian,* April 17, 2009.

9. World Bank in Russia, *Russia Economic Report* 18 (March 2009).

10. A. E. Kramer, "A $50 Billion Bailout in Russia Favors the Rich and Connected," *New York Times*, October 30, 2008.

11. S. Johnson, "The Quiet Coup," *Atlantic*, May 1, 2009, 1.

12. C. G. Gaddy and B. W. Ickes, "Russia After the Global Financial Crisis," *Eurasian Geography and Economics* 51, no. 3 (2010), 281–311.

13. J. Conrad, "Russia in the Financial Crisis and Beyond," Deutsche Bank Research, December 11, 2009.

14. "The Financial Crisis in Russia," Stratfor, October 28, 2008, https://www.stratfor.com /analysis/financial-crisis-russia.

15. World Bank in Russia, *Russian Economic Report* 17 (November 2008).

16. S. Crowley, "Monotowns and the Political Economy of Industrial Restructuring in Russia," *Post-Soviet Affairs* 32, no. 5 (2016), 397–422.

17. J. Jungmann and B. Sagemann, eds., *Financial Crisis in Eastern Europe: Road to Recovery* (Wiesbaden: Gabler, 2011), 433.

18. M. Korostikov, "Russia and China: Against the Storm," *Journal of Communist Studies and Transition Politics* 27, no. 3-4 (2011), 605–631.

19. Gaddy and Ickes, "Russia After the Global Financial Crisis," 281–311.

20. *Russian Analytical Digest* 63 (July 7, 2009), http://www.laender-analysen.de/russland /rad/pdf/Russian_Analytical_Digest_63.pdf.

21. S. Fortescue, "Putin in Pikalevo: PR or Watershed?," *Australian Slavonic and East European Studies* 23, nos. 1–2 (2010), 19–38.

22. Sakwa, *The Crisis of Russian Democracy*, 332–341.

23. D. Medvedev, "Go Russia!," September 10, 2009, http://en.kremlin.ru/events/president /news/5413.

24. D. Medvedev, "Speech at Meeting of Council of Legislators," December 28, 2009, http:// en.kremlin.ru/events/president/transcripts/6497.

25. P. P. Pan, "Medvedev Calls for Economic Changes," *Washington Post*, November 13, 2009.

26. For a salutary stress on diversity across the region see E. Berglöf, Y. Korniyenko, J. Zettelmeyer and A. Plekhanov, "Understanding the Crisis in Emerging Europe," (European Bank for Reconstruction and Development (Working Paper No. 109, 2009).

27. Danske Bank Research, "Euro Area: Exposure to the Crisis in Central and Eastern Europe," February 24, 2009.

28. EBRD Transition Report 2015–2016 (London: EBRD, 2016), 12.

29. I. Kaminska, "The EE Mortgage," *Financial Times*, October 24, 2008.

30. L. Thomas Jr., "Politics Add to Economic Turmoil in Hungary," *New York Times*, April 1, 2009.

31. FOMC meeting, October 28–29, 2008.

32. Ibid.

33. S. Vallée, "Behind Closed Doors at the ECB," *Financial Times*, March 30, 2010.

34. R. A. Auer, S. Kraenzlin and D. Liebeg, "How Do Austrian Banks Fund Their Swiss Franc Exposure?," *Austrian National Bank Financial Stability Report* (2012), 54–61.

35. L. Andor, "Hungary in the Financial Crisis: A (Basket) Case Study," *Journal of Contemporary Central and Eastern Europe* 17, no. 3 (2009): 285–296; L. Calmfors et al., "The Hungarian Crisis," *EEAG Report on the European Economy* (2012), 115–130; and T. Egedy, "The Effects of Global Economic Crisis in Hungary," *Hungarian Geographical Bulletin* 61, no. 2 (2012), 155–173.

36. S. Lütz and M. Kranke, "The European Rescue of the Washington Consensus? EU and IMF Lending to Central and Eastern European Countries," *Review of International Political Economy* 21, no. 2 (2014), 310–338.

37. "Days of New Flats, Cars and Generous State Benefits Over as Currency Collapses," *Guardian*, October 28, 2008.

38. J. A. Cordero, "The IMF's Stand-by Arrangements and the Economic Downturn in East-ern Europe: The Cases of Hungary, Latvia, and Ukraine," CEPR, September 2009.

39. IMF, "Review of Recent Crisis Programs," September 14, 2009.

40. L. Barber, C. Giles, S. Wagstyl and T. Barber, "Zoellick Urges EU to Help East Europe," *Financial Times*, February 18, 2009.

41. "Keep Calm and Carry On," *Economist*, February 19, 2009.

42. A. Evans-Pritchard, "Failure to Save East Europe Will Lead to Worldwide Meltdown," *Telegraph*, February 14, 2009. Z. Kudrna and D. Gabor, "The Return of Political Risk: Foreign-Owned Banks in Emerging Europe," *Europe-Asia Studies* 65(3) (2013), 548–66.

43. Z. Darvas, "The EU's Role in Supporting Crisis-Hit Countries in Central and Eastern Europe," *Bruegel Policy Contribution* No. 2009/17 2009.

44. E. Hugh, "Let the East into the Eurozone Now!," February 20, 2009, http://fistfulofeuros .net/afoe/let-the-east-into-the-eurozone-now/.

45. S. Wagstyl, "IMF Urges Eastern EU to Adopt Euro," *Financial Times*, April 5, 2009.

46. R. De Haas et al., "Foreign Banks and the Vienna Initiative: Turning Sinners into Saints?" (IMF Working Paper 12-117, 2012). The effectiveness of the initiative is sug-gested in Berglöf, Korniyenko, Zettelmeyer and Plekhanov, "Understanding the Crisis," who find that cross-border bank ownership helped to stabilize lending.

47. EBRD, EIB and World Bank, *Final Report on the Joint IFI Action Plan* (March 2011). According to officials of the German finance ministry they undertook action at a na-tional level to hold the German lenders in line.

48. Blustein, *Off Balance*, Kindle location 1816.

49. C. Dougherty, "Sweden Aids Bailout of Baltic Nations," *New York Times*, March 12, 2009.

50. "Latvia: Will It Start a Dangerous Domino Effect?," May 6, 2009, http://www.econo monitor.com/analysts/author/mstokes/.

51. L. Nyberg, "The Baltic Region in the Shadow of the Financial Crisis," *BIS Review* 105 (2009); and Y. Koyama, "Economic Crisis in the Baltic States: Focusing on Latvia," *Economic Annals* 55, no. 186 (2010), 89–114.

52. A. Evans-Pritchard, "Latvian Debt Crisis Shakes Eastern Europe," *Telegraph*, June 3, 2009.

53. O. J. Blanchard, M. Griffiths and B. Gruss, "Boom, Bust, Recovery: Forensics of the Latvia Crisis," *Brookings Papers on Economic Activity* 2 (2013), 325–388.

54. Darvas, "The EU's Role."

55. J. Sommers and C. Woolfson, *The Contradictions of Austerity: The Socio-Economic Costs of the Neoliberal Baltic Model* (New York: Routledge, 2014).

56. J. Brundsen, "Brexit Gives Valdis Dombrovskis Big Sway over Banks," *Financial Times*, June 30, 2016.

57. D. Arel, "Ukraine Since the War in Georgia," *Survival* 50, no. 6 (2008), 15–25.

58. A. Mayhew, "The Economic and Financial Crisis: Impacts on an Emerging Economy Ukraine" (SEI Working Paper 115, 2010).

59. A. Åslund, "Ukraine: Worst Hit by the Financial Crisis," George Washington University, February 23, 2009, https://www2.gwu.edu/~iiep/assets/docs/aslund_ukraine_23feb09 .pdf.

60. A. Åslund, "Ukraine's Financial Crisis, 2009," *Eurasian Geography and Economics* 50, no. 4 (2009), 371–386.

61. R. Connolly and N. Copsey, "The Great Slump of 2008–9 and Ukraine's Integration with the European Union," *Journal of Communist Studies and Transition Politics* 27, no. 3-4 (2011), 541–565.

62. K. Westphal, "Russian Gas, Ukrainian Pipelines, and European Supply Security: Les-sons of the 2009 Controversies," SWP research paper, September 11, 2009.

63. T. Alloway, "Domino Theory, Eastern Europe Edition," *Financial Times*, February 16, 2009.

CHAPTER 10: THE WIND FROM THE EAST: CHINA

1. A. Tsygankov, "What Is China to Us? Westernizers and Sinophiles in Russian Foreign Policy," *Russia.Nei.Visions* 45 December 2009.
2. D. W. Drezner, "Bad Debts: Assessing China's Financial Influence in Great Power Politics," *International Security* 34, no. 2 (2009), 7–45.
3. "Fannie, Freddie Failure Would Be World 'Catastrophe,'" Bloomberg, August 22, 2008, reported by https://mises.org/blog/fannie-freddie-failure-would-be-world-catastrophe.
4. J. Fallows, "Be Nice to the Countries That Lend You Money," *Atlantic*, December 2008, https://www.theatlantic.com/magazine/archive/2008/12/be-nice-to-the-countries -that-lend-you-money/307148/.
5. Drezner, "Bad Debts."
6. W. M. Morrison and M. Labonte, "China's Holdings of US Securities: Implications for the US Economy," *Current Politics and Economics of Northern and Western Asia* 20, no. 3 (2011), 507.
7. "A Truer Picture of China's Export Machine," *McKinsey Quarterly* (September 2010), http://www.mckinsey.com/business-functions/strategy-and-corporate-finance/our -insights/a-truer-picture-of-chinas-export-machine.
8. "The Decoupling Debate," *Economist*, March 6, 2008.
9. J. Yardley, "China to Streamline Government into 'Super Ministries,'" *New York Times*, March 11, 2008.
10. S. Minggao and H. Yin, "Macroreview: Crisis Tests Strength of China's Export Muscle," http://english.caijing.com.cn/2009-08-19/110227250.html.
11. For this rough figure, see S. Fardoust, J. Yifu and L. X. Luo, "Demystifying China's Fiscal Stimulus," World Bank (Policy Research Working Paper 6221, 2012). For a more detailed treatment, see C. Fang and K. Wing Chan, "The Global Economic Crisis and Unemployment in China," *Eurasian Geography and Economics* 50, no, 5 (2009), 513–531.
12. B. Naughton, "Understanding the Chinese Stimulus Package," *China Leadership Monitor* 28, no. 2 (2009), 1–12.
13. D. Schmidt and S. Heilmann, "Dealing with Economic Crisis in 2008–2009," *China Analysis* 77 (January 2010), www.chinapolitik.de; see also http://knowledge.ckgsb.edu .cn/2015/12/14/china/the-party-planners-five-year-plans-in-china/.
14. For this and the following quotes, see Naughton, "Understanding the Chinese Stimulus Package," 1–12.
15. C. Sorace, "China's Vision for Developing Sichuan's Post-Earthquake Countryside: Turning Unruly Peasants into Grateful Urban Citizens," *China Quarterly* 218 (2014), 404–427.
16. J. Kirkegaard, "China's Experimental Pragmatics of 'Scientific Development' in Wind Power: Algorithmic Struggles over Software in Wind Turbines," *Copenhagen Journal of Asian Studies* 34, no. 1 (2016), 5–24.
17. H. Yu, "Universal Health Insurance Coverage for 1.3 Billion People: What Accounts for China's Success?," *Health Policy* 119, no. 9 (September 2015): 1145–1152.
18. Naughton, "Understanding," 8.
19. G. Ollivier, J. Sondhi and N. Zhou, "High-Speed Railways in China: A Look at Construction Costs," *World Bank China Transport Topics* 9 (July 2014).
20. So much so that Obama's enthusiasm attracted critical attention. "Obama Needs to Get Over His China Envy," *Baltimore Sun*, November 5, 2011, http://www.baltimoresun.com /news/opinion/bal-obama-needs-to-get-over-his-china-envy-20111104-story.html.
21. S. Breslin, "China and the Crisis: Global Power, Domestic Caution and Local Initiative," *Contemporary Politics* 17, no. 2 (2011), 185–200.
22. IMF, "Survey: China's Difficult Rebalancing Act," September 2007, http://www.imf.org /en/News/Articles/2015/09/28/04/53/socar0912a.
23. A. Wheatley, "Calculating the Coming Slowdown in China," *New York Times*, May 23, 2011.
24. "China Seeks Stimulation," *Economist*, November 10, 2008.

25. Fardoust, Yifu and Luo, "Demystifying China's Fiscal Stimulus."
26. Naughton, "Understanding," 10.
27. Fardoust, Yifu and Luo, "Demystifying China's Fiscal Stimulus," figure 2.
28. B. Naughton, "Reading the NPC: Post-Crisis Economic Dilemmas of the Chinese Leadership," *China Leadership Monitor* 32 (2010), 1–10.
29. Naughton, "Understanding," 3.
30. A. Szamosszegi and C. Kyle, *An Analysis of State-Owned Enterprises and State Capitalism in China,* US-China Economic and Security Review Commission (October 2011), 1–116.
31. C. E. Walter and F. J. T. Howie, *Red Capitalism* (Singapore: Wiley, 2012).
32. N. Lardy, *Sustaining China's Economic Growth* (New York: Columbia University Press, 2012).
33. A. Collier, *Shadow Banking and the Rise of Capitalism in China* (Singapore: Palgrave Macmillan, 2017).
34. N.-L. Sum, "A Cultural Political Economy of Crisis Recovery: (Trans-) National Imaginaries of 'BRIC' and Subaltern Groups in China," *Economy and Society* 42 no. 4 (2013), 543–570.
35. Schmidt and Heilmann, "Dealing with Economic Crisis in 2008–2009."
36. C. Wong, "The Fiscal Stimulus Program and Problems of Macroeconomic Management in China," 2011, https://www.oecd.org/gov/budgeting/48143862.pdf; and C. Wong, "The Fiscal Stimulus Programme and Public Governance Issues in China," *OECD Journal on Budgeting* 2011/3, https://www.oecd.org/gov/budgeting/49633058.pdf.
37. Fardoust, Yifu and Luo, "Demystifying China's Fiscal Stimulus."
38. D. Shambaugh, "Coping with a Conflicted China," *Washington Quarterly* 34, no. 1 (2011), 7–27.
39. G. Qian, "How Should We Read China's 'Discourse of Greatness,'" *China Media Project,* http://cmp.hku. hk/2010/02/23/4565/ (accessed December 8, 2010).
40. "In Wake of Stronger Growth, More Americans and Europeans Say US Is Top Economic Power," July 2, 2015, http://www.pewresearch.org/fact-tank/2015/07/02/in-wake-of -stronger-growth-more-americans-and-europeans-say-u-s-is-top-economic-power/.
41. T. M. Cheung, "Dragon on the Horizon: China's Defense Industrial Renaissance," *Journal of Strategic Studies* 32, no. 1 (2009): 29–66.
42. "What Does China Really Spend on Its Military?," http://chinapower.csis.org/military -spending/.
43. T. Shanker and M. Mazzetti, "China and US Clash on Naval Fracas," *New York Times,* March 10, 2009.
44. "UPDATE 3-Geithner Tells China Its Dollar Assets Are Safe," *Reuters,* May 31, 2009.
45. Shambaugh, "Coping with a Conflicted China."
46. National Intelligence Council Global Trends 2025 (Washington, DC, 2008); and K. Liao, "The Pentagon and the Pivot," *Survival* 55, no. 3 (2013), 95–114.
47. J. Fallows, "Be Nice to the Countries That Lend You Money."

CHAPTER 11: G20

1. C. Pereira and J. A. de Castro Neves, "Brazil and China: South-South Partnership or North-South Competition?" Brookings Policy Paper Number 26, March 2011.
2. A. Ahuja and M. S. Nabar, "Investment-Led Growth in China: Global Spillovers" (IMF Working Paper 12/267, 2012).
3. OECD, Maddison Project database, http://www.ggdc.net/maddison/maddison-project /data.htm.
4. J. R. Blöndal, I. Hawkesworth and H.-D. Choi, "Budgeting in Indonesia," *OECD Journal on Budgeting* 9, no. 2 (2009), 49.
5. A. Doraisami, "Macro-Economic Policy Responses to Financial Crises in Malaysia, Indonesia and Thailand," *Journal of Contemporary Asia* 44, no. 4 (2014), 581–598.

6. M. Fackler, "South Koreans Reliving Nightmare of Last Financial Crisis," *New York Times*, October 24, 2008.

7. H. Cho, *South Korea's Experience with Banking Sector Liberalisation* (research report, Amsterdam, 2010); and T. Kalinowski and H. Cho, "The Political Economy of Financial Liberalization in South Korea: State, Big Business, and Foreign Investors," *Asian Survey* 49, no. 2 (2009), 221–242.

8. H. Cho, *South Korea's Experience with Global Financial Crisis* (Ontario: North-South Institute, 2012), 10.

9. J. Ree, K. Yoon and H. Park, "FX Funding Risks and Exchange Rate Volatility–Korea's Case" (IMF Working Paper 12-268, 2012).

10. B. Eichengreen, *Exorbitant Privilege: The Rise and Fall of the Dollar and the Future of the International Monetary System* (Oxford: Oxford University Press, 2010), 168.

11. H. C. Chung, "The Bank of Korea's Policy Response to the Global Financial Crisis," *Bank for International Settlements Paper* 54 (2010), 257.

12. J. Chomthongdi, "Thailand and the World Financial Crisis: How Will Civil Unrest Further Damage Thailand's Economic Position?," April 20, 2009, http://www.theglobalist .com/thailand-and-the-world-financial-crisis/; and S. Chirathivat and S. Mallikamas. "Thailand's Economic Performance and Responses to the Global Crisis," Proceedings of Asia After the Crisis Conference, 2010.

13. M. Z. Abidin and R. Rasiah, "The Global Financial Crisis and the Malaysian Economy: Impact and Responses" (Kuala Lumpur: UNDP Malaysia, 2009).

14. K. Sangsubhan and M. C. Basri, "Global Financial Crisis and ASEAN: Fiscal Policy Response in the Case of Thailand and Indonesia," *Asian Economic Policy Review* 7, no. 2 (2012), 248–269.

15. M. C. Basri and S. Rahardja, "Mild Crisis, Half Hearted Fiscal Stimulus: Indonesia During the GFC," *Assessment on the Impact of Stimulus, Fiscal Transparency and Fiscal Risk (*ERIA Research Project Report 1,2010), 169–211.

16. E. Chew, "Malaysia Stimulus Tops $16 Billion," *Wall Street Journal*, March 11, 2009.

17. A. Maierbrugger, "1MDB Scandal: Next Suspect Goldman Sachs Banker," February 15, 2016, http://investvine.com/1mdb-scandal-next-suspect-goldman-sachs-banker/.

18. "Chronology of Korean Responses to the Financial Crisis," *New York Times*, October 19, 2008.

19. N. Baba and I. Shim, "Policy Responses to Dislocations in the FX Swap Market: The Experience of Korea," *BIS Quarterly Review*, June 2010.

20. T. Kalinowski, "The Politics of Market Reforms: Korea's Path from Chaebol Republic to Market Democracy and Back," *Contemporary Politics* 15, no. 3 (2009), 287–304.

21. T. Kalinowski, "Crisis Management and the Diversity of Capitalism: Fiscal Stimulus Packages and the East Asian (Neo-)Developmental State," *Economy and Society* 44, no. 2 (2015), 244–270.

22. FOMC meeting, October 28–29, 2008.

23. R. H. Wade, "Emerging World Order? From Multipolarity to Multilateralism in the G20, the World Bank, and the IMF," *Politics & Society* 39, no. 3 (2011), 347–378.

24. J. Kirton, *G20 Governance for a Globalized World* (Farnham, UK: Ashgate, 2013).

25. "Norway Takes Aim at G-20," *Spiegel Online*, June 22, 2010.

26. Culminating in the UN Conference at the Highest Level on the World Financial and Economic Crisis and Its Impact on Development, June 2009, http://www.un.org/ga /president/63/interactive/uneconference.shtml.

27. Darling, *Back from the Brink*, 193.

28. Seldon, *Brown at 10*, 45.

29. Washington press conference with Gordon Brown and Alistair Darling, Saturday, November 15, 2008, http://webarchive.nationalarchives.gov.uk/20090330160949; http:// www.number10.gov.uk/Page17514.

30. Seldon, *Brown at 10*, Kindle locations 7411–7417.

31. J. Beale, "Lofty Ambitions for Obama's Visit," *BBC News*, March 31, 2009.

32. Seldon, *Brown at 10*, Kindle locations 7660–7663.

33. For a discussion, see E. Helleiner and J. Kirschner, eds., *The Great Wall of Money* (Ithaca, NY: Cornell University Press, 2014). For the original, see "Zhou Xiaochuan: Reform the International Monetary System," March 23, 2009, http://www.pbc.gov.cn/english/130724/2842945/index.html.

34. J. Zhongxia, "The Chinese Delegation at the 1944 Bretton Woods Conference: Reflections for 2015," https://www.omfif.org/media/1067515/chinese-reflections-on-bretton-woods-by-jin-zhongxia.pdf.

35. M. P. Dooley, D. Folkerts-Landau and P. Garber, "The Revived Bretton Woods System," *International Journal of Finance and Economics* 9, no. 4 (October 2004), 307–313.

36. On the China rebalancing effort, see B. Setser, "The Balance of Financial Terror, Circa August 9, 2007," https://www.cfr.org/blog/balance-financial-terror-circa-august-9-2007.

37. UN, "Report of the Commission of Experts of the President of the United Nations General Assembly on Reforms of the International Monetary and Financial System," New York, September 2009.

38. G. C. Chang, "China's Assault on the Dollar," March 26, 2009, https://www.forbes.com/2009/03/26/zhou-xiaochuan-geithner-renminbi-currency-opinions-columnists-dollar.html.

39. J. Kollewe, "Global Currency Flies with Push from Russia and Slip from Timothy Geithner," *Guardian*, March 26, 2009.

40. A. Lane, "In Defending US Currency, Bachmann Distorts Geithner's Comments About Dollar," April 1, 2009, http://www.politifact.com/truth-o-meter/statements/2009/apr/01/michele-bachmann/defending-dollar-bachmann-distorts-geithners-comme/.

41. E. S. Prasad, *The Dollar Trap: How the US Dollar Tightened Its Grip on Global Finance* (Princeton, NJ: Princeton University Press, 2014).

42. H. Cooper, "On the World Stage, Obama Issues an Overture," *New York Times*, April 2, 2009.

43. Joint press conference with Angela Merkel and Nicolas Sarkozy, April 1, 2009, https://ca.ambafrance.org/Joint-press-conference-with-Angela.

44. For the following, A. Rawnsley, *The End of the Party* (London: Penguin, 2010).

45. P. Blustein, *Laid Low: Inside the Crisis That Overwhelmed Europe and the IMF* (Waterloo, Ontario: CIGI, 2016), 75.

46. N. Woods, "Global Governance After the Financial Crisis: A New Multilateralism or the Last Gasp of the Great Powers?," *Global Policy* 1, no. 1 (2010), 51–63.

47. For the following, Rawnsley, *The End of the Party*, ibook location 4218–4351.

48. "Transcript: Obama's G20 Press Conference," April 2, 2009, https://www.cbsnews.com/news/transcript-obamas-g20-press-conference/.

49. A. Sparrow, K. Baldwin and H. Stewart, "Today's G20 Deal Will Solve Financial Crisis, Claims Gordon Brown," *Guardian*, April 2, 2009.

50. M. Rosie and H. Gorringe, "What a Difference a Death Makes: Protest, Policing and the Press at the G20," *Sociological Research Online* 14, no. 5 (2009), 4.

51. "King Warns Against More Spending," *BBC News*, March 24, 2009.

52. P. Aldrick, "Failed Gilt Auction Stokes Fears over UK Economy," *Telegraph*, March 25, 2009.

53. M. Gove, "Coyote Ugly: G20 Finally Pushes Prudence into the Abyss," *Scotsman*, March 28, 2009.

54. P. Wintour and N. Watt, "Gordon Brown: A Statesman Abroad, Under Fire Back Home," *Guardian*, March 25, 2009.

55. "London Summit—Leaders' Statement," April 2, 2009, https://www.imf.org/external/np/sec/pr/2009/pdf/g20_040209.pdf.

56. N.-L. Sum, "A Cultural Political Economy of Crisis Recovery."
57. Germany's modest discretionary stimulus in early 2009 would later rise due to tax cuts following the elections of September 2009.

CHAPTER 12: STIMULUS

1. S. Erlanger and S. Castle, "European Leader Assails American Stimulus Plan," *New York Times*, March 25, 2009.
2. A. White, "EU Presidency: US Stimulus Is 'The Road to Hell,'" *San Diego Tribune*, March 25, 2009.
3. Rawnsley, *End of the Party*, ibook location 4309.
4. N. Sheiber, *The Escape Artists: How Obama's Team Fumbled the Recovery* (New York: Simon & Schuster, 2012), 96.
5. R. Lizza, "The Obama Memos," *New Yorker*, January 30, 2012, http://www.newyorker.com/magazine/2012/01/30/the-obama-memos.
6. M. Grunwald, *The New New Deal: The Hidden Story of Change in the Obama Era* (New York: Simon & Schuster, 2012).
7. D. Loewe, "Obama's Blues Agenda," *Guardian*, February 13, 2009.
8. J. Green, "The Elusive Green Economy," *Atlantic*, July/August 2009, https://www.theatlantic.com/magazine/archive/2009/07/the-elusive-green-economy/307554/.
9. M. Grabell, *Money Well Spent? The Truth Behind the Trillion-Dollar Stimulus, the Biggest Economic Recovery Plan in History* (New York: PublicAffairs, 2012).
10. B. Dupor, "The Recovery Act of 2009 vs. FDR's New Deal: Which Was Bigger?," https://www.stlouisfed.org/publications/regional-economist/first_quarter_2017/the-recovery-act-of-2009-vs-fdrs-new-deal-which-was-bigger.
11. F. Reichling, "Estimated Impact of the American Recovery and Reinvestment Act on Employment and Economic Output from October 2011 Through December 2011," Congressional Budget Office, Washington, DC, 2012. This broadly concurs with T. G. Conley and B. Dupor, "The American Recovery and Reinvestment Act: Solely a Government Jobs Program?," *Journal of Monetary Economics* 60.5 (2013), 535–549.
12. Council of Economic Advisers, "The Economic Impact of the American Recovery and Reinvestment Act Five Years Later" (final report to Congress, February 2014).
13. P. Krugman, *End This Depression Now*; and Eichengreen, *Hall of Mirrors*, 297–301.
14. C. Romer and J. Bernstein, "The Job Impact of the American Recovery and Reinvestment Plan," January 9, 2009, https://www.economy.com/mark-zandi/documents/The_Job_Impact_of_the_American_Recovery_and_Reinvestment_Plan.pdf.
15. N. Barofksy, *Bailout: An Inside Account of How Washington Abandoned Main Street While Rescuing Wall Street* (New York: Free Press, 2012).
16. The figure of 9.3 million homes lost is an estimate by the National Association of Realtors cited in L. Kusisto, "Many Who Lost Homes to Foreclosure in Last Decade Won't Return," *Wall Street Journal*, April 20, 2015. See also "The End Is in Sight for the US Foreclosure Crisis," December 3, 2016, https://www.stlouisfed.org/publications/housing-market-perspectives/issue-3-dec-2016/the-end-is-in-sight-for-the-us-foreclosure-crisis.
17. "Lawrence Summers on 'House of Debt,'" *Financial Times*, June 6, 2014.
18. R. Suskind, *Confidence Men*.
19. R. E. Rubin, P. R. Orszag and A. Sinai, "Sustained Budget Deficits: The Risk of Financial and Fiscal Disarray," AEA-NAEFA Joint Session, Allied Social Science Associations Annual Meetings, 2004.
20. P. Mauro, M. A. Horton and M. S. Kumar, "The State of Public Finances: A Cross-Country Fiscal Monitor," IMF, 2009.
21. "Budget of the US Government Fiscal Year 2011," https://www.gpo.gov/fdsys/pkg/BUDGET-2011-BUD/pdf/BUDGET-2011-BUD.pdf.
22. IMF, *Fiscal Monitor*, Washington, DC, May 2010.

23. Editorial, "The Bond Vigilantes," *Wall Street Journal,* May 29, 2009.

24. Scheiber, *Escape Artists,* 151; and Suskind, *Confidence Men,* 516.

25. Scheiber, *Escape Artists,* 150.

26. A. P. Lerner, "Functional Finance and the Federal Debt," *Social Research* (1943), 38–51.

27. D. Gabor and C. Ban, "Banking on Bonds: The New Links Between States and Markets," *Journal of Common Market Studies* 54, no. 3 (2016), 617–635.

28. Bastasin, *Saving Europe,* 110–111.

29. D. Gabor, "The ECB and the Eurozone Debt Crisis" (ND), https://www.academia.edu/868218/The_ECB_and_the_European_Debt_Crisis, and D. Gabor, "The Power of Collateral: The ECB and Bank Funding Strategies in Crisis," May 18, 2012, available at SSRN: https://ssrn.com/abstract=2062315 or http://dx.doi.org/10.2139/ssrn.2062315. To supplement the LTRO operations the ECB also operated a smaller scheme to support the covered bond market.

30. IIF, "Interim Report on the Cumulative Impact on the Global Economy of Proposed Changes in the Banking Regulatory Framework," June 2010, 26.

31. M. Dettmer, D. Kurbjuweit, R. Nelles, R. Neukirch und C. Reiermann, "Diebische Freude," *Spiegel,* January 12, 2009.

32. OECD, *Public Debt Markets: Trends and Recent Structural Trends* (Paris: OECD, 2002).

33. "Konjunkturpaket II," *Spiegel,* January 27, 2009.

34. "Konjunkturpaket," *Spiegel,* January 6, 2009.

35. C. Reiermann, "Goldener Zuegel," *Spiegel,* February 9, 2009.

36. F. Gathmann, "Einigung zur Schuldenbremse," *Spiegel,* February 6, 2009; and "Finanzhilfen für ärmere Länder," *Spiegel,* February 13, 2009.

37. "Foederalismusreform," *Spiegel,* March 27, 2009.

38. "Fuehrende Oekonomen verteufeln die Schuldenbremse," *Handelsblatt,* February 13, 2009; and S. Dullien, "Kommentar," *Spiegel,* February 9, 2009.

39. "Schlacht um die Schuldenbremse," *Manager Magazin,* January 16, 2009.

40. D. Hawranek, et al., "Gipfel am Abgrund," *Spiegel,* March 30, 2009.

41. Kuttner, *Presidency in Peril,* 78–79.

42. Suskind, *Confidence Men,* 656.

43. Scheiber, *Escape Artists,* 150.

44. IMF, *Fiscal Monitor,* Washington, DC, November 2010.

CHAPTER 13: FIXING FINANCE

1. OECD, *Economic Outlook No. 85* (June 2009).

2. "Acquisition of Merrill Lynch by Bank of America," June 5, 2009, https://www.federalreserve.gov/newsevents/testimony/bernanke20090625a.htm.

3. "Citigroup Stock Sinks to an All-Time Low of 97 Cents," May 4, 2009, http://www.huffingtonpost.com/2009/03/05/citigroup-stock-sinks-to_n_172167.html.

4. P. Wintour and J. Treanor, "RBS Bonuses to Reach £775m Despite Treasury Tough Talk," *Guardian,* February 17, 2009,

5. B. White, "What Red Ink? Wall Street Paid Hefty Bonuses," *New York Times,* January 28, 2009.

6. G. Farrell and J. Macintosh, "Merrill Delivered Bonuses Before BofA Deal," *Financial Times,* January 21, 2009.

7. "Obama's Statement on AIG," *New York Times,* March 16, 2009.

8. K. Guha and E. Luce, "Greenspan Backs Bank Nationalization," *Financial Times,* February 17, 2009.

9. "Nationalization: Is It the Only Answer to Save Banks?," February 15, 2009, http://abcnews.go.com/WN/Economy/story?id=6885587.

10. "Obama: Swedish Model Would Be Impossible Here," February 11, 2009, http://www.businessinsider.com/obama-swedish-model-would-be-impossible-here-2009-2.

11. J. Cassidy, "No Credit Timothy Geithner's Financial Plan Is Working—And Making Him Very Unpopular," *New Yorker*, March 15, 2010, http://www.newyorker.com/magazine/2010/03/15/no-credit-2#ixzz0haHEOfV7.

12. Suskind, *Confidence Men*, 397–464.

13. Bair, *Bull by the Horns*, Kindle location 3032.

14. S. Johnson and J. Kwak, *13 Bankers: The Wall Street Takeover and the Next Financial Meltdown* (New York: Pantheon Books, 2010).

15. Suskind, *Confidence Men*, 455–460, 695. Geithner issued a public denial: "Press Briefing by Press Secretary Jay Carney, Treasury Secretary Tim Geithner, and OMB Director Jack Lew," September 19, 2011, https://obamawhitehouse.archives.gov/the-press-office/2011/09/19/press-briefing-press-secretary-jay-carney-treasury-secretary-tim-geithne.

16. E. Javers, "Inside Obama's Bank CEOs Meeting," *Politico*, March 4, 2009, http://www.politico.com/story/2009/04/inside-obamas-bank-ceos-meeting-020871.

17. Geithner, *Stress Test*, 376.

18. DealBook, "Geithner Haunted by a Goldman Past He Never Had," *New York Times*, August 19, 2010.

19. Geithner's calendar: https://www.nytimes.com/interactive/projects/documents/geithner-schedule-new-york-fed.

20. A. Clark, "Diary Shows Geithner-Darling Contact During Crisis," *Guardian*, October 11, 2009.

21. Scheiber, *Escape Artists*, 38.

22. J. Anderson, "Calm Before and During a Storm," *New York Times*, February 9, 2007.

23. Suskind, *Confidence Men*, 455.

24. Federal Reserve, "The Supervisory Capital Assessment Program: Design and Implementation," April 24, 2009, https://www.federalreserve.gov/newsevents/press/bcreg/bcreg20090424a1.pdf. As Kuttner, *Presidency in Peril*, 151, points out, the stress test team was grossly underpowered given the complexity of the businesses they were examining.

25. Geithner, *Stress Test*, 345–350.

26. D. Enrich, D. Fitzpatrick and M. Eckblad, "Banks Won Concessions on Tests," *Wall Street Journal*, May 9, 2009.

27. Bair, *Bull by the Horns*, Kindle location 2843; and F. Guerrera and J. Eaglesham, "Citi Under Fire over Deferred Tax Assets," *Financial Times*, September 6, 2010.

28. Scheiber, *Escape Artists*, 128.

29. On Citi, Kuttner, *Presidency in Peril*, 129.

30. SIGTARP, "Exiting TARP: Repayments by the Largest Financial Institutions," September 29, 2011.

31. Bair, *Bull by the Horns*, Kindle location 3686.

32. D. Baker and T. McArthur, "The Value of the 'Too Big to Fail' Big Bank Subsidy," CEPR, 2009.

33. An outstanding road map to the passage of Dodd-Frank can be found in A. S. Blinder, *When the Music Stopped: The Financial Crisis, the Response and the Work Ahead* (New York: Penguin, 2013), 263–366. For contending political accounts, see Geithner, *Stress Test*, 388–438; Bernanke, *Courage to Act*, 435–466; and S. Bair, *Bull by the Horns*, Kindle location 3223–4339.

34. "Dodd-Frank Wall Street Reform and Consumer Protection Act," Public Law 111–203, July 21, 2010, https://www.gpo.gov/fdsys/pkg/PLAW-111publ203/pdf/PLAW-111publ203.pdf.

35. US Treasury, "Financial Regulatory Reform: A New Foundation," Washington, DC, 2009.

36. Geithner, *Stress Test*, 399.

37. Pew Research Center, "Americans' Views of Fed Depend on Their Politics," December 16, 2015, http://www.pewresearch.org/fact-tank/2015/12/16/americans-views-of-fed-depend-on-their-politics/.

38. "Ben Bernanke," *Time*, December 16, 2009.

39. Bernanke, *Courage to Act*, 430–434.

40. S. A. Binder, "Ben Bernanke's Second Term as Chairman of the Federal Reserve," January 30, 2010, https://www.brookings.edu/opinions/ben-bernankes-second-term -as-chairman-of-the-federal-reserve/; and S. Chan, "Senate, Weakly, Backs New Term for Bernanke," *New York Times,* January 28, 2010.

41. Bernanke, *Courage to Act*, 445–447.

42. Geithner, *Stress Test*, 404.

43. Ibid., 432.

44. Ibid., 398.

45. "The United States Residential Foreclosure Crisis: Ten Years Later," March 2017, http:// www.corelogic.com/research/foreclosure-report/national-foreclosure-report-10 -year.pdf.

46. "Life After Lehman," September 13, 2013, http://www.institutionalinvestor.com/Article /3254651/Life-After-Lehman-A-Look-at-How-6-Prominent-Players-Have-Fared.html# .Wavm3ZOGN0s.

47. S. Grocer, "Banks Set Record for Pay," *Wall Street Journal,* January 14, 2010.

48. T. M. Tse, "Goldman Sachs Earns \$13 bn in 2009," *Washington Post,* January 22, 2010.

49. Gasparino, *Bought and Paid For,* 6.

50. Bair, *Bull by the Horns,* Kindle location 3924–3971.

51. D. Polk, "Dodd-Frank Progress Report." July 2013, https://www.davispolk.com/files /Jul2013_Dodd.Frank_.Progress.Report.pdf.

52. Blinder, *After the Music Stopped,* 314–319.

53. B. Protess and P. Eavis, "At the Finish Line on the Volcker Rule," *New York Times,* December 10, 2013.

54. PWC, "Volcker Rule Clarity: Waiting for Godot," May 2014, http://www.pwc.com/us/en /financial-services/regulatory-services/publications/volcker-rule-clarity-waiting-for -godot.html.

55. B. Protess, "Jamie Dimon Shows Some Love for Volcker Rule," *New York Times,* May 21, 2012.

56. P. Clement, "The Term 'Macroprudential': Origins and Evolution 1," *BIS Quarterly Review,* 2010, 59.

57. D. Skeel, *The New Financial Deal: Understanding the Dodd-Frank Act and Its (Unintended) Consequences* (Hoboken, NJ: Wiley, 2010).

58. Federal Reserve, "The Supervisory Capital Assessment Program, May 2009, https:// www.federalreserve.gov/newsevents/files/bcreg20090507a1.pdf.

59. Federal Reserve, "Dodd-Frank Act Stress Test 2013: Supervisory Stress Test Methodology and Results," March 28, 2013, https://www.federalreserve.gov/bankinforeg/stress-tests /appendix-b.htm.

60. "Rules and Regulations," *Federal Register* 76, no. 231 (December 1, 2011), https://www .gpo.gov/fdsys/pkg/FR-2011-12 01/pdf/2011-30665.pdf.

61. Federal Reserve, "Federal Reserve Board Issues Final Rule on Annual Capital Plans, Launches 2012 Review," https://www.federalreserve.gov/newsevents/pressreleases /bcreg20111122a.htm.

62. P. Jenkins and P. J. Davies, "Thirty Financial Groups on Systemic Risk List," *Financial Times,* November 30, 2009.

63. See the collective letter "Healthy Banking System Is the Goal, Not Profitable Banks," *Financial Times,* November 8, 2010; and A. Admati and M. Hellwig, *The Bankers' New Clothes* (Princeton, NJ: Princeton University Press, 2013).

64. IIF, "Interim Report on the Cumulative Impact on the Global Economy of Proposed Changes in the Banking Regulatory Framework Institute of International Finance," June 2010.

65. Bair, *Bull by the Horns,* Kindle location 4731–4748.

66. FSB, "Policy Measures to Address Systemically Important Financial Institutions," November 4, 2011.

67. The High Level Group on Financial Supervision in the EU chaired by Jacques de Larosière, Report, February 25, 2009, http://ec.europa.eu/internal_market/finances /docs/de_larosiere_report_en.pdf.
68. A point I owe to Shahin Vallée.
69. M. Goldstein and N. Véron, "Too Big to Fail: The Transatlantic Debate" (Bruegel working paper 2011/03, 2011).
70. A. S. Posen and N. Véron, "A Solution for Europe's Banking Problem," *Bruegel Policy Brief* (2009).
71. IMF, *Global Financial Stability Report* (April 2009).
72. "Bafin beziffert Kreditrisiken auf 816 Milliarden Euro," *Spiegel*, April 24, 2009.
73. Eichengreen, *Hall of Mirrors*, 323.
74. Geithner, *Stress Test*, 425–426.

CHAPTER 14: GREECE 2010: EXTEND AND PRETEND

1. In full agreement with Sandbu, *Europe's Orphan*; E. Jones, "The Forgotten Financial Union: How You Can Have a Euro Crisis Without a Euro," in *The Future of the Euro*, ed. M. Matthijs and M. Blyth (New York: Oxford University Press, 2015); and D. Mabbett and W. Schelkle, "What Difference Does Euro Membership Make to Stabilization? The Political Economy of International Monetary Systems Revisited," *Review of International Political Economy* 22.3 (2015), 508–534.
2. J. M. Brown, "Things Fall Apart," *Financial Times*, January 15, 2009; and C. Lapavitsas et al., *Crisis in the Eurozone* (London: Verso, 2012), 58.
3. Z. Darvas, "The EU's Role in Supporting Crisis-Hit Countries in Central and Eastern Europe," *Bruegel Policy Contribution* (December 17, 2009).
4. S. Kalyvas, *Modern Greece: What Everyone Needs to Know* (Oxford: Oxford University Press, 2015).
5. G. Papaconstantinou, *Game Over: The Inside Story of the Greek Crisis* (Athens: George Papaconstantinou, 2016).
6. On the politics of creditor-led, as opposed to debtor-led, default, see Lapavistas et al., *Crisis in the Eurozone*, 126–135.
7. M. Walker, C. Forelle and B. Blackstone, "On the Secret Committee to Save the Euro, a Dangerous Divide," *Wall Street Journal*, September 24, 2010.
8. Papaconstantinou, *Game Over*.
9. V. Acharya and S. Steffen, "The Banking Crisis as a Giant Carry Trade Gone Wrong," *VoxEU*, May 23, 2013.
10. S. Wagstyl, "Greeks Search for Hint of Daylight Between Schäuble and Merkel," *Financial Times*, February 19, 2015.
11. For an interpretation that sees it as the key to the entire policy of Merkel's government, see H. Thompson, "Germany and the Euro-Zone Crisis: The European Reformation of the German Banking Crisis and the Future of the Euro," *New Political Economy* 20, no. 6 (2015), 851–870.
12. B. Benoit and T. Barber, "Germany Ready to Help Eurozone Members," *Financial Times*, February 18, 2009.
13. T. Koukakis, "Josef Ackermann: The Secret 2010 Financial Support Plan for Greece and Why It Was Sunk," http://www.tovima.gr/en/article/?aid=639539.
14. R. Zohlnhöfer and T. Saalfeld, eds., *Politik im Schatten der Krise. Eine Bilanz der Regierung Merkel 2009–2013* (Wiesbaden: Springer VS, 2015).
15. A. Tooze, "After the Wars," review of *The Age of Catastrophe: A History of the West 1914–45*, by Heinrich August Winkler, *London Review of Books* 37.22 (2015), 15–17, December 7, 2017, https://www.lrb.co.uk/v37/n22/adam-tooze/after-the-wars.
16. For the quote see I. Traynor, "Angela Merkel Dashes Greek Hopes of Rescue Bid," *Guardian*, February 11, 2010.
17. BVerfG, Judgment of the Second Senate of June 30, 2009—2 BvE 2/08—paras. 1–421.

18. "Merkel sagt Griechenland Milliarden-Hilfe zu'," *Die Welt*, April 26, 2010; and "Union will Bankenbeteiligung prüfen," *Die Zeit*, April 27, 2010.

19. J. Schönenborn, "Griechenland-Hilfe nur mit Bankenbeteiligung," April 4, 2010, ARD-DeutschlandTrend Mai 2010, www.tageschau.de.

20. Bund der Steuerzahler, "Keine Steuerzahlergarantien ohne Bankenbeteiligung," May 5, 2010, https://www.steuerzahler.de/.

21. W. Schäuble, "Why Europe's Monetary Union Faces Its Biggest Crisis," *Financial Times*, March 11, 2010; "Proposal for European Monetary Fund Wins EU Support," *Spiegel Online*, March 8, 2010; and "Why Is Germany Talking About a European Monetary Fund?," *Economist*, March 9, 2010.

22. The second edition of the proposal from May 2010 is available at https://www.ceps.eu /system/files/book/2010/02/Nopercent20202percent20EMFpercent20e -versionpercent20updatepercent2017percent20May.pdf.

23. M. Feldenkirchen, C. Reiermann, M. Sauga and H.-J. Schlamp, "Merkel Takes On the EU and Her Own Finance Minister," *Spiegel Online*, March 22, 2010.

24. "Issing zur Lage Griechenlands: IWF-Hilfe ist die einzige Alternative," February 10, 2010, www.tagesschau.de; and "Man muss den Griechen auf die Finger schauen," March 2, 2010, www.deutschlandfunkkultur.de.

25. Blustein, *Laid Low*, 26–31.

26. IMF Country Report 13/156, May 20, 2013, written up dramatically by A. Evans-Pritchard, "IMF Admits Disastrous Love Affair with the Euro, Apologises for the Immolation of Greece," *Telegraph*, July 28, 2016.

27. "EZB warnt vor IWF-Hilfen für Griechenland," *FAZ*, March 24, 2010.

28. Papaconstantinou, *Game Over*, Kindle locations 1465–1470.

29. C. Volkery, "Merkel's Risky Hand of Brussels Poker," *Spiegel Online*, March 26, 2010; and "Deutschland hilft den Griechen, wenn der IWF hilft," *FAZ*, March 25, 2010.

30. Gabor, "The Power of Collateral," 23.

31. D. Gabor and C. Ban, "Banking on Bonds: The New Links Between States and Markets," *Journal of Common Market Studies* 54.3 (2016), 617–635.

32. For a summary of the argument, see the case brought against the ECB in 2015 to the German supreme court "Verfassungsbeschwerde," October 22, 2015, https://www .jura.uni-freiburg.de/de/institute/ioeffr3/forschung/papers/murswiek/verfassungs beschwerde-qe-anleihenkaeufe-gauweiler.pdf.

33. Gammelin and Löw, *Europas Strippenzieher*, 70.

34. Papaconstantinou, *Game Over*, Kindle locations 1529–1536.

35. J. White, "Emergency Europe," *Political Studies* 63.2 (2015), 300–318.

36. A. Evans-Pritchard, "Europe Agrees IMF-EU Rescue for Greece," *Telegraph*, March 25, 2010.

37. Papaconstantinou, *Game Over*, Kindle location 1677.

38. "Irish Deficit Balloons After New Bank Bail-Out," *BBC News*, September 30, 2010.

39. H. Smith, "Super-Wealthy Investors Move Billions out of Greece," *Guardian*, February 6, 2010; and F. Batzoglou, "Anxious Greeks Emptying Their Bank Accounts," *Spiegel Online*, December 6, 2011.

40. "Euro Zone Readies Giant Rescue Package for Greece," *Reuters*, April 11, 2010.

41. Evans-Pritchard, "Europe Agrees IMF-EU Rescue for Greece."

42. T. Barber, "Saving the Euro: Dinner on the Edge of the Abyss," *Financial Times*, April 22, 2010.

43. Bundesfinanzministerium, "Chronology: Stabilisation of the Economic and Monetary Union," http://www.bundesfinanzministerium.de/Content/EN/Standardartikel/Topics /Europe/Articles/2010-06-04-Chronologie-Euro-Stabilisierung.html?__act=render Pdf&__iDocId=199342.

44. K. Connolly, "Greek Debt Crisis: IMF Chief to Woo Germany over Bailout Deal," *Guardian*, April 28, 2010.

45. "Transcript of Statements to the Media by Angela Merkel and Strauss-Kahn in Berlin," April 28, 2010, https://www.imf.org/en/News/Articles/2015/09/28/04/54/tr042810.
46. Bastasin, *Saving Europe*, 203.
47. J. Pisani-Ferry, "Tim Geithner and Europe's Phone Number," *Bruegel* (blog), February 4, 2013.
48. Papaconstantinou, *Game Over*, Kindle locations 2186–2188.
49. "Regierungserklärung von Bundeskanzlerin Merkel zu den Hilfen für Griechenland," May 5, 2010, https://www.bundesregierung.de/ContentArchiv/DE/Archiv17/Regierung serklaerung/2010/2010-05-05-merkel-erklaerung-griechenland.html. For the wider implications of TINA see A. Séville, "There Is No Alternative," *Politik zwischen Demokratie und Sachzwang* (Frankfurt: Campus, 2017).
50. "Deaths Place Greece on 'Edge of Abyss,'" May 6, 2010, www.ekathimerini.com.
51. Gabor, "The Power of Collateral," 25.
52. "Findings Regarding the Market Events of May 6, 2010," Report of the staffs of the CTFC and SEC to the Joint Advisory Committee on Emerging Regulatory Issues, http://www.sec.gov/news/studies/2010/marketevents-report.pdf.
53. "Preliminary Findings Regarding the Market Events of May 6, 2010," Report of the staffs of the CFTC and SEC to the Joint Advisory Committee on Emerging Regulatory Issues, https://www.sec.gov/sec-cftc-prelimreport.pdf.
54. Bastasin, *Saving Europe*, 202.
55. For this and the following see T. Barber, "Saving the Euro: Dinner on the Edge of the Abyss," *Financial Times*, April 22, 2010.
56. Barber, "Saving the Euro."
57. Bernanke, *Courage to Act*, 481. Bernanke held a private briefing of the Senate Banking Committee to ensure there was no negative reaction.
58. Gammelin and R. Löw, *Europas Strippenzieher*, 75–86.
59. Bastasin, *Saving Europe*, 214–215.
60. Bastasin, *Saving Europe*, 218; Papaconstantinou, *Game Over*, Kindle location 2707.
61. The IMF's own devastating postmortem is IEO, *The IMF and the Crises in Greece, Ireland, and Portugal* (Washington, DC: IMF, 2016), 15–18.
62. Blustein, *Laid Low*, 136.
63. M. Blyth, *Austerity: The History of a Dangerous Idea* (Oxford: Oxford University Press, 2013), 73.
64. "John Lipsky Biographical Information," https://www.imf.org/external/np/omd/bios/jl.htm.
65. Blustein, *Laid Low*, 64.
66. Ibid., 139; and IMF, *Greece: Staff Report on Request for Stand-By Arrangement* (IMF Country Report No. 10/110, 2010).

CHAPTER 15: A TIME OF DEBT

1. For this and the following, see http://www.foxnews.com/story/2010/02/12/glenn-beck-is-us-doomed-to-follow-greece-into-crisis.html.
2. C. M. Reinhart and K. Rogoff, *This Time Is Different, Eight Centuries of Financial Folly* (Princeton, NJ: Princeton University Press, 2009); and C. M. Reinhart and K. S. Rogoff, "Growth in a Time of Debt" (NBER Working Paper 15639, 2010).
3. J. Cassidy, "The Reinhart and Rogoff Controversy: A Summing Up," *New Yorker*, April 26, 2013.
4. C. Reinhart and K. Rogoff, "Why We Should Expect Low Growth Amid Debt," *Financial Times*, January 28, 2010.
5. "Germans Say Euro Zone May Have to Expel Greece: Poll," *Reuters*, February 14, 2010.
6. Irwin, *The Alchemists*, 237–238.
7. G. Osborne, "The Threat of Rising Interest Rates Is a Greek Tragedy We Must Avoid," *Telegraph*, December 21, 2009.

8. P. Habbard, "The Return of the Bond Vigilantes," March 7, 2012, http://www.ituc-csi .org/IMG/pdf/1203t_bond.pdf; and S. Johnson, "Bond Fund Managers Brave 'The Ring of Fire,'" *Financial Times*, February 7, 2010.

9. A. Stratton, "Top Economists Attack Labour Plan to Tackle Britain's Budget Deficit," *Guardian*, February 14, 2010.

10. Lord Skidelsky et al., "Letter: First Priority Must Be to Restore Robust Growth," *Financial Times*, February 18, 2010.

11. P. Wintour, "Mervyn King Shaped Tough Deficit Policy—But Was It Political Bias?," *Guardian*, November 30, 2010.

12. D. Laws, *22 Days in May: The Birth of the Lib Dem-Conservative Coalition* (London: Biteback Publishing, 2010); and Irwin, *The Alchemists*, 244.

13. P. Wintour, "Mervyn King: I Gave Nick Clegg No New Information on Debt Crisis," *Guardian*, July 28, 2010.

14. S. Wren-Lewis, "The Austerity Con," *London Review of Books* 37, no. 4 (2015), 9–11.

15. Irwin, *The Alchemists*, 248–249.

16. P. Krugman, "More on Invisible Bond Vigilantes," *New York Times* (blog), November 10, 2012.

17. N. Watt, "David Cameron Makes Leaner State a Permanent Goal," *Guardian*, November 12, 2013.

18. ONS, "Statistical Bulletin: Public Sector Employment, UK: September 2016," https:// www.ons.gov.uk/employmentandlabourmarket/peopleinwork/publicsectorpersonnel /bulletins/publicsectoremployment/september2016.

19. T. Crewe, "The Strange Death of Municipal England," *London Review of Books* 38, no. 24 (2016), 6–10. For a dramatic summary of the impact of austerity on the British welfare state see the essays in V. Cooper and D. Whyte, eds., *The Violence of Austerity* (London: Pluto Press, 2017).

20. Clark, *Hard Times*, 180–191.

21. Editorial, "The Risks and Rewards of George Osborne's Austerity," *Financial Times*, July 21, 2015.

22. S. Stein, "Peter Orszag, Former Top Obama Adviser, Takes Issue with Portrayal in New Book," *Huffington Post*, February 24, 2012, www.huffingtonpost.com.

23. Kuttner, *Presidency in Peril*, 207.

24. "Obama's State of the Union Transcript 2010: Full Text," *Politico*, January 27, 2010.

25. P. Krugman, "Obama Liquidates Himself," *New York Times*, January 26, 2010.

26. J. Geraghty's *National Review* blog quoted in "How the Austerity Class Rules Washington," *Nation*, October 19, 2011.

27. H. Yeager, "Circling Back on the Orszag Story," *Columbia Journalism Review* 9 (January 2010).

28. Bernanke, *Courage to Act*, 504; and L. Elliott, "It's Too Soon for Austerity, Ben Bernanke Tells Congress," *Guardian*, July 22, 2010.

29. E. Luce, "US Deficit Key to Orszag Departure," *Financial Times*, June 25, 2010.

30. T. Skocpol and V. Williamson, *The Tea Party and the Remaking of Republican Conservatism* (Oxford: Oxford University Press, 2012).

31. G. C. Jacobson, "The Republican Resurgence in 2010," *Political Science Quarterly* 126, no. 1 (2011), 27–52.

32. S.-A. Mildner and J. Howald, "Jumping the Fiscal Cliff: The Political Economy of Fiscal Policy-Making under President Obama," *CESifo Forum* (June 2013).

33. T. E. Mann and N. J. Ornstein, *It's Even Worse Than It Looks: How the American Constitutional System Collided with the New Politics of Extremism* (New York: Basic Books, 2016), 9–10.

34. Q. Peel, "Merkel Spells Out €80bn Spending Cuts," *Financial Times*, June 8, 2010.

35. OECD, "Budget Deficits: What Governments Are Doing" (2010), http://www.oecd.org /germany/budgetdeficitswhatgovernmentsaredoing.htm.

36. "German Government Agrees on Historic Austerity Program," *Spiegel Online*, June 7, 2010.
37. Peel, "Merkel Spells Out €80bn Spending Cuts."
38. D. Mara and A. Bowen, "German Government Unveils Unprecedented Austerity Plan," *Deutsche Welle*, June 7, 2010.
39. A. Beattie and Q. Peel, "Scene Set for G20 Battle over Fiscal Strategy," *Financial Times*, June 24, 2010.
40. W. Schäuble, "Maligned Germany Is Right to Cut Spending," *Financial Times*, June 23, 2010.
41. L. Summers and T. Geithner, "Our Agenda for the G-20," *Wall Street Journal*, June 23, 2010.
42. J. Calmes and S. Chan, "Leaders at Summit Turn Attention to Deficit Cuts," *New York Times*, June 26, 2010.
43. OECD, "Employment: Job Creation Must Be a Top Priority in Months Ahead, Says OECD's Gurria," July 7, 2010, http://www.oecd.org/newsroom/employmentjobcreation mustbeatoppriorityinmonthsaheadsaysoecdsgurria.htm.
44. H. Zimmermann, "A Grand Coalition for the Euro: The Second Merkel Cabinet, the Euro Crisis and the Elections of 2013," *German Politics* 23, no. 4 (2014): 322–336.
45. Bastasin, *Saving Europe*, 221–235.
46. Papaconstantinou, *Game Over*, Kindle locations 2352–2365.
47. IMF Country Report 11/68 (March 2011).
48. Bank of Greece, "The Chronicle of the Great Crisis: 2008–2013, http://www.bankof greece.gr/BogEkdoseis/The%20Chronicle%20Of%20The%20Great%20Crisis.pdf.
49. CEBS, "EBA Aggregate Outcome of the 2010 EU Wide Stress Test," July 23, 2010, https:// www.eba.europa.eu/documents/10180/15938/Summaryreport.pdf/95030af2-7b52 -4530-afe1-f067a895d163.
50. A. Blundell-Wignall and P. Slovik, "The EU Stress Test and Sovereign Debt Exposures" (OECD Working Papers on Finance, Insurance and Private Pensions, no. 4, OECD Financial Affairs Division, 2010).
51. The fact that Europe's bank stress tests lacked the backing of clear recapitalization facilities is highlighted by T. Santos, "El Diluvio: The Spanish Banking Crisis, 2008–2012," manuscript (2017), Columbia Business School, Columbia University.
52. L. Thomas Jr., "Greek Bonds Lure Some, Despite Risk," *New York Times*, September 28, 2011.
53. Bastasin, *Saving Europe*, 259.
54. Acharya and Steffen, "The Banking Crisis as a Giant Carry Trade Gone Wrong."
55. B. H. Cohen, "How Have Banks Adjusted to Higher Capital Requirements?," *BIS Quarterly Review*, 2013, 25.
56. *Report of the Joint Committee of Inquiry into the Banking Crisis*, Houses of the Oireachtas (Inquiries, Privileges and Procedures) Act, 2016.
57. C. Gleeson, "Ireland's Austerity Budgets," *Irish Times*, December 13, 2013.
58. Blustein, *Laid Low*, 157.
59. G. Wiesmann, "Merkel Seeks to Pull Bondholders into Rescues," *Financial Times*, November 24, 2010.
60. K. Bennhold, "At Deauville, Europe Embraces Russia," *New York Times*, October 18, 2010.
61. C. Forelle, D. Gauthier-Villars, B. Blackstone and D. Enrich, "As Ireland Flails, Europe Lurches Across the Rubicon," *Wall Street Journal*, December 27, 2010.
62. Zimmermann, "A Grand Coalition for the Euro."
63. L. Barber and R. Atkins, FT interview transcript: Mario Draghi, *Financial Times*, December 18, 2011.
64. A. Mody, "The Ghost of Deauville," *VoxEU*, January 7, 2014.

65. *Report of the Joint Committee of Inquiry into the Banking Crisis* (Dublin: Houses of the Oireachtas, 2016), https://inquiries.oireachtas.ie/banking/.
66. L. O'Carroll, "Ireland's Central Bank Governor Confirms IMF Loan on Its Way," *Guardian*, November 18, 2010.
67. "Jean Claude Trichet Letter to Brian Lenihan," *Irish Times*, November 6, 2014.
68. Editorial, "Was It for This?," *Irish Times*, November 18, 2010.
69. Sanbu, *Europe's Orphan*, 104.
70. A. Chopra, "Lessons from Ireland's Financial Crisis," 2015, https://www.youtube.com /watch?v=6XDomfai7DY.
71. P. Spiegel, "Draghi's ECB Management: The Leaked Geithner Files," *Financial Times*, November 11, 2014.
72. *Report of the Joint Committee of Inquiry into the Banking Crisis*, Houses of the Oireachtas.
73. M. Matthijs and M. Blyth, "When Is It Rational to Learn the Wrong Lessons? Technocratic Authority, Social Learning, and Euro Fragility," *Perspectives on Politics* (2017): 1–17.
74. Eichengreen, *Hall of Mirrors*, 302–311.
75. Bernanke, *Courage to Act*, 482–496.
76. See the sharp retrospective analysis by N. Kocherlakota of the Minneapolis Fed, "The Fed's Unspoken Mandate: It Wants to Be 'Normal,' and That's Bad for Most Americans," June 13, 2017, https://www.bloomberg.com/view/articles/2017-06-13/the -fed-s-unspoken-mandate.
77. "Fed Doubted QE2 Impact, Worried over 'Currency War' Perception," *Reuters*, January 15, 2016.
78. G. Beck, transcript, Fox News, November 3, 2010; Irwin, *The Alchemists*, 409; and Blinder, *After the Music Stopped*, 248–256.
79. D. Morgan, "Palin Tells Bernanke to 'Cease and Desist,'" *Reuters*, November 8, 2010; and C. Asness et al., "Open Letter to Ben Bernanke," *Wall Street Journal*, November 15, 2010.
80. J. Wheatley and P. Garnham, "Brazil in 'Currency War' Alert," *Financial Times*, February 27, 2010.
81. Irwin, *The Alchemists*, 257.
82. "Interview with German finance minister Schäuble, The US Has Lived on Borrowed Money for Too Long," *Spiegel Online*, November 8, 2010; and "Global Anger Swells at US Fed Actions," *Reuters*, November 5, 2010.
83. R. Atkins, "Germany Attacks US Economic Policy," *Financial Times*, November 7, 2010.
84. B. S. Bernanke, "Federal Reserve Policy in an International Context," *IMF Economic Review* 65, no. 1 (2017), 5–36.
85. "UPDATE 2-Geithner: Beijing Supportive of G20 Rebalancing Effort," *Reuters*, November 8, 2010.
86. Morgan, "Palin Tells Bernanke to 'Cease and Desist.'"
87. R. Neil, "Non-US Banks' Claims on the Federal Reserve," *BIS Quarterly Review*, March 2014; and C. Choulet, "QE and Bank Balance Sheets: The American Experience," BNP Paribas, *Conjoncture* 7 and 8 (July/August 2015), 3–19.

CHAPTER 16: G-ZERO WORLD

1. P. Krugman and R. Wells, "Where Do We Go from Here?," *New York Review of Books*, January 13, 2011; P. Krugman, "The Intimidated Fed," *New York Times*, April 28, 2011; and P. Krugman, "Against Learned Helplessness," *New York Times*, May 29, 2011.
2. P. Krugman, "The Mistake of 2010," *New York Times*, June 2, 2011.
3. "Playboy Interview: Paul Krugman," *Playboy*, February 15, 2012.
4. A. Etzioni, "No Marshall Plan for the Middle East," *Prism* 3, no. 1 (2011), 75–86.

5. T. Duncan, "The Federal Reserve Is Causing Turmoil Abroad," *Wall Street Journal*, February 23, 2011.

6. "Blood on Bernanke's Hands," *Mish's Global Economic Trend Analysis*, January 27, 2011, http://globaleconomicanalysis.blogspot.com/2011/01/blood-on-bernankes-hands -riots-in-egypt.html.

7. P. Krugman, "Droughts, Floods and Food," *New York Times*, February 6, 2011.

8. I. Bremmer and N. Roubini, "AG-Zero World: The New Economic Club Will Produce Conflict, Not Cooperation," *Foreign Affairs* 90 (2011), 2.

9. J. M. Magone, "Portugal Is Not Greece," *Perspectives on European Politics and Society* 15.3 (2014), 346–360.

10. S. Hessel, *Indignez-Vous!* (Paris: Indigène éditions, 2010).

11. E. Castañeda, "The Indignados of Spain: A Precedent to Occupy Wall Street," *Social Movement Studies* 11.3–4 (2012), 309–319.

12. "'We Are Not Goods on Politicians and Bankers' Hands'—A Letter from Spain," June 13, 2011, http://www.fondation-bourdieu.org/index.php?id=20&tx_ttnews%5Btt _news%5D=40&.

13. J. M. Antentas, "Spain: The Indignados Rebellion of 2011 in Perspective," *Labor History* 56.2 (2015), 136–160.

14. A. A. Ellinas, "The Rise of Golden Dawn: The New Face of the Far Right in Greece," *South European Society and Politics* 18, no. 4 (2013), 543–565.

15. N. Hughes, "'Young People Took to the Streets and All of a Sudden All of the Political Parties Got Old': The 15M Movement In Spain," *Social Movement Studies* 10, no. 4 (2011), 407–413; and M. Kaika and K. Lazaros, "The Spatialization of Democratic Politics: Insights from Indignant Squares," *European Urban and Regional Studies* 23, no. 4 (2016), 556–570.

16. E. Romanos, "Evictions, Petitions and Escraches: Contentious Housing in Austerity Spain," *Social Movement Studies* 13, no. 2 (2014), 296–302.

17. Borrowing from protests in Argentina designed to unmask the torturers of the military regime, S. Kaiser, "Escraches: Demonstrations, Communication and Political Memory in Post-Dictatorial Argentina," *Media, Culture & Society* 24, no. 4 (2002), 499–516.

18. W. Streeck, *Buying the Time: The Delayed Crisis of Democratic Capitalism* (London: Verso, 2014), 116.

19. M. Kaldor and S. Selchow, "The 'Bubbling Up' of Subterranean Politics in Europe," *Journal of Civil Society* 9, no. 1 (2013), 78–99.

20. For a sharp analysis of Tsipras's new rhetoric of the people see J. B. Judis, *The Populist Explosion* (New York: Columbia Global Reports, 2016), Kindle location 1516–1517. For a view from the far left see K. Ovenden, *Syriza: Inside the Labyrinth* (London: Pluto Press, 2015).

21. C. Delclós, *Hope Is a Promise* (London: Zed Books, 2015).

22. D. Hancox, "Why Ernesto Laclau Is the Intellectual Figurehead for Syriza and Podemos," *Guardian*, February 9, 2015.

23. P. Iglesias, *Politics in a Time of Crisis: Podemos and the Future of European Democracy* (London: Verso, 2015), 61.

24. Paul Krugman, "The Expansionary Austerity Zombie," *New York Times*, November 20, 2015.

25. C. Forelle and M. Walker, "Dithering at the Top Turned EU Crisis to Global Threat," *Wall Street Journal*, December 29, 2011.

26. Papaconstantinou, *Game Over*, Kindle locations 3083–3095.

27. Bastasin, *Saving Europe*, 223.

28. R. Atkins, "ECB Raises Rates for First Time Since 2008," *Financial Times*, April 7, 2011; and R. Atkins, "ECB Raises Interest Rates to 1.5%," *Financial Times*, July 7, 2011.

29. J. Stark, "ECB Must Favour No Nation," *Financial Times*, March 30, 2011.

30. Bastasin, *Saving Europe*, 268; Gabor, "Power of Collateral," 27; and D. M. Woodruff, "Governing by Panic: The Politics of the Eurozone Crisis," *Politics & Society* 44.1 (2016), 81–116.
31. Bank of England, *Financial Stability Report* (December 2011).
32. P. Garheim, "Traders 'Short' Dollar as Currency Loses Attraction," *Financial Times*, March 7, 2011; and C. Comstock, "Check Out the Hedge Funds Profiting Off Big Europe Shorts," *Business Insider*, August 5, 2011.
33. For clear-headed dissection of the argument see Sandbu, *Europe's Orphan*, 118–122, and Schelkle, *Political Economy of Monetary Solidaity*, 266–302.
34. For an admirably comprehensive and multilingual bibliography of the debate, see Professor Sinn's Web site, http://www.hanswernersinn.de/en/controversies/TargetDebate.
35. W. Jacoby, "Germany and the Eurocrisis: The Timing of Politics and the Politics of Timing" (ACES Cases, no. 2014.3, 2014).
36. C. Forelle and M. Walker, "Dithering at the Top," *Wall Street Journal*, December 29, 2011.
37. C. Reiermann, "Greece Considers Exit from Euro Zone," *Spiegel Online*, May 6, 2011; and "Bailing Out the Bail-out," *Economist*, May 9, 2011.
38. C. Forelle, "Luxembourg Lies on Secret Meeting," *Wall Street Journal*, May 9, 2011; and V. Pop, "Eurogroup Chief: 'I'm for Secret, Dark Debates,'" April 21, 2011, https://euob server.com/economic/32222.
39. Blustein, *Laid Low*, 201.
40. "No Country Is an Island: Ireland and the IMF," *IMF* (blog), July 14, 2011, https://blogs .imf.org/2011/07/14/no-country-is-an-island-ireland-and-the-imf/.
41. N. Véron, "The IMF's Role in the Euro Area Crisis: Financial Sector Aspects" (*IEO Background Paper* BP/16-02/10, IMF, 2016).
42. D. Strauss-Kahn, "Crisis Management Arrangements for a European Banking System" (speech, Brussels, March 19, 2010), https://www.imf.org/en/News/Articles/2015/09/28 /04/53/sp031910.
43. P. J. Williams, "L'Affaire DSK: Presumption of Innocence Lost," *Nation*, May 24, 2011.
44. P. Wilkinson, "Sarkozy Party Chief Denies DSK 'Plot Claim,'" CNN, November 28, 2011.
45. M. Naß, "USA wollen mehr deutsche Verlässlichkeit," *Die Zeit*, June 5, 2011.
46. IMF Country Report 11/175 (July 2011).
47. A. Faiola and H. Schneider, "Debt Crisis Threatens Italy, One of Euro Zone's Biggest Economies," *Washington Post*, July 12, 2011; and S. Castle, "Italian Debt Adds to Fears in Euro Zone," *New York Times*, July 10, 2011.
48. O. Helgadóttir, "The Bocconi Boys Go to Brussels: Italian Economic Ideas, Professional Networks and European Austerity," *Journal of European Public Policy* 23, no. 3 (2016), 392–409; and M. Blyth, *Austerity: The History of a Dangerous Idea* (Oxford: Oxford University Press, 2013), 170–171.
49. A. Friedman, *Berlusconi: The Epic Story of the Billionaire Who Took Over Italy* (New York: Hachette, 2015).
50. S. Braghiroli, "The Italian Local Elections of 2011: Four Ingredients for a Political Defeat," *Bulletin of Italian Politics* 3, no. 1 (2011), 137–157.
51. "Helmut Kohl rechnet mit Merkels Europapolitik ab," *Spiegel Online*, July 17, 2011.
52. T. Alloway, "Goldman Answers 10 Questions on Italy," *Financial Times*, July 18, 2011.
53. Bastasin, *Saving Europe*, 313.
54. ETF, "Market-Implied Default Probabilities and Credit Indexes," December 30, 2011, http://www.etf.com/publications/journalofindexes/joi-articles/10605-market-implied -default-probabilities-and-credit-indexes.html?nopaging=1.
55. L. Thomas Jr., "Pondering a Dire Day: Leaving the Euro," *New York Times*, December 12, 2011.

56. R. De Bock, "What Happens in Emerging Markets If Recent Bank and Portfolio Inflows Reverse?," IMF, April 15, 2012.
57. J. Barthélémy, V. Bignon and B. Nguyen, "Illiquid Collateral and Bank Lending During the European Sovereign Debt Crisis," *Mimeo*, 2017.
58. Bastasin, *Saving Europe*, 293.
59. G. Wearden, "European Debt Crisis Meeting," *Guardian*, July 21, 2011.
60. Blustein, *Laid Low*, 227.
61. A boast confirmed by economic analysis that suggests that the haircut was, in fact, minimal. J. Zettelmeyer, C. Trebesch and M. Gulati, "The Greek Debt Restructuring: An Autopsy," *Economic Policy* 28, no. 75 (2013), 513–563.
62. For this and the following, "EU Leaders Must Now Persuade Investors That New Drive Can Work," July 22, 2011, http://business.financialpost.com/news/economy/eu-leaders -must-now-persuade-investors-that-new-drive-can-work.
63. R. Milne and J. Wilson, "Deutsche Bank Hedges Italian Risk," *Financial Times*, July 26, 2011.
64. V. Damiani, "Italian Prosecutor Investigates Deutsche Bank over 2011 Bond Sale," *Reuters*, May 6, 2016.
65. T. E. Mann and N. J. Ornstein, *It's Even Worse Than It Looks*, 2nd ed. (New York: Basic Books, 2016).
66. US Treasury, "As US Reaches Debt Limit, Geithner Implements Additional Extraordinary Measures," May 16, 2011, https://www.treasury.gov/connect/blog/Pages/Geithner -Implements-Additional-Extraordinary-Measures-to-Allow-Continued-Funding -of-Government-Obligations.aspx.
67. G. Sargent, "Nonstop Chatter About Deficit Does Nothing to Reassure People About Economy," *Washington Post*, April 28, 2011.
68. P. Wallsten, L. Montgomery and S. Wilson, "Obama's Evolution: Behind the Failed 'Grand Bargain' on the Debt," *Washington Post*, March 17, 2012.
69. "Trillion Dollar Coin," https://en.wikipedia.org/wiki/Trillion_dollar_coin.
70. "Debt Limit Analysis," July 2011, http://cdn.bipartisanpolicy.org/wp-content/uploads sites/default/files/DebtLimitAnalysis.pdf.
71. N. Krishnan, A. Martin and A. Sarkar, "Pick Your Poison: How Money Market Funds Reacted to Financial Stress in 2011," *Liberty Street Economics* (blog), 2013.
72. D. A. Austin and R. S. Miller, "Treasury Securities and the US Sovereign Credit Default Swap Market," *CRS Report for Congress*, no. 7-5700, 2011.
73. K. Drum, "Quote of the Day: Hostages and Ransom Demands," *Mother Jones*, August 3, 2011, http://www.motherjones.com/kevin-drum/2011/08/quote-day-hostage-and-ransom -notes.
74. *Washington Post* staff, "Origins of the Debt Showdown," *Washington Post*, August 6, 2011.
75. "US Credit Rating Downgraded," *Economist*, August 3, 2011.
76. "Research Update: United States of America Long-Term Rating Lowered to 'AA+,'" August 6, 2011, http://www.standardandpoors.com/en_AP/web/guest/article/-/view /sourceId/6802837.
77. US Treasury, "Just the Facts," August 6, 2011, https://www.treasury.gov/connect/blog /Pages/Just-the-Facts-SPs-2-Trillion-Mistake.aspx.
78. M. Walker, D. Paletta, and B. Blackstone, "Global Crisis of Confidence," *Wall Street Journal*, August 13, 2011.
79. "FBI Documents Reveal Secret Nationwide Occupy Monitoring," December 21, 2012, http://www.justiceonline.org/fbi_files_ows.
80. "Media Coverage of Occupy vs. Tea Party," October 21, 2011, http://www.journalism .org/numbers/tale-two-protests/.
81. M. A. Gould-Wartofsky, *The Occupiers: The Making of the 99 Percent Movement* (Oxford: Oxford University Press, 2015).

82. E. Addly, "Occupy Movement: From Local Action to a Global Howl of Protest," *Guardian*, October 17, 2011.
83. J. Zeley and M. Thee-Brenan, "New Poll Finds a Deep Distrust of Government," *New York Times*, October 25, 2011; and "Americans' Approval of Congress Drops to Single Digits," *New York Times*, October 25, 2011.

CHAPTER 17: DOOM LOOP

1. "Pressestatements," September 1, 2011, https://www.bundesregierung.de/ContentAr chiv/DE/Archiv17/Mitschrift/Pressekonferenzen/2011/09/2011-09-01-merkel-coelho .html.
2. V. A. Schmidt and M. Thatcher, "Why Are Neoliberal Ideas So Resilient in Europe's Political Economy?," *Critical Policy Studies* 8, no. 3 (2014): 340–347.
3. Q. Peel, "Germany and the Eurozone: Besieged in Berlin," *Financial Times*, September 26, 2011.
4. "Merkel im Bundestag: Die größte Belastungsprobe, die es je gab," *Die Zeit*, October 26, 2011.
5. Classically articulated by F. Fukuyama, *The End of History and the Last Man* (New York: Free Press, 1992).
6. As argued forcefully in W. Streeck, *Buying Time*.
7. G. Dinmore and R. Atkins, "ECB Letter Shows Pressure on Berlusconi," *Financial Times*, September 29, 2011.
8. E. Lobina and R. Cavallo, "The Campaign Against Water Privatisation in Italy," 2011, https://research.ncl.ac.uk/media/sites/researchwebsites/gobacit/Emanuele%20Lo bina.pdf.
9. G. Angiulli, "The State of Emergency in Italy" (University of Trento, 2009) mimeo, http://www.jus.unitn.it/cocoa/papers/PAPERS%204TH%20PDF%5CEmergency%20It aly%20Angiulli.pdf.
10. G. Tremlett, "Spain Changes Constitution to Cap Budget Deficit," *Guardian*, August 26, 2011.
11. Cited in G. Hewitt, *The Lost Continent: The Inside Story of Europe's Darkest Hour Since World War Two* (London: Hodder & Stoughton, 2013), 184.
12. "Financial Markets in Early August 2011," ECB, *Monthly Bulletin*, September 2011.
13. Bastasin, *Saving Europe*, 306; and V. Constancio, "Contagion and the European Debt Crisis," *Financial Stability Review* 16 (2012), 109–121.
14. M. Schlieben and L. Caspari, "Merkels Mehrheit für einen Tag," *Die Zeit*, September 29, 2011.
15. J. Ewing and N. Kulish, "A Setback for the Euro Zone," *New York Times*, September 9, 2011.
16. S. Fidler, "EFSF Leverage: A Rundown," *Wall Street Journal*, September 27, 2011.
17. IMF, *Global Financial Stability Report* (Washington, DC: IMF, 2009).
10. C. Lagarde, "'Global Risks Are Rising, But There Is a Path to Recover,'" August 27, 2011, https://www.imf.org/en/News/Articles/2015/09/28/04/53/sp082711.
19. IIF, *The Cumulative Impact on the Global Economy of Changes in the Financial Regulatory Framework* (September 2011).
20. B. Masters and T. Braithwaite, "Tighter Rules on Capital: Bankers Versus Basel," *Financial Times*, October 2, 2011.
21. "Federal Reserve Aid to the Eurozone: Its Impact on the US and the Dollar," https:// archive.org/stream/gov.gpo.fdsys.CHRG-112hhrg75083/CHRG-112hhrg75083_djvu .txt.
22. Bespoke Investment Group, "A Look at Bank and Broker Credit Default Swap Prices," seekingalpha.com, February 15, 2017.
23. Geithner, *Stress Test*, 474.
24. M. Krupa and J. Riedl, "Ach, die Maria!," *Die Zeit*, June 21, 2012.

25. Geithner, *Stress Test*, 473.
26. "EFSF Leverage Explained," October 28, 2011, https://www.macrobusiness.com.au/2011/10/efsf-leverage-explained/.
27. J. Chaffin, A. Barker and K. Hope, "Geithner Warns EU of 'Catastrophic Risk,'" *Financial Times*, September 17, 2011.
28. S. Castle, L. Story, "Advice on Debt? Europe Suggests US Can Keep It," *New York Times*, September 16, 2011.
29. C. Giles, "Financial Institutions Stare into the Abyss," *Financial Times*, September 22, 2011.
30. L. Summers, "The World Must Insist That Europe Act," *Financial Times*, September 18, 2011.
31. H. Stewart, "Eurozone Ministers Under Pressure as Debt Crisis Dominates IMF Summit," *Financial Times*, September 24, 2011.
32. "IMF Survey: Lagarde Urges Collective Action to Restore Confidence," September 15, 2011, http://www.imf.org/external/pubs/ft/survey/so/2011/NEW091511A.htm.
33. N. Whitbeck, "Dexia—Rise and Fall of a Banking Giant," *Les Etudes Du Club* no. 100, 2013.
34. Acharya and Steffen, "The Banking Crisis as a Giant Carry Trade Gone Wrong."
35. M. Sparkes and A. Wilson, "Debt Crisis: As It Happened," *Telegraph*, October 5, 2011.
36. A. Lucchetti, "MF Global Told to Boost Capital," *Wall Street Journal*, October 17, 2011; and Cause of Action, "The Collapse of MF Global: Summary & Analysis," https://causeofaction.org/wp-content/uploads/2013/06/MF-Global-Summary-and-Analysis1.pdf.
37. "Regierungserklärung," October 26, 2011, https://www.bundesregierung.de/Content Archiv/DE/Archiv17/Regierungserklaerung/2011/2011-10-27-merkel-eu-gipfel.html.
38. Bastasin, *Saving Europe*, 332; the remarkable blow-by-blow blog "Debt Crisis as It Happened," *Telegraph*, October 26, 2011; and Papaconstantinou, *Game Over*, chapter 19.
39. R. Donadio and N. Kitsantoni, "Thousands in Greece Protest Austerity Bill," *New York Times*, October 19, 2011.
40. A. Visvizi, "The Crisis in Greece, Democracy, and the EU," December 10, 2012, https://www.carnegiecouncil.org/publications/ethics_online/0076/:pf_printable.
41. For the narrative of the Cannes meeting see P. Spiegel, *How the Euro Was Saved* (London: Financial Times, 2014).
42. "Lucas Papademos: A Man Who Tried to Rescue Greece," *BBC News*, May 25, 2017.
43. Blustein, *Laid Low*, 271–276.
44. P. Spiegel, "Draghi's ECB Management: The Leaked Geithner Files," *Financial Times*, November 11, 2014.
45. Geithner, *Stress Test*, 476.
46. For an account stressing the death of Berlusconi's premiership from natural causes and the legitimacy of Napolitano's role see A. Benvenuti, "Between Myth and Reality: The Euro Crisis and the Downfall of Silvio Berlusconi," *Journal of Modern Italian Studies* 22.4 (2017), 512–529.
47. M. Walker, C. Forelle and S. Meichtry, "Deepening Crisis over Euro Pits Leader Against Leader," *Wall Street Journal*, December 30, 2011; and "Kissinger: 'I Tell You What Napolitano Did in 2011 and 2014,'" November 26, 2015, http://www.ilgiornale.it/news/cronache/kissinger-vi-dico-cosa-ha-fatto-napolitano-2011-e-2014-1198786.html.
48. Friedman, *Berlusconi*, 207–237.
49. "Profile: Mario Monti," *BBC News*, February 18, 2013.
50. G. Pastorella, *Technocratic Governments: Power, Expertise and Crisis Politics in European Democracies* (Ph.D. thesis, London School of Economics and Political Science, 2016).
51. S. Foley, "What Price the New Democracy?," *Independent*, November 18, 2011.
52. Interview with Hans Knundani, September 2017.

53. P. Spiegel, "It Was the Point Where the Eurozone Could Have Exploded," *Financial Times,* May 11, 2014.

54. E. Kuehnen and A. Breidthardt, "ECB Should Stay Out of EFSF Leveraging: Buba Chief," *Reuters,* September 17, 2011.

55. Spiegel, "It Was the Point Where the Eurozone Could Have Exploded."

56. "Klare Umfragemehrheit für Rot-Grün," *Die Zeit,* December 16, 2011.

57. P. Spiegel, "If the Euro Falls, Europe Falls," *Financial Times,* May 15, 2014.

58. T. Durden, "Presenting Deutsche Bank's Pitchbook to the ECB to Go 'All In,'" *Zero Hedge* (blog), November 15, 2011.

59. *Spiegel* staff, "Germany's Central Bank Against the World," *Spiegel Online,* November 15, 2011.

60. "Germany Suffers 'Disaster' at Bond Auction," *Telegraph,* November 23, 2011.

61. R. Sikorski, "Poland and the Future of the European Union," November 28, 2011, http://www.mfa.gov.pl/resource/33ce6061-ec12-4da1-a145-01e2995c6302:JCR.

62. Bastasin, *Saving Europe* (2nd ed.), Kindle location 6847–7544.

63. C. Giles and G. Parker, "Osborne Urges Eurozone to 'Get a Grip,'" *Financial Times,* July 20, 2011; and A. Woodcock and D. Higgens, "Eurozone Crisis: David Cameron Calls for Action," *Independent,* December 2, 2011.

64. I. Traynor et al., "David Cameron Blocks EU Treaty with Veto, Casting Britain Adrift in Europe," *Guardian,* December 9, 2011.

65. Bastasin, *Saving Europe,* 342–351.

66. *Rapport Annuel de la Banque de France* (Paris, 2011), 37, 92.

67. J. Daley, "Eurozone Crisis: The US Has to Ride to the Rescue Once Again," *Telegraph,* December 3, 2011.

68. Spiegel, "If the Euro Falls, Europe Falls."

69. "FT Person of the Year: Mario Draghi," *Financial Times,* December 13, 2012; and A. Verdun, "Political Leadership of the European Central Bank," *Journal of European Integration* 39, no. 2 (2017), 207–221.

70. L. Barber and R. Atkins, *FT* interview transcript: Mario Draghi, *Financial Times,* December 18, 2011.

71. ECB, "Introductory Statement by Mario Draghi," December 1, 2011, https://www.ecb.europa.eu/press/key/date/2011/html/sp111201.en.html.

72. B. Blackstone, M. Karnitschnig and R. Thomson, "Europe's Banker Talks Tough," *Wall Street Journal,* February 24, 2012; for more extended comments by Draghi on unemployment, see M. Draghi, "Unemployment in the Euro Area," https://www.kansascityfed.org/publicat/sympos/2014/2014Draghi.pdf.

73. For this and the following see Barber and Atkins, *FT* interview transcript: Mario Draghi.

74. Bastasin, *Saving Europe,* 343–345.

75. E. Kuehnen, "ECB Wall of Cash Averts Credit Crunch," *Reuters,* February 27, 2012, http://uk.reuters.com/article/us-ecb-m3/ecb-wall-of-cash-averts-credit-crunch-idUSTRE81Q0XP20120227.

76. J. Cotterill, "Keep On Carrying On LTROs," *Financial Times,* October 7, 2011; and "ECB Announces Details of Refinancing Operations from October 2011," http://www.ecb.europa.eu/press/pr/date/2011/html/pr111006_4.en.html.

77. R. Atkins and T. Alloway, "ECB Launches New Support for Banks," *Financial Times,* December 8, 2011.

78. Barber and Atkins, *FT* interview transcript: Mario Draghi.

79. P. Jenkins, M. Watkins, and R. Sanderson, "Draghi's Cash Tonic Makes Bank Smile," *Financial Times,* March 1, 2012.

80. J. Plender, "Beware Sovereign Stress If ECB Backdoor Bet Backfires," *Financial Times,* February 28, 2012.

81. G. Wiesmann, P. Spiegel and R. Wigglesworth, "S&P Downgrades France and Austria," *Financial Times*, January 14, 2012.

82. "Merkel: World Needs a Decade to Recover from the Crisis," November 7, 2011, https://www.newsmax.com/t/finance/article/417090.

CHAPTER 18: WHATEVER IT TAKES

1. K. Hughes and L. Rojas, "G20 Pushes for Extra Steps from Europe on Crisis," January 21, 2012, http://www.livemint.com/Politics/JVBm6ECtqt9oBlHCDcRZ2L/G20-pushes-for-extra-steps-from-Europe-on-crisis.html.

2. "IMF Note on Global Economic Prospects and Policy Changes," February 25, 2012, https://www.imf.org/external/np/g20/022512.htm.

3. S. Böll et al., "European Politicians in Denial as Greece Unravels," *Spiegel Online*, January 30, 2012.

4. P. Spiegel, "Inside Europe's Plan Z," *Financial Times*, May 14, 2014.

5. B. McLannahan and K. Hille, "China and Japan Unite on IMF Resources," *Financial Times*, February 19, 2012.

6. S. Foxman, "European Firewall Capacity Raised to €800 Billion," *Business Insider*, March 30, 2012, http://www.businessinsider.com/european-firewall-capacity-raised-to-800-billion-2012-3.

7. For an excellent dissection of the Greek negotiations in early 2012, see K. H. Roth, *Greece: What Is to Be Done?* (Winchester: Zero Books, 2013).

8. G. Wiesmann and Q. Peel, "Berlin Split on Bail-out for Greece," *Financial Times*, February 16, 2012.

9. The following is based on J. Zettelmeyer, C. Trebesch and M. Gulati, "The Greek Debt Restructuring: An Autopsy," *Economic Policy* 28, no. 75 (2013), 513–563.

10. Y. Mouzakis, "Where Did All the Money Go?," *Macropolis*, January 5, 2015, http://www.macropolis.gr/?i=portal.en.the-agora.2080.

11. For the following, J. Schumacher and B. Weder di Mauro, "Diagnosing Greek Debt Sustainability: Why Is It So Hard?," *Brookings Papers on Economic Activity* (2015).

12. CADTM, "Evolution of the Greek Public Debt During 2010–2015," http://www.cadtm.org/Evolution-of-the-Greek-public-debt.

13. FRED, "Current Price Gross Domestic Product in Greece," https://fred.stlouisfed.org/series/GRCGDPNADSMEI.

14. Spiegel, "Inside Europe's Plan Z."

15. E. Dinas and L. Rori, "The 2012 Greek Parliamentary Elections: Fear and Loathing in the Polls," *West European Politics* 36, no. 1 (2013), 270–282.

16. P. Spiegel, "Greeks Urged to Run Poll as Vote on Euro," *Financial Times*, May 17, 2012.

17. B. Clift, "Le Changement? French Socialism, the 2012 Presidential Election and the Politics of Economic Credibility Amidst the Eurozone Crisis," *Parliamentary Affairs* 66, no. 1 (2013), 106–123; and N. Hewlett, "Voting in the Shadow of the Crisis: The French Presidential and Parliamentary Elections of 2012," *Modern & Contemporary France* 20, no. 4 (2012), 403–420.

18. F. Hollande, *Le Changement C'est Maintenant* (Paris: Libération, 2012).

19. S. Erlanger, "Socialists' Victory in France Buttresses Hollande's Power," *New York Times*, June 17, 2012.

20. C. Ban, "Austerity Versus Stimulus? Understanding Fiscal Policy Change at the International Monetary Fund Since the Great Recession," *Governance* 28, no. 2 (2015), 167–183.

21. D. Leigh and O. J. Blanchard, "Growth Forecast Errors and Fiscal Multipliers" (IMF Working Paper 13/1, Washington, DC, 2013).

22. C. Luther, "Mit Hollande wird es Merkel nicht leicht haben," *Die Zeit*, May 16, 2012.

23. S. Bajohr, "Die nordrhein-westfälische Landtagswahl vom 13. Mai 2012: Von der Minderheit zur Mehrheit," *Zeitschrift für Parlamentsfragen* (2012), 543–563.

24. "Landtag beschließt Neuwahlen in NRW," *Die Zeit*, March 14, 2012.

25. "Ein Sommer ohne Sonne," http://cicero.de/innenpolitik/ein-sommer-ohne-sonne/51299.
26. Economic Research St. Louis Fed, "Spain: Unemployment and the Crisis," https://research.stlouisfed.org/dashboard/770.
27. A. Cárdenas, "The Spanish Savings Bank Crisis: History, Causes and Responses" (*IN3 Working Paper Series*, 2013); Santos, "Antes del Diluvio" (2017) and above all the indispensable account in T. Santos, "El Diluvio: The Spanish Banking Crisis, 2008–2012," manuscript (2017), Columbia Business School, Columbia University.
28. F. Ortiz, "Newsmaker Rajoy Leans on Abrasive Economist in Spanish Crisis," CNBC, October 25, 2012, https://www.cnbc.com/id/100046357.
29. V. Mallet and M. Johnson, "The Bank That Broke Spain," *Financial Times*, June 21, 2012.
30. IMF, "Global Economic Prospects and Policy Changes," February 25–26, 2012, https://www.imf.org/external/np/g20/pdf/022512.pdf.
31. R. Minder, N. Kulish and P. Geitner, "Spain to Accept Rescue from Europe for Its Ailing Banks," *New York Times*, June 9, 2012.
32. G. Tremlett, "Spain Issues Dramatic Messages of Impending Eurozone Doom," *Guardian*, June 14, 2012.
33. J. Pisani-Ferry, "Tim Geithner and Europe's Phone Number," *Bruegel*, February 4, 2013.
34. "G20 Summit: Leaders Alarmed over Eurozone Crisis," *BBC News*, June 19, 2012.
35. "Can This Man Save Europe?," *Time*, February 20, 2012.
36. N. Véron, "Tectonic Shifts," *Finance & Development* 51, no. 1 (March 2014).
37. Spiegel, "If the Euro Falls, Europe Falls."
38. Dinas and Rori, "The 2012 Greek Parliamentary Elections."
39. Michael Kaczmarek, "SPD-Troika: Fiskalpakt nicht antasten, aber ergänzen," May 15, 2012, http://www.euractiv.de/section/wahlen-und-macht/news/spd-troika-fiskalpakt-nicht-antasten-aber-erganzen/.
40. Bastasin, *Saving Europe*, Kindle location 8460.
41. D. G. Smith, "Merkel's Hard Line 'Could Kill the Euro,'" *Spiegel Online*, June 28, 2012.
42. J. A. Emmanouilidis, "The Prospects of Ambitious Muddling Through," July 2, 2012, http://www.epc.eu/documents/uploads/pub_2765_post-summit_analysis_-_2_july_2012.pdf.
43. *Spiegel* staff, "German Dominance in Doubt After Summit Defeat," *Spiegel Online*, July 2, 2012.
44. C. Volkery, "Monti's Uprising," *Spiegel Online*, June 29, 2012.
45. "Spanish Bank Borrowings from ECB Continue Parabolic Rise," August 14, 2012, http://www.zerohedge.com/news/spanish-bank-borrowings-ecb-continue-parabolic-rise.
46. S. P. Chan and R. Cooper, "Debt Crisis: As It Happened," *Telegraph*, July 24, 2012.
47. A. Monaghan, "Sir Mervyn King Admits Policymakers Made 'Major Mistakes' in Financial Crisis," *Telegraph*, July 27, 2012.
48. Confiding to a friend, Draghi used a more colorful Italian expression. See Bastasin, *Saving Europe*, Kindle location 8731. The hostility and incomprehension displayed by the Anglophone commentariat toward the euro project was also raised by Jorg Asmussen a few weeks before Draghi's appearance in London. See J. Asmussen, "Building Trust in a World of Unknown Unknowns—Central Bank Communication Between Markets and Politics in the Crisis," speech at the European Communication Summit 2012, Brussels, July 6, 2012.
49. ECB, "Verbatim of the Remarks Made by Mario Draghi," July 26, 2012, https://www.ecb.europa.eu/press/key/date/2012/html/sp120726.en.html.
50. For this and the following see P. Carrel, N. Barkin and A. Breidthardt, "Special Report: Inside Mario Draghi's Euro Rescue Plan," *Reuters*, September 25, 2012.
51. "No Time to Lose," *Spiegel Online*, July 30, 2012.
52. 'Schäuble Unmoved by Geithner's Pleas," *Deutsche Welle*, July 31, 2012, and G. Heller, "Geithner, Schaeuble Discuss Euro on Windy German Island," *Reuters*, July 30, 2012.
53. Geithner, *Stress Test*, 483.

54. "Draghi's ECB Management: The Leaked Geithner Files."

55. Geithner, *Stress Test*, 483.

56. P. Carrel, N. Barkin and A. Breidthardt, "Special Report: Inside Mario Draghi's Euro Rescue Plan," *Reuters*, September 25, 2012.

57. Gammelin and Löw, *Europas Strippenzieher*, 96–97.

58. Gammelin and Löw, *Europas* V. Pop, "China Urges Germany and France to Solve Euro-Crisis," August 30, 2012, https://euobserver.com/china/117376.

59. D. Lombardi, "The European Central Bank's Bond Buying Program," September 25, 2012, https://www.brookings.edu/opinions/the-european-central-banks-bond-buying-program-is-berlin-the-greatest-beneficiary/amp/.

60. Bastasin, *Saving Europe*, Kindle locations 8910–8912.

61. ECB, "Technical Features of Outright Monetary Transactions," September 6, 2012, https://www.ecb.europa.eu/press/pr/date/2012/html/pr120906_1.en.html.

62. FOMC press conference, September 13, 2012, https://www.federalreserve.gov/monetarypolicy/fomcpresconf20120913.htm.

63. Bernanke, *Courage to Act*, 532.

64. A. Hall, "EU Summit: How Germany Reacted to Merkel's 'Defeat,'" *Telegraph*, June 30, 2012.

65. E. Helleiner, *The Status Quo Crisis: Global Financial Governance After the 2008 Meltdown* (Oxford: Oxford University Press, 2014).

66. D. W. Drezner, *The System Worked: How the World Stopped Another Great Depression* (Oxford: Oxford University Press, 2014).

67. The initiator was T. J. Sargent's Nobel Prize lecture of December 2011. T. J. Sargent, "Nobel Lecture: United States Then, Europe Now," *Journal of Political Economy* 120, no. 1 (2012), 1–40. See also H. James and H.-W. Sinn, "Mutualisation and Constitutionalisation," *Vox EU*, February 26, 2013.

68. "Obama: US 'The One Indispensable Nation in World Affairs,'" May 23, 2012, http://www.voanews.com/a/obama_tells_air_force_academy_us_is_one_indispensable_country_world_affairs/940158.html.

69. S. G. Brooks, G. J. Ikenberry and W. C. Wohlforth, "Don't Come Home, America: The Case Against Retrenchment," *Quarterly Journal: International Security* 37, no. 3 (Winter 2012–2013), 7–51; and S. M. Walt, "More or Less," http://foreignpolicy.com/2013/01/02/more-or-less-the-debate-on-u-s-grand-strategy/.

70. B. Eichengreen, *Hall of Mirrors*.

71. https://www.facebook.com/notes/randy-fellmy/transcript-of-larry-summers-speech-at-the-imf-economic-forum-nov-8-2013/585630634864563/.

CHAPTER 19: AMERICAN GOTHIC

1. https://www.youtube.com/watch?v=nY_T-JIDJ-c.

2. T. J. Sugrue, *The Origins of the Urban Crisis: Race and Inequality in Postwar Detroit*, 2nd ed. (Princeton, NJ: Princeton University Press, 2014).

3. L. Deng, E. Seymour, M. Dewar and J. Manning Thomas, "Saving Strong Neighborhoods from the Destruction of Mortgage Foreclosures: The Impact of Community-Based Efforts in Detroit, Michigan," *Housing Policy Debate* (2017), 1–27.

4. C. MacDonald and J. Kurth, "Foreclosures Fuel Detroit Blight, Cost City $500 Million: Risky Loans Contribute to Swaths of Empty Homes, Lost Tax Revenue," *Detroit News*, June 2015.

5. C. S. Chung, "Zombieland/The Detroit Bankruptcy: Why Debts Associated with Pensions, Benefits, and Municipal Securities Never Die and How They Are Killing Cities Like Detroit," *Fordham Urban Law Journal* 41 (2014): 771–848.

6. J. Zeitz, "Born to Run and the Decline of the American Dream," *Atlantic*, August 24, 2015.

7. S. Lemke, *Inequality, Poverty and Precarity in Contemporary American Culture* (New York: Palgrave, 2016).

8. For this and the following quotes from Summers, see the transcript at D. Vinik, "Larry Summers Gave an Amazing Speech on the Biggest Economic Problem of Our Time," *Business Insider,* November 17, 2013.

9. Reinhart and Rogoff, *This Time Is Different.*

10. P. Krugman, "The Big Fail," *New York Times,* January 6, 2013.

11. L. H. Summers, "US Economic Prospects: Secular Stagnation, Hysteresis, and the Zero Lower Bound," *Business Economics* 49, no. 2 (2014): 65–74.

12. For an outstanding elaboration of the breadth of Summers's argument see B. DeLong, "Three, Four . . . Many Secular Stagnations," *Grasping Reality with Both Hands* (blog), January 7, 2017, http://www.bradford-delong.com/2017/01/three-four-many-secular -stagnations.html.

13. L. H. Summers, "The Inequality Puzzle: Piketty Book Review," *DEMOCRACY: A Journal of Ideas* 32 (Spring 2014).

14. E. Saez, "Striking It Richer: The Evolution of Top Incomes in the United States (Updated with 2012 Preliminary Estimates)," UC Berkeley, September 3, 2013 http://eml.berkeley .edu//~saez/saez-UStopincomes-2012.pdf.

15. T. Piketty and E. Saez, "Income Inequality in the United States, 1913–1998," *Quarterly Journal of Economics* 118 (2003): 1–39.

16. Saez, "Striking It Richer."

17. The distortion was caused by the extremely wealthy taking advantage of a Bush-era tax loophole to log their incomes in 2012. By 2015 the share of the top 1 percent in the recovery was down to 52 percent. Gary Burtless, "Income Growth Has Been Negligible But (Surprise!) Inequality Has Narrowed Since 2007," *Brookings,* July 22, 2016.

18. *Politico* staff, "President Obama on Inequality (Transcript)," *Politico,* December 4, 2013.

19. G. Beauchamp and L. Nelson, "The Opioid Epidemic: A Brief History," June 2017, Pain andPSA.org.

20. Centers for Disease Control and Prevention, "Vital Signs: Overdoses of Prescription Opioid Pain Relievers—United States, 1999–2008," *Morbidity and Mortality Weekly Report* 60 (2011): 1487–1492.

21. A. Case and A. Deaton, "Rising Morbidity and Mortality in Midlife Among White Non-Hispanic Americans in the 21st Century," *Proceedings of the National Academy of Sciences* 112, no. 49 (2015), 15078–15083.

22. See, for instance, R. Reich, *The Work of Nations: Preparing Ourselves for 21st Century Capitalism* (New York: Vintage, 2010).

23. W. Kimball and R. Scott, "China Trade, Outsourcing and Jobs," Economic Policy Institute, briefing paper 385, December 11, 2014. More recent estimates put the number for job losses closer to 2 million. See David H. Autor, David Dorn and Gordon H. Hanson, "The China Shock: Learning from Labor-Market Adjustment to Large Changes in Trade," *Annual Review of Economics* 8 (2016), 205–240.

24. D. Card and J. E. DiNardo, "Skill-Biased Technological Change and Rising Wage Inequality: Some Problems and Puzzles," *Journal of Labor Economics* 20.4 (2002), 733–783.

25. R. Shapiro, "The Politics of Widening Income Inequality in the United States, 1977 to 2014," CBPP, Georgetown University, October 2017.

26. G. Sargent, "'There's Been Class Warfare for the Last 20 Years, and My Class Has Won,'" *Washington Post,* September 30, 2011.

27. M. J. Lee, "Buffett: My Plan to Tax the Rich," *Politico,* November 15, 2011.

28. J. Hayward, "The Smith Project," *Breitbart,* February 3, 2016, http://www.breitbart .com/big-government/2016/02/03/the-smith-project-a-look-at-the-new-american -insurgency/.

29. M. Phelan, "Building the House of Breitbart," *Jacobin,* November 5, 2016.

30. "The Corruption in Academic Economics: INET's Interview with Charles Ferguson," StopForeclosureFraud.com, November 25, 2012.

31. P. Krugman, "Challenging the Oligarchy," *New York Review of Books*, December 17, 2015.

32. P. Krugman, "Why Inequality Matters," *New York Times*, December 15, 2013.

33. Excerpt from R. B. Reich, *Saving Capitalism: For the Many, Not the Few* (New York: Vintage, 2015), 19.

34. "Bernanke, Trichet, Brown Join Pimco Advisory Board," *Reuters*, December 7, 2015.

35. C. Goodhart and D. Schoenmaker, "The United States Dominates Global Investment Banking: Does It Matter for Europe?" *Bruegel*, March 7, 2016.

36. A. Schechter, "Market Power and Inequality: How Big Should Antitrust's Role Be in Reducing Inequality?," *ProMarket*, July 14, 2016; and E. Porter, "With Competition in Tatters, the Rip of Inequality Widens," July 12, 2016. And the panel debate documented by A. Schechter, "Is There a Connection Between Market Concentration and the Rise in Inequality?," 5 May, 2017, https://promarket.org/connection-market-concentration -rise-inequality/.

37. "Too Much of a Good Thing," *Economist*, March 26, 2016.

38. J. Furman and P. Orszag, "A Firm-Level Perspective on the Role of Rents in the Rise of Inequality" (presentation at "A Just Society" Centennial Event in Honor of Joseph Stiglitz at Columbia University, October 16, 2015), http://gabriel-zucman.eu/files/teaching/ FurmanOrszag15.pdf.

39. H. M. Schwartz, "Wealth and Secular Stagnation: The Role of Industrial Organization and Intellectual Property Rights," *Russell Sage Foundation Journal* 2.6 (2016): 226–249.

40. J. Kollewe, "'Political Crap': Tim Cook Condemns Apple Tax Ruling," *Guardian*, September 1, 2016.

41. P. Thiel, "Competition Is for Losers," *Wall Street Journal*, September 12, 2014.

42. Piketty, *Capital in the Twenty-First Century* (Cambridge, MA: Harvard University Press, 2014).

43. R. Reich, "Income Inequality in the United States" (testimony before the Joint Economic Committee, US Congress, January 16, 2014).

44. E. McMurry, "Fox's Hasselbeck Knocks Obama's 'Class Warfare' Speech: 'He *Is* the System' He Criticizes," *MEDIAite*, December 5, 2013.

45. Mildner and Howald, "Jumping the Fiscal Cliff."

46. R. T. Meyers, "The Implosion of the Federal Budget Process: Triggers, Commissions, Cliffs, Sequesters, Debt Ceilings, and Shutdown," *Public Budgeting & Finance* 34.4 (2014), 1–23.

47. http://www.fixthedebt.org/.

48. P. Orszag, "Too Much of a Good Thing," *New Republic*, September 14, 2011.

49. R. Kuttner, "Destroying the Economy and the Democrats," *American Prospect*, April 5, 2013.

50. "Public Goals, Private Interests in Debt Campaign," *New York Times*, January 9, 2013.

51. "Stacking the Deck: The Phony 'Fix the Debt' Campaign," *Nation*, February 20, 2013.

52. "To Understand the Budget Debate, You Need to Understand the Sequester: Here's a Quick Primer," *New Republic*, September 29, 2013; and Mildner and Howald, "Jumping the Fiscal Cliff."

53. N. Confessore, "Senate Passes First Budget in Four Years," *Washington Post*, March 23, 2013.

54. J. Bendery, "John Boehner on Debt Ceiling: Let's Pay China First, Then US Troops," *Huffington Post*, May 8, 2013.

55. J. Cohn, "Don't Blame the Tea Party for the Shutdown. Blame Boehner," *New Republic*, September 30, 2013.

56. S. M. Burwell, "Impacts and Costs of the Government Shutdown," White House archives, November 7, 2013.

57. R. Radosh, "Steve Bannon, Trump's Top Guy, Told Me He Was 'a Leninist,'" *Daily Beast*, August 22, 2016.

58. A. Crooke, "Steve Bannon's Apocalyptic 'Unravelling,'" *Consortium News*, March 9, 2017.
59. G. Steinhauser, "Europe Enjoys 'Shutdownfreude' over US Debt Troubles," *Wall Street Journal*, October 16, 2013.
60. M. Hujer and D. Sander, "US Fumbling Puts China at Risk," *Der Spiegel*, October 22, 2013.
61. D. Roberts, "China's State Press Calls for 'Building a de-Americanized World,'" *Bloomberg Businessweek*, October 14, 2013..
62. M. Park, "US Shutdown: How the World Reacted," *CNN*, October 1, 2013.
63. R. McGregor, "Congressional Impasse on IMF Shows the Tight Spot Obama Is In," *Financial Times*, January 27, 2014.
64. J. Mayer, *Dark Money* (New York: Doubleday, 2016).
65. N. Hemmer, "The Chamber of Commerce Is Fed Up with the Tea Party," *U.S. News & World Report*, December 31, 2013.
66. P. Hamby, "Company Men: The US Chamber Flexes Its New Political Muscle," *CNN*, July 22, 2014, http://cnn.it/1tMAhvT.
67. E. Eichelberger, "How the Tea Party Is Causing Big Business to Back Democrats," *Mother Jones*, September 15, 2014.
68. A. Altman, "The US Chamber of Commerce Is Saving the GOP Establishment at Ballot Box," *Time*, July 14, 2014.

CHAPTER 20: TAPER TANTRUM

1. "Federal Reserve Board Announces Reserve Bank Income and Expense Data and Transfers to the Treasury for 2015" (press release, Board of Governors of the Federal Reserve System, January 11, 2016).
2. For a careful econometric analysis using global data see M. Fratzscher, M. Lo Duca and R. Straub, "On the International Spillovers of US Quantitative Easing," *Economic Journal* (2016), doi:10.1111/ecoj.12435.
3. "A Marriage of Convenience Comes to an End," *Financial Times*, October 17, 2014.
4. On the importance of the interaction of interest rate and exchange rate movement see B. S. Bernanke, "Federal Reserve Policy in an International Context," *IMF Economic Review* 65.1 (2017), 5–36.
5. R. N. McCauley, P. McGuire and V. Sushko, "Dollar Credit to Emerging Market Economies 1," *BIS Quarterly Review* (2015), 27.
6. "Zambia Raises $750 mln in Debut 10-Year Eurobond," *Reuters*, September 13, 2012.
7. R. Wigglesworth, "Zambia Makes Bond Market Return," *Financial Times*, April 7, 2014.
8. "The Dollar's Strength Is a Problem for the World," *Economist*, December 3, 2016.
9. K. Miyajima and I. Shim, "Asset Managers in Emerging Market Economies," *BIS Quarterly Review*, September 14, 2014.
10. IMF, "The Asset Management Industry and Financial Stability: Chapter 3," *Global Financial Stability Report: Navigating Monetary Policy Challenges and Managing Risks*, April 2015.
11. IMF, *Global Financial Stability Report*, April 2015.
12. "The Never-Ending Story," *Economist*, November 14, 2015.
13. On the global credit cycle see the highly influential paper by Hélène Rey, originally delivered in August 2013 at Jackson Hole, "Dilemma Not Trilemma: The Global Financial Cycle and Monetary Policy Independence" (NBER Working Paper 21162, May 2015). On the evolution of the IMF's view on capital controls see IMF Survey, "IMF Adopts Institutional View on Capital Flows," December 3, 2012, http://www.imf.org/en/News/Articles/2015/09/28/04/53/sopol120312a.
14. "Just in Case: Capital Controls Are Back as Part of Many Countries' Financial Armoury," *Economist*, October 13, 2013.

15. C. Jones, R. Wigglesworth and J. Politi, "Fed Fights Back Against 'Feral Hogs,'" *Financial Times*, June 24, 2013.
16. P. da Costa and A. Bull, "Bernanke Says More Progress Needed Before Stimulus Pullback," *Reuters*, May 22, 2013.
17. "The Dollar's Strength Is a Problem for the World."
18. Miyajima and Shim, "Asset Managers in Emerging Market Economies."
19. K. Forbes, "Don't Rush to Blame the Fed," *New York Times*, February 5, 2014.
20. "Just in Case."
21. See the forceful restrospective defense of Fed policy offered by B. S. Bernanke, "Federal Reserve Policy in an International Context," *IMF Economic Review* 65.1 (2017), 5–36.
22. J. Frankel, C. Reinhart and B. Zoellick, "The Fed and Emerging Markets: Another Crash?," Belfer Center, Harvard Kennedy School, May 15, 2014.
23. B. Eichengreen and P. Gupta, "Tapering Talk: The Impact of Expectations of Reduced Federal Reserve Security Purchases on Emerging Markets," CEPR's Policy Portal, December 19, 2013.
24. "Raghu's Reality Check," *Economist*, September 20, 2013.
25. C. Tugal, *The Fall of the Turkish Model: How the Arab Uprisings Brought Down Islamic Liberalism* (New York: Verso, 2016), Kindle locations 3–5.
26. "Turkish Police Use Water Cannon to Disperse Remembrance Gathering," *Guardian*, June 22, 2013; and D. Dombey, "Erdogan Hits at Financiers in Effort to Quell Turkey Protests," *Financial Times*, June 10, 2013.
27. D. Dombey, "Erdogan Says Same Forces Behind Brazil and Turkey Protests," *Financial Times*, June 23, 2013.
28. M. Champion, "Is Erdogan's Turkey the Next Putin's Russia?," *Bloomberg*, June 5, 2013.
29. "Fed Officials Rebuff Coordination Calls as QE Taper Looms," *Livemint*, August 26, 2013.
30. R. Harding et al., "India's Raghuram Rajan Hits Out at Unco-ordinated Global Policy," *Financial Times*, January 30, 2014.
31. "Fed Officials Rebuff Coordination Calls as QE Taper Looms."
32. R. Harding, "Why Emerging Markets Are Unlikely to Sway the Fed," *Financial Times*, February 2, 2014.
33. "Federal Reserve Won't Consider Problems Abroad," *Boston Globe*, August 26, 2013.
34. P. da Costa, A. Bull, "Fed Surprises, Sticks to Stimulus as It Cuts Growth Outlook," *Reuters*, September 18, 2013.
35. A. Fontevecchia, "Bernanke Keeps the Printing Press at Full Speed as Taper Decision Likely to Fall on Yellen," *Forbes*, October 30, 2013.
36. K. Lansing and B. Pyle, "Persistent Overoptimism About Economic Growth," *Federal Reserve Bank of San Francisco Economic Letter*, February 2, 2015.
37. A. Kaletsky, "The Markets and Bernanke's 'Taper Tantrums,'" *Reuters*, September 19, 2013.
38. "BlackRock's Fink Says There Are 'Bubble-Like Markets' Again," October 29, 2013, http://www.pionline.com/article/20131029/ONLINE/131029857/blackrocks-fink-says-there-are-bubble-like-markets-again.
39. "BlackRock Admits the Fed Is Causing 'Tremendous Distortions,'" *ZeroHedge* (blog), August 19, 2013.
40. W. Gross, "Survival of the Fittest?," *Investment Outlook*, Pimco, October 2013.
41. Gross, "Survival of the Fittest?"
42. T. Alloway, "A Marriage of Convenience Comes to an End," *Financial Times*, October 17, 2014.
43. Ibid.
44. D. Ranasinghe, "Best Performing Currency in September? India's Rupee," *CNBC*, October 8, 2013.
45. "Federal Reserve and Other Central Banks Convert Temporary Bilateral Liquidity Swap Arrangements to Standing Arrangements," Board of Governors of the Federal Reserve System, October 31, 2013.

46. The deepest exploration of its logic is P. Mehrling, "Elasticity and Discipline in the Global Swap Network," *International Journal of Political Economy* 44.4 (2015), 311–324.

47. T. Nakamichi, "Japan to Double Indonesia, Philippines Swap Lines," *Wall Street Journal*, December 6, 2013.

48. "Fed Officials Rebuff Coordination Calls as QE Taper Looms," *Livemint*, August 26, 2013.

49. E. Macaskill and G. Dance, "The NSA Files," *Guardian*, November 1, 2013.

CHAPTER 21: "F*** THE EU": THE UKRAINE CRISIS

1. S. G. Brooks, G. J. Ikenberry and W. C. Wohlforth, "Don't Come Home, America: The Case Against Retrenchment," *International Security* 37, no. 3 (Winter 2012–2013), 7–51; and S. M. Walt, "More or Less: The Debate on US Grand Strategy," *Foreign Policy*, January 2, 2013.

2. M. Landler, *Alter Egos: Hillary Clinton, Barack Obama, and the Twilight Struggle over American Power* (New York: Random House, 2016); and K. Campbell, *The Pivot: The Future of American Statecraft in Asia* (New York: Twelve, 2016).

3. G. Resnick, "Inside the New Hillary Clinton Emails: All the Secretary's Yes Men," *Daily Beast*, September 1, 2015.

4. G. J. Ikenberry, "The Illusion of Geopolitics," *Foreign Affairs* (May/June 2014).

5. "Political Staple," *Economist*, December 2, 2013. For the background of strategic competition in East Asia see the valuable overview by G. Rachman, *Easternization: Asia's Rise and America's Decline* (New York: Other Press, 2016).

6. J. Xi, "Gut für China, Europa und die Welt," *Frankfurter Allgemeine*, March 28, 2014.

7. S. Farrell, "City of London Boosted by China Currency Trading Move," *Guardian*, June 18, 2014.

8. N. Watt, P. Lewis and T. Branigan, "US Anger at Britain Joining Chinese-Led Investment Bank AIIB," *Guardian*, March 12, 2015.

9. G. Rachman, "China's Money Magnet Pulls in US Allies," *Financial Times*, March 16, 2015.

10. G. Dyer and G. Parker, "US Attacks UK's 'Constant Accommodation' with China," *Financial Times*, March 12, 2015.

11. Ibid.

12. G. Parker, A.-S. Chassany and G. Dyer, "Europeans Defy US to Join China-Led Development Bank," *Financial Times*, March 16, 2015.

13. A. Stent, *The Limits of Partnership: U.S.-Russian Relations in the Twenty-First Century* (Princeton, NJ: Princeton University Press, 2014).

14. A. Clark, "Dmitry Medvedev Picks Silicon Valley's Brains," *Guardian*, June 23, 2010.

15. T. Kaplan, "Russia Blocks Yogurt Bound for US Athletes," *New York Times*, February 5, 2014.

16. R. Korteweg, "Mogherini's Mission: Four Steps to Make EU Foreign Policy More Strategic," Centre for European Reform, January 19, 2015.

17. *Spiegel* staff, "How the EU Lost Russia over Ukraine: Four Thousand Deaths and an Eastern Ukraine Gripped by War," *Der Spiegel*, November 24, 2014.

18. A. Åslund, "Ukraine's Choice: European Association Agreement or Eurasian Union?," *Policy Brief* (2013), 13–26.

19. R. Sakwa, *Frontline Ukraine: Crisis in the Borderlands* (New York: I. B. Tauris, 2015), 76

20. Ibid.

21. R. Youngs, *Europe's Eastern Crisis: The Geopolitics of Asymmetry* (Cambridge: Cambridge University Press, 2017), 54.

22. "How the EU Lost Russia over Ukraine"; and "The Eu-Ukraine Association Agreement and Deep and Comprehensive Free Trade Area: What's It All About?," http://eeas.europa.eu/archives/delegations/ukraine/documents/virtual_library/vademecum_en.pdf.

23. Åslund, "Ukraine's Choice."

24. "'We Want to See the Euro Zone Flourish,'" *Der Spiegel*, May 16, 2012; and K. Gebert and U. Guerot, "Why Poland Is the New France for Germany," *European Council on Foreign Relations*, October 19, 2012.

25. K. Gebert, "Reinventing Europe: Poland and the Euro Crisis," European Council on Foreign Relations, February 7, 2012.

26. Kudrna and Gabor, "The Return of Political Risk."

27. S. Lambert, "The Orban Government and Public Debt," *The Orange Files: Notes on Illiberal Democracy in Hungary,* https://theorangefiles.hu/the-orban-government-and-public-debt/.

28. "Hungary's Orban Wants Deal with IMF, Cbank Cuts Rates," *Reuters*, April 26, 2010.

29. J. Johnson and A. Barnes, "Financial Nationalism and Its International Enablers: The Hungarian Experience," *Review of International Political Economy* 22 (2014): 535–569.

30. A. Deak, "The Putin-Orban Nuclear Deal: A Short Assessment," *Green Political Foundation*, January 27, 2014.

31. O. Sushko, "A Fork in the Road? Ukraine Between EU Association and the Eurasian Customs Union," *PONARS Eurasia*, September 2013.

32. "How the EU Lost Russia over Ukraine."

33. A. Wilson, *Ukraine Crisis: What It Means for the West* (New Haven, CT: Yale University Press, 2014).

34. B. Steil, "Taper Trouble," *Foreign Affairs* (July/August 2014).

35. Wilson, *Ukraine Crisis*, 16.

36. I. Traynor and O. Grytsenko, "Ukraine Aligns with Moscow as EU Summit Fails," *Guardian*, November 28, 2013.

37. E. Piper, "Special Report: Why Ukraine Spurned the Eu and Embraced Russia," *Reuters*, December 19, 2013.

38. "How the EU Lost Russia over Ukraine."

39. "Press Release: Statement by IMF Mission to Ukraine" (IMF press release no. 13/419, October 31, 2013), https://www.imf.org/en/News/Articles/2015/09/14/01/49/pr13419.

40. Wilson, *Ukraine Crisis*, 64–65.

41. Piper, "Special Report: Why Ukraine Spurned the Eu and Embraced Russia."

42. D. M. Herszenhorn, "Ukraine Blames IMF for Halt to Agreements with Europe," *New York Times*, November 22, 2013; and A. Evans-Pritchard, "Historic Defeat for EU as Ukraine Returns to Kremlin Control," *Telegraph*, November 22, 2013.

43. "Merkel Still Open to Ukraine Cooperation," *Der Spiegel*, November 28, 2013.

44. "Poll: Ukrainian Public Split over EU, Customs Union Options," *Kyiv Post*, November 26, 2013.

45. "Ukraine Crisis: Transcript of Leaked Nuland-Pyatt Call," *BBC*, February 7, 2014.

46. A. Higgins and A. E. Kramer, "Ukraine Leader Was Defeated Even Before He Was Ousted," *New York Times*, January 3, 2015.

47. Plans were first drawn up after the war in Georgia in 2008: Wilson, *Ukraine Crisis*, 108.

48. D. Chollet, *The Long Game: How Obama Defied Washington and Redefined America's Role in the World* (New York: Hachette, 2016).

49. K. Rogov, "What Will Be the Consequences of the Russian Currency Crisis?," European Council on Foreign Relations, December 23, 2014.

50. A. Evans-Pritchard, "US Hits Russia's Oil Kingpin Igor Sechin with First Energy Sanctions," *Telegraph*, April 28, 2014.

51. Wilson, *Ukraine Crisis*, 202.

52. M. Feldenkirchen, C. Hoffmann and R. Pfister, "Will It Be America or Russia?," *Der Spiegel*, July 10, 2014.

53. 13-26, "Deutsche trauen den USA nicht mehr," July 18, 2014, https://www.tagesschau.de/inland/deutschlandtrend-116.html.

54. I. Traynor et al., "Ukraine Crisis: US-Europe Rifts Surfacing as Putin Tightens Crimea Grip," *Guardian*, March 4, 2014.
55. A. Yukhananov, "Ukraine Could Borrow More If IMF Reforms Passed—US," *Reuters*, March 4, 2014.
56. Y. Kwon, "The IMF, Ukraine, and the Asian Financial Crisis Hangover," *Diplomat*, March 17, 2014.
57. S. Schadler, "Ukraine: Stress at the IMF," CIGI policy brief no. 49, October 2014.
58. D. Tolksdorf, "The European Union to Ukraine's Rescue," *Politique Etrangere* 3 (2014): 109–119; and S. Erlanger and D. M. Herszenhorn, "IMF Prepares $18 Billion in Loans for Ukraine," *New York Times*, March 27, 2014.
59. A. Yukhananov, "IMF Approves $17 Billion Bailout for Ukraine amid Big Risks," *Reuters*, April 30, 2014.
60. "IMF Survey: Ukraine Unveils Reform Program with IMF Support," IMF, April 30, 2014.
61. P. Shishkin, "US Sanctions over Ukraine Hit Two Russian Banks Hardest," *Wall Street Journal*, March 5, 2015.
62. OSW Report, "The Economic and Financial Crisis in Russia—Background, Symptoms and Prospects for the Future," Centre for Eastern Studies, June 2, 2015.
63. N. Buckley and M. Arnold, "Herman Gref, Sberbank's Modernising Sanctions Survivor," *Financial Times*, January 31, 2016.
64. K. Rogov, "Can Putinomics Survive?" ECFR policy memo, June 5, 2015.
65. Dmitry Zhdannikov and Alex Lawler, "Saudi Oil Policy Uncertainty Unleashes the Conspiracy Theorists," November 18, 2014, https://www.reuters.com/article/opec/refile-saudi-oil-policy-uncertainty-unleashes-the-conspiracy-theorists-idUSL6N0T73VG20141118.
66. M. Mazzetti, E. Schmitt and D. D. Kirkpatrick, "Saudi Oil Is Seen as Lever to Pry Russian Support from Syria's Assad," *New York Times*, February 3, 2015.
67. Rogov, "Can Putinomics Survive?"
68. Courtney Weaver and Jack Farchy, "Russian Economy: An Asset to the State," *Financial Times*, June 15, 2015.
69. A. Mercouris, "Sberbank CEO Confirms Russia Came Under Financial Attack in December—Was US Involved?," *Russia Insider*, May 29, 2015.
70. Buckley and Arnold, "Herman Gref, Sberbank's Modernising Sanctions Survivor."
71. OSW Report, "The Economic and Financial Crisis in Russia—Background, Symptoms and Prospects for the Future."
72. A. E. Kramer, "S&P Cuts Russian Debt One Notch to Junk Level," *New York Times*, January 26, 2015.
73. Rogov, "Can Putinomics Survive?"
74. On the continuities between 2008 and the domestic "war coalition" of 2014, see K. Gaaze, "The Accidental Formation of Russia's War Coalition," Carnegie Moscow Center, June 22, 2017, http://carnegie.ru/commentary/71340.
75. M. Birnbaum, "Putin's Approval Ratings Hit 89 Percent, the Highest They've Ever Been," *Washington Post*, June 24, 2015.
76. A. Stepanyan, A. Roitman, G. Minasyan, D. Ostojic and N. Epstein, "The Spillover Effects of Russia's Economic Slowdown on Neighboring Countries," IMF, 2015.
77. M. Dabrowski, "Currency Crises in Post-Soviet Economies—A Never Ending Story?," *Russian Journal of Economics* 2 (2016), 302–326; and M. Dabrowski, "It's Not Just Russia: Currency Crises in the Commonwealth of Independent States," *Bruegel*, February 2015.
78. "Contagion," *Economist*, January 15, 2015.
79. D. Trilling, "Remittances to Central Asia Fall Sharply, as Expected," *Eurasia Net*, April 21, 2015.

80. S. Schadler, "Ukraine and the IMF's Evolving Debt Crisis Narrative," CIGI policy brief no. 68, November 2015.
81. R. Olearchyk, "War-Torn Ukraine's Currency Collapses," *Financial Times*, February 5, 2015; and L. Kinstler, "Ukraine Is Heading for a Total Economic Collapse," *Quartz*, February 12, 2015.
82. "Tinkering Around the Edges," *Economist*, August 29, 2015.
83. A. Gabuev, "A 'Soft Alliance'? Russia-China Relations After the Ukraine Crisis," ECFR policy brief, 2015.
84. I. Koch-Weser and C. Murray, "The China-Russia Gas Deal: Background and Implications for the Broader Relationship," US-China Economic and Security Review Commission Staff Research Backgrounder, June 9, 2014.
85. "America's Seven-Decade History as Asia's Indispensable Power," *Economist*, April 20, 2017.
86. M. Sieff, "Why Is the US Failing to Honor Russia's Victory Day Anniversary?," *Nation*, May 7, 2015.

CHAPTER 22: #THISISACOUP

1. "Russia's Friends in Black," *Economist*, April 19, 2014; and B.-H. Lévy and G. Soros, "Save the New Ukraine," *New York Times*, January 27, 2015.
2. N. Véron, "Tectonic Shifts," IMF, *Finance & Development*, March 2014; and A. Posen and N. Véron, "Europe's Half a Banking Union," Bruegel, *Europe's World* 15, September 2014.
3. H. Thompson, "The Crisis of the Euro: The Problem of German Power Revisited," SPERI paper 8 (2013).
4. "The Merkel Plan," *Economist*, June 15, 2013.
5. "Germany's Current Account and Global Adjustment," *General Theorist*, July 6, 2017.
6. U. Jun, "Der elektorale Verlierer der Regierung Merkel II: Gründe für den Absturz der FDP," *Politik im Schatten der Krise* (Wiesbaden: Springer Fachmedien, 2015), 113–135.
7. D. Bebnowski, *Die Alternative für Deutschland: Aufstieg und gesellschaftliche Repräsentanz einer rechten populistischen Partei* (Wiesbaden: Springer Fachmedien, 2015).
8. "Schäuble: Die Schwarze Null ist kein Selbstzweck," *FAZ*, September 9, 2014.
9. "Europe's Deflation Risk," OECD Observer, October 2014.
10. T. Winkelmann, "Infrastrukturpolitik im Zeitalter von Austerität," *Austerität als gesellschaftliches Projekt*, R. Sturm, T. Griebel and T. Winkelmann (eds.) (Wiesbaden: Springer Fachmedien, 2017), 155–179.
11. N. Kwasniewski, "ECB Rate Drop Shows Draghi's Resolve," *Der Spiegel*, November 8, 2013; and A. Evans-Pritchard, "Dam Breaks in Europe as Deflation Fears Wash Over ECB Rhetoric," *Telegraph*, October 10, 2014.
12. "Public Opinion in the European Union," European Commission, December 2014.
13. "Européennes 2014: Comprendre le Vote Des Français," *Ipsos*, May 25, 2014.
14. J. Pavia, A. Bodoque and J. Martin, "The Birth of a New Party: Podemos, a Hurricane in the Spanish Crisis of Trust," *Open Journal of Social Sciences* 4 (2016): 67–86.
15. A. Higgins, "Populists' Rise in Europe Vote Shakes Leaders," *New York Times*, May 26, 2014; C. Mudde, "Jean-Claude Juncker and the Populist Zeitgeist in European Politics," *Washington Post*, December 30, 2014; and T. Barber, "European Democracy Must Keep Rightwing Populism at Bay," *Financial Times*, September 16, 2014.
16. F. Wesslau, "Putin's Friends in Europe," European Council on Foreign Relations, October 19, 2016.
17. J. Goldberg, "Is It Time for the Jews to Leave Europe?," *Atlantic*, April 2015.
18. Eurostat, "At-Risk-of Poverty Rate Anchored at a Fixed Moment in Time (2008), 2014 and 2015," http://ec.europa.eu/eurostat/statistics-explained/index.php/File:At-risk-of_poverty_rate_anchored_at_a_fixed_moment_in_time_(2008),_2014_and_2015_(%25).png.

19. "Society at a Glance 2014 Highlights: Greece The Crisis and Its Aftermath," OECD, March 2014.

20. H. Smith, "Young, Gifted and Greek: Generation G—the World's Biggest Brain Drain," *Guardian*, January 19, 2015.

21. V. Petsinis, "Syriza and ANEL: A Match Made in Greece," *OpenDemocracy*, January 25, 2017.

22. Y. Varoufakis, *Adults in the Room: My Battle with Europe's Deep Establishment* (New York: Vintage, 2017).

23. S. Kornelius, "Six Things You Didn't Know About Angela Merkel," *Guardian*, September 10, 2013.

24. "The Plan for Italy," *Economist*, November 13, 2014.

25. "Yiannis Stournaras: A Brief Bio of the New Finance Chief," *Ekathimerini*, June 26, 2012.

26. P. Mason, "The Inside Story of Syriza's Struggle to Save Greece," *Nation*, December 18, 2015; and Tyler Durden, "Greece Suffers Biggest Bank Run in History: January Deposits Plunge to 2005 Levels," *ZeroHedge* (blog), February 26, 2015.

27. S. Nixon, "ECB's Draghi Takes a Gamble on QE-lite," *Wall Street Journal*, September 7, 2014.

28. "Opinion of Advocate General Cruz Cillalon," January 14, 2015, http://curia.europa.eu/juris/document/document.jsf;jsessionid=9ea7d0f130ded7290bd15b9341dcab778007656336d9.e34KaxiLc3eQc40LaxqMbN4ObhiRe0?text=&docid=161370&pageIndex=0&doclang=en&mode=req&dir=&occ=first&part=1&cid=205645.

29. "ECB Announces Expanded Asset Purchase Programme," European Central Bank, January 22, 2015.

30. The idea in its basic outline was already spelled out in 2012. Y. Varoufakis, "An Emergency Program for Greece," *Yanis Varoufakis: Thoughts for the Post-2008 World* (blog), November 5, 2012, https://www.yanisvaroufakis.eu/2012/11/05/an-emergency-program-for-greece/.

31. A. Higgins, "Greece Steps Back into Line with European Union Policy on Russia Sanctions," *New York Times*, January 29, 2015.

32. Varoufakis, *Adults*, 237.

33. A. Evans-Pritchard, "Europe's Manhandling of Greece Is a Strategic Gift to Russia's Vladimir Putin," *Telegraph*, April 8, 2015.

34. Varoufakis, *Adults*, 274.

35. Ibid., 185–187.

36. Blustein, *Laid Low*, 384.

37. The IMF developed a particular preoccupation with Greece's pharmacies. IMF Country Report 14/151 (June 2014).

38. M. Walker and G. Steinhauser, "Germany's Merkel Intervenes in Greek Rift with Creditors," *Wall Street Journal*, March 19, 2015.

39. "Barack Obama Signals Support for Greece's Call to Loosen Austerity Programme," *Telegraph*, February 2, 2015.

40. C. Giles et al., "IMF Knocks Greek Debt Rescheduling Hopes," *Financial Times*, April 16, 2015.

41. S. Nixon, "Can US Bring an End to Greek Drama?," *Wall Street Journal*, May 31, 2015; and I. Talley and G. Steinhauser, "IMF Official Sees Greek Bailout Needing Several More Weeks of Talks," *Wall Street Journal*, April 17, 2015.

42. ThePressProject, "Clinton Emails Give Away Schäuble Plans in 2012—Exclusive Commentary by Varoufakis," https://www.thepressproject.gr/article/91399/Clinton-Emails-Give-Away-Schauble-Plans-in-2012—-Exclusive-Commentary-by-Varoufakis.

43. S. Meunier, "A Tale of Two Ports: The Epic Story of Chinese Direct Investment in the Greek Port of Piraeus," Council for European Studies, December 14, 2015.

44. Varoufakis, *Adults*, 321.

45. S. Jones, K. Hope and C. Weaver, "Alarm Bells Ring over Syriza's Russian Links," *Financial Times*, January 28, 2015.
46. Varoufakis, *Adults*, 348.
47. M. Gilbert, "Bond Markets Bet on Grexit," *Bloomberg*, March 20, 2015, http://www.greekcrisis.net/2015/03/bond-markets-bet-on-grexit.html.
48. J. Cox, "Greek Government Bonds Plunge," *Wall Street Journal*, April 16, 2015; and C. Giles, S. Fleming and P. Spiegel, "Christine Lagarde Dashes Greek Hopes on Loan Respite," *Financial Times*, April 16, 2015.
49. S. Fleming and C. Giles, "Draghi Says Eurozone Has Tools to Deal with Greece Crisis," *Financial Times*, April 18, 2015.
50. P. Spiegel and K. Hope, "Frustrated Officials Want Greek Premier to Ditch Syriza Far Left," *Financial Times*, April 5, 2015.
51. Ibid.
52. "One Economist Just Delivered a Scathing Indictment of the New Greek Government," *Bloomberg*, April 1, 2015, http://www.greekcrisis.net/2015/04/one-economist-just-delivered-scathing.html.
53. T. Barber, "Don't Bank on Tsipras Dumping Syriza's Leftwing Diehards," *Financial Times*, April 14, 2015.
54. S. Wagstyl, P. Spiegel and C. Jones, "Greek Bailout Monitors Hold Emergency Summit," *Financial Times*, June 1, 2015.
55. M. Walker, "Greece's Creditors Draft Final Offer for Bailout Aid in Bid to Break Stalemate," *Wall Street Journal*, June 2, 2015.
56. Y. Palaiologos, "Running Out of Options on a Deal with Greece," *Wall Street Journal*, June 4, 2015.
57. W. Munchau, "Greece Has Nothing to Lose by Saying No to Creditors," *Financial Times*, June 14, 2015.
58. P. Spiegel and K. Hope, "Greece Central Ban Warns of 'Painful' EU Exit If No Deal Reached," *Financial Times*, June 17, 2015.
59. P. Mason, "The Inside Story of Syriza's Struggle to Save Greece," *Nation*, December 18, 2015.
60. K. Hope, "Knives Out for Tsipras as Syriza Hardliners Threaten Mutiny," *Financial Times*, June 23, 2015.
61. "Sorry, No Extensions," *Economist*, April 16, 2015; and G. Steinhauser and M. Dalton, "Germany Signals It's Open to a Greek Referendum on Bailout Program," *Wall Street Journal*, May 11, 2015.
62. P. Spiegel, S. Wagstyl and H. Foy, "Tsipras Announces Referendum on Creditors' Bailout Demands," *Financial Times*, June 27, 2015.
63. See more at P. Mason, "Greece Referendum: Did The Euro Just Die at 4pm?" *Channel4*, June 28, 2015.
64. R. Christie, C. Ruhe and J. Stearns, "Euro Area Pushes Greece to Open Books as Talks Resume," *Bloomberg*, March 9, 2015.
65. M. Gilbert, "Greece's True Deadline May Be May 29," *Bloomberg*, May 19, 2015.
66. J. Black, K. S. Navarra and N. Chrysoloras, "ECB Said to Reject Supervisory Move on Greek Banks," *Bloomberg*, March 19, 2015.
67. Blustein, *Laid Low*, 429.
68. O. Blanchard, "Greece: A Credible Deal Will Require Difficult Decisions by All Sides," *IMFBlog*, June 14, 2015.
69. See more at P. Mason, "Greece Crisis: A Failure of Economics in the Face of Politics," *Channel4*, July 3, 2015, https://www.channel4.com/news/by/paul-mason/blogs/greece-crisis-failure-economics-face-politics.
70. P. Taylor, "Exclusive: Europeans Tried to Block IMF Debt Report on Greece: Sources," *Reuters*, July 3, 2015.

71. H. Mahoney, "The EU Parliament's Big, Fat Greek Moment," *EUObserver*, July 10, 2015; and "Greece: MEPs Debate the Country's Situation with Prime Minister Tsipras," *Europarl*, July 8, 2015.

72. "Schäuble's Push for Grexit Puts Merkel on Defensive," *Der Spiegel*, July 17, 2015.

73. G. Davet and F. Lhomme, *Un président ne devrait pas dire ça* (Paris: Stock, 2016).

74. A.-S. Chassany, A. Barker and D. Robinson, "Greece Talks: 'Sorry, But There Is No Way You Are Leaving This Room,'" *Financial Times*, July 13, 2015.

75. "Europe's Religious War Failure and Its Consequences," *Economist*, August 26, 2015.

76. Chassany, Barker and Robinson, "Greece Talks."

77. A. Kassam, "#ThisIsACoup: How a Hashtag Born in Barcelona Spread Across the Globe," *Guardian*, July 13, 2015; and W. Ahmed, "Amplified Messages: How Hashtag Activism and Twitter Diplomacy Converged at #ThisIsACoup—and Won," *Democratic Audit UK*, January 14, 2016.

78. K. Hope and T . Barber, "Syriza's Covert Plot During Crisis Talks to Return to Drachma," *Financial Times*, July 24, 2015.

79. P. Spiegel, "Donald Tusk Interview: The Annotated Transcript," *Financial Times*, July 16, 2015.

80. P. Oltermann, "Merkel 'Gambling Away' Germany's Reputation over Greece, says Haberman," *Guardian*, July 16, 2015.

81. S. Wagstyl and C. Jones, "Germany Blames Mario Draghi for Rise of Rightwing AfD Party," *Financial Times*, April 10, 2016.

82. M. Matthijs and M. Blyth, "When Is It Rational to Learn the Wrong Lessons? Technocratic Authority, Social Learning, and Euro Fragility," *Perspectives on Politics* (2017), 1–17.

83. L. Orriols and G. Cordero, "The Breakdown of the Spanish Two-Party System: The Upsurge of Podemos and Ciudadanos in the 2015 General Election," *South European Society and Politics* 4 (2016), 469–492.

84. D. Finn, "Luso-Anomalies," and C. Martins, "The Portuguese Experiment," both in *New Left Review* 106 (July-August 2017).

85. A. Evans-Pritchard, "Eurozone Crosses Rubicon as Portugal's Anti-Euro Left Banned from Power," *Telegraph*, October 23, 2015.

86. "DBRS Confirms Portugal's BBB (Low) Rating, Stable Trend," *Reuters*, November 13, 2015.

87. "Eurozone Crosses Rubicon."

88. J. Henley, "Portugal Faces Political Crisis as Leftists Vow to Topple New Government," *Guardian*, October 26, 2015.

89. A. Khalip and A. Bugge, "Socialist Costa to head Portuguese Government with Uneasy Far-Left Backing," *Reuters*, November 24, 2015.

90. Katharine Dommett, "The Theory and Practice of Party Modernisation: The Conservative Party Under David Cameron, 2005–2015," *British Politics* 10.2 (2015), 249–266.

91. M. A. Orenstein, "Paranoid in Poland," *Foreign Affairs* (September 2017).

CHAPTER 23: THE FEAR PROJECTS

1. G. Morgan, "Supporting the City: Economic Patriotism in Financial Markets," *Journal of European Public Policy* 19, no. 3 (2012), 373–387.

2. C. Berry and C. Hay, "The Great British 'Rebalancing' Act: The Construction and Implementation of an Economic Imperative for Exceptional Times," *British Journal of Politics and International Relations* 18, no. 1 (2016), 3–25.

3. https://www.youtube.com/watch?v=jS4ytmMDQME.

4. H. Jones, "London Stung by US Attack on Bank Regulation Record," *Reuters*, June 20, 2012.

5. "Deutsche Bank Capital Concerns in US Far from Over, According to UNITE HERE Report," *Business Wire*, September 5, 2012, https://www.businesswire.com/news/home

/20120905005476/en/Deutsche-Bank-capital-concerns-UNITE-Report; T. Braithwaite and S. Nasiripour, "Deutsche Bank Avoids US Capital Rules," *Financial Times*, March 21, 2012; and "Balkanised Banking: The Great Unravelling," *Economist* 20, no. 4 (2013).

6. J. Gapper, "Europe Needs Deutsche Bank as Its Champion," *Financial Times*, April 22, 2015.

7. R. Florida, "According to at Least One Index, New York Has Overtaken London as the World's Leading Financial Center," *City Lab*, March 20, 2014.

8. J. Green, " The offshore city, Chinese finance and British capitalism," *The British Journal of Finance and International Relations*, October 2017.

9. G. Osborne, "Britain Issues Western World's First Sovereign RMB Bond, Largest Ever RMB Bond by Non-Chinese Issuer," HM Treasury, Gov.UK, October 14, 2014.

10. N. Watt and R. Mason, "David Cameron Calls for New EU-China Free Trade Agreement," *Guardian*, December 2, 2013.

11. "Why We Need to Question the Influence of the City on UK Plc," *The Conversation*, April 20, 2015.

12. G. Archer, "Local Elections: The Capital Fails to See the Heartache and Pain Beyond," *Telegraph*, May 23, 2014.

13. S. Hinde, "Brexit and the Media," *Hermès, La Revue* 77 (2017): 80–86.

14. P. Whyte, "Britain, Europe and the City of London: Can the Triangle Be Managed?," Centre for European Reform, July 2012.

15. H. Clarke, M. Goodwin and P. Whiteley, *Brexit: Why Britain Voted to Leave the European Union* (Cambridge: Cambridge University Press, 2017), 61–85.

16. H. Thompson, "Competing Political Logics: The Political Intractability of London and the EU" (ND), available from http://speri.dept.shef.ac.uk/wp-content/uploads/2016/04/Thompson_DraftPaper_Workshop.pdf; also see the essential inside view of I. Rogers, "The Inside Story of How David Cameron Drove Britain to Brexit," *Prospect* 25, November 2017.

17. H. Thompson, "How the City of London Lost at Brexit: A Historical Perspective," *Economy and Society* 46, no. 2 (2017): 211–228.

18. See the *Spiegel* reaction: "The Failure of a Forced Marriage," *Der Spiegel*, December 10, 2011.

19. A. Gamble, "Better Off Out? Britain and Europe," *Political Quarterly* 83, no. 3 (2012): 468–477.

20. N. Copsey and T. Haughton, "Farewell Britannia? 'Issue Capture' and the Politics of David Cameron's 2013 EU Referendum Pledge," *Journal of Common Market Studies* 52 (2014), 74–89.

21. "Could the Netherlands Provide the Beginnings of a Coalition for EU Reform?," *Open Europe* 11 (January 2013); R. Korteweg, "Will the Dutch Help Cameron to Reform the EU?," *CER Bulletin* 91 (August/September 2013); and R. Korteweg, "Why Cameron's Timing on EU Reform Is Off," CER, March 26, 2014.

22. J. Springford and S. Tilford, "Why the Push to Install Juncker Is So Damaging," CER, June 23, 2014.

23. A. Möller, "The British-German Misunderstanding," ECFR, November 4, 2015.

24. C. Grant, "A Five-Point Plan for Cameron to Win an EU Referendum," CER, May 8, 2015.

25. T. McTague, A. Spence and E.-I. Dovere, "How David Cameron Blew It," *Politico*, June 25, 2016.

26. G. Van Orden, "Britain's Departure from 'Ever Closer Union' Is of Great Significance," http://blogs.lse.ac.uk/brexit/2016/04/28/britians-departure-from-ever-closer-union-is-of-great-significance/.

27. J. Springford and S. Tilford, "The Great British Trade-off: The Impact of Leaving the EU on the UK's Trade and Investment," CER, January 2014.

28. A. Spence, "David Cameron Unleashes 'Project Fear,'" *Politico*, February 26, 2016.
29. N. Vinocur, "Jim Messina to Advise David Cameron's EU Referendum Campaign," *Politico*, February 24, 2016.
30. S. Swinford and B. Riley-Smith, "Military Leaders to Warn Against a Brexit," *Telegraph*, February 21, 2016.
31. V. Chadwick, "David Cameron to Nigel Farage: No 'Neverendums,'" *Politico*, May 17, 2016.
32. L. Fedor, "EU Referendum: City of London Corporation Signs Off on Campaigning for the UK to Remain in the EU," *City A.M.*, March 3, 2016.
33. F. Guerrera and T. McTague, "City May Be Gagged in Brexit Vote," *Politico*, April 17, 2016.
34. "Breathe Easy Brussels, UK Will Stay in EU," *Politico*, May 4, 2016.
35. A. Mody, "EU Referendum: Why the Economic Consensus on Brexit Is Flawed," *Independent*, May 31, 2016; and K. Allen and A. Asthana, "IMF Says Brexit Would Cause 'Global Damage,'" *Politico*, April 12, 2016
36. A. Asthana, "Brexit Would Pose 'Serious Risk' to Global Growth, Say G7 Leaders," *Guardian*, March 27, 2016.
37. T. McTague, "11 Things You Need to Know About George Osborne's Brexit Warning," *Politico*, April 18, 2016; and T. McTague, "George Osborne: Brexit Would Leave UK 'Permanently Poorer,'" *Politico*, April 18, 2016.
38. "Remain Campaign 'Not Conspiracy, but Consensus,' says George Osborne," *Daily Mail*, May 16, 2016.
39. M. Arnold, "UK Banks Back Staying in EU but Remain Reluctant to Speak Out," *Financial Times*, March 24, 2016.
40. W. Watts, "'Financial Contagion' Biggest Risk to US from Brexit: Goldman," *MarketWatch*, June 29, 2016.
41. J. Treanor, "JPMorgan Backs Campaign to Keep Britain in the EU," *Guardian*, January 21, 2016.
42. S. Farrell, "JP Morgan Boss: Up to 4,000 Jobs Could Be Cut After Brexit," *Guardian*, June 3, 2016.
43. T. McTague, "Boris Johnson Slaps Down 'Part-Kenyan' Barack Obama over Brexit Push," *Politico*, April 22, 2016.
44. T. McTague, "9 Takeaways from Barack Obama's Brexit Intervention," *Politico*, April 22, 2016; and B. Gurciullo, "Obama to the British People: Just Say No to Brexit," *Politico*, April 22, 2016.
45. S. Watkins, "Oppositions," *New Left Review* 98 (2016).
46. T. McTague, A. Spence and E.-I. Dovere, "How David Cameron Blew It," *Politico*, June 25, 2016.
47. S. Chan, "Boris Johnson's Essay on Obama and Churchill Touches Nerve Online," *New York Times*, April 22, 2016.
48. McTague, Spence and Dovere, "How David Cameron Blew It."
49. G. Younge, "Brexit: A Disaster Decades in the Making," *Guardian*, June 30, 2016.
50. "Breathe Easy Brussels, UK Will Stay in EU."
51. S. Becker, T. Fetzer and D. Novy, "Who Voted for Brexit? A Comprehensive District-Level Analysis" (CESifo Working Paper 6438, April 24, 2017).
52. E. Kaufmann, "It's NOT the Economy, Stupid: Brexit as a Story of Personal Values," *LSE European Politics and Policy* (blog), July 9, 2016.
53. L. Elliott, "Brexit Is a Rejection of Globalization," *Guardian*, June 26, 2016; J. Tankersely, "Britain Just Killed Globalization as We Know It," *Washington Post*, June 25, 2016; *Deutsche Welle*, "Brexit—the End of Globalization?," June 30, 2016, http://www.dw.com/en/brexit-the-end-of-globalization/a-19369680; T. Guénolé, "La victoire du Brexit est un vote contre la mondialisation," *Figaro*, June 24, 2016.

54. "Theresa May's Brexit Speech in Full: Prime Minister Outlines Her 12 Objectives for Negotiations," *Independent*, January 17, 2017.
55. R. Blitz and L. Lewis, "Pound Tumbles to 30-Year Low as Britain Votes Brexit," *Financial Times*, June 24, 2016.
56. H. Lash and E. Krudy, "World Stocks Tumble as Britain Votes for EU Exit," *Reuters*, June 23, 2016.
57. Blitz and Lewis, "Pound Tumbles to 30-Year Low."
58. M. Carney, "Uncertainty, the Economy and Policy," Bank of England, June 30, 2016.
59. A. Mody, "Stop Being So Gloomy About Brexit," *Bloomberg*, July 13, 2016.
60. L. Meakin, "Carney's Stimulus Questioned as BoE Faces Pro-Brexit Lawmakers," *Bloomberg*, September 5, 2016.
61. C. Giles, "Brexit Experts, Confess to Your Errors and Carry On," *Financial Times*, January 4, 2017.
62. M. Hall, "WRONG! And WRONG Again—The Utterly Useless 'Forecasters' We Should Stop Listening To," *Express*, October 28, 2016.
63. A. Posen, "Dangers of Following the Path to an Offshore Britain," *Financial Times*, June 21, 2016.
64. W. Davies, "Home Office Rules," *London Review of Books* 38, no. 21 (2016), 3–6.
65. A. Mody, "Don't Believe What You've Read: The Plummeting Pound Sterling Is Good News for Britain," *Independent*, October 10, 2016.
66. "Brexit and the Pound" (speech given by Ben Broadbent, deputy governor of Monetary Policy, Imperial College, London, March 23, 2017).
67. R. Skidelsky, "Why Sterling's Collapse Is Not Good for the UK Economy," *Guardian*, October 21, 2016.
68. J. Kirkup, "Fiona Hill and Nick Timothy: The Story Being Told About Theresa May's Top Advisers Is Inaccurate and Unfair," *Telegraph*, June 10, 2017.
69. M.Bearak, "Theresa May Criticized the Term 'Citizen of the World.' But Half the World Identifies," *Washington Post*, October 5, 2016.
70. J. Pickard and K. Allen, "Theresa May Sets Out Post-Brexit for a Fairer Britain," *Financial Times*, October 5, 2016.
71. "Theresa May Brexit Speech: Economic Experts React," *Independent*, January 17, 2017.
72. P. Campbell, "Nissan Boss 'Confident' After Downing Street Talks," *Financial Times*, October 14, 2016.
73. P. Jenkins and J. Ford, "City of London Lobby Group Wants 'No Change' Brexit Deal," *Financial Times*, November 7, 2016.
74. H. Sants, M. Austen, L. Naylor, P. Hunt and D. Kelly, "The Impact of the UK's Exit from the EU on the UK-Based Financial Services Sector," Oliver Wyman, 2016.
75. "Goldman Sachs' Chief Takes Theresa May to Task over Brexit," *Irish Times*, January 29, 2017.
76. J. Ford, "City of London Lobbying Group Drops Demand for EU 'Passports,'" *Financial Times*, January 11, 2017.
77. M. Savage, "Germany Industry Warns UK Not to Expect Help in Brexit Negotiations," *Guardian*, July 9, 2017.
78. T. Gutschker, "The Disastrous Brexit Dinner," *Frankfurter Allgemeine Zeitung*, May 3, 2017.
79. G. Parker, J. Ford and A. Barker, "Is Theresa May's Brexit Plan B an Elaborate Bluff?," *Financial Times*, January 19, 2017.
80. A. Withnall, "UK Could Become 'Tax Haven' of Europe If It Is Shut Out of Single Market After Brexit, Chancellor Suggests," *Independent*, January 15, 2017.
81. "Professor Mario Draghi Joins Goldman Sachs," Goldman Sachs Press Release, 2002, http://www.goldmansachs.com/media-relations/press-releases/archived/2002/2002-01-28.html.

82. A. Monaghan, "Juncker Questions Barroso's Decision to Join Goldman Sachs," *Guardian,* September 15, 2016.

83. G. Steinhauser, "'Brexit' Would Be Europe's Lehman Brothers Moment, Finnish Minister Says," *Wall Street Journal,* June 16, 2016.

84. Z. Radionova, "Moody's: Political Contagion Across European Union Is Greatest Brexit Risk," Moody's Investors Service, July 8, 2016.

85. K. Forster, "Brexit Vote Met with Celebrations from Far-Right Groups Across Europe," *Independent,* June 24, 2016.

86. "Moody's: Political Contagion Across EU Is Greatest Brexit Risk, Moody's Says," *Independent,* July 8, 2016.

87. "What If the French Second Round Pits Melenchon Against Le Pen?," *Economist,* April 11, 2017.

88. P. Anderson, "The Center Can Hold," *New Left Review* 105 (May/June 2017).

89. A. Parker, "Donald Trump, in Scotland, Calls 'Brexit' Result 'a Great Thing,'" *New York Times,* June 24, 2016.

CHAPTER 24: TRUMP

1. "Full Text: Donald Trump 2016 RNC Draft Speech Transcript," *Politico,* July 21, 2016.

2. D. Diaz, "Ivanka Trump Markets Her Look After RNC Speech," *CNN,* July 22, 2016.

3. K. Reilly, "Read President Obama's Remarks on Donald Trump's Convention Speech," *Time,* July 22, 2016.

4. D. W. Drezner, "My One Contribution to the Autopsies of the 2016 Presidential Election," *Washington Post,* May 2, 2017.

5. The question of whether young white men—the so-called Bernie bros—dominated the Sanders coalition stirred passions on the left long after the election. See T. Cahill, "A New Harvard Study Just Shattered the Biggest Myth About Bernie Supporters," April 19, 2017, http://resistancereport.com/politics/harvard-poll-bernie-supporters/.

6. M. Talbot, "The Populist Prophet," *New Yorker,* October 12, 2015.

7. J. Kasperkevic and G. Wearden, "Federal Reserve Puts Rate Rise on Hold—As It Happens," *Guardian,* September 17, 2015.

8. N. Confessore and S. Craig, "2008 Crisis Deepened the Ties Between Clintons and Goldman Sachs," *New York Times,* September 24, 2016.

9. T. Gabriel, "Hillary Clinton–Bernie Sanders Schism Grows on 'Too Big to Fail' Banks," *New York Times,* April 13, 2016.

10. M. Taibbi, "The Great American Bubble Machine," *Rolling Stone,* April 5, 2010.

11. L. Fang et al., "Excerpts of Hillary Clinton's Paid Speeches to Goldman Sachs Finally Leaked," *The Intercept,* October 7, 2016.

12. P. Lawrence, "A New Report Raises Big Questions About Last Year's DNC Hack," *Nation,* August 9, 2017.

13. H. Levintova, "Hacks, Leaks, and Tweets: Everything We Now Know About the Attack on the 2016 Election," *Mother Jones,* May 30, 2017.

14. G. Miller, E. Nakashima and A. Entous, "Obama's Secret Struggle to Punish Russia for Putin's Election Assault," *Washington Post,* June 23, 2017.

15. T. Dickinson, "Meet the Right-Wing Rebels Who Overthrew John Boehner," *Rolling Stone,* October 6, 2015.

16. Mayer, *Dark Money.*

17. For an outstanding investigation of the dynamics of the primary race, see T. Ferguson and B. I. Page, "The Hinge of Fate? Economic and Social Populism in the 2016 Presidential Election, a Preliminary Exploration," prepared for delivery at the INET Conference, Edinburgh, UK, October 20–23, 2017, https://www.ineteconomics.org/uploads/papers/Ferguson-and-Page-Scotland-Paper-revised-for-Conference.pdf.

18. C. Laderman and B. Simms, *Donald Trump: The Making of a Worldview* (London: Endeavour Pess, 2017).

19. K. W. Capehart, "Hyman Minsky's Interpretation of Donald Trump," *Journal of Post Keynesian Economics* 38.3 (2015): 477–492

20. F. Norris, "Trump Sees Act of God in Recession," *New York Times*, December 4, 2008.

21. Soopermexican, "Trump on TARP and Stimulus Sounds More Like a Crony Capitalist Than a Conservative," *The Right Scoop* (blog), August 15, 2015, http://therightscoop .com/trump-on-tarp-and-stimulus-sounds-more-like-a-crony-capitalist-than-a -conservative/.

22. Southern constitutionalist, "Trump Has Supported Nearly All of Obama's Economic Policy Agenda," *RedState* (blog), August 27, 2015.

23. J. Green, *Devil's Bargain: Steve Bannon, Donald Trump, and the Storming of the President* (New York: Penguin Press, 2017), 96–103.

24. M. Grunwald, "Trump's Love Affair with Coal," *Politico*, October 15, 2017, https:// www.politico.com/magazine/story/2017/10/15/trumps-love-affair-with-coal-215710.

25. Pew Research, "Clinton, Trump Supporters Have Starkly Different Views of a Changing Nation," August 18, 2016, http://www.people-press.org/2016/08/18/5-issues-and-the-2016 -campaign/.

26. R. Rubin and N. Timiraos, "Donald Trump Shows GOP's Economic Pillars Are Loosening," *Wall Street Journal*, July 19, 2016.

27. J. Creswell, "Trump and US Chamber of Commerce Pull No Punches on Trade Policy," *New York Times*, July 11, 2016.

28. B. White, "Wall Street Shuns Trump's Cleveland Convention," *Politico*, July 13, 2016.

29. T. Mak, "Major Corporate Sponsors Are Scaling Back Support for GOP Convention," May 6, 2016, https://www.thedailybeast.com/major-corporate-sponsors-are-scaling -back-support-for-gop-convention.

30. H. Paulson, "When It Comes to Trump, a Republican Treasury Secretary Says: Choose Country Over Party," *Washington Post*, June 24, 2016.

31. Ibid.

32. S. Bannon, *Generation Zero* film, https://www.youtube.com/watch?v=bsqu9gh6xhk.

33. D. Johnson, "Trump Nominates Goldman Sachs 'Alligator' Jay Clayton to Run SEC," *TruthOut*, March 29, 2017.

34. A. Greenspan, "Ich bin im falschen Jahrhundert geboren," *Zürcher Tages-Anzeiger*, September 19, 2007.

35. M. Adday, "Alan Greenspan Doesn't Want 'Crazies' to Undermine the U.S.," *Fortune*, September 15, 2016.

36. Editorial, "Who's Greenspan Calling Crazy?," *New York Sun*, September 14, 2016, http:// www.nysun.com/editorials/who-is-greenspan-calling-crazy/89716/.

37. "Trump Says US Interest Rates Must Change as Fed Weighs Rate Hike," *Reuters*, September 5, 2016; "Trump Finally Got It Right on the Fed's 'False Economy'—but Will We Listen?," *Guardian*, September 8, 2016; "Donald Trump Says Federal Reserve Chair Janet Yellen 'Should Be Ashamed of Herself,'" *Washington Post*, September 12, 2016.

38. *Esquire* editors, "The Untold Stories of Election Day 2016," *Esquire*, November 5, 2017, http://www.esquire.com/news-politics/a13266971/election-2016-behind-the-scenes/.

39. C. E. Lee and N. Stamouli, "Trump's Win, Brexit Vote Stem from Mishandling of Globalization, Obama Says," *Wall Street Journal*, November 16, 2016.

40. N. Carnes and N. Lupu, "It's Time to Bust the Myth: Most Trump Voters Were Not Working Class," *Washington Post*, June 5, 2017.

41. R. Blendon, L. Casey and J. Benson, "Public Opinion and Trump's Jobs and Trade Policies," *Challenge* 60 (2017), 228–244.

42. A. Guisinger, "Americans' Views of Trade Aren't Just About Economics. They're Also About Race," *Washington Post*, August 16, 2016.

43. M. Davis, "The Great God Trump and the White Working Class," *Jacobin*, February 7, 2017; and Ferguson and Page, "The Hinge of Fate?"

44. D. Drezner, "My One Contribution to the Autopsies of the 2016 Presidential Election," *Washington Post*, May 2, 2017.

45. M. Crowley, "The Deep State Is Real," *Politico*, September/October 2017; and T. Porter, "Deep State: How a Conspiracy Theory Went from Political Fringe to Mainstream," *Newsweek*, August 2, 2017.

46. J. Winter and E. Groll, "Here's the Memo That Blew Up the NSC," *Foreign Policy*, August 10, 2017.

47. B. Leubsdorf, E. Morath and J. Zumbrun, "Economists Who've Advised Presidents Are No Fans of Donald Trump," *Wall Street Journal*, August 25, 2016.

48. B. Casselman, "Why Trump's Carrier Deal Isn't the Way to Save US Jobs," *FiveThirtyEight* (blog), December 5, 2016, https://fivethirtyeight.com/features/why-trumps-carrier-deal-isnt-the-way-to-save-u-s-jobs/.

49. D. Griswold, "Trump's Carrier 'Success' Signals a Retreat of US Business in Global Markets," *Mad About Trade*, December 2, 2016.

50. S. Liesman, "Optimism on Economy, Stocks Surges Since Trump Election: CNBC Survey," CNBC, December 9, 2016.

51. P. Domm, "How Donald Trump Blew Up the Bond Market and Changed Everyone's View of Interest Rates," CNBC, November 14, 2016.

52. D. Dayen, "Donald Trump Isn't Even Pretending to Oppose Goldman Sachs Anymore," *The Intercept*, March 15, 2017.

53. M. Grunwald, "The Trade Deal We Just Threw Overboard," *Politico Magazine*, March/April 2017.

54. "Brad Delong: The Democrats' Line in the Sand," *Economist's View*, June 30, 2008, http://economistsview.typepad.com/economistsview/2008/06/brad-delong-the.html.

55. "Kentucky Residents Express Dissatisfaction with GOP Efforts to Dismantle Obamacare," *All Things Considered*, NPR, July 18, 2017, https://www.npr.org/2017/07/18/537948591/kentucky-residents-express-dissatisfaction-with-gop-efforts-to-dismantle-obamaca.

56. H. Fingerhut, "Support for 2010 Health Care Law Reaches New High," Pew Research Center, February 23, 2017.

57. R. Savransky, "Poll: Support for ObamaCare Repeal-Only Plan at 13 Percent," *The Hill*, July 19, 2017.

58. R. Berman, "The Republican Majority in Congress Is an Illusion," *Atlantic*, March 31, 2017.

59. M. Sheetz, "Treasury Secretary Mnuchin Extends Measure to Hold Off Debt-Limit Default," CNBC, July 28, 2017.

60. M. Grunwald, "Mick the Knife," *Politico*, September/October 2017.

61. E. D. Kleinbard, "The Debt Ceiling Crisis Is Real," *New York Times*, August 7, 2017.

62. R. Savransky and J. Fabian, "Trump: US 'Needs a Good Shutdown,'" *The Hill*, May 2, 2017, http://thehill.com/homenews/administration/331512-trump-us-needs-a-good-shutdown.

63. R. Bade, B. Everett and J. Dawsey, "Trump Sides with Democrats in Debt Limit, Funding, Harvey Deal," *Politico*, September 6, 2017. The far bigger disaster in Puerto Rico turned out to be of little concern to Washington.

64. I. Millhiser, "Memo to the *New York Times*: Donald Trump Is a Republican," *Think Progress*, September 11, 2017.

65. M. Yglesias, "The Looming Debt Ceiling Fight, Explained," *Vox*, August 9, 2017.

66. "How the Republican Tax Bill Compares with Previous Reforms," *Economist*, December 9, 2017.

67. A. Rappeport, "Ahead of Vote, Promised Treasury Analysis of Tax Bill Proves Elusive," *New York Times*, November 30, 2017. For the one-page memo summarizing the Treasury's claims about the growth impact of tax cuts see "Analysis of Growth and

Revenue Estimates Based on the U.S. Senate Committee on Finance Tax Reform Plan," December 11, 2017, https://www.treasury.gov/press-center/press-releases/Documents /TreasuryGrowthMemo12-11-17.pdf.

68. P. Baker, "Arthur Laffer's Theory on Tax Cuts Comes to Life Once More," *New York Times*, April 25, 2017.

69. A. Simpson and E. Bowles, "A Moment of Truth for Our Country's Financial Future," *Washington Post*, November 29, 2017.

70. R. Rubin, "Analysis: How Consensus for Corporate Rate Cut Turned into Partisan Tax Brawl," *Wall Street Journal*, December 22, 2017.

71. K. Zernike and A. Rappeport, "Heading Toward Tax Victory, Republicans Eye Next Step: Cut Spending," *New York Times*, December 2, 2017.

72. "Tax Reform Plan a 'Bid to Make US Inequality Champion,'" Al Jazeera, December 16, 2017, https://www.aljazeera.com/news/2017/12/tax-reform-plan-bid-champion-inequality -171216105649640.html.

73. CBO, "Analysis of the Long-Term Costs of the Administration's Goals for the Military," December 2017, https://www.cbo.gov/publication/53350.

74. L. Summers, "Sugar High Is Right Diagnosis, Tax Cuts Are the Wrong Prescription," December 10, 2017, http://larrysummers.com/2017/12/10/sugar-high-is-right-diagnosis -tax-cuts-are-the-wrong-prescription/.

75. J. Hilsenrath and D. Harrison, "Yellen Cites Benefits to Running Economy Hot for Some Time," *Wall Street Journal*, October 14, 2017.

76. L. Summers, "Three (Almost) Inexplicable Parts of the Republican Tax Plan," *Washington Post*, November 5, 2017.

77. C. Collins, "House Republican: My Donors Told Me to Pass the Tax Bill 'or Don't Ever Call Me Again,'" November 7, 2017, https://www.vox.com/policy-and-politics/2017/11 /7/16618038/house-republicans-tax-bill-donors-chris-collins.

78. "What Donald Trump's Election Means for Government-Bond Markets," *Economist*, December 3, 2016.

79. J. Sommer, "Clouds Are Forming over the Bond Market," *New York Times*, June 30, 2017.

80. S. Oh, "Treasury Yields Rise as Roadblock to Tax Bill Removed," December 15, 2017, https://www.marketwatch.com/story/treasury-yields-inch-higher-as-tax-bill-set-for -unveiling-2017-12-15.

81. IMF, *World Economic Outlook* (Washington, DC: IMF, 2017), 19, Figure 1.13, panel 4.

82. Americans for Financial Reform, "How Americans View Wall Street and Financial Regulation," August 2017, http://ourfinancialsecurity.org/americans-view-wall-street-financial -regulation-august-2017/.

83. J. Mason and S. N. Lynch, "Trump's Message to Bankers: Wall Street Reform Rules May Be Eliminated," *Reuters*, April 11, 2017.

84. J. Dizard, "The Trump Era of Light-Touch Regulation Dawns," *Financial Times*, July 2, 2017.

85. H. Levintova, "House Republicans Are Trying to Pass the Most Dangerous Wall Street Deregulation Bill Ever," *Mother Jones*, June 7, 2017.

86. G. Bennett, "House Passes Bill Aimed at Reversing Dodd-Frank Financial Regulations," *NPR*, June 8, 2017.

87. "A Financial System That Creates Economic Opportunities: Banks and Credit Unions— Core Principles for Regulating the United States Financial System," US Treasury report to President Donald J. Trump, Executive Order 13772 (June 2017).

88. J. Dizard, "The Trump Era of Light-Touch Regulation Dawns," *Financial Times*, July 2, 2017.

89. A. Scaggs, "Save the OFR," *Financial Times*, June 15, 2017.

90. B. Jopson, "US Regulator Moves to Loosen Volcker Rule," *Financial Times*, August 2, 2017.

91. R. Tracy, "Trump Team to Recommend Keeping Dodd-Frank Liquidation Power," *Wall Street Journal*, November 29, 2017.

92. For Greenspan's defense see A. Greenspan, "The Crisis," *Brookings Papers on Economic Activity*, Spring 2010, 202–250. For media coverage, see Dealbook, "Greenspan: The Fed Failed to Gauge the Bubble," *New York Times*, March 18, 2010.

93. B. Bernanke, "Shrinking the Fed's Balance Sheet," *Brookings*, January 26, 2017.

94. V. Guida and B. White, "Trump Dumps Yellen, Picks Powell in Biggest Economic Move," *Politico*, November 2, 2017, https://www.politico.com/story/2017/11/02/trump-picks-powell-fed-chair-244475.

95. See Powell's bio at the Bipartisan Policy Center, https://bipartisanpolicy.org/person/jerome-powell-0/.

96. B. Applebaum, "In Choice of Fed Chairman, Trump Downgrades Deregulation," *New York Times*, October 29, 2017.

97. D. A. Irwin, "Mr. Trump's Trade War," *Wall Street Journal*, December 15, 2017.

98. D. Lawder, "G20 Ministers Give Mnuchin Space to Define Trump Trade Agenda," *Reuters*, March 20, 2017.

99. C. Jones and S. Fleming, "G20 Drops Vow to Resist All Forms of Protectionism," *Financial Times*, March 18, 2017.

100. Ibid.

101. A. Parker, P. Rucker, D. Paletta and K. Deyoung, "Inside Donald Trump's Sudden Reversal on NAFTA," *Chicago Tribune*, April 27, 2017.

102. J. Mason and D. Lawder, "Trump Says Was 'Psyched to Terminate NAFTA' but Reconsidered," *Reuters*, April 26, 2017.

103. "Inside Donald Trump's Sudden Reversal on NAFTA."

104. M. Grunwald, "The Trade Deal We Just Threw Overboard," *Politico Magazine*, March/April 2017.

105. D. A. Irwin, *Clashing over Commerce: A History of US Trade Policy* (Chicago: Chicago University Press, 2017), Kindle location 9115–10214.

106. G. Shaffer, M. Elsig and M. Pollack, "The Slow Killing of the World Trade Organization," *Huffington Post*, November 17, 2017, https://www.huffingtonpost.com/entry/the-slow-killing-of-the-world-trade-organization_us_5a0ccd1de4b03fe7403f82df.

107. P. Levy, "Robert Lighthizer's Global Trade Governance Critique," *Forbes*, December 12, 2017.

108. "US Broadside Leaves WTO Meeting in Tatters," *Deutsche Welle*, December 12, 2017.

109. K. McNamara, "Trump Takes Aim at the European Union: Why the EU Won't Unify in Response," *Foreign Affairs*, January 24, 2017.

110. E.-K. Symons, "Steve Bannon Loves France," *Politico*, March 22, 2017, and C. Alduy, "The Novel That Unites Marine Le Pen and Steve Bannon," *Politico*, April 23, 2017.

111. D. Frum, "Trump's Trip Was a Catastrophe for US-Europe Relations," *Atlantic*, May 28, 2017.

112. J. Henley, "Angela Merkel: EU Cannot Completely Rely on US and Britain Any More," *Guardian*, May 28, 2017.

113. R. Haass, Twitter, May 28, 2017.

114. Sorbonne speech of Emmanuel Macron, full text/English version, http://international.blogs.ouest-france.fr/archive/2017/09/29/macron-sorbonne-verbatim-europe-18583.html.

115. Remarks by President Trump to the people of Poland, July 6, 2017, https://www.whitehouse.gov/briefings-statements/remarks-president-trump-people-poland/.

116. "Schäuble Defends German Trade Surplus in the US," April 20, 2017, http://www.dw.com/en/sch%C3%A4uble-defends-german-trade-surplus-in-the-us/a-38525267.

117. T. Fairless, "Schäuble Defends Germany's Trade Surplus," *Wall Street Journal*, April 20, 2017.

118. B. W. Setser, "G-3 Coordination Failures of the Past Eight Years? (A Riff on Cœuré and Brainard)," *Follow the Money* (blog), August 23. 2017, https://www.cfr.org/blog/g-3 -coordination-failures-past-eight-years-riff-coeure-and-brainard.

119. See the remarks by the director general of the WTO, R. Azevedo, "Remarks: The Evolution of Trade, Technology, and Globalization: How to Foster Inclusive Growth," November 8, 2017, https://www.wto.org/english/news_e/spra_e/spra198_e.htm.

120. C. Constantinescu, A. Mattoo, and M. Ruta, "The Global Trade Slowdown: Cyclical or Structural?," International Monetary Fund, No. 15–16, 2015.

121. See the powerful critique in S. J. Evenett and J. Fritz, *Will Awe Trump Rules? The 21st Global Trade Alert Report* (London: CEPR, 2017).

122. B. W. Setser, "Dark Matter. Soon to Be Revealed?," *Follow the Money* (blog), February 2, 2017, https://www.cfr.org/blog/dark-matter-soon-be-revealed.

123. National Security Strategy of the United States (Washington, December 2017), 37, https://www.whitehouse.gov/wp-content/uploads/2017/12/NSS-Final-12-18-2017 -0905.pdf.

124. D. A. Graham, "The Wrong Side of 'the Right Side of History,'" *Atlantic,* December 21, 2015, https://www.theatlantic.com/politics/archive/2015/12/obama-right-side-of-history /420462/.

125. IMF, *World Economic Outlook,* October 2017, 23, 187, 204.

CHAPTER 25: THE SHAPE OF THINGS TO COME

1. N. Barkin and E. Piper, "In Davos, Xi Makes Case for Chinese Leadership Role," *Reuters,* January 17, 2017.

2. "President Xi's Speech to Davos in Full," *World Economic Forum,* January 17, 2017.

3. E. Wong and C. Buckley, "Stock Market Plunge in China Dents Communist Party's Stature," *New York Times,* July 9, 2015.

4. C. Walter and F. Howie, *Red Capitalism: The Fragile Financial Foundation of China's Extraordinary Rise* (Singapore: Wiley, 2011).

5. "China Forex Reserves Fall $512.66 Billion in 2015, Biggest Drop on Record," *Reuters,* January 7, 2016.

6. "China's Yuan Carry Trade, an Anchor and a Risk for Asia," *Reuters,* January 30, 2014; and "Is the $1tn China Carry Trade Imploding?," *Financial Times,* February 5, 2015.

7. "Highlights of the BIS International Statistics," BIS, December 7, 2014.

8. R. N. McCauley, "Capital Flowed Out of China Through BIS Reporting Banks in Q1 2015," BIS, September 13, 2015.

9. "The World Economy Is Picking Up," *Economist,* March 18, 2017.

10. "China's Slowdown and Cheap Oil," BBC, August 26, 2015.

11. "Timeline of China's Attempts to Prevent Stock Market Meltdown," *Reuters,* August 28, 2015.

12. "The World Economy Is Picking Up."

13. S. Fischer, "The Federal Reserve and the Global Economy," Board of Governors of the Federal Reserve System, October 11, 2014.

14. "Janet Yellen Invokes China 16 Times in 1 Hour," CNN, September 18, 2015.

15. "Fed Should Not Raise Interest Rates Just Yet: China FinMin," CNBC, October 12, 2015.

16. "Fed's Focus on China Unnerves Some Investors," *Reuters,* September 18, 2015.

17. "Fed Raises Key Interest Rates for First Time in Almost a Decade," *New York Times,* December 16, 2015.

18. B. Setser, "Too Chinese (and Russian) to Fail?"

19. "The View of the Eurozone Crisis from China," *Chicago Policy Review,* April 16, 2012; and "China's Fears Grow over Eurozone Crisis," *Telegraph,* August 20, 2012.

20. V. Dombrovskis and P. Moscovici, "Reflection Paper on the Deepening of the Economic and Monetary Union" (Brusssels: European Commission, 2017).

21. "Initiative for Europe: A Sovereign, United, Democratic Europe" (speech by Emmanuel Macron, Sorbonne, Paris, September 26, 2017).

22. A. Lerner, "The Economics and Politics of Consumer Sovereignty," *American Economic Review* 62 (1972), 258–66.

23. The two most significant contributions being C. Clark, *Sleepwalkers* (London: Penguin Press, 2013); and J. Leonhard, *Pandora's Box* (Cambridge, MA: Harvard University Press, 2017).

24. M. Mann, *Sources of Social Power*, vol. 2, 2nd ed. (Cambridge: Cambridge University Press, 2012), is a remarkable social theoretic reconstruction.

INDEX